Moonshine, Murder & Mayhem
In Georgia

Co-written, Compiled and Edited
By
Olin Jackson
B.A., M.Ed.

Published by Legacy Communications, Inc.
200 Market Place, Suite 100
Roswell, Georgia, 30075

International Standard Book Number (ISBN):
1-880816-15-6

For additional copies:
Legacy Communications, Inc.
Post Office Box 127
Roswell, Georgia 30077-0127
Tel: (770) 642-5569

Dedicated To

The writers and researchers
who have painstakingly
pieced together
the articles in
North Georgia Journal
and
Georgia Backroads
magazines for over twenty years.

Acknowledgements

The articles, facts and photographs on the pages which follow are a compilation of information carefully researched and painstakingly collected over a period of approximately twenty years. This volume of information is not designed as nor intended to be a comprehensive history of Georgia. It, rather, is a compilation of captivating historic subjects personally selected by the editor and publisher of *North Georgia Journal* and *Georgia Backroads* magazines. Special attention was accorded to those articles involving subjects pertaining to particularly unusual and captivating incidents in the history of the state of Georgia.

All research involved in the preparation of this book was conducted by skilled historians and dedicated researchers/students of history. All material contained herein is – to the best of our knowledge – factual and accurate.

Grateful appreciation is hereby extended to the following writers and researchers without whose assistance this book would not have been possible:

Anne Dismukes Amerson
Jimmy Anderson
Harry Bartlett
Herbert Buffington
Ray Chandler
J. Timothy Cole
Robert S. Davis, Jr.
Lisa A. Ennis
David Godfrey
Kathryn Gray-White
Joe Griffith
Hugh T. Harrington
Sylvia Gailey Head
Marion Hemperley
Nancy Bearden Henderson
Jackie Kennedy
Edward Jordan Lanham
Deborah Malone
Sara Hines Martin
Wayne McDaniel
Morton R. McInvale
Sybil McRay
Martin Register
Daniel M. Roper
Gordon Sargent
Rev. Philip P. Scott
Glovis Gore South
Karen Spears Zacharias

Contents

Baldwin County
Milledgeville's Unusual Kenan-Strother Shootings . . . 1
The Finney-Stanley Shooting . . . 8
The Killing Spree Of Marion Stembridge . . . 10

Bartow County
Tales Of Indians, Slaves And Mayhem In Old Folsom, GA . . . 24
The Called Him 'Pretty Boy' . . . 31
Tales Of Tiny Taylorsville . . . 37

Bibb County
The Terrible Woolfolk Murders . . . 45

Carroll County
The Assassination Of Chief William McIntosh . . . 56

Cherokee County
The Life & Hard Times of Augustus 'Gus' Coggins . . . 65

Clarke County
The 1918 Road Lab Murders At The University Of Georgia . . . 74

Cobb County
Mobster Benjamin 'Bugsy' Siegel's Girl . . . 84

Dawson County
Dawson County 'Moonshine' Racers From Yesteryear . . . 92
The Rambling Russell Brothers From Leathers' Ford . . . 98

Fayette County
Fayette County Moonshining And The Murder Of James Langston . . . 106

Floyd County
The 1913 Rosedale Twister . . . 111
The Calhoun-Williamson Duel In North Georgia . . . 116
The Graves At Farmer's Cemetery . . . 124

Forsyth County
The Murder And Burial Of Cherokee Chief James Vann . . . 132

Fulton County
Atlanta's Big Fire Of 1917 139

Gilmer County
Gunfight At Doublehead Gap 147
Anthony Goble And The Brown Murder Of 1876 150

Gordon County
Marked For Death: The Story Of Stand Watie 156

Habersham County
The Tallulah Falls Disaster Of 1921 167

Hall County
The 1909 Clermont Tornado. 172
The Terrible Gainesville Tornado Of 1936 176
The Capture & Last Days Of Old West Bandit Bill Miner 182
The Trial Of George Corn Tassels 191

Haralson County
Tallapoosa Law Enforcement Tragedies. 199

Heard County
West Georgia 'Law And Order' And Old Heard County Jail 202
Night Of Terror At Merrill's Mill 207

Jones County
Fateful Day At Griswoldville: The Georgia Militia's Last Hurrah 211
The Griswoldville Battlefield Today 222

Lowndes County
In Search Of Doc Holliday In Valdosta, Georgia. 223
Susan McKey Thomas On The Acquaintances Of Doc Holliday 229

Lumpkin County
The Great Dahlonega Bank Robbery Of 1913 233
The Branch Mint Building Fire And Price Memorial Hall. 240
Grandpa Was An Outlaw. 248
Axe Murders In North Georgia: The Baxter Family Slayings 254

North Georgia
The Life & Times Of John A. Murrell 264
The North Georgia Moonshine War Of 1876-77 268
A Former 'Moonshiner' In The Mountains 275
Guerrilla Fighter John Gatewood And A Notorious Livestock Theft 282
Forgotten Union Guerrillas Of The North Georgia Mountains 287

Paulding County
Early Northwest Georgia Railroad Disasters 299

Pickens County
Last Days Of The Civil War In Pickens County 305
The Last Raid Of Lee Cape 311
Murder In Pickens County 318
The Murder Of Narcissa Fowler Revisited 329
Pickens County In The Civil War 332
The 1923 Pickens County Jail Break 336
The Cherokee Village At Long Swamp Creek 339
The Night Riders Of Pickens County 345
The Whitestone Disaster Of 1938 348

Polk County
The Amazing Polk County 'Pot Plane' 352
The Wreck Of The *Royal Palm* And The *Ponce de Leon* 359
Frontier Gunslingers: The Asa Prior Family 366
Moonshine And Murder At Esom Hill 377
Murder And The Aragon Mill Strikes 384

Rabun County
Murder At The Old Fisher Place 389

Spalding County
'Doc' Holliday's Early Life In Georgia 393
John Henry Holliday's Travels In The West 397
The Last Days Of John Henry Holliday 404
Where Lie The Bones Of John Henry 'Doc' Holliday? 412

Troup County
Moonshining, And The Murder Of Sheriff William Shirey 416

White County

The Last Hanging In White County 422
Nacoochee Valley's 'West End,' And The James Hall Nichols Family 427

Whitfield County

The Murder Of Joseph Standing 434
The Mysteries Of Old Gordon Springs. 438

Wilkes County

Mystery Of The Gold Coins At Chenault Crossroads 443
The Chase And Capture Of Jefferson Davis 456

Subject Index 465

Full Name Index 479

Milledgeville's Unusual Kenan–Strother Shootings

Both John Strother and Lewis Kenan were married, and both apparently had ladyfriends with whom they consorted outside their marriages. In a confusing web of events involving these ladies and the hardships surrounding the days following the War Between The States, Kenan was gunned down in the streets of Milledgeville and Strother was later murdered on a lonely road in Louisiana.

Prior to 1866 John R. Strother and Lewis Holmes Kenan of Milledgeville had been friends. However, a series of mysterious personal insults, coupled with political differences stemming from the chaos of the Reconstruction years in the late 1860s and early 1870s would changed this relationship permanently. On the evening of July 3, 1871, one man was killed in the street across from the Georgia Governor's Mansion and his assailant became a fugitive from justice in a strange series of events which had started months earlier.

On a warm spring afternoon on May 9, 1871, John Strother and Judge Peter Fair had stopped their buggy in front of Moore & Co.'s store on Wayne Street in Milledgeville. At this same time, Lewis Kenan suddenly emerged from the store carrying a double-barreled shotgun which he aimed and fired at Strother. Just as Kenan pulled the trigger another man – a Mr. Stevens – reportedly pushed the barrel of the weapon suddenly upward so the charge flew above Strother, lodging in a house across the street.

As Kenan prepared to fire a second time at Strother, the buggy's horse lurched sending Strother and Fair sprawling on the ground. The second shot missed the falling men but hit an unnamed black man on the opposite sidewalk.[1]

By the time the second shot had echoed down the street, a crowd had begun forming and further violence was avoided. John Strother was bruised and battered, but otherwise uninjured. He expressed surprise to those around him, claiming to have no idea why Kenan would want to kill him.

Lewis Kenan was arrested and subsequently posted a $2,500 bond, a significant sum for 1871. According to an article in the Milledgeville *Southern Recorder* which reported the incident, neither of the men's

A photo of downtown Milledgeville circa 1870s at the approximate time of the murder of Lewis Kenan. (Photo courtesy of Special Photo Collections, Georgia College & State University)

A view of Wayne Street in the 1870s. It was at the northeast corner of Wayne and Hancock Streets that John Strother began stalking Lewis Kenan moments before fatally wounding him. (Photo courtesy of Special Photo Collections, Georgia College & State University)

Another view of Wayne Street in downtown Milledgeville. (Photo courtesy of Special Photo Collections, Georgia College & State University)

friends knew why Kenan had fired at Strother but the same article also stated the men's friends were worried *"that another meeting between these gentlemen will result fatally to one..."*[2]

Judge Iverson L. Harris attempted to settle the matter by having both men sign an agreement stating *"that neither one, by word or deed, in any manner whatever, was to attempt to revive the hostilities."*[3] Kenan reportedly no longer carried any weapons, *"not even a knife,"* after signing Judge Harris's agreement for fear he would *"violate his honor."*[4]

However, less than two months later, on Monday July 3, 1871 around 7:00 p.m, Strother broke the agreement. According to a report of this incident, Lewis Kenan had started home after chatting with friends at Clark's Drug Store on the southeast corner of Wayne and Hancock Streets. Carrying an armload of packages he had walked west on the south side of Hancock Street. He was unaware that John Strother was watching him from the northeast corner of Wayne and Hancock Streets. Strother was in front of the Masonic Hall which still stands at that location today.

Walking along the north side of Hancock Street, Strother began following Kenan. As Strother passed a relative's house he ducked inside where he retrieved a carbine rifle.[5] As Kenan neared the corner of Clark and Hancock, he started to cross diagonally across Hancock Street. When Kenan had reached the middle of Hancock Street, Strother – now only about fifteen feet away – fired the carbine.

The round from the rifle hit Kenan in the back, entering just below the right shoulder blade, piercing his lungs and heart, exiting through his left armpit, and lodging in the wooden fence surrounding the Governor's Mansion. A witness, Mrs. C.W. Compton who was about 60 feet away, heard Lewis Kenan's last words, "John, I did not think you would treat me so," was all he was able to say.[6]

After the shooting John Strother left the scene immediately, and disappeared into the evening shadows of the south Georgia countryside. The county sheriff was unable to locate him. Friends and relatives vouched for his appearance at a trial, *"confident of his acquittal, as they regard the homicide perfectly justifiable."* [7] Strother, however, never appeared, and was nowhere to be found.

Georgia Governor James M. Smith, issued a proclamation offering a reward of $250 *"for the apprehension and delivery, to the Sheriff or Jailer of said county, the body of said Strother..."* [8] Despite the reward Strother was not apprehended and remained a fugitive from justice. He reportedly had departed Georgia, gaining help from several friends who amazingly shipped him by railroad – inside a crate – to relatives in Louisiana.[9] He never again returned to Georgia.

Relatives and friends and the authorities remained perplexed at the motives involved in the two shootings. What had caused emotions to boil over into a tempest of gunplay?

Both Kenan and Strother were active in Milledgeville politics and society but the Kenan family was known all over Georgia. Local newspaper accounts from reporters and eyewitnesses provide clues to the events and possible motives leading to the fatal July 3rd shooting. What emerges is a vivid personal picture of the complicated web of allegiances and relationships in Reconstruction Georgia.

When Kenan had reached the middle of Hancock Street, Strother – now only about fifteen feet away – fired the carbine.

Lewis Holmes Kenan, born January 18, 1833, was the son of Henrietta Alston and Augustus Holmes Kenan. The elder Kenan was one of the state's most prominent lawyers and politicians of that day. He had served in the Seminole and Creek Indian Wars and represented Baldwin County in both the House and Senate in the Georgia State Legislature. Augustus, however, was a firm Unionist, voting against secession thirteen times. Despite this initial loyalty to the Union, Augustus supported the Confederacy after the secession ordinance was passed, but when he signed the final draft of the ordinance, he immediately threw the pen away in obvious disgust. He was one of the nine Georgia delegates to travel to Montgomery, Alabama, to draft a Confederate constitution, and he served in the Confederate Congress.[10]

Lewis Kenan followed in his father's footsteps as both a lawyer and military man. The younger Kenan served as the elected captain of Company I of the 1st Georgia Regulars and was wounded at John's Island, South Carolina.[11] His political career included terms as Milledgeville's mayor, state senator, and secretary of the Georgia Senate.[12]

Less is known about John Strother – born on May 18, 1834 – and his family. He had served in the Confederate Army, and had even seen stints as Milledgeville's sheriff, tax collector of Baldwin County, and town alderman.[13] He was tall – almost six

The governor's mansion in Milledgeville, photographed in 1877, shows the picket fence in which the bullet that killed Lewis Kenan was embedded. (Photo courtesy of Special Photo Collections, Georgia College & State University)

The shooting scene was photographed above in 2002. This view was photographed from the point at which Strother was standing when he fired at Kenan in the middle of what then was a dusty dirt street. The old governor's mansion is visible in the background. (Photo by Hugh T. Harrington)

feet – and about 150 pounds in weight, with hazel eyes and light brown hair. He also was a man who was acquainted with violence.[14]

Elected as sheriff of Baldwin County in January of 1866, he shot and killed a man named W.A. Roberson on the streets of Milledgeville on March 24 of 1866 *"as the result of some private misunderstanding."* [15] As the shooting was not done under the auspices of his duties as sheriff, Strother resigned his position. Whether this was done voluntarily or under duress is unknown today. A special election was held on June 6th to obtain a new sheriff, and Obadiah Arnold – Strother's brother in law – won the post.

Sheriff Arnold, fortunately, was not forced to face the unpleasant task of arresting Strother, since the fugitive had fled Milledgeville. On June 2, Governor Charles J. Jenkins issued a proclamation offering a reward of $200 for the apprehension of Strother.[16]

Surprisingly, Strother reappeared in Baldwin County some years later, and apparently was not arrested or indicted for the Roberson shooting. It is unclear today how the former sheriff was able to obtain exoneration for Roberson's death.

In 1869 Strother was listed among those Confederate veterans who were relieved of liability for their actions during the War Between The States.[17] His return to Baldwin County seems to coincide with the establishment of the Radical Reconstruction Government in Georgia.

The first inklings of trouble between Kenan and Strother came in 1866. Interestingly, in an anonymous letter written by a "well known" person of high standing in Milledgeville to the *American Union* on July 27, 1871, both men were described as having *"unlawful loves."*[18]

Kenan married Sarah Davidson –

called "Sallie" – on September 30, 1858, but apparently also had an interest in a woman named Liz Willis. Strother reportedly made an insulting comment about Willis and the two men launched into a fistfight over the words.[19] Bystanders soon broke up the fight, but the embers of anger apparently continued to smolder.[20]

In the Old South, honor and pride were central to the Southern psyche and in the years following the War Between The States, Southerners clung to the traditions of the South tenaciously. They had lost everything else. The Reconstruction Period was an extremely bitter time for the South. Voting rights were temporarily denied; an entire way of life and means of livelihood was eliminated; property taxes were raised; and an entire culture was forced to struggle for survival. One's honor and dignity were extremely difficult to maintain during this period, and many times, the circumstances degenerated to violence.

Duels often occurred over words uttered in anger. The offended party had to counter or risk being labeled a coward.[21] Kenan had already defended his honor once in a duel, and it is quite possible that he demanded satisfaction from Strother following Strother's unflattering comments about the female, Willis.[22]

According to the letter written July 27, 1871 to the *American Union*, the day after Kenan fired on Strother with the shotgun, he (Kenan) told Drs. Hertz and Case that he *"had tried to get Strother to fight him time and again, and Strother would not fight him, and he got so damned mad that he intended to have satisfaction anyhow."*[23]

Strother's "unlawful love" is never named. Today, one can only speculate on his female acquaintances. However, there are some fairly obvious possibilities.

One possibility was Sarah Barnes Kenan, whom Strother married. Augustus

Masonic Hall on the northeast corner of Wayne and Hancock streets was the site at which John Strother was standing when he began following Lewis Kenan just prior to killing him. (Photo by Hugh T. Harrington)

The comfortable home built in the 1800s by Augustus Holmes Kenan, father of Lewis Kenan, still stands in Milledgeville. Following the death of Augustus Kenan, this domicile became the home of his widow, Sarah Barnes Kenan, who later married John Strother. Strother then took up quarters in this home. (Photo by Hugh T. Harrington)

Kenan's marriage to Sarah Barnes was his second. Augustus's first wife and Lewis's mother was Henrietta Alston, whom Augustus had married June 19, 1828, and then subsequently divorced.[24] Augustus remarried August 30, 1864 at age fifty-nine to nineteen-year-old Sarah Barnes.

Augustus and Sarah remain married until Augustus died June 2, 1870. Less than a year later Sarah Barnes Kenan was married to John Strother in a ceremony held in her house. Lewis Kenan apparently did not attend the marriage, and it was not reported in the area newspapers.[25] Could Sarah Barnes – while she was still married to the elder Kenan – have been Strother's "unlawful love"? If Strother had fostered a relationship with Sarah while she was married to Augustus Kenan – and if Lewis had known of this clandestine relationship – it surely could have contributed to an already tense situation.

Evidence also points to another area of difficulty between the two men – politics. As Strother was relieved of liability for his Confederate service, he became involved with the Radical Republicans. In order for former Confederates to re-obtain the right to vote and hold public office, they were required to swear allegiance to the Union. Strother apparently did swear this allegiance, but Kenan's name, does not appear on the list.

Kenan, on the other hand, represented the Old South. The *Federal Union* reported that Kenan *"was possessed of many of the qualities of his late lamented and gifted father, Col. A.H. Kenan – Nature and education had lavished their gifts upon him, making him a most genial and fascinating companion and accomplished gentleman. Warm-hearted, fearless, an unflinching supporter of what he thought right – impatient of opposition, jealous of his honor, quick to resent an injury, but magnanimous and forgiving – a true friend, a dangerous foe – a genuine type of Southern chivalry and the spirit of the age."*[26] His funeral attracted a large crowd as *"business was very generally suspended and the people turned out en masse."*[27]

The *Federal Union* in covering Kenan's funeral, gives a clue to the nature of the conflict between Kenan and Strother. While saying that *"without expressing any opinion as to the unfortunate difficulty which resulted in his death,"* the editor continues with a very strong denunciation of *"the growing tendency of the age among our people to right their wrongs with their own right arms instead of appeal to the law."* The article includes the interesting statement, *"we appeal to our young men and old men and ESPECIALLY TO OUR WOMEN (boldface added) in the future, to discourage, by every means in their power, the too common disposition to trample under foot the laws of God and man."*[28]

> *Strother's "unlawful love" is never named. Today, one can only speculate on his female acquaintances.*

One integral aspect of the murder of Lewis Kenan – particularly as involves the suggestions from anonymous letter writers about "unlawful loves" – is the unusual 40-year difference in age between Augustus Holmes Kenan and his young wife, Sarah. Sarah became the wife of John Strother less than six weeks before Strother killed Kenan.

In its comments,

the *Federal Union* article seems to be urging restraint – especially among the women of that era – in an effort to stop the violence as if it were known locally that a particular woman was either not using restraint on Strother or was even encouraging him toward violence.

Interestingly, on October 27, 1874 Sarah Kenan, age 30, the young widow of Augustus Holmes Kenan and wife of John Strother, reportedly died. Her death is not mentioned in the newspapers. The report of the sexton of the city cemetery lists her as *"Mrs. Sarah Kenan."* The cause of death portion of the report was left blank. It is unknown today if she died a violent death, or was claimed by disease or some happenstance injury.[29]

As fate would have it, John R. Strother did meet a violent death. Since he was a fugitive from justice, he always carried a rifle, but that didn't help him on an autumn day in November of 1888. As he was riding down the road on that fateful day in Claiborne Parish, Louisiana, he was ambushed and shot from his horse. After he had fallen from his mount, he was shot again in the top of the head with buckshot. Someone wanted to – and did – make an example of him.[30]

According to family tradition, "Long John" Strother, as he was called, was a ladies man and felt superior to most people in the Louisiana community in which he was then residing. He was hated by some and feared by many.

Strother apparently had insulted yet another local man's honor, taunting him and boasting that the unborn baby the man's wife was carrying was actually the product of a union between the man's wife and himself (Strother). A few days later this outraged husband and several other men ended Strother's days on earth forever.

ENDNOTES

1/ *Southern Recorder*, 16 May, 1871.
2/ *Southern Recorder*, 16 May, 1871.
3/ *Southern Recorder*, 11 July, 1871.
4/ *Southern Recorder*, 11 July, 1871.
5/ A carbine is a short, lightweight rifle.
6/ *Southern Recorder*, 11 July, 1871, and *Macon Telegraph & Messenger*, 9 July, 1871.
7/ *Southern Recorder*, 11 July, 1871.
8/ *Southern Recorder*, 23 April, 1872.
9/ Correspondence from relative, Edward L. Strother, to the authors dated 20 February, 2002.
10/ *Federal Union, 7 June, 1870 and Register, Alvaretta Kenan, The Kenan Family* (self-published, 1967) p. 99.
11/ Henderson, Lillian, *Roster of Confederate Soldiers of Georgia, 1861-1865* (Hapeville, GA, Longina & Porter, 1964.)
12/ *Federal Union*, 12 July, 1871.
13/ *American Union*, 27 July, 1871, *Union Recorder*, 6 December, 1870, and *Union Recorder*, 24 April, 1866.
14/ *Southern Recorder*, 5 June, 1866.
15/ *Southern Recorder*, 10 April, 1866.
16/ *Southern Recorder*, 6 June, 1866.
17/ *Southern Recorder*, 21 December, 1869.
18/ *American Union*, 6 July, 1871.
19/ *American Union*, 27 July, 1871.
20/ *American Union*, 27 July, 1871 and Bonner, James C., *Milledgeville, Georgia's Antebellum Capital.* (Athens: UGA Press, 1978) pp 211-212.
21/ Bertram Wyatt-Brown. *Honor and Violence In The Old South* (New York: Oxford University Press, 1986): 149-153.
22/ Seawright, "Ghost Fry."
23/ *American Union*, 27 July, 1871.
24/ The Kenan Family
25/ Harrington, Hugh T., editor, *Methodist Church Record Books, Milledgeville, Georgia, 1811-1876*, Milledgeville, Boyd Publishing, 1997, p. 158.
26/ *Federal Union*, 12 July, 1871.
27/ *Federal Union*, 12 July, 1871.
28/ *Federal Union*, 12 July, 1871.
29/ Harrington, Hugh T. and Susan J. Harrington, ed. *The Dead Book: Burials In The City Cemetery, Milledgeville, Georgia, 1869-1904*, (Milledgeville, GA, Boyd Publishing Co, 1998) p 90.
30/ *Union Recorder*, 25 December, 1888.

The Finney-Stanley Shooting

An incident of arrogant bullying led to a rash response which scarred two Milledgeville families for over half a century.

Hancock Street in downtown Milledgeville was the scene of a hailstorm of bullets Saturday afternoon November 19, 1898. One man was left dead on the sidewalk and five others were wounded. The cause of the gunfight, as is often the case, proved to be nothing more than arrogance and wounded pride.[1]

According to an account of the incident, the trouble began about noon at the restaurant of 18-year-old Thomas Finney. Bill Stanley, 30, accompanied by his 24-year-old brother, Julian, was not satisfied with his food. The two had eaten soup, broiled steak, pork, sausage and coffee, as well as light bread and biscuits.

After he had finished his meal, Bill Stanley said he had been served only half a dinner. Thomas Finney told Stanley that he had been served exactly what he ordered. Bill Stanley responded by telling Finney it was a "damned lie."

Young Thomas Finney tried to explain and reportedly offered to give the Stanleys anything else they wanted. Bill Stanley, however, further complicated the incident by calling Finney "a son of a bitch," and then slapping him in the face. The Stanleys then left the restaurant.

Thomas Finney, angry and humiliated, put a .32 caliber Iver Johnson pistol in his pocket and reportedly announced "if he slaps me again I will kill him." Finney then went across the street to the wheelwright shop of his father, W.O. "Bill" Finney.

Upon hearing the story, Bill Finney went out onto Wayne Street and located policeman Lawrence whom he brought back to the restaurant so that the younger Finney could repeat his story to the lawman. Bill Finney then demanded the arrest of Bill Stanley.

As a result of the complaint, Stanley was indeed arrested. He subsequently posted bond for his appearance before the mayor on Monday morning. Policeman Lawrence then reported to Bill Finney that he had arrested Stanley in the hope that it would calm the Finneys' hot tempers.

An arrest, however, apparently was not good enough for the Finneys. Bill Finney was extremely angry, saying that Stanley "had cursed his son and had to apologize or one of them would have to die."

The Finneys then began a search for the Stanleys, walking up and down crowded Hancock Street. In front of the store of L.H. Thomas, just west of the intersection of Hancock and Wayne streets, the Finneys suddenly saw their antagonizers coming toward them.

Bill Finney wasted no time. He walked straight up to Bill Stanley and announced, "You called my boy a son of a bitch," and then quickly shot Stanley once in the chest with a .38 Iver Johnson revolver.

Severely wounded, Bill Stanley grabbed Finney's arm while pulling his own revolver, a .38 Smith & Wesson, and fired six shots at Bill Finney, mortally wounding him.

Standing nearby, Thomas Finney immediately fired four shots from his .32 Iver Johnson at the Stanleys. His fire was met by only one shot from Julian Stanley's

.32 Smith & Wesson.

Policemen Lawrence and Terry were on the scene immediately. After order was restored, the two officers found that all the participants in the incident were wounded and one was dying.

Bill Finney was lying on the sidewalk leaking his lifeblood onto the concrete. Upon seeing the policemen, Bill Stanley came out of a store with his empty pistol still in his hand. Julian Stanley was inside the store bleeding from a wound to his face.

Thomas Finney was shot in the leg and side. Two stray bullets had struck a black man and a black woman inflicting minor wounds.

The body of Bill Finney was taken to his home on South Wayne Street. Thomas Finney was taken to Carrington's Drug Store on the southwest corner of Wayne and Hancock streets where his wounds were treated.

The Stanleys were initially treated at the store of L.H. Thomas on Hancock Street and later were taken to the Harper House Hotel where they remained for several days, recovering from their wounds.

The day following the shooting, a coroner's jury investigated the incident. After hearing the evidence, they brought the following verdict:

"That W.O. "Bill" Finney came to his death from pistol wounds inflicted by W.B. "Bill" Stanley, and that Stanley killed Finney in self defense."

Bill Stanley's chest wound healed, but the bullet within him ultimately ended his life anyway. During his treatment, the bullet was never located in Stanley's body and therefore never extracted. Stanley later survived a bout of typhoid fever during the summer of 1899, but sometime in late December of that same year, the elusive bullet in his chest brought on a case of blood poisoning which Stanley's body could not overcome. He died on January 2, 1900,[2] and was buried at Salem Baptist Church Cemetery.[3]

Bill Finney is buried in Milledgeville's Memory Hill Cemetery. He is in East side, Section A, Lot 18, Grave #1.[4] A few graves away, in the same lot, is his son, Thomas, who died October 14, 1961, almost 63 years after the shooting.

GUNFIGHT SCENE FROM YESTERYEAR –The southwest corner of Hancock and Wayne streets in Milledgeville as it appears today. The Finney-Stanley gunfight took place where the newspaper boxes are located. In 1898, the building on the corner was Carrington's Drug Store where Thomas Finney was taken for treatment of his wounds following the shooting. (Photo by Hugh T. Harrington)

Julian Stanley is also buried in Memory Hill Cemetery. He is in East side, Section D, Lot 85, Grave #1.[5] The grave of Julian Stanley is within sight of the graves of the Finneys.

The simple disagreement over a lunch and the subsequent wounded honor cost two men their lives and caused serious injuries to two others, not to mention the infliction of wounds on two innocent bystanders. The families, both highly respectable, lived with the consequences of that fateful day for over sixty years until the last of the participants found peace in death.

ENDNOTES

1/ *Union Recorder*, November 22, 1898.
2/ *Union Recorder*, January 9, 1900.
3/ Salem Baptist Church, 8.4 miles west of Baldwin County Courthouse on Route 49, south on Salem Church Road .3 of a mile.
4/ Harrington, Susan J., Hugh T. Harrington, Floride Moore Gardner, eds., *Historic Memory Hill Cemetery, Milledgeville, Georgia, 1804-1997*, Milledgeville, Boyd Publishing Co., 1998.
5/ Harrington, Susan J., Hugh T. Harrington, Floride Moore Gardner, eds., *Historic Memory Hill Cemetery, Milledgeville, Georgia, 1804-1997*, Milledgeville, Boyd Publishing Co., 1998.

The Killing Spree Of Marion Stembridge

A half century ago, a businessman in this small mid-Georgia town shocked the state with a bizarre series of murders.

Saturday, May 2, 1953 was the day all Milledgeville had eagerly awaited. The town was poised to celebrate its sesquicentennial marking the city's founding in 1803 as Georgia's capital. Red, white and blue bunting draped the buildings of the downtown like Spanish moss. Many men and women walked about in the fashions of the 1800s, some of the men wearing full beards and carrying makeshift muskets in which they were setting off firecrackers. A parade was on tap for the afternoon, with a grand ball to follow that evening. A full slate of parties, picnics and pageants had been arranged for all the next week, one day of which would include an appearance by Governor Herman Talmadge. Little did all these participants know that they were about to receive the shock of a lifetime.[1]

At a little after 10 a.m., Milledgeville resident and businessman Marion Stembridge walked past those lined up to see the western, *Dead Man's Trail* at the Campus Theater on Hancock Street, the town's main thoroughfare. He started up the stairs leading to the suite of offices above the theater. The 61-year-old banker and grocer appeared as he always did, wearing a neatly-pressed suit and a soft felt wide-brimmed hat pulled down low over his eyes. As usual, he was stone-faced, unsmiling, peering out at the world through thick glasses that distorted his eyes and gave him a look described as "cold and crazy."[2]

Crazy indeed was how most Milledgevillians would have described Marion Stembridge. Over the past five years – if the stories circulating about his peculiar lifestyle were true – his status had degenerated from merely eccentric to almost certainly insane.

Crazy indeed was how most Milledgevillians would have described Marion Stembridge.

Stembridge's so-called banking enterprise was nothing more than a loan-sharking operation, and he was well-known for a mean streak as wide as a country mile. He had been convicted of manslaughter four years earlier in an incident stemming from his loan-sharking, but had mysteriously avoided serving any time in jail.

Just the previous Monday in federal court in Macon, Stembridge had been convicted of tax evasion and attempting to bribe federal agents. An account in the Milledgeville *Union-Recorder* that week had reported all the seamy details, as well as the fact that Stembridge was to report to court the following Monday for sentencing. This situation apparently put Marion Stembridge "over the edge," sending him spiraling downward into the vortex of depravity and precipitating the horrible crime which was about to occur on this happy day of celebration.[3]

With his insane task partially completed in the offices above The Campus Theater, Stembridge hurried back out into the street. A six-year-old youngster waiting with his mother told her excitedly "That man has a gun." The woman assured her young charge that the pistol in the man's hand was just a toy, like the muskets the other men were carrying, but she was uneasy nonetheless.

Meanwhile, Stembridge hurried by the two and ran up the steps of the Sanford Building next door to the theater. Some he passed later recalled that he tipped his hat politely as he went by. A few moments later, a woman shouted hysterically from a window above the theater that attorney Marion Ennis had been shot.[4]

Soon thereafter, city police, the county sheriff and his deputies began to converge on the downtown, sirens blaring. Rumors of what had happened spread like wildfire in dry grass and the streets filled with people. Local historian Louis Andrews remembered one man riding up and down Hancock Street in his car, tires squealing, horn blowing, trying to alert everyone about the shooting.

The home once owned by Marion Stembridge still stands on Columbia Street in Milledgeville. (Photo by Ray Chandler)

The store/office building once owned by Marion Stembridge was photographed here circa 1950. Stembridge's name can faintly be read on the signage above the front door.

A view of downtown Milledgeville taken in 2002 looking toward the scene of the Stembridge murders. (Photo by Ray Chandler)

In 1953, the building which today houses Ryals Bakery on Wayne Street in Milledgeville was owned by Marion Stembridge and was the site at which he no doubt planned the murders of 1953. (Photo by Ray Chandler)

Marion Stembridge murdered Marion Ennis in his law offices above the Campus Theater on Hancock Street. This building, photographed here in 2003, still stands as of this writing. (Photo by Ray Chandler)

The county courthouse stands next to the old Campus Theater building. In 1953, the Sanford Building in which attorney Pete Bivens' offices were located stood on this site. Bivens was Stembridge's second murder victim. (Photo by Ray Chandler)

"He was so excited he couldn't even talk," Andrews recalled. Streets near the scene quickly became so congested that people had to park blocks away and walk into the downtown area. "It was one terrible morning," Andrews added.[5]

Responding To Gunfire

Eugene Ellis, active and razor-sharp at 89, was the Milledgeville police chief in 1953, and for him, the events of that morning 50 years ago are as crystal clear as any he can recall from a lifetime of law enforcement.

"I got a call that there had been a shooting at the Campus Theater," Ellis explained in a recent interview. "When I got there, Sheriff Dennis Cox told me that Marion Stembridge had killed Marion Ennis in his law office and had gone into the Sanford Building.

Responding to the situation, the officers started up the stairs of the Sanford Building. Ellis advised Cox that if they rushed up the stairs, they would be "sitting ducks," and he urged the men to proceed cautiously.

Halfway up the stairs, the men heard what sounded like a pop from a handgun. When Ellis crept near the top and peered up into the hallway leading off the stairs, he saw Stembridge lying facedown in front of the office of Judge Edwin Sibley. Ellis approached slowly, his gun drawn.

As he reached the prostrate Stembridge, Ellis saw a gun in the man's hand and thought the wily unpredictable Stembridge might be "playing possum," despite the blood pooling around his head. He put one foot on Stembridge's wrist and kicked the gun away with his other foot.

Stembridge, however, had been dead from the moment he hit the floor. Apparently, after hearing the approach of Ellis and Cox up the stairs and seeing no chance of escape, he had put the barrel of a

.38 caliber revolver into his mouth and pulled the trigger. Before killing himself, Stembridge – to the horror of Ellis and Cox – had committed a second murder, killing attorney Stephen "Pete" Bivens.

As Ellis knelt over Stembridge's body, he felt a hand on his shoulder. It was that of local state solicitor Shep Baldwin. "To this day," said Ellis, "I don't know how he got there. I don't remember hearing him walk up on me. He just said, 'It's over now, ain't it boy.'"[6]

The fears and troubles of those whose lives had unfortunately become entangled with that of Marion Stembridge were indeed over. Stembridge had ended all that with his suicide, but not before also ending the lives of two of Milledgeville's most prominent citizens – two of many the crazed man apparently had intended to kill.

James Jossey, a retired captain from the Milledgeville Police Department and now (as of this writing) chief of detectives for the Baldwin County Sheriff's Department was 10 years old at the time of the murders, and was in a drugstore down the street that morning looking at comic books after his weekly haircut. "I remember seein' 'em bring Ennis's and Bivens's bodies out," he said. "They were covered in sheets, but the sheets looked like somebody had dumped a bucket of blood over 'em. Those were the first murdered people I ever saw." [7]

Pete Dexter who had grown up in Milledgeville hearing stories about the terrible event ultimately immortalized the incident in a popular novel – *Paris Trout* – published in 1989. And then, in 1991, the terrible day was sensationalized once again in the movie version of the book, starring Dennis Hopper in the title role. Many in Milledgeville didn't take kindly to the movie or the book, looking upon them as the reopening of an old wound.

Stembridge's Earlier Life

Marion Wesley Stembridge was born in 1892 into a prominent and prosperous Baldwin County family. "They were nice people," said Eugene Ellis, "easy to get along with – all except for Marion."

Evidently, whatever shaped young Marion into what he later became had started early in his life, and even seemed to have been apparent to some of his family members. When Marion was 19, his older brother, Roger, and a sister attempted to have him committed to the state mental hospital in Milledgeville. Marion's mother, however, was opposed to the move, insisting that her son was completely normal.

For the rest of his life, Marion hated his brother for that act, and in fact, alienated himself from all his family except for his mother and two sisters. When his mother eventually went to live with Roger and his wife near the state hospital where Roger headed the sanitation department, Marion would often come to visit his mother, but refused to set foot in Roger's home. Instead, mother and son would talk through a side window. For a time, the widow Stembridge also apparently provided Marion with financial support – a benefit which he seemed to think was his due. As his sister-in-law later described him, "He thought he was the crown prince of the family."[8]

Whatever quirks the younger Marion Stembridge had exhibited, he was regarded as extremely intelligent, even "brilliant, bordering on genius." He was graduated from the University of Georgia School of Law, but never applied for admission to the Georgia Bar. He entered the Army during World War I, but was discharged for medical reasons. Years after his death, his sister-in-law revealed the belief within the family that whatever had happened to him in the Army had exacerbated whatever mental

Eugne Ellis was an officer with the Milledgeville Police Department in the autumn of 1948 when he arrested Marion Stembridge for manslaughter involving the death of Emma Johnekin. On New Year's Day in 1949, Ellis became chief of police in Milledgeville. Photographed here in 2003, he holds the strange suicide note left by Stembridge in his apartment prior to the murders of 1950. (Photo by Ray Chandler)

The gravesite of Marion Ennis at Memory Hill Cemetery in Milledgeville. Ennis was Stembridge's first murder victim on May 2, 1953. (Photo by Ray Chandler)

problems he may already have had. In the 1930s, Stembridge actually did voluntarily spend several months in a mental institution. He never revealed the reasons, not even to his family.[9]

In the 1920s, Stembridge started a mail order business that allowed him to amass capital reputed to be in the range of $160,000, a large sum for that day. In time, he parlayed that stake into a complex and varied array of financial interests. He came to own a mercantile and grocery store near downtown Milledgeville; a timber, pulpwood and lumber yard on the outskirts of town; several houses and parcels of real estate around town and out in the country; and his "banking" business.

The Stembridge Banking Company, a private unincorporated bank that Marion ran out of the rear of his store, most readily reflected his darker side to the community of Milledgeville. As later became clear, the bank was little more than a front for loansharking, an endeavor aimed primarily at the poorer members of the black community in town. Marion's tactics habitually included the use of written contracts that took advantage of the illiterate.

At the time of his death, Stembridge's fortune was estimated at approximately $750,000, with well over half of that in the assets of the bank. Marion's dealings in this business set in motion the course of events that ultimately led to the fateful Saturday that Milledgeville has never forgotten.[10]

The Dark Side Of Marion

During his years as a businessman in Milledgeville, the residents in the community came to know several facets of Marion Stembridge. Those who dealt with him in his store or wood products businesses knew a hard-nosed businessman, reserved and decidedly uncongenial but always polite, with almost courtly manners. However, those who borrowed money from him found him to be a ruthless individual, one to be despised and feared.

"Marion just didn't have any small talk for anybody," was how former State Court Judge Robert Green described him. As a young lawyer and a county magistrate, Green came to know Stembridge during those years. He handled many routine legal matters (usually small claims court proceedings) for Stembridge, remembering the man's banking business as "just inside the law."[11]

Stembridge was also known to be armed on a regular basis. This was not especially unusual, except that Marion always carried several handguns. He habitually carried a German Army-issue 9mm Walther P-38 automatic in his coat pocket and, according to Eugene Ellis, at least two other handguns in a briefcase that he carried with him religiously.

As a result of his poor eyesight, Marion painted the sight blades of his guns white for easier aiming. Locals who previously had judged him to be harmless would come to a different verdict during the last five turbulent years of Stembridge's life, as his private quirks became more public and mounting legal problems brought to light his darkest side.[12]

In July of 1947, Stembridge surprised many Milledgevillians by marrying Sarah Jordan Terry, a one-time English teacher at the Women's College of Georgia (present-day Georgia College & State University). The new Mrs. Stembridge was described by many who knew her as "big and mean as sin." It was suspected that she would be a good match for the mercurial Marion.

The marriage however, apparently was far from a happy one, and when Sarah Stembridge filed for divorce in the spring of 1953, her allegations provided townspeople more of a glimpse at the odd private life and darker side of Marion Stembridge. This divorce suit also piled more troubles onto those already plaguing Marion at this time, and undoubtedly was a factor when he finally snapped mentally.[13]

Loan-Sharking Mayhem

Officer Eugene Ellis had joined the Milledgeville Police Department in 1946, fresh out of the Army where he had served in the military police at Camp Wheeler near Macon. He had served with and come to know many native Milledgevillians while there, and had decided to remain in Georgia rather than return to his native Maine where he had been a deputy sheriff. Ellis would become chief of the Milledgeville Police Department on New Year's Day, 1949.

The downfall of Marion Stembridge actually began in the fall of 1948, with an event that brought him into contact with Officer Ellis for the first time.

"That very day," Ellis recalled, I got a call that there had been a shooting at a house off South Wayne [Street], in the colored section near the creek. We drove out there and found two women had been shot. . . . And there stood Marion Stembridge and Sam Terry, and Terry had a gun in his hand."

Terry, the son of a former Baldwin County sheriff, had once been the county coroner. Since losing the coroner job, he had worked for Marion Stembridge as "muscle" to help with loan collections. Interestingly, Terry's brother had been Sarah Stembridge's first husband.[14]

After arriving at the scene, the Ellis and his partner discovered two women had been shot. One of them was deceased and the other was seriously wounded. The circumstances leading to the shooting remained murky even at Stembridge's ensuing trial.

According to records, Stembridge had loaned Richard Cooper $800 to buy a 1941 Chevrolet. Stembridge had tacked an additional $227 onto the loan, ostensibly to pay for insurance for the car. Cooper's mother, Emma Johnekin, and brother had co-signed the note.

According to the terms of the note, Cooper was to pay Stembridge $70 per month for 18 months, and the mother and brother were to pay an additional $15 monthly. After a couple of months, Cooper's car was severely damaged in an accident, and he approached Stembridge to have it repaired with the insurance. Stembridge, however, hadn't bothered to take out insurance and refused to repair Cooper's car.

In retaliation, Cooper ceased making payments on the car, and Stembridge repossessed the car and resold it. Then, despite the fact that he had repossessed and sold the car, Stembridge intended to continue collecting payments on the original loan. That day, he had driven out to confront Cooper about these payments, taking along Terry.

Cooper wasn't home, so Stembridge confronted the mother. He apparently threatened her with the seizure of her furniture and other property if the payments weren't continued immediately. In the ensuing argument, Stembridge reportedly pulled out his handgun and opened fire, hitting Emma Johnekin four times and her sister once. When he noticed Ellis approaching, Stembridge quickly handed the gun to Terry.

"I later asked Terry why he had taken it (the gun)," Ellis said. "He said 'With Marion, what would you have done?'"[15]

Even more surprising, Stembridge claimed Terry had shot the women, but Ellis's investigation gave the state solicitor, Shep Baldwin, reason to think otherwise. Both Stembridge and Terry, nevertheless, were indicted for murder. That brought Stembridge and Ellis head-to-head for the second time.

A Manslaughter Conviction

"When I walked into his office that day, he just looked at me," Ellis continued. "He had crazy eyes that could stare right through you, but I could always stare him down. . . . I told him, 'Mr. Stembridge, I've got a warrant for your arrest.' He said, 'Can I see the warrant?' When I showed it to him he pulled a gun out of his desk."

Almost taken off guard, Ellis leaped for Stembridge, wrestling the gun away and handcuffing him. He then hustled him off to jail.

"He was raising hell the whole time," Ellis added, "saying how his rights were being violated . . . Shep Baldwin later told me the biggest mistake I ever made was not killin' him right then and there when he pulled the gun."

Stembridge later was released on bond, and Ellis kept a sharp eye out for him. "I knew he hated my guts," Ellis continued. "Crazy as he was, from then on he always beared watchin'."[16]

Marion Stembridge went to trial in July, 1949, with Shep Baldwin prosecuting and Judge George Carpenter presiding. Marion Ennis defended Stembridge, having been persuaded to take the case by Roger Stembridge whose wife was Ennis's cousin.

Ennis, 42 at the time, was one of the most prominent attorneys and civic leaders in Milledgeville. Besides being a star in the courtroom, he was a former and future state legislator, considered a worthy successor to Milledgeville's renowned legislator Culver Kidd. He was so highly respected that he was even spoken of as a potential candidate for governor. Though his brother still was not speaking to him, Roger Stembridge had obtained one of the best legal representatives available in the state for Marion.

Due to the circumstances of this case, however, no lawyer in Georgia at that time would have been able to get Stembridge an acquittal. The evidence against him was simply too damning. The best Ennis and his co-counsels – Jimmy Watts and Frank Evans – could manage was to concede to a charge of voluntary manslaughter. Stembridge was convicted and sentenced to from one to three years in prison.

To say the least, Marion Stembridge was outraged. He appealed immediately, and dropped Ennis as his attorney. The appeals dragged on for three years and their finale would add yet another odd chapter to the strange saga of Marion Stembridge. Sam Terry, interestingly, disappeared before the court date and was never tried.[17]

The Pressure Mounts

Out on bond and awaiting his appeal, Marion Stembridge abandoned his wife after a bare two years of marriage. He apparently could not deal with both her and his mounting legal problems at the same time. As Sarah Stembridge later charged in her divorce filing, her husband had continued to pay part of the utilities on the house they shared, but she was forced to take a series of jobs – at the state mental hospital and later teaching in nearby towns – to survive. Marion, meanwhile, moved into the top floor of the Baldwin Hotel downtown in Milledgeville, where more facets of his eccentricity slowly began to bubble to the surface.

After he moved into the hotel, Marion felt his room needed additional security. He had the door fitted with no less than a dozen deadbolts and locks, and would not allow the maids to clean the room unless he was present.

Inside the room, Marion kept a large refrigerator which was padlocked. Rumors gradually spread – probably stemming from the maids – that he had put sheets of glass on the floor to guard against someone trying to electrocute him, and that he had put thin sheets of lead between the mattresses of his bed because he feared someone trying to kill him with x-rays.

Robert Green, Stembridge's sometime attorney, also then lived at the Baldwin Hotel which his brother, J.C. owned and managed. Green attested to one of Stembridge's minor oddities.

"Newspapers were five cents apiece down at the front desk," Green explained, "but Marion wanted his to be in his letterbox. If it wasn't, he would go up to his room and send down for one, always giving the bellhop 25 cents for it. . . . Marion always wanted things his way."[18]

The next round of trouble for Stembridge was a lawsuit that also stemmed from his loan-sharking. The owner of the local brickyard sent one of his workers to attorney Eva Sloan with the request that she look into the man's case. Sloan worked with Marion Ennis at the time, first as his secretary, and then, after passing the Bar, as his associate.

The brickyard worker apparently had borrowed $50 from Stembridge and after making payments for some time, had stopped. Stembridge had sued in small claims court to have the man's wages garnished. The man had never been served with court papers, but Stembridge insisted on going ahead with the garnishment.

To her surprise – or possibly not – Sloan discovered that as a result of the payments he had made, the man had already paid $550

Almost taken off guard, Ellis leaped for Stembridge, wrestling the gun away and handcuffing him.

on a $50 loan. She counter-sued on the man's behalf and won. Stembridge was ordered to pay back the full $500 plus court costs. It was another blow to Stembridge's dubious banking procedures, and put Eva Sloan on Marion's hit list.

To Stembridge, losing the case was more than enough reason to hate both Eva Sloan and Marion Ennis. Ennis had, by his association with Sloan, earned his second black mark in Stembridge's eyes. The first black mark had been earned when Stembridge held Ennis accountable for his conviction in the manslaughter case.[19]

Beating The System

In July of 1952, the U.S. Supreme Court rejected Stembridge's last appeal, and what followed continues to baffle Milledgevillians even today. On September 6, the obviously-deranged man traveled with two lawyers – Victor Davidson of Irwinton and George Jackson of Gray – to Wrightsville in Johnson County where, at high noon, Stembridge presented Sheriff Dewey Hall with papers assigning him to serve his sentence at that county's work camp. Under ordinary circumstances, Stembridge should have been assigned to the state penitentiary, but Sheriff Hall found that the Georgia Department of Corrections had indeed sent Stembridge's paperwork to Johnson County.

Immediately after Stembridge surrendered to Hall, Stembridge's lawyers filed a request with Johnson County Superior Court Judge Roy Rowland stipulating Stembridge be released on grounds of *habeas corpus*, charging the testimony that convicted him was perjured. The judge set the hearing for 2:00 p.m. and the five men – Stembridge, his lawyers, the sheriff, and the judge – went to lunch, together. At 2:00 p.m., Judge Rowland granted *habeas corpus* and Marion Stembridge, amazingly, was released as a free man.

After Stembridge's death, the circumstances of this strange case provoked an inconclusive investigation by the Georgia Bar Association and various committees of the Georgia State Legislature which pronounced the strange release to be "unheard-of before in Georgia." To some Milledgevillians, the release seemed to indicate the awesome degree to which Stembridge could use his wealth to buy influence at high levels. "I don't think they ever figured out how he did it," said Eugene Ellis. Stembridge seemed to be a man who could get away with anything – even murder, or so he thought.[20]

That arrogance, by whatever means motivated, was the springboard for Stembridge's next round of problems. By late 1952, his various dealings had attracted the attention of the Internal Revenue Service. IRS investigators determined that Stembridge had not filed tax returns some years, and when he had filed, he had substantially underreported his income. In late December, IRS agents Julian Odum and Yancey Edwards approached Stembridge in his store and informed him he was to be charged with tax evasion.

According to their later testimony at his trial, the two men said Stembridge offered them $10,000 to make the problems disappear. The officers told Stembridge they would consider the matter and give him a response later. On January 6, 1953, the two men returned and told Stembridge they had mulled it over and would cover up his evasion for $10,000 each. Stembridge claimed he didn't have that kind of money, but when the men appeared to be leaving, he went into the back of the store and came out with $20,000 in two stacks.

Unfortunately for Stembridge, the two men were wearing microphones. He had charged headlong into their sting operation. He was arrested for tax evasion and attempted bribery. His trial was set for the April term of federal court in Macon.[21]

Marked For Death

In the midst of all his other legal problems, Marion Stembridge was sued for divorce. Sarah had engaged a law firm in a neighboring town to handle her case, but the firm had hired Milledgeville attorney Stephen "Pete" Bivens to handle the case.

Bivens, 27, was a star graduate of Milledgeville's Georgia Military College and of Cornell University. He was widely regarded as one of the city's rising leaders. He was familiar with Marion since he had taken a case for a client contesting one of Stembridge's mortgage foreclosures. Stembridge had evidently sworn a false oath in the course of filing the foreclosure and Bivens had pressed for an indictment for perjury. As a result of his handling the divorce proceedings for Sarah Stembridge, Marion now had a second reason to hate Bivens. The young attorney had now also become marked for death.

According to Judge Green, at least four attorneys in Milledgeville had warned Bivens to "go easy on Stem" because he was unstable. Bivens's answer in each case was that he carried a Colts .45 in his pocket and wasn't worried about Marion Stembridge.[22]

In April, Marion Stembridge went on trial in Macon's federal court for the tax evasion and bribery charges. During the proceedings, Stembridge loudly denounced the "courthouse crowd" in Milledgeville, claiming they were "all against him" and responsible for his troubles. On Monday, April 27, a jury deliberated only 50 minutes before convicting Stembridge on both charges. Judge A.B. Conger gave him one week to get his affairs in order and ordered him to report the following Monday, May 4, for sentencing.

Stembridge filed his own appeal for the two convictions, and then, according to Judge Green, "holed up in his room for three days." On Friday, May 1, he mailed two large bound and locked suitcases to a sister in Washington, D.C. He also made several unannounced visits to Marion Ennis's office, but Ennis was away in Macon on a trip to promote Milledgeville's sesquicentennial celebration, set to begin the next day.[23]

Aside from Ennis, Sloan and Bivens, Marion Stembridge apparently had marked several other people for death as well. On that last morning, before he went up to Marion Ennis' office, he borrowed the car of a woman who sometimes worked as his secretary. He drove first out of Milledgeville to the home of Shep Baldwin who had prosecuted him when he was convicted of manslaughter in 1949.

When Stembridge drove up to Baldwin's home, Shep was inside watching television. He saw Stembridge drive into the yard. The businessman had paused, but never emerged from the car. A short time later, he simply drove away. Interestingly, Baldwin's wife had driven his car into town that morning, and Baldwin later realized that Stembridge, not seeing the car in the yard, must have assumed Baldwin was not at home. Shep Baldwin was a lucky man.

Stembridge returned to town and parked in the lot at the Piggly Wiggly grocery across from the courthouse and behind the Sanford Building. He left the car's door open and the engine running, possibly in readiness for a quick getaway. He next walked to the courthouse where some later recalled he looked at the closed windows of the office of Judge George Carpenter who was the presiding judge when Marion was convicted of manslaughter.

Probably assuming the closed windows

of the judge's quarters meant he was not in his office, Marion again departed with his mission unaccomplished. Judge Carpenter later revealed that on several occasions prior to that morning, he had received anonymous telephoned death threats and he suspected they had come from Marion Stembridge.[24]

Stembridge next went to the office of J.C. Cooper, clerk of the superior court who had handled all the paperwork for the many legal proceedings against him. Cooper was in. When Marion entered the office, Cooper looked up from his desk and said, "Hello Mr. Stembridge." Marion reportedly focused his baleful stare upon Cooper, but said nothing. He simply propped open the door and left. Cooper later suspected – probably correctly – that Stembridge had marked him for death too, but evidently had pegged him as a lower priority than his other intended victims.[25]

Two Tragic Victims

Marion Ennis and Eva Sloan, to their misfortune, were in their offices that morning too, and they were very high on Stembridge's hit list. However, while Ennis took a telephone call, Sloan stepped up the hall to the office of attorney Lee Parttiss. This completely random act quite probably saved her life.

Ms. Sloan, coincidentally, was discussing Marion Stembridge's conviction of five days earlier, when Parttiss suddenly put his finger to his lips, instructing her to be quiet. He had just seen Stembridge walk down the hall toward Ennis's office.

Suddenly and without warning, several loud pops were heard in Ennis's office. Surprisingly, neither Eva Sloan or Lee Parttiss were surprised. They both simply thought the noise was the sound of firecrackers being set off in some of the toy muskets in the streets below. Meanwhile, Marion Stembridge, his killing spree just begun, apparently did not notice Eva in Parttiss' office, and quickly departed the scene.

When she walked back down to Ennis's office, Eva Sloan in no way expected what she found. There, lying on his stomach, Marion Ennis was bleeding and dying. He had been shot three times. As the coroner's inquest would later show, Stembridge's first bullet had hit Ennis in his shoulder. The second had ripped through his stomach. After Ennis had collapsed on the floor, Stembridge then had stood over him and fired another .45 caliber slug at point-blank range into his back.

The panicked Sloan knelt over the dying Ennis. He raised his head and tried to speak, but blood gushed from his mouth. He died grasping Sloan's arm. She had to pry his hand loose in order to rise. Everyone in the office suites was alerted now. A woman screamed to the street below that Ennis had been shot. A chiropractor later reported seeing Stembridge run by his office toward the stairs.[26]

The panicked Sloan knelt over the dying Ennis. He raised his head and tried to speak, but blood gushed from his mouth.

Robert Green saw Stembridge soon after his sometime client had entered the Sanford Building. A woman had walked into Green's office looking for the chiropractor's office and Green was directing her to the offices above the Campus Theater when he saw Stembridge outside his door. Green thought that was odd. Stembridge had never come to his office before, always sending the paperwork when he had work for Green. Stembridge, however, walked on past without so much as even a glance. Pete Bivens's office was down the hall. Unbeknownst to Green, Pete Bivens was Stembridge's objective.[27]

When Stembridge entered Bivens's office, the attorney was dictating a letter to his secretary, Jean Stockum. According to Stockum's later testimony to the coroner's jury, when Bivens saw the deranged man, he offered a courteous "Good morning Mr. Stembridge. What can I do for you?"

Without a word, Stembridge opened fire on the hapless attorney. In the hail of bullets, Bivens rose and started for Stembridge but the crazed man held his ground and continued firing. He emptied his .45 automatic at Bivens, hitting him four times in the chest.

When Bivens reached Stembridge, the murderer was frantically trying to slam another magazine into his weapon. Though quickly dying, Bivens somehow managed to wrest the handgun and ammunition from Stembridge, but slumped to the floor after reaching the hallway, the gun pinned beneath him. Stembridge then hurried out of Bivens's office toward the stairs leading down to the back door.[28]

Meanwhile, Robert Green and his accidental visitor had heard the gunshots and Stockum's screams. Green's visitor became hysterical and Green shoved her under his desk and began telephoning the police and an ambulance. In an instant, he had correctly sized up the situation. Then, Green heard another gunshot. He did not know it at the time, but that loud report had ended the life of one Marion Stembridge.

When it seemed the gunfire was over, Green entered the hallway. He first saw Bivens lying face-down with a local doctor kneeling over him. Green was met by Deputy Sheriff Buford Lingo, who told him what had happened and that he should take the woman downstairs.[29]

From the time Marion Stembridge had walked up the stairs of the Campus Theater building, the whole terrible murderous scenario had played out in less than 20 minutes. For Police Chief Eugene Ellis, however, the end of the shooting was only the beginning of the horrible crime.

A Descent Into Madness

Ellis was responsible for getting to the bottom of what had just happened. One of the places on which he focused his attention was Stembridge's room at the Baldwin Hotel. After managing to get beyond the Fort Knox of locks on the door, Ellis found the room as the many rumors had described it. He found more too.

In each corner of the room were loaded guns and ammunition. On the nightstand beside Stembridge's bed was a *Bible* and – something that gives Ellis an ironic chuckle even to this day. It was a copy of the book *How To Win Friends and Influence People.*

It wasn't until Ellis went to Stembridge's office, however, that he actually began piecing together the puzzle. On the man's desk he found a handwritten suicide note:

To whom it may concern:

I just do not care to be sentenced for another crime I did not commit. In this connection, I will not be able to do my full duty. I can only do the best that I can.

Marion W. Stembridge

I was convicted by tampering with the jury.

What Stembridge evidently saw as his "duty" was the attempt to kill as many of his perceived tormentors as he could before he met his own end. Certainly he wanted to kill Ennis and Bivens, and Eva Sloan lived only because she had momentarily accidentally eluded the killer.

The exact number of other people Stembridge wanted to kill is unknown today. Shep Baldwin and Judge Carpenter almost certainly were on the list. Cooper possibly was on the list too, perhaps Sarah Stembridge and maybe even Eugene Ellis.

"He would have killed me if he could," Ellis said. "He hated me enough."

One clue to Stembridge's full plan may be the fact that when his body was discovered, he had eight spare magazines for his .45 in his pockets, plus the .38 revolver. Over the weeks that followed, a rumor circulating around Milledgeville maintained that Stembridge had a "death list" naming those he planned to kill, but according to Ellis, no such list was ever found.

Despite the fact that he had left his car running, Stembridge clearly never thought he could run very far or for very long. Coupled with his previous visits to Ennis's office, the Friday date on the suicide note indicates he likely had intended to carry out the murders the previous day.[30]

The parade scheduled for that Saturday afternoon was canceled, but the grand ball went on as planned. Both Ennis and Bivens had been on the sesquicentennial planning committee and their families agreed both men would have wanted the revelries to go on. The full week of festivities were observed as scheduled, interrupted only by the three funerals.

The funeral service for Marion Stembridge was sparsely attended. According to Eva Sloan, the murders were little discussed during the sesquicentennial because "everyone was trying hard to make the celebration perfect." Dealing with the tragedy could come afterward.[31]

Part of dealing with it all was the cleaning up of the details, which included pulling the final wrappings off Marion Stembridge's life. In Stembridge's store, Ellis and others found five locked safes. Locksmiths were called in to crack the safes. Fearing that they might be booby-trapped, Ellis and Dennis Cox blocked off the downtown streets as a precaution.

When the safes were opened, some of them contained jars and jugs of urine bearing Stembridge's name and dates, and instructions that if he should die, the samples were to be tested for poisons. Rusty nails and parts of guns were found in some of the other safes. Milledgeville jeweler John W. Grant opened one safe and found an M-1 carbine rifle inside.

What was not found was Stembridge's money. Later, townspeople speculated that what cash Stembridge had packed away he had mailed to his sister in the two locked suitcases. This, however, was never confirmed.[32]

A few days after the killings, J.C. Green, owner of the Baldwin Hotel, delivered to his brother Robert a letter posted from Stembridge which Stembridge had instructed be delivered to his relatives. According to Robert Green, J.C. Green was one of the few people Marion Stembridge had ever seemed to trust. The Stembridge family never revealed the contents of the letter.[33]

When Stembridge's will was probated, his wife was left

In Stembridge's store, Ellis and others found five locked safes.

$1.00, the absolute minimum under Georgia law, though later in court she was awarded the house she had shared with Stembridge. She remained in Milledgeville for a short time before moving away.

The remainder of his estate Stembridge left to his sisters. When the property inside the store was auctioned, Eugene Ellis bought Stembridge's desk, the same desk that Stembridge had been sitting behind the day Ellis had arrested him and almost lost his life. "For some reason, I just wanted that desk," Ellis said.[34]

(Grateful appreciation is extended to all those whose efforts and cooperation made this article possible: James Jossey, chief of detectives, Baldwin County Sheriff's Department; Baldwin County Sheriff Bill Massee; Dr. Bob Wilson, associate professor of history, Georgia College & State University; Patti Wright, GC&SU graduate assistant; Nancy Bray, archivist, GC&SU; Hugh Harrington; John W. Grant; and most of all, Eugene Ellis.)

ENDNOTES

1/ The plans for the sesquicentennial and the description of Milledgeville on the morning of May 2 are drawn from the April 30 edition of the *Milledgeville Union-Recorder* and the May 1-3, 1993 weekend edition of the same paper.

2/ The *Union-Recorder,* May 1-3 edition, 1993, "Murder-Suicide Shocked Milledgeville In 1953." The description of Stembridge's appearance, habits, and eyes are from the author's interview with Eugene Ellis.

3/ Drawn from synopsis of notes of Patti Wright , Georgia College & State University student who interviewed several of the surviving principals in the Stembridge case some years ago. The characterization of Stembridge is drawn from her interview of Judge Robert Green. The notes are found in the GC&SU archives.

4/ The *Union-Recorder,* May 1-3, 1993, "Murder-Suicide Shocked Milledgeville In 1953."

5/ *Macon Telegraph,* May 13, 1991, "Paris Trout Is About Milledgeville Murders."

6/ Narrative drawn from author's interview of Eugene Ellis, hereafter denoted as "Ellis."

7/ From author's interview of James Jossey.

8/ Summary drawn from notes of Patti Wright, GC&SU archives. Quote of Stembridge's sister-in-law is from the *Union-Recorder,* May 1-3 edition, 1993, "Murder-Suicide Shocked Milledgeville In 1953."

9/ Notes of Patti Wright, GC&SU archives. Characterization of Stembridge is from transcript of Judge Robert Green interview.

10/ Wright notes, GC&SU archives.

11/ Wright notes, GC&SU archives.

12/ Wright notes, GC&SU archives.

13/ Wright notes, GC&SU archives.

14/ Ellis interview.

15/ Details of loan are from transcript of Wright interview of Eva Sloan. Quote from Ellis interview.

16/ Narrative from Ellis interview.

17/ Wright notes, GC&SU archives

18/ Drawn from Wright notes, GC&SU archives; divorce papers filed by both Sarah and Marion Stembridge, April 1953, and transcript of Green interview, GC&SU archives.

19/ From transcript of Eva Sloan interview, GC&SU archives.

20/ The *Union-Recorder,* Oct. 8, 1953.

21/ Wright notes, GC&SU archives

22/ Wright notes, transcript of Robert Green interview, both in GC&SU archives, and the *Union-Recorder,* May 7, 1953.

23/ Wright notes, GC&SU archives

24/ Wright notes, GC&SU archives, and interview with Ellis.

25/ Wright notes, GC&SU archives

26/ Wright notes, and transcript of Eva Sloan interview, both in GC&SU archives

27/ Transcript of Robert Green interview, GC&SU archives

28/ Wright notes, GC&SU archives

29/ Transcript of Green interview, GC&SU archives

30/ Interview with Ellis

31/ The *Union-Recorder,* May 1-3 edition, 1993, "Murder-Suicide Shocked Milledgeville in 1953," transcript of Eva Sloan interview, GC&SU archives, and interview with Ellis.

32/ Wright notes, GC&SU archives; Ellis interview; interview with John W. Grant

33/ Transcript of Robert Green interview, GC&SU archives

34/ Copy of Marion Stembridge's Last Will & Testament and Wright notes, both in GC&SU archives, and interview with Ellis.

Tales Of Indians, Slaves And Mayhem In Old Folsom, GA

Today, one can drive through the little hamlet of Folsom and never know it. This rural north Bartow County community – though only a shadow of its former liveliness today – experienced an interesting array of incidents in pioneer days.

Driving on Georgia Highway 140 through northern Bartow County, travelers pass through the tiny community of Folsom – usually without even realizing it. Only one or two faded and dilapidated old storefronts mark the site of this crossroads hamlet today, but it's history is substantially more captivating than one might imagine.

Many of today's citizens are descendants of the early settlers of this area who moved into this vicinity from the Carolinas, traveling on the old Alabama roads and other pioneer trails following the Cherokee Indians' removal in the late 1830s. The pioneers settled on small subsistence farms and practiced the various crafts needed to support themselves and their families.

The township on the site was originally called Salacoa, but in the latter portion of the nineteenth century was renamed Folsom in honor of Frances Folsom Cleveland, wife of U.S. President Grover Cleveland.[1]

The old Federal Road was an early trail which mail carriers and travelers used between Washington, D.C. and the Gulf of Mexico. The portion of this road between Athens, Georgia, and Spring Place, Georgia, was intersected by many of the trails which passed through the Folsom area. This portion of the old Federal Road was actually a spur of the Washington to Milledgeville to New Orleans Highway.[2]

Native Americans At Salacoa

Today, it is unknown exactly when the first settlement was established at Salacoa (Folsom). Prior to inhabitation by European-Americans, the site was occupied by Native Americans. The many pottery fragments and stone implements found over the years by farmers in their plowed fields attest to this inhabitation.

In the early 19th century, two Indian trade routes intersected at present-day Folsom. One trail extended from Head-of-Coosa (present-day Rome, Georgia) to eastern points in what today are Oconee and Pickens counties, South Carolina. The other trail was a north-south route which crossed the Etowah River near the old Hightower Mission west of Cartersville, and proceeded north to Spring Place where it intersected with the Federal Road.

Salacoa experienced its share of Indian/white settler hostilities. They provide a vivid and sometimes gruesome picture of the early days of the community.

One incident involved the murder of a family by the name of Bowman. On December 15, 1832, James L. Bowman, his wife, Bersheba, their infant daughter, Martha, and Bersheba's blind mother, Elizabeth Holcombe, were all slaughtered, reportedly by a renegade Cherokee or Cherokees in the area. The native Cherokees were the most friendly and possibly the most intellectually-advanced of all the Native Americans of North America. But just as with the whites, there were also criminal Indians.

The heinous murder of the Bowman family raised the indignation of the white community and prompted a petition to Georgia's Governor Wilson Lumpkin for a military unit to come *"drive the Indians of the Salacoe [sic] Settlement into submission."* On December 18, 1832, this petition bore the names of *Jacob R. Brooks, Nathan Rice, Benjamin Bowman, John Hambleton* [sic], *J.H. Stokes, William Grant, Sherred Bowman, Joseph Hambleton* [sic], *John Bowman, William Hambleton* [sic], *Nath'n Wofford,* and *Hiram Bright.*[3]

It is unknown today whether the petition brought protection to Salacoa. One thing, however, is certain. Two years later, a traveler near Salacoa was robbed, murdered and burned. This time, the resident whites sought help from General John Coffee who had been with Andrew Jackson at the Battle of Horseshoe Bend.[4]

The Savage George Took

Ultimately, an infamous Cherokee by the name of George Took, was captured by Cass County Sheriff Lewis Tumlin. Took was known to be a renegade and outlaw of the highest order. Incidents of his hatred of whites were well-established long before his capture.

On one occasion, John Seaborn, a North Carolinian, was camped with a party of surveyors on the banks of the Etowah River in the 17th District, reportedly a mile and a half from the Bartow County landmark known as Salt Peter Cave.

Seaborn had no family and a roving disposition. He traveled the countryside with a huge brindle dog for his companion. By a peculiar whistle between his fingers, he could call the dog from a good distance.

Near the camp of the surveyors, a missionary station had been established by the Moravians. Seaborn had planned to visit the station. He had gone approximately one-half mile when the sound of voices attracted his attention.

With caution acquired by experience in the hostile countryside, Seaborn stepped behind a bush and listened attentively. Two figures soon came into view – one an Indian of gigantic size, and the other a beautiful white girl.

The young girl was seated on a jet-black pony and the Indian held the bridle with one hand and a war ax in the other. Suspecting that the young lady was not a voluntary companion, Seaborn maintained his concealment. His suspicion was confirmed when the girl tried to escape but was roughly restrained by the Indian.

In recapturing the girl, the Indian raised a war ax to threaten her, and the uplifted motion caused a violent start of the pony which resulted in the young lady being thrown from the saddle.

With an impulse of rage and a heart

Rebecca Franklin Scott and her extended family were photographed circa 1880. They lived in the Salacoa (Folsom) community. Seated to Mrs. Scott's left is Henry Bomer Scott holding his baby daughter. As a boy, Henry lost his beloved horse when Union Army soldiers took it from him during the U.S. Civil War. "Old Jack" (foreground) was said to be the best rabbit dog in the community.

A lonely headstone marks the grave of a female killed by a slave. She was buried in Glade Cemetery. The slave was hung in Cassville. Violence was commonplace in rural north Georgia during the years of the Civil War and shortly thereafter. (Photo by Rev. Philip P. Scott)

throbbing with excitement, Seaborn reportedly sprang from his place of hiding with a yell that so startled the Indian that he instantly released the girl and ran towards the woods.

When he realized he was confronted by only one person, however, the Indian stopped and turned. "Mount quick and fly!" Seaborn reportedly shouted to the girl. She needed no further urging. The pony was near at hand.

As she moved off, Seaborn faced the Indian who later was identified as George Took, known among the Cherokees as "Unakayah-wah" or "white man killer." He had tremendous size and strength, and stood with obvious hatred in his eyes. Seaborn realized for the first time that he was at an immense disadvantage.

Seaborn, however, was also in the prime of his life. . . muscular and of fair stature himself. With a step backward, he planned to lure the Indian in the direction of his camp where he might obtain the assistance of his companions. As he turned to run, he whistled loudly thru his fingers for his dog.

George Took, however, had other plans. Fearing that he might be drawn into ambush, he hurled his war ax at Seaborn. It knocked the young surveyor's cap off and stunned him, but did not seriously harm him. It whistled on beyond him and buried itself in a tree some feet away.

With his foe upon him, Seaborn turned and took a swing at the Indian's head. Evading the blow with a side-step, Took rushed Seaborn and tried to throw him over his head. The two punched, kicked, gouged, bit and pounded each other for many long minutes.

Seaborn had a knife in his belt, but had been unable to grasp it while protecting himself from the Indian's furious assault. Finally, in desperation, he grabbed the handle of the weapon. At about this same time, "Bruno," Seaborn's dog, suddenly appeared and with almost primal rage, sunk his teeth into the shoulder of the savage and began ripping and tearing at the Indian.

The attack from the dog caused Took to lose his hold on Seaborn, and in an instant, Seaborn raised his knife and sunk in into Took's arm. As Seaborn raised his arm to repeat the blow, Took reportedly yelled "Enough! Enough!" in the Indian tongue and in broken English exclaimed "Take dog off quick. Brave white man. No kill chief!"[5]

The desperate struggle ended in the capture of the Indian. The disposition of this crime is unknown today. However, the ultimate demise of this particular Indian is well-documented.

In 1835, Took had murdered a white family for revenge. He set fire to their home, and when a little girl of the family recognized him and ran to him for rescue, he reportedly picked her up and threw her into the flames.

In this instance, Took was pursued by Sheriff Lewis Tumlin of Cass County. After being tracked down by Tumlin, the Indian confronted his pursuer in a vicious fight. In the melee that ensued, Took was severely wounded in the shoulder. The injury caused Took to surrender once again. His wound turned out to be so traumatic that the arm had to be amputated prior to the Indian's trial.

The trial resulted in a conviction of Took for murder. He was hanged in Cassville, Georgia in 1835, under the judgeship of John W. Hooper.[6]

Settlers in the Salacoa area ultimately took more precautions for their safety from marauding Indians. According to the late Mrs. Ida Edwards, who died at the age of 101 and lived as a child at Folsom, the spring to the north of the Marshall Lewis home in Folsom was once the site of a block house where white families gathered in a highly-protective structure to sleep at night when circumstances necessitated.[7]

Mysteries Of The Cherokees

Indian stories about Salacoa (Folsom) have persisted into the 20th century. Many of the legends involved the presumed return

Reba McClure was a resident of Salacoa and was often seen riding in her "Amish-style" buggy.

Vaccination Day – Dr. Howard Felton is shown conducting a public vaccination in Folsom. Dr. Felton's father, Dr. William Felton, was not only a physician, but a United States congressman as well. When Dr. Felton's mother was appointed to the U.S. Senate to fill an unexpired term, she became the first female to serve in the Congress of the United States.

of native Cherokees seeking items of value they had buried prior to their forced removal to reservations in the American West.

Mrs. Tom McDaris and her sister, Mrs. Theodore Hamby, grew up on the old Scott farm near Folsom. Before their deaths, they often related the story of an Indian from the West who camped for a time in a cemetery near their childhood home.

One night, their father, Jeff Scott, reportedly noticed a lantern burning through the night on the cemetery hill.

When Scott went to check on the Indian the next morning, the stranger was gone.

At the site of the Indian's camp, Scott discovered a hole in the ground. It the bottom of the hole, the imprint of a box or some other such container was clearly visible in the clay.

Some area residents speculated the Indian may have exhumed valuables his family had hidden in the ground many years earlier when they were relocated to Oklahoma. However, the Indian may also have merely been removing the last remains of one of his ancestors to take home with him to the West.

A similar story has been passed down for generations. It involved an Indian who supposedly unearthed something on the Frank Carson homeplace and who then vanished. The Indian supposedly had told Carson in a joking manner before he left that he (Carson) was "rich and didn't even know it."[8]

Following the Indian removal to the West, the lands in north Georgia were distributed by lottery. Benjamin Scott, due to his service in the War of 1812, was given the chance to draw for a land lot. The property he drew is located where Cedar Creek Church is located today on Georgia Highway 140.[9]

Slaves In Salacoa

Small manufacturing and agricultural enterprises existed in Folsom throughout the 19th century. The Mosteller and Pinson families had grist, lumber, carding, and ginning mills run by water power. The economy of Salacoa and its environs, however, was ultimately built upon yeoman agriculture. The land did not lend itself well to plantation agriculture, but was ideal for the production of hogs, corn and wheat.

Despite this fact, there were some slave-holders in the area. There was only one businessman in the Salacoa vicinity, however, which could have been considered a member of the "planter class." This was Felix Denman who owned 28 slaves in 1840. William Wyley, who held 14, was the second-largest slave-holder in the community that year.[10]

Evidence of slavery can yet be found in Folsom. In the Glade Cemetery east of Folsom, there is a memorial stone to Mary Ann Camp Morris who, along with her family, moved to Cass County from Henry County, Georgia. In March, 1836, Mrs. Morris was murdered by a slave who, like George Took, met his fate in Cassville at the end of Judge Hooper's rope. The memorial stone states that he was *"lawfully hung."*

In an honored place in the Hays Cemetery in Folsom, a short little obelisk is etched with the word, *"Ex-Slaves."* This is the resting place of Frank and Henrietta Carson who were known as "Uncle Frank" and "Aunt Connie" to the local population. "Aunt Connie" was warmly loved by many residents in the Folsom area at the turn of the century, and "Uncle Frank" worked on the farms of a number of the local farmers.

The Carsons were held in high esteem until their deaths: Henrietta in 1921 and Frank in 1926. Their graves are still well-kept by a community which holds valuable the memories of this devoted couple.

The Civil War In Folsom

Folsom is also not without its Confederate veterans. On a hilltop in the Hays Cemetery, the remains of George Mosteller sleep for eternity. George was a member of the 40th Georgia Infantry and served at the siege of Vicksburg, Mississippi. He finally was killed at Missionary Ridge, and his body was brought home and placed near his parents-in-law in the Hays Cemetery.[11]

Salacoa witnessed its share of Yankees during the "Late Unpleasantness" too.

Henry Bomer Scott was a lad of eight years of age, when William T. Sherman's Union Army forces came through the community. Elements of Schofield's Army of the Ohio and Hooker's Army of the Cumberland made their way through Salacoa in the spring of 1864.

William Scott had presented his son, Henry Bomer with a horse as a gift shortly before the arrival of the Yankees. Little Henry, however, would not enjoy his gift long, for the Union Army requisitioned it. As it was led off, a tearful little barefooted boy rained rocks on the soldiers in blue.

Surprisingly, with very few exceptions, the Folsom area's residents continued with little hardship after the U.S. Civil War. Census records indicate that few families lost their lands after the war and continued the lifestyle of the antebellum years. Such was the resiliency of the yeoman farmer lifestyle.

This, however, was in sharp contrast to the white and black populations of the plantation districts which experienced massive hardships. With no slaves to plant, maintain and harvest the hundreds of acres of each planter family; with the ruined monetary system and decimated production centers, the planter families experienced the worst deprivations of all. And the slaves, freed from their oppressive owners, suddenly found themselves with no homes, food, or subsistence. It was a strange new world which greeted both of these groups.

In contrast, the Folsom family enterprises were able to begin producing wheat, corn, pigs, wool and lumber – the staple crops of the area – relatively easily. These small to medium-sized enterprises fared well, practically picking up where they had left off prior to the war.

Another Troubling Incident

Interesting and oft-times troubling incidents continued in Folsom after the war as well. One such story was related to this writer by Ida Edwards in 1981. Mrs. Edwards told me of the unusual death of Matt Denman after the Civil War.

It seems that Denman and his wife lived not far east of Folsom. Mr. Denman needed to drive his team (wagon) to Cartersville for supplies. He took along with him a girl who had been living with the Denmans since her father had been killed in the war and her mother had recently died.

At the time of this incident, Mrs. Denman was ill and in bed, and the young girl was accompanying Mr. Denman to do Mrs. Denman's shopping. When Denman and the girl returned quite late, it was obvious that the girl was very upset.

Either that night, or a few nights later, the girl arose from her bed after the others were asleep and killed Mr. Denman. The young murderess was kept in jail until the baby came. She was then released and never charged with a crime.[12]

Growth In Folsom

The late 1890s witnessed the erection of three stores in Folsom which furnished the community with general merchandise, clothing, and food. These stores, Lewis and Sons, J.B. Adcock & Brothers, and Mosteller & Scott, were all locally owned.

This partnership with Henry Scott was not the first mercantile effort by a Mosteller in Folsom. The 1860 census indicates that Jacob Mosteller was in business at the crossroads and also operated a corn and wheat mill.

The Mostellers were famous in the area for their ability to construct and operate water-powered mills. David Mosteller, a man of some means ($18,900 in real estate and cash according to the census) was listed on the census as a master millwright.

Folsom folks have always been highly religious in nature. Most individuals in town have subscribed to the Baptist persuasion over the years.

Cedar Creek, established in the 1840s, is the oldest church in the community, but the Glade and Plainview Baptist churches can claim their places in the community as well.

Some medical doctors left records of their Folsom practices, providing a small window of information on medical science in the community in days gone by. The earliest doctor located on the census material is Dr. Henry Bomer.

Dr. Bomer practiced his healing talents to the degree he could, given the state of medical practice in his day. He must have been quite popular, especially with the female "ladies in waiting" for there were Henry Bomer Scott and Henry Bomer Stokes and Henry Bomer Barton and a number of other "Henry Bomers" as well.

Besides Dr. Bomer, Folsom had other physicians over the years. The community's Dr. Dykes delivered this writer's father, and the town's Dr. Richard Bradley delivered my mother. On August 8, 1910, she was born at the home of her grandparents, Mr. and Mrs. S.G.H. Barton, with respiratory complications. Dr. Bradley came to her aid by alternately dipping her in cold and warm water until her breathing became normal. Due to Dr. Bradley's ministrations, my mother was born (and this was subsequently made possible.).

Like most communities in the old South, Folsom and its environs established small one-room schools within walking distance of the greatest number of students. School houses were sometimes in short supply so churches were often used during weekdays for the instruction of the young.

Today, the old two-room Folsom School still stands, but is badly in need of repair. The structure was closed when Pine Log, Adairsville and Cassville became the centers for elementary and secondary education in northern Bartow County.

In the 1950s, the old school enjoyed a brief resurrection of sorts when it was used as a movie theater – of all things. Today, the old building – sadly in disrepair – is a silent sentinel to those bygone days when generations of youth found a knowledge of letters and numbers inside its confines.

Today, as the Atlanta to Chattanooga corridor continues to expand in population, Folsom will probably experience a new day of prominence. More and more new families and construction are in evidence. Who knows. The old school may be reawakened from its peaceful sleep once again.

ENDNOTES

1/ Cartographic Division, National Archives, Washington, D.C.

2/ Georgia State Archives, Cherokee Letters, Atlanta, Georgia, (Coulter, 251)

3/ Warren, Mary B. and Weeks, Eve B., ed., *Whites Among The Cherokees, Georgia, 1828-1838.* Danielson, Georgia. Heritage papers, 1987, (p 110), and Georgia State Archives, Cherokee Letters, Atlanta, Georgia, (p 385).

4/ Georgia State Archives, Cherokee Letters, p 385, Atlanta, Georgia.

5/ Cunyus, Lucy Josephine, *History Of Bartow County, Georgia,* (1933), pp 7-9.

6/ Cunyus, Lucy Josephine, *History Of Bartow County, Georgia,* (1933), pp 7-9, and Correspondence of Ida and William Edwards to Father Philip P. Scott, (April, 1987).

7/ Cunyus, Ludy Josephine, *History Of Bartow County, Georgia,* (19330, pp 7-9, and Correspondence of Ida and William Edwards to Father Philip P. Scott, (April, 1987).

8/ Scott family tradition; Related by Mrs. Alton Adcock of Folsom.

9/ Surveyor General's Records, Georgia State Archives, Atlanta; Scott Family Papers; Barton Family Papers.

10/ U.S. Census, 1840, 1850, and 1860, Cass County, Georgia, Sixth District.

11/ Confederate Military Service Records, Georgia State Archives, Atlanta; George Mosteller gravestone data.

12/ Correspondence of Ida and William Edwards to Father Philip P. Scott, 1981.

They Called Him 'Pretty Boy'

Though little-known today, one of America's most infamous criminals was born and lived his early years in the town of Adairsville, Georgia.

Despite the fact he lived most of his life in Oklahoma and died in a hail of gunfire in Ohio, one of the most notorious criminals in U.S. history was born in the sleepy north Georgia town of Adairsville. Indeed, the roots and family heritage of Charles Arthur "Pretty Boy" Floyd run deep in the north Georgia area.

The house in which Floyd was born still stands (as of this writing) at 102 Railroad Street[1]. Many members of the Floyd, Murphey, Pinson, Echols, Gaines, and other families of the Adairsville area are related to the outlaw. These families came to Cass (now Bartow) County from South Carolina shortly after the removal of the Cherokees in 1838.[2]

Family Roots

Charles Floyd's great-great-great-grandfather, Roger Murphey, Jr., migrated to Cass from Laurens County, South Carolina. He and his father had both held property in Laurens, giving them a financial base from which to acquire land in the Georgia counties of Forsyth, DeKalb, and Cass.[3]

From a review of his real estate investments, his interest in acquiring slaves, and his attempt at large-scale agriculture, it would appear that Roger made an earnest attempt to join the planter elite, but never quite succeeded. He used slaves to farm his Cass County farm, but he and his children apparently were required to perform manual labor right alongside the slaves, to maintain production output. Such was the case with many yeoman farmers during pre-Civil War times.

When Roger died in 1854, his estate was divided among his children. His home and property were purchased by his son, John, who used a portion of the slaves to continue farming.[4]

According to tradition, John Murphey's wife, Frances, has been described as a hearty individual. According to accounts of her life, she often saddled up her horse and rode the many miles back to South Carolina to visit relatives and friends. This was no easy trek, particularly for a woman in the mid-19th century, and the fact that she accomplished it alone makes it even more amazing.[5]

When John and Frances Murphey died, their farm was purchased by a daughter and son-in-law, Redding and Katherine Murphey Floyd. Redding was the son of Samuel and Patience Pinson Floyd. The

Charles Arthur "Pretty Boy" Floyd, became a poster boy following an arrest in Colorado. (Photo courtesy of Western History Collections, University of Oklahoma Library)

Pinsons were of the Particular Baptist faith. A number of Pinson family members worked as millwrights in South Carolina and continued their tradition in Cass County, Georgia, constructing a number of water-powered mills in the area.[6]

Hard Times

The Floyd clan began moving away from Cass County prior to the U.S. Civil War. "Pretty Boy" Floyd's great-grandfather, Redding Floyd, had two brothers – Newport and Jasper – who migrated to Arkansas in the last years of the 1850s. According to one family story, when Newport and Jasper arrived in Arkansas, they stopped at a cabin to ask directions to Fort Smith. An elderly gentleman who lived in the cabin provided them with the appropriate instructions.

After explaining the route, the old man inquired about the travelers' names and their former home. Newport and Jasper replied that they were Floyds from Cass County, Georgia. The elderly gentleman then reportedly stunned the two men by explaining that he was their father – Samuel Floyd.

Years before, Samuel and Patience Pinson Floyd had split up. Samuel had moved away and the family had never heard from him again. The old gentleman apparently accompanied Newport and Jasper to their new home, because the 1860 Census of Arkansas indicates that he was living in Newport's household at that time.[7]

Meanwhile, back in Georgia, Redding Floyd had decided to remain behind, farming the old Murphey place. At the time of the Civil War, he owned three slaves and the farm, which apparently produced a reasonable living for his family.

In November of 1862, Redding enlisted in Kingston, Georgia, joining Company F of the 12th Georgia Cavalry. His brother-in-law, Matthias Murphey, wrote a letter to Redding on January 18, 1863, not knowing that Redding had already enlisted. His letter, in part, indicates that even at that early date, morale was a definite problem within the Confederate forces.:

"... I understand that you have a couple of heirs (referring to Redding's recently born twins) at your house and I wish you great sicess (sic) in raising of them. . . Red, between me and you and the Gait post we have got the meanest Colonel in the confederate service. I never shall like Abda Johnson (later mayor of Cartersville, Georgia) *any more as long as I live. . . . Red the Soldiers are all getting very tired of this war and if it is not stopt shortly they will stop it themselves by throwing down their muskets and going home. I am going to stay til July and if they don't let me come home*

on fair terms I am coming on fowl terms. This is the worst place we have been camped at yet – bad water bad beef and bad weather.[8]

Starting Anew In The West

Row crop agriculture – the predominant occupation of many of the Floyds and Murpheys in north Georgia – was decimated by the changes and devastation associated with the U.S. Civil War. Following the war, many Southerners – the Floyds and Murpheys included – yearned for a new beginning and struck out for the West.

From Anderson County, Texas in 1870, C.M. Murphey wrote to his brother-in-law, Redding Floyd, in Bartow County, Georgia. Murphey described the great promise of post-war Texas:

"Texas looks like a world of cotton. People kill all their meat out of the woods as fat as they are in georgia when we feed them 10 bushels of corn apiece. use cast plows never sharpen them cheaper than iron plows on Georgia. Water better than I expected to find."[9]

Redding Floyd received the same kind of mail extolling the virtues of Pike County, Arkansas from his brother, Jasper. This love affair with the West continued in the Floyd and Murphey families, but Redding was never enticed to leave his Bartow County farm.

One reason Redding never departed was his elderly mother for whom he cared. He reportedly did not want to uproot her and take her on the long, dangerous journey westward.[10]

A second wave of emigration of Floyds and their allied kin occurred around the turn of the century, continuing until around 1915. This relocation was ignited by the opening of the Indian territory and the opportunity to acquire fertile agricultural lands at limited or no cost.

Formative Years Of "Pretty Boy"

One of the families that went West during this second exodus (around 1912) was that of Redding's grandson, Walter Floyd.[11] Within this family was included young Charles Arthur Floyd, called "Charlie" by the family. He had been born in Adairsville on February 3, 1904, living most of his formative years in the community.

The house where Charles Arthur Floyd was born still stands (as of this writing) at 102 Railroad Street in Adairsville.

The home once owned by Redding Floyd still stands in Folsum, Georgia. Redding and his wife, Kathryn, are buried near the home in Macland Cemetery.

Charles' mother's family – the Echols – lived in the Towes Chapel area of Bartow County near Cassville. Like the Floyds, the Echols were farmers who made an adequate but hard living off the lands they owned.

Walter Floyd had married Mamie Echols in 1897 in Bartow County. Mamie's mother – Emily Elizabeth Gaines Echols – wife of Elmer Echols – hailed from one of the South's most illustrious families – the Gaines – of Culpepper County, Virginia.[12]

"Pretty Boy" Floyd is remembered primarily as a bank robber in the annals of U.S. criminal history. From time to time, however, he is also anointed with the mantle of a folk hero. He was referred to occasionally as "the Robin Hood of the Cookson Hills."

While robbing banks in that area, Floyd reportedly tore up first mortgages, hoping they had not been recorded. This act, if true, freed many of the destitute Depression-era families from loan obligations when hard cash was almost nonexistent.[13]

Today, the official FBI file on the career of "Pretty Boy" Floyd is in excess of 15,000 pages. Books, magazine articles, and movies have chronicled his life and times, often substituting fiction for fact to embellish circumstances.

One of the little-known ironies of the "Pretty Boy" Floyd story is the fact that his brother, E.W. Floyd, served many terms as sheriff of Sequoyah County, Oklahoma, and was highly respected in the law enforcement community.

A cousin, Duff Floyd, was a famed revenue officer of north Georgia. On one occasion when he was asked what he would have done had "Pretty Boy" crossed his path, Duff reportedly replied "I would have arrested him like any other criminal."[14]

Today, it is unknown for certain whether or not Charles "Pretty Boy" Floyd ever returned to Georgia to the land of his youth. According to folklore, however, he did once hide out in a house on Montgomery Street in Cartersville, Georgia.

Beginning A Life Of Crime

Floyd's first run-in with law enforcement personnel occurred in Akin, Oklahoma, in 1922. According to accounts of the incident, he took $350 in pennies from the post office there. He was convicted and sentenced to probation.

For a short period of time, Charles apparently attempted to follow "the straight and narrow," moving to Sallisaw, Oklahoma, where he found work as a plumber and baker. Two years later, he married 16-year-old Wilma Ruby Hardgrave. It was a lifestyle, however, to which Charles obviously felt he could never adjust.

It wasn't long before Floyd was back up to his old tricks. In 1925, he and an accomplice robbed a St. Louis, Missouri Kroger store of $11,984. Floyd was ultimately arrested at his home in Sallisaw. He was eventually convicted of the crime and sent to the Missouri State Penitentiary at Jefferson City for five years.

While Charles was in prison, Ruby gave birth to their only son, Jack Dempsey Floyd. Though she loved their son, Ruby apparently had given up on Charles, and divorced him shortly after Jack's birth. Later, the couple reconciled for a short period of time – without "benefit of clergy," – but then separated permanently.

After he was released from the state penitentiary, Charles resumed his criminal lifestyle. He and a friend, Bert Walker, stole a car and robbed a bank in Sylvania, Ohio.

By coincidence, while making a raid on a Kenmore Boulevard home, Officer Sherman Gandee of the Akron Police encountered Floyd and Walker. During an ensuing gun battle, Officer Harland F. Manes was shot dead by Walker.

A phone number discovered in the Kenmore Boulevard house led to another house on Lodi Street in Akron where Floyd and Walker were subsequently captured. Walker eventually earned an appointment with the electric chair for his deeds. Meanwhile, Floyd, on his way to the Ohio State Penitentiary, jumped out of a train window and successfully escaped.

The First Murders

"Pretty Boy" eventually found his way to Toledo, Ohio where two brothers, William and Wallace Ash, befriended him. It was a friendship, however, that apparently was not reciprocated by Floyd. The Ash brothers were later discovered dead from gunshot wounds to the head. Their wives and Floyd had left town and later turned up in Kentucky.

Bowling Green, Kentucky, was the scene of Charles' next crime spree. He, William "Baby Face Billy" Miller, and the Ash women were at a Bowling Green hardware store when Officer Ralph Castner reportedly approached their car. Witnesses, who later identified Floyd, stated he opened fire on the policeman who was killed in the fray along with Miller. A ballistics analysis later matched the bullets in the policeman with those from the heads of the Ash brothers.

By this time, Floyd was now a suspect in three murders. In his career, he stands accused of killing 12 men, ten of whom were officers of the law.

From May through December of 1931, Floyd allegedly committed some 15 bank robberies in Missouri, Kansas, and Oklahoma. When the governor of Oklahoma posted a $1,000 reward for Floyd's capture, the daring criminal promptly sent the good governor a letter.

"You either withdraw that $1,000 at once or suffer the consequences," Floyd penned. *"No kidding, I have robbed no one but moneyed men. Floyd."*

Despite the reward (which was not withdrawn), Floyd was not caught. From June through December of 1932, he continued his odyssey, staging robberies in some 40 additional banks.

On June 16, 1933, Floyd, Adam "Eddy" Richetti, and Vern Miller, allegedly made an unsuccessful attempt to free their friend, Frank Nash, who was being transferred to a federal prison. The effort, which was made at Union Station in Kansas City, resulted in a shoot-out between federal officers and Floyd and his accomplices. Agent Raymond J. Caffrey of the Federal Bureau of Investigation lived just long enough to identify his attackers as a group led by "Pretty Boy" Floyd.

Kansas City Massacre

Following the "Kansas City Massacre," as it came to be known, the Kansas City Police received a postcard from the ever-colorful Floyd.

"Dear Sirs:

"I, Charles Floyd, want it made known that I did not participate in the masacree (sic) of officers at Kansas City. Charles Floyd."

The postcard had been mailed in Oklahoma which prompted Gov. Murray to send the National Guard into Floyd's old lair in the Cookson Hills again. They did indeed flush the criminal out, but the ever-wily criminal escaped once again.

Floyd next turned up in Cresco, Ohio. The police in Cresco also cornered Charles, but he shot his way out to freedom once again. Accompanied by two women, he and Adam Richetti reunited and made their way to Wellsville, Ohio, where their car developed mechanical problems.

While the two women took the car to be repaired, Floyd and Richetti hid out in the nearby hills. A suspicious local resident spotted the two men and reported them to the Wellsville Police Department. Chief John Fultz, along with his deputy, Grover Potts, went to investigate. A gun battle ensued. Richetti was captured, but Floyd escaped once again. He had lost his machine gun, but he still had his two .45 caliber pistols.

His Last Day

On Monday, October 22, 1934, Mrs.

Ellen Conkle was scrubbing her floors when she noticed a man in her driveway. She did not know it at the time, but she was face-to-face with one of the most notorious criminals of all time.

Floyd said he needed a ride into Youngstown, and Mrs. Conkle replied that her brother could oblige. Floyd was already seated in the car with Mrs. Conkle's brother when two other cars drove up the driveway.

Realizing that the cars contained police officers, Floyd jumped out and ran for cover behind the Conkles' corn crib. East Liverpool officer, Chester Smith, saw Charles and advanced on the corn crib. Floyd ran again, and Smith fired two shots at the elusive outlaw. One of the rounds hit Floyd in the back and knocked him off his feet.

The account of what next transpired depends upon what one wishes to believe. According to one respected account, FBI agent Melvin Purvis closed in on Floyd, who was seriously wounded in the shoulder, and disarmed him. He then reportedly ordered an agent named Hawless to go ahead and shoot Floyd again, which the agent did, firing point-blank into his chest.

The life and bloody career of Charles "Pretty Boy" Floyd thus ended on a lonely Ohio farm, a long way from the criminal's north Georgia roots. In an ironic twist of fate, most modern-day references to Floyd list his hometown as Akin, Oklahoma, and it was to that locale that his body was conveyed for burial.

Today, no historic marker identifies the house (which still stands) in which Floyd was born and in which he lived during his early years in Adairsville, Georgia. As of this writing, an effort is underway to identify the site at which Floyd died in Ohio.

ENDNOTES

1/ Interview with Mrs. Bessie Darby, March, 1995. Also, telephone interview with city clerk, city of Adairsville, Georgia, March, 1995.

2/ Early deed books in the office of the Clerk of the Superior Court of Bartow County indicate many titles recorded to these families in the 1830s and '40s. See also the 1840 U.S. Census Population Schedule for Cass County, Georgia.

3/ See land title records, Laurens County, South Carolina and Forsyth, Dekalb and Cass counties, Georgia. The Murphey farming operation in DeKalb County seems to have been conducted by Roger's son, Charles, while the farm in Cass County was managed primarily by Roger and John. Little is known about the Forsyth County Land.

4/ Letters of Administration, Administration Returns, and Inventories for 1855-56, Office of the Probate Judge, Bartow County, Georgia.

5/ Fannie Mae Floyd Moss interview, 1983. Fannie Mae Floyd Moss owned the old Redding Floyd farm until her death. She was the custodian of the old farm, and also was an unofficial repository of a wealth of folklore and stories involving the family line of Charles Arthur Floyd.

6/ Pinson genealogical data in the files of the author.

7/ Pike County, Arkansas population schedule for the 1860 and 1870 Censuses of the United States.

8/ Fannie Mae Floyd Moss papers. Photo copy in the collection of the author.

9/ Fannie Mae Floyd Moss papers in the custody of Katheryn Floyd, Ed.D.

10/ Fannie Mae Floyd Moss interview, 1983.

11/ Dale Floyd interview (Walter Floyd's grandson), 1992. As of this writing, Mr. Floyd resides in Oklahoma and is the nephew of Charles Arthur Floyd.

12/ Mary Kathryn Gaines Korstian, *"History Of The Gaines Family,"* Rome, Georgia: Brazelton-Wallis, 1973.

13/ Sandy Lesberg. *"A Picture History Of Crime,"* New York: Haddington House, 1976, pp 109-110. Most of the material concerning Charles Arthur Floyd's career after he left Georgia was drawn from an extensive feature in the Sunday Magazine of the "Akron Beacon Journal," Akron, Ohio, October 20, 1974.

14/ Telephone interview with Katheryn Floyd, Ed. D., daughter of Duff Floyd. The author personally recalls hearing Mr. Floyd recount this statement once at a family reunion.

Tales Of Tiny Taylorsville

Many travelers never notice and most have never even heard of the tiny community of Taylorsville, Georgia, as they drive down Highway 113 between Cartersville and Rockmart, Georgia. Beginning in the 1930s, however, the little bank in this town was a mainline financial institution for the many farmers in the rural southwest corner of Bartow County. Because of its isolated and relatively unprotected circumstances, this bank was also a favorite target of bank robbers.

They are the two words which can instantly strike fear into the hearts of the unfortunate victims of this crime – "bank robbery." The tiny rural fiefdom of Taylorsville, Georgia in southwest Bartow County became a favorite target of bandits during the desperate years of the 1930s and '40s, and even as late as the 1970s. More often than not, however, the events which transpired during these offenses more often resembled a comic opera than vicious and violent acts, and many area residents can still chuckle in remembrance of the circumstances of one or more of these occasions.

Taylorsville is tiny. There's no mistaking that. It also is a very historic site. Native aborigines had villages on and near this spot in prehistoric times. Later, during the U.S. Civil War, Union troops passed through and camped in the vicinity. It therefore is paradoxical that the vicinity is remembered not for its history, but as a repeated target for bank robbers.

With its isolated location, lively bank, and limited law enforcement personnel, Taylorsville, from all appearances, was a natural opportunity ripe for picking. Today, intensive security precautions and beefed up law enforcement have eliminated the bank's reputation as an easy mark for criminals, but locals still like to talk about the "shoot-outs" in the old days.

Early Stick-Ups

One manager – Mr. M.A. Perry – who came to the Taylorsville bank in the early 1930s, was forced to endure two robberies under his watch. His son, W.J. "Bill" Perry, was six or eight years of age at the time, and, in an interview in the 1990s, recalled the incidents endured by his father.

"The first robbery Dad experienced at Taylorsville was about 1933," the younger Perry explained. "The gunman locked Dad in the vault and he was lucky to have survived it with the lack of oxygen in there. Dad was the only person in the bank in those days, so he was all alone.

"Fortunately, an individual named Mr. Bob Taylor, who was a bank director, made it his business to check on the bank every day," Perry continued. "He was the only other person in town who knew the combination to the vault, and he just happened to stop by shortly after the robbery. He heard Dad banging on the inside of the vault, and he hurriedly opened the large door.

"The second robbery during Dad's time in Taylorsville occurred sometime around 1936 or '37," Perry added. "Dad had a .38 caliber "Police Special" that he kept for protection. One day, a man drove up to the bank in a 1934 or '35 Chevy. He walked in and pulled a gun on Dad and ordered him back inside the vault, only this time, Dad wasn't locked inside. The gunman took all the money and put it into a washtub, then told Dad 'You get on the floor. If you come out, I'll kill you.'

"Well. . . Dad laid on the floor until he heard the motor start in that old Chevy. He then grabbed his gun and ran outside and emptied all six rounds at the fleeing car. The car never slowed up though. A few days later, the thief was brazen enough to phone in and explain that Dad 'couldn't hit the side of a barn.' It sure wasn't from a lack of trying though."

A Run On The Bank

As could be expected, Bill Perry describes the early 1930s as desperate times. He says that aside from the bank robberies, there was also a "run" on the Taylorsville Bank during this period (about 1932), but that some clever work by another bank director saved the day.

"Many of the farmers in the area got the idea the bank was about to fail," Perry continued. "When people started lining up to withdraw their money, Dad called Mr. W. D. Tripp, who was a stockholder and on the board of directors.

"Mr. Tripp told Dad to stall as long as possible and pay out just as slowly as possible until he (Mr. Tripp) had a chance to get there. Mr. Tripp went to another bank with which he was associated in Bartow County and borrowed $2,000 – all in one-dollar bills – and put it all in a big bag. He rushed back to the Taylorsville Bank, then walked calmly inside, dumped the $2,000 in bills out on a counter and announced 'I understand some people want their money.'

"Well, in 1932, that $2,000 looked like a million dollars today. Most of the accounts there were only eight and ten-dollar accounts. Before you knew it, people began walking away, and that was the end of the crisis."

A Move To Rockmart

Crises at a little bank, however, were not the foundation upon which Mr. Perry wished to build his career, so after the second bank robbery in Taylorsville, he began looking around for employment elsewhere.

He soon moved to what he expected to be a more secure situation in nearby Rockmart in Polk County.

Ironically, two years later (about 1939), that bank also was robbed – the only hold-up on record for the Rockmart bank. This time, however, the elder Perry had gone home for lunch, and thankfully missed all the excitement.

As with many of the offenses at Taylorsville, the Rockmart robbery also involved a comic element. After the hold-up, the bandits jumped into their getaway car and were prepared to race away from the town. To their despair, they discovered the car would not crank.

Just as the robbers were about to flee

the scene on foot, one of the friendly Rockmart citizens – completely unaware of the circumstances into which he had stepped – assisted the criminals in starting the troublesome vehicle and kindly waved as the bandits smiled broadly and drove away.

Memories of yet another episode of thievery also survive – undoubtedly with some embellishment – from a 1940 Taylorsville robbery. The bank manager of that time, William Dorsey, was victimized one morning just as the bank opened for business. The bandits tied him to an old pot-bellied stove, a humiliating act to which Mr. Dorsey took great exception.

Years later, Dorsey always reacted rabidly when reminded of the event. "There wasn't no need for that – they had no business tying me to that stove," he often growled. (And no, the stove wasn't hot.)

Today, it's easy to find humor in bank robberies which went awry, but the situation is anything but funny for a bank teller gazing down the business end of a loaded revolver. Long after one particularly disturbing robbery, one bank official expressed his feelings thusly: "I was always thankful that they did get away, especially after I found out who they were."

Bartow County Sheriff Jim Wheeler (l) confers with several FBI agents following a robbery in 1976 at the Peoples Bank of Bartow County in Taylorsville, Georgia. (Photo courtesy of Golden Memory Photos)

As a diversion in the 1976 Taylorsville bank robbery, the conspirators planted dynamite with a delayed fuse beneath historic Euharlee Presbyterian Church. The detonation was designed to occur at the same time as the robbery, serving to draw law enforcement personnel away from downtown Taylorsville.

Planning A Robbery

It is the last robbery inflicted on the little bank in Taylorsville – in 1976 – that is remembered by many area residents today, mainly because it was one of the most unusual. It also emphasized the fact that the Taylorsville Bank was no longer "an easy mark."

The two "masterminds" of the '76 hold-up reportedly were experienced professionals. According to later courtroom testimony, they arrived in the Cartersville area from their home base in Indianapolis, Indiana, and settled into a combination truck-stop, pool hall and boarding house on U.S. Highway 41.

One of the men, Leon Johnson, walked with a distinctive limp. The other, Donald Anderson, had "rotten teeth." The bank employees at Taylorsville would remember these identifying features years after the crime.

The duo became a trio when they met up with Marvina Satterfield, described as an individual who more resembled a man with long hair. The three still later were joined by a fourth accomplice – an attractive blonde named Charmaine Garrett – who witnesses would also easily recall and later identify.

The four partners in crime all had one thing in common: They all needed money and intended to obtain it – violently if necessary.

It wasn't long before this quartet of criminals began forging a plan to accomplish their goal. They no doubt took their time, observing the rural countryside, plotting which bank would surrender the most loot with the least risk.

Clayton J. Harris, bank manager at the Taylorsville Bank in 1976, says the initial plan of the gang was to rob the First National Bank of Cartersville. Their scheme involved kidnapping bank manager Russell Archer, taking his family hostage, then threatening harm to them unless Archer opened the bank vault. This plan was squelched, however, when Marvina Satterfield objected, explaining that she might be recognized by the Archer family.

The crooks therefore had to cast about for a new target bank. Taylorsville, with its isolated location soon drew their attention. Its well-known history of robbery and burglary may even have been learned by the group.

Despite an obvious lack of security and law enforcement personnel in the vicinity of the bank, the bandits decided a diversion would increase their margin of safety. Their plan called for the creation of an emergency situation – such as a bombing – a short distance away, to draw away any police in the area.

The conspirators located a church several miles away in the little community of Euharlee in Bartow County. They decided to blow it up with dynamite, using a delayed fuse.

"Their plan didn't work, however," recalled church member Bill Thomason. "The fuse wasn't attached properly and fell out. The dynamite remained unexploded."

The newspapers of that day reported many details of the robbery, as well as the subsequent manhunt, but there was not a single word describing the deadly explosives at Euharlee. Bank manager Clayton Harris, however, does recall the FBI informing him of the discovery of the dynamite three or four weeks later.

One can only imagine the somber congregation singing and praying in the little church on Sunday, completely unaware of the deadly explosives poised for destruction beneath the church floor.

Harris says he was infuriated when he learned of the proposed wanton destruction of the historic religious structure. "I really didn't get mad about that robbery – you know, angry, angry mad – until I found out about that church deal. The money they stole from the bank was unimportant compared to the destruction of the church."

To make their plan as effective as possible, the conspirators scouted the back roads and made practice driving runs for a number of days prior to the crime. They had to time the driving routes; select a discreet rendezvous point where they could abandon their "hot" car; and select a drop-off point where the men could hide out with the money

She dropped a handful of hundred-dollar bills into the bag then froze in fear.

overnight while the two women evaded roadblocks.

The criminals decided to steal a car for their getaway vehicle which they would abandon as soon as possible following the robbery. This tactic ultimately proved successful in temporarily stymieing area police who were hot in pursuit.

The stolen car – a 12-year-old Ford Galaxie – was snatched in Marietta. The criminals "hot-wired" the car to get it started. Before traveling back to Taylorsville, they stopped in Kennesaw where they stole a Michigan license plate, using it to replace the Georgia plate on the Galaxie.

Now the group had two vehicles: the Galaxie for the actual robbery, and a 1970 or '71 "dirty-brown" Ford or Chevrolet, owned by one of the members and which would be used for an escape after abandoning the Galaxie.

The Hold-Up of '76

Thursday, March 11, 1976, was the appointed day for the crime. The thieves' first act was to set the explosives beneath the Presbyterian Church at Euharlee and then go on to the bank.

At approximately 10:00 a.m., the group arrived in Taylorsville, and parked the stolen car directly in front of the bank. Charmaine Garrett remained at the wheel with the engine running, while the others quickly prepared themselves for the robbery.

The two men – Johnson and Anderson – carried pistols and pulled ski masks over their faces. They took pillow cases to use in the collection of the bank notes.

The men burst through the front door of the bank, and to their surprise, found themselves facing tellers who were protected behind bullet-proof glass (since the bank management had obviously begun taking precautionary measures for the robberies being suffered). Despite this fact, the door leading through the bullet-proof glass was quickly and easily penetrated by the gunmen, according to Clayton Harris.

Harris explained he was escorting two Boy Scout executives out after a meeting in his office. "I was still chatting with them as I opened the door, when these robbers came bouncing in the front door and got the drop on us." It was a lucky break for the bandits.

Harris said Johnson pushed him back inside the secure area, then went from one teller to the next with his pillow cases in a villainous sort of "trick-or-treat." Tellers Glenn Williams and Shelva Campbell scooped up the greenbacks and dumped them into the bags.

Johnson reached one flustered teller and reportedly yelled "Big money!" She dropped a handful of hundred-dollar bills into the bag then froze in fear. Johnson promptly prodded her for more with his gun.

Meanwhile, the other bandit, Donald Anderson, stationed himself next to the security door. Assistant Vice President Jackie Smith was sitting at her desk beneath Anderson's gaze, desperately trying to think of what she could do to save the diamonds she was wearing. She stealthily slipped them into the garbage can at her desk. The robbers, however, were not bothering with jewelry or coins that day. They were too busy bagging $22,000 in large denominations.

Harris remembered that one customer in the bank, Marron Haas, began to edge slowly towards the front door. Anderson turned his gun on him and stated matter-of-factly that if he took one more step, he would blow him in half.

"That got me right back up to the counter and got both my hands on the counter just like they were supposed to be," Haas later recounted. "I didn't make another move."

The right front tire of the Ford Galaxie used as an escape vehicle reveals the damage done by shots fired by Charles Ford, a bystander at the bank who attempted to stop the bandits. (Photo courtesy of Golden Memory Photos)

It was at this aged creaky iron bridge on Davistown Road that bandits Leon Johnson and Donald Anderson were picked up by their female accomplices in the early morning hours the morning after the Taylorsville bank robbery in 1976. The two men had spent the night in the woods in an attempt to elude the authorities. (Photo by Gordon Sargent)

Calling In The Cavalry

It was about this time that the gunmen's luck began to fade. Ray Hughes, a repairman, was working on a faulty air conditioner next to the bank's side door. He had been making frequent trips in and out of the bank, and had wedged a small screwdriver in the side door to keep it from locking.

It was on one of his trips from the air conditioner back into the bank that he suddenly noticed the masked men with guns, and he quickly and quietly backed out the door, unseen. He ran across the street to Wolfe's convenience store, instructing them to call the police and report the robbery.

Next in the fast-moving sequence of events, a bank customer drove up and parked around the corner from the front door. He was near Ray Hughes who had run back to the side of the bank. Either Hughes or a bystander reportedly shouted, "They're robbing the bank!"

When he learned the circumstances unfolding around him, the newly-arrived customer – Charles Ford – ran to his pick-up truck and grabbed a .22 caliber, two-shot derringer. He looked around quickly and thought he recognized the get-away car in which Charmaine Garrett sat. He started toward the getaway car, intending to confront the driver with his derringer, but thought better of it (which may have been wise, since Garrett had a sawed-off shotgun in the car with her).

Just as Ford returned to his pickup, the masked bandits dashed from the bank and jumped into their car. Garrett gunned the stolen Galaxie around the corner past Ford and his derringer, past Ray Hughes, the air conditioner repairman, and down the road leading to a rendezvous site three miles east of town.

As the vehicle roared past Charles Ford, he fired two shots at the front tire of the getaway car. The fleeing bandits fired back as they sped away, but the shots went wild and no one was hit. When the car was found later, the right front tire was flat with two bullet holes.

Meanwhile, the planned diversion – the detonation of the explosives beneath Euharlee Presbyterian Church – never happened. And with no diversion, the forces of law and order were able to collectively focus upon the bank theft. More bad luck for the bandits.

The charming 1853 Presbyterian

Church, unchanged in more than a century, was spared. It was weeks, however, before anyone even knew of the existence of the hidden dynamite. All this time, church members were lifted spiritually as they sat in their lovely old sanctuary each Sunday morning. Little did they know at that time how close they were to being lifted "physically" by the dynamite. Prayers in this house of worship undoubtedly took on a new dimension following discovery of the explosives.

Pursuit Of The Criminals

Meanwhile, the alarm had gone out to law enforcement contingents in a three or four county area following the report from the convenience store. Police forces quickly mobilized and concentrated on the shaken little community as well as on every back road in the county. Within ten minutes, Georgia State Patrol aircraft, including a helicopter, were overhead scouring the area.

According to press reports of that day, "Every available road leading out of Bartow County was covered. Shortly after the robbery, nearby Georgia State Patrol officers from Cartersville, Canton, Rome, Cedartown and Polk County, plus the Cedartown and Cartersville police departments, assisted in the investigation."

In a race with destiny, the stolen getaway car careened down the road from town, crossing GA Highway 113 and ignoring the stop sign. The bank robbers headed along Davistown Road for their appointed rendezvous. R.C. Free was traveling in the opposite direction towards Taylorsville. He noticed the reckless driving of the bandits and he was able to get a good look at the occupants of the car. He later assisted in their identification.

The bandits eventually reached their pre-planned rendezvous spot where they awaited the second car driven by Marvina Satterfield. During all the excitement, Satterfield had been constantly circling the back roads. A nearby resident noticed that she stopped beside the getaway car, picked up its occupants, then drove off. The bandits' carefully laid plans did not take into consideration the attentive eyes of curious bystanders.

An hour later, area police discovered the abandoned getaway car, its engine still running. They took fingerprints and searched for any clues.

The bandits meanwhile had continued to follow their plan, with the two men hiding out in the woods overnight, and the two women driving on alone to pass through the roadblocks. That night, weather forecasters had predicted scattered showers by morning and a low in the mid to upper 40s. Both Anderson and Johnson, no doubt, were soggy and quite cold by the time the women returned in the early hours of Friday morning to the little creaking bridge over Floyd Creek to pick them up.

Despite the uncomfortable circumstances, the criminals undoubtedly were feeling a little better about their odds for escape by this time. They headed south on GA Highway 61, and reportedly stopped to hide in an American Legion building for the remainder of the night.

Upon arrival in Paulding County, Donald Anderson, surprisingly, stopped

As the vehicle roared past Charles Ford, he fired two shots at the front tire of the getaway car.

to have his decayed teeth repaired by a dentist. He presumably used a portion of the stolen money to pay his bill. The bank notes were soon traced by the FBI, and Anderson was the first of the gang arrested, betrayed by a toothache.

In a continuing comedy of errors, the remaining bandits apparently boldly traveled back to Bartow County to Cartersville where they purchased a Lincoln Continental at City Motors. According to Clayton Harris, Johnson, Satterfield, and Garrett brazenly made a down payment with some of the stolen money, then had the audacity to visit the First National Bank (their original robbery target) where they sought a loan to finance the car.

The bandits' movements in Georgia after that point are unknown, but several weeks later, Charmaine Garrett was located and arrested by FBI agents. Following an intensive interrogation, she confessed to her part in the crimes. A few weeks later, Johnson also was caught, as was Marvina Satterfield. All, except Johnson, were quick to plea-bargain in exchange for lighter sentences.

The Trial

At this time, a federal trial for armed bank robbery in Cartersville, Georgia, would have taken place in Rome, but the defendants were considered too dangerous for the Rome jail. Also, Leon Johnson's brother, Morris, who was in the custody of federal agents in New Orleans at the time, was subpoenaed by the defense to testify on his brother's behalf. Both of the Johnson brothers had previously escaped from jail, and Morris Johnson, amazingly, had twice escaped from the Atlanta Federal Penitentiary, a feat which remains a record to this day.

Morris Johnson also was the proud owner of yet another record – that of making the FBI's *"10 Most Wanted"* list. Atlanta, therefore, with its more secure incarceration facilities, was chosen as the site for the trial.

Five months after the bank robbery, Leon Johnson was tried for his part in the crimes. He was the only defendant to plead "Not Guilty." Morris Johnson and five witnesses testified that Leon was home in Indiana at the time of the holdup.

Interestingly, Morris claimed it was he, not Leon, who had masterminded the Taylorsville job. His comments were carried in an article in the *Atlanta Constitution*:

"When the prosecutor asked Johnson if he committed the robbery, he answered, 'I pulled it. Yes.' "

The jury in the trial, however, was unmoved by the subterfuge. The trial lasted only a few days. On August 6, 1976, the jury took just 33 minutes to return a verdict of "Guilty" for Leon Johnson.

In September when the bandits were sentenced, Johnson drew a total of 50 years, Satterfield six years, Garrett ten years, and Anderson 15 years.

Bank robberies in recent years have increased at a pace not seen since the 1970s. One FBI official offered a surprising explanation for the increase:

"Lots of bank robbers convicted in the late 1970s and early 1980s are now back on the streets (because of liberal parole policies in use at the time)."

If Leon Johnson was paroled after serving a third of his sentence, the entire Taylorsville Bank robbery gang may all be freely circulating again someplace in the United States.

Meanwhile, back at the Taylorsville Bank, the window tellers in the tiny facility say they still keep a nervous eye on the front door as each customer enters today.

The Terrible Woolfolk Murders

On a hot August night in 1887, one of the most heinous mass murders in the history of the state of Georgia was carried out in the hinterlands of Bibb County.

When I passed through the gate and entered Rose Hill Cemetery, I was stunned by its utter vastness. Impressive cathedral-like monuments stood on hill after hill in the huge burial ground. What had begun as a simple task had now become a formidable project. How would I manage to find nine unmarked graves among the acres of obelisks, angels and mausoleums before me?

I backed my car up to the caretaker's house. He was out, but I found a map of the cemetery posted on the outside of the small building. Fortunately for me, it identified points of historical interest, and shortly thereafter, I stood for the first time in front of the nine simple graves which would haunt my dreams in the weeks ahead.

The burial plot was unobtrusive. The simplicity of the site begged for (and received) almost total anonymity, causing me to feel even more like just another intruder. These red brick-covered graves have been visited by thousands since 1887: curiosity seekers, newspaper reporters from across the United States, historians, and even a few brave descendants of the Woolfolk family – the source of this tragic story.

I was aware I was not the first to be haunted by the story of the Woolfolk family murders. For over one hundred years, the tragedy of what occurred on August 6, 1887, in Bibb County, has become the 20th century bane of the present-day Woolfolk family's existence.

I was aware I was not the first to be haunted by the story of the Woolfolk family murders.

The story of this horrible incident originates in Athens, Georgia, on the city's Pulaski Street, just off Prince Avenue. It is a street more known for its flowering dogwoods, homes of antebellum aristocrats, and towering houses of God, than the beginnings of a murder story. In the 1860s, this prestigious avenue witnessed the nurturing of a person who has become known as one of the most notorious villains in Georgia's criminal history. Tom Woolfolk – or as the nineteenth century press dubbed him, "Bloody Tom."

Beginnings

"Woolfolk, Woolfolk, see what you've done.

You've murdered your whole family and never fired a gun."

Tom Woolfolk's father, Richard Franklin Woolfolk[1] (pronounced WOOL-FORK) was graduated from the University of Georgia in Athens in 1854. He was married shortly thereafter to Susan Moore, daughter of Thomas Moore, who was superintendent of the Georgia Factory in Athens.

Susan and Richard began their life on a plantation in Bibb County just north of Macon, Georgia. *(Author's Note: Richard's father, Thomas Woolfolk, was from a prominent North Carolina family. Thomas had migrated to the Macon area during the initial settlement days of this community. He purchased a one hundred-acre tract of land and played a prominent role in Macon's early growth. Richard undoubtedly returned to his father's plantation following his marriage to Susan to manage the family business.)*

From the union of Susan and Richard came three children – two girls and a boy. The two females were named Floride and Lillie. The little boy – Thomas G. Woolfolk – was born on June 18, 1860.

Unfortunately, Susan died soon after her son's birth, and was buried in the yard of the Woolfolk plantation. A holly bush reportedly was planted at the spot to mark the grave.

Young Tom was sent to Athens shortly thereafter, quite probably when the U.S. Civil War called his father away. Tom was raised by his aunt, Fannie Moore Crane. Aunt Crane had married John Ross Crane, a builder of some renown in Athens prior to the war.[2]

Tom spent the first seven years of his life on Pulaski Street in a house that Crane built in 1842. Today, this structure still stands and is occupied by the University of Georgia chapter of Sigma Alpha Epsilon (SAE) fraternity.[3]

Dressed in her Victorian finery, Aunt Crane quite likely pushed the infant Tom in a carriage down Prince Avenue, past the Taylor-Grady house and other well-known Athens edifices during the early days of the Civil War.

And while Aunt Crane nurtured the infant, Richard Woolfolk fought in the war. During Georgia's Reconstruction days, Tom undoubtedly played happily and innocently with other children on the great lawn of the Crane home, with never a hint of his dark future in his daily activities.

Following the close of the war, Richard Woolfolk apparently remarried, his bride being Mattie E. Howard, a graduate of the Forsyth Female Collegiate Institute in Monroe County. Richard and Mattie began a new family which by 1887 included six more children – two boys and four girls.[4]

At age seven, young Tom was sent to the Woolfolk plantation twelve miles outside Macon to join his father and stepmother in a new life. *(Author's Note: Many people today maintain the old plantation site is reached via Bonnie Gilbert Road; others say Thomaston Road. No remains of the planta-*

tion exist today.) He apparently was a problem child from the outset. He reportedly never liked his stepmother Mattie. More accurately, he resented her tremendously. He returned many times to Athens, a place where he obviously felt most comfortable, to visit his Aunt Crane. His final visit was in June of 1887, just before the terrible night.

First Failures

Upon reaching manhood, Tom sought a profession, attempting numerous business endeavors, undoubtedly with the aid of his father. He, however, was a miserable failure in each one, including stints at running a plantation, managing a store, driving a streetcar in Macon, and owning a grocery store.

Despite his shortcomings, money and property became an obsession with Tom. He told friends that he hoped to get his father's estate. However, as more children were born to his father and Mattie, it became increasingly obvious this dream of an extravagant inheritance quite likely would never be fulfilled. As a result, Tom became embittered toward his father, and was increasingly unpleasant and cold toward his stepmother, choosing to blame her for depriving him of his opportunity for wealth.

At age 27, Tom married Georgia Bird, the daughter of a well-to-do farmer. In a rather strange ceremony, Tom and Georgia boarded a train passing south to Macon and were married in the aisle as the train proceeded full-speed ahead. Georgia lived near Holton, Georgia, (Jones County), and the couple apparently boarded at the train station there.

Following the wedding, Tom promised his new bride that he would take her to a fine mansion in Macon. He, however, had nowhere to take her except to the home of his sister. The marriage lasted all of three weeks.

Strange behavior, however, had become the norm for Tom. Prior to his wedding, he had already attracted considerable attention to himself in Athens. He had also begun carrying a pistol, even when visiting his aunt.

Following his failed attempt at marriage, Tom told one acquaintance that everybody was against him, and that he had no friends. He also said that he was a fool for marrying Georgia since she was no good, and that he might have *"to frail her out."*

The Murders

After his professional failures, Tom returned to the Woolfolk plantation where he was reduced to working for nine dollars a month for his father. His labors in this capacity undoubtedly were a rude awakening – far from the privileged life he craved. It is unknown today, but at some point shortly after beginning his ministrations at the plantation, it is believed by many that Tom's anger, jealousy and resentment boiled over early one fateful morning, sending his life careening into a dark void from which he would never recover.

On Saturday, August 6, 1887, between 2 and 4 a.m., Tom knocked on the door of a local cabin where he awoke Green Locket, a black man who worked for the family. He told Green that something awful had happened. "Someone got into the house and killed my family," he reportedly blurted.

Upon their arrival at the Woolfolk plantation, Tom tried to persuade Locket to enter the house to investigate. Locket, however, apparently decided discretion was the better part of valor, and chose instead to go get neighbors for help.

When the neighbors of Hazzard District of Bibb County arrived, Tom repeated his story of someone entering the house and murdering the Woolfolk family. He said he had escaped by jumping through a window.

In what may have been a tragic twist of fate, later testimony indicates one of the neighbors who had gathered on the scene that night had remarked that he heard a noise in the house. Tom, reportedly, immediately reentered the house alone to investigate, remaining inside for twenty to thirty minutes, according to eyewitnesses. When he returned, he told the men outside that he could find no one alive.

The following is an account of the murder scene as published in the October 30, 1890 issue of the *Macon Telegraph*.[5] It undoubtedly was a reprint of the original news report of 1887. This account is provided in an abbreviated format, since the full account is considered far too graphic.

"Finally it was decided to make an investigation, and not until then was the whole horror of the butchery discovered. In the back room on the left of the hall the bodies of Capt. Woolfolk and his wife were found lying on the bed with their skulls crushed by fearful blows. Across the foot of the same bed was the body of the baby (eighteen months), also with its head crushed by fearful blows. Across the foot of the same bed and half on the floor was Miss Pearl (age 17). She had dreadful cuts on the back of the neck as well as on the hand, which showed that she had defended her life with desperate courage, and the position of the body showed that her murderer had killed her either in another room or in the hall and then had dragged the body across the floor and thrown it where it was found.

"Just inside the door of the same room, the body of Charles H. Woolfolk, a small boy (age 5) was found. It was evident that he had entered the room and a single blow had crushed in his skull and his body had been left lying where it fell.

"A little further in the room was the body of Richard Woolfolk, Jr., a young man of 20, and it was evident that he, too, had made a struggle for life and had not been killed easily. His forehead and part of his face was disfigured with numerous small gashes, which gave rise to the theory that he had seized the axe in the hands of the murderer and had held to it until the sharp edge had pushed into his face so often that he became blinded with his own blood and could struggle no longer with his opponent. The coup de grace was delivered in the top of the head, crushing the skull . . .

"Across the hall was the body of Mrs. Temperance West,[6] an aged lady who was on a visit, and those of Rosebud, aged 7 years, and Annie, aged 10, were found (as well). Mrs. West had been struck while asleep and one hand still rested under the head which was horribly crushed. On the floor, little Rosebud was stretched, and near the window, half covered with a sheet, was Annie. It was evident that Annie had been the last victim, and that she had dragged the sheet from the bed in a wild

From the outset, most individuals suspected Tom as the guilty party.

effort to hide herself, and that while crawling to the open window to make her escape, she had been overtaken by the murderer and slaughtered like the rest of her family by blows from an axe."

Convincing Evidence

From the outset, most individuals suspected Tom as the guilty party. According to the *Macon Telegraph* newspaper, the neighbors, even before law enforcement officials arrived, had gone to Tom and *"with hard-set faces and determined voices, told him that he was under arrest for murder, and if he attempted to escape he would be killed like a dog."*

Daylight brought hundreds of curious people to the scene and every clue at the investigation continued to point at Tom.

Bloody footprints were found in all the rooms of the house. Tom acknowledged they were his.

In the room that Tom shared with his brothers, it was found that the floor had been scrubbed with soap and water within a few hours of the murders. Tom said he had washed his feet because they were bloody and he had then wiped up the floor. However, it was apparent to all that had anyone else been in the house, they could not have avoided leaving bloody foot marks and Tom's were the only tracks found.

The gathering crowd also noticed that Tom had on a dirty shirt and trousers which were much too large for him. Later, the clothes were proven to be the property of his murdered brother. Tom refused to explain what had become of his own clothes.

Remarkably, from the first summons for help, Tom had displayed an unusual calm. As news of the terrible crime spread and more people began arriving, Tom, reportedly, sat beneath a tree, totally emotionless. No tears were shed and "not a muscle quivered in agitation.

In one strange turn, Tom asked that a china cup be filled with water from the well and brought to him. When the water arrived, however, Tom reportedly looked at the cup for a second, touched it to his lips, and then strangely dumped the water on the ground.

Local tradition maintains that it was this clue which caused Sheriff Cooper to discover the critical evidence which was used against Tom. According to one version of this story, Cooper went to the well and drew a bucket of water, offering Tom a drink. When Tom became visibly repulsed at the offer, it aroused Cooper's suspicions. He reportedly sent a man down into the well where Tom's blood-stained clothes were discovered.

Newspaper accounts, however, offered a slightly different variation of the story. In these reports, a Sheriff Westcot is credited with the discovery.

"A bundle of clothes, soaked in blood, was brought up," the news article explained, *"and they were identified beyond the peradventure of a doubt as having belonged to Tom. There was a shirt, an undershirt, a pair of trousers, and a pair of drawers. They were all dyed a deep red, except the drawers and even they were terribly stained. They had been rolled up in such a way that the water had not been able to soak it (the blood) out and on the leg of the drawers, just above the knee, on the inside, was the imprint of a hand, with the fingers pointing up, just as they would have been if a struggling person had grasped the murderer by the leg."*

Following the discovery of the clothes, Sheriff Westcot immediately removed Tom to the Macon jail, because the incensed crowd was threatening to lynch him on the spot. Upon arrival at the jail, Tom was stripped and searched, and on the inside of his leg, in exactly the same spot which corresponded with the hand mark on his underclothing, was a similar imprint dyed into his flesh. Tom argued that he had rested his hand when it was wet with his own blood on his leg. It soon became obvious, however, that in order for him to have successfully placed his hand on his leg in such a manner, he would have been *"obliged to assume an acrobatic posture, as the fingers pointed up instead of down."*

Coroner Hodnet conducted an inquest that same day. Tom was stripped to reveal the bloody handprint to the coroner's jury. They, as a result, became convinced there was enough evidence to try Tom for capital murder. He was moved shortly thereafter from Macon to Atlanta to prevent mob violence.

19th Century Journalism

The *Atlanta Constitution* played up the Woolfolk murders and the story eventually was reported in papers as far away as the *Cincinnati Enquirer* and even on the front page of the *New York Times*. The *Times* called it *"the bloodiest, blackest chapter in Georgia criminal history."* Other papers called it a *crime "without parallel in the criminal history of the South if not the world"* and *"the bloodiest tragedy in the annals of crime."* It was the press which first labeled the accused murderer as *"Bloody Tom."*

It, however, was a Macon photographer who captured the true grisliness of the crime. Traveling to the Woolfolk home the morning following the crime, before even any part of the scene had been disturbed, he photographed the mangled corpses and blood-stained walls and furniture. The photos were sold on the streets and mailed out to various newspapers.

None of the photos taken in 1887 are known to still be in existence today. A copy of the October 29, 1890 issue of the *Macon Evening News*, however, offered a glimpse of the carnage of the terrible crime scene, with sketches likely drawn from the photos taken by the photographer. The illustrations show a very bloody murder scene, offer a vivid reminder that Annie, the child of ten, had tried desperately to escape. The sketch shows how she made it to the window, but no farther, as the terrible blows from the ax rendered her unconscious, her hands still clutching the open window sill.

The *Evening News* also detailed the layout of the home. It was described as a one-story four-room structure with a porch of six columns. It had a central hallway with three bedrooms and a parlor.

The boys slept in the front bedroom on the left, across the hallway from the parlor which was on the right. Captain and Mrs. Woolfolk occupied the back bedroom on the left. The baby's cradle was in their room too. The girls and the guest, Mrs. West, slept in the third bedroom in the right rear portion of the house. Six of the victims were found in one room and three in another.

According to reports, a Macon undertaker was the individual responsible for going to the scene of the tragedy and preparing the bodies for burial. The task took longer than expected, and it was Sunday morning around 6:00 a.m. when the funeral procession left the plantation and headed to Rose Hill Cemetery.

As I traveled the twelve desolate miles west of Macon, I tried to imagine the hot August morning when five hearses followed by wagons and carriages bearing equipment and people moved slowly toward Macon. Along the route, the procession was joined by more carriages, buggies, wagons, carts, men on horseback, and people on foot, until, according to reports, the line of mourners had become a mile long before the hearses reached Macon. Others who did not join the procession, lined up along the road to watch.

When the procession passed through the streets of Macon, the people became so frenzied that an outbreak of violence was feared by local law enforcement officials.

The nine murdered Woolfolk family members were laid to rest in two rows under an ancient tree on a hill just above Macon's Civil War veterans. The Ocmulgee River flows peacefully in the background.

The Woolfolk graves are topped by rectangular brick and are unmarked. Only the name *"Woolfolk"* on the steps that lead down to the graves identifies the plot.

According to reports, the five adults were buried in black coffins and lie in one row. The only indication of who rests beneath each of the brick coverings may be discerned by a slight difference in the length of the last two brick overlays. The slightly shorter overlays obviously indicate where Richard Jr. and Pearl were placed. These rectangles also suggest the order of the first row (from left to right): Richard F. Woolfolk, Mattie H., Temperance West, Richard Jr., and Pearl. The four small children undoubtedly lay in the second row, probably also in order of age: Annie, Rosebud, Charles, and the baby, Mattie. Tom and his two older sisters were not buried with the family.

The Trials

I made a point of visiting Aunt Crane's grave at Oconee Hill Cemetery in Athens. She and Tom's sisters – Floride Woolfolk Edwards Shackelford and Lillie Woolfolk Cowan – stood by Tom to the very end. The sisters greeted Tom with a kiss upon their arrival in court each day. When someone in the audience shouted "Hang him! Hang him!" during the closing arguments of the first trial, Tom's sisters threw their arms around him as if to protect him from the mob in the courtroom. Tom, however, was found guilty by a Bibb County jury in twelve minutes.

John C. Rutherford, Tom's lawyer, asked for a new trial. And Aunt Crane, as devoted as ever, was there to pin a bouquet of violets on Tom in 1889 when he was granted the new trial. The three stood by Tom during the proceedings of the first trial in Bibb County, the second trial in Houston County, and during hearings in the Georgia Supreme Court for a third trial. The three always arrived with flowers, fruit and a kiss, and all three testified to Tom's affection for the whole family.

As for his own demeanor, Tom apparently exhibited a total disinterest as well as disdain for the trial proceedings. During the second trial, he resorted to outright disrespect by spending most of his time reading Joel Tyler Headley's *Napoleon And His Marshals.*

Tom had hired John C. Rutherford of Athens as his lawyer. The Rutherfords were prominent Athenians as were the Cranes. John C.'s father had been a professor at the University of Georgia. John's sister, Mildred, was principal of The Lucy Cobb Institute on Milledge Avenue in Athens. The historic structure in which the Institute once existed still stands as of this writing in Athens.

During his defense of Tom in the Bibb County trial in December of 1887,

Rutherford was unable to blame the slaughter on anyone else, and though the evidence in law terms was "circumstantial," it was also considered very strong. There simply was no one else at which to direct the vehemence of those wishing to convict Tom, and he did make a very convincing target.

Many believed it was Green Locket that had foiled Tom's original plan for an alibi. Most believed it was Tom's intention to get Locket inside the house that night, kill him, and then accuse him of committing the heinous butchery. During the trials, there were several attempts to blame the murders on tramps or blacks.

In the account of the murders in the *Macon Evening News*, it was speculated that Pearl was the individual who had revived early that morning after the neighbors arrived. She quite likely made the noise that drew Tom so quickly back into the house. Many believed that she received the initial blows from the axe in the hallway, but since her body was found lying across the foot of the bed on which her father and mother lay, she had revived from the early blows and had made it to the bed, and was struggling there when Tom returned to finish her.

Tom reportedly showed no nervousness or anxiety during the first trial. His calmness was recorded repeatedly in news accounts.

The Georgia Supreme Court ordered a new trial in February of 1889. He was being re-tried for the murder of his father, and was warned by the judge that even if he were found *"Not Guilty,"* there were eight other indictments on which he could be tried.

The new trial took place in Perry in May of 1889. Once again, in less than an hour, the Houston County jury brought back the verdict of *"Guilty."*

Some ladies in Macon sent Tom flowers, fruits, and *"delicacies"* after the second *"Guilty"* verdict. His wife, however, was more direct. She divorced him and took back her maiden name – Bird.

Undeterred, Rutherford filed for a third trial. It was denied. Rutherford then appealed to the Georgia Supreme Court. Some said Rutherford was a determined lawyer and would take the case all the way to the United States Supreme Court if he lost the appeal.

The Georgia Supreme Court heard arguments in June of 1890. In July of 1890, the Court upheld the second conviction of Tom Woolfolk and refused to order another trial. Rutherford became ill soon afterward and was unable to handle Tom's case any further. Many believed at the time that if Rutherford had not become ill, Tom would never have been hanged for the murders. However, such was not the case, and Tom was finally sentenced, and his date of execution was set for October 29, 1890.

Closing Moments

Tom was finally sentenced, and his date of execution was set for October 29, 1890.

One stop on my Macon to Perry to Hawkinsville swing during research for this article, was to locate the Dr. A.C. Hendrick Memorial Bridge in Perry. This structure which connects with the General Courtney Hodges

Boulevard, is about a mile west of the Houston County Courthouse, and spans a valley where Big Indian Creek joins Fanny Gresham Branch.

I turned off the bridge to the right and parked my car in a churchyard on the hill. As cars whizzed over the bridge, I followed an old road-bed down to the valley underneath. I stopped near the place I thought the gallows had stood that day on October 29, 1890, and tried to imagine the event which had transpired on this site.

On the day of the execution, a reporter from the *Macon Telegraph* wrote that a *"noticeable feature of the day is the immense number of ladies and children in attendance."* Local folklore maintains some of the onlookers even munched on 'possum sandwiches as they awaited the fateful event.

The *Telegraph* report continued by explaining that *"the Perry Rifles, who had recently won a prize at a state drill in Atlanta, marched to the jail under the command of Capt. W.C. Davis, and formed a line in front. Soon, Sheriff Cooper and Deputy Sheriff Riley escorted Tom Woolfolk to a carriage waiting in front. Under the escort of the Rifles, the carriage moved to the scene of death, moving past the red brick courthouse. The crowd, estimated at from 7,000 to 10,000, followed."*

The *Telegraph* reporter also described the appearance of the execution site, a spot at which I was now standing some 103 years after the event. *"Meanwhile, as the hour of noon came near, the multitude began to gather about the gallows, which had been erected in a little valley half a mile from the courthouse and on the Central road. A small stream flowed through the depression which was surrounded by hills almost shutting it in on all sides and forming a natural coliseum. On the one side was the railroad crossing the brook on a low trestle. On the other was the town cemetery. It was on a hill top, looking down upon the scene with its white monuments confronting the victim as he stood upon the scaffold. Three negro churches crowned the hill tops around. The white gallows stood in the middle of the little valley.*

"A circular space of 150 feet had been roped off at the scaffold for those who had tickets, around 200 people. The military marched inside the enclosure and with fixed bayonets assisted the deputies in keeping the mass of people from pressing upon the reserved space. Tom Woolfolk declared his innocence from the scaffold and prayed with his head upraised toward heaven. A few seconds before the drop fell, Tom said 'God bless you all.'"

According to reports, Tom Woolfolk became one of the unfortunate souls of that day whose necks did not break after dropping through the scaffold to the end of the rope. When this happened, there was nothing to do but wait until the body ceased twitching and jerking, and it often was a long painful wait too.

In Tom's case, the noose had slipped from its proper position under the right ear. The trauma had partially torn the black death cap from Tom's head, revealing his stretched neck.

Seven minutes later, Woolfolk's pulse reportedly was still beating. Every ten or twenty seconds, his breast heaved and his shoulders drew up. Eleven minutes later, however, there was no pulse. He was pronounced dead at 1:58 p.m. The body was cut down, placed in a coffin, and sent by hearse to Hawkinsville.

Final Resting Place

I received no unusual looks when I stopped in at the Hawkinsville Courthouse to ask directions to Orange Hill Cemetery. An elderly gentleman asked who I was looking for and when I told him, he recounted several stories about Tom Woolfolk, including the inevitable one about how for decades people have seen a strange light near Tom's grave.

Tom is buried next to his older sister, Floride Shackelford. The tombstone appears to have been vandalized at one time and repaired. The name Thomas G. Woolfolk is barely legible today.

Prior to his death, Tom had been concerned about his place of burial. It was he (not another family member) that had asked not to be buried in Macon with his murdered family. He had also asked that no one view the body except his brother-in-law, Mr. Cowan, husband of Lillie Cowan. His grave was dug in Orange Hill Cemetery, the body placed therein, and walled with brick and cemented.

Tom never admitted to the murders. However, even Aunt Crane and one sister admitted to his strange behavior just prior to the murders. In an interview in the *Athens Weekly Banner-Watchman* shortly after the crime, Floride and Aunt Crane said they had discussed Tom and had agreed that he must be losing his mind. Floride said she had told her father of their conclusion but that Captain Woolfolk had not agreed.

Today, Millie Stewart, an avid researcher and family historian, has doubts about Tom's guilt. "My grandmother said he was mean enough, but I don't think he did it," she explains.

Some evidence, revealed years after Tom's execution, may lend credence to her doubts. Strange confessions to the murders were forthcoming from other individuals. Articles in the August 6, 1987 issue of the *Telegraph* and in the August 7, 1987 issue of the Anderson (SC) *Independent-Mail* revealed that ten years after Tom's execution, a criminal named Simon Cooper had been lynched in South Carolina and a note found in his diary explained ominously: *"Tom Woolfolk was mighty slick, but I fixed him. I would have killed him with the rest of the damn family, but he was not at home."*

In 1893, a letter appeared in the *Pittsburgh Dispatch* which stated that the writer of the letter had met a tramp who killed not only the Borden family of Massachusetts in that highly publicized crime, but a farm family near Macon. The tramp confessed that he and some friends were in Macon a few years earlier where they had trouble with a farmer. He said they went into the farmer's house and killed all but one son that had escaped. They said they took some of his clothes and threw them, with blood on them, into the well.

A reprint of the article appeared in the *Macon Telegraph* on August 28, 1893. It identified the similarities of the two crimes. Both Tom Woolfolk and Lizzie Borden were at odds with their parents over money; both had stepmothers; both exhibited extraordinary self-control during the investigations; both murders included an axe, and both occurred in early August. The Bordens were murdered on a Thursday, August 4.

There is also one other similarity – the massive publicity on both murders which contributed to the outcome of both trials. However, in the case of Lizzie Borden, positive newspaper coverage quite possibly contributed to a *"Not Guilty"* verdict. Tom Woolfolk, by comparison, received considerable negative publicity before his trial, and quickly received *"Guilty"* verdicts in both of his trials. He was virtually convicted in newspapers all over the state prior to his trial.

To many of the Woolfolk descendants today, the Woolfolk murders story is wearisome. "It doesn't bother me. I'm a genealogist," Millie Stewart concludes, "but it did bother my parents and grandparents.

Millie's attitude undoubtedly is fortunate. She says at least once a year, someone knocks on her door investigating the Woolfolk murders.

After the hanging, Tom's sisters, Floride and Lillie, sold the old Woolfolk plantation. Millie Stewart has found deeds which state the land was divided between the two sisters.

The old house where the violent murders took place stood vacant for many years. In 1909, it became, for a short while, the headquarters of the Macon Auto Club. Then it stood vacant again for a number of years.

In 1964, Merton E. Coulter, professor of history at the University of Georgia, visited the site when writing an article for the *Georgia Historical Quarterly*. He described *how "nothing was left except two large piles of brick and stones, marking the chimney places; a depression, appearing to have been the cellar; a well nearly filled up near a cedar tree; some shrubbery; and a large holly tree, undoubtedly marking the spot where Susan M. Woolfolk, Tom's mother, was buried."*

When I visited the spot commonly identified today as the former Woolfolk plantation, I found, as suspected, that nothing whatsoever remains of the now infamous site. Some individuals think the locale has been covered over by a new housing development. Others believe it to be permanently buried beneath the dark waters of Lake Tobesofkee.

ENDNOTES

1/ Richard F. Woolfolk was one of four sons born (1832) to Thomas Woolfolk.

2/ John Ross Crane was responsible for the construction of the University Chapel (1832) and New College (1832) on the old campus of the University of Georgia; the First Presbyterian Church and several homes, including the Ferdinand Phinizy house (1857) in Athens.

3/ Several previous articles have stated that Tom Woolfolk grew up on Prince Avenue in the John Ross Crane home. This structure supposedly was located at 716 Prince, and was described as having been demolished. However, following research on the work of John Ross Crane in Athens, I discovered that his home still exists (built in 1842) on Pulaski Street (an extension of Prince). In 1924, the house was sold out of private ownership to the Athens Lodge and then again in 1929 to Sigma Alpha Epsilon (SAE) fraternity. It continues to serve as the fraternity house today. Crane died in 1866, leaving the home to Fannie Moore Crane. In Longstreet's *Annals Of Athens*, there is a reference to a Mrs. Ross Crane. She was living on Prince in the home of a Col. Billups. This house, destroyed by fire, was not the fine home built by John Ross Crane (as previous articles have indicated). Research indicates Fannie Crane sold her large home on Pulaski Street following her husband's death in 1866, moving into the Billups home shortly thereafter. Former writers undoubtedly were confused by the recorded fact that Mrs. Ross Crane's last known residence (which was quite near the 1842 home built by her husband), was destroyed by fire, deducing they were one and the same. It is therefore quite likely that Tom Woolfolk was raised for seven years in the fine structure which today houses SAE fraternity in Athens. It was shortly after John Ross Crane's death in 1866, that young Tom was sent back to Macon. Therefore, when he visited Athens from that point forward, he may indeed have stayed with Aunt Crane at her home (the old Billups house) on Prince Avenue, but it and the 1842 house on Pulaski Street were not one and the same.

4/ In 1887, the day of the murders, Richard F., Jr., was age 20, and Charles age 5. The girls included Pearl, age 17, a student at Wesleyan Female College; Anne, age 10; Rosebud, age 7; and Mattie, eighteen months.

5/ The account was republished in the Wednesday, October 29 1890 issue of the *Macon Telegraph* following the hanging.

6/ Temperance West was Mattie Howard's aunt.

The Assassination Of Chief William McIntosh

On a spring night in 1825, Creek warriors set ablaze the home of William McIntosh on the Chattahoochee River near present-day Carrollton, Georgia, and then summarily executed the famed leader during the final days of the Creek Nation in the Southeast.

Were the songbirds silent along the banks of the Chattahoochee River on Saturday, April 25, 1825, as the fatal day dawned at the home of Creek Indian Chief William McIntosh in present-day Carroll County, Georgia? Even the wildlife around the wilderness home must have been unaware of approaching danger – or else the very silence of the forest might have aroused the soon-to-be victims to consciousness, keenly accustomed as they were to hear the first sounds of a new day. On that morning – some 166 years ago – the Creek Indians of Alabama murdered or legally executed (according to which side one takes in the issue) one of their major chiefs – William McIntosh – and two others, all of whom had participated in the signing of the Treaty of Indian Springs.

The Indians' rage could be understandable. As a result of the treaty – signed on February 12, 1825 – the last remaining Creek Indian lands in Georgia were ceded to the U.S. Government for the use of Georgia. The negotiations for the ratification of that treaty had been in progress for a number of years, because Georgia had been pressing for more land to enable the expansion of her frontiers westward. The Creeks, on the other hand, viewing with alarm their diminishing homeland in what today are Georgia and Alabama, were reluctant to part with another strip of ground to land-hungry pioneers and settlers.

Caught in the vortex of these negotiations were Georgia Governor George Troup and his cousin – mixed-blood Creek Indian Chief William McIntosh. The two were related through Governor Troup's mother who was a sister of McIntosh's father, making the two leaders first cousins. Both men were astute politicians in their own domains, and both conspired to cede the Creeks' last vestige of lands in today's Georgia to the encroaching whites.

In the 1820s, despite the constant immigration of colonists into the region, most of Georgia was still a frontier; and the native Indians, by and large, still lived by their own code of ethics and morals. Warnings had been sounded through the years by other chiefs in the Creek Nation, extolling to all who would listen, the punishment which would be meted out to any member of the Nation involved with any further diminishment of the Nation's land. But McIntosh, with his cousin in the position as head of the rapidly growing white government in Georgia, chose to ignore these threats, thus sealing his fate.

On February 12, 1825, McIntosh, along with a large number of lower chiefs, signed the now infamous "Treaty of Indian Spring," so-called because the signing was conducted at the site of McIntosh's home/inn which still stands as of this writing in present-day Butts County, Georgia. This fine structure, though unprotected and unpreserved in later years, somehow managed to survive intact to the 21st century, and is currently preserved and maintained at Indian Spring by the Butts County Historic Society.

In payment for signing the treaty, the U.S. Government agreed to pay the Creek Nation (McIntosh) the sum of $200,000 "as soon as practicable after ratification of this treaty." McIntosh received other considerations as well, including his large reservation on the Chattahoochee River in present-day western Georgia.

For years, a pervading myth has maintained that McIntosh was paid the $200,000 in person and in gold. One tale even relates how many wagons were necessary to transport the gold back to McIntosh's Chattahoochee River plantation. No evidence, however, has ever surfaced to substantiate these stories, and no mention of gold was made in the language of the treaty. Despite this fact, rumors persist to this day, and searches continue for "McIntosh's gold" all along the road from Indian Spring in Butts County to the site of McIntosh's Chattahoochee River home.

Immediately after the treaty was signed, the Creek chiefs who had opposed the signing met in secret at several sites in the Creek towns of east-central Alabama, where they began discussion of retaliation against those individuals who had signed away the tribal lands. It was decided that William McIntosh would die, as would his son-in-law, Samuel Hawkins. Hawkins lived on the Tallapoosa River near the Creek towns which once existed in today's central Alabama.

Within the secret meetings, detailed and careful instructions were provided to a group of the tribe's warriors on how they were to meet and march to McIntosh's plantation in today's Carroll County (on the Chattahoochee River) in Georgia. The exact number of Creeks involved in this group of executioners is unknown today; best estimates range from 170 to 400, according to several different sources which recorded events at that time.

The group, principally from Ocfuskee and Tookabatchie – both large Indian towns in east-central Alabama – met and marched on foot and in single file toward Georgia. They traveled so silently that they were undetected on their journey, reaching the neighborhood of McIntosh's Chattahoochee plantation near the evening of the second day. They reportedly stationed themselves on both sides of an intersection, about one mile northwest of McIntosh's home, and awaited wee hours of early morning to carry out their assignation.

It was on the evening of their arrival, that an ironic incident befell the warriors. According to accounts of the day, McIntosh and his son-in-law Samuel Hawkins – both of whom were slated for execution by the Creeks – met at the very intersection where the Indians were concealed, totally unaware of the vengeful warriors surrounding them. The two remained upon their mounts as they conversed at length. The Indians were so quiet that, even though they could

Shortly before his murder in 1825, Chief William McIntosh sat for his portrait. His formal clothing seems to reflect both his Native American as well as his Scottish heritage.

This early postcard shows a Seminole Indian of Florida, photographed circa 1916. The clothing and outfittings of the Seminoles were similar to that of their Creek cousins of Alabama.

almost have reached out and touched the two unsuspecting men, they remained undiscovered. The warriors could easily have killed the two men on the spot, but had been instructed to execute McIntosh "in his own yard, in the presence of his family, and to let his blood run upon the soil of that reservation which the Georgians had secured to him in the treaty which he had made with them."

After concluding his meeting with McIntosh, Hawkins reportedly turned and headed home, with McIntosh riding a short distance beside him. Turning back toward his own home shortly thereafter, McIntosh again passed right through the hidden Indians, and again they had an opportunity to kill him, but did not. As Hawkins continued westward to return to his farm on the Tallapoosa River (near present-day Talladega, Alabama), a chosen few of the warriors separated from the main group and silently followed him, intent upon an equally bloody demise for him.

The main body of the Creek warriors reportedly remained in the woods until about 3:00 a.m. of the fateful morning, at which time, they gathered "fat lighter" (the flammable resinous heart-wood of aged pine trees) to use to burn McIntosh's house. They quietly surrounded the house, and at daybreak, set the structure ablaze to force McIntosh and his family outside.

For a number of years, McIntosh (as did several other prominent Indian chiefs during this period in Georgia history) had operated an inn as well as a ferry near his home on the Chattahoochee River. The inn provided accommodations for travelers using the "Alabama Road" which passed beside the site. Inside this inn on the night of the attack, five persons were sleeping, including Chilly McIntosh, son of the doomed William. Chilly, upon hearing the commotion in the yard, leaped from a back window and swam the Chattahoochee, escaping with his life. He apparently had immediately recognized the situation in the yard nearby, and, as he was also one of the signers of the ill-fated treaty, knew his life was also in grave danger.

The Creek warriors, meanwhile, had had the presence of mind to bring a white man (named Hudman or Hutton; records differ on the spelling of the name) with them, in order to certify that no harm had come to any whites in the inn. There were whites sleeping there, including one white peddler. Accounts of the day maintain that the peddler "became a most wretched man" after the commotion began, until Hutton reassured him that no harm would come his way. The Indians, true to their word, left the peddler unharmed, but destroyed his wares, along with everything else in sight.

However, another of the signers of the treaty, a minor Creek chief named Toma Tustinugee who was also sleeping in the inn, was not so lucky. The warriors, totally unexpecting this additional prize, removed Toma to the yard, where, in the light of the burning building, they executed him summarily by firing some fifty bullets into his body.

McIntosh, in the meantime, was having problems of his own. The flames from his home threw a bright light over the yard, giving his astonished family a clear view of the painted warriors surrounding the house. To the warriors' credit, they allowed McIntosh's two wives and his children to remove themselves from the burning house; no harm befell them. They, however, did not allow the women or children to remove any articles with them from the burning structure. Consequently, the women were wearing only their night clothes, and the children were naked.

After the women and children were removed, McIntosh reportedly barricaded his front door and stood near it until it was forced open. He then retreated to the second floor, guns in his hands, returning the fire from the warriors.

Shouting "McIntosh! We have come! We have come! We told you, if you sold the land to the Georgians, we would come!," the Creeks continued to discharge their weapons into the burning house. McIntosh's wives, in the meantime, were imploring the assailants to spare their husband, or at least to remove him from the burning house before shooting him. They told the Creeks that McIntosh was an Indian like themselves, and, as a brave man, did not deserve to die in the flames.

In short order, the burning house forced McIntosh to return to the first floor, where he was met by a hail of bullets. He fell to the floor and was seized by the legs and dragged to the yard outside by the warriors. While lying in the yard, and while blood coursed from numerous wounds, he reportedly raised himself on one arm and surveyed his murderers with a look of defiance. At that moment, an Ocfuskee Indian plunged a long knife to the hilt into McIntosh's breast. It is recorded that he took one long breath before collapsing and dying.

The Indians, however, were far from finished. Their appetites had only been whetted and their wrath was far from depleted. They proceeded to plunder the out-houses and to kill every domesticated animal in sight. Anything they could not carry with them, they destroyed with vehemence. Hogs were shot and left lying in the yard beside the dead men. All the peddler's goods were removed from the inn and destroyed.

One of McIntosh's wives went to the warriors and requested that they give her a white suit in which to bury her husband. This request was quickly refused. McIntosh

Because he moved in both the white man's and the red man's world, Chief William McIntosh was able to see opportunities for financial gain where other Indians could not. The inn at Indian Spring built by McIntosh in 1823 is a good example. (Illustration by John Kollock. Reprinted with permission. All rights reserved.)

EARLY INN – Known originally as the McIntosh Inn, the structure known today as Indian Spring Inn was built by Chief William McIntosh and his cousin, Joe Baillie, in 1823 at Indian Spring. A westward travel route in that vicinity had become known as the McIntosh Trail, and was a much used route by early white settlers and Indians alike in the late 18th and early 19th centuries. By the early- to mid-20th century, the inn had fallen into disrepair, but was completely renovated and returned to its original design by the Butts County Historic Society in the 1990s. (Photo courtesy of Butts Co. Historic Society)

was scalped and left lying in the yard where he had died. He later was buried in the yard a short distance away.

After looting and destroying the plantation, the Indians returned to their Alabama homes, carrying McIntosh's scalp with them. It later was exhibited in the public square at Ocfuskee. The scalp was a warning to others who might be tempted to take similar measures with the remaining Creek lands.

Samuel Hawkins suffered a similar fate. After following Hawkins home to Alabama, the Creek warriors assigned to him quietly surrounded his farmhouse where they remained until daybreak. Following instructions, Hawkins was not killed out-right, but was taken prisoner until the fate of McIntosh became known. About 3:00 p.m., after word had been received of McIntosh's death, Hawkins also was killed and scalped. The latter trophy was displayed with that of McIntosh in Ocfuskee Town.

The resulting repercussions of these killings were felt all the way to the halls of Congress. Called "murder" by the whites, and "a legal execution" by the Indians, the incident was actually an act of desperation by a nation of people quickly being displaced from their homeland by an on-rushing tide of white settlers. It would only be a short ten years before the state and federal governments would remove the Indians completely from their remaining lands in Alabama, shipping them west to present-day Oklahoma.

Today, one can visit the site of the McIntosh killing in a Carroll County park located about four miles southwest of Whitesburg. It is a beautiful, quiet and secluded spot overlooking the scenic Chattahoochee River.

The remains of a later house built on or near the site of McIntosh's burned home stood until the late 20th century. The later structure was almost completely destroyed by greedy "treasure hunters" and vandals, many of whom were ridiculously searching for McIntosh's mythical gold. As of this writing, a replica of McIntosh's burned home has been reconstructed at the site, and is preserved there today.

If one visits the intersection of the park road with GA Highway 5, just north of the old home-place, he or she will be in the exact spot where McIntosh and Hawkins conversed on that fateful night so long ago.

For those who desire to retrace the original McIntosh Road westward from Indian Spring, the following directions are provided:

Leaving Indian Spring in a southwestwardly direction, the old road passed just north of Mt. Vernon Church and by Elgin and Liberty Churches, before going through an area once known as "Sandy Plains."

The road next passed through the old ghost town of Waltham, before reaching Spalding County on today's GA Highway 16. It continued by Union and Ringgold Churches to the intersection of GA Highways 16 and 156. At that crossing there was once a well-known stagecoach stop known as "Double Cabins" (the Militia District today retains the name: "Cabin District").

Double Cabins was due north of present-day Griffin and the McIntosh Road in running through the former town, missed Griffin completely. Along that stretch, the old road was once known as the "Old Madison Alabama Stage Road," and also as "Upper Cabin Road."

Passing on through the upper fringes of Experiment, the McIntosh Road took the left fork at McIntosh School, before going through Rio and Vaughn and crossing the Flint River into Fayette County. It ran on westward through Brooks and Senoia, passing just north of Turin to go through Sharpsburg and Raymond, close on GA Highway 16, before reaching Newnan on McIntosh Street, a name obviously retained from the original McIntosh Road.

From Newnan, the old thoroughfare turned northwest to cross the Chattahoochee River near the mouth of Pearsons Creek. At that stream, the McIntosh Road crossed over McIntosh's Ferry into present-day Carroll County where it reached the settlement of William McIntosh.

As of this writing, there is an area on McIntosh's old reservation just west of the Chattahoochee River where an abandoned remnant of the old original roadway is still discernible. Turning up the hill from the river, the road passes the site at which McIntosh's home and inn once existed – the site of his murder.

Continuing northward for a short distance, the old road reached an intersection just west of today's Rotherwood. It was at that intersection that William McIntosh and Sam Hawkins conversed while the silent Indians surrounded them.

From this point, the McIntosh Road turned directly westward to run on GA Highway 5 all the way into Alabama, passing through Lowell, Roopville, and Tyrus along the way. It was along the latter stretch that Sam Hawkins made the final trip to his home in Alabama before dying at the hands of his Creek brethren.

Today, there is a great interest in the McIntosh saga. In Peachtree City, just north of the actual route of the road, there is a McIntosh Opry as well as a McIntosh High School. In fact, all along the way from Indian Spring in present-day Butts County westward, remnants of the name are retained, and many persons living today along the old route are familiar with details

Still visible in some spots in the woodlands of middle Georgia, the aged McIntosh Trail may yet be traversed if one knows where to find it. Parts of the old trail have also become portions of today's modern roadways. Chief William McIntosh and other members of his family regularly traveled this route between Indian Spring and the Creek Indian Nation in Alabama.

The large reserve McIntosh obtained for himself in presentday west Georgia (Whitesburg) was one of many items of valuable consideration perceived by his Creek Indian brethren as a "sell-out" of the Creek Nation in Georgia. As a result of this and his endorsement of the Treaty of Indian Spring in 1825, McIntosh was murdered by the Creeks that same year. A recreation of the home in which McIntosh lived when murdered is visible in the background, rebuilt on the site of the original structure which was burned by the Creeks in 1825. Following his murder, McIntosh was buried in the yard outside his home (left foreground).

concerning the McIntosh legend.

Though he has departed this earth, and though the worldly possessions of Chief William McIntosh have been scattered and lost, the historic milestones of this once-prominent member of the Creek Indian Nation live on . . . as does McIntosh's legend.

Today, archived at the University of Georgia Libraries are two letters, one written by two of the three wives of Chief William McIntosh, and another written by the daughter of the third wife. The letters were written immediately following McIntosh's murder.

The letters were sent to white leaders of that day in 1825. They represented the McIntosh family's desperate pleas for help. These plaintive documents vividly describe the horror and anguish suffered by Peggy and Susannah McIntosh (two of the wives), and of Jane Hawkins (a daughter of the third wife). The letters also provide a clear indication of the oftentimes harsh and unforgiving circumstances encountered by 19th century American Indian leaders (and, subsequently, their families) who dared to negotiate with and bargain away tribal lands to the U.S. government. These letters are maintained in the Telamon Cuyler Collection at UGA Libraries, and are provided in their entirety below.

May 3, 1825. Line Creek, Fayette Co.
To Col. Duncan G. Campbell and
Major James Meriwether U.S. Commss

Gentlemen,

When you see this letter stained with the blood of my husband the last drop of which is now spilt for the friendship he has shown for your people, I know you will remember your pledge to us in behalf of your nation, that in the worst of events you would assist and protect us. And when I tell you that at day light on Saturday morning last, hundreds of the Hostiles surrounded our house, and instantly murdered Genl McIntosh & Tom Tustunnugge, by shooting near one hundred balls into them (Chilly and Moody Kennard making their escape thro' a Window) they then Commenced burning and plundering in the most unprincipled way, so that here I am driven from the ashes of my smoking dwelling, left with nothing but my poor little naked hungry children, who need some immediate aid from our white friends, and we lean upon you white, you lean upon your government.

About the same time of the morning that they committed the horrid act on the General, another party caught Col Saml Hawkins, and kept him tied until about 3 o'clock when the chiefs returned from our house and gave orders for his execution in the same way, and refused to leave his impliments to cover his body up with, so that it was left exposed to the Fowls of the Air and the beasts of the Forest, and Jinny and her child are here, in the same condition as we are – this party consisted principally of Oakfuskies, Talledegers & Muckfaws, tho' there were others with them – The Chiefs that appeared to head the party were Intockunge of Muckfaw, Thloc-co-cos-co mico of Arpachoochee, Munnawho, but I know not where he was from, who said they were ordered to do it by the Little prince and Hopoeth Yoholo, and that they were supported and encouraged in it by the Agent and the chiefs that were left after the Big Warriors Death in a council at Broken Arrow where they decreed that they would murder all the Chiefs who had any hand in selling the Land, and burn & destroy and take away all they had, and then send on to the President that he should not have the Land – I have not heard of the murder of any others but expect all are dead that could be catchd.

But by reason of a great freshet in the Chattahochee they could not get Col Miller nor Hogey McIntosh nor the Darisaws, and they and Chilly are gone to the Governor. Our country is in a most ruined State so far as I have heard (tho' by reason of the high waters word has not circulated fast) all have fled from their homes in our parts and taken refuge among their white friends, and I learn there are now at Genl Wares (near this place) from 150 to 200 of them who are afraid to go to their homes to get a grain of what little corn they have to eat, much more to try to make any more, and if You and Your people do not assist us, God help us – we must die either by the Sword or the famin.

This moment Genl. Ware has come in and will in a few minutes start with a few men and a few friendly Indians to try to get a little something for us to eat. I hope so soon as you read this, You will lay it before the Governor and the President that they may know our miserable condition, & afford us relief as soon as possible, I followed them to their camp about one and one-half miles to try to beg of them something to cover the dead with, but it was denied me. I tryed also to get a Horse to take my little children and some provisions to last us to the White Settlements which was given up to me and then taken Back – and had it not have been for some White men who assisted in burying the Dead and getting us to the White Settlements, we should have been worse off then we were if possible – before I close I must remark that the whole of the party so far as I knew them were hostile during the War.

Peggy & Susannah McIntosh
Fayett County, 3rd May, 1825

Col. Campbell and Major Meriwether,

My dear friends, I send you this paper, which will not tell you a lie, but if it had ten tongues it could not tell you all the truth. On the Morning of the 30th of April at break of day, my Fathers house was surrounded by a party of Hostile Indians, to the number of several hundred, who instantly fired his dwelling, and Murdered him, and Thomas Tustunnuggee by shooting more than one hundred balls into them, and took away the whole of Fathers money and property which they coud carry off, and destroyed the rest leaving the family no clothes (some not one rag) nor provision. – Brother Chilly was at Fathers and made his escape through a Window under cover of a Travelling white man who obtained leave for them to come out that way, It being not yet light, he was not discovered.

While those hostiles were Murdering my beloved Father, they were tying my Husband (Colo Saml. Hawkins) with Cords, to wait the arrival of Itockchunga, Thloccocoscomicco and Munnawwa, who were the commanders at Fathers, to give orders for the Colos execution also, which took place about 3 oclock the same day. And these barbarous men, not content with spilling the blood of both my Husband and Father to attone for their constant friendship to both your Nation and our own; refused my hands the painful previledge of covering his body up in the very ground which he lately defended, against those Hostile Murderers, and drove me from my home, stript of my two best friends in one day, Stript of all my property my provision, and my clothing, with a more painful reflection than all these, that the body of my poor murdered husband should remain unburied, to be devoured by the birds, and the beasts. (Was ever poor woman worse off than I?).

I have this moment arrived among our white friends, who altho they are very kind, have but little to bestow on me, and my poor helpless infant, who must suffer befor any aid can reach us from you, but I can live a great while on very little, besides the confidence I have on you, and your government. For I know by your promise, you will aid and defend us, as soon as you hear from our situation.

These Murderers are the very same Hostiles who treated the whites 10 years ago as they have now treated my husband and Father, who say they are determined to kill all who had any hand in selling the land, and when they have completed the work, of Murdering, Burning, plundering and destruction, they will send the President word that they have saved their Land, and taken it back and that he and the white people never shall have it again. Which is the order of the heads of the Nation, by the advice of the Agent.

We expect that many of our best friends are already Killed, but have not heard, by reason of the waters being too high for word to go quick, which is the only reason Colo Miller and others on his side of the River were not Killed. We are in a dreadful Condition, & I dont think there will be one ear of corn made in this part of the Nation, for the whole of the friendly party have fled to Dekalb and Fayett Counties two much alarmed to return to their houses to get a little grain of what corn they left, for themselves and their families to subsist on, much more to stay at home to make more, and we fear every day that what little provision left will be destroyed.

I am afraid you will think I make it worse, but how can that be, for it is worse of its self than any pen can write, my condition admits of no equal, & mocks me when I try to speak of it. After I was stript of my last Frock but one, humanty and duty called on me to pull it off and spread it over the body of my dead Husband, (which was allowed no other covering) which I did, as a Farewell witness of my Affection, I was 25 miles from any friend (but sister Catharine, who was with me) and had to stay all night in the woods, surrounded by a thousand hostile Indians, who were constantly insulting and affrighting us. And now I am here with only one old coat to my back, and not a Morsel of Bread to save us from perishing, or a rag of Blanket to cover my poor little boy from the sun at noon or the due at night, & I am a poor distracted orphan and Widow.

Jane Hawkins

The Life & Hard Times Of Augustus 'Gus' Coggins

Fortune smiled often on his business endeavors, creating in time an enterprise which was reaching national proportions. Fate, however, was waiting in the wings, as changing times and intrigue lingering from the U.S. Civil War ended the career of one of Cherokee County's most promising favorite sons.

Driving northward today along Georgia Highway 5 in Canton, travelers often notice the very impressive Georgian Revival-style home set back off the road on a crest above the Etowah River. And on the opposite side of Highway 5, a large and imposing stone barn exists, silently enduring the years. To the unenlightened, these two structures may not even arouse a second glance, but to natives of the area, they are the remnants of the once-proud enterprises of one of the most successful and yet tragic figures in Cherokee County history.

Augustus "Gus" Lee Coggins, didn't begin his life in Canton. He was born in north Georgia's Gilmer County on September 24, 1868, only three years after the close of the U.S. Civil War. His father, Alfred B. Coggins, was a Confederate veteran and the father of nine children.

The plantation economy and lifestyle of the South in general was devastated by the U.S. Civil War.

Following the war, north Georgia was virtually lawless, and educational opportunities for children were even more nonexistent. For these and other reasons, Gilmer County was not the best locale in which to raise children, and Alfred Coggins therefore moved his family southward to Canton. There, he became a successful merchant, and the seeds for the entrepreneurial genius of his son were sown.

Many historians today find it ironic that Coggins moved to Canton to escape the lawless bands of renegades which pervaded north Georgia after the war. The same evil element had infected Cherokee County as well, and despite his son's amazing business successes later in life, it was these very forces which were at least partly responsible for the tragic professional demise of Cherokee County's Gus Coggins.

The plantation economy and lifestyle of the South in general was devastated by the U.S. Civil War. Most whites formerly associated with the planter economy were totally disenfranchised by the war, and therefore became a desperate segment of an already desperate society. Negroes who formerly had been slaves, suddenly found themselves free men, and they were willing, indeed eager, to accept paid laborer positions many of which formerly had been the exclusive domain of whites. And even in those labor positions which traditionally had been occupied by blacks, the desperate disenfranchised whites could not find opportunities, because Negro laborers could be employed at much lower salaries and subsistence levels than could whites.

In a backlash against this depressed economy and lack of employment opportunities, angry whites formed vigilante and outlaw groups whose sole purpose of existence became that of punishing the whites who were hiring blacks. Gus Coggins, being the adept businessman that he was, hired large numbers of blacks for his many businesses. He provided exceptional housing and living conditions for his workers, and therefore had no problem attracting some of the best talent in the region. However, as a result of these business practices, he also was constantly plagued by unexplainable losses due to fire, undoubtedly the work of angry area whites. It, quite likely, was for this reason that Coggins decided a stone barn was a much better investment than a wooden one.

A "barn," according to *Webster's New Dictionary*, is *"a building used especially to store farm products and to shelter livestock."* Gus Coggins knew this better than most men.

Virtually the entire financial foundation of Coggins' enterprises – businesses which leaned heavily in the direction of livestock breeding and sales – was based upon the housing of livestock. And it is the huge old structure which still stands today on Highway 5 in Canton, which, more than anything else, bears mute testimony to this fact, and which therefore, is a fitting final reminder of Coggins' former existence in the area. Known locally as "the Rock Barn," this immense building was constructed in 1906 by Coggins who had purchased the acreage on which it was built in 1903.

On January 3, 1894, Gus Coggins married Daisy Ryman of Nashville, Tennessee. Her father, Thomas Green Ryman, owned and operated the Ryman Steamboat Lines. He also constructed a large auditorium in Nashville which is familiar to millions of people today as Ryman Auditorium, home of "The Grand Ole Opry."

Daisy's younger sister, Pearl Ryman, married Thomas Raleigh ("Rol") Coggins, Gus's younger brother. Shortly thereafter, Gus and Rol entered into business together under the name "Coggins Brothers," and the stage was set for one of the most prolific business enterprises ever developed in Cherokee County. Gus Coggins, shortly after the turn of the century, was a well-known Canton farmer, horse-breeder and businessman who possessed an uncanny knack for entrepreneurial success.

The 7,000-square-foot Rock Barn is just one example of Coggins' persistent and determined desire to succeed in whatever he pursued, regardless of the circumstances. It is, quite likely, the only stone barn of its age remaining in the state, and its historic significance has been duly noted by its enlistment on the *National Register of Historic Places.*

The property on which Coggins centered his enterprises enjoys an amazing history all its own. It includes broad fertile river bottomlands most of which are encircled by the Etowah River in a broad crescent shape, earning it the name "Crescent Farm."

Rising above these fertile fields is a promontory called Mount Etowah, a spot known to have been occupied (with villages) by aboriginal man dating back to prehistory. The first known inhabitants of this spot for which any record exists were the Cherokee Indians.

Elizabeth Coggins Jones, the daughter of Gus and Daisy Coggins, remembers her childhood at the family home intimately. The historic significance of both it and the business endeavors of her father are vivid memories.

"According to legend, the area around Mount Etowah was an Indian village site, and records appear to confirm this," Mrs. Jones explained in an interview in the late 1980s. "A Chief Still, sometimes referred to as 'Old Still,' is mentioned as an inhabitant of this site."

When the first frame house was built upon Mount Etowah in the 1880s by Robert F. Maddox, family tradition maintains that an Indian grave was discovered during the excavation of the cellar of the home. The artifacts discovered therein reportedly were sent to the Smithsonian Institute in Washington, D.C.

"Looking back, it's easy to believe there was a village or community of some kind there," Mrs. Jones continued. "Two paths from the top of the hill led to the Etowah River below. The one on the right passed a pile of loose flat rocks (Possibly one of the unexplained prehistoric stone cairns which still are occasionally found today across north Georgia.). Another path on the left led down to connect with the larger path

Augustus "Gus" L. Coggins as a young man.

GUS COGGINS HOME (Circa 1896) – Built in the early 1880s, this structure was first owned and occupied by Robert F. Maddox who was instrumental in bringing the railroad to Cherokee County in the 1870s. Gus Coggins purchased Crescent Farm and moved into the structure above with his bride – Daisy Ryman – in 1903. When this home burned mysteriously in 1917, Coggins replaced it with the structure on the site today – Edgewater Hall – built of fire-resistant red clay bricks.

CANTON, GA – During and immediately following the U.S. Civil War, the mountainous counties of north Georgia were short on law enforcement and long on lawlessness. For this reason, and because he wished to provide his nine children with good educational opportunities, Alfred B. Coggins moved his family to Canton shortly after the war. Augustus L. (Gus) and his son Lee Rol Coggins were photographed here in front of the Canton livery stable circa 1915. The A.B. Coggins (Gus' father) home is just visible at right. This structure was razed in 1969 for construction of a parking lot for the Canton Textile Mills.

FAMED RACER (1922) – "Abbedale" was a name renowned in racing circles in the 1920s. Raised and owned by Gus Coggins, this thoroughbred is pictured here as she wins the race at Columbus, Ohio, with a winning time of 2:01 and one-quarter (a record at that time). Mr. Walter Cox was the trainer and driver.

that descended to the river from the Rock Barn. This path veered left across fields and a stream to connect with the road crossing the bridge over the river. A large rock projected into the river at the base of Mt. Etowah and a fish trap was located there."

The first known structure built by whites on "Crescent Farm" is believed to have been built by James McKinney who purchased the property in 1840 from Felix Moss. Deeds to this property in 1868 and 1877 refer to it as "The McKinney Plantation."

Robert F. Maddox was the next owner of the Crescent Farm property, and it was he who constructed the first frame house (circa 1880s) on Mount Etowah. He and Major Campbell Wallace were instrumental in bringing the railroad to Canton in 1879. A newspaper clipping from August 21, 1884, states in part that *"Col. R.F. Maddox and family are spending the summer at their lovely villa across the river at Mount Etowah."*

Maddox sold the farm to Major Wallace in 1887. Gus Coggins leased the farm from the Wallace estate in the mid-1890s, and then purchased it in 1903.

"This was my parents' home when I was born in 1899," remembered Mrs. Jones. "The house was a one-story Victorian with a porch on three sides. The north side opened onto a court. On one side of the court was the kitchen and on the other side was the carding and quilting room. A screen porch connected the two and was full of shelves with cedar water buckets, lamps to be cleaned and filled, kindling wood, and coal bins."

Coggins built his domain steadily over the years. Crescent Farm was a working plantation with departmental heads managing each segment of its operations.

"In my day, Pete Green, a black man with a very imposing appearance was in charge of mules and livestock," Mrs. Jones continued. "John Heard, another black man, was in charge of the vegetable garden and orchard. He also attended to the personal riding horses and family buggy and surrey.

"A white overseer was responsible for planting and raising crops. The first one I remember was Mr. Ruth Collins from Salacoa and the last one was Bill Richardson. He coordinated with the livery stable in town which was headed by a manager. Turkeys, guineas, sheep, pure-bred Jersey cattle, hogs, dogs, walking horses, and race horses were raised with crops of hay, cotton, corn and some molasses cane."

Gus Coggins traveled extensively, especially by railroad, to coordinate his business enterprises. He was perhaps best-known for his engagement in the sales and marketing of mules and other livestock. This aspect of his business empire carried him to Missouri, Texas, Tennessee, and numerous other states where he purchased large numbers of mules and livestock. He owned livery stables in Canton and in Atlanta, and maintained a large mule brokerage business extending across the United States and even to foreign countries.

"A white man, Mr. Harve Barnes, was the office manager and was in charge of the office and business operations at the livery stables on Main Street in Canton," Mrs. Jones continued. "The office was known as 'The Tack Room,' and this was the place where many of the farmers, businessmen and other citizens would gather to swap stories and keep up with cotton and livestock prices and current events."

Perhaps the greatest enjoyment ever experienced by Gus Coggins involved the raising, breeding and racing of horses. Mr. J.B. Hill of Tate, Georgia, was a close friend and contemporary of Rube Jones, the nephew of Gus Coggins. "I remember once when Rube and I were there with him, and Mr. Coggins said 'The prettiest sight I've ever seen is a pacer coming around the last curve and coming down the home stretch.'"

"The men of our community were interested in horseback riding, and my father and many of our farm workers were great enthusiasts of harness racing and the training and showing of fine horses," Mrs. Jones continued. "There, however, was also a very strict code of conduct for the people living in Cherokee County, as well as most of north Georgia back then. Some people were known as 'Round Heads' and others as 'Cavaliers.' The Round Heads were opposed to horse racing and they thought that this pursuit was accompanied with gambling and other types of misconduct."

SIXES GOLD MINE, 1883 – Judge Jonathan Lilly Coggins (with white beard) was the grandfather of Gus Coggins. Also shown in the photo are Gus Coggins and Mrs. A.B. Coggins (next to Judge Coggins). Daughter Margaret (b. 1878) is at her knee. A.B. Coggins does not appear in this photo. Judge Coggins was judge of the Inferior Court of Gilmer County in the 1850s.

CANTON, GA (Circa 1905) – The pace was slow in Canton at the turn of the 19th century. B. Frank Coggins was Gus Coggins younger brother.

Gus Coggins ran his various businesses and constantly lived within the vortex of the whirling social codes in Canton. "My father did not belong to any church although he did join the Methodist Church shortly before he died," Mrs. Jones added. "He had a strict code of ethics, but his lifestyle did not conform to that of many people of that era. He was a very practical person, and had good ideas. I remember that he once said 'if you want to lay out and plan a good road, then watch where the cows go. Follow their paths, because they always select a path that is well-drained, has a firm foundation, and that is not too steep and has a good grade.'"Aside from their good business sense, both Gus Coggins and his brother, Rol, apparently had a sense of humor too. Lee Rol and his cousin Tom Coggins, according to Mrs. Jones, had a pet monkey named "Sally Gal" which they kept around the old Rock Barn for many years. It, understandably, was not only a novelty in the area, but an endless source of entertainment for all involved.

"Rufus Childers had a grocery store on Railroad Street in Canton, just across the river from our home," Mrs. Jones related. "He'd get in a supply of bananas, and the monkey invariably would escape and could be found on a banana stalk that was hanging in front of the Childers Store. We'd retrieve the monkey and bring it back to the barn."

It was another pet, however, with which Gus had the most fun. "Yes, father also kept a pet bear," Mrs. Jones laughed. "It was a rather large animal, and it could terribly frighten an unsuspecting person just by its presence. It was kept at times at the Rock Barn, and sometimes at the livery stable in Canton. It was probably a better protector of property than any watch-dog; even better than an armed guard, because the bear seemed to enjoy making sudden appearances when no one even knew it was around."

The last overseer or superintendent that worked for Gus Coggins at Crescent Farm was William E. "Bill" Richardson. In an interview in the late 1980s, his son, Jack, recalled an incident involving his father which the elder Richardson undoubtedly remembered the rest of his life.

"My father went into the barn one night about dusk, and there, of course, were no lights. It apparently was very dark in the barn. My father said he was feeling his way around looking for some gear, when all of a sudden, the bear pounced on him, and gave him a big bear hug. My father always said he wasn't hurt by the bear, but he was so scared, and lunged so violently to escape, that he injured himself in his fear." One can only imagine the terror which must have been struck into the heart of Bill Richardson on that fateful night.

Fun and games aside, it was the raising of horses for harness racing which gave Gus Coggins the most pleasure. Crescent Farm was perhaps best-known in racing circles for "Abbedale," its world-class race horse. Abbedale brought fame and fortune to Crescent Farm, and has been listed in the Harness Racing Hall of Fame in Goshen, New York. Abbedale also earned recognition in the book, *Harness Racing* by Phillip Pines.

Sunday afternoons were especially pleasurable times for Coggins and his family. Gus had laid out and constructed a one-quarter-mile race track near where, as of this writing, Cherokee County High School is located today. When horses weren't being run on this track, Gus and other members of his group were traveling about the Southern circuit, trading and racing horses across the Southeast.

A Mr. George Stiles in Rome, Georgia, owned a prominent training track. A Mr.

Walter Candler also had a beautiful and elaborate track at Lullwater Farms in Atlanta (present-day home of the president of Emory University in Atlanta). These facilities were frequently used by the Coggins trainers and horses.

Gus Coggins was a firm believer in the value and beauty of many forms of livestock, not the least of which were his fine race horses and the mules which he traded and bartered over much of the United States. It was for the housing and care of these great numbers of livestock that he constructed the numerous barns he owned, not only in Canton, but in Atlanta as well. And it was these "wooden" barns which proved to be a weak link in the Coggins Brothers' business affairs. Devastating fires plagued these and other wooden structures owned by Coggins throughout his career.

The first Coggins barn for which there was any record of destruction was burned in February of 1900. In this fire, the fine race horse "Queen Nab" was destroyed, as well as seven head of cattle. The cause of this fire was never discovered.

"All the other horses in this barn were saved except Queen Nab," remembered Mrs. Jones. "She had won the $6,000 derby in Macon in 1891, and had taken purses in Knoxville and at the state fair in 1891."

A newspaper account published in the *Cherokee Advance* in Canton described the event as follows: *"It's often been said that you cannot get a horse out of a burning building, but 'Hannah,' Mrs. Coggins' buggy horse broke out of her stable, jumped over the lot fence, and ran all the way over to town, and had to be carried back to the farm. 'Queen Nab,' the mare that was burned, was one of the best race horses in the state, and was considered the best animal in the barn."*

It was about this time in 1906, that Gus Coggins decided a safer structure was needed to house his valuable race horses, and the next barn he built was the Rock Barn. "I am certain that the Rock Barn was built for his fine race horses and were not for the Coggins mules," said Mr. J.B. Hill, a close friend and contemporary of Rube Jones, nephew of Gus Coggins.

A third barn was built to replace the earlier one which had been destroyed by fire. On December 3, 1915, both this new barn as well as an adjacent barn also burned, destroying some 162 mules and approximately 15,000 bushels of corn. This time, however, credit for the destruction was blatantly claimed by a vigilante group known as "The Night Riders." This organization, as previously explained, was terrorizing employers of blacks in north Georgia.

According to the Atlanta newspapers, *"In two instances, notes had been left by 'Night Riders' and in two other instances, no word had been received. The 'Night Riders' operating in Cherokee County are charged with destruction of property valued at approximately ninety thousand dollars during the past two days, following the receipt of mysterious unsigned notes, cautioning employers of Negroes against the pretension of these employees. The heaviest sufferers in a series of fires were Coggins Brothers whose immense barns and granaries, located less than a mile west of Canton, were destroyed with a loss of about seventy-five thousand dollars. Rol Coggins of Atlanta, one of the men interested in the business Monday was unable to state the amount of insurance carried, although he did not believe that it would cover the loss. A message from Canton, however, was to the effect that insurance amounted to less than twenty-five thousand dollars."*

The newspaper accounts explained that other barns and livestock had been similarly destroyed at the property of Otto Sherman, located six miles east of Canton, and at the Freeman Bell farm. The news accounts stated that all of the fires seemed to have been started from the interior of the buildings, since the fires were always well-advanced prior to being discovered. On the side of one of the burned buildings, a five-gallon oil can was discovered.

Speaking of the loss in this fire by Coggins Brothers, the newspapers stated that *"It is learned that 162 horses and mules were burned, together with a large quantity of foodstuffs and farming implements. All cattle were saved by the employees of the concerned owners. Coggins Brothers deal extensively in horses, mules and cattle, and operate a large farm in connection with their barns. . . They also employ a large number of workmen, about 75 of whom are Negroes."*

It was in 1917 that the Coggins' home was destroyed. "We found the silver flatware in a melted lump in the cellar," Mrs. Jones explained. "Father built our two-story red brick home (which is on the site today) in 1922."

A third barn which was a mule barn, burned in the 1920s. It was located just south of the intersection of Highways 5 and 140, across from the spot where, as of this writing, the present-day McDonald's, Hardee's and several other restaurants are located. A large number of mules were lost in this fire.

Over the years, most of the wooden barns built on the Coggins properties were destroyed by fire at one time or another. As a result of the hazards involving fires in that day and time, it is reasonable to conclude that Gus Coggins built the Rock Barn for the protection of his highly-prized race horses. It apparently was a wise precaution too, because the Rock Barn is one of the few Coggins structures which never fell victim to fire.

Another fact will also not escape the perceptive evaluator. . . When Gus Coggins rebuilt his home on Mount Etowah, he built it not of wood, but of brick. The two most important structures in his life were built of the most fire-resistant material he could find. This new family home was named "Edgewater Hall."

The Rock Barn's existence today is directly attributable then to the violence and fear which was woven into the fabric of life in post-Civil War north Georgia. The valuable race horses housed in the Rock Barn almost certainly would have been the target of the Night Riders in 1915, had not the barn been constructed of stone. This edifice stands today not only as a monument to a determined entrepreneurial spirit, but also as a reminder of the social injustice which existed in north Georgia at that time.

Despite his determination and sharply-honed business acumen however, Gus Coggins was no match for the combination of events which finally felled his businesses. Many of the culminating events were simply beyond his control. More than anything else, Coggins was a victim of the times – swiftly changing social and industrial practices and trends.

The Coggins practice of hiring blacks was very unpopular in north Georgia, and Gus suffered as a result. The destruction of the huge mule barn by the Night Riders in 1915 was a severe blow. The loss of horses, mules, and grain was estimated at $75,000, a huge sum at that time.

It was also at approximately this time that the cotton market fell. Cotton was a major commodity produced on Crescent Farm. This income loss was also substantial.

One of the most devastating blows, however, was the totally unanticipated loss of a huge mule market – one on which Gus apparently had decided to "roll the dice." Gus and Rol had obtained large government contracts to supply Allied troops in

Europe with mules during World War I. German U-Boats controlled the shipping channels to Europe however, leaving no available transportation for a huge stock of mules which Gus was therefore forced to maintain in stockyards. And following the Armistice in 1918, the market for the mules for the troops was suddenly gone, and worse yet, the new age of the automobile and automotive power had arrived, replacing the market for horses and mules. Coggins Brothers, as a result, was forced to absorb huge unprojected losses from unsaleable livestock.

The fourth and final blow came in the form of the banking system – particularly the chain system of banks to which Gus's bank – The Bank of Cherokee – belonged. At that time, there was no Federal Deposit Insurance Corporation or any other safeguards to protect against the possibility of heavy losses suffered by large inventory businessmen such as Gus and Rol Coggins. The factors described above, combined with the economic panic of the early 1900s, ignited the Bankrupt Sale of 1928. All Coggins holdings, including Crescent Farm and Edgewater Hall, were sold at auction. The Coggins business empire was completely and unequivocally dissolved. Over the years since 1928, rumors to the effect that Gus Coggins escaped from this disaster as a wealthy man have persisted. Nothing, in fact, could have been further fom the truth.

Gus Coggins, as a result of the humiliation and danger of remaining in Canton, was forced to relocate out of the state. He moved to Colorado where he lived until the last few months of his life.While he lived in Colorado, several of his friends visited him there, and over time, all have confirmed that his living circumstances there were exceptionally simple and humble, in no way indicative of a wealthy man.

During Gus's final year of life, he struggled against leukemia to survive. Mrs. Jones, his daughter, brought him back to Georgia on the L&N Railroad to live out his final months. The San Francisco – Chicago run connecting with the L&N made a special stop for the man who at one time had shipped more mules by rail than any other customer.

On the Sunday that he arrived back in Canton, Gus Coggins was greeted by one hundred sixteen old friends who came to welcome him home. He died only a few months later at age 84, and was buried in the family plot in Canton.

Since 1928, much of the acreage which formerly comprised Crescent Farm has been redeveloped with various new buildings and other enterprises. Cherokee County High School, Canton Elementary School, a Georgia State Patrol office, the National Guard Armory, just to name a few. Edgewater Hall and the Rock Barn remain as the lone sentinels to the glory days of Gus Coggins and some of the finest harness and race horses ever produced in Georgia.

The Rock Barn was donated to the Cherokee County Historical Society in the late 1980s for renovation and use as a combination museum and conference center. Donations – either in cash or in pledges – were sought for this project.

Noted preservationist architect C. Gregory Chupp, A.I.A. was retained and supervised the contracting activities. In 1989, the Society received a substantial grant from the National Trust for Historic Preservation. Other grants and gifts followed.

When completed, the project will be an even more permanent testament to an era in time and a way of life truly "gone with the wind."

The 1918 Road Lab Murders At The University of Georgia

The somber historic structures on the old campus at the University of Georgia in Athens, Georgia, have nobly served academia for many years – some for over 150 years. On a cold, blustery night in January of 1918, however, one of the oldest of these buildings was the site of a heinous activity far removed from normal college pursuits.

In 1918, a scandal which rocked both Athens and Jefferson, Georgia, took place on the campus of the University of Georgia (UGA) in Athens. It brought so much pain and embarrassment that almost 80 years later, descendants of the relatives of those involved are still reluctant to speak of it.

My efforts to uncover information regarding this unusual incident were thwarted at almost every turn. One Jackson County historian even discouraged me in my attempt to locate the relatives of the victims in order to verify written reports. There were many others, too, who failed to see the importance of chronicling this story of the first capital crime[1] to take place on the University of Georgia campus.

Despite the roadblocks, however, I finally located someone who, though very young at the time of the incident, at least remembered the terrible deed. And though this person had no details to add and had never read the 1918 *Athens Banner* newspaper articles, my informant verified what I had already concluded. . . "They kept it quiet."[2]

In 1918, Americans were singing *"Over There,"* a tune that reflected the mood of the day. Thousands of young men, including the brother of the young Jefferson woman involved in the terrible incident, were fighting a world war in France. During these uncertain economic times, entrepreneurs in small-town Athens, Georgia, attracted customers by eliciting an image of sophistication. College Avenue boasted the Manhattan Cafe and East Clayton Street the New York Cafe and the Holland Hotel.

During this era on the UGA campus, however, it was a different story. Most of the buildings, including the building that had housed the first scientific library – the Road Laboratory Building – showed signs of considerable deterioration. First named Philosophical Hall, the Road Lab as well as the Old College building and even the remodeled Academic building were all described as decrepit, cold, unsanitary and even dangerous.[3]

By 1918, the second floor of the Road Lab Building was being used as a dormitory.[4] For the 1917-1918 academic year, students Tom Holliday, Howard Dadisman and Alva Pendergrass were living there. They not only were roommates, but had grown up together in Jefferson in Jackson County.

From the outset, the cold winter evening of Tuesday, January 29, 1918, was a routine weekday night. After preparing for the next day of class, the young men were just going to sleep when a midnight knock on the door interrupted their slumbers. The three students were surprised to find another Jefferson friend, James E. Johnson, standing outside. And as surprised as they were to see him, they were even more surprised to see he was accompanied by a seventeen-year-old female companion – Belle Hill – at this late hour on the all-male campus.[5]

The three students debated whether or not to allow Johnson and his companion to stay the night in their dorm room. After some discussion, they arrived at a decision. It proved to be a fatal one that would haunt them to their graves.

Almost eighty years after that terrible choice was made, I visited the graves of the four men at the substantial Woodbine Cemetery in Jefferson. James E. Johnson is buried on a hill near an old cedar tree not far from his three comrades. His death date was January 30, 1918. And the three roommates, who died years apart, surprisingly were buried within site of each other.

I also visited the grave of Belle Hill at Thyatira Church Cemetery just outside of Jefferson. Her death date was incorrectly engraved upon her headstone. It records January 22, 1918, as the date of her murder.

Barely discernable at the top of the obelisk headstone on Belle's grave was the word *"Hope."* Later, as I inspected the graves of other members of her family, I turned around and was surprised to find on the rear of Belle's monument these words: *"We trust our loss will be her gain. And that with Christ she's gone to reign."*

Belle was a beautiful young woman who, according to official reports, met death at the hands of a young man she apparently trusted and loved. She had nothing to fear the night she left the Manhattan Cafe and strolled down the University's "Campus Walk" toward the Road Lab Building alongside James E. "Jamie" Johnson.

Today, all the details of the events which transpired inside the Road Lab Building – the terrible details which collectively led to Belle Hill's sudden journey into eternity – are not known. In fact, the questions far outnumber the answers.

James E. Johnson

Death came wholesale in 1918. A world war was winding down, but during the preceding three and one-half years, 8.5 million people had died, 21 million would return home scarred for life. An influenza epidemic took hold throughout the world and 22 million would die before it was eradicated in 1920. Perhaps that's why the murder of a young girl on the campus of the University of Georgia would send shock waves through the community but then be quickly forgotten. Or perhaps it was as my informant had said: It was simply kept quiet!

"Jamie" was born in 1897. He was named after his grandfather, James E. Johnson, who had died at age 87 in April prior to Jamie's birth in October. His father, Robert David Johnson, was born the

A view up College Avenue in Athens taken in 1920. It was down this street that Belle Hill and Jamie Johnson walked on the night of January 29, 1918, as they hurried to the Road Lab Building. Notice the old watering trough for horses which remains in the center of the intersection.

Woodbine Cemetery overlooking the community of Jefferson, Georgia, was photographed in 1996. The Johnson family plot is visible in the foreground, with the grave of James E. "Jamie" Johnson at the far end. (Photo by Kathryn Gray White)

"Campus Walk" on North Campus at the University was photographed in the mid-1990s. (Photo by Kathryn Gray-White)

year the South had been plunged into civil war. He died at age 53, seventeen days before Jamie's sixteenth birthday.

By age 21, Jamie was said to have been *"a clever young man and had many friends."*[6] Three of those many friends would be present as Jamie drew his last breath. And it would be these three friends who would live the rest of their lives with the decision that led to their involvement in the bizarre events which transpired on the morning of January 30, 1918.

Jamie had left Jefferson on Tuesday afternoon on the south-bound passenger train to Athens. Belle Hill was also on that train. The two were seen together at "supper"[7] Tuesday night at the New York Cafe. They were also seen together at the Holland Hotel. Late that evening, around 11:00 p.m., they were seen at the Manhattan Cafe and then finally on campus.

Many questions haunt the curious individuals trying to piece together the details of January 29, 1918, as Jamie and Belle spent their last moments on earth. Why were they in Athens in the first place? Why didn't they overnight at the Holland Hotel where they would have been less likely to have been recognized? Did they run out of time and options, or were they just two star-crossed lovers destined for a fatal end? Perhaps we'll never know now.

A Terrible Decision

According to records, on the fateful night, Jamie's three friends had been torn between turning him away and letting him and his companion spend the night. Jamie was not a University student, and as such was not allowed in University dormitory quarters after hours. And his female companion most certainly was prohibited from access to the room under any circumstances. However, it was late, the frigid January weather had taken a turn for the worse, and Jamie was a hometown boy.

Jamie told his friends that he and Belle were planning to go on to Atlanta on the early Seaboard train. The students reluctantly agreed that the couple could stay if they left by 3:30 a.m. Later, as Tom provided a report of the incident to the local authorities, he added one important detail to the initial conversation between he and Jamie. According to official records, Tom stated that, *"They came up here about twelve o'clock and knocked, and I opened the door and said 'Come in Jamie.'"*

The record further notates that Jamie responded with *"Mike (sic) I want to stay with you up here. . . was afraid to go to the hotel."*[8]

After Jamie and Belle were allowed into the dorm room, the couple, apparently exhausted, laid down across a bed, and in the warmth of the coal-heated dorm room, they all fell asleep except for Howard, who said he could not sleep for a while.

At approximately 2:00 a.m., Jamie suddenly awakened everyone as he searched for a pencil and paper. He explained his anxiousness by saying that he *"had to"* write a letter *"tonight."* He also said it had been on his mind for some time.

Alva reluctantly left his warm bed to find stationery and a pencil. Tom and Alva then went back to sleep. Howard said he also fell asleep at this point.

In the chilly early morning hours, Jamie Johnson began his horrible descent into homicide. He sat at a table and wrote out what would be his last words. It was a somewhat cryptic letter addressed to his mother, sister and brother. The letter did not contain what could be described as mournful or regretful words, rather an almost moralistic justification for his mind-numbing crime. When he had finished the letter, Jamie picked up his revolver.

The old Road Lab Building is known as Rusk Center at Waddell Hall today. (Photo by Kathryn Gray-White)

"Campus Walk" was photographed here in 1920, approximately two years after the Road Lab deaths. (Photo courtesy of Hargret Rare Book and Manuscript Library, University of Georgia)

"Beautiful Belle" – Ollie Belle Hill

Belle Hill, a "very handsome and attractive person,"[9] was only seventeen years old on the night of Tuesday, January 29th, 1918. She worked in an Atlanta restaurant.

Belle had left Jefferson on Tuesday morning on the south-bound train to Athens where she planned to connect with a train to Atlanta. Though it was not stated whether or not they were traveling together, Jamie was also on that Jefferson train.

Later that day, according to newspaper accounts, the couple both registered at the Holland Hotel. This was not Belle's first stay in Athens. She, reportedly, had been in town two weeks earlier, spending a night or two at a local hotel. Inclement weather could have played a role in this stay-over, for it was at about this same time, on January 16, that the *Athens Banner* reported that a blizzard had raged through Dixieland and Athens had been cut off from the rest of the world by an ice storm.

Later on – after the terrible deed – there would also be reports in the newspaper of *"occurrences at the Holland Hotel – where the couple is said to have registered as man and wife."* [10] Under a column entitled *"Happenings At Hotel,"* the occurrences were not discussed in detail nor were they explained in the published investigations. However, most likely, the couple had fled the hotel because of these incidents, stopped by the Manhattan Cafe to collect themselves, and from there had decided, in desperation, to seek shelter with Jamie's friends on the UGA campus.

A Flight To The Afterlife

By the time he finished his letter to his mother, Jamie Johnson apparently had decided his fate, as well as that of the beautiful Belle. He placed his letter on a table, took his pistol over to the bed where Belle slept, then quickly shot her once squarely through the heart. Then, just as quickly, he somehow fired not one, but two blasts into his own heart.

The first of the three shots immediately awoke Alva, and he reportedly bolted upright just in time to see Belle reel up off the bed and then fall to the floor. He also reportedly saw her clothes strangely burst into flames.

According to reports, Tom and Alva rushed to put out the flames on poor Belle. Howard, sleeping soundly, awoke only as the last shot was fired, and saw his two shocked friends placing Belle's limp body back upon the bed.

The three young men couldn't believe their eyes! Belle was dead! Jamie was dying! They were horrified, and could think of nothing to do but run for help.

The men first rushed to the local Young Men's Christian Association (YMCA)[11] to summon Dr. A.C. Holliday. This prominent Athens physician, whose testimony would be most important at the Coroner's Inquest, interestingly, was the uncle of all three young men living in the dorm. After sending word for Dr. Holliday, the students then went to the nearest telephone at the New York Cafe to call police and wait for the doctor to arrive.

Authentic Suicide Letter?

When the authorities arrived at the dorm room, Policeman C.H. Almond found Jamie's letter on a table and the pistol on the floor. Alva Pendergrass later testified that *"we picked up the pistol after Dr. Holliday got there. Then we went and got Col. Snelling (C.M. Snelling, Dean of the University)."*

Jamie's letter was published in the February 1, 1918 issue of the *Athens Banner*. It read as follows:

Dear Mother sister and brother:

Please let me ask you all to pardon me for the way I have done. I feel like that I am doing my duty in doing this deed. The country is better off without such cattle. I just have the nerve to die before disgracing my good people. I wouldn't to of been in this place if it hadn't to of been for showing my man – I knew that no body couldn't run over me.

Read all of this to the public and let them know how I stand.

Please don't lay any of the blame on any-

body up there and tell brother to get to business and make a man of himself not to do like me and others have done. To make a man. And please train sister right – don't let her make a thing in this world that is what brought us to a close.

Please try to get brother and sister to get to business and make something of themselves that you and them too will be proud of.

Well good bye dear old Mother, good bye brother, good bye dear little sister, for God's sake make something of yourselves and for mine too.

My burden is so great I can't go with it any further.

Tell brother to get you all of the wood he can he may have to go to war and you all cant get anybody to get you any. Well good bye to all of my friends.

P.S. Well that is all I will say about that – so don't you all worry about me; its all right. You all pay Cousin Gus for me and $100.00; keep the rest of my part for yourselves; give brother his part and then if he spends all of his part in 5 years dont give him any of the part but if he makes good give him about one thousand dollars, it will help him some if he is a good business boy. I owe Emory a little and Allen (Wedell) $1.75; make everything I have all right and tell folks that I am doing my duty and don't worry about me. And give Mrs. Turner about $15.00 to buy something to eat with; she told me today she didn't have anything to eat.

I am sorry for the way I have done but don't you all bother yourselves – before I would let folks say that I disgraced my folks I will die. Tell all of my friends good-bye for me, and tell them I am not crazy – it is nerve.

I am asking everybody to forgive me for the way I have done and I will forgive them; dont lay this trouble on anybody but the one's that is going to ride the same train that I ride.

I hope that God will forgive me for doing this good deed for the country."

The funds described in Jamie's letter were found in his clothing, as were two pocket knives and one Elgin watch and chain. It was never stated whether or not the pistol had belonged to Jamie.

Jamie's actions sent his mother, Mamie Johnson, her family and even her descendants into a century-long spiral of agony and embarrassment. Mamie was fifteen years younger than her first husband, Robert David Johnson, who had died five years earlier. She eventually remarried, and died 38 years after this tragedy in 1956. She was 81 years old.

Lawrence Herndon Hill – Belle's brother – would later die in World War II and be recognized as a Carnegie Hero. In 1918, however, he was interviewed by an *Athens Banner* reporter, and explained that his sister was between 17 and 18 years of age, and had been married early the previous autumn to a man named Cochran from Chattanooga who, at the time of her death, was serving with the U.S. Expeditionary Forces in France![12] He added that her friends and acquaintances did not know of her marriage.

It was never stated whether or not the pistol had belonged to Jamie.

Jamie's letter is tinged with images of a world at war and a young man at odds with his own existence. It also includes a darker element – that of an individual bent upon playing judge, jury and executioner to what many

Philosophical Hall, also known as the Road Laboratory Building, was photographed at the turn of the century. Built in 1821, this structure originally was a repository for books and scientific equipment. Belle Hill was murdered on the second floor of this building in 1918. (Photo courtesy of Hargret Rare Book and Manuscript Library, University of Georgia)

would say was a jilting lover.

Jamie's words *". . .don't lay this trouble on anybody but the one's that is going to ride the same train that I ride. I hope that God will forgive me for doing this good deed for the country."* appears to indicate a possible motive for his actions.

Could Jamie Johnson have discovered Belle's secret and have acted in vengeance as his letter seems to indicate? Or could he have acted in a fit of insane jealousy after discovering the young woman he loved was about to jilt him, just as she had done her husband who was dutifully away at war? Perhaps we'll never know the true details.

In contrast, it is interesting to note how the editor of the *Jackson Herald* interpreted Jamie's letter:

"A note was found on the table, written by Mr. Johnson to his mother, Mrs. Mamie Johnson, telling her of his purposes and intentions. In the note he stated he was tired of life was why he meant to terminate his own experience, but gave no reason why he took the life of Miss Hill." [13]

North Campus at the University of Georgia was photographed circa 1920s.

Last Remains

On Wednesday, January 30, a crowd gathered outside the W.F. Dorsey Funeral Parlor on East Clayton Street as the cold body of "Beautiful Belle" underwent preparation for burial. The remains were viewed by many local curiosity seekers prior to the coffin being closed. However, the pressing crowd was not allowed to see the $3 stuffed carefully into Belle's stocking, her burned clothing, the hole in her young heart – or the ring that hung around her neck.

The first reports of the murder/suicide disputed the statement by the three students that the shooting occurred around 3:00 a.m. Some individuals believed the shooting had occurred earlier, because several residents near the campus had heard gunshots near the scene between ten and eleven o'clock. These reports, however, were ignored by the authorities because at approximately five o'clock when the police and news reporters arrived, the bodies were *"hardly cold, in fact were limp as the body of a person asleep."*

Jamie's note to his mother was also questioned as to its authenticity at first. Later, however, newspaper reports indicate that relatives agreed it was genuine and that the letter indicated that Jamie was just *"tired of life."* But what about Belle? The question remains. . . Why did Jamie take the life of beautiful Belle?

At 1:30 p.m. on Wednesday afternoon of January 30, Belle was buried two miles outside Jefferson at Thyatira Church. The family farm was once located in this old Jackson County community.

When I visited the family plot located on a hill above the red-roofed 1796-built church, I found that this tragedy was just one of many the Hill family had faced. In March of 1917, barely a year before Belle's death, the Hills had suffered the loss of a son, Henry Hoyt Hill at age 19. Jewell T. Hill died five months after Belle, "Over There." At age 24, he was one of thousands to fall on "a foreign field" in France. William Thomas Hill died in an airship in 1933 at age 30, and Lawrence Herndon Hill, who was awarded the Carnegie Medal posthumously, died at age 54 during World War II.

The deaths of Jamie Johnson and Belle Hill, to be certain, were a tragedy. And just as in most extraordinary incidents of this nature, there were many rumors about the Road Lab Building deaths, which, according to news accounts, were *"founded on only slight circumstance and later found unfounded in tangible fact."*

However, these same news accounts also implied that some information was concealed. *"Some facts in the case, known to the jury investigating the affair and to those who visited the scene and saw the bodies of the dead couple, were passed over – in deference to decency and good taste."*

Two official investigations took place. The Coroner's Inquest the morning of the killings, and an investigation by the Clarke County Grand Jury which was held on Tuesday, February 5. The *Athens Banner* also stated the University would conduct its own investigation.

The Three Roommates

The three University students involved in the incident – Tom, Alva and Howard, testified at the Inquest. They were three of only twelve privileged youths from Jackson County attending college that year.

Tom Cecil Holliday was 19 years old and a freshman in the school of commerce (business). He identified the bodies for the police. *"Shots woke me up," he stated. "The boy is Jamie Johnson, Jefferson, Georgia, and the girl Belle Hill, Jefferson, Georgia."*

Alva Wesley Pendergrass was 20 years old and a sophomore majoring in science. Alva said *"We picked up the pistol after Dr.*

Holliday got to the dorm. The gun had three loaded and three unloaded cartridges. It was a S and W (Smith & Wesson) Special, 32 caliber."

Howard Dean Dadisman was 19 years old and a freshman in the school of commerce. He testified that he had opposed Jamie and Belle staying in the dorm, but relented because of the weather. He also said he heard only one shot, the last blast. He also witnessed Pendergrass and Holliday placing Belle's body back on the bed.

The details of the Clarke County Grand Jury investigation of the incident were reported in the *Athens Banner* under the headline *"Jackson County Young Men Exonerated From Any Criminal Connection With Recent Tragedy," and went on to say that "A great many witnesses were examined and exhaustive testimony was taken in the investigation which resulted in the absolute exoneration of the three young men, Messrs. Holliday, Pendergrass and Dadisman, occupants of the room in which Jamie Johnson shot and killed Miss Belle Hill and then turned the weapon upon himself and committed suicide."*

Dr. A.C. Holliday described the wounds. Johnson had two bullet holes. One on the left side of the breast bone, two and a half inches above the nipple. The other right in the middle of the breast bone. One bullet passed through the body. The other lodged just under the skin. The wounds were two inches apart and either one would have been fatal. Belle Hill's wound was just a little to the left of the breast bone, just over the heart. The shot entered her heart.

Following the investigations, reports in the *Athens Banner* indicated the three young men were not dismissed from school as might have been anticipated. Nor were they even suspended. However, their names did not appear in *The Pandora*, the University yearbook, in 1919 or 1920.

From the time Tom, Howard and Alva shared the same dormitory room in 1918 to the point they all had burial plots in the same general vicinity on the hill overlooking the city of Jefferson in 1989, the Road Lab Murder bound these three men together with tragedy. Tom C. Holliday died just two years after the murder in 1920. Howard D. Dadisman died 33 years later in 1951. And Alva W. Pendergrass carried the memory of that terrible night for 71 years. He died in 1989 at age 91.

The University – 1918 To Present

In the early 1900s, Athens still contained remnants of the old 19th century agricultural South, as well as hints of the coming "New South" so strongly touted by preeminent leaders such as Henry Grady.

"Best Western Mules" were advertised for sale in the newspaper and a watering trough for horses and mules still stood at the intersection of Broad Street and College Avenue. In January of 1918, The Strand theater advertised a silent film starring Douglas Fairbanks – *The Three Musketeers!* Some things in Athens have changed very little since the Road Lab deaths. Others have changed dramatically.

In July of 1996, just before the Olympic Games, I parked at the University Bookstore near the section of the campus once referred to as "the Cow College" (for its agricultural curriculum) but known today as south campus.

Near the stadium, there was an air of excitement as the colorful Olympic banners moved in the hot breeze.

Up the hill, the old campus was less active. Near the aged Road Lab Building – which still stands as of this writing and is known today as Rusk Center – only a few people walked the pathways that thousands have traversed for almost two centuries in search of an education. The front door to the structure was open for workers who were relocating the Rusk Center offices to another building on campus.

Though empty on this day, the old Road Laboratory Building undoubtedly did not remain vacant for very long. Space is a precious commodity on this campus of around 30,000 students, and there is always a clamor for an empty building – even the second-oldest on campus.

By the time of this printing, the historic North Campus structure will have undergone yet another metamorphosis on the interior, and its name will have changed yet another time. For me, however, it will always be the 1918 Road Lab Building and I will never pass this austere edifice without thinking of Jamie and Belle, and their last walk on this campus – and on this earth.

ENDNOTES

1/ Unless otherwise stated, all details of the 1918 suicide-murder are from various reports in the *Athens Banner* from the period January 31 through February 6, 1918.

2/ In the books written on the history of the University and Clarke County and examined by this writer, nothing was said about the murder-suicide which occurred in this historic building in 1918. The only newspaper article on the subject, outside of those written at the time of the murder, was published in the *Athens Observer* in May of 1992. The article was written by University of Georgia law professor Donald E. Wilkes.

3/ Philosophical Hall or the Road Laboratory Building was built in 1821, Old College in 1806 and the Academic Building underwent remodeling in 1905. Thomas G. Dyer discusses the impoverished turn-of-the-century campus in *The University of Georgia, A Bicentennial History, 1785-1985.*

4/ The building was originally called Philosophical Hall because it housed books and equipment for scientific research which at the time was known as "natural Philosophy." It is the second-oldest building on campus and initially was used as a chapel and the second floor as a library. It has also been used as a classroom, boarding house, dormitory, lunchroom, gymnasium, the residence of Registrar Thomas W. Reed (1906-1950), storage, a lunchroom, a speech therapy center, headquarters for a program for exceptional children, home of he University Press and, until July of 1996, as the Dean Rusk Center for International and Comparative Law. After it was remodeled in 1955-56 for speech therapy, the building was renamed for Dr. Moses Wadel, president of the University from 1818 to 1829. [Wadel spelled his name with one l, but his son added another (Wadell).] The building has also been known as Agricultural Hall, the Reed House, and in 1918, an Athens map listed it as the Road Lab Building.

5/ In January of 1918, it was unusual for a woman to be found on campus at the University, even during the day. The trustees of UGA did not endorse the admission of women until September of that year. Various organizations, including the Daughters of the American Revolution, argued for coeducation at the University as early as 1899. Women were allowed to attend classes during summer sessions in 1903, but this was not considered formal admission. Later in the year in 1918, women were formally admitted, but were confined to programs in education and home economics for a number of years.

6/ This description of Jamie Johnson is from "Two Tragic Deaths," published in *Jackson Herald* on Thursday, January 31, 1918, p. 1.

7/ *Jackson Herald*, "Two Tragic Deaths," Thursday, January 31, 1918, p. 1.

8/ "Motive of Double Tragedy On The Campus Yesterday Morning Is Still Mystery To Those Interested In Case," *Athens Banner*, Thursday, January 31, 1918, p. 1.

9/ The *Jackson Herald* gave the only description of Belle Hill. "Two Tragic Deaths," Jackson Herald, p. 1.

10/ "Motive Of Double Tragedy On The Campus Yesterday Morning Is Still Mystery To Those Interested In Case," p.1.

11/ The Y.M.C.A. became a part of the campus club movement in the late 1800s.

12/ "Motive Of Double Tragedy On The Campus Yesterday Morning Is Still Mystery To Those Interested In Case," p. 1.

13/ "Two Tragic Deaths," p. 1.

14/ "Motive Of Double Tragedy On The Campus Yesterday Morning Is Still Mystery To Those Interested In Case," p. 1.

15/ "Motive Of Double Tragedy On The Campus Yesterday Morning Is Still Mystery To Those Interested In Case," p. 1.

16/ It is believed that this investigation never took place. No records exist and no reference to the tragedy is made in official historic records. The University did not have a campus police force in 1918.

17/ *The Pandora*, the University yearbook, included a map of Georgia in 1918 with the number of students from each county identified in the appropriate area.

18/ Tanyard Branch near the Tate Center marked the boundary line between north and south campuses. The liberal arts faculty on the hill and the agricultural faculty south of the branch were friendly rivals.

19/ The Dean Rusk Center for International and Comparative Law relocated to the new Rusk Building on north campus in July of 1996.

Mobster Benjamin 'Bugsy' Siegel's Girl

In 1933, an attractive teenage girl left north Georgia to seek her fortune in Chicago. In short order, she became the darling of some of America's most powerful criminals. The public knew her as a Hollywood starlet and an associate of mobsters. Her friends and neighbors in Marietta, Georgia, however, knew her simply as "Miss Virginia."

Bill Kinney is old enough to remember Marietta, Georgia, when it was still a relatively young community. Not that Kinney is in his dotage, by any means. It's just that Marietta retained much of its flavor as a quiet, picturesque little town in the foothills of the north Georgia mountains well into the 1960s (prior to the mega-development which has occurred since that time).

With a touch of wistfulness, Kinney, a long-time reporter and editor for the *Marietta Daily Journal* newspaper, speaks of the days of cotton wagons and street trolleys, the old courthouse on the square, and daring youths swimming in the water tank by the railroad tracks. Then, with a twinkle in his eye and a smile on his lips, Kinney launches into the story of Virginia Hill – the saucy, curvaceous, red-headed bombshell that burst upon Marietta's serenity during the hard times of the Great Depression.

Beginnings

At a time when the virtues of chasteness, modesty and piety characterized polite society in the rural South, Virginia Hill stood out like Elvis at a deacon's meeting.

"In those days, women were just getting around to wearing one-piece bathing suits," Kinney recalls. "Virginia Hill wore only a halter-top and short, short-shorts. She would ride her horse down Church Street into Marietta, around the square, and back up Cherokee Street to her house dressed just like that – and barefoot to boot."

Born in 1916 to Margaret and Mack Hill, Virginia spent her earliest years in Bessemer, Alabama. Her father, an itinerant blacksmith and horse-trader, later moved the family to the little Cobb County hamlet of Acworth, no doubt as a result of substantial mule-raising, selling and trading which was concentrated in that vicinity at the time. Although Mack Hill's daughter did not receive much formal education (going no further than the eighth grade), she later proved that she had plenty of street smarts and savvy to go with her good looks.

She also was very independent. Prior to her 18th birthday, Virginia Hill left Georgia and eventually found employment as a "shimmy dancer" at the 1933 World's Fair in Chicago. There, she hooked up with

Joe Epstein, a prominent bookkeeper and advisor for the notorious criminal, Alphonse "Al" Capone.

Epstein soon discovered that Hill's assets went far beyond her physical beauty... She possessed a good business mind as well, and was loyal and reliable. Using these characteristics to advantage, Epstein employed Hill as a courier to transport large sums of cash between gang headquarters in places like Chicago, St. Louis and Miami.

Through Epstein, Virginia Hill tapped into a lifestyle that a poor country girl undoubtedly found alluring. She suddenly had easy access to large sums of money, bright lights and powerful men.

"Joe Epstein ran the gambling business around Chicago," Kinney says. "Of course, the races at the tracks were fixed. Epstein, Virginia Hill, Joe Adonis and other racketeers made a lot of money placing bets on those races. But," he added, "we didn't know all of this until much later."

Moving Up In The Mob

During her heydays from the 1930s to the 1950s, Hill enjoyed a succession of roles as the "kept woman" of prominent gangland leaders like Epstein, Adonis and Benjamin "Bugsy" Siegel. Despite her growing notoriety, few people back home knew of her ties to crime. They just knew that she was very attractive and had lots of money.

It, therefore, should not be surprising that Hill received a mixed reception whenever she returned to Marietta to visit. "When Virginia Hill came to town," Kinney smiles, "all the women would tell their husbands 'now you stay away from that hussy.' But all of us young fellows stood there on the square at the corner of Hodge's Drug Store anyway, waiting for her. We were all out on 'Virginia Watch.'"

"We thought," Kinney remembers,

A publicity print of Virginia Hill during her days as a Hollywood starlet. (Associated Press photo courtesy of Bill Kinney)

The old Flamingo Hotel in Las Vegas was the creation of Bugsy Siegel, with some assistance from a lady named Virginia Hill. The historic structure was destroyed in the late 20th century to make way for new real estate. (Associated Press photo courtesy of Bill Kinney)

Sometime around 1937, Virginia Hill began a relationship with Benjamin "Bugsy" Siegel, a noted mobster and hitman for mob boss Charles "Lucky" Luciano. (UPI photo, reprinted with permission)

Corner Hangout – "Shop Til You Drop" is the successor to Hodge's Drug Store which once existed at this site on the town square in Marietta. It was at this spot that Bill Kinney and other young men passed the hours on "Virginia Watch" in the 1930s. (Photo by Daniel M. Roper)

This Polk Street house reportedly was the first residence ever purchased by Virginia Hill for her mother (Margaret Hill). (Photo by Daniel M. Roper)

Bill Kinney stands beside the Church Street residence in Marietta which Virginia Hill purchased for her mother from Dr. and Mrs. Ralph Fowler. (Photo by Daniel M. Roper)

"that she was an actress or rich heiress or that she had married very well into money. As a result, the people around here didn't ask many questions about Virginia, because she was so good for all of us."

Although she must have known that her activities were, at worst, illegal, and, at best, of interest to law enforcement authorities, Hill never went to great lengths to conceal them from the home folks. Bill Kinney recalls a typical incident one hot summer day in the late 1930s.

"Virginia was enjoying a game of bridge with several friends on the front porch of her Church Street apartment awaiting a delivery from Epstein," Kinney says. "In the middle of the game, the postman arrived with a package labeled 'hand lotion.' Virginia opened the package and pulled out $5,000 to $10,000 cash money."

Visits Back To Georgia

Even though much of so-called polite society never fully accepted Virginia Hill, she achieved a surprising degree of popularity with the folks at home – especially, but not exclusively, among young men.

"She was sort of our economy back in those days," Kinney grins. "She was our roving branch bank. She carried a roll of hundred dollar bills at a time when you could throw down a twenty dollar bill and ring every cash register on the square in Marietta."

As one source put it: "She paraded around with money to burn – with hundred dollar bills that filled her purses and her pockets – paying for a champagne party in a nightclub or for barefoot rumba dancing."[1]

"One night," says Kinney, recalling an instance of Hill's lavish ways, "we were having a little party at her mother's house and ran out of soft drinks. Virginia gave one young man – Ralph Fowler, Jr. (who later became a Marietta pediatrician) – a hundred dollar bill to get some Coca-Cola down at Holbert's store. When he got back with the drinks and tried to give her the change, she said 'Oh, just keep it.' That was the typical Virginia Hill way of life."

Hill could also open doors usually closed to a youth from the "rural" side of town. "One time, Virginia decided to carry us all night-clubbing in Atlanta," Kinney recounts. "We drove down the four-lane (old U.S. 41) stopping at roadside inns along the way. We would just pay a little visit and leave. We ended up at the Paradise Room at the Henry Grady Hotel in Atlanta. There we were," Kinney smiles in remembrance, "just a bunch of rag-tag country boys from Marietta. The maitre de refused to seat us, but Virginia just heaved her hefty bosoms and showed him a roll of hundred dollar bills. It wasn't long before we were sitting down front. While we were there, Virginia introduced us to the performer Red Skelton. She knew him because he had previously appeared at her club in New York."

Money didn't always open doors for Hill, but even when it didn't, Virginia used it as a whip to lash her detractors. On one occasion, she decided to give a party for her brothers, Chick and Cotton Hill. "She thought that the Marietta Country Club would be a good place to have that party," Kinney relates, "and so she went to see the club president, Rob Northcutt."

"'Well, Miss Virginia,'" Northcutt announced, "'you know that you have to be a member to hold a party out here, don't you?'"

Unimpressed, Virginia reportedly replied, "Well, I own the Hurricane Club up in New York City. How much do you want for this sorry outfit?"

"You know," says Kinney, "she probably could have bought it too."

Devoted To Friends & Family

Those who helped Hill also benefited from her largess. Kinney says he remembers one incident in particular which also turned out to be a bit humorous.

"Virginia stopped in Marietta for a few days after taking a load of money down to Miami," Kinney says. "She decided that she wanted to ride her horse around town as she had done many times in the past. Unfortunately, the horseback-riding caused an ailment – probably hemorrhoids – to flare up. Virginia went limping in to Dr. Murl Haygood's office and he got her fixed up in short order.

"In payment, Virginia took out her roll of hundred dollar bills and said, 'Well, Dr. Haygood, how much do I owe you?'

"The good doctor replied 'Oh, Miss Virginia, about $20 I guess.'

"Virginia said, 'Here's a hundred dollar bill. Put it toward Mama's account.' Then she added, smiling broadly, 'You know, this is the cheapest that anybody has ever seen my hind parts.'"

Years later, after he had become a reporter, Kinney says he too benefited handsomely from his friendship with Hill. "She became a frequent topic for New York City newspaper columnists," he recalls. "They wanted a picture of her grandmother, Miss Reed, chopping cotton on her farm out on the Due West Road. I made the photograph for them and the *New York Times* paid me $150. That was two weeks salary then at the *Marietta Journal*.

As her income increased, Hill began to upgrade her mother's living quarters. First, she bought her mother a house on Polk Street, a structure which still stands to this day. Later, a house (which was demolished in recent years) on the corner of Griggs and Marietta streets became her home.

Finally, Hill set her sights on a house owned by Dr. Ralph Fowler, Sr. and his wife Irma. "Dr. Fowler," Kinney recounts, "didn't want to sell to her and raised the asking price from $10,000 to $11,500. That, however, didn't faze Virginia Hill. She promptly paid cash for the property."

It is unknown today whether or not this acquiescence to the higher price gained Virginia favor in the Fowler household. Whatever the circumstances, the Fowlers did begin heartily defending her, and Bill Kinney says he learned this first-hand.

"I made an uncomplimentary remark about Virginia in print," Kinney relates. "I instantly felt Irma Fowler's wrath for my misdeed. She called me on the telephone and said, 'Let me tell you something, Billy Kinney. . . People like Virginia Hill who do good things for their brothers and mother and relatives – they go to heaven. Folks like you go straight to hell.'"

Another woman, however – Virginia Watkins – didn't feel so solicitous toward Hill. Watkins, who had the same first name as Hill, and who lived in the house next to Virginia Hill, was sometimes a victim of mistaken identity.

One day, John Carroll, a famous 1930s-era Hollywood actor drove his 16-cylinder Cadillac convertible into Marietta. He and Virginia were involved in a relationship, and, while looking for Hill's house, Carroll mistakenly arrived at the house of Virginia Watkins.

"When Watkins answered Carroll's knock," Kinney notes with a wry laugh, "she didn't know whether to be pleased to meet the movie star, or mortified at the fact that people were mistaking her for Virginia Hill." Worried that mobsters might make the same mistake and unwittingly target her for some nefarious punishment intended for Virginia Hill, Kinney says Virginia Watkins thereafter promptly identified herself as "Mrs. Watkins" whenever she answered the door and telephone.

Meanwhile, Virginia Hill was oblivious to the effect her reputation was having upon her neighbors. Had she known, however, she probably would have found a way to relieve them of their concerns. Among her other qualities, she had a thoughtful and kind disposition too.

In fact, Virginia seemed to have a knack for excelling at most everything she did. "She was even a good athlete," remembers Kinney. "She would skate down Church Street early in the morning and that was something to see. She'd also go over to Brumby Center (a former recreation center which no longer exists today) where they had a swimming pool and do high dives."

Hill also excelled at the culinary arts. "She was a gourmet cook and loved to prepare dinner for us," Kinney reminisces.

The Mobster Bugsy Siegel

According to many sources, Virginia Hill found the true love of her life when she linked up with renowned mobster Benjamin "Bugsy" Siegel in the early 1940s. Siegel, a prominent figure in the New York City underworld, got his start in organized crime as a heroin pusher for Charles "Lucky" Luciano. He ultimately advanced to cold-blooded murder.

In 1936, top New York mafia leaders had learned that other organized crime figures were planning to move west into California to take over the rackets there, particularly in Hollywood. Ben Siegel and several others were sent to seize control of as much of the illicit opportunities there as possible, particularly in Los Angeles.

Virginia Hill apparently traveled to Hollywood at about this same time. Bugsy Siegel had grown up (literally) with famed Hollywood actor George Raft in New York's "Hell's Kitchen." As a result, Siegel was introduced to many of the movers and shakers in the Hollywood arena at that time, and even fancied himself as an actor at one point.

According to one report,[2] Virginia Hill

had ingratiated herself to Samuel Goldwin, and had landed a plum role opposite Gary Cooper and Barbara Stanwyck in the big-screen production, *Ball Of Fire*. Whether she earned her acting roles via the assistance of mob figures or via the "casting couch," or indeed by her own acting talent is unknown today. Whatever the circumstances, her relationship with Siegel and his contacts within the Hollywood movie industry undoubtedly did her no harm. In fact, on a professional basis, she blossomed during this period.

Birth Of A Deadly Idea

It was also at this time that the war was coming to an end, and the public – particularly the wealthy public – had a growing desire for escapism and entertainment. Siegel, by chance, traveled through a sleepy, dusty little one-horse town in nearby Nevada called Las Vegas, and came up with what eventually was a hugely-successful money-making idea. Unfortunately, it would cost Bugsy his life before it became a successful venture.

"Siegel decided to build a nightclub and hotel right in the middle of the desert," Kinney explained. His scheme was to build the largest hotel-casino in the United States in a place where gambling and alcoholic beverages would be legal.

"He named the opulent hotel after Virginia Hill, whom he called his 'flamingo,' because flamingos have long, slender legs and so, he said, did Virginia," Kinney continued. "That, reportedly, is how the Flamingo Hotel in Las Vegas got its name."

In December of 1946, the long-awaited and highly-heralded hotel-casino finally was ready, but Siegel had fallen victim to huge cost overruns. Underworld crime figures develop friendships just like anyone else, and Benjamin Siegel had advanced high enough in the hierarchy to earn him-

"Virginia kept her horse here in this old garage behind the house that she purchased from the Fowlers for her mother," Kinney says. (Photo by Daniel M. Roper)

House Of Repute – Back in the 1930s, the structure above was known as "Mrs. Abbott's Boarding House." It was here that Virginia Hill stayed when she returned to Marietta for a visit. It was also at this residence that Hill, who was a mob courier, once received a package of cash worth thousands of dollars which was labeled simply as "Hand Lotion." (Photo by Daniel M. Roper)

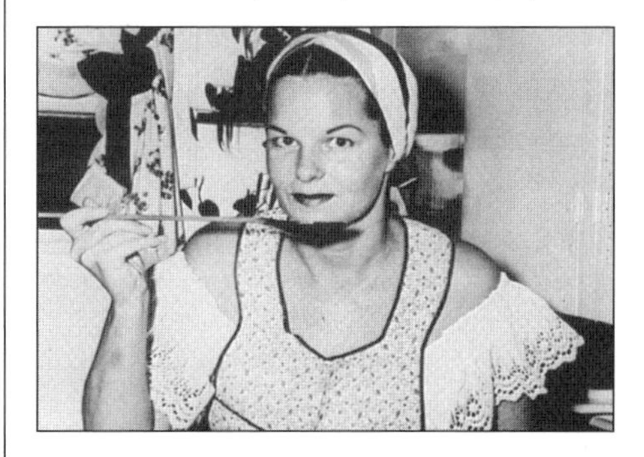

Somethin's Cookin' – When she returned home, Virginia Hill liked to prepare meals for some of her friends. "She was a gourmet cook," says Kinney. (Associated Press photo courtesy of Bill Kinney)

The Beverly Hills, California mansion rented by Virginia Hill. It was in this house on the night of June 20, 1947, that mobster Benjamin "Bugsy" Siegel was murdered. (Associated Press photo courtesy of Bill Kinney)

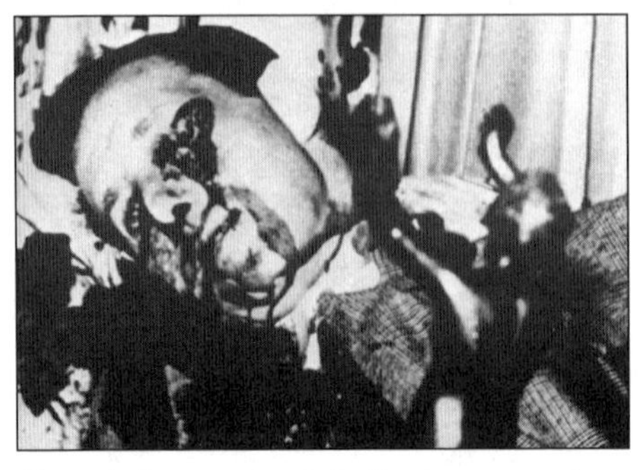

Sprawled on a couch in the lower quarters of Virginia Hill's Beverly Hills mansion, mobster Benjamin Siegel was shot to death by an unknown assailant. Hill was away from the home on the night of the murder.

self a measure of patience from the persons to whom he answered, but that patience only went so far. . . Business was business. The relationships Siegel had cultivated in the New York mafia – most notably with Lucky Luciano – eventually became strained to the breaking point. Siegel had confidently estimated that he could build the Flamingo for two million dollars, but the final price-tag – $6,000,000 – was a huge sum in those days, and is still a lot of money even today. Compounding the problem was the fact that Siegel was showing signs of spending even more money on the project.

"Rumors swirled that Bugsy and Virginia had skimmed off a lot of money," Kinney observes. "But I don't know, and I don't think anyone will ever know for certain."

Threats On Siegel's Life

Even with the rumors and the dangerous circumstances under which he was forced to function, Siegel refused to take even normal precautions like drawing the drapes on the windows of a room in which he was sitting at night. And brushing aside Virginia's concerns about threats on his life which he had begun receiving, Siegel assured her according to some accounts with the response that "I'm the killer and I will do the killing." He apparently believed that no one would dare harm one of Lucky Luciano's henchmen.

According to reports, Virginia Hill packed up and left Las Vegas in the spring of 1947 following a lover's quarrel there with Siegel. She had rented a Spanish-Moorish estate at 810 Linden Drive in Beverly Hills. Siegel, unwilling to lose her, reportedly trailed after her in an attempt at reconciliation.

On the night of June 20, 1947, Siegel, once again, took not even the simplest precautions to protect himself. While he was seated on a couch reading the *Los Angeles Times* newspaper on the ground floor of Virginia's mansion in Beverly Hills, Bugsy Siegel was shot dead. A gunman fired through a window of the home, hitting Siegel multiple times in the head. He died instantly.

Hill was not at home at the time of the slaying. Four days earlier, she had flown to Paris, France, supposedly to purchase furniture for the Flamingo. Some sources claimed she had gone to Europe to see Luciano (who had recently been deported to Italy) to plead for Bugsy's life. More cynical reports suggested she simply wished to be out of harm's way when the shooting began.

Regardless of the circumstances, the

chapter of her life dealing with Benjamin Siegel was ended forever on that summer night. His baby-blue eyes would never tempt her again. He was buried in Beth Olam Cemetery near RKO Studios in Hollywood, which, like Siegel, would soon be dead too.

Life After Siegel

As a result of the renown of Siegel and Hill, America was temporarily captivated by their lives and their tragic deaths. Hollywood, quick to recognize the possibility of a money-making venture, retold their story on the silver screen, most recently in the major motion picture *Bugsy*, starring Warren Beatty and Annette Bening.

In 1950, Americans witnessed Hill at her best when Senator Estes Kefauver summoned her to testify before a U. S. Senate committee investigating organized crime. Many onlookers expected Hill to retaliate against those who had killed Bugsy Siegel by freely divulging her knowledge of gangland activities. Hill, however, persistently denied any knowledge of criminal activity by Siegel and his associates.

Hill also displayed a sharp wit and tart tongue in reply to probing questions from the Senate committee. Bill Kinney recounts her testimony with a chuckle.

"When she was asked by Kefauver whether she was a 'kept woman,' " Kinney smiles, "she simply retorted 'Senator Kefauver, if you put every kept woman in this country in jail, you wouldn't have any room for anybody else.' When asked whether she herself was a criminal, she said 'No. All of the criminals are in Washington.' "

Kinney believes that Hill tried to "go straight" after Siegel's death. She married a renowned Austrian ski instructor and spent much of the rest of her life in Europe. United States authorities, however, did not believe that she had changed her ways. Rumors persisted that she couriered mob money to banks in Switzerland. The Internal Revenue Service initiated several investigations of Hill and eventually seized a home she still owned in Spokane, Washington.

"They also sold all of her furs and possessions that she didn't hide out on Due West Road with her mother, too," Kinney comments. "They even sold her wedding ring after it was discovered in a container of flour."

As with much of her adult life, Virginia Hill's death is shrouded by intrigue and mystery. She died of an overdose of drugs while on a ski slope in Salzburg, Austria, in 1966. Whether she had taken the drugs voluntarily or had been force-fed them is not known today.

According to Kinney, some individuals believe that Hill kept a diary filled with intimate details about her lovers, money, sex and the crimes of the men in her life. "So," Kinney continues, "one theory holds that she used the diary to threaten the mob and that Joe Adonis had her bumped off anyway."

A second theory maintains that Hill's death was a genuine suicide. "She didn't have any money left, and she'd lost her beauty at age 48," Kinney relates. The illness of depression may well have been Virginia Hill's killer.

Whether she died by her own hand or not, the attractive, outspoken red-head whose looks once mesmerized powerful men in powerful places, will long be remembered in the history of mobsters in America, and certainly by the handful of people still alive who grew up with the little Hill girl from Marietta, Georgia.

ENDNOTES

1/ Sifakis, Carl, 1987. *The Mafia Encyclopedia, Facts on File*, Inc., New York, New York; pp. 152-3.

2/ Anger, Kenneth, 1975. *Hollywood Babylon*, Stonehill Publishing Co., Simon and Schuster; pp. 242-7.

Dawson County 'Moonshine' Racers From Yesteryear

"Awesome Bill From Dawsonville" – Bill Elliott of NASCAR fame – is the latest and greatest racecar driver from Dawson County in north Georgia, but he is not the only racing champion to emerge from this colorful locale, nor was he the first – not by a long shot.

If you travel to Dawson County today, you'll enter a land of many paradoxes. Small family farms, mountain cottages and upstart businesses line Georgia Highways 9 (old U.S. 19) and 53 which intersect at Dawsonville, the seat of the county's government. Nearby, along Georgia 400 Highway, office buildings, a big new shopping center, and other new developments vie for space as growth continues its way up this burgeoning artery. Not far away, beautiful Amicalola Falls attracts thousands of visitors annually to that scenic locale. And in the lonely graveyard overlooking Dawsonville with its pioneer courthouse silhouetted against a steel-gray winter sky, the tombstone of Lloyd Seay stands in mute testimony to one of the numerous racing legends for which the county has become familiar.

Not every early racing champion in the South honed his driving skills by outrunning state or federal revenue agents, "but a good many of them did," explained Dawsonville businessman and racing historian Gordon Pirkle in an interview in the 1990s. And according to many, Dawson County led the pack when the sport of stock car racing was in its infancy and "moonshine" was still king in the mountains.

Pirkle, as of this writing, owns the Dawsonville Poolroom, which is a paradox in itself. The moment you walk into this place of business, you realize instantly that it isn't just another pool hall in yet another slow-paced Georgia town. To the contrary, Mr. Pirkle's place is quite literally a museum and a shrine.

"This place ain't about pool," Pirkle intones. "It's about racing."

And indeed, every wall in the building is covered with information about the sport. Newspaper clippings and pictures stretch from ceiling to floor, attesting to the fame of not only local and national hero, Bill Elliott, but to a number of other Dawson County notables from yesteryear as well, including Gober Soseby, Lloyd Seay, and Roy Hall, to mention a few.

"Lloyd and Roy were both known to

run liquor," said Pirkle with a smile. "I don't know if Gober ran any or not, but man, he burned those backroads and race-tracks plumb up."

A visit to the Dawsonville Poolroom is not complete without viewing at least one of the many films of old races Pirkle has collected over the years. He has hundreds, and will gladly play the race of your choice on one of half a dozen TV screens scattered around his place of business.

The races of choice, according to Pirkle, most often are those that were run half on low tide beach sand and half on the paved surface of Atlantic Avenue in Daytona Beach, Florida, during the early years of the famed Daytona 500.

And while you're watching the race, Pirkle recommends you try the house specialty – a bacon cheeseburger "with the works." It seems the Poolroom has earned a reputation not only as a site of racing memorabilia, but for tasty food as well.

The guest register at the front door of the Poolroom includes testimonial after testimonial from satisfied customers too. The addresses there represent racing fans from all across the U.S., and even the world. Somehow, they have sought him out in little downtown Dawsonville for decades.

Their comments reflect their enthusiasm for both his hobby and his fare: "The best ol' fashion burger in the state, if not the world." "Go Big Bill." "Super fries and burgers, just like when I was a kid." "Bill is back!"

Page after page of the comments alternate between praise for the homemade burgers and fries and encouragement for Dawson County's favorite son. No mention is ever made of the game of pool.

"We serve hundreds of burgers every day," Pirkle explained with a flourish. "We do it the old-fashioned way. We pat out the fresh beef patties several times a day and fry them on the grill. The fries are hand-cut from big ol' Idaho baking potatoes."

On the evening I visited the Poolroom, a special guest – Charley Weems – strolled through the doors, as if magically summoned for an old-time get-together and stroll down memory lane. Weems, a former ATF (Alcohol Tobacco And Firearms) agent for the U.S. Treasury Department in the 1950s and '60s, was active during the same time that many of the racing legends were in their heydays in Dawson County. The stories of his adventures quickly fill the night air, just as they fill the pages of his two books: *A Breed Apart* and *Agents That Fly.*

"I was alone one night," Weems explained as he described one incident from his colorful career, "and I came up behind a vehicle I recognized. You know the man that was in it," he said to Pirkle with a smile, whispering the name to him. "He was from around here.

"I ran him down and he jumped out of the passenger side and tumbled down a kudzu-covered bank in the dark. I didn't want him to get away, so I just jumped out into the night and landed smack on top of him. I knew the minute I landed that I had hold of a big, strong man, and that I was in trouble."

"Yeah," Pirkle agreed. "He was real stout. He's in prison right now and he calls me sometimes. He gets out in August. You'll have to come back and visit when he's free. Did you catch him?"

"Well, I weighed about 165 pounds in those days," Weems continued. "I knew I either needed a real good plan, or I was about to get one heck of a beating. I hollered out, 'It's okay Coppe! I've got him,' to suggest to the fellow I'd just landed on that I wasn't alone," Weems added with a smile. "Every violator in the state at that time knew Carl Coppe. You might say he was very dedicated (as a law enforcement

The Dawsonville Poolroom in Dawsonville, Georgia, is a popular stop for many locals and racing enthusiasts in general.

officer) and most of the liquor law violators respected and feared him.

"When we got back up the bank, my prisoner asked 'Where's your partner?' I just told him that he was over at the car and behind the lights.

"It wasn't until I got him cuffed and secured in the car that he finally figured out that I was alone," Weems smiled.

Talk in the Dawsonville Poolroom just naturally seems to drift back and forth between great car races, racecar drivers and illegal whiskey "daytrippers" who transported the coveted spirits down to Atlanta and elsewhere. As often as not, the race driver and tripper were the same person.

"There's plenty of folks around here try to separate the racing from the whiskey-makin' and transportin'," Pirkle grinned. "To me, that's just so much wishful thinkin'."

The production of illegal or untaxed liquor of course evolved in north Georgia generations before the days of stockcar racing. Immigrants from the Ulster region of what today is Northern Ireland brought their liquor distilling skills to America, spreading the craft throughout the Appalachians as they settled in the region.

Pirkle credits two incidents in the history of our nation for the evolution of "moonshining" as a big-time illegal money-making enterprise.

"It was the Depression and Prohibition that done it," he explains without hesitation. "The poultry industry and tourism were (still far away) in the future; the forests were gone (eliminating the timber industry); the ground wouldn't grow good crops; and there just wasn't many other ways to make a livin'."

There is obvious pride in Pirkle's voice when he speaks of Bill Elliot, racing champion and multi-winner of that premier stock car race, the Daytona 500.

"Visitors will ask me if Bill is the first Dawson County driver to win at Daytona, or they'll ask if he was the only one from around here, and I'll tell them 'Neither.' He's the latest, but about the sixth to win it.'

"There was Gober Sosebee. He won it three times. 'Course we're talking about the '40s and '50s, when it was the Daytona Beach Race, and it was run at low tide, half on the beach and half on Atlantic Avenue. It was some race in them days.

"Then there was Lloyd Seay and Roy Hall, Bernard G. Long, and a lady (believe it or not) by the name of Carleen Rouse. All in all, Dawson County drivers have won at Daytona more than ten times."

It was at this point that Pirkle enjoyed explaining a peculiarity of big city sports reporting involving Dawson County racers. "Whenever one of our drivers won a race anywhere," he smiled, "the Atlanta papers used to always declare 'Atlanta driver wins at so and so.' But just let that same driver get caught running white likker the next week, and those same papers would all say 'Dawson County violator arrested.'"

Perhaps one of the most charismatic of the early Dawson County racers was a handsome and lead-footed devil-may-care driver known as Lloyd Seay.

"Lloyd could drive," Pirkle agreed.

"The law couldn't catch him at all. There's no tellin' how far he could have gone as a race driver if he had 'alived."

Unfortunately, Lloyd Seay didn't live beyond his 21st birthday, and the manner of his death shocked and disgusted the world of racing in the 1940s.

It was about sugar – a large amount of the sweetener that Seay reportedly had purchased for the family's whiskey-making enterprise. He apparently had used a cousin's line of credit – without obtaining the obligatory permission – to buy the sugar. That just wasn't done in the moonshine business, and Woodrow Anderson, his cousin, was upset.

The previous day, Seay had won the prestigious Lakewood 100 in Atlanta on the old Lakewood Speedway. It was Labor Day, 1941, and Seay had won in his newly-numbered open-top '39 Ford roadster. He had always run with #7 painted on the side of his racer, but on the day of the Lakewood 100, for unknown reasons, Seay painted #13 on his doors – an unlucky omen of the events which would transpire in less than 24 hours.

After the race, Seay had gone to the tiny hamlet of Burtsboro, between Dawsonville and Dahlonega, to spend the night at the house of his brother Garnett Seay. Early the next morning, Anderson appeared at the home, insisting that Seay "go with him to settle up."

Anderson said they would go to the house of another family member – an aunt to all three of them – who was respected by all and who would settle the dispute. Lloyd Seay, his brother Garnett, and Anderson, left together, but they never reached Aunt Monnie's house.

After stopping briefly at his own house, Anderson drove to the house of his father, Grover Anderson, "to put water in the car radiator." At this point, Woodrow invited

Dawsonville native Gober Sosebee posed beside his 1939 Ford in 1994. He raced it to victory in the 1950 and '51 Daytona 500. In 1949, he also finished first in the heralded Daytona race, but was disqualified after his mechanic jumped inside his car to refuel it as Gober drove to victory.

The headstone on the grave of early Dawsonville racer Lloyd Seay in the city graveyard in Dawsonville. Seay was only 21 years of age when he was murdered during a dispute over moonshine supplies. The day before his death on Labor Day of 1941, the young racer had won the Lakewood 100 at Lakewood Speedway in Atlanta.

Garnett Seay to get out of the car "if you don't want to get mixed up in somethin'."

According to court records, Garnett's account of the incident sent Woodrow Anderson to prison for life. He (Garnett) testified that when he refused to get out of the vehicle, Anderson jumped on Lloyd and began striking him with his fists.

"Then he pulled a gun out of the bib of his overalls and shot me in the neck," Garnett explained in his court testimony. "He shot Lloyd right through the heart and told me he would finish me off if I ever said anything about it."

Lloyd Seay's funeral drew friends, relatives, and fans in numbers never previously witnessed in the little town of Dawsonville. Seay's tombstone in Dawsonville City Cemetery was purchased by Raymond Parks who owned the cars that Seay raced. Parks also was one of Seay's biggest fans, and the flamboyance of the tombstone clearly reflects this admiration.

"You can go see it now, if you want to," Pirkle added. "It's only a block or so from here."

I realized what they were talking about after visiting the gravesite. Carved into the stone is the requisite image of a racecar of the 1940s. It has a large #7 (not #13) on the door. At the wheel of the vehicle sits Lloyd Grayson Seay, his photograph frozen forever in a block of crystal, smiling his best winning smile back to his fans for eternity.

Back at the Poolroom, talk drifts on to other racers. "Hey Gordon," exclaims Charley Weems, "I've always been a big fan of Gober Sosebee. Do you think we could go over a see him?"

A quick telephone call by Gordon confirmed that Gober indeed was at home, and "would truly enjoy" talking about the early days of Southern stockcar racing.

The twenty-minute backroad trip to the Sosebee residence rekindled memories for both Weems and Pirkle as they pointed out first a former "still" location and then the home of a former moonshiner.

"That's old Snuffy's place," says Pirkle.

"I remember him," Weems replied. "We just passed over the place back there where his son, Clifton, had a head-on collision with Doug Denney and James Stratigos (former ATF agents). Three people died from that, counting the boy riding with Clifton. James was nearly killed too, but he managed to survive."

We shortly pulled up at the Gober Sosebee home. "I'm glad you fellers could come," Sosebee greeted, as we emerged from the car. "Ya'll come on in the house and sit a spell."

The living room of the Sosebee home looks like a trophy hall. Nearly 100 huge racing trophies fill the long rows of specially-built trophy cabinets which line the walls.

"We had nearly this many more in that building over yonder," Sosebee laments, "but somebody broke in and stole 'em. Don't have no value for anybody 'cept me and my family. Guess they did it just for meanness. You know how some people are nowadays."

It is difficult, upon meeting Gober Sosebee, to understand the nickname "Wild Injun" being applied to him in earlier days. A gentler looking, more soft-spoken gentleman would be difficult to imagine. After hours of conversation, however, an inkling of what he must have been like in the late 1940s and early '50s began to emerge.

"Those were the early days of racing," Sosebee explained. "They were the best days too. There were the Flocks – Tim, Fonty and Bob – and lots of other good drivers back then. I could hold my line with any of them," he said, unabashedly.

A quick scan of the list of entries for any of these races will reveal names that excite the imagination of anyone who knows anything about racing. Fireball Roberts, Crash Waller, Lee Petty, Pee Wee Martin, and the Flocks show up again and again. Not coincidentally, many of the names of race drivers also appear in ATF case histories of the same time-period.

It is also interesting to note that the vast majority of top cars in these races were

1939 Fords. This was also the car of choice for many trippers as they ran their loads of illegal "shine" from the hills of north Georgia into Atlanta.

"I won at Daytona Beach in both 1950 and '51," Sosebee continues. "I came in first in '49 too, but they disqualified me. I still say I won that race."

The record set by Sosebee that day still stands and is unchallenged. It, in fact, is what led to his disqualification. He made what is still known in racing circles as the fastest pit stop in racing history.

"All the front runners were low on fuel," recalls Sosebee. "I had my fuel tank mounted inside the car, behind the seat. When the others went in to refuel, I just slowed down and my mechanic jumped in with a can of gas and we kept goin'. He just trickled it in by hand as we finished the race."

At that time, there was no rule which prohibited the tactic, but Bill France, founder of NASCAR, wasn't about to allow a technique as volatile as that to gain acceptance. He disqualified Sosebee and Gober didn't take the news well at all.

Upon learning of France's ruling, Sosebee had some choice words for the venerated race organizer. "I knew your mother to be quite a lady," Sosebee says he told France. "That must make you a self-made son-of-a-bitch."

The next day, Sosebee says, the rule books had been changed. There would be no question in the future that mechanics belonged in the pits and not in the back of a race car. And needless to say, from that day forward, Gober Sosebee and Bill France no longer considered each other as friends.

Today, however, Sosebee fondly remembers many of his racing contemporaries from that era.

"Lloyd Seay was a gentleman on the track," Sosebee continued. "They're always trying to paint him as reckless, but I felt fine with him driving on my outside, whether it was into a curve or on a straightaway. There's plenty of others you can't say that about. They'd try and put you into the rail first chance they got."

"Gober," someone asks, "Most of the Dawson County drivers of your day got their start running white liquor. Did you ever do any of that?"

The spark came back into the gentle eyes of the former racer for just an instant – or was it a twinkle?

"I won't say one way or another," he smiled, "but there's some around here will claim that I did."

Before we left his home, Sosebee wanted to show us a car. To my amazement, it was the original 1939 Ford that he had raced to so many victories over half a century earlier. The little car is a sparkling black with an Indian chief painted on the side to represent the Atlanta battery shop that was his sponsor. It was the origin of his nickname – "Wild Injun."

As the old Ford thundered around Sosebee's big circle drive, the years seemed to fall away, and instead of the silver-haired octogenarian at the wheel, the original "Wild Injun" almost seemed to be reincarnated, if only for just a moment.

I wonder why Gober never made it into the Racing Hall Of Fame?" asks Weems. "There's plenty of men in there who can't hold a candle to him and who never won Daytona – not even once."

"It sure don't seem right," agrees Pirkle. "I'm sure that for many years, it was because of hard feelings on (Bill) France's part, and now, so many years have gone by."

As we prepared to leave, the white-haired racing legend stopped his car and bade us a wistful farewell.

"You fellers come back anytime and visit," he called after us. "We'll talk a spell more about racin' then."

The Rambling Russell Brothers From Leathers' Ford

The Russell Brothers sought gold in the hills and streams across the United States. They were adventurers of the first order, surviving Indian battles, the U.S. Civil War, disease, injuries and numerous other deprivations, to become wealthy men. They began their quest for gold in the north Georgia mountains.

It is generally acknowledged today that the first major gold rush in the United States took place in a little community north of Atlanta called Auraria. It isn't generally known however, that a family from this town is credited with initiating the Pike's Peak gold rush and the founding of Denver, Colorado. It is no coincidence that the community which was created at the site of the Georgia gold rush and the city of Denver once shared the same name – "Auraria."

It is a name, when translated, that loosely means "golden place," and it was intentionally bestowed upon the Colorado locale by the Georgia miners in memory of their old home. But who were these early roving gold-seekers from the peach state?

It was in February of 1858, that a rough-shod group of miners was organized by the Russell brothers (William Greenberry "Green", Levi, and Joseph Oliver) from Leather's Ford near present-day Dahlonega, Georgia. Despite the fact that gold mining was still active in the north Georgia mountains, all the "easy gold" had been reached by the mid-1800s, and the Georgia miners had long since begun looking elsewhere for opportunities.

The Russells had learned the trade of gold mining from their father, James Russell. James had supplemented his gold mining income with income from various surveying jobs. Both professions were difficult work in the 1830s. In 1835, a fatal illness suddenly claimed James' life, and Green became the patriarchal head of the household, a position he would hold for the rest of his life.

"Go West Young Man"

The Russell brothers were lured west by Indian and fur-trader accounts of sightings of gold in the peaks and valleys of the present-day Rocky Mountains. The Russells had intermarried with and befriended the Cherokees in north Georgia, and it is believed today they learned of the possible location of the precious yellow metal in the Rockies from their Cherokee brethren who themselves traveled and traded widely with other Native Americans and trappers across the West.

On the appointed day, the Russells – led by brother Green – reportedly set out up old Gold Diggers Road (the present-day course of Georgia Highway 9 from Auraria to just north of Dahlonega where its course has been abandoned across the mountains) for the journey. Green was highly admired and respected by his brothers, of which there were actually four (another brother, John, who is described in some references as being older than Green and in some others as younger, did not accompany the group to Colorado to prospect). It was the lure of gold, newly discovered in California in 1848, which had aroused the interest of the brothers, and which ultimately sent them packing for Colorado after they heard rumors of the presence of the precious yellow metal there.

A trip across the wilds of the West was not a novel undertaking for the Russells. Green and John had been among the first 35,000 gold seekers to travel overland to California in 1849 for the gold rush there. By the end of the year, they had amassed a sizeable fortune and had returned to Georgia by way of the Isthmus of Panama and New Orleans.

From this venture, Green was able to pay (according to written accounts) $10,000 cash for the 540-acre Savannah Plantation on the Etowah River, one of the most beautiful parcels of land in present-day Dawson County, 20 miles from his family's old Leathers' Ford home. (Savannah Plantation would be the seat of the family activities for the next 20 years.) John was able to purchase a mercantile business and a place of his own too.

The quest for gold and lure of prospecting ran deepest in Green. Before the end of 1850, he had returned to California a second time – a remarkable achievement in that day and time when Indians and deprivations abounded – this time with his two younger brothers – Levi and Oliver.

The men remained in the gold fields roughly two years before returning home to Georgia, and again, were lucky in their efforts. Levi had acquired enough to pay for his tuition and costs for medical school at the Pennsylvania College of Medicine and Surgery from which he was graduated in 1856 (training which served him well later during the group's trips into the Kansas Territory and their encounters with hostile Indians).

Interestingly, little more than 15 years after Levi's graduation from the medical school in Pennsylvania, another Georgian who would earn lasting fame out West – Dr. John Henry "Doc" Holliday – also was graduated (1872) from this same institution. He too would be lured out West, but not for the same reasons as the Russell brothers. Holliday was diagnosed with tuberculosis shortly after his graduation, and was advised to reside in a dryer climate in the West for health reasons. In order to support himself, he lived in numerous mining towns in Kansas, Arizona and Colorado, plying the gambling trade at which he was an adept player. He ultimately died in the mining town of Glenwood Springs, Colorado in 1887 (Readers please see *A North Georgia Journal of History, Volume IV* and *Volume V*).

Colorado Prospecting

After the California gold rush trips, and with a seemingly secure future, Green and his brothers eased into a life of leisure in Georgia. At Savannah Plantation, Green became a typical small Southern planter. He is listed as a member of the Blue Mountain Masonic Lodge (an affiliation which served him well more than once during his adventures out West). His brothers enjoyed similar success in other professions. John was a merchant, and Levi practiced medicine *(Editor's Note: Until the 1980s, Levi's old doctor's office still stood near the site of Green's Savannah Plantation. The office, unfortunately, was not protected, and eventually succumbed to weathering, collapsing into a pile of rubble.)*

Except for the money panic of 1857

William Greenberry Russell

immediately prior to the U.S. Civil War, the Russells' interest in gold prospecting might well have been ended with the California trips. Green and Oliver however, were both reportedly overextended in various investments. They planned a trip to what was known as "Kansas Territory" to invest in cheap land and to investigate the source of rumors they were encountering from trappers and Cherokee Indian friends about sightings of gold in this region.

There apparently was never any thought of leaving Georgia permanently at this point, for the brothers' families remained at home with the various farming and business enterprises there. A quick dollar and new investment opportunities seemed to be the only motive for the trip.

This initial trip ultimately focused upon what later became the vicinity of present-day Denver, Colorado (then part of the Kansas Territory). It, however, apparently resulted in little more than an exploration of the area and minor investments in land in the region. (Despite their nearness to the bloody border wars raging along the Smokey Hill River near present-day Manhattan, it does not appear that the Russell brothers were involved in any of the violent activities there.).

This trip did however, introduce the brothers to a half-breed Baptist preacher named John Beck, who was to rekindle their interest in their quest for gold in the region. Beck had been a member of a party led by Lewis Ralston seven years earlier to California. In the Rocky Mountains area, Beck remembered discovering promising signs of gold and was able to interest Green in returning to the site to search it more closely.

It wasn't long thereafter that the group was organized. Ralston's Creek in Colorado was the stated objective. Led by Green, the group of 104, nineteen of which were from Georgia, 27 picked up in Missouri, and others from various other states including approximately 50 Cherokees from the Cherokee Nation, set out on the trek. The wives of both Green and John Russell were of Cherokee descent and the Russell family accordingly enjoyed close ties to the Cherokees.

Leaving Georgia with Green, Oliver, and Levi, were six other men: Lewis Ralston, William Anderson, Joseph McAfee, Solomon Roe, Samuel Bates, and John Hampton. Just as they had ten years earlier in the trip to California, the group moved up old Gold Diggers Road.

A Courageous Leader

A trip across America in the mid-1800s was not a simple affair, as one might well imagine. The trip to Kansas Territory (present-day Colorado) proved to be an arduous undertaking, rife with sickness and hostile Indians. After arriving in the Rockies, the group's luck didn't change much either, at least initially. They panned and prospected for weeks with little success.

Despite their close ties with the Cherokee Indians, the Russells' group was not welcomed in Kansas Territory in 1858. The region was the home of the Cheyenne and Arapahoe Indians and was not considered "open for settlement." The white men were considered invaders, and as a result, skirmishes with the Indians of the area were not unusual, a situation which often required Levi to put his medical training to good use, once even on himself, when he, amazingly, had to cut an arrow from his own hip.

By late June of 1858, the disappointment was beginning to take its toll. Luke Tierney, the self-proclaimed journalist of the group wrote: *"On the twenty-sixth, most of the men spent the day prospecting. On their return to camp, the spirits were very much depressed . . . The prospect was so far short of their expectations and feverish hopes, that many began to show signs of mortification. They no doubt expected to find lumps of gold like hailstones, all over the surface."*

According to Tierney, it wasn't long before most of the group decided to head back home . . . all of them that is, except Green Russell.

"Gentlemen," he reportedly said, "You can all go, but I will stay if but two men will stay with me. I will remain to satisfy myself that no gold can be found."

This statement remained indelibly imprinted for the remainder of their lifetimes in the memories of the twelve men who decided to stay on with Green, for their decision to remain loyal to him proved to be a fortuitous one. Green Russell apparently possessed an uncanny sense of knowing "where to pan" for gold. He also had received a good education in the profession of gold mining from his father.

To his good fortune – and that of the twelve men who remained behind with him in the wilds of the Kansas Territory in 1858 – Green Russell ultimately did discover gold in Colorado. The rest is history. In the process, he initiated the Pike's Peak gold rush, ushering in the beginnings of the his-

Joseph Oliver Russell

Dr. Levi Jasper Russell

The former home of Green Russell still stands (as of this writing) on Etowah River road in Dawson County, photographed here in 1987. (Photo by Olin Jackson)

Known today as "McClure Cemetery," this early graveyard exists a short distance to the rear of the historic Silas Palmour-Green Russell home site in Dawson County. Many of the Russell family members are interred here, including the matriarch of the Russell brothers, Elizabeth M. Russell (1793-1855) (foreground); Green's wife, Susan (1827-1893); two of Green's sons, Thomas (1856-1859) and Benjamin H. (1858-1859); Levi's son, Charlie (1858-1858); and John's daughter, Francis (1855-1859). (Photo by Olin Jackson)

tory of the state of Colorado.

Green Russell very likely, was the only man in U.S. history connected with all three gold rushes of the last century. His first strike in Colorado was at Little Dry Creek, located in the present-day Denver suburb of Englewood. His discovery of the rich mining section known as "Russell's Gulch" nearby in Colorado is credited with starting the settlement of Central City, Colorado, once described as *"the richest square mile on earth."*

The gold rush was on, but so was another event of epic proportions in America at that time – The U.S. Civil War. With the outbreak of the war, the Russells decided to return to Georgia. Their investments and mines in Colorado had made them wealthy men for their day and time.

Bringing The Fortune Back To North Georgia

In September of 1859, a Denver newspaper reported that Green Russell and three of his men were in Denver City, dispatching 103 pounds of gold back home to Georgia. A packet of 103 pounds of gold was quite a fortune in the 1850s, and certainly nothing to be sniffed at today as well. A year later, 22 men from the Russell Gulch area headed back to "the states" with three wagons hauling what then amounted to $110,000 in gold bullion.

Despite a rising tide of anti-Southern sentiment in Colorado in 1859, Green and Levi returned to the region once again the following year, to divest themselves of their mining interests there, which were many and varied. Oliver had remained in Colorado over the winter, and reportedly had endured *"dynamitings"* to mining properties and other property damages. The Russell brothers' strong Masonic ties with many of the Union partisans apparently staved off serious problems until the brothers could sell off their holdings (reportedly at a rate far below market value) and return home to Georgia.

Deciding to leave the Colorado Rockies was one matter. However, actually being able to leave proved to be an entirely different situation. Almost all customary routes to the South were, by this time, held by Union forces, a situation which promised trouble for the Southerners. The best route, the Russells felt, lay through New Mexico and Texas on the Fort Smith Road known then as *"the back door to the Confederacy."*

In the end, this route proved to be flawed too. In the Texas panhandle, some 200 miles from present-day Las Vegas, the group was detained and imprisoned by a troop of Union cavalry under the command of a Lieutenant Shoup. On February 14, 1863, having found no legitimate reason to hold the Russells further, Lt. Shoup ordered that the men be released and their property restored.

Once again, the Masonic ties of the Russells apparently had been advantageous. They had been instrumental in the development of good relations with the Union commander and his men, and ultimately resulted in the release of the Russells and the restoration of their property – which amazingly included their gold!

The harsh trip to Georgia still remained ahead for the Russells, but it proved to be much less troublesome than it could have been. The Russell luck was still holding.

The brothers subsequently took a stagecoach to St. Joseph. They were granted passes as far as Louisville, Kentucky, by a Union soldier. From the Ohio River however, they had to hide by day and travel by night, and often within earshot of both Confederate and Union soldiers. The trip, which should have taken but a couple of weeks, reportedly was stretched to several additional weeks in length.

Amazingly, the Russells, somehow reached Savannah Plantation with their gold intact. Reports indicate that Green, an ardent Democrat, spent much of his Colorado gold outfitting a Confederate cavalry company. On August 11, 1863, Captain William Green Russell's company, Georgia Cavalry, was mustered at Dawsonville, Georgia. Oliver Russell was named a lieutenant, and even Green's 16-year-old son John joined as a trooper.

The company reportedly never numbered more than 50, nor is it likely they saw service outside of Georgia. Accounts indicate Captain Russell's company spent most of its time rounding up deserters and recruiting new men, duties which did not earn him or his brothers great popularity in the region at this time.

Civil War Desolation

When the South surrendered in 1865, things became even worse. The uncertain and quickly-unraveling circumstances in Georgia at this time undoubtedly were the impetus for the brothers' decision to leave Georgia again shortly after 1865. Also, Georgia at that time was terribly impoverished, and the Russells undoubtedly realized that the restoration of order and prosperity would be long in coming.

Green was eager to return to Colorado, this time permanently with his family. Levi had become disinterested in gold mining and Colorado altogether. He wanted to go to Texas. Oliver's wife, Jane, had relatives in Texas, and wished to go there too. John's wife, Frances, being part Cherokee, had friends and relatives in the Cherokee Indian Territory in Oklahoma which she longed to see. She also was entitled to land there as a result of her heritage, so this became

Green Russell very likely, was the only man in U.S. history connected with all three gold rushes of the last century.

their destination. (Green's wife, also of Cherokee lineage, decided to accompany Green back to Colorado.)

Though saddened to be separating from his brothers with whom he had experienced so much over the years, Green nonetheless was irresistibly attracted back to Colorado and the Huerfano Valley where he owned a ranch. Many of his old Georgia friends and prospectors had recently returned to the valley for similar reasons, so he knew he would hardly be lonely there.

The Colorado country reportedly was beautiful that fall, especially on Apache Creek where Green lived. For the first two years, Green and his son John, now 25, turned most of their attention to building a cattle and horse ranch in the valley. Mrs. Russell and the six younger children soon came to share the men's enthusiasm for the region.

The End Of The Line

It wasn't long however, before it became apparent that the Russell luck was running out. John was killed in a tragic mining accident in 1874. (Green and his son apparently could never fully abandon the urge to mine gold.) Grasshopper plagues and droughts depleted cash reserves needed for ranching. A change was inevitable.

Green eventually decided to move nearer to his brother John in the Cherokee Indian Territory (in Briartown) in present-day Oklahoma. Green's wife and six children, as a result of their Cherokee blood, had land title rights in the territory.

In the winter of 1877, with John's help, Green selected 600 acres on the Canadian River three miles southeast of Briartown, and settled down for a new life there. The bad luck continued however. The following June, malaria, perhaps complicated with typhoid, struck every member of the family.

By this point, Green apparently had had his fill of the Oklahoma climate. He reportedly longed for the cool crispness of the north Georgia mountains. Unfortunately, he never made it back to his beloved north Georgia mountains.

On August 14, William Greenberry Russell suffered a massive stroke or some type of similar affliction, possibly a heart attack, while chopping wood in his yard. Ten days later, he died. He was buried in Briartown Cemetery.

As one of the most colorful figures in the gold rush history of the United States, and a pioneer of the early explorations of the American West, the contributions of Green Russell have been largely overlooked. He has been called the "Sutter of Colorado," and was sought out for counsel by the likes of Kit Carson (when he was sent into the Kansas Territory by the United States government to form a pact with the Arapaho and Ute tribes); Horace Greeley (when he came to Colorado in 1859 researching his book *An Overland Tour To San Francisco* which is crowded with material furnished by Russell); and many others.

Demise Of The Brothers

According to records, Dr. Levi Russell became a practicing physician in Texas and died and was buried in Menardsville in 1908. Joseph Oliver Russell, apparently believing there was more money in the cattle business than in gold mining, moved to Texas also, and became a rancher, dying there in 1906.

After Green's death, John decided to stay in the Cherokee Nation in Oklahoma where he owned a fine ranch. He and his wife lived a long and fruitful life together, and are buried there.

Interestingly, Green's wife, Susan, moved her family back to Georgia to live again at Savannah Plantation in Dawson County, where it had all begun for the Russells. The old family home still stands there today, and remains as part of the legacy earned through all the hardships suffered by Green Russell and his brothers.

In the family cemetery near the original homesite rest the remains of many of the descendants of the Russell family, pioneers in the truest sense, and history-making adventurers recorded in the annals of at least five states.

In an ironic twist of fate, the Colorado State Historic Society corresponded with the county historian near Auraria, Georgia in 1931, requesting information on the Russell brothers. (A historic marker in Confluence Park in downtown Denver, Colorado commemorates that site as the spot where the Russells discovered gold and began the gold rush culminating in the founding of Denver.). The fortunes of Auraria, Georgia had sunk so low by 1931, that the former gold rush town had all but disappeared. There was no information available there on the Russells. Adding insult to injury, *Webster's Geographic Dictionary*, published in 1949 either did not know of the community, or just decided to ignore it. The listing for Auraria that year read: *"First settlement in Colorado; established in 1858."*

Aaron Palmour/Dr. Levi Russell Home -Once located at the intersection of Seed Tick and Etowah River Roads in Dawson County, this fine example of a pioneer log cabin was relocated to a new site on Ridge Road in Dawson County in the latter portion of the 20th century. Built circa 1830 by Aaron Palmour (b. ca. 1771), this structure was designed as a part of the original fort-type compound constructed by the Palmour family when they first arrived in Dawson (then Lumpkin) County. It stood originally in the flood plain near the Etowah River, and later reportedly was moved up to the intersection of Seed Tick and Etowah River roads by Levi Russell in the mid-1800s. (Photo by Jimmy Anderson)

This attractive country home is known today as the home to which Susan Russell returned to live in 1877 after her husband – Green Russell – had passed away in Oklahoma. (Photo by Olin Jackson)

Fayette County Moonshining And The Murder Of James Langston

On a crisp morning in 1922, a U.S. postman was methodically murdered on a backroad just south of Atlanta. The perpetrators – all revenge-minded moonshiners – were pleased with their vendetta, until they realized they had killed the wrong man.

"Neither snow or rain nor heat or gloom of night shall stay these couriers from their appointed rounds." That well-known U.S. Postal Service motto was intended to include many unattractive circumstances, but not the horrible act which interrupted mail delivery on October 28, 1922 in Fayette County, Georgia.

James C. Langston had been a U.S. Postman for a number of years. According to the late Marvin Rivers, he was a tall, popular man who resided in downtown Fairburn. He also was known for his big feet – so big – that the foot peddles on his Ford automobile had to be specially rebuilt for him by a local blacksmith.

On a Saturday morning in late October, Langston knew nothing of the fate awaiting him as he left the Fairburn Post Office on his rural mail route. He stepped into his Ford, adjusted the clutch with his special peddle, and drove off on his route. It was a trip from which he would never return.

Deadly Chain Of Events

A series of events had been set into motion in late September of 1922 which unavoidably destined Langston for doom. Fayette County Sheriff Tom Kerlin and U.S. Revenue Agents Milam and T. B. Harris had raided an illegal liquor ("moonshine") distillery ("still") just off Kite Bridge Road in upper Fayette. They were accompanied on their mission that night by at least one other person – Abner (Ab) Davis – a peddler who lived in the nearby Kenwood community about two miles east of the still site.

The moonshine distillery itself (remnants of which still exist as of this writing) had a 50-gallon capacity, and was located on the property of John Waller just off Kenwood Road on Kite Road. John and his brother – Charlie – were well-known bootleggers in the illicit trade and enjoyed a steady business in the countryside south of Atlanta. They were also shrewd criminals.

When buyers approached the Wallers

for moonshine, they (the Wallers) instructed the clients to walk back into the garden and look under a certain cabbage plant. A bottle of "shine" would be awaiting pick-up there.

An informant eventually alerted law-enforcement officials to the presence of the Waller brothers' operations – an action which culminated in the night raid by Sheriff Kerlin. Ab Davis was with the officers and assisted in the destruction of the still.

As the party was leaving the still site, they were observed from cover by another moonshiner – Ora Whittle – who was quick to note Ab Davis' presence in the group. Davis was well-known in the area because he often peddled his wares along the road.

Word of Davis' involvement in the incident spread quickly in the close-knit community. On the following Sunday morning, a group of the moonshiners consisting of Ora Whittle, John and Charlie Waller, and Rainey Cauthen, met at the home of John Waller. They discussed plans to punish Davis for his actions.

According to later court testimony, John Waller wanted to "whip Davis," but Charlie Waller and Ora Whittle said it "would be better to kill him." The argument reportedly continued until the men eventually reached an agreement whereby they would pay Cauthen approximately $125 to "whip Davis."

The more the men pondered this punishment, however, the more they felt it to be inadequate. Another meeting eventually was scheduled at John Waller's house the following Wednesday and at this session, the plans were changed from whipping Davis to killing him. The deed was set to be accomplished the next Saturday morning, since Davis was known to travel down

The former home of Postman Jim Langston still stood in downtown Fairburn as of this writing.

Kite Road each Saturday.

The men originally planned to use a firearm of some sort to murder Davis. However, after further consideration, it was decided that a gun would make too much noise, and an axe and a maul were selected instead, since they were silent in their deadliness.

By this time, a total of eight moonshiners were included in the group conspiring to kill Davis. According to later news accounts and courtroom testimony, the murderous group was ultimately enlarged to include Arthur Alexander, Melvin Brown, Oscar Dutton, and Melvin Windham.

The Murder Site

Kite Bridge Road, Kite Lake Road, or South Kite Road as the route is variously known today, turns northward from Kenwood Road and immediately begins a gentle downhill descent to a small tributary of Morning Creek before continuing up the next hill. A bridge at the bottom of the hill was to be the site of the killing, and an ambush was carefully planned for that spot. Today, this site is well-developed with attractive homes, but in 1922, it was a very secluded spot with no residences near the bridge or creek.

John Waller's home, located approximately 150 yards up the hill, was the nearest residence to the creek. Today, in retrospect, the selection of an ambush and murder site so near to the headquarters of the perpetrators was an infantile decision. It was one of many aspects of this gruesome crime which defied logic, and which remain unexplained today.

Long-time Fayette residents still remember the very good spring which once existed at the bottom of the hill. Travelers often stopped at the spot for a cool drink. Fayette native Woodrow Harris said the postman always stopped at that spring for a drink and usually ate his lunch there. This, however, somewhat contradicts the murderers' testimony.

According to courtroom testimony, just before 11:00 a.m. on the appointed day of October 28, 1922, Postman Jim Langston crested the hill in his Ford automobile, his bag of mail in the seat beside him. He drove on down the slope and was surprised when Rainey Cauthen stepped out of the bushes along the roadside and flagged him to a stop. Langston immediately informed Cauthen that he was unable to provide him with transportation, saying, "I'm a government man and can't give you a ride."

It was at this point that Langston's heart must have jumped into his throat, because Melvin Brown jumped out into the road and covered the by now dumbfounded Langston with his shotgun.

"What are you fellows going to do with me?" Langston reportedly implored.

"We're going to teach you how to report stills," Cauthen reportedly responded, as Ora Whittle, an axe in his hands, and Oscar Dutton, hefting a large wooden maul, jumped menacingly from their hiding spots nearby.

Despite the fact that Langston obviously was not the intended victim (Ab Davis), the men, for some unknown reason, nonetheless proceeded with their grisly plans. Were they simply so eager for revenge that they were willing to exact retribution from Langston (a federal official) too? Or were they simply too eager, mistakenly stopping Langston, and then fearing he would later implicate them if they released him and then subsequently committed the ill deed on Davis? The true circumstances likely will never be known.

The Murder

"You're not going to kill me for nothing?" the by-now terror-stricken Langston reportedly croaked, realizing the men had a bloodthirsty gleam in their eyes. These words, reportedly, were the last ever uttered by Jim Langston.

By this point, Rainey Cauthen must have begun having second thoughts, because he reportedly instructed the group to "Let the man go. We were going to whip him, not kill him."

"Alright," Whittle replied deceivingly. He and Dutton reached in and pulled Langston over the car door and out of the vehicle, obviously indicating they had no intention of halting their actions.

Again Cauthen repeated "We weren't

Whittle struck Langston viciously in the back of the head with his axe.

going to hurt anyone, but whip Ab Davis."

It was at this point that Windham said to Dutton and Whittle "Turn him loose."

Langston, apparently thinking he might escape unharmed after all, went around to the front of his car to re-crank it. It was the last move he ever made.

According to courtroom testimony – and for reasons still unknown today – Whittle struck Langston viciously in the back of the head with his axe. Langston fell to his knees. Dutton, his thirst for violence unquenched, then struck Langston again with his heavy maul, crushing the entire top of Langston's head. The mailman collapsed to the ground, instantly dead.

It must have been about this time (if at all) that reality began to dawn upon the murderers. If they had not previously noticed the mail bag, and if for some unknown reason they still believed that Langston was Davis, the existence of the mail must have tipped them off to their mistake.

Accounts differ somewhat as to the actions of the men immediately following the murder. Newspapers of that day state that all the men ran in different directions and later met at Kite's Lake, trying all the while to disguise their trails with a turpentine and camphor mixture which they spread liberally behind them to confuse the bloodhounds they knew would follow shortly.

It would almost seem comical today, had not the crime been so heinous. Before departing the murder scene, Whittle hid the axe in nearby woods. No mention of the disposition of the wooden maul was ever made in courtroom testimony.

All the murderers (again defying logic) met at approximately 12:00 or 12:30 at John Waller's house (near the top of the hill and just a short distance from the murder site). At this point, according to later testimony, John Waller stated "Well, we got the wrong man," to which Whittle replied "Yes, but it's too late to pray after the devil's done got you."

The Murder Investigation

Meanwhile, Rosa Porch, sometimes known as "Lizzie," was a black lady who lived on the corner of Kenwood and Kite Roads, just above John Whittle. It was she who informed Fayette County Sheriff Tom Kerlin of the murder. Kerlin immediately contacted U.S Department of Revenue Officer T. B. Harris before speeding to the crime scene.

When Kerlin arrived, he noted Langston's car on the bridge in the center of the road with Langston stretched out in front of the automobile, his skull crushed and the U.S. Mail bag and its contents strewn in the road along the side of the car.

By 3:00 p.m., Revenue Agent Harris had arrived from his office in Newnan, Georgia. He began assisting in the investigation. U.S. Postal Inspector J.W. Cole also aided in the investigation. He was replaced sometime later by Inspector Frank Ellis, who in turn was assisted from time to time by Inspectors J.R. Smith and W.W. Hodge.

No records remain today of the investigation conducted by the federal government, and none of the men involved in the murder were ever charged with any federal crimes, although a number of charges could have been brought against the men for interference with the U.S. mails. The U.S. Postal Service officials apparently were content to allow local officials to investigate, arrest and prosecute the perpetrators solely for the crime of murder, which is a state, not a federal offense.

The authorities instantly suspected the Waller brothers. After all, they were known bootleggers and John lived almost within sight of the murder scene.

John and Charles Waller, as well as George B. Samuels, were all arrested the following week on suspicion of murder. Samuels was "a Spaniard who had been in the World War" and who lived with Lula Waller, daughter of John. All these men denied any knowledge of the crime and were released.

Over the span of the next two years, Ora Whittle and John Waller were both arrested, but were only charged with possession of intoxicants. They were both subsequently found "Not guilty" and released.

Despite the difficulties involved in solving this case, the local authorities did not give up. Finally, in May of 1925, Oscar Dutton and Ora Whittle were arrested as suspects in the case. Dutton was sent to the Coweta County Jail in Newnan and Whittle was held in Atlanta, both probably for safekeeping. Both men had flatly denied any connection with the murder and openly proclaimed their innocence. While in jail, however, Dutton eventually confessed and implicated some of the others, including John Waller who was promptly arrested.

The Trial & Sentences

A special June session of Superior Court was called in 1925 to try Whittle and Dutton for the murder of Jim Langston, and also to try John Waller as an accessory before the fact of the murder. The *Fayette County News* reported that despite a June heat wave, large crowds attended the trial and the Fayette County Courthouse was completely filled. Overflow spectators surrounded the building, hoping to hear some of the trial through the open windows.

All three men were found "Guilty" on July 3, 1925, but surprisingly were given life sentences with recommendations for mercy. Existing records are not clear as to how the other perpetrators were implicated in this case, but by December, all eight men involved had been tried and found "Guilty." Melvin Brown, Rainey Cauthen, Arthur Alexander, Melvin Windham, Oscar Dutton and Ora Whittle were also given life sentences with recommendations for mercy for the murder. John and Charlie Waller drew the same sentence for being accessories to the others.

All eight men were sent to different prison camps to serve out their sentences. Some long-time Fayette County residents today can still remember Dutton and Whittle serving on the local "chain gang," once located just east of Fayetteville.

Despite the blood-thirsty nature of the crime, most of the men served relatively short sentences. Charlie Waller was paroled in July of 1932, and his brother, John, in November of 1935. Melvin Windham received a parole in September of 1933, and Oscar Dutton was granted parole in January of 1935. No record has been located for the release date of Ora Whittle, Melvin Brown, Arthur Alexander or Rainey Cauthen.

Meanwhile, Ab Davis, the object of all the hatred and vicious blood-letting on an October morning in 1922, continued peacefully in the produce business and in later years ran a store in Kenwood. He lived out his life without incident.

Author's Note: *Information on the murder of Jim Langston is a matter of public record in the Fayette and Spalding County courthouses, the Georgia Department of Archives and History, and the archives of the local newspapers. Special thanks is hereby extended to Jon Wolleat, the author's mailman, for details involving the murder of Jim Langston.*

The 1913 Rosedale Twister

On the evening of March 13, 1913, a deadly twister which has practically been forgotten today, struck a very sparsely-populated area in Floyd County. This huge tornado obliterated everything in its path for nearly 20 miles, and when the terror had ended, 13 people – mostly children – had been killed, and dozens more were injured. This is their story.

Thick gray clouds rolled overhead as I walked through the old Mt. Vernon Baptist Church cemetery in northern Floyd County. A brisk east wind buffeted the graveyard's oak trees, tossing about gnarled limbs cloaked with resurrection fern. The U.S. Weather Service has just issued an alert for severe thunderstorms and flash floods, and thunder rumbled in the distance. It must have been much like this, I thought, the day the tornado swept across Turkey Mountain and laid waste to the tiny community of Rosedale.

I have always enjoyed old cemeteries like this one. They are peaceful places, frequently quite beautiful, and they often contain useful historical and genealogical information. But Mt. Vernon cemetery is a melancholy place. Although it is pleasantly situated on a tree-covered knoll across from the newly-painted church building, it contains an appalling number of children's graves. Fully one-third of Mt. Vernon's 120 graves are those of babies, infants and youths.

While infant mortality was a common occurrence in rural communities at the turn of the century, judging from its cemetery, this community suffered more than its fair share of these losses. An area on the cemetery's west side is particularly telling. Seven children are buried there in close proximity to one another: Stella, Henry, Viley, Ruth and Frank Bolt, John Reed and Loucille Martin. Each of these children died on March 13, 1913 – victims of a tornado that Rome's *Tribune-Herald* newspaper called at that time *"the most disastrous storm in the history of Floyd and Gordon counties."*

Rosedale

In the early years of the century, Rosedale was a bustling little community at the intersection of the Dalton and Rosedale roads, fourteen miles north of Rome. Many of its residents farmed the bottomlands of the nearby Oostanaula River and the town boasted a store, school and a church. Other than the troop movements of both Union and Confederate armies during the U.S. Civil War, nothing much had ever happened in Rosedale until that fateful night in 1913.

The John B. Davis house was one of the tornado's first victims. The fierce storm destroyed all but the front two rooms and porch. Afterwards, the damaged house served as an emergency morgue and the bodies of seven victims were laid out on its front porch. As of this writing, the home belongs to Davis's son, Fred Davis.

Shortly after 9:00 p.m. on March 13, 1913, the immense tornado swept across Turkey Mountain (background) and almost destroyed the John Davis home. The tornado then crossed the pasture (foreground) and leveled the L.M. Bolt residence. This photo was taken from the site of the old Bolt home. (Photo by Daniel M. Roper)

Harsh weather during the first days of March that year perhaps foreshadowed the terror which was enroute. The *Tribune-Herald* grumbled day after day about heavy rains, unseasonably cold temperatures and spring weather that seemed to have *"a hard time getting out of the almanac."* On March 12, the weather-weary newspaper observed that *"March has played the dickens so far. There has been all kinds of weather at all kinds of time."*

Eighty-two years later, Bobby Pierce still remembered the unusual weather conditions on the evening of March 13, 1913, even though he had been a child of just seven years of age at the time. "We lived in a house about seven miles north of Rosedale," Pierce recalled in a 1995 interview just before he passed away. "As night fell," he continued, "there was an eerie stillness. Then the wind picked up and the thunder and lightning were awful. My father knew something bad was coming and he moved us all into the front room of the house."

Fortunately, the tornado inflicted only minor damage on the Pierce farm which stood on the fringe of the storm's path. Neighbors of the Pierces to the south and east, however, would not be so lucky.

The terrible tornado formed at roughly 9:00 p.m. in Texas Valley, some ten miles west of Rosedale. According to accounts in the *Tribune-Herald*, it moved east, cutting a swath a mile wide and 20 miles long *"as clean as a hound's tooth"* through the countryside. It struck glancing blows at the little towns of Armuchee and Everett Springs, but it did not fully unleash its destructive fury until it crossed Turkey Mountain.

The John B. Davis farm was one of the first hit by the huge twister. Kay Davis, John Davis's granddaughter, grew up hearing about the vicious storm. "The tornado," she remembers, "smashed and demolished all but the front rooms and porch of the house."

John Davis and his family, who fortunately were in a front room at the time, escaped injury. The badly-damaged house then faced another danger when coals scattered from a fireplace set the wood flooring ablaze. Davis, undoubtedly dazed by the concussive impact of the twister and the devastation around him, still had the presence of mind to grab a churn of milk and douse the flames.

The next house in the path of the storm was the L.M. Bolt residence on top of a small ridge just across the pasture from the Davis farm. "The Bolts," Kay Davis recalls, "had just tucked six young children into bed and apparently had no warning that a tornado was approaching."

A direct hit on the Bolt home killed five of the sleeping children and demolished the house – shattering it into small kindling wood according to newspaper reports. "All that remained," Davis says sadly, "were a few items on the floor, some jars of fruit preserves, and the children's shoes that had been neatly tucked underneath their beds."

Wreckage and the bodies of the dead and injured littered the hillside. The powerful winds cast the lifeless forms of little Frank and Stella Bolt into the family well, seriously wounded another child, and hurled their mother into an oak tree. L.M. Bolt, fortunately uninjured, found his wife hanging there by her arm, unconscious. (According to granddaughter Christina Bolt Boyd, Mrs. Bolt never fully recovered from this injury and continued to have trouble with the arm right up until her death in 1954.)

The bodies of little Frank and Stella Bolt were soon located but it took nearly a week to find and recover the remains of Ruth, Viley and Henry. Finally, on March 21, the *Tribune-Herald* sadly reported that *"the three Bolt children, pinned underneath debris which was covered by back water* (of the flooding Oostanaula River), *were found yesterday, their bodies swollen and decayed almost beyond recognition."*

The W.M. Martin house just south of the Bolt residence also stood squarely in the path of the tornado. Unlike the Bolts, the Martin family apparently knew the twister was approaching. According to news accounts, W.M. Martin *"yelled a warning to his wife and ran for a storm pit, where he escaped death."* With tragic results and for reasons unknown today, Mrs. Martin refused to follow her husband. The house was *"blown to atoms"* and a falling rafter killed the baby Mrs. Martin was holding in her arms.

The Rosedale twister's tremendous size and strength is apparent from this photo, taken shortly after the tornado had passed. Notice the absence of any substantial trees to the rear of the individual pictured here. This rare picture is one of only two photos taken of the storm's aftermath. (Photo courtesy of Clara Green)

A second view of destruction caused by the twister.

The killer tornado, by this point an immense vortex at least three-quarters of a mile wide, careened northeastward through the Oostanaula River valley chewing up everything in its path. Just south of Rosedale, its deadly winds obliterated the house of Monroe Barnett, knocking him senseless, killing his wife, and seriously injuring their four children. Upon regaining consciousness, Barnett reportedly *"crawled to his well, where he grasped the form of one of his children. The child was climbing from the well into which it had been blown and from which it had climbed using the stone curbing for a foothold."*

Rosedale also took a direct hit. The tornado totally destroyed the one-room schoolhouse and ripped off the roof and walls of nearby New Hope Baptist Church. Remarkably, amidst the debris of the church, an open *Bible* remained on the pulpit undisturbed. With a sense of wonder, eighty-eight-year-old Ted Barton still remembers a verse from a page to which the *Bible* was open: *"Heaven and earth shall pass away, but my words shall not pass away."* (Matthew 24:35)

Curryville

Continuing on its destructive path, the storm next battered the Gordon County community of Curryville. There, in a desperate gamble to save her three young children from the approaching twister, Bob Walraven's wife locked her little ones in a large trunk. The vicious power of the tornado blew the house to pieces and seriously injured both she and her husband. Amazingly, the trunk came through the storm undamaged and Mrs. Walraven, upon recovering her senses, found her children inside uninjured. One can only imagine, however, the horror experienced by the youngsters as they lay confined in the trunk, listening to the roar of the twister and feeling the terrible vibrating and buffeting of the trunk as their house disintegrated around them.

Jasper Walraven was another tragic victim. The tornado destroyed his house and barns and hurled his wife more than 100 yards into a ravine. The force of the impact crushed her skull. *"Late Friday afternoon,"* the *Tribune-Herald* reported, *"with broken arm, bleeding vitals and the vacant stare of a madman, he* (Jasper) *was administered to, but there is little hope for his recovery, and even if he does, it is not improbable that he will be an insane man."*

The death of Curryville's Lester Walraven was perhaps the final fatality of the freak of nature. He, his wife and three children were seated inside their house when the violent windstorm struck. According to news reports, *"the chimney gave way and fell in a solid mass like a felled tree, crushing the father like a man of paper."* Afterwards, Walraven's lifeless body was taken to the Curryville schoolhouse – the only building left standing in the ravaged community. His wife and children, though tossed about and bruised, escaped serious injury.

Aftermath

Even after the twister disappeared, the ordeal was not yet over for the storm victims. The injured and dying desperately needed medical attention, but flood-waters and impassible roads hampered relief efforts. Sudden heavy rains had pushed already swollen creeks and rivers out of their banks. The raging waters of Johns Creek swept away the bridge at Barnett's Mill and left the area isolated from Rome and Calhoun. *"Automobile parties by the score started out on both the Dalton and Summerville roads,"* the newspaper reported, *"but bridges across Armuchee Creek were covered and could not be crossed."*

Finally, a party including eight physicians and the Floyd County sheriff managed to cross Armuchee Creek and succeeded in getting to Armuchee where they hired teams and eventually reached Rosedale. They found the stricken region in ruins. *"A number of Romans,"* the *Tribune-Herald* chronicled on March 18, *"visited the district scwept (sic) by the cyclone, Sunday, and report awful devastation which it left in its wake."*

The list of victims and damage was extensive and included the following as reported: *"Mrs Delia Hendricks, widow, terribly injured, will die, lost everything, three children bruised; J. W. White, two houses and barn gone, damage about $2,000; Elwood Dickson, colored, lost all he had; Jack Reed, self and wife bruised, son killed, five children hurt, damaged about $250; New Hope Church, value about $500 and school house, value about $600, both completely blown away."*

In addition to 13 fatalities and dozens of injuries, estimates placed property damage in the devastated area as high as $100,000 – an enormous sum at that time. Today, one would expect a nationwide response to a disaster of this magnitude. The people of Floyd and Gordon counties, however, came from a proud, independent, rugged stock. They fully intended to see to their neighbors' needs themselves.

The people of Floyd ultimately gave more than $3,000 to the storm sufferers: a public meeting at the courthouse in Rome raised $400; Lindale residents collected $241; and Floyd County contributed $1,000 from the county treasury. In Gordon County, the people donated clothing, food and shelter. *"Some people,"* the *Tribune-Herald* declared proudly, *"thought of asking help from Atlanta and Chattanooga, but it has been decided not to do this. . . . Rome and Floyd County have shown that they can take care of their own people and neighbors."*

Today, eighty-five years later, only a few individuals remain who remember the 1913 Rosedale cyclone. Perhaps because it occurred in a sparsely-settled, remote region, the event quickly disappeared from the public eye. In fact, it is not even mentioned in George Magruder Battey's *A History Of Rome And Floyd County* – a large volume published in 1922.

Following the terrible storm however, those who suffered through it made certain they would have a semblance of protection if such a freak of nature ever reappeared in the future. Evidence of this preparedness still dots the countryside. Storm shelters can still be seen in the yards of homes in many spots along the highway connecting Rosedale and Curryville.

Kay Davis notes that her grandfather, John Davis, was very particular about adding a storm cellar when he rebuilt his house. And every time thereafter when a storm approached, Kay's grandparents insisted that everyone seek shelter there.

Although the cyclone occurred prior to the advent of modern weather tracking equipment, it is still possible to get a sense of the tornado's magnitude. A glance at a county road map can provide one measure. A line drawn on the map from the site of the Bolt residence to Rosedale to Curryville forms a right angle. The first side of the angle is three-quarters of a mile long and the second is two miles long. Since news reports described a single storm swath through the countryside – a description confirmed by old-timers – the tornado had to be nearly a mile wide for its path to encompass each of these places.

One quirk of the storm provides yet another measure of its might. Its powerful winds scattered debris from W.M. Martin's house across the countryside. Among the missing items was a trunk filled with Martin's personal papers, including an old bank note. A week later, a Whitfield County farmer found the note in his cotton patch – 30 miles from Rosedale!

Time has now erased every sign of devastation from the tornado. Rosedale and Curryville are still peaceful rural communities nestled between the green ridges of Johns, Turkey and Horn mountains. But when storm clouds gather over the mountains to the west, those who remember the 1913 Rosedale cyclone glance apprehensively at the sky wondering if it could ever happen again.

The Calhoun-Williamson Duel In North Georgia

A well documented formal duel between two angered men degenerated into comic adventure before becoming the last such event in the state's history.

On August 8, 1889, two men in Atlanta, Georgia, exchanged words that threatened to change their lives forever. The events that led to the duel between Pat Calhoun and Captain John D. Williamson are virtually forgotten today, but they caused quite a stir at the time in north Georgia.

Captain Williamson was the president of the Chattanooga, Rome and Columbus Railroad Company. Pat Calhoun was general counsel and a director of the Central Railroad and Banking Company of Georgia. Young Pat enjoyed the added distinction of being the grandson of famed South Carolina statesman and former vice-president of the United States John C. Calhoun. Both men were highly respected in their professions.

At the time of the incident, Captain Williamson resided part-time in Rome at the Armstrong Hotel, located on Howard Street (present-day Second Avenue) in Rome. Pat Calhoun was from the Atlanta area.

The trouble between the two men began at a legislative committee hearing at the Georgia state capitol in Atlanta. Williamson was in favor of a bill that would prevent the consolidation of competing railroad companies. He assured the committee that his Chattanooga, Rome & Columbus Railroad was and would remain an "independent line."

Pat Calhoun, however, representing a company that was actively consolidating railroads in the South, strongly opposed the bill. At some point in the discussions of the new bill, Calhoun, referring to Captain Williamson, reportedly remarked, "The gentleman knows that the first project he had in the building of this road was to unload it on the Central. That would have been done had I not stood in the way."

Captain Williamson took umbrage at the remark, bounding to his feet and countering, "When Mr. Calhoun states that it was my purpose to unload on the Central, he states what is unqualifiedly false. . . I never had any talk with Mr. Calhoun on the subject, and never made any proposition of the kind he indicates."

With this dangerous charge of falsehood, a deafening silence fell over the committee room. In times past, it had not been uncommon for words of this nature to be followed with the challenge of a duel, and this day would prove to be no exception. Without any further exchange and in an attempt to stem the anger between the two men, the committee meeting was immediately terminated, but the fateful words had already been spoken.

After leaving the meeting, neither man hesitated to attain a representative – known as "a second" – to handle any correspondence between them. Mr. Calhoun sent for his friend Captain Henry Jackson, while Captain Williamson telegraphed Jack King of Rome, Georgia, to represent him.

If there had been any hope that this confrontation between the two men could be halted, it was soon shattered. On the evening of August 8th, Pat Calhoun sent a letter to Captain Williamson which read as follows:

Dear Sir:

Before the railroad commission of the house of representatives this afternoon, in the discussion of the Olive bill, you characterized certain statements which had been made by me as false. I request an unqualified retraction of this charge.

This communication will be handed to you by my friend, Mr. Henry Jackson, who is authorized to receive the reply, which you may see proper to make.

Respectfully,
Pat Calhoun

That same evening, Williamson responded to Calhoun's letter as follows:

Dear Sir:

Your note of this evening has been delivered to me by Mr. Henry Jackson. You stated before the committee that I had solicited you to act as a general counsel of the Chattanooga, Rome and Columbus Railroad Company, and that my purpose was to unload that road upon the Central Railroad Company of Georgia through your influence.

This statement carried with it a reflection upon myself. It was without foundation, and I promptly pronounced it false. So long as this

Patrick Calhoun as he appeared in his later years.

Despite John D. Williamson's accomplishments in life, little more than a course illustration of him has been located to date. At this time, no photograph is known to exist.

The Armstrong Hotel in which Captain John D. Williamson once resided burned in 1932, and was rebuilt. The stonework around the lower level of the structure in this photo is original to the Armstrong which once stood on this site. (Photo by Deborah Malone)

At the time of the duel, Captain John D. Williamson, president of the Chattanooga, Rome & Columbus Railroad Company, resided part-time at the Armstrong Hotel on Howard Street (present-day Second Avenue) in Rome, Georgia. (Photo courtesy of Rome Area History Museum)

language, used by you, is not withdrawn, I must decline to make any retraction, which you request.

This will be handed to you by my friend, Hon. J. Lindsay Johnson.

Respectfully,
J.D. Williamson

After several additional communications, the last written correspondence between the two men names the time and place for the duel.

Dear Sir:

My friend, Mr. J. King of Rome, Georgia, has arrived and has been put in possession of contents of the correspondence between us. In conformity with your request in your last note delivered at 1:05 p.m. today, I will meet you in Alabama, at Cedar Bluff, on the Rome and Decatur Railroad, tomorrow (Saturday) afternoon at 5 o'clock. Unless I hear to the contrary, I shall expect to find you there at that hour.

My friend, Mr. King, will deliver this note.

Respectfully,
J.D. Williamson

Word had gotten out that there was to be a duel, and a substantial attempt was made by government officials to intercept the principals to avoid bloodshed. Governor John B. Gordon of Georgia, sent telegrams to the governors of Tennessee and Alabama asking them to stop the duel and arrest the principals. The same request was sent out to law officers at Rome and Cedartown, as well as to Anniston, Alabama. Alabama's Governor Tom Seay did the same for likely points in his state.

The *Atlanta Constitution* as well as the *Atlanta Journal* (separate newspapers at that time) eventually learned of the details of the duel. E.W. Barrett from the *Constitution* was assigned to the Williamson party and Edward C. Bruffey was assigned to the Calhoun group. Gordon N. Hurtel from the *Journal* was given orders to stick with Williamson and his party until a resolution was reached or until the duel had occurred.

As a result of the publicity surrounding the scheduled duel, the task of actually reaching the appointed meeting place was no easy chore for either party. Friday night, August 9, Captain Jackson met Pat Calhoun and both departed on a sleeping car from Union Station in downtown Atlanta. They overnighted at the Anniston Inn in Anniston, Alabama. The next morning, they slipped out the rear door of the inn.

According to Bruffey's newspaper account of the incident, while Williamson and his party were making their way to the duel site, Jackson had taken Pat Calhoun out for some target practice. Jackson reportedly tossed a coin in the air and instructed Calhoun to hit it. After five shots had been fired, the results showed three of the rounds had hit the mark – a somewhat amazing feat.

After witnessing Calhoun's accuracy with the pistol, Jackson reportedly remarked, "That's good Pat. Now, if we can't have peace and must have war, and you can do that – well, you will come home alive."

Calhoun spent the next couple of hours napping at a friend's house. The two men had sent for their luggage at the hotel, but reportedly were forced to abandon the property when they saw lawmen following the carriage conveying the luggage.

When they went to catch the 11:00 o'clock train, Jackson recognized the Anniston city police chief at the depot, so a quick decision was made to backtrack through the woods to nearby Leathertown to board the train there. After having lunch in Gadsden, the men boarded a Rome and Decatur train to be on their way to the site of the duel.

Meanwhile, Captain Williamson's trip to the meeting place was turning out to be quite an adventure as well. Gordon Hurtel, the *Journal* reporter, was able to give a detailed account because he faithfully followed the Williamson party.

Hurtel left Union Station in Atlanta at 8:00 a.m. He boarded a west-bound Western & Atlantic train to find that Williamson and his party were occupying the parlor car. His party consisted of Mr. Jack King, Williamson's second; Judge H.B. Tompkins; and Major C.B. Lowe. Dr. Henry Battey boarded the train in Rome.

The men then set out for Kingston, Georgia, where Williamson's private car was waiting. The private car was coupled to the engine and the train set out for Rome.

Hurtel, the *Journal* reporter, was a determined news correspondent, but he suspected that his ride would be short-lived because he had been spotted. He believed that Rome would be his place of departure from the group and he was not far off the mark.

"As I expected," Hurtel explained in his article, "the special car was uncoupled [from the other cars behind it] and run through town at the rate of twenty miles an hour. Two miles the other side of Rome, Mr. Jack King discovered me hiding on the steps [of the car]. The train was stopped and I was put off like a tramp, and had to count the cross-ties for two miles through the hot sun [back to Rome]."

Little did Williamson and Hurtel know, however, that fate would bring them together again where they would become allies. With the help of E.W. Barrett, who had been put off the train along with Hurtel, the two men were able to get an engine and engineer (W.T. Dozier) to drive a locomotive for them.

After procuring the locomotive

The Farill homeplace in Farill, Alabama, just over the Georgia state line, was the site at which the duel took place. The Rome & Decatur Railroad tracks once existed beside this structure. A depot (demolished in years past) once was located to the left of the home. (Photo by Debbie Malone)

Both Pat Calhoun and Capt. John D. Williamson departed for the dueling site from old Union Terminal in downtown Atlanta, pictured here in 1889. In time, bridges and viaducts were built over this railroad gulch, hiding it from sight. The buildings to the right in this photo lay dormant for decades, until a popular entertainment complex known as "Underground Atlanta" brought them renewed life.

"Daniel S. Printup" from the Forrestville Station in north Rome, the men set out in hot pursuit of Williamson and his party. They encountered them sooner than expected.

Roughly two or three miles down the track, Captain Williamson's train had been sidetracked at the Rome & Decatur junction for lack of an engineer who knew the route. Seizing the opportunity, Hurtel offered the men his engineer in exchange for the privilege of riding along with them. Williamson took Hurtel up on the offer and the men were welcomed into his private car.

While in the private car, Barrett and Hurtel were given a fine lunch, cigars and champagne. Hurtel later noted, "This was the same car from which I had been fired like a tramp an hour earlier."

While Williamson was awaiting the departure of his party, the men went into the nearby woods in order to allow the captain an opportunity to practice with his revolver. The target practice was short-lived, however, because a runner alerted the men that a sheriff from Floyd County, with a deputy, was coming down the tracks. In order to elude the sheriff, Captain Williamson and Jack King ran through the woods to a point a couple of miles down the track where they re-boarded the private car.

After picking the two men up, the train

E.W. Barrett, a reporter with the *Atlanta Constitution* and Gordon N. Hurtel, reporting for the *Atlanta Journal*, were able to secure the locomotive "Daniel S. Printup" (above) from the Forrestville Station in north Rome, to chase Captain John Williamson and his party to the site of the duel.

was once again on its way to Cedar Bluff, Alabama. It reached its destination about 4:00 p.m. in the afternoon. At Cedar Bluff, the train was side-tracked for an east-bound passenger train, and no sooner had the cars come to a halt when someone called out, "Here comes the sheriff!" The men all scrambled to get back on the private car.

According to a vivid description provided by journalist Hurtel, "We were in Cherokee County, Alabama, and the sheriff was one of those bushy, black-whiskered fellows with a broad-brimmed hat who meant business."

Hurtel went on to explain that Williamson's private car did not get far before it was caught and returned to the sheriff. Williamson, however, was nowhere to be found.

Meanwhile, Pat Calhoun and Henry Jackson had been on the regular passenger train coming from Atlanta by way of Anniston. The train stopped and Calhoun got off and was promptly arrested by the sheriff who said "Mr. Williamson, consider yourself under arrest."

If not for Captain Seay – who was known by the sheriff and attested that Mr. Calhoun was not Captain Williamson – the situation might have become even more confusing. Calhoun, however, was released and the Chinese fire-drill continued.

The sheriff would not give up easily, however. He swore he would find Williamson, never realizing he had just released the other principal, Mr. Calhoun. Both trains were searched, but the men were not found. Pat Calhoun and Captain Jackson were locked up in a closet in the private car. Captain Williamson and Jack King were hidden in a closet on the regular passenger train. These two men were determined to end the day with a duel, come hell or high water.

When the passenger train was finally released, it carried Captain Williamson, Mr. King, Dr. Battey, Captain Williamson's private secretary, Captain Seay and Gordon Hurtel. The train continued down the tracks to Raynes' Station, five miles closer to Rome. Calhoun's train also arrived at Rayne's Station and it seemed the two duelists might be about to effect their stated mission.

Debbie Malone stands on the former roadbed of the Rome & Decatur Railroad at Farill, Alabama. The duelists traveled on the line to this site.

The bushy-bearded sheriff, however, was a determined man, and also proceeded to Raynes' Station. He was then led to believe that both of the dueling parties were on the train and that apologies had been made and everything was settled.

After the sheriff – being convinced that everything was alright – had departed, the men all got off the train. The seconds were arranging preliminaries and Hurtel was wiring the *Journal*. About that time, four men, believed to be deputies, riding mules and brandishing shotguns, came clamoring up and one of them shouted, "If anybody moves, I'll shoot." One has to wonder at this point if the lawmen were going to kill someone to avoid a killing.

Taking their chances, the men scrambled for the train. The engineer ducked down in the cab and pulled the throttle wide open. The previously somber preparations for a duel were quickly taking on the appearance of comical hijinks.

The train sped away from the lawmen. Three miles down the tracks, the men once again disembarked and the seconds began conferring. It was already beginning to get dark. As Jackson and King were talking someone yelled, "Look out! Everybody on the train!"

The warning had come just in time. The four men with the shotguns seemed to be just as determined as the black-whiskered sheriff. Once again, everyone jumped aboard the train which again headed down the tracks. About four or five miles nearer to Rome, the men stopped again to prepare for the duel.

The final destination for the duel was Farill, Alabama, on the Farill Plantation (about three miles east of the location where General Nathan Bedford Forrest captured Col. Streight's men in the battle of 1863). A small natural clearing in an oak grove was selected for the duel.

Captain Seay made one last futile attempt to stop the affair, but the men had come too far to abandon the fight now. Captain Williamson, having the choice of weapons, chose the hammerless Smith & Wesson five shooter. By this time, it was well into dusk, and the light was fading as the moon rose over the treetops in the east.

The two seconds, Mr. King and Captain Jackson, were attempting to load the pistols for their principals. Captain Jackson, being unfamiliar with this pistol, was having trouble loading his. Mr. Bruffey, a journalist with the *Constitution*, spoke up, "I can help Cap."

Within seconds, an explosion broke the silence in the dark woods. "There, my finger's gone!" Mr. Bruffey suddenly shouted, walking off and holding up a bloody hand. A part of the third finger of his right hand had been torn away by the ball.

"Let me dress it," said Dr. Cooper who was standing by. "Oh, go on with the fight," Bruffey huffed as he wrapped a handkerchief about his wounded finger. "A finger don't amount to anything."

Captain Jackson then loaded Mr. Calhoun's pistol and handed it to him. As the two men were preparing to face off with each other, Captain Seay made one last desperate attempt to put a stop to the duel. "As a citizen of Georgia and in the name of the Governor of Alabama" cried out Seay, "I call upon you to stop!" Seay obviously didn't know which state he was in, so he was covering all the bases.

His pleas, however, fell upon deaf ears once again.

"Gentlemen, are you ready?" called out Mr. King. The men acknowledged their readiness. The paces were counted off and the command to "Fire!" was given.

Six rapid shots followed the command. The deed was done. All the men held their breath, waiting to see which duelist crumpled to the ground. Both seconds ran to their principals to see if they were injured and discovered they were not.

There had been some confusion as to the procedure that was to be used. Captain Williamson had thought that all shots were to be fired in succession, so he had fired all five of his shots at once. Pat Calhoun, however, had fired only once, thus leaving four balls remaining in his weapon. What would Calhoun do with those remaining shots?

"Mr. Williamson," Calhoun intoned, "I have four remaining balls which I have the right to fire at you. I now ask if you will withdraw the statement you made before the legislative committee."

"I will," Williamson responded, "provided you will say that you meant no personal reflection upon me."

It quickly became apparent that despite the circumstances, Captain Williamson was still refusing to unequivocally retract his statement. And even though he had braved the hail of bullets from Captain Williamson, Pat Calhoun, to his credit, had no further desire to fire at his opponent.

After a short additional verbal exchange between the two men, Pat Calhoun spoke these words: "Mr. Williamson, in my remarks before the legislative committee you personally did not enter my mind." Calhoun then raised his pistol in the air and fired his remaining four balls into the air.

"Since you have stated you meant nothing personal in your remarks," Williamson said, "I now withdraw the statement I made before the committee." The two men shook hands and ended the matter.

The party retired to the train and celebrated with cigars and champagne. They arrived in Rome a few minutes after 9 p.m. News of the results was telegraphed to Atlanta.

According to records, this duel was the last such formal incident associated with Georgia, and since it actually occurred in Alabama, it may have been the final such occurrence there as well. If so, it was a dramatic final curtain for an old custom, despite the somewhat comical circumstances under which this incident took place.

Several of the sites mentioned in this incident still exist today. Captain Williamson's residence – the Armstrong Hotel – burned in 1932, but was rebuilt as the Greystone Hotel. The Greystone, which still exists today, boasts some of the original stonework from the Armstrong, and is listed on the National Register of Historic Places.

Much of downtown Rome remains the same as it was in 1889, with many of the buildings being from that era. Howard Street, known today as Second Avenue, does not have a trolley track down the center any longer, but it is just as busy as it was a hundred years ago.

The Forrestville Station no longer exists, but the Rome & Decatur junction where Williamson's car was side-tracked is still in use today.

A trip to Farill, Alabama, where the duel took place, proved to be an adventure. After talking with several of the residents there, I met Judy Smith and her husband who live next to the old Farill homeplace. Judy had lived in the Farill house herself at one time, and showed me the old roadbed where the railroad once had existed beside the house. Even though the exact location of the duel is unknown today, I sensed that it must be very near.

It is unknown today if Captain Williamson and Pat Calhoun lived long fruitful lives, but it is known that on a hot August night in 1889, their lives were spared, and happiness reigned supreme once again – at least for the moment.

ENDNOTES

1/ Battey, George Magruder; *A History of Rome and Floyd County*, Cherokee Publishing Company, Marietta, Georgia, (1922).

The Graves at Farmer's Cemetery

Several unusual graves in a small north Georgia cemetery lead to the origins and devastation wrought by the world-wide influenza epidemic that tortured our nation in 1918-1919.

I recently took a walk through the New Armuchee Baptist Church cemetery near Rome, Georgia and stopped to read the tombstones of a husband and wife:

J.T. Holder
Sept. 17, 1888 to Jan. 8, 1919
Thy will be done

Emmie L. Holder
Nov. 5, 1895 to Feb. 19, 1991

These epitaphs piqued my curiosity because J.T. Holder was only thirty years old when he died and Emmie, a widow for 72 years, apparently had never remarried. I couldn't help but wonder how her husband had died.

The solemn inscription on his grave marker – *Thy will be done* – seemingly indicated a resigned acceptance of some tragic ending for the young husband. Could he have been a victim of the Spanish influenza epidemic that swept the country in 1918-19, a battlefield casualty of World War I, or had an accident claimed his life?

After jotting down information from the Holder tombstones and taking a few pictures, I found another interesting marker near the crest of the hill:

Ragland Bergwall
Pvt. 1st Class
H.Q. Co. 167th Infantry U.S.A.
Beloved Son of John
&
the Late Matilda Bergwall
Born Feb. 14, 1897
Died Jan. 26, 1919:
He left his home in perfect health
He looked so young and brave
We little thought how soon he'd be
Laid in a soldier's grave

The Bergwall surname was unfamiliar to me. I had not previously come across the name in research for my Floyd County writings nor are there any Bergwalls listed in Rome's telephone directory today. Where had this family lived? Had Ragland died in combat? Did any of his family reside in the community today?

The only other information I had to go on came from the nearby tombstones of Ragland's father, John Bergwall (who died in 1933), Eric Bergwall (a younger brother who also served in the army in World War I and died in 1976), and Mrs. Ellen A. Bergwall (his step-mother who died in 1934).

Several days later, I visited the Sara Hightower Regional Library in Rome to look for information about the Holders and Bergwalls in microfilmed copies of Rome's newspapers. I got off to a good start when I found Emmie Holder's 1991 obituary in the Rome *News Tribune.*

I learned that Emmie had been a life-long resident of Floyd County; that her parents were Oscar and Loretta Touchstone; and that a son, Frank Holder, survived her. Oddly enough, the obituary did not mention her marriage to "the late J.T. Holder."

Later that day I was pleasantly surprised when I looked in the Rome telephone book and found a listing for a Frank Holder. When I dialed the telephone number, Louise Holder answered and told me that her husband Frank was not home. I identified myself and told her that I was interested in information about J.T. and Emmie Holder.

"They were Frank's mother and father," Louise replied matter-of-factly. During our brief conversation, Mrs. Holder explained that J.T. Holder succumbed to Spanish influenza when Frank was just 11 months old; Emmie had never remarried, and thereafter Emmie and little Frank went to live with Emmie's parents on the Touchstone family farm in Armuchee. She told me that Frank spent most of his adult life out west, returning to Rome just a few months before his mother's death in 1991.

It looked like Frank Holder would be my best and perhaps only source of information about his father because the other resources I checked had little to offer. The Rome *Tribune-Herald* did not publish his obituary. In that era, I found, newspapers typically ran "necrologies" only for the "notable" people of rural communities like Armuchee. I concluded that J.T. Holder might have been a laborer or farmer whose demise did not rate mention under the customs of the time.

Other library and county records revealed little beyond the fact that J.T. Holder had married "Miss Emmie Touchstone" on Christmas Eve 1916, and they had never held title to any real property in Floyd County. The records also revealed that a John Holder worked at an Armuchee sawmill in the early 1900s. (Shortly thereafter, Louise Holder confirmed that the Holders had indeed been in the lumber business in the Armuchee area at that time).

The little town of Armuchee, I already knew, had just come into existence in J.T. Holder's day. The establishment of the Rome & Northern Railroad in 1909 helped turn the quiet agricultural area into a promising commercial location. The railroad linked iron mines at Taylor's Ridge with foundries in Rome and brought new businesses to northern Floyd County. By 1919, the so-called "Valley City" had its own depot, electricity provided by a water-powered generator on Armuchee Creek, a pants factory, cooperage mill, telephone exchange, auto court, and at least four sawmills.

The Spanish influenza epidemic sweeping the country in early 1919 was big news.

While I had found out frustratingly little about J.T.

"Nothing, much less a Boche (German soldier)," boasts the caption to this U.S. Army photograph, "will be able to withstand a charge such as is being demonstrated by the 250 non-commissioned officers of the 28th Keystone Division who are being taught by the English officer to use the deadly bayonet with telling effect." (Courtesy U.S. Army Military History Institute)

Doughboys at Augusta's Camp Hancock trained for all contingencies of war including enemy attacks employing mustard gas and other debilitating chemicals. Unfortunately, however, these masks did not offer any protection against the Spanish influenza epidemic that hit Camp Hancock hard in October 1918. (Courtesy U.S. Army Military History Institute)

Holder's life beyond the fact that he probably worked at one of those Armuchee sawmills, I came across plenty of information about the illness that resulted in his death.

The Spanish influenza epidemic sweeping the country in early 1919 was big news. The epidemic began in early 1918 and continued for more than a year, killing 675,000 people in the United States and 40 million worldwide (far more than had died in World War I from 1914 to 1918).

Prior to the November 1918 armistice, wartime censors anxious to protect public morale rigorously suppressed news of the epidemic in America and many other western nations. As a result, the press in neutral Spain was the first to report the fast-spreading sickness, thus unwittingly giving the flu its name. Ironically, Spanish influenza probably actually started in the United States at an army base in Kansas.

Government concern about morale was justified. Fear bordering on outright panic gripped the hardest hit areas – including most of the eastern seaboard of the United States – as tens of thousands of new cases erupted each day with some large cities reporting cataclysmic death rates exceeding 10,000 per day. Just imagine the abject panic today, if some of our largest cities were experiencing 10,000 deaths per day.

Given the flu's extraordinary mortality rate, the speed with which it struck down healthy individuals in the prime of their life, and its brutal effects on the human body, the hysteria was understandable. Symptoms included high fever, nausea, severely aching muscles, back, head, and joints, and wild bouts of delirium. To make matters worse, virulent cases of pneumonia frequently followed on the flu's coattails. This lethal one-two punch was highly contagious and struck those in the twenty- to forty-year-old age range especially hard. This meant trouble for America's military bases where four million young men were living in close quarters training for war.

Indeed, the flu first showed up in Georgia at Camp Hancock, an army base in Augusta. It struck with a vengeance. On September 30, 1918, Camp Hancock had just two soldiers in the base infirmary. A near-stampede took place the next morning when 716 men answered sick call with flu-like symptoms. By the fifth day, three thousand Camp Hancock "Doughboys" had been stricken and 52 were dead.

The flu spread quickly across the state. Desperate public officials took drastic action to stop the epidemic. In Atlanta, the city counsel imposed a quarantine and declared that all public gathering places – including schools, libraries, churches, and theatres – would be closed for two months.

On October 8, Fulton County schools sent pupils home with their books for the duration of the quarantine. In Athens, the University of Georgia took similar measures and suspended classes indefinitely, as did Rome's Shorter College.

Tift College in Forsyth, Georgia took less drastic action according to 104-year-old alumnus Dr. Leila Denmark. Dr. Denmark amazingly retired from the medical profession in Alpharetta, Georgia, in January of 2002, after a distinguished 74-year career as a pediatrician and researcher.

"There were 400 of us girls [at Tift] at the time," she recalled in a recent interview. "We didn't go anywhere. We ate at school and we always walked under cover of shelter from our dormitories to the cafeteria to our classes." These simple precautions proved effective. "We didn't have a single person in that college develop influenza," she notes.

Denmark, who later became the third woman in the state to attend medical school

The hey days for the little farming community of Armuchee lasted from the turn-of-the-century through the 1930s. At the time this photograph was taken circa 1930, the town had several prosperous looking businesses. Later, however, the town fell on hard times, beginning with the failure of the Rome & Northern Railroad in the early 1920s. Today Armuchee is a quiet, mostly rural community north of Rome. (Courtesy Herman Yarbrough)

BERGWALL FAMILY – John and Matilda Bergwall immigrated to the United States in 1906 undoubtedly expecting that a fresh start in the "New World" would bring happiness and prosperity. Sadly, though, from the outset bad luck, disease, and death plagued the family. This photograph was taken in their new hometown of Rome, Georgia, circa 1908, shortly before Matilda, who succumbed to tuberculosis, became the first in the family's long list of casualties. Featured in the photo (seated, left to right) are Eric, Everett, John, Ernest, Matilda, Sigrid and (standing, left to right), Carl, Ragland, Oscar and Signa. (Photo courtesy of Louise Mathis)

TROOPS ASSEMBLE – Soldiers of the 167th Infantry, American Expeditionary Forces, assemble at Vitry-la-Ville, France on their way to the front in June 1918. (Courtesy U.S. Army Military History Institute)

J.T. Holder worked in the lumber business before he succumbed to Spanish influenza and pneumonia in early 1919. Pictured here is one early Floyd County sawmill much like the one at which J.T. Holder labored. (Courtesy Sara Hightower Regional Library)

Leila Denmark – (Left) As a student at Forsyth, Georgia's Tift College, Leila never came down with Spanish flu, but she lost a sister-in-law in the awful epidemic. She later became the third woman in the state to attend medical school and has devoted her life to medicine. (Right) Dr. Denmark at 104-years-of-age. (Photos courtesy of Dr. Leila Denmark)

and graduated from the Medical College of Georgia in 1928, observes that it was exposure to the elements that led to most influenza related deaths.

"Influenza was very contagious," she points out. "The first day you just had chills and you felt sick and stayed in bed. The next day, you felt the same. The third day, patients were feeling much better. Then, about the fourth day, they went out to milk the cows or feed the hogs. Their resistance was down to nothing and they developed pneumonia and died."

Interestingly, a few days after my conversation with Dr. Denmark, I learned from Louise Holder that J.T. Holder's death corresponded exactly with that scenario: "Frank's father," she told me, "had been feeling better, went outside to take care of a prize horse, took ill with pneumonia and died."

Today, Dr. Denmark is well-known in medical circles. In 1936, she invented the vaccine for whooping cough.

No doubt motivated in part by the death of a sister-in-law in the 1918-19 epidemic, Dr. Denmark turned her attention to an influenza vaccine. This time, however, the results were not satisfactory.

"Immunization was the greatest thing ever created and I tried for eleven years, but it didn't work," she explained. "The first year, we would give 12 shots, the next year six, and I continued that way for a long time. But it didn't do any good. Certain things – like strep throat – you can't immunize against because the body doesn't build antibodies. I think influenza is one of them."

Until the development of penicillin and other antibiotics years later, common sense precautions like those taken at Tift College were the best weapons available to combat Spanish influenza. "The people just learned that when they got sick they didn't get up and get out and do something on the fourth day," summarizes Dr. Denmark. "They took care of themselves and the thing went away."

By late 1918, the crisis in Georgia seemed to have passed. Reports of new influenza cases were down considerably and state and local governments began to relax or lift onerous quarantine rules restricting public gatherings. In November, the Great War ended, censorship ceased, and people throughout the state and country began to look forward to a new year that undoubtedly would be far better than the troubled one about to be ushered out.

On New Year's Day, 1919, the Rome *Tribune-Herald* announced that Shorter College would reopen. A week later, the newspaper proclaimed happily, "...the great epidemic of influenza that swept this county during the fall and early winter of last year has subsided."

This optimism, however, proved sadly to be premature. The very next day, the Tribune-Herald reported that "another influenza epidemic is feared" as two deaths (presumably one was that of J.T. Holder who died on January 8) and many new cases had occurred in Floyd county over the past 48 hours.

This second round of Spanish influenza took the lives of many more Georgians. The toll included all five members of one family who were staying at the Salvation Army house in Rome. The first to die was the husband and father, Thomas Howard, on January 14, 1919. His widow and 5-year-old daughter Lucille died three days later.

"With no ministering hand to cool fevered brows mother and tot follow husband and papa to grave," the *Tribune-Herald* reported. Then the Howard's six-month old baby girl expired on the 20th, followed a day later by 3-year-old Margaret. "Death kisses down weary eyelids of last Howard baby, nurses shed tears," lamented the newspaper.

Later that spring the epidemic finally ended, but its bitter legacy is an abundance of tombstone epitaphs in Georgia cemeteries (and elsewhere) bearing dates of death during the period between April 1918 and April 1919. A surprising percentage of these victims were people like J.T. Holder struck down in the prime of life.

The little New Armuchee Cemetery (once called Farmer's Cemetery after a prominent Civil War era family who lived nearby) where J.T. is buried has at least five or ten other graves of men and women from 20- to 40-years old who also died between October 1918 and January 1919.

So what about Ragland Bergwall, who died shortly after J.T. Holder and who is buried just up the hill? For more than a month, my efforts to discover his fate were unsuccessful. Many promising leads led only to frustrating dead ends. I spent hours at an old microfilm projector cranking through Rome *Tribune-Herald* newspaper issues from January through September of 1919 (since it often took weeks or months for news of the death of a soldier to reach home), but I did not find anything even though a soldier's death was always a newsworthy event.

This second round of Spanish influenza took the lives of many more Georgians.

I then turned to other sources. The City of Rome directories from 1899 through the 1990s, John Bergwall's 1933 obituary, Floyd

Soldiers from a 167th Infantry Regiment patrol pose with German prisoners at Meurthe et Moselle, France on September 12, 1918. Descendants of John and Matilda Bergwall have identified the soldier on the right as Carl Bergwall. Carl and Ragland Bergwall were both headquarters company messengers when they swam the chilly waters of a French river in late 1918 to avoid capture. Ragland was thereafter hospitalized with tuberculosis and died before Carl could get leave to visit his ailing brother. (Courtesy U.S. Army Military History Institute)

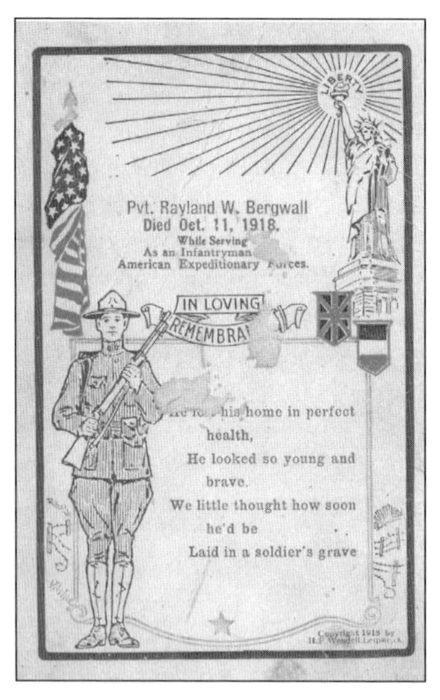

After the Armistice in November 1918, the United States government sent condolence postcards to the families of deceased soldiers. The grieving Bergwall family selected the postcard poem as a suitable epitaph for young Ragland. (Courtesy Louise Mathis)

County real estate records, and other genealogical resources disclosed a few additional facts about the Bergwall family. I learned that they had immigrated to the United States from Sweden, settled in Rome in 1906, that John Bergwall was a carpenter, and that the family had rented living quarters on the north side of town. Probate records further indicated that John Bergwall received a $2,813 death benefit check for Ragland from the U.S. Veterans Bureau in 1925 and divided the money between two of his sons, Ernest and Everett.

A newspaper article mentioned that Ragland's unit (the 42nd "Rainbow" Division) was still in France when he died in January 1919, but since his demise followed the armistice by two months, I doubted that he had been a battlefield casualty. A suspicion began to build that Ragland Bergwall, like J.T. Holder, might have been a victim of Spanish influenza. To my surprise, I discovered that my hunch was wrong when I finally tracked down a member of the Bergwall family.

"Ragland and his brother Carl served together in France as messengers," explained Rome's Louise Mathis over the phone one evening in August 2002. I had gotten Mrs. Mathis's name from Olaf Bergwall, one of Ragland's nephews who I had finally located in Atlanta after a sometimes exasperating search that took a month. He had, in turn, suggested that I contact Mrs. Mathis, a family historian whose mother Sigrid was Ragland's younger sister.

"My mother told me that the Germans overran the American troops at one point," Louise Mathis continued telling me the story over the telephone. "Ragland and Carl were cut off and the only way to avoid capture was to swim across a river. They made it, but the water was bitterly cold. Ragland took sick and was admitted to an army hospital, I believe with tuberculosis.

He died before Carl could get permission to return to the hospital."

The *Georgia State Memorial Book*, a large volume published in 1921 and adopted by the state as the "Official Record by the Military Department, State of Georgia," provided further confirmation of Mrs. Mathis's account. Ragland Bergwall's entry reads: "After receiving his preliminary military training, Private Bergvall embarked for over-sea service, attached to Headquarters Company, 167th Infantry, 42nd (Rainbow) Division. Private Bergvall contracted tuberculosis, which resulted in his death at Base Hospital in France, January 26th 1919."

Sadly, Ragland's premature death was just one of many setbacks the family had experienced in connection with their decision to immigrate to America. Their journey to the New World had gotten off to an inauspicious start when Swedish authorities denied Matilda permission to embark since she was far along in pregnancy. In all likelihood, she would deliver her baby enroute, a port official said, and the newborn child thus would not have the proper papers for entry into the United States.

John Bergwall found himself in a difficult situation. He could not remain in Sweden because he had already quit his job, sold his house, and had a job waiting in Rome, Georgia. He and Matilda therefore decided to temporarily part ways. He and the oldest children would proceed to America while Matilda and the youngest children would stay with her brother until the baby was born. Immigration records (using their "un-Americanized" names) reflect that Johan (age 34), Signe (12) and Karl (11) departed Gothenburg, Sweden for America on October 31, 1906. Mathilda (38), Ragnar (9), Erik (7), Bror (5), Ture (2) and Sigrid ("age 0") followed on January 25, 1907.

Two years after their arrival in America, the Bergwall family experienced the first in a series of premature deaths when Matilda died of "white plague" (tuberculosis) in August of 1908. John Bergwall thereafter married Ellen Saul and their only child, three-year-old Elizabeth, died in 1914. A few years later, Signa, who had married in 1917, lost a daughter and then died in the Spanish influenza epidemic. Finally, 21-year-old William Saul, John Bergwall's stepson, died of a ruptured appendix in 1925. Given this run of luck, it is no wonder that Louise Mathis often heard her mother, Sigrid, say that the family would have been better off staying in Sweden.

All of my questions had now been answered save one. Why, I asked Mrs. Mathis, did the family bury Ragland in Armuchee when the Bergwalls did not have any apparent ties to the community?

"That too is a sad story," she replied. "My grandfather (John Bergwall) purchased ten lots in Rome's Myrtle Hill Cemetery when Matilda died in 1908. He had Ragland's body shipped home from France for burial beside his mother, but he could not get permission to bury Ragland there because he did not have a deed to his Myrtle Hill plots. He therefore had Ragland buried in nearby Armuchee until he could get the matter straightened out. Unfortunately, that never happened and Ragland's grave remained in the Armuchee cemetery."

Ironically, itinerant worker Howard Thomas, the ill-fated Salvation Army tenant whose entire family died in the influenza epidemic, was buried in Myrtle Hill cemetery while local war-hero Ragland Bergwall was not. Instead, Ragland was laid to rest near J.T. Holder in the little tree-covered hilltop cemetery north of Rome where the simple headstone epitaphs do not explain the dreadful conditions in 1918 and 1919 when disease cut short the lives of so many, from Armuchee lumbermen to soldiers at the front.

The Murder And Burial Of Cherokee Chief James Vann

On a cold night in the winter of 1809 in north Georgia, an assassin's bullet ended the life of James Vann II, condemning one of the most historically acclaimed chiefs of the Cherokee Nation to an unmarked grave at an unknown site.

"Here lies the body of James Vann, who killed many a white man. At last by a rifle ball he was felled, and the devil dragged his soul down to hell!"
Author Unknown

As local folklore goes, the verse above was supposedly inscribed upon a marker which at one time existed upon the grave of Cherokee Chief James Vann at a site in present-day Forsyth County. Both the marker and grave however, have strangely eluded official identification for well over a century, and the murder occurred approximately 200 years ago.

Today, many Georgians – especially those familiar with the history of the state – are aware of the legacy of Vann. Descriptions of his stately mansion at Spring Place (near present-day Chatsworth, Georgia), stories of his wealth and widespread business affairs, and finally, his murder at Buffington's Tavern near the present-day Forsyth/Cherokee County line in Georgia, have been handed down from generation to generation. But how many people really know the actual site of Vann's burial? I'll tell you how many . . . Not a single person.

Much of the problem in obtaining the actual facts involving Vann's murder and in locating his grave site, stems from a tendency of the general public to perpetuate myths and fanciful stories created in the absence of factual information.

Historians (and indeed much of the public) are well aware of Vann's identity as a leader of the Cherokees in the Southeast in the early 1800s, and of his impressive plantations, complete with slaves, and extensive business enterprises. The development of the Federal Road between Athens, Georgia, and Nashville, Tennessee – formally permitted by the Cherokees in the Treaty of Tellico in 1805 – created tremendous commercial opportunities for Vann, and he quickly took advantage of them, achieving enormous wealth for that day. In addition to his previously-mentioned endeavors, he operated a stagecoach stop on the Federal Road near Eton, Georgia, including a trading post and tavern. He operated a ferry and public house where the Federal Road crossed the Chattahoochee River in present-day Forsyth County, and a second plantation near that same vicinity. He also owned another ferry where the road crossed the Conasauga River just west of Spring Place, as well as a mill on Vann's Mill Creek (a tributary of the Conasauga; the Federal Road crossed the Conasauga on Lot #149, District 9, Section 3, according to the 1832 surveys of old Cherokee County by David Duke, D.S., June, 1832).

Though described variously throughout most of the two centuries since it occurred, Vann's murder took place at Buffington's Tavern (the site of which is a controversy unto itself today, and which may or may not still be in existence today). Many individuals have, for years, identified an old log structure across the road from the former site of the Sherrill home on the old Federal Road in Forsyth County as the remains of Buffington's Tavern, but nothing could be further from the truth, according to Forsyth County Historian Don L. Shadburn.

"That's true," Shadburn says. "Vann was killed at Buffington's Tavern, and Buffington's Tavern was on the old Federal Road not far from the Sherrill Place, but it (the tavern) isn't the old structure across the road from Sherrill's. That structure is part of what used to be Lewis Blackburn's Public House built around 1820. It (Blackburn's Public House) is very historic in its own right, but it is not Buffington's Tavern."

Constructed with log timbers 20" x 6" x 32', Blackburn's Public House is immensely sturdy, accounting for its endurance over the years. It and the property on which it exists (as of this writing) are privately-owned today. It is awe-inspiring to stand in the doorway of this building and understand the history that has both passed and entered its doorstep. It is shameful that the structure is not in some way identified as an official historic site and protected for posterity in some manner.

"Part of the confusion between Buffington's Tavern and Blackburn's Public House centers around the fact that Lewis Blackburn married Tom Buffington's widow after Tom died," Shadburn added. "Lewis and the former Mrs. Buffington lived at Buffington's Tavern for a short while before moving to Blackburn's Public House at the site of the present-day Sherrill homeplace. Buffington's Tavern actually existed on up the old Federal Road from the Sherrill Place, and was on the right, just across the Cherokee County line."

Shadburn said another myth involving Vann and his death included Vann's sister – Nancy Falling (also spelled "Fawling") – who supposedly lived across the road from Buffington's Tavern. "That's just another case in which the facts have been embellished and twisted," he explained. "Nancy lived south of Spring Place at Vann's home near present-day Chatsworth."

For years, local folklore has maintained that Nancy's supposed residence across the road from Buffington's Tavern in some way connected her with Vann's death. Vann was, in fact, responsible for the death of Nancy's husband – John Falling – but no definite connection between her and Vann's death has ever been established. Most historians today do agree however, that it quite possibly was Falling's family which was responsible for Vann's death, as was the Cherokee custom at that time.

Blackburn's Public House is very historic in its own right, but it is not Buffington's Tavern.

Despite his enterprising and peaceful nature when sober, James Vann has been characterized by histo-

James Vann II, a wealthy and prominent leader of the Cherokees of the late 18th and early 19th centuries, lived in this impressive home which he built in 1804 at Spring Place in present-day Murray County. While traveling from this home to his tavern and ferry across the Chattahoochee River in present-day Forsyth County, Vann was fatally wounded by an unknown assailant at Buffington's Tavern. (Photo by Daniel M. Roper)

Pictured above is the structure some historians claim was the site of the murder of James Vann in 1809. Most Georgia historians, however, agree this structure, in fact, was Lewis Blackburn's Public House, and early maps of this vicinity appear to support this contention. This structure originally stood on the opposite side of the Old Federal Road. It was moved in the 20th century to its current location across the road from the Ernest Sherrill homeplace (right rear in photo) in Forsyth County. (Photo by Olin Jackson)

rians as a very violent, arrogant, and abusive person when under the influence of alcoholic beverages which he reportedly consumed in ever-increasing quantities during his later years in life. It was during one of Vann's fits of anger, that he reportedly was responsible for the death of Falling.

It is ironic that history has chosen to characterize Vann as violent and abusive. An argument could be made for the fact that he was the victim of circumstances beyond his control in a quest to best portray his section of the Cherokee Nation as law-abiding and socially acceptable in the face of an advancing tide of white settlers who were by this time openly seeking reasons to displace the Cherokees.

It is well documented that Vann ordered the use of such devices as painful whippings, etc., for the punishment of criminals, a practice which no doubt enhanced his reputation as a man of cruelty. The fact not so well documented, is that Vann was carrying out Cherokee law as decided by the entire Cherokee Nation. Indeed, in the *Laws of the Cherokees*, published in the *Cherokee Advocate* at Tahlequah, Oklahoma in 1852, a glimpse into Indian life on the frontier is provided. One of the laws (in an order from the chiefs and warriors in National Council at "Broom's Town" on September 11, 1808, the year prior to Vann's murder) provided for the formation of "regulating companies" of one captain, one lieutenant and four privates each, for the purpose of arresting horse thieves and protecting property. The penalty for stealing a horse was 100 lashes on the bare back of the thief, be it man or woman, and fewer lashes for things of less value; and if a thief resisted the regulators with gun, axe, spear or knife, he or she could be killed on the spot. This law was signed by Black Fox, principal chief; Charles Hicks, secretary to the Council; Path Killer; and Toochalar.

Even more interesting, this same National Council barely a year and a half later on April 10, 1810 (a year after Vann's death) passed the following law: *"Be it known that this day the various clans and tribes which compose the Cherokee Nation have agreed that should it happen that a brother, forgetting his natural affection, should use his hand in anger and kill his brother, he shall be accounted guilty of murder and suffer accordingly; and if a man has a horse stolen, and overtakes the thief, and should his anger be so great as to cause him to kill him, let his blood remain on his own conscience, but no satisfaction shall be demanded for his life from his relatives or the clan he may belong to."*

One of the more enlightened and enduring achievements of Vann was his association and support of Moravian missionaries which he allowed to establish a mission near his home at Spring Place. It is from the diaries kept by the Moravians that one of the most reliable accounts of Vann's murder is described. On February 21, 1809, the following entry was made:

"We received the startling news of the murder of Mr. Vann. Here and there, he and his had punished Indians for stealing. When one of them refused to surrender, Vann ordered him to be shot.

"For a few days thereafter, Vann stopped at the tavern of a half-breed, Tom Buffington, about 56 miles from here. While there, he drank heavily and became involved in altercations with some of his friends for whom he had taken a violent dislike. He feuded with them, was most abusive, and made violent threats.

"Toward midnight, Vann stepped out of the tavern and stood before the open door, when suddenly, a shot was fired from without which pierced his heart. He fell lifeless to the floor without his perpetrator being seen.

"After hearing the shot, Joseph, his son, and a Negro rapidly gathered up the belongings of father and son, including Vann's 'pocketbook' with a considerable amount of cash and bank notes. Wrapped in a blanket, Joseph with the Negro fled to his father's plantation on the Chattahoochee River, 13 miles from Buffington's Tavern.

"At the crack of dawn, Mrs. Vann and other members of the family fled to Buffington's but before they arrived, Vann's body had been buried in the woods not far from the road."

It was this and similar descriptions which have led historians and residents to believe that Vann's grave was located in present-day Blackburn Cemetery, situated not far from the old tavern site.

"That's right," Shadburn continued. "There's no doubt that Blackburn Cemetery or its general vicinity is the burial site. In October of 1818, an individual by the name of Ebenezer Newton was traveling on the Federal Road from Athens, Georgia to Tennessee. In a journal describing his trip, he details how his travels led him to Vann's Tavern on the Chattahoochee River. The following morning, he describes how he continued on up the road toward Tennessee, crossing the Hightower (Etowah) River, suddenly encountering a grave on the right *'on an eminence, paled in (to keep out livestock), and painted, with a headboard and inscription which read: 'Here Lies The Body Of James Vann Who Departed This Life February, 1809, Aged 43.'* Newton's description of the location of Vann's grave almost perfectly fits the description of present-day Blackburn Cemetery."

But in the 1960s, when a team of what has been described as "amateur archaeologists" and a descendant of Vann – J. Raymond Vann of Mt. Vernon, New York – exhumed what they and many others assumed to be the remains of Vann, they received a surprise.

According to the *Atlanta Journal*, of August 29, 1962:

"Dalton archaeologist Wayne Yeager has confirmed that he removed the skeleton of Chief Vann from his grave near Ball Ground, Georgia, and brought the remains to a local funeral home which he declined to name.

"The local archaeologist said it took seven

hours to exhume the remains from the old Blackburn family cemetery on the Etowah River between Ball Ground and Cumming. Mr. Yeager said the skeleton is in good condition considering that it has been 153 years since Chief Vann's death.

"Mr. Yeager said he is positive that he has the right skeleton because of several factors. No. 1 is that local residents pin-pointed the grave from local common knowledge, although it was not marked. No. 2, the upper right arm bone had been fractured as if by a bullet. Mr. Yeager said Chief Vann fought a political duel from horseback with his brother-in-law, John Falling (sic ?) (Fawling?) shortly before his death, and accounts of the duel say that Falling was killed and Chief Vann was hit in the right arm by a bullet. No. 3, Mr. Yeager has compared the shirt buttons found in the grave and the buttons of a shirt of the same era, and found them to be the same. The shirt used for comparison belonged to Tarleton Lewis, an ancestor of Mr. B.J. Bundy, (a Dalton historian).

"Mr. Yeager said the grave was located on property owned by Mr. and Mrs. Ernest Sherrill, and that Mr. Sherrill's 94-year-old aunt, known only as "Becky", stated that she could remember when the grave was marked with a wooden slab.

"In fact, after the Georgia Historical Commission established the location of the grave, Mr. Sherrill piled brush over it and refused to tell curious historians where it was located in fear that they might dig into the grave.

"However, Mr. Sherrill did show the grave to Raymond Vann and Mr. Vann secured an order from Forsyth County Ordinary A.B. Tollison to exhume his ancestor. Mr. Tollison acted as an official witness during the excavation.

"Found in the grave were seven glass buttons, approximately 50 nails from the coffin, and a belt buckle. Mr. Yeager said the bottom of the grave was in the exact shape of the old-time wooden coffins.

"Mr. Yeager (also) said two gold rings were discovered on the hands of the skeleton, and these rings are now being cleaned by Jack Zbar, another Dalton archaeologist and chemist. The rings appear to be inscribed, but the cleaning process has not been finished."

What then was officially established by this exhumation of the supposed grave of James Vann? Were the remains really those of James Vann . . . or were they the remains of someone else?

Clifford Ruddel, interviewed in 1988, had lived in the vicinity of Blackburn Cemetery most of his life, and he well remembered the day the remains were removed from the grave site. He was one of the diggers hired to perform the labor.

"We dug for a good long while, and then all of a sudden, we were into the bones," he explained. "They told us to get out of the hole, and they jumped in with all these little tools and brushes.

"Eventually, when they had collected all they wanted from the grave; they put it in bags and then left," he continued. "I don't remember exactly how long it was, but later on, they came back, and I think they put the bones or something back into the grave, and then they covered it all back over. That always struck me as kinda strange."

Strange indeed. For far from ending a controversy, the exhumation of this grave actually began spawning additional ones.

In the *Dalton Daily News* of August 29, 1962, a bold headline proclaimed *"Vann Excavation Stirs Controversy."* The article went on to describe how state and local officials were casting considerable doubt on the findings of Yeager and Zbar as well as their credentials. The article stated:

". . . Dalton amateur archaeologist Wayne Yeager has stirred a controversy among historians and archaeologists throughout the state. Doubt has been expressed on the part of at least one archaeologist, Clemens deBaillou, as to whether the remains of Chief Vann have actually been found.

"However, on the other hand, the Rev. Mr. Yeager, a Baptist minister, said today that an

inscription uncovered on one of the gold rings found on the hands of the skeleton (leaves no) doubt in his mind that he found Chief Vann.

"The Rev. Mr. Yeager said one of the plain, gold rings was inscribed with a 'V', and he doubts very much that anyone else buried in the Blackburn Cemetery in Forsyth County near Ball Ground would have had a name starting with the letter 'V'."

Ironically, the proclaimed discovery of the ring with the "V" inscribed in it greatly complicated (rather than simplified) the issue of identification of the remains. In the April 25, 1971 issue of the *Chattanooga News-Free Press*, Dalton Historian Mrs. B.J. Bandy said that her investigation of the census records of that time-period indicated no one in that area had a name starting with a "V" except the Vanns. Therefore, the likelihood of anyone but James Vann being in possession of, not one, but two gold rings, particularly a ring inscribed with a "V," would have been extremely remote.

Imagine the surprise and disappointment then of all involved, when the analysis of the remains – which were supposed to have been James Vann's bones – indicated that the bones were Negroid.

". . . the man appointed by the Georgia Historical Commission had been against the whole thing from the start," Mrs. Bandy continued. "He was determined that it wasn't Vann. He insisted it was a slave, although I never heard of a slave with a gold ring. He turned in a documentary report against it, so there was nothing we could do.

"I was just sick," Bandy added, "but when you have done all you can, you can't do anything else. I took the bones back and re-buried them where we got them (in Blackburn Cemetery)."

Where then rest the remains of Cherokee Chief James Vann? Do they lie

According to historic records, James Vann II was murdered at Buffington's Tavern on the old Federal Road near the present-day Forsyth-Cherokee County line. In 1818, a traveler – Ebenezer Newton – was making his way along the Federal Road in this vicinity, when he notated a description of Vann's burial site in his diary. Rev. Charles Walker, a noted historian and illustrationist of historic landmarks in north Georgia, recreated this historically-accurate depiction of Vann's grave on the Federal Road, based upon Newton's description.

Like Buffington's Tavern, Blackburn's Public House was one of the earliest such structures on the Georgia frontier in the early 1800s, and as such, was well over 180 years old when this photo was made in 1988. It is characteristic of the public houses built along the Federal Road to facilitate travelers. (Photo by Olin Jackson)

Clifford Ruddell, photographed here in 1988 at the age of 82, was a member of the team which exhumed what some historians believed to have been the remains of James Vann II in 1962. Ruddell stands at the site of the exhumation and what has been believed by generations of area residents to be the gravesite of Vann. An official analysis of the remains recovered from this site identified them as those of a slave, despite the discovery of two gold rings on the fingers of the deceased, one of which was inscribed with a "V." (Photo by Olin Jackson)

moldering still in some unmarked grave in or around Blackburn Cemetery? Or were those really James Vann's bones unearthed on a hot summer in August of 1962?

Could James Vann have been part Negro, thus accounting for the bone analysis? Or could there have been a misinterpretation as Negroid instead of Mongoloid?

"At the very least, I am convinced those were definitely not the bones of Vann exhumed in 1962," explained Forsyth County Historian Don Shadburn. "There were just too many conclusive facts to the contrary. Even the nails used in the coffin were of a type not in existence in 1809. I've seen that report, (by the Georgia Historic Commission done in 1962) and their conclusions were very thorough."

Archaeologists Yeager and Zbar and Historian Bandy later returned to Forsyth County seeking another court order from County Ordinary A.B. Tollison for the exhumation of yet another grave believed to be Vann's, but by that time, Mr. Tollison had had enough. He denied their request.

The exact location of Vann's grave may never be known now, other than the fact that it is somewhere in or near Blackburn Cemetery in Forsyth County. On the other hand, there may be a person or persons who know exactly where the grave site is, but who, in the interest of preservation, have withheld the information in order to protect the site.

It's probably just as well, that Vann be remembered for his remarkable achievements, such as the home at Spring Place, and the nurturing of the Moravian Mission there which provided the diaries revealing the style and substance of pioneer life in north Georgia in the early 1800s.

And as for the location of the grave containing the remains of a man who may or may not have had a passion for violence, it's probably just as well that it remain in obscurity.

Atlanta's Big Fire Of 1917

It began so quietly, the actual source of the horrific fire of 1917 in Atlanta was never determined. Before it was brought under control, however, a large swath across the city had been destroyed, and if the winds had not turned, the total damage might have been even more unbelievable.

The United States had been at war with Germany for hardly one month during World War I when all hell broke loose in Atlanta, Georgia. Not since General William T. Sherman's men torched the town in 1864 had there been such a big fire, and the damage to the city was devastating.

Starting after noon at the corner of Decatur and Fort Streets on the east side of Atlanta, a fire began to spread in a northerly direction, and was whipped up into a raging inferno up Jackson Street and Boulevard by a brisk wind. The fire was two to five blocks wide at various times, and crossed Ponce de Leon Avenue before its rampage ceased just short of Greenwood Avenue south of Piedmont Park.

In its wake, the fire left 73 square blocks destroyed, and some 10,000 people homeless and destitute. It reportedly caused millions of dollars in damage in a day and time when that was an almost unbelievably large sum of money. It wiped out everything in its path, leaving nothing but the stark brick chimneys marking the sites of the former homes.

"Just the chimneys," remembered Stella Smith, who lived in the area at the time, "just the chimneys. Best as I could refer to how it looked, was like a cemetery."[1]

A "Fire Wind" Comes To Atlanta

It was May 21, 1917. It had been a dry spring and a brisk hot wind was blowing steadily from the South – a "fire wind" as firefighters called it. They knew the danger of wildfires increased greatly when that weather condition existed.

Franklin Garrett, the late distinguished Atlanta historian, was a young witness to the events of that day. He recalled that it was a Monday and a clear, warm sunny day with a strong breeze blowing from the south. He says it became a bad day when within about one hour, four fires broke out in widely separated sections of the city.

"The area was as devastated as any bombed out town in World War I, which the United States had just joined at the time," Garrett recalled. As a boy of ten, he watched in horror from his house near Piedmont Park while flames and smoke boiled into the sky a mile to the southeast. As an adult, he included six pages on the fire in his book, *Atlanta And Its Environs.*[2]

At 11:39 a.m., the first fire was reported in the Candler Warehouse on Murphy Avenue. These flames were brought under control with the loss of a few bales of cotton.

A few minutes later, however, at 11:43, an alarm was sounded at York and Ashby Streets in West End. This second fire was more serious and several houses were damaged here. And at 12:15 p.m., a third alarm was sounded from the corner of Woodward Avenue and King Street behind the state Capitol building. In this fire, about a dozen houses were destroyed before these flames were brought under control.

By that time, the Atlanta Fire Department had committed all of its mostly horse-drawn fire engines with their steam-driven pumps to fight those three fires. In 1917, less than half of the fire engines in the department were motorized.[3] Just when things seemed to be returning to normal at 12:46 p.m., a fourth alarm was sounded, and devastation was at the doorstep.

This fourth alarm was for a fire on the roof of a storage depot at Grady Hospital located just north of Decatur Street between Fort and Hilliard Streets. Since all the fire-fighting equipment was currently deployed in other sections of the city, a simple supply truck was sent to answer this fourth alarm.

Upon reaching the scene of this fire, the firemen found a stack of burning mattresses at the depot. Since they had no hose or pumper they could not put water on the fire. They could only watch as that strong wind from the south whipped the flames into an inferno which quickly spread northward over the wood shingled roofs of the frame houses and business buildings in the neighborhood between Edgewood Avenue and Houston Street. The Atlanta "big fire" was just getting started and heading north.[4]

Atlanta fireman Hugh McDonald was one of the first men with firefighting equipment to fight the fire. He described what he found when he arrived on the scene: "And when they sent us over there, Old Wheat Street had already got away. The way I understand it, they didn't have the equipment to send. Woodward Avenue, that's where the fire apparatus were. They didn't have no water to put it out, because they didn't have a pumper or hose wagon. That's where it just spread."[5]

Fire Rages Northward

Within twenty minutes after it started, the fire was beyond control and an hour later it had crossed Houston Street eating its way into the more affluent residential section of the city. The fire department was having little effect on the fire as the firemen moved from house to house. Before they could even begin defensive measures, the flames were being carried ahead of them by sparks and burning debris in the wind. Sometimes, they had to keep moving just to save themselves because the flames were quickly becoming a firestorm. They abandoned their hoses to the fire.

Problems for the firefighters were mounting too. The fire horses pulling the equipment were exhausted and their hooves reportedly were bloody from galloping over the Belgian block and brick pavement and streetcar tracks along the streets that were paved. Also, the water pressure from the hydrants was very low or, at times, nonexistent, and there was no water available from nearby lakes or streams.

Eventually, even the supply of coal needed to heat the water in the boilers of the steam pumpers was exhausted. That made the equipment useless and the firemen had no choice but to abandon this equipment too. Therefore, despite the valiant efforts of the firefighters to stop the blaze, by late afternoon, it had reached Ponce de Leon Avenue.[6]

The fire had moved so fast that most of the residents south of Houston Street had seen their houses crumble in the flames before the owners could get anything out at all. Farther up Boulevard, however, the residents in the path of the fire had some warning and were trying desperately to remove as many things from their houses as possible. Household goods were stacked on lawns and sidewalks in the hope that by some miracle they could be hauled away to safety. Unfortunately, most of it burned with the

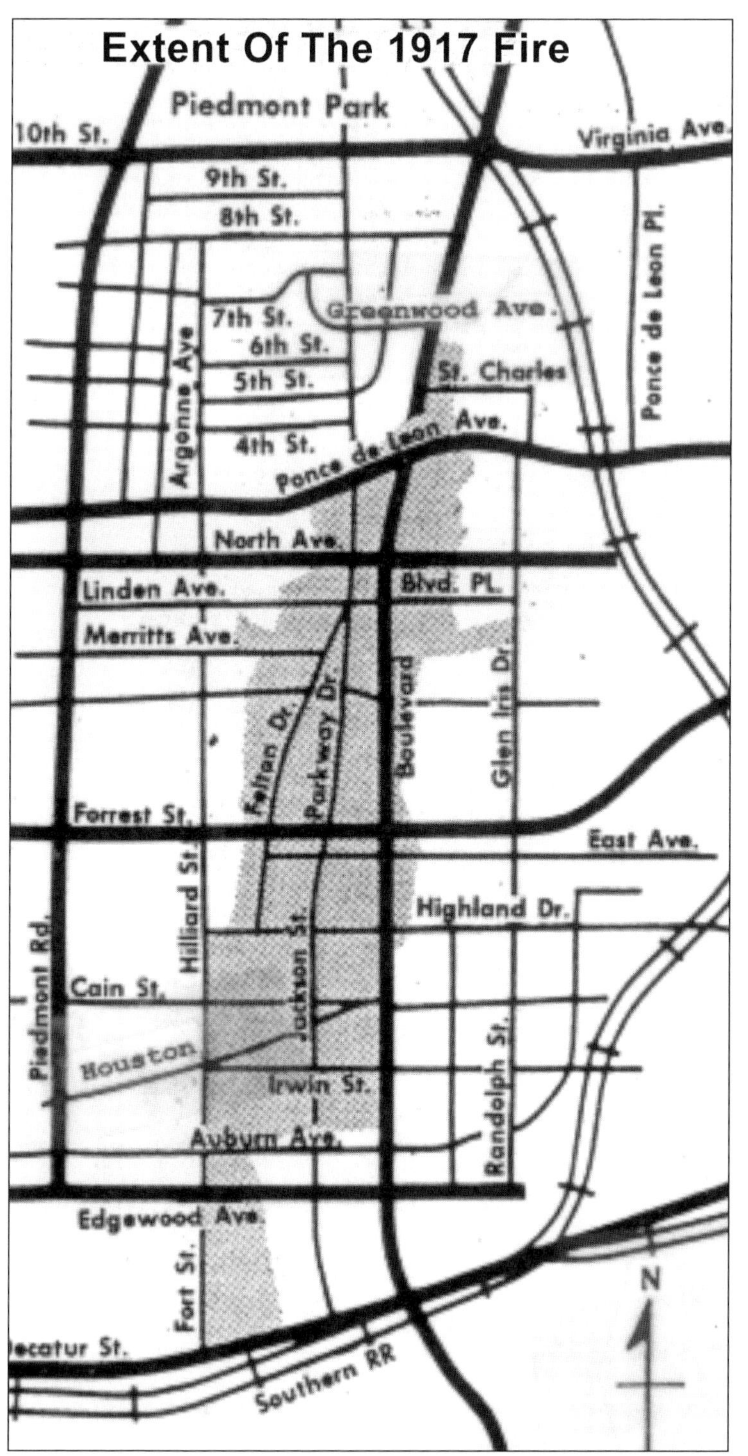

Roaring to life shortly after 12:00 noon on May 21, 1917 at the corner of Decatur and Fort Streets on the east side of Atlanta, the great fire of 1917 raged northward, carried by a brisk wind. It moved up Jackson Street and Boulevard, and was two to five blocks wide at times. It crossed Ponce de Leon Avenue before it stopped its rampage around midnight just short of Greenwood Avenue south of Piedmont Park.

homes when they were engulfed in the flames. In most instances, there was no place to drag anything clear of the path of the blaze.[7]

Other residents were directing feeble sprays of water from garden hoses onto the wood shingle roofs of their homes in a futile attempt to provide some measure of protection from the flying embers and burning debris. However, the wind and dry heat quickly negated any wetness on the structures and they fell victim nonetheless.

Prominent Witnesses

Twenty-seven year-old William B. Hartsfield – later a prominent mayor of Atlanta – lived on Jackson Street (present-day Parkway Drive) directly in the path of the roaring flames. He later wrote, *"Practically all of my stuff was burned that I had taken out back, excepting a few things I threw down the high bank and dragged two blocks down into Ponce de Leon Woods* (present-day Ponce de Leon Park area where the old Sears parking lot was later constructed and where, ironically, Atlanta City Hall East is located today), *including our trunk, sewing machine, phonograph and some blankets. Of course all our heavy furniture in the house went up."*

Taking refuge from the fire in the woods were hundreds of people carrying cherished items they had saved from their homes. In his memoirs, Hartsfield expressed surprise in the fact that people would hang on to little cheap statuary, pitchers, and bowls and leave more important things to burn.[8]

Fire companies from other communities were rushed to Atlanta to aid in the fight. Firemen from East Point reportedly were among the first to arrive at 1:30 p.m., and were sent into service against the raging inferno. Ten minutes later, a unit from Decatur arrived and was quickly dispatched to duty by Atlanta Fire Chief W.C. Cody. Others arrived during the afternoon, but many were too late to have an impact on the rapidly spreading fire.

The city quickly mobilized to aid the refugees from the fire.

Margaret Mitchell, author of *Gone With The Wind*, was a sixteen-year-old junior at the Washington Seminary, a private school in Atlanta, at the time of the fire. She experienced the devastation of the flames first-hand, when her childhood home, a two-story Victorian house on Jackson Street, eleven houses owned by her Grandmother Stephens, and her Grandmother Mitchell's old house on Boulevard, were all burned to the ground by the fire. Luckily, in 1912, when Margaret was eleven, her family had moved from Jackson Street into a new house on Peachtree Street. That elegant colonial-style home was not in the path of the fire, and avoided the disaster.

The city quickly mobilized to aid the refugees from the fire. A tent city was set up at Piedmont Park to house the homeless, and the City Auditorium served in a similar capacity downtown.

Civic-minded, Maybelle Mitchell went to the auditorium soon after the fire began to volunteer to help the homeless and took her daughter Margaret along with her. At midnight, Mrs. Mitchell was still there helping to feed and comfort the terrified victims of the disaster.

During the afternoon and evening, rescuers had picked up furniture, clothing, and other possessions abandoned in the streets and taken them to the auditorium. Soon, the big hall took on the look of an enormous rummage sale with lost children wandering among the piles of rescued possessions.

Finding there was no plan in place to handle such an emergency, Margaret became the coordinator of rescued furniture and lost children. Sitting on one of the rescued desks looking much like a young child herself with her pigtails and middy blouse, Margaret began matching lost children with their parents and lost goods with owners. She reportedly worked diligently at her job throughout the night and continued the next day and beyond.

Margaret's efforts to help the refugees allowed her to witness all aspects of a disastrous fire first-hand. The pall over the city; the terrifying explosions; martial law with soldiers deployed throughout the city; terrified men, women and children running for their lives; homes and cherished belongings destroyed; and the bewildered homeless seeking food and shelter, all were indelibly etched in the mind of this young woman. The horrible memories of this tragic event no doubt were very helpful to her later when she penned her epic novel, a book which ultimately became one of the best-selling literary works in history.[9]

At 3:00 p.m., Atlanta Mayor Asa Candler called Colonel Charles R. Noyes of the Seventh U.S. Infantry and the Officers Training Camp at Fort McPherson, requesting help from the military. The colonel responded by sending 2,000 soldiers loaded on streetcars to the fire-fighting mobilization point at Peachtree and Baker streets, arriving there by 4:30 p.m.

The King Hardware Company's trucks also arrived there loaded with buckets to be used by the soldiers to form old-fashioned bucket brigades to fight the flames. The streetcars were again loaded to transport the soldiers – buckets in hand – to their firefighting locations along the perimeter of the fire.

In addition to the regular Army soldiers from Fort McPherson, Mayor Candler requested National Guard assistance from the Governor. The Fifth Regiment and the Governor's Horse Guard were called from their camp at Lakewood Park and arrived at the mobilization point shortly after the regular soldiers. After conferring with Mayor

Atlanta's Station No. 10 was one of many fighting the fire on May 21, 1917. It served the southeastern portion of the city and was located at the corner of Oakland Avenue and Bryan Street. The pump on the horse-drawn engine was powered by steam generated in the upright boiler. The firefighters and hose went to the fire on a separate "hose wagon." The engines were capable of pumping 600 gallons of water per minute, but proved woefully inadequate in the conflagration of 1917. A year later, in 1918, the Atlanta Fire Department was completely motorized.

This stark photograph made after the fire was halted shows a view of Ponce de Leon Avenue. The area to the left (the south side of the avenue) shows where dozens of homes were dynamited into oblivion to provide a fire break in a desperate attempt to stop the fire from crossing the street and burning farther northward. In the foreground, large pieces of debris are visible which were blown onto the avenue by the explosions. A soldier stands guard on the left to prevent looting. The man seated in the rocking chair beside the car in the distance apparently is taking comfort in possibly all he has left from the disaster.

Almost 2,000 structures were destroyed in the big fire. Churches, commercial buildings, and many private residences were swallowed in the maelstrom as smoke boiled into the sky casting a deathly pall over the city of Atlanta.

Fueling the disaster were the many wood-shingled roofs of the frame houses of Butter Milk Bottoms photographed above on the day of the fire. A strong wind kept the fire moving steadily, and had not the direction of the wind flow shifted that night, much more of the city might have been lost.

Some homes in the path of the blaze amazingly survived partially intact. Most, however, were reduced to little more than smoldering ruins. According to reports of the incident, women were fainting, children were screaming, and confusion reigned supreme as the devastation raged.

Candler, and determining the situation was out of control, Colonel Noyes declared the city to be under martial law.

The National Guard soldiers were separated into detachments and sent to several points in the fire zone, arriving at their posts at about 5:00 p.m. They were used in handling fire hoses, patrolling and guarding exposed property to prevent looting, directing traffic, and acting as messengers.

The Hospital Corps set up tents in Piedmont Park which were staffed by Red Cross personnel, the Salvation Army, the Y.M.C.A., and Boy Scouts, to administer to the refugees from the fire. The fire zone had become very congested and the military was effective in clearing the area of those not engaged in fighting the fire.[10]

Dynamiting – The Horror Grows

At some point in the afternoon, it became apparent to Mayor Candler that the only way to defeat the wind and stop the fire from spreading further, would be to eliminate the material fueling the fire. Candler and his advisors decided to clear a large fire-break ahead of the fire by using dynamite.

One can only imagine the heartbreak and trauma experienced by the poor residents whose homes were selected for demolition in this fire-break. The fire had not yet reached these structures, and the residents undoubtedly had hopes that their homes might escape the disaster entirely. When they learned that their homes and possessions were to be destroyed by dynamite right before their very eyes, the realization must have been devastating.

Interestingly, Mayor Candler was so involved in the process that he reportedly personally helped to transport the explosives in his automobile from the Du Pont Powder Company in Atlanta.

After a section of the city was selected to be erased by the dynamite, soldiers began ordering the unfortunate families living in the sacrificial houses to immediately leave. They were allowed to carry with them only their most cherished possessions which could be easily transported.

When the houses were vacant, demolition crews began placing dynamite in the front parlor fireplaces. Shortly after 4:00 p.m., dynamiting began at designated houses on Pine Street, but those blasts proved to be ineffectual in halting the flames, as the wind, to the horror of the firefighters, continued to spread the terrible fire.

Trying their best to keep ahead of the flames, the demolition teams continued dynamiting the homes at a rapid rate. Soldiers were forced to continuously warn residents to evacuate the demolition area to avoid the deadly missiles hurled by the dynamite. Many terrified residents began fleeing west to safety on Peachtree Street.

Despite their best efforts, the fire-fighters were losing hope the dynamiting would stop the fire. The flames continued to spread along North Avenue and Ponce de Leon as far as Kennesaw Avenue, about two blocks from the baseball park. To the west, however, the dynamiting was halting the flames, and at the corner of Jackson Street and Ponce de Leon Avenue, the fire was prevented from spreading farther along the avenue.[11]

When the fire reached Ponce de Leon Avenue, William B. Hartsfield and the others gathered in the woods to the east were surrounded in a sort of semi-circle of flames. He recalled the sensation: "*. . . the roar of it sounded just like the roar of a heavy surf pounding, although it was punctuated with frequent dynamite explosions, and we could see the pieces of some fine houses go up into the air and fall again.*"[12]

"*I imagine about ten o'clock that night,*" recalled Hugh McDonald, "*they come out there and blowed up those houses up there on Ponce de Leon Avenue just before you get to Ponce de Leon Park. It kept it from jumping over. A man from DuPont came in and put charges in the fireplace. Those houses flattened as soon as it hit. I had to dodge one of the boards coming over. I was running the pump, close to it, and one of the one-by-twelves comes – I had to duck out behind the machine. And the last I remember the soldiers were playing water on those houses to keep them wet down, keep it from jumping over there. So, that's the way it ended.*"[13]

In point of fact, however, the end was not yet at hand. Unbeknownst to Mr. McDonald, the relentless fire jumped and crossed the wide Ponce de Leon Avenue yet again a short time later, and swept up Boulevard (now Monroe) to just short of Greenwood.

Finally, notwithstanding the courageous firefighting and desperate dynamiting of houses, only a reversal of the direction of the wind ultimately created an environment which stopped the fire in its tracks at about midnight. With the wind now blowing from the opposite direction, the fire

This view shows a portion of the destroyed area which was photographed several days after the fire. Pictured is the vicinity of Angier Avenue to Houston Street, along Forrest Avenue (present-day Ralph McGill Boulevard), Boulevard and Jackson Street.

could not spread back over its own blackened path of devastation to the south.

Aftermath

When the fire was over, an area of 300 acres and 1,938 buildings, of which 47 were brick and 1,891 were frame, had been burned, leaving 10,000 people homeless. Property losses, including dwellings, outbuildings, businesses, churches, schools and warehouses, as well as public services such as the streetcar system, electric and telephone lines, were estimated to be as high as $5,500,000, of which $3,500,000 was covered by insurance.

Remarkably, no one died in this horrific fire, but two people later died as a result of the fire. Bessie Dodd Hodges died of an apparent heart attack soon after the shock of seeing her home on North Boulevard go up in flames. The second death – that of Son White – occurred when Mr. White was shot dead by Corporal Forrest Shear after Mr. White reportedly pulled a pistol on Shear who was standing guard against looters.[14]

Since 1,682 of the 1,938 buildings destroyed had wood shingle roofs, an ordinance was passed forbidding the construction of any new buildings in Atlanta with wooden shingles. Instead, the homes and other buildings would be covered by some kind of unspecified fire-resistant material. In addition, public reaction to the tragic fire expedited the call to modernize the Atlanta Fire Department and replace all remaining horse-drawn equipment with motorized vehicles. This modernization was completed one year later on May 21, 1918.[15]

How did the fire start? It was rumored at the time that the German espionage agents started the conflagration. After all, the United States had just entered World War I, and it seemed reasonable to fear that German spies had been sent to this country to destroy things. Others speculated that someone in the Grady Hospital neighborhood had set the mattresses on fire in the depot. The exact location of the start of the main fire was never known.

In the end, most individuals agreed that the flames had probably been started by an ember carried northward on the wind over the Georgia Railroad from the Woodward Avenue fire. Whether it was sabotage, arson or simply a burning ember riding on a fire wind, the day of the big fire was a bad day in the history of Atlanta.[16]

ENDNOTES

1/ Clifford M. Kuhn, Harlon E. Joye, and E. Bernard L. Lomax. *Living Atlanta: An Oral History Of The City, 1914-1948* (Athens, GA: The University Of Georgia Press, 1990), 20, 26.

2/ *Atlanta Journal*, "Disaster! The Great Atlanta Fire, May 21, 1917," 8 December, 1976; *Atlanta Journal and Constitution*, "Atlanta's Other Great Fire," 17 May, 1987.

3/ Franklin M. Garrett. *Atlanta & Environs: A Chronicle Of Its People And Events* (Athens, GA: University Press, Reprinted 1969, Original 1954), 700.

4/ *Ibid*

5/ Clifford M. Kuhn, *Living Atlanta*, 21.

6/ Franklin M. Garrett, *Atlanta & Environs*, 702.

7/ Steve B. Campbell, "The Great Fire Of Atlanta, May 21, 1917," *The Atlanta Historical Bulletin, Vol. 13, No. 2* (June, 1968): 28-29.

8/ William B. Hartsfield, "The Atlanta Fire Of 1917," *The Atlanta Historical Bulletin, Vol. 13, No. 2* (Fall, 1977): 53-60.

9/ Finis Farr. *Margaret Mitchell Of Atlanta: The Author Of Gone With The Wind* (New York: William Morrow & Company, 1965), 35-36; Jane Bonner Peacock, ed. *Margaret Mitchell: A Dynamo Going To Waste* (Atlanta, GA: Peachtree Publishers, Ltd., 1985), 11-15; Darden Asbury Pyron. *Southern Daughter: The Life Of Margaret Mitchell* (New York: Oxford University Press, 1991), 74-75.

10/ Steve B. Campbell, "The Great Fire Of Atlanta," 29-32.

11/ Franklin M. Garrett, *Atlanta & Environs*, 703-704.

12/ William B. Hartsfield, "The Atlanta Fire Of 1917," *The Atlanta Historical Bulletin, Vol. 21, No. 3* (Fall, 1977): 53-60.

13/ Clifford M. Kuhn, *Living Atlanta*, 25-26.

14/ *Atlanta Journal*, "Disaster! The Great Atlanta Fire, May 21, 1917," 8 December, 1976; Franklin M. Garrett, *Atlanta & Environs*, 705.

15/ Clifford M. Kuhn, *Living Atlanta*, 27.

16/ *Atlanta Journal & Constitution*, "Atlanta's Other Great Fire," 17 May, 1987; Clifford M. Kuhn, *Living Atlanta*, 27-28; Franklin M. Garrett, *Atlanta & Environs*, Endnote 22.

Gunfight At Doublehead Gap

Though Texas, California and parts westward have been acknowledged as "the wild West" in early American history, many of the first cowboys, gunfights and legendary lawmen actually originated in Georgia along the southern colonial frontier.

The events which culminated in the gunfight at Doublehead Gap in Gilmer County in 1884 span a period of time in history from the U.S. Civil War through Reconstruction and on to the "Moonshine Wars" which followed. Today, this period is recognized by many as a bench-mark for the last days of the frontier South.

A principal figure in this era was Walter Webster "Web" Findley of Pickens and later Fannin County, Georgia. Findley was born in Gilmer County on May 20, 1841. He was the son of James R. and Catherine Findley.

The Findley family members were ardent secessionists, and well-connected politically in the Democratic Party. Web Findley's brother was Col. James Jefferson Findley, a Dahlonega, Georgia resident well-known for his unsympathetic and often hostile sentiments involving Unionists during the Civil War.

Web Findley had served as a second lieutenant in the Gilmer County militia during the Civil War, and had also gained a reputation as a pugnacious adversary of his pro-Union neighbors in the mountainous portions of north Georgia. A sometime lawman, Findley won fame and fortune by tracking down and bringing to justice Jackson County murderer Sanford Pirkle in 1875, Fannin County killer Ayers Jones in 1876, and Pickens County murderess Kate Southern in 1877.

Findley's home was frequently used as a headquarters by revenue agents during raids on illegal liquor ("moonshine") distilleries in north Georgia. Findley himself served on many of their raids. His career as a lawman might have been even more extensive had he learned to read and write.

Interestingly enough, however, Findley, as did many mountaineers during this period, occasionally worked the other side of "the straight and narrow" too.

Both men drew pistols and began firing at each other at the murderous range of only fifteen to thirty feet.

During the U.S. Civil War and for a time thereafter, north Georgia was a lawless and sometimes virtually uncivilized environment. Kinship and friendship, rather than the U.S. legal system, often determined the actions and allegiances of area residents. This apparently was a motivating factor for Findley's illegal actions which ultimately resulted in the shoot-out at Doublehead Gap.

The production and sale of home-produced corn liquor were considered a "God-given" right by mountaineers, and the income derived from moonshine was important to the very limited incomes of these hardy sons of the pioneers. Any tampering with these rights – especially by the U.S. government – was serious business.

John A. Stuart, a north Georgia Unionist during the war, was the Deputy Collector of Internal Revenue following the war, and quickly earned a reputation as an effective lawman. In a massive raid during one period of time, he led posses which destroyed fourteen illegal liquor distilleries in Fannin, Towns, and Union counties.

The "moonshiners," led by none other than Walter Webster Findley, retaliated by attacking Stuart's farm in the early hours of April 6, 1880, burning the storehouse and slightly wounding Stuart's son when the attackers fired upon Stuart's home.

Twenty men were later indicted for the attack, including both former Union and Confederate soldiers. Those arrested were: Benjamin M. Tilly, John D. Fricks, S.J. Simmons, Cub Newberry, J.W. Vandergriff, Bud Hill, J.F. Bingham, William Crisp, James Findley, Samuel White, Jasper .

Long, Charles Smith, Walter W. Findley, Jackson Bearden, R.V. Hughes, Bud Roberts, William Teague, Milton Dill, Wilson Bryant, and George Sparks.

The two Findleys, Bearden and Sparks were the first of the group to be tried. All but Sparks were found "Guilty" in federal court in Atlanta on October 14, 1882.

Amazingly, following the reading of the verdict, the Findleys (who, incidentally, were father and son) and Bearden brandished pistols and ran. Bearden was quickly subdued, but James escaped (he was recaptured in Gilmer County in 1886). Walter W. Findley had an injured hip, and, not being able to run, surrendered.

Findley was sentenced on February 10, 1883. He received two years in the Erie County Penitentiary in Buffalo, New York. After he had served six months of his sentence, Findley made application to the President of the United States (a Democrat) for a pardon. To strengthen his plea, a petition campaign calling for his release came from Lumpkin, Fannin, Gilmer, Hall, Pickens, White, and Forsyth counties, as well as from the prison authorities themselves. Both of Georgia's U.S. senators and a congressman wrote letters of endorsement and several members of the Georgia State Legislature signed a pro-Findley petition.

At the same time, however, another petition signed by church members, ministers, and the Fannin County sheriff, requested the President not release Findley, a plea seconded by the United States Attorney General. The anti-pardon campaign was led by Robert P. Woody (1838-1901), a native north Georgian and a Union Army officer during the Civil War.

Woody was injured during the war, and was receiving a federal pension as a disabled veteran. He had assisted the prosecution in its conviction of Findley. Although Woody and Findley held opposing political views, they had once been friends.

The President, however, surprisingly granted the pardon over the objections of his attorney general. The trial judge and the U.S. Pardon Attorney had recommended the pardon, pointing out that Findley's sentence had nearly expired anyway, counting the time that he had spent in jail in Atlanta. The U.S. Attorney for North Georgia consented because of reports of Findley's poor health.

Following Findley's release, he and Woody, though residing in the same locale, refused to greet or even acknowledge each other in passing. As time passed, their hatred of each other grew more pronounced.

Finally, on Sunday, September 28, 1884, their grievances "came to a head" as the pair met at Mt. Pleasant Church, Doublehead Gap, near the Gilmer-Fannin County Line.

Woody had traveled to the site with his wife for a church meeting. Night had fallen by the time they reached the church, but a full moon provided reasonably-good visibility. Woody was bringing up his ox-drawn wagon when he was greeted by several friends who later stated they knew trouble was brewing when they smelled liquor on Woody's breath.

According to Woody's version of the events which transpired that night, he was helping his wife out of the wagon when Findley loudly remarked: "By God, roll her out Woody." Mrs. Woody was overweight, but Findley later claimed that his remarks were not directed toward her, but to Jesse Bailey and a saddle blanket. Woody, in fairness, was very nearly deaf, and could have mistaken Findley's comments.

Whatever the circumstances, Woody, in response to Findley's remarks, angrily replied, "By God, I'll roll you down," and then cursed Findley as a thief, house-burner, and a jailbird. Findley responded in kind, calling Woody a "lie swearer."

Both men drew pistols and began firing at each other at the murderous range of only fifteen to thirty feet. Several shots were exchanged as the two men drew even nearer, and both attackers, in their anger, ignored the several individuals between them who were attempting to stop the fight.

Woody was wounded in the hand on the first exchange, but he managed to get off a second shot. Findley's second shot passed harmlessly through Woody's vest and Woody's third shot nicked Findley's shirt. Woody's pistol then began misfiring, and Findley wounded him again – this time seriously – in the stomach.

Both men fell to the ground – Findley, apparently because someone had hit him in the head with a rock. A bystander – William Kimsey – lay with them, mortally wounded before he was able to evade the gunfire.

That neither Findley nor Woody was killed in the exchange is not nearly as amazing as the fact that more bystanders were not hit. The pistols of that day often were crude and inaccurate instruments, so much so, that even renowned marksmen such as Wyatt Earp often preferred to use pistols to club rather than shoot an opponent.

When order was restored, Woody was arrested. He subsequently was found guilty of assaulting Findley and served one year in the Georgia State Penitentiary. He and Findley were both tried for the murder of Kimsey and were acquitted.

Findley later successfully gathered information which caused Woody's Disability Pension to be revoked as fraudulent. Woody, however, gained a measure of satisfaction after being appointed U.S. postmaster at the community of Dial.

The feud between the two men, surprisingly, ended without further bloodshed. According to a Woody relative – Willis Rackley – Woody eventually tired of Findley's public insults (mainly in the form of public snubs). On one such occasion shortly after the gunfight at Doublehead Gap, he demanded that Findley either have the courtesy to speak to him in public and treat him civilly, or the two of them would end the matter once and for all. From that day forward, the feud ceased to exist.

Walter W. Findley died in Fannin County on June 9, 1910.

ENDNOTES

1/ A transcript of a pro-Woody official report of the events leading to the gunfight is available in Lawrence L. Stanley's *A Little History Of Gilmer County*, (1975), and in the Robert Barker Collection, Knoxville Public Library.

2/ A transcript of the Woody trial (The State versus Robert Woody) is available in the Gilmer County Court Case Papers, Record Group 161-12-11, Box 24, Georgia Department of Archives and History.

3/ Information on Robert P. Woody came from Willis Rackley and an article by William C. Farmer in *Facets Of Fannin: A History Of Fannin County, Georgia*, (1989).

4/ Findley's pardon papers are on record in the National Archives, Washington, D.C., in Record Group 204.

Anthony Goble And The Brown Murder Of 1876

The only legal execution in Gilmer County history closed the books on what had been a particularly grisly mountain murder.

If one takes the words of politicians and country music singers literally, a century ago capital punishment was dispatched quickly and frequently. The reality of the situation, however, was very different. Individuals did die in public hangings in the late 1800s, but even then, the legal process inevitably involved a long road from the crime to the gallows, and the proceedings could be stretched out by numerous appeals. Reform movements of that day argued strongly against the spectacle of public executions and even the value of capital punishment.

The story of the hanging of Anthony "Tone" Goble is a classic example of the reality of the death penalty in Georgia at that time. Despite the poverty, rural lifestyle, and the harshness of the Reconstruction Era in Gilmer County during the 1870s, Goble's hanging represents the only instance in which an individual was executed by a Gilmer County court decree.

Goble, ironically, did almost everything imaginable to facilitate his eventual execution, but his case was still not easily resolved. Had he made a significant effort to save himself, he quite likely would have been spared by the court of that day.

The circumstances of this public hanging included many classic elements of the era in which it occurred – prejudices from the U.S. Civil War, whiskey, and mountain feuds.

On November 2, 1876, Wofford L. Brown of Gordon County and William Gentry went to the government-licensed distillery of Mart Barnes near Ellijay in Gilmer County. A group of people had gathered there that day, not just buying whiskey, but also drinking it – "freely."

According to details of the incident, Brown – well-intoxicated – approached an individual who was observing a card game in progress. Brown asked the man if his name was Goble. The man replied that his name had "passed for it." Pressing on, Brown (obviously unaware of the jeopardy in which he was placing himself) charged that during the Civil War, Goble's father had stolen meat from his (Brown's) father, and that he (Anthony Goble) had helped eat it.

"Tone" Goble was known to be a tremendously-strong individual, and a very dangerous man to insult. He did not deny the charge made by the man facing him, but pointed out that since he was only a boy during the war, he was not familiar with the details of the situation described by Brown.

The day progressed without further incident, and Brown reportedly apologized for his actions and comments. The two men seemed to have become friends. In reality, however, nothing could have been further from the truth – at least not as far as Tone Goble was concerned.

That afternoon, Brown asked Goble to show him the route to a Mr. Watkins' house. The two were seen leaving together on foot, laughing and talking, without the slightest indication of the horrible crime that was shortly to occur.

William Gentry accompanied the two men a short distance, but then parted company with them at approximately 1:30 p.m. on Round Top Mountain Road. Gentry, according to reports, continued on across Barnes Mountain to the Oak Hill community. According to later testimony, he remembered noticing Goble pick up and pocket a rock at that time.

Over the next six hours, the two men proceeded only three miles, around Round Top, bearing to the right on the Round Top – Pea Ridge Road, and then to a washed-out gully on the property owned (as of this writing) by Homer and Glen Reece. It was here that the life of Wofford L. Brown was snuffed out.

Shortly after 8:00 p.m. that night, Tone Goble appeared at the door of the house of a Mrs. Tuck (also identified as the Kell House). Mrs. Tuck reportedly invited Goble inside, where to her surprise, Goble confessed to her his shame of having been fighting and having killed a man. At this point, he held out his hands to show the blood on them.

Mrs. Tuck, no doubt, was disturbed by this as well as by the blood on Goble's shoes. But she and several other people present at her home at this time all initially assumed that this was some type of joke, and that the blood simply came from recently-butchered meat. However, seeing the doubt in their eyes and to prove his grizzly account, Goble proceeded to pull whiskers out of his pocket and announced, "Here's the damned rascal's whiskers, and if you will give me a dollar apiece for them, I will go and stick them back."

Undoubtedly horrified by this point, Mrs. Tuck inquired about his victim and whether or not he had put up a fight. According to accounts, Goble replied: "No, he never offered to strike me, but begged like a damned puppy, and I made him pay manfully."

Mrs. Tuck asked if Goble was certain the man was dead. Goble replied that if he wasn't dead, he would be by the time they got to him.

Several people were assembled shortly thereafter, and they followed Goble to the site of the crime. There, they found Wofford Brown, lying just as Goble had claimed they would, with his left arm beneath his body. Most witnesses were horrified by what they saw.

"Tone" Goble was known to be a tremendously-strong individual, and a very dangerous man to insult.

According to an article in the

In the 1870s, government-licensed distilleries operated legally in Georgia and other states. These were often a place of congregation for area residents. On a crisp autumn morning in 1876, Wofford L. Brown of Gordon County interrupted a card game outside the distillery near Ellijay to accuse one of the participants of a theft several years earlier. (Illustration by Walter Hunt)

MURDER SITE – Ellijay resident Raymond Davis (l) and Sam Morgan (r) pause at the spot at which Wofford L. Brown was murdered by Anthony Goble near Round Top Mountain in 1876. This spot, photographed here in 1991, undoubtedly appears much as it did the day of the murder. (Photo by Robert S. Davs, Jr.)

Dahlonega Signal And Advertiser, a witness at Goble's trial remarked that the sight that awaited the crowd following Goble *"was the worst mangled body that was ever heard of, and the murder one of the most atrocious ever committed in a civilized community, and stands without a parallel."*

To the surprise of the group which approached the mangled body that day, Brown still appeared to cling to life when turned face-up.

"Thank God. He is not dead yet!" exclaimed Mrs. Tuck.

Brown, in actuality, was in the final throes of death, and was apparently still feebly attempting to crawl away from his attacker. Upon this realization, Goble proceeded to kick and further beat Brown, before being restrained by members of the group.

Goble was arrested soon thereafter and sent to the Cobb County Jail in Marietta for confinement, secure from any possible rescue by his family and friends.

An investigation later revealed that Wofford Brown's head had been crushed, and he had been severely beaten and choked prior to his death. He was buried in his family cemetery near East Damascus Church in Ryo, Georgia.

Anthony Goble was brought before the Superior Court of Gilmer County on May 14, 1877. He pleaded "Not Guilty" to murder. Unable to afford an attorney, several lawyers were appointed to defend him: Charles H. Phillips, Gilmer County Ordinary J.C. Allen, and newly-elected Congressman Hiram P. Bell.

Despite the efforts of this defense team, Goble not only made no effort to defend himself, but "was utterly defiant, ugly and callous" to the court. No one was called upon to testify on his behalf, but the prosecution produced a parade of witnesses. Goble, subsequently was found guilty and sentenced to die.The execution was set for June 22, 1877. Goble's attorneys announced they would make an appeal, but none was ever filed.

At this point, Sheriff William Jones must have realized he was facing a dilemma. Since the Civil War and the struggles against the U.S. Department of Revenue, official law and order had largely ceased to exist in the mountains of north Georgia. Justice, such as it was, was dealt out by family feuds and personal vendettas. Jones apparently did not wish to become the victim of a blood feud through his action in this execution, so he resigned on May 29, 1877, rather than hang Anthony Goble.

Many others also declined the duty. The responsibility eventually fell to Dr. James R. Johnson who, ironically enough, was the county coroner. He was an old friend of Goble's, but apparently did not want to resign his job.Security for the execution was tight. Two rows of guards surrounded the log jail where Goble was held, to prevent any rescue of the condemned man. Even members of the news media were not allowed to see Goble.

Meanwhile, Tone Goble, to the surprise of many, was far from depressed. He even joked openly about the need for a rope strong enough to hold his weight.

On the morning of June 22, Goble was converted to and baptized in the Methodist faith (prayer meetings on his behalf had been held repeatedly in the jail). At 11:00 a.m. that day, dressed in a white robe, Goble was placed in a wagon for the trip to the gallows.

The scaffold had been erected in Pump Spring Hollow, a natural amphitheater selected by County Ordinary J.C. Allen, because of the proximity to Ellijay's only licensed liquor shop. According to local legend, Goble rode to the site atop his coffin, with John Irvin Patton Smith

During his trial in 1877, Anthony "Tone" Goble was incarcerated in the basement of the Gilmer County Jail, a log structure which once stood across from the present-day First Baptist Church. As of this writing, the old jail site (above) is occupied by a machine shop between Dalton and Sand streets. (Photo by Robert S. Davis, Jr.)

Rather than risk his own life by starting a blood feud by hanging Anthony Goble, the elected sheriff of Gilmer County – William Jones - resigned his position. With no one else willing to do the job, it fell to County Coroner J.R. Johnson (above). Following the execution, Johnson knew his days in Gilmer County were numbered, so he gathered his possessions and moved out of the state.

HANG HOLLOW, ELLIJAY – The scaffold for the execution of Anthony Goble was erected in a natural amphitheatre selected because of its proximity to Ellijay's only licensed liquor shop. At 11:00 a.m. on the morning of June 22, 1877, Goble, dressed in a white robe with his hands bound behind him, rode in a wagon atop his casket to the execution site just outside Ellijay. (Illustration by Walter Hunt)

BURIAL SITE - Raymond Davis (l) and Sam Morgan stand before the grave of Anthony Goble in the Ellijay Town Cemetery. (Photo by Robert S. Davis, Jr.)

driving the wagon.

A fifty-man posse had been assembled by Ordinary Allen to prevent any rescue attempt of Goble on the way to the gallows. A reporter for the *Dahlonega Signal* wrote that at least half of the population of Gilmer County was on hand for the execution, in addition to the people from other counties. Some individuals had traveled fifteen to twenty miles just to witness the event.

The crowd included many women and children. The Dahlonega reporter described the spectacle as *"more barbarous than the scenes within the amphitheater at Rome in the days of Nero."*

The last ride of Tone Goble is difficult to reconstruct today. Ellijay was and is still today a community built upon hillsides and winding streets (narrow trails at that time). Floods, fires and "Father Time" have eliminated the old buildings, and even the streets have been changed.

Raymond Davis, a resident of the area, studied the Goble hanging, as well as the history of Ellijay, for many years. In an interview in the late 1980s, he maintained that Goble was incarcerated in the basement of the old jail which stood across from the present-day First Baptist Church in Ellijay, a lot occupied (as of this writing) by a machine shop between Dalton and Sand Streets.

The street down which Goble's execution wagon traveled no longer exists. (It was in the hollow, to the left of modern Corbin Hill Road.) To get to the execution site today, one has to travel up Sand Street, then north on Spring Street to Corbin Hill Road, thence to Charles Street and then down into the natural arena called "Hang Hollow." The courthouse, gallows, and cemetery were within a circle with a diameter of less than a mile. However, the maze of twisted streets undoubtedly made the journey long and torturous for Goble.

At the gallows, according to accounts, the wagon drove beneath the prepared noose and halted. A Rev. Edwards read several verses of scripture, including Ezekiel 18:23 (King James version of the *Bible*): *"Have I any pleasure at all that the wicked should die? saith the Lord God: and not that he should return from his ways and live?"*

Rev. Edwards then read a confession Goble had dictated, blaming his end upon whiskey, cards, women, and bad company. Goble stated that he had never had religious training and that he had only once attended school.

Dr. Johnson then announced that this was a sad duty, but that he had tended Goble every kindness. Goble acknowledged Johnson's statement. The coroner then allowed friends and relatives – more than 500 people – to come to the wagon where Goble was sitting, to say their goodbyes.

Goble asked each person in turn to meet him in heaven. Only with some of his relatives did the condemned man show strong emotion.

At last, Tone Goble was led up the steps of the gallows. He shook hands with Dr. Johnson and his hands were then bound behind his back while a white hood was placed over his head. A witness at the event – Mary Louise Logan – later remembered that a small thunderstorm rolled through the mountains during the execution, but the hanging proceeded anyway. After the noose was adjusted, all but one support was removed from the gallows. The trap nearly collapsed beneath Goble's weight.

"Tone, are you ready?" asked Dr. Johnson. "Yes sir," was the reply in a firm voice. The coroner then gave several strong jerks to the rope tied to the trigger beneath the trap, even cutting his wrist at one point, but the trap held firm. Johnson then reportedly wrapped the rope around his wrist and, pulling with both hands and digging in with his feet, gave the trigger one last great heave. The trap fell and Goble dropped five feet into eternity.

The trap fell and Goble dropped five feet into eternity.

Goble's relatives did not bury him at Round Top. Instead, interment took place just outside the town cemetery, with the body facing north-south, instead of the traditional east-west. The gallows was not demolished following the execution, but was left, undisturbed, to rot.

Gilmer County's one official execution slowly faded into legend over the years. Almost all of the buildings and most of the streets of the Ellijay of 1877 – including the courthouse, the jail, and Dr. Johnson's house – have all now disappeared. The latter stood on the site of the present-day courthouse. The courthouse in Goble's day stood on the site of the present-day veterans monument on the town square in Ellijay.

Wofford Brown's family moved away shortly after his murder. Dr. James Johnson, a prominent citizen of Ellijay and twice grand master of the local Masonic Lodge, also moved out of state.

Law and order as we know it today in north Georgia was still a number of years in the future in 1877. The issues of capital punishment and the merits thereof were argued in 1877, contrary to popular myth, much as they are today.

Marked For Death: The Story Of Stand Watie

In the 1830s, he advocated a treaty between his tribe and the American government which would relocate his tribe from the southeastern United States to the West. He knew – as a result of Cherokee law – that his support for this treaty meant almost certain death for himself. Amazingly, he survived the Cherokee death squads sent to execute him. Later, he rose to the rank of brigadier general in the Confederate Army. Today, the courage of this unusual Cherokee is unquestioned, yet he has been virtually forgotten by the modern-day residents of his former homeland.

In 1995, the United States Post Office issued a set of commemorative stamps featuring distinguished individuals and battles of the United States Civil War. In the foreground on one of those stamps, the image of a Cherokee Indian who also was a brigadier general in the Confederate Army, is prominently displayed riding on horseback. This nondescript Native American is one of the least heralded leaders of the Cherokee Nation, yet he played a pivotal role in the destiny of the Cherokees, and amazingly escaped almost certain death at the hands of his misguided brethren.

In the distant background on this same commemorative postage stamp, smoke can be seen rising from the burning hulk of the Federal steam-driven ferryboat – the *J.R. Williams* – on the Arkansas River. Watie and his men ambushed this vessel during the U.S. Civil War on June 15, 1864.

While the *J.R. Williams* was steaming upriver on its way to Fort Gibson in the western Indian Territory, the vessel was fired upon and disabled by Watie's artillery. The Indians fired from behind bushes on a bluff overlooking the river. Blasted out of control, the boat ran aground on a sandbar on the north side of the river.

The outnumbered Federal soldiers aboard the boat were taken completely by surprise. Those who survived the ambush fled on foot southward back toward Fort Smith from whence they had come. The boat's crew deserted to the Confederates.

Watie's men swarmed over the captured vessel. Composed mostly of Creeks and Seminoles, the Indians began looting the boat of its cargo of commissary stores, quartermaster supplies and sutler's goods intended for Fort Gibson.

After they had gathered up what booty they could carry, most of the Indians fled the scene to rejoin their destitute families who were living along the Red River in Texas where they had taken refuge from the invading Union Army. Watie loaded up as much of the supplies as he and his remaining Cherokee soldiers could carry away with them, then set fire to the boat. He then departed for his camp on the Limestone Prairie in the Cherokee Nation, because he knew a strong Federal reaction force would be arriving at the site of the burned ferryboat in short order.[1]

The Stand Watie stamp commemorates this amazing leader's many years of perseverance and devotion to both the Cherokee Indian and Confederate American lost causes. As a three-quarter-blood Cherokee aristocrat, prosperous slaveholding planter, and leader of his mixed-blood allies, he somehow survived the many years of bloody tribal feuding in both the East and the West. As a Confederate Army Brigadier General, he also survived this conflict despite regular service in combat situations. He was the highest-ranking Native American to fight in the Civil War – on either side.[2]

Stand Watie (1806-1871), was the brother of Buck Watie (Elias Boudinot). He was a plantation owner in Cass County and also a member of the Treaty Party. By a stroke of luck, he was absent from his home the day Major Ridge, John Ridge and Buck were assassinated. He later became the highest ranking Indian officer in the U.S. Civil War, rising to the rank of brigadier general in the Confederate Army. (Image courtesy of Western History Collection, University of Oklahoma Library)

Stand Watie's Early Life

Stand Watie was born on December 12, 1806.[3] Kenny A Franks, in his autobiography of Stand Watie, writes that he was born "at the town of Oothcaloga, south of New Echota in the Cherokee Nation, an area later organized into Cass County, Georgia. . . . [where he] spent his boyhood years along the creek that flowed gently through the pleasant valley."[4]

He was named Ta-ker-taw-ker at birth, which meant "to stand firm," and formally by tribal custom as De-gado-ga, which meant "he stands on two feet." He was later baptized into the Moravian Church and given the Christian name Isaac. Still later, his name evolved to a combination of a shortened form of the English translation of his Cherokee name, "to stand firm," and a contraction of his father's last name, Oo-Wa-tie, which ultimately led to the name "Stand Watie."[5]

In his youth, Stand Watie lived in a comfortable home built in the 1790s by his father, David Watie (the double Oo, as in "Oo-Wa-tie" was, at some point, dropped from his name). In addition to the income from his plantation, David operated a ferry on the Hightower (Etowah) River from 1825 to 1831.

By this point in time, the Cherokees had adopted many of the ways of the white settlers in the area. The assumption of these customs included the custom of owning

Buck Watie, also known as Elias Boudinot (1802-1839), was editor of the Cherokee Phoenix newspaper. His support for the Removal Treaty caused him to be replaced as editor of the paper, and later, to be brutally murdered at his new home in Park Hill, Arkansas. (Image courtesy of Western History Collection, University of Oklahoma Library)

Major Ridge was speaker of the lower house in the Cherokee Council. He also was chief of the Cherokee police, a close advisor to Chief John Ross, and a strong supporter of the treaty being urged by the United States government which would cede the Cherokee lands to the whites. His advocation for this treaty eventually cost him his life.

black slaves to work the plantations. Young Stand Watie was raised by his father to work alongside the slaves in the fields, but after his chores were done for the day, he often went hunting in the forest to bring in fresh meat for the family.[6]

When he was only six or seven years of age, Stand Watie's father, David, was appointed as a captain in a regiment of 600 Cherokee volunteers – mostly mixed-bloods – commanded by his brother, Major Ridge. Under the overall command of Andrew Jackson, the regiment was a portion of a larger force sent to fight the Red Stick faction of the Creek Nation in present-day Alabama.

In March of 1814 at the Battle of Horseshoe Bend on the Tallapoosa River, the Andrew Jackson forces crushed the Red Stick uprising, quite nearly killing all of the Red Stick Creeks in the process. It was during that campaign that Major Ridge acquired his first name when he was commissioned as a major in the United States Army by Andrew Jackson.[7]

Stand Watie, who spoke only his native tongue until he was twelve, learned to speak, read, and write English at the Moravian Mission Schools, attending classes at both the school at Spring Place and another at Brainerd, Tennessee. Young Watie was especially interested in sports. He was small in stature, but reportedly was an outstanding athlete and an excellent rider. He was considered one of the best players in the games of ball in the "challenge" competitions in the Cherokee Nation.[8]

Stand Watie had a brother who was four years older than he named Kilakeena, meaning "stag" or "male deer." He was commonly known as "Buck" Watie. In time, the two boys were joined by other siblings for a total of eight children – four boys and four girls.

Buck Watie and his cousin, John Ridge (the son of Major Ridge), were sent to complete their education at the American Board of Commissioners for Foreign Mission

Schools at Cornwall, Connecticut. While there, in addition to a higher education, Buck gained a new name, and both Buck and John gained New England girls as their wives.

According to a common practice at the time, as a tribute to someone held in high esteem, Buck Watie adopted the name of his white benefactor – Elias Boudinot – who was a Philadelphia philanthropist. In 1827, Buck (now called Elias Boudinot) married Harriet Gold and brought her home to live at New Echota.[9]

The Cherokee Nation In The East

In 1819, the sprawling Cherokee settlement of New Town was established on the south bank of the Oostanaula River just below the confluence of the Coosawattee and Connasauga rivers. In 1820, at New Town, a law was passed by the tribal council dividing the Cherokee country of Georgia, Alabama and Tennessee into eight territorial and judicial districts. Although Stand Watie and Major Ridge lived 30 miles apart, they both lived within the Coosewattie District.[10]

In 1825, New Town was designated as the new Cherokee National Capital and renamed New Echota (Echota being the Cherokee term for "town"). New Echota was (and a portion of its historic remnants still are) located east of present-day Calhoun, Georgia, in Gordon County, off GA Highway 225 at the present-day locus of New Echota State Historic Site.[11]

About eight miles south of New Echota, the Indian town of Oothcaloga once stood in the Oothcaloga Valley. Christianity was strongly held in the community as witnessed by a large number of converts made during the revivals held there in 1819-20. Soon thereafter, a prominent group of Cherokee leaders requested that a Moravian Mission be established in their neighborhood to conduct regular church services.

Major Ridge, his wife, Susanna, and their son, John, were among the first to invite the Moravians to come to the valley. In addition, David Watie and his wife, Susannah, and their sons, Elias Boudinot and Stand Watie, encouraged the establishment of both a church and a school. Thus, from 1822 to 1833, the Oothcaloga Mission Station was operated by the Moravian Church in the valley.[12]

John Ross (1790-1866), principal chief of the Cherokee Nation from 1828 until his death, appeared to have much more white blood than Cherokee blood. He was an eighth-blood Cherokee. He also was unflinchingly opposed to the treaty which would cede the Cherokee lands to the whites. (Photo courtesy of Western History Collection, University of Oklahoma Library)

According to the *Cherokee Constitution* adopted on July 26, 1827, the Cherokee Supreme Court was authorized to appoint a clerk to a term of four years. Stand Watie was appointed as clerk in 1828, and at age 22, began a long career in legal work that eventually gained him a license to practice law in the Cherokee Nation.[13]

The Watie Family

During the time of his residence in the East, Stand Watie married three of the four wives with whom he was associated during

On June 29, 1995, the U.S. Post Office issued a set of 20 commemorative stamps showing 16 individuals and 4 battles of the U.S. Civil War. Brigadier General Stand Watie (1806-1871) was one of the individuals selected to appear on the stamps. He is pictured here, on horseback, following a raid on a Union river boat.

his lifetime. These first three wives all had Christian names and there were no children from any of these marriages.

His first wife was Elizabeth "Betsy" Fields, who died in childbirth, as did the child in late March of 1836.

His second marriage – in September of 1836 – was to the former wife of a deceased Cherokee neighbor Eli Hicks. Her name was Isabella Hicks. She had a son by the previous marriage.

Watie's third marriage was to Eleanor Looney. No details of this marriage are known today.

Stand Watie married his fourth wife – Sarah (Sallie) Carolina Bell – after he was a resident in the western Indian Territory in 1843. With Sarah, Stand Watie had five children – three sons and two daughters.[14]

When they reached maturity, the three cousins – Stand Watie, Elias Boudinot and John Ridge, along with the older Major Ridge, came to be not only a tight family group, but, in 1832, the leadership core of a pro-treaty party favoring the removal of the tribe to the West. They were seeking to gain control in the Cherokee Nation over the anti-treaty faction, which opposed the tribe's removal. The anti-treaty faction was led by the principal chief of the Cherokees, John Ross.[15]

Over time, the Ridge-Watie-Boudinot family group had realized that it was futile to attempt to staunch the never-ending flow of Europeans settling in the Cherokee Nation. There simply were too many whites flocking to the eastern seaboard of the then-fledgling United States. For this reason, the pro-treaty faction advocated selling the tribe's lands in the East (and moving to new lands in the West) before the eastern lands were simply taken away by the whites.

After Andrew Jackson and the state of Georgia recognized the pro-treaty faction as the legitimate delegation of the Cherokee Nation, they (the pro-treaty faction) took the lead in negotiating the Treaty of New Echota in 1835, surrendering the Cherokees' ancestral homes in the Southeast for new lands in the West.[16]

On December 29, 1835, at Elias Boudinot's house at New Echota, the Watie-Ridge-Boudinot-led faction signed the Treaty of New Echota. They gave up all claims to their land in the East in return for new land west of the Mississippi River and just compensation for any improvements made on their land in the East.

Other Cherokees, however – led by John Ross – were not present for the signing of this treaty, and bitterly opposed it and the removal of the tribe. They vowed to exact retribution from the Watie-Boudinot-Ridge pro-treaty faction. The United States Senate quickly ratified the treaty and three years later, the United States army enforced the Cherokee removal in what was called the "Trail of Tears."[17]

The Cherokee Nation In The West

In the spring of 1837, the Stand Watie, Elias Boudinot and Ridge families began their migratory journey to the Indian Territory in the West. Upon arrival, they joined forces with the "Old Settlers," those Cherokees who had removed to the Indian Territory in 1817 long before the signing of the Removal Treaty.

Contrary to their expectations, the Watie-Boudinot-Ridge families and their allies among the Old Settlers were unable to gain leadership over the Cherokee Nation in the West. Their old treaty opponent – John Ross – who had arrived in the West in mid-March of 1839 in the wake of the forced removal – still retained the allegiance of the majority of the Cherokees.[18]

On June 21, 1839, at Double Springs in the Indian Territory, a secret meeting of the Cherokees who had opposed the removal treaty was held to judge those who had violated the "blood law," and, without authorization, sold Cherokee land. A verdict of death was passed against all the signers and endorsers of the Treaty of New Echota.

On the next day on June 22, the sentences were being carried out by execution squads and three of the most prominent signers – Major Ridge, who was Stand Watie's uncle; John Ridge, who was Stand Watie's cousin; and Elias Boudinot, who was his brother – were all brutally murdered. Stand Watie, however, who was also marked for execution, was warned about the death squads, and managed to escape the assassins.[19]

For his protection, Stand Watie organized a band of warriors at Old Fort Wayne as a personal bodyguard. The next few years were a time of murderous internal feuding between the two treaty factions. Relations between the factions bordered on civil war, with many acts of vengeance and retaliation carried out by both sides.

Eventually, a restless calm emerged in the Indian Territory, and Stand Watie, who

This historic structure stands on the Bray Farm near Calhoun, Georgia in Gordon County. Local lore maintains that the core of this home is an aged log cabin built by David Watie in the 1790s. David was the father of Stand Watie and Elias Boudinot, and it is generally believed they both were born in this cabin. (Photo by Joe Griffith)

Major Ridge, the uncle of Stand Watie, departed for the West in 1837. The structure in this photograph has an Indian log cabin at its core which was Ridge's home while he resided in Indian Territory in what today is Rome, Georgia. Ridge also operated a ferry and several other business endeavors at this site in the 1820s and '30s. Today, this structure is called Chieftains Museum, and is a National Historic Landmark dedicated to the preservation of the heritage of the Cherokees. (Photo by Joe Griffith)

Following the removal of the Cherokees in 1838, the town of New Echota fell into ruin and the land reverted to agricultural usage. In the foreground in this photo, the last remains of the Buck Watie aka Elias Boudinot home are visible. Buck was the older brother of Stand Watie and served as the first editor of the Cherokee Phoenix newspaper. Buck constructed a large two-story home on this site in 1827. Nothing remains of the home today except a few foundation stones and the outline of the old well. (Photo by Joe Griffith)

Pictured here is a reproduction of the print house which once stood on the grounds of New Echota in Gordon County. Elias Boudinot, aka Buck Watie, was the brother of Stand Watie. He also was the editor of the Cherokee Phoenix and published this Cherokee language newspaper in this structure. Stand Watie assisted his brother with the paper from time to time, and was acting editor in 1832 during his brother's absence. (Photo by Joe Griffith)

had attained prominent social and political stature in the territory, joined the Tribal Council where he served from 1845 to 1861. During that time, he participated in the leadership of the Cherokee Nation until the beginning of the War Between The States.[20]

The U.S. Civil War

In the spring of 1861, the Union abandoned all its military posts in the Indian Territory. The Confederates quickly occupied them.

As a prosperous planter and slave owner, Stand Watie was sympathetic to the Southern cause, but his dedication had little to do with his loyalty to the Southern states. He, no doubt, saw the war as an opportunity to get rid of his old treaty party enemies – the John Ross regime.

When Confederate emissaries approached him for his support, he agreed to organize a cavalry unit. With the outbreak of the war, Stand Watie was made a colonel in the Confederate army and he raised a regiment of mostly mixed-blood, pro-slavery soldiers known as the Cherokee Mounted Volunteers.[21]

As a military unit, the Cherokee Mounted Volunteers fought as a band of very irregular cavalry. They wore odd colored shirts and pants, moccasins, and hats with feathers sticking out of them. They had no reliable source of supply, so they depended upon captured Union supplies and equipment for their logistical support.

In cold weather, the Cherokee Mounted Volunteers were known to wear captured pieces of Yankee blue uniforms and overcoats. Watie and his men, armed mostly with shotguns, knives and tomahawks, preferred to fight on horseback, conducting slashing raids on unsuspecting enemies in the tradition of the guerrilla tactics of Francis Marion, the "Swamp Fox," in South Carolina during the American Revolution. Thus, Stand Watie led his men with dash and daring as they ambushed wagon supply trains, steamboats, and military escorts during the war.[22]

It is a matter of record, however, that Watie and his men did participate in one traditional infantry battle. On March 7-8, 1862, his unit was part of Confederate Major General Earl Van Dorn's 16,000-man army in the vicinity of Fayetteville, Arkansas. Van Dorn was trying to encircle the right flank of Major General Samuel R. Curtis' Union Army of 12,000 men.

Curtis was deployed in the defense on good ground about 30 miles to the northeast of Fayetteville at a place called Pea Ridge. He was prepared for an attack and managed to fight off the Confederates in two days of battle, sending Van Dorn's forces into retreat in complete disarray.[23]

Ironically, in that defeat, Stand Watie's reputation as a fierce fighter and capable combat leader was assured. In a driving snow storm, Colonel Stand Watie's men, who were for the first time being employed on foot as regular infantry, were aligned with other units on the left flank of the attacking force. During the attack, Watie's men charged a Union artillery battery of three guns protected by dismounted Union cavalry.

As they ran across the open field screaming a blood-curdling Rebel yell and brandishing the cold steel of their weapons, Watie's men caused the startled Yankees to break from their positions and flee in terror. In the process, three cannons were captured – an accomplishment considered a great victory at that time. As a result of this courage in the face of terrible fire, Watie and his men were cheered by the other Confederate units.[24]

Interestingly, despite the great victory in the capture of the cannons, Watie had no horses or harnesses to move the cannons to the rear. He therefore directed his men – still under hostile fire from other Union artillery units – to drag the captured pieces into the woods where they were secured. Unfortunately, Watie's advanced position became untenable as other Confederate forces in the line began retreating, and he was forced to withdraw with them.

Thus, Watie and his men had fought in their one and only battle deployed as traditional infantrymen. They had been successful, but at the end of the day, the battle became a crushing defeat for the Confederates.[25]

Following the defeat at Pea Ridge, John Ross – who initially had supported the Confederacy – became a turn-coat and suddenly switched sides. He realigned his Cherokee supporters with the Union army and cause. A short time later, a Union force – with the cooperation of Ross and his people – invaded the Indian Territory. This invasion divided the Cherokee Nation into its former treaty factions once again.

As a result, pro-Union Cherokees battled pro-Confederate Cherokees, with the Ross faction once again bitterly fighting the Watie faction. Following four years of violence based almost entirely upon tribal animosity rather than U.S. Civil War conflicts, the Cherokee homeland in the West was generally laid to waste.

Ultimately, the victory of the Union over the Confederacy returned John Ross to his position of control over the Cherokee Nation. Factional violence within the Nation essentially ended upon the culmination of the U.S. Civil War, but bitterness and hatred endured well into the next century.[26]

On May 6, 1864, Stand Watie was promoted to the rank of brigadier general, becoming the highest ranking Indian to fight in the Civil War. On June 23, 1865, over two months after General Lee's surrender, Stand Watie became the last Confederate general to surrender his forces.

Following the war, Watie tried unsuccessfully to rebuild his fortune. He died on September 9, 1871, at his home on Honey Creek in Delaware County, Oklahoma, near the northwest corner of Arkansas.[27]

Vestiges Of Stand Watie In Georgia Today

Back at Stand Watie's old home-site in

what today is northwest Georgia, there is no commemorative marker of any type at the birth-site of this amazing Cherokee. The only recognition of any type whatsoever is found in the form of The Sons Of Confederate Veterans, General Stand Watie Camp #915 in Calhoun, Georgia which honors his name. If one knows where to look, however, there are still vestiges of Watie's former existence in the area.[28]

The first site of interest undoubtedly would be the spot where Stand Watie was born in 1806. The actual location of this site, however, may be in question.

The *Calhoun Times and Gordon County News* reported on March 11, 1998, that "The site [the Bray farm] includes a historic home-place historians estimate was built around 1796 by Oo-Watie [David Watie], 'The Ancient One,' brother of Major Ridge. [David Watie's sons] Elias Boudinot and Stand Watie, a leading family of the Cherokee Nation, were both born on the site."[29]

Others claim the old home place at Bray Farm (also known as "Daffodil Farm"), was built by a Methodist minister, Bannister Bray in 1837. For example, Jewell B. Reeve in her book *Climb The Hills Of Gordon* writes, "There, near a grove of oak and cedar trees surrounding three springs, he built a house of logs covered with white clapboard and faced with a row of six majestic white columns."[30]

Regardless of the circumstances, a historic farmhouse is located on Land Lot 119, District 15, Section 3, about five miles south of downtown Calhoun, Georgia, in Gordon County. The farm on which this structure exists was purchased by Dr. J. Brent Box in the year 2000.

According to Dr. Box, he has investigated the claim that Stand Watie was born in the house on his property, but to date, no evidence has been found to confirm or deny this claim. Dr. Box, however, says he has researched the construction of the house, and has been informed that the current structure actually has an earlier log structure at its core, similar in style to that of the Cherokee dwellings of the early 19th century.[31]

Another historic house of interest is the large two-story home of Stand Watie's uncle – Major Ridge. This structure is well-preserved in Rome, Georgia, beside the Oostanaula River, approximately 30 miles south of New Echota.

"The Ridge," as he was called, reportedly migrated to the Oothcaloga Valley in what today is north Georgia as a young man. He was one of the first Cherokees to adopt the farming and herding methods of the white man. He acquired black slaves and established an efficient plantation.

As a National Historic Landmark, his former home presently houses the Chieftains Museum, an interesting repository of memorabilia and artifacts relating to the Cherokee Indian culture of the 18th and 19th centuries. At the core of this house – which has been renovated numerous times – is the original four-room "dog-trot style" log structure which was built by Ridge after 1794. In the museum is a small wall exhibit with a photograph and information about the life of Ridge's famous nephew, Stand Watie.[32]

If one knows where to look, however, there are still vestiges of Watie's former existence in the area.

The site of the home of Stand Watie's older brother – Elias Boudinot – is located at the northwest corner of the New Echota town square on the New Echota State Historic Site near Calhoun, Georgia. Boudinot served as the first editor of the *Cherokee Phoenix* newspaper, and a short distance from the printing shop where he published the paper, he built a two-story frame house in 1827.

It was at Boudinot's house that, on December 29, 1835, the *Treaty of New Echota* was signed by twenty Cherokees, including Major Ridge and Elias Boudinot. Stand Watie and John Ridge later signed the treaty in Washington City (D.C.) on March 1, 1836. Sadly, today, only corner stones and an abandoned well remain to mark this historic site.

The New Echota State Historic Site has a visitors center and a museum, and is open daily for a self-guided tour of the historic buildings and archaeological sites.[33]

According to James F. Smith in his book *The Cherokee Land Lottery*, Stand Watie's personal property as an adult was located in the 14th District, 3rd Section in present-day Gordon County, Georgia. Specifically, the property was located in and adjacent to the town of New Echota near the confluence of the Coosawattee and Connasauga rivers. Survey notes indicate that most of Watie's improvements (e.g. buildings, outbuildings and orchards) were located astride the convergence of Land Lots 92, 93, 124 and 125. In addition, some improvements were scattered along a line between Land Lots 93 and 94.

To date, the actual site upon which Stand Watie's home (during his adult years in the Southeast) once stood has not been located or identified. He may possibly have lived near his brother, Elias Boudinot, at New Echota. Land Lottery records indicate Stand Watie owned 95 additional acres of improved land in the Oothcaloga Valley as a part of Land Lot 156 in the 15th District and 3rd Section of present-day Gordon County, Georgia. This property might also possibly have been the site of his home in his adult years in the Southeast.

Land Lot 156 is located approximately six miles south of downtown Calhoun, Georgia. Oothcaloga Creek runs north through this tract of land which is just west of the present-day intersection of Hwy. 41 and Taylor Bridge Road about a mile north of the lower Gordon County line. On November 15, 1836, his improvements were appraised at $2,392 by the land lottery surveyors.[35]

Interestingly, Isabella Watie, Stand Watie's third wife, did not migrate with him to the West, and claimed separate improvements on Oothcaloga Creek. These improvements included 80 acres of improved land, buildings, and orchards for which she was paid $3,095. This property quite possibly was owned by Isabella's first husband – Eli Hicks – and willed to her following his death.[36]

As previously mentioned, the site at which Oothcaloga Mission Station once stood may be viewed today approximately three miles to the northeast of the Stand Watie property. The mission was located on Land Lot 209. The Ridge and Watie families attended church there from 1822 to 1833.

To visit the Oothcaloga Mission Station site, start at the intersection of present-day Highway 41 and Taylor Bridge Road. Proceed north on Highway 41 approximately 1.8 miles to Union Grove Road. Turn right and proceed eastward one mile to Belwood Road and turn left. Proceed north for approximately two-tenths of a mile to a site overgrown with trees and brush on the left side of the road.

The structures at historic Oothcaloga Mission Station no longer exist. Sadly, the two-story frame main building fell into ruin in recent years and has virtually disappeared.

At this same location, but on the opposite side of the road, is a dirt road. Approximately 100 yards up that road to the east is old Morrow Cemetery. John Gambold, the first Moravian missionary at Oothcaloga Mission Station in 1822, was buried in this cemetery in 1827. Gambold not only was a missionary, but also the only known Revolutionary War veteran buried in Gordon County.[37]

Vestiges Of Stand Watie In The West

In the former Indian Territory in the West, historic monuments, markers and national historical sites honor Stand Watie in present-day Oklahoma, Arkansas, Missouri and Texas.

The courageous Cherokee's grave may be visited in old Ridge Cemetery (later known as Polson Cemetery) in present-day Delaware County, Oklahoma. Outside the cemetery, a historical marker provides details of his life for travelers.

There are additional markers and monuments at Honey Creek, Old Fort Wayne, Park Hill, Cabin Creek and Doaksville. Three miles east of present-day Gore, Oklahoma, at the original capital of the Cherokee Nation in the West, there is an exhibit honoring the Watie, Boudinot and Ridge families at Tahlonteskee Museum. At Sequoyah's home in Sequoyah County, Oklahoma, there is an exhibit honoring Stand Watie and his cousin John Ridge.

At the Pea Ridge Civil War Battleground in Arkansas, there is an exhibit commemorating Stand Watie's participation in that famous battle.

ENDNOTES

1/ Kenny A. Franks, *Stand Watie and the Agony of the Cherokee Nation* (Memphis, TN: Memphis State University Press, 1979), 160-164.
2/ George Magruder Battey, Jr., *A History of Rome and Floyd County* (Atlanta, GA: Cherokee Publishing Company, 1979), 47.
3/ Don L. Shadburn, *Cherokee Planters In Georgia, 1832-1838* (Roswell, GA: W.H. Wolfe Associates, 1990) 25.
4/ Frank Cunningham, *General Stand Watie's Confederate Indians* (Norman, OK: University of Oklahoma Press, 1998), 2-4.
5/ Ibid, 4.
6/ Franks, *Stand Watie*, 2-3.
7/ Ibid, 3.
8/ Roger Aycock, "Stand Watie Strong Leader In Times Of War And Peace," Rome (Georgia) News-Tribune, 10 October 1971, 8-B.
9/ Franks, *Stand Watie*, 4.
10/ Battey, *A History Of Rome*, 27, 51.
11/ Ibid, 27.
12/ William G. McLoughlin, *Cherokees and Missionaries, 1788-1839* (New Haven, CN: Yale University Press, 1984), 146.
13/ Battey, *A History Of Rome*, 26-28; Franks, *Stand Watie*, 10-12; James F. Smith, *The Cherokee Land Lottery*, "Field Notes" (Atlanta, GA: Records of the Georgia Surveyor-General Department, nd), 256-263.
14/ Battey, *A History Of Rome*, 211-212; Cunningham, *Confederate Indians*, 16; Franks, *Stand Watie*, 8, 37, 9-41; Gary E. Moulton, ed., *The Papers Of Chief John Ross, Volume II, 1840-1866* (Norman, OK: University of Oklahoma Press, 1984), 738.
15/ Franks, *Stand Watie*, 2-3.
16/ Ibid, 13, 14-36.
17/ Franks, *Stand Watie*, 26-27; Shadburn, *Cherokee Planters*, 17-19.
18/ Franks, *Stand Watie*, 8.
19/ Battey, *A History Of Rome*, 89-90.
20/ Franks, *Stand Watie*, 96-97.
21/ Ibid, 114-118.
22/ Cunningham, *Confederate Indians*, 1-3.
23/ Franks, *Stand Watie*, 124-125.
24/ Ibid.
25/ Ibid.
26/ Ibid, 126-212 passim.
27/ Ibid, 159, 180-182, 208.
28/ The Sons of Confederate Veterans, General Stand Watie Camp #915 of Calhoun, GA.
29/ "Bray Farm To Hold Annual Open House," *The Calhoun Times and Gordon County News*, 11 March 1998.
30/ Gordon County Bicentennial Committee, *A Historical Tour of Gordon County Celebrating 1976, American's Bicentennial Year* (Calhoun, GA: Published by GCBC, 1976), 1-3; Jewell B. Reeve, *Climb The Hills Of Gordon* (Easley, SC: Southern Historical Press, 1979, c 1962), 218-225.
31/ Telephone conversation between Joe Griffith, the author, and Dr. J. Brent Box, the current owner of the Bray farm, 26 January 2002.
32/ Battey, *A History Of Rome*, 37, 50; Sesquicentennial Committee of the City of Rome, *Rome and Floyd County: An Illustrated History* (Charlotte, NC: The Delmar Company, 1986), 14-15; McLoughlin, *Cherokees and Missionaries*, 1788-1839, 85.
33/ New Echota State Historic Site, *New Echota Self-Guiding Trail Guide*, Calhoun, Georgia.
34/ Franks, *Stand Watie*, 10-12; Shadburn, *Cherokee Planters*, 34; Gary E. Moulton, ed., *The Papers Of Chief John Ross, Volume II, 1840-1866* (Norman, OK: University of Oklahoma Press, 1984), 738.
35/ Franks, *Stand Watie*, 39; Shadburn, *Cherokee Planters*, 34, 38.
36/ Franks, *Stand Watie*, 39-41; Shadburn, *Cherokee Planters*, 13, 34.
37/ Kenneth W. Boyd, *The Historical Markers of North Georgia* (Atlanta, GA: Cherokee Publishing Company, 1993), 84-87, 89-90; John M. Brown, ed., *Yesterdays 1830-1977* (Calhoun, GA: Gordon County Historical Society, Inc., 1977), 8.

The Tallulah Falls Disaster Of 1921

In the early 1900s, Tallulah Falls in northeast Georgia rivaled such attractions as Niagara Falls in popularity. In one fell stroke on a cold winter night in 1921, however, the entire town was virtually erased and its tourism industry destroyed – quite possibly forever.

"Oh my God! How could this have happened to us?" The thought raced through Cora Ledbetter's mind as she witnessed the devastation wrought by the terrible fire that burned the mountain community of Tallulah Falls to the ground in 1921. It was a devastating blow to the acclaimed resort – one from which it has never recovered.

Cora, interviewed for this article in the early 1990s, was a student at Tallulah Falls School at the time. During the night of the fire, she was at home in Toccoa. She saw what was left of the community the next afternoon. Perhaps unaware of it at the time, she unwittingly also witnessed the end of an era for the once-mighty falls.

It was a devastating blow to the acclaimed resort – one from which it has never recovered.

The Early Days

No description of the devastating fire of 1921 would be complete without an accounting of the four decades of immense development which had preceded the fire. Tallulah Falls had blossomed as a tourist mecca from 1882 – the year the Tallulah Falls Railroad first chugged into town – until 1921, the year of the fire. Though other factors were already negatively impacting the town's tourism economy by 1921 (such as the dams built on the Tallulah River by Georgia Power Company), the community of Tallulah Falls had continued to persevere because of its grand hotels which had beckoned invitingly from the mountainsides.

Tucked away in the northeast corner of the state, the popularity of Tallulah Falls had grown progressively, thanks to word-of-mouth publicity and writers such as David Hillhouse whose account of the falls was widely published in the United

States. Additionally, a new trail cut through the forested mountainsides of northern Habersham County, had gradually attracted increasing numbers of visitors curious about the phenomenal stories of a huge gorge and mighty falls emptying into the precipice.

Despite the lure of the site, many travelers found they needed a guide just to help them find their way to the falls, but still they came – in droves. According to researcher and educator Dr. John Saye in *his The Life And Times Of Tallulah . . . the Falls, the Gorge, the Town* (available in shops in Tallulah Falls*), "By 1840, visits to the falls by groups of men, women, and even children had become quite common."* By conservative estimates, nearly 2,000 visitors reportedly had journeyed to the falls in the remote corner of north Georgia by 1877.

Perhaps Tallulah Falls' resort era actually began in 1870 with the construction of the Shirley Hotel on the brow of the gorge. Just a year later, the hotel began expanding to handle the increasing numbers of visitors. With two more hotels built during the 1870s, the resort's popularity as a travel destination began in earnest.

Arrival Of The Railroad

The next decade witnessed the arrival of a convenience which brought "boomtimes" to the town of Tallulah Falls – the railroad. By the 1880s, travelers no longer were required to brave the rough trip to the falls via a mountain trail. The Tallulah Falls Railroad had been completed to the rim of the gorge, making the destination even more appealing.

Travelers came by train from Atlanta and Athens to Cornelia, Georgia, where they boarded the Tallulah Falls train. An hour and fifteen minutes later, they stepped off at Tallulah Falls.

A variety of hotels offered accommodations for travelers. Author John Saye describes it this way:

"At its peak, there were seventeen hotels and boarding houses in and around town. Guests could stay in a large, grand hotel, or in a small, intimate establishment. They could stay in the heart of the bustling little town, or in the peaceful forest surrounding Tallulah Falls."

Until 1904, the railroad ended at Tallulah Falls, and the area's tourist industry thrived. However, some seventeen years later in 1921, the lifeblood of the community literally went up in smoke.

A Fire In A Windstorm

"I have never seen nor heard the wind blow so hard as it did that night," said Bertha Burrell, a Tallulah Falls resident. "That wind carried burning bark and shingles as far away as Tugalo." Bertha had arrived home from Athens Normal School for the holidays and hadn't even unpacked.

Drucy Turpen remembered the fire all too well too. "We lived on a hill on the other side of town. I was sleeping in the front room. Granny Harvey lived just below us. She came up to the house hollering that the town was burning," Drucy said sadly, tears filling her eyes at the memory. "We stood on the porch and watched it. It was just awful. It even burned the railroad trestle and my daddy's store."

Valiant town residents and businessmen did what they could to save their community. Some rang dinner bells to awaken the sleeping citizens. Others fired shots from rifles and pistols.

"Most everybody lost everything," recalled a still-distraught Gussie Harvey. Her father lost a store and a car in the fire. The Maplewood Inn and the Robinson Annex and some dozen other hotels went up in flames – reduced to ashes in a matter of hours.

Photographed shortly after the tremendous fire at the town of Tallulah Falls in 1921, the devastation of the community is clearly visible. It is believed this photo was made from the porch of the Cliff House, which somehow miraculously escaped the holocaust. The Tallulah Falls Railroad trestle (left in photo) was also completely destroyed, but it had been rebuilt shortly before this photograph was made.

Terrible Devastation

The actual cause of the inferno is still a matter of conjecture today. Several differing accounts exist.

One story maintains that a man whose car had become stuck in the mud had stopped at a local garage for help. The garage was on the street level of a three-story building. The owner, who lived upstairs, reportedly told the chilled stranger to come back in the morning.

It was shortly after those remarks that the town went up in flames. Apparently angry at the lack of help, the stranger with the mired car is suspected of having torched the town.

"He broke into the garage to steal what tools he needed to repair his car," says Drucy Turpen. "He set fire to the garage to cover up the break-in."

Ironically, according to local sources, some years later, this same individual was himself consumed by flames when he mistakenly used gasoline instead of what he thought was kerosene to start a fire.

Regardless of the cause of the conflagration, the results were horrible by all accounts. A barn with livestock was consumed. "I remember the screaming, mooing, and braying of those poor animals," recalled Bertha Burrell. "It was terrible." Most of the animals perished. Some were more fortunate, breaking out of the barn and racing up Main Street.

"There was no fire department in those days, and certainly no water mains," Bertha

The Cliff House in Tallulah Falls was a popular summer resort for many years. It was located across the railroad tracks from the old Tallulah Falls Railroad Depot. Though it escaped the fire of 1921, it was destroyed itself by a fire in the 1930s.

Engine #77, a coal-burning steam engine, regularly transported travelers to the falls. This engine, and the automobile parked beside the depot, clearly date this photo as post-1921. The front corner of the Cliff House, one of the few structures to survive the 1921 fire, is visible at left.

added. "People had spring water for their own use, but little else. There was nothing to do but watch the town burn. We saved our house by putting bags of cottonseed meal on the roof."

Gussie Harvey recalled the destruction of the railroad. "About half of the trestle was burned, stopping passenger service to Clayton, Georgia and Franklin, North Carolina," she explained, still wide-eyed at the memory. "There was a freight train that came down from Franklin, so benches were put in some of the freight cars for passengers.

"I remember," continued Gussie, "my father went to town in his bare feet. He came back the next day with badly blistered feet. To try and save the store, he had poured Coca-Cola syrup on it, but the fire was just too hot for the syrup."

Gussie's sister remembered that the livestock ran up and down the street – many until they dropped dead from exhaustion. "Some of the animals were on fire," she said.

After The Fire

Little, if anything, was rebuilt after the fire. None of the hotels were reconstructed. Although the fire was a death blow to the town, other factors contributed to its ultimate demise.

The extension of the railroad to Clayton and Franklin, North Carolina, inevitably lured visitors deeper into the mountains, causing many of them to by-pass Tallulah Falls. "Many people had been coming here from South Georgia for health reasons," explains Jim Turpen, a local Methodist minister. "Once they realized they could go even further into the mountains, they did."

The construction of the massive dam

just above the falls and at other sites farther upriver also changed the town's character. The once-mighty falls were virtually extinguished, eliminating much of the original attraction and beauty of the site. The focus of leisure pursuits then shifted from the falls to fishing and lifestyles around the various lakes created behind the dams.

Cost was another reason for the town's demise. In those days, few people had insurance coverage on their homes and property, and the cost of rebuilding the hotels was prohibitive.

By the mid- to late-1930s, all of the grand hotels had completely disappeared from the brow of Tallulah Gorge. If the 1921 fire didn't get them, another fire or destructive element did.

By the 1950s, passenger service had been discontinued on the Tallulah Falls Railroad, further depleting service to the resort. And in 1961, the railroad itself ceased to exist – a victim of its own success. The transportation system which had made all of the original growth at the falls possible, had outlived its usefulness. It had made possible the construction of the dams which choked off the beautiful falls; it had transported the felled trees from the area until the logging industry expired; and it had brought in the building materials necessary for the construction of U.S. Highway 441. With the advent of the highway, trucking firms could then transport products and materials more economically and precisely than the railroad. Each year, the revenues from the Tallulah Falls Railroad became less and less until bankruptcy was inevitable.

By the mid- to late-1930s, all of the grand hotels had completely disappeared from the brow of Tallulah Gorge.

The Future

Today, despite its decline, Tallulah Falls still vies for a slice of the tourism pie dollars in Georgia. Travelers still want to view the beautiful gorge and the remnants of the scenic little town.

A new state park was established within Tallulah Gorge in the 1990s, to preserve as much of the gorge as possible for posterity. Area residents are hopeful the new park will facilitate new growth in the little town.

The community of fewer than two hundred residents still welcomes tens of thousands of visitors who pause to admire the gorge, and perhaps reminisce a bit about the glory days of the town of yesteryear.

The old Tallulah Falls Railroad depot, which somehow survived the firestorm of 1921, also escaped serious damage during a devastating tornado in the 1990s. It serves today as a crafts store, displaying the wares of local mountain craftspersons.

Tallulah Falls School still attracts students from throughout Georgia and other states for its excellent programs. The area also boasts a rehabilitation center and an adult education center.

However, unless the falls are freed once again to crash and roar unrestrained into the gorge, recreating the wonderland which caused Indians to anoint the site as a sacred place and tourists to flock to the falls by the trainload, it is highly unlikely that this scenic spot will ever again be the tourism destination it was prior to a terrible fire in the winter of 1921.

The 1909 Clermont Tornado

The violent storm struck suddenly and with a vengeance on a warm spring day early in the 20th century. It was an incident which affected many individuals in the small community of what today is Clermont in north Hall County. One former resident who lived there as a child remembers the fateful event.

Tornadoes – especially the large destructive ones – have fascinated mankind since the beginning of time. However, the number of individuals who have observed them up close and personal and survived the encounter is relatively small. Sylvia Gailey Head, 94 years of age as of this writing, of Athens, Georgia, has lived through two of them.

On April 29, 1909, a tornado with a path approximately one mile in width, swept across north Hall County and the site known today as Clermont, Georgia. Mrs. Head, who was only six years of age at the time, says she remembers the terrible event distinctly.

"Our home, built three or four years earlier (in 1905-06) was completely destroyed," she explained, "but the Whelchel home about one-quarter of a mile north survived. It still stands today, and is the home of Jane and Kermit Crumley. Following the tornado, the road between these two sites was blocked by uprooted trees. I remember how difficult it was for me to climb over the large trunks in our flight after the storm.

"Uncle Gilbert Barrett of White County was returning from Gainesville and reached our house just in time to hitch his horses to a tree across the road," Sylvia continued. "He took refuge with us (Mother and four little children; Father was at work) in Mother's flower pit.

The tornado picked up their six-year-old daughter, Vallie, and gently put her down in a field a short distance away.

"After the tornado had passed, Uncle Gibb quickly carried my younger siblings,

Birdie and Briton (Mother had baby James in her arms; I was on my own), to Mrs. Whelchel's home.

"I can still remember how the home of a neighbor about one mile south of us was destroyed in the twister," Sylvia added. "The Johnnie DeLongs lived there with three little children and his invalid mother. We learned later that when it became evident that the tornado was upon them, the grandmother said, 'Take the children and get in the ditch beside the road. I'll be all right.'"

The DeLongs reportedly did as their invalid grandmother directed. There wasn't enough time for them to return for her before the storm hit. When it was over, Sylvia says the entire house had disappeared – all except for the floor supporting their elderly grandmother's bed and a leaning wall beside it. According to an account of the incident, the aged lady was sitting up in her bed after the storm had passed, trying to smother sparks in the bed covers with her hands, seemingly oblivious to the fact the rest of the house had disappeared.

"There were two other houses between the DeLong house and ours that were also destroyed," Sylvia continued. "The families in these homes found shelter in ditches. The Jim Hulsey house nearly one-half mile south of our home was badly damaged. The tornado picked up their six-year-old daughter, Vallie, and gently put her down in a field a short distance away. It took her anguished family a while to find her.

"Not even the chimneys of our house were left standing and our barn across the road was flattened," Sylvia remembered, with a pained look on her face, "but Uncle Gibb's wagon between our house and the

James Z. Hudgins and son in the Hudgins general merchandise store in Clermont in 1930. This structure once stood on the town square.

The town square in Clermont, photographed in the early 1990s. This vicinity (foreground) was once occupied by the James Z. Hudgins store.

Students at Chattahoochee High School in Clermont pose for a photo in 1919. This facility, which was a center for education in northeast Georgia in the early 1900s, luckily was not in the direct path of the storm.

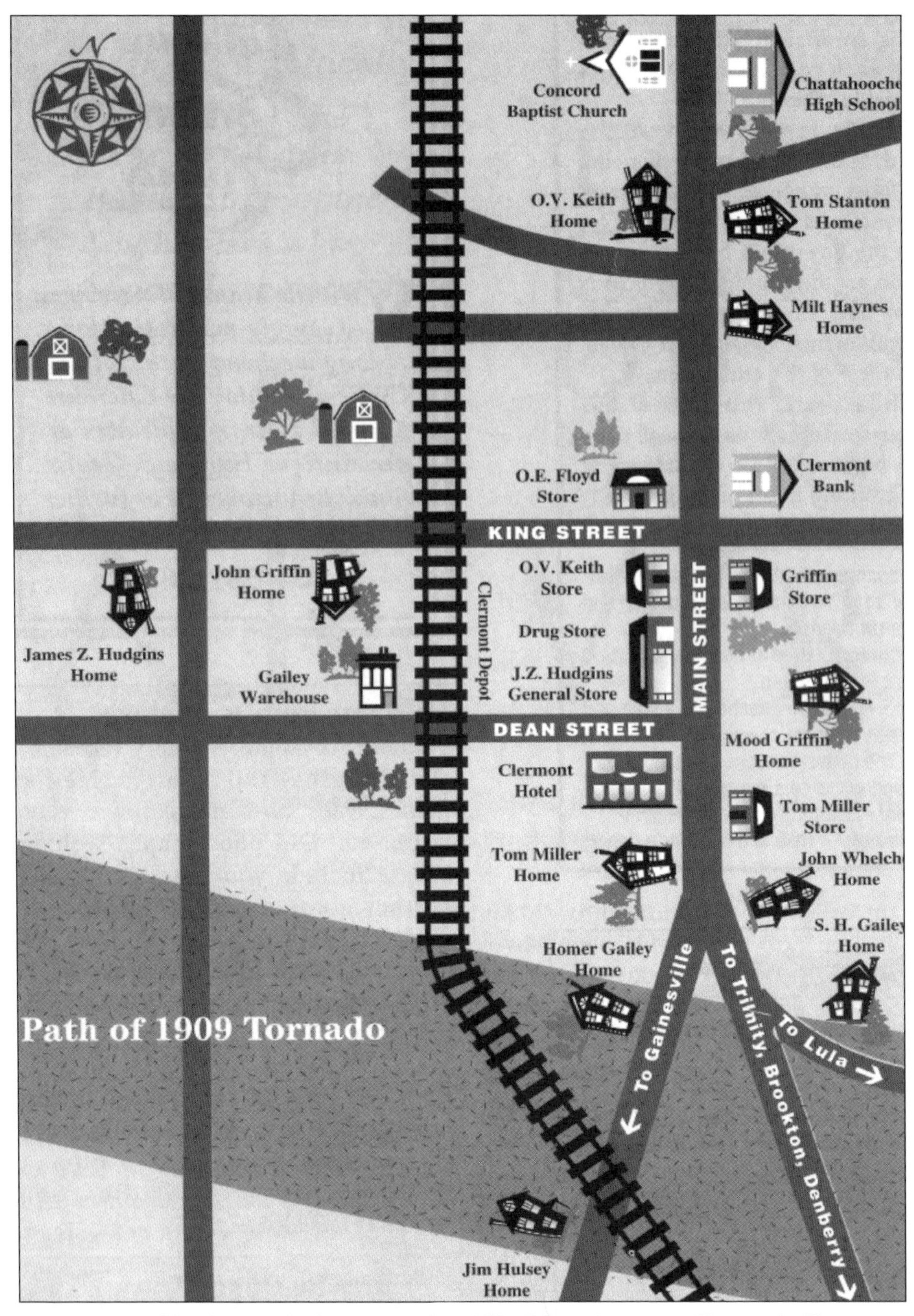

The homes and businesses in the community of "Dip" (later known as Clermont). The tornado destroyed a wide swath just south of what later was downtown Clermont. At least one person was killed.

barn still had the bowframe and sheet intact, and the tree holding the horses was still upright."

Sylvia says that none of her family's possessions were recovered except the headboard of a wooden bed with "Homer M. Gailey" (her father) written on the back, and a framed picture of Grandpa and Grandma Gailey with their dog, Betsy. The headboard was discovered approximately ten miles away.

"Other homes were lost too," Sylvia said, "but I can remember only one person that was killed. After reaching his storm shelter safely, the gentleman, Jake Faulkner, ran back into his house at the last moment to retrieve some money he had hidden there, and he was killed."

Sylvia says that despite the horror of the tornado, she has lots of good (and humorous) memories of the little community of Clermont too.

"There was never a theater of any kind in Clermont," she continued with a smile. "Everybody just depended on the school (Chattahoochee High) for entertainment, and it didn't let them down. There were plays and debates several times each year which ended with three days and nights of 'Commencement.' Everybody came in the morning bringing food for 'Dinner On The Ground,' and ate the leftovers for supper. Why get in the buggy or surrey to go home to eat when you were just going to turn right around and come back for the night program?

"Mr. T.C. 'Tom' Miller was one of Clermont's most colorful individuals," Sylvia smiled in remembrance. "He purchased the first automobile in town. After he had bought it, he realized he needed someone to drive and maintain it, so he hired an even more colorful individual – J.D. 'Shug' Matthews – from the Athens, Georgia area to keep it operating properly.

"Later on, when he went into business for himself, Shug bought a little truck from which he sold candy and chewing gum. The vehicle was emblazoned with his name, and also with the words 'Watch Me Grow!' on the side panel. (Mr. Matthews was never at a loss for words. . .)

"Shug eventually opened a little sporting goods store in a hole-in-the-wall shop in Gainesville," Sylvia continued. "He told me that when he sold anything, he would put the empty box back up on his shelves so that it would always appear that he had a full stock of goods. One day, while looking for an item for which he had a buyer, he discovered – to his shock – that all of his boxes were empty. Thunderstruck, he wandered out into the middle of the street, threw up his hands and yelled 'Bankrupt by God!'"

Undeterred, however, the one-time chauffeur built his business back up after a period of time, ultimately growing to a store one block deep with a sign outside which read, *"Ask For It. We Have It."* His colorful store offered everything from elephant harness to chocolates.

"Thunderstruck, he wandered out into the middle of the street, threw up his hands and yelled 'Bankrupt by God!' "

The Terrible Gainesville Tornado Of 1936

Sylvia Gailey Head is a writer and historian who currently lives in Athens, Georgia. As of this writing, she is among a rapidly-diminishing number of people who experienced the disastrous tornadoes on the morning of April 6, 1936, that destroyed downtown Gainesville, Georgia.

The spring and early summer months in Georgia are some of the most dangerous for the state, weather-wise. Strong weather fronts move across the state, many times spawning violent killer tornadoes, such as the one which struck Gainesville, Georgia, in the spring of 1936.

As of this writing, Sylvia Gailey Head is 96 years of age, but she clearly remembers the incidents surrounding this incredible event which completely destroyed the downtown area of Gainesville that fateful day. The horrible freak of nature descended upon the community shortly after 8:00 a.m. on April 6 of 1936. By the time it had expended its fury, some 200 individuals are believed to have been killed (the exact number is unknown today). The National Weather Service still officially lists the death toll at 203, with 950 identified as injured.

Ominous Foreboding

In 1936, a Sylvia Gailey Head, recently widowed, was living in an apartment in the home of the Wallace family a few blocks up Green Street in Gainesville. "That Monday morning, (as) I came out the front door (I remember saying) to the maid sweeping the porch, 'A tornado is coming,'" she said.

"I felt I was speaking from experience," Mrs. Head explained, "because that was my second such storm. The first one (had) razed our home (in Clermont in 1909). Although I was only six years old at the time, the stillness of that day (had) remained in my subconscious mind . . . As I walked to work (in Gainesville), I watched the clouds and felt they were the same as those on the day of the tornado in 1909."

Mrs. Head said she walked a block out of her way to ask her cousin and good friend, John Rogers of Pruitt-Barrett Hardware, to go with her into the open countryside outside town, so that they might be able to see the tornado coming and be able to find a suitable ditch in which to hide. At the last minute, she said she decided against asking him, but did stop to discuss the possibility of a place of refuge in the city – ruling out the manholes in the street.

Explaining that the Wallace family was out of town and that she would be alone, Sylvia apparently made clear her fears involving the coming storm. "I will check on you tonight," she said Rogers reassured her. A few big rain drops began falling suddenly, and Sylvia says she then scurried on to work.

"Realizing I had not replied to his offer, I turned from across the street and said to him – still standing in the door – 'Do.'" That simple word was the last one Sylvia ever spoke to John Rogers. In a matter of minutes, he was dead.

Sylvia said she walked on to her place of employment at J.D. Matthews where she was a bookkeeper. "A man working near the door at J.D. Matthews laughed when I told him, 'A tornado is coming,'" Sylvia smiled in remembrance.

"I (remember removing) my rain coat and (had hardly) reached the office in the back of the store, when I put it back on again (so that I could go back outside to watch for the storm). A man working there (outside the back door) grinned when he asked, 'Are you going somewhere?' Hearing the roar of the tornado at that point, I ran the length of the store on my way back to Pruitt-Barretts.

Terrible Destruction

"Out in the street, debris was swirling about me," Sylvia recalled with fear. "(I remember) someone calling out 'Get back inside!' I did, but we could not close the doors. (Later) some people said that both doors being open saved the building. Others thought it was protected by the stone wall of the building next door. Sylvia, however, maintains that she thinks a "higher order" was responsible for the path of the

Devastation caused by the Gainesville Tornado of 1936.

The Gainesville town square as it appeared shortly after the tornado had passed. Notice how the tops of many of the automobiles had been ripped off.

The train yard of the Gainesville-Midland Railroad is pictured above. The old depot in the background somehow weathered the storm and still stands as of this writing in downtown Gainesville. Railroad boxcars (foreground) were tossed about like toys.

An aerial view of the devastation. Notice how many of the major buildings in the downtown area were totally destroyed.

Pruitt-Barrett Hardware Company and the C.V. Nalley Company were both devastated by the tornado and the fires that raged afterwards. It was in Pruitt-Barrett Hardware that Gainesville resident John Rogers lost his life.

More than 100 workers lost their lives in the Cooper Manufacturing Company building.

twister which missed the store by a scant six inches.

"When the tornado hit, I put my arms around a sobbing girl who I thought was Miss Mickey Matthews, until she said, 'Oh, my poor children.' In a moment, I saw that it was Agnes Palmour Wade who was married. That just goes to show how intensely dark it was as the tornado struck. It was like darkness.

An official weather bureau map from 1936, shows the terrible storm as a "triplet" (three tornadoes). The first of the gigantic twisters reportedly came in from the west, striking Brenau College a short distance from the town square at 8:27 a.m., before moving on to the mill community of New Holland where more destruction occurred. No deaths were recorded from this tornado. Meanwhile, two other more deadly funnels were approaching the city – one from the west along the Dawsonville Highway (GA 53) and the other from the southwest along the Atlanta Highway.

Mrs. Head says the tornadoes were over in moments, but she was aghast at the devastation they left behind. "I ran to the door, jumping over a man rising from the floor. I saw at once that the two-story building so recently Pruitt-Barrett Hardware Company was a mass of rubble with smoke rising from it. On my way there, I saw that the three buildings south of us were also piles of brick. I thought immediately 'Oma Rogers (who worked at Frierson-McEver store) is dead.' When I met her a few days later, I was sure I was seeing things."

Struggle For Survival

This was just a small fraction of the destruction wrought by the tornadoes. "A heap of bricks blocked the Pruitt-Barrett

Bradford Street entrance," Sylvia related, still disturbed by many of the memories. "I could see an iron safe holding back a pile of rubble which had a man's hand sticking through some plow handles. When I called out, the man begged 'Please help me.' A fire had already started and I told him I would get help."

Nearby, Sylvia says a man was digging in the rubble that had been Wrights Ice Cream Company. "I screamed 'There's a fire here and I need help,' but the man just dug on. I grabbed at another man running past me, but he ran on. I then saw Ed Roper of the Gainesville Bank standing in front of that building. I ran across the street and asked him for help too. He just stood there, like the monument of the Confederate soldier facing him. I later heard that he said it never happened."

Returning to the spot where the man was buried beneath the bricks, Sylvia said she noticed for the first time that there was a man sitting in a car at the curb. "I opened the door and pulled him out. It was then that I saw the trapped man climbing out of the bricks. He said, 'They are all in there.'"

According to a description of the events unfolding, Sylvia ran north along Bradford Street to Citizen's Bank on the next corner where John Roger's father worked as a vice-president. That building was still intact and some men were inside. "(As I was) telling them about the fire from which only one man had escaped, one fellow asked me to describe the fellow. I said 'red hair and wore glasses.' The man was laughing and crying at the same time when he said, 'That's my brother.' Later, I learned that his name was Harold Head."

W. M. Brice was the Gainesville correspondent for The *Atlanta Constitution* and the *Associated Press* at the time of the tornadoes. According to his book, *A City Laid Waste,* there were many freaks of violence caused by the tornadoes. *"One of the most striking examples of the power of this storm was exhibited in the destruction of the courthouse,"* Brice wrote. *"The one-ton bronze bell in the courthouse tower which had spoken in deep, mellow tones for the past fifty-three years was carried through the air, across South Green Street, across East Spring Street, and deposited against a corner of the home of Mrs. Nell M. Pope, more than three hundred yards from the spot where it had been hung."*

The disaster had such an impact, that it even prompted a stop-over by U.S. President Franklin D. Roosevelt three days later on April 9. Roosevelt spoke from a platform at the rear of the train, extending his condolences to the many Gainesville residents who had lost family and friends in the storm, and promising every available element of federal support.

Otto F. Bading, of Atlanta, visited Gainesville on Thursday, following the tornadoes. He had also been in San Francisco, California, at the time of the killer earthquake there, and reported that the Gainesville tornadoes were more destructive than even the killer quake, but that the quake, coupled with the fires (which came after the quake) cumulatively caused more total damage.

The disaster had such an impact, that it even prompted a stop-over by U.S. President Franklin D. Roosevelt.

Relief Workers

Sylvia Gailey Head says she went home after stopping at Citizen's Bank. "While I was home, the C.C.C. (Civilian Conservation Corps) parked their trucks to walk to the ruins," she continued. "The C.C.C. never stopped in their rescue efforts. At some point, I told Ranger Woody (who led many of the men) *(Readers please see "The Life And Times Of Ranger Arthur Woody," A North Georgia Journal Of History, Volume II)* that the place where I ate lunch had nothing to cook on and he sent them a wood-burning range.

Later that night, Sylvia says she and other grieving friends were at the home of John Rogers's parents – Ruth and Dr. Lee Rogers. "During the night, Ruth said 'I can't take any more. Let's get out for awhile.'

In walking past the First Methodist Church, we saw much activity and walked in to find it was the Red Cross headquarters. A woman manning a telephone asked me to relieve her for a moment. I did, and she never returned.

Most of the telephone calls came from people seeking information about loved ones. (In one report), a woman had heard the same name as her brother's who had fought in World War I and had never been heard from again. She wanted to know if this could be he.

"I took names and phone numbers, promising to investigate and call back. In the morning, I turned over my notes to a Red Cross official, who asked if I could type. He gave me a list of the dead and injured, saying, 'Show it to no one.' I was there days and into the nights, pulling manilla folders, cutting my cuticles until I learned to protect them with tape. Once, the director asked me to come to his desk and get on the payroll. I never got there, but he later informed me that I was an employee. That was their way of preventing volunteers from walking out when they could take no more.

"In about three weeks, the W.P.A. (Works Progress Administration) completed a rough building on Maple Street to house the Red Cross. It resembled a warehouse with very little partitioning."

In this new building, Mrs. Head says she became secretary to the case workers, typing and filing their findings. "Before they had finished, I was moved to the bookkeeping department where I remained until the Red Cross left Gainesville," she added. "At the end, there were four of us – the Red Cross official, Jim Downey Brewer (a college student), and a girl about my age whose name I have forgotten. We still worked into the nights. One night, my coworker put her head on the desk and cried. I told the boss that if he didn't want to lose her he had better take her home for some rest. He took both of us home.

Today, the terrible disaster in Gainesville is little more than a footnote in history to most of the residents.

Tears For Fears

"I remember crying only once during all of this. Marie Ward, R.N., told of a make-shift hospital where patients were put on blankets on the floor. On one pallet were two little girls. Ms. Ward explained how one of the little girls said, 'That's my sister, but she's asleep.' (Ms. Ward told me it was at that point that she realized) the little girl was dead. We both cried."

Even months after the tragic event, Sylvia said other events associated with the tornadoes occurred. "Before a year had passed, I was subpoenaed to appear in court," she added. "The insurance companies did not want to pay for damages from the fires caused by the tornadoes where there was no tornado insurance. This (fires caused by the tornadoes), however, was the situation in most, if not all, of the Gainesville losses. The fine line was: 'Which came first? The falling of the walls, or the beginning of the fires?' It ultimately was decided that one case would be tried and that case would be used to govern all the others. The one case selected (ironically) was Pruitt-Barrett Hardware Company. I panicked. I had never (even) seen a court trial. Being (selected as) a witness was terrifying to me.

"(My father, however, reassured me.) He told me just to answer the questions of the lawyers without volunteering anything. He came to court as a spectator and said he thought they would never get anything out of me. Congressman Frank Whelchel said that I was a good witness, which was somewhat calming for the re-trials – one in a higher court in Atlanta. The final verdict was in favor of the plaintiff(s) – the businesses of Gainesville."

Today, the terrible disaster in Gainesville is little more than a footnote in history to most of the residents. The few who remember it, however, look to the west with fear and trepidation each time the weather fronts of spring and early summer begin moving across the state.

Resolute against the maelstrom, the Confederate soldier monument on the Gainesville town square escaped with little damage.

Stunned residents survey the damage along West Spring Street in Gainesville.

The Capture & Last Days Of Old West Bandit Bill Miner

One of the most notorious bandits of the Old West robbed his last train near Gainesville in 1911. He turned out to be one of the more colorful villains ever captured in Georgia.

For generations of Americans, the exciting sagas of train robberies in the old West have fueled the imaginations of young and old alike. Despite the violence of their circumstances, these events almost invariably were added to the pantheon of American folklore, and often became the romantic subject of song, story, and motion pictures.

For this reason, the circumstances surrounding the events of February 18, 1911, in Gainesville, Georgia, are considered even more incredible. Here, in a rarely disturbed little backroads community in the foothills of the north Georgia mountains, one of the most notorious outlaws of all time committed his last robbery.

Born George Anderson in Jackson County, Kentucky, in 1843, Bill Miner used a variety of names to get through life: George Morgan, California Billy, George Edwards, George Bud, and Louis Colquhoun, to name a few. He was the son of a schoolteacher mother and fly-by-night father who abandoned his family before the boy was 10 years old. Young George quickly earned a reputation as a dare-devil and an irresponsible youth, traits by which he would live for the rest of his life.

Shortly before the U.S. Civil War, George left home for the gold fields of California where he landed a job as a pony express rider. He apparently decided early in life, that an honest job just wasn't the method he wanted to use to make a living. He soon began robbing stagecoaches, igniting the life of crime from which he never wavered.

The nation watched in interest, as young Billy the Kid, Jesse James, Black Bart, Cole Younger, the Daltons and the other notorious outlaws of the old West rose to prominence and then faded into the mists of time. George, who gradually had become infamous under the name Bill Miner, was cut from the same mold and is considered by many modern-day historians to have been even more notorious than his counterparts. He was one of the last surviving members of this fraternity, and was still robbing trains well into the 20th century.

Early on a cold February morning of 1911, he held up Southern Railway's Train No. 36 near the White Sulphur station north of Gainesville. Because of his advancing years, Miner may have known that he was nearing his last days of crime, as this final episode of his life of theft began unfolding.

According to reports, at approximately 3:15 a.m. on the appointed morning, engineer David J. Fant of Atlanta might have cursed had he not been known as a railroad evangelist. Southern Railway No. 36 was already late when he took it out of Atlanta at 12:15 that morning. On this, of all mornings, Fant had H.E. Hudgens, general superintendent of the railroad on board in a private car at the rear, and now someone was flagging down the train, further delaying things.

As Fant peered through the darkness and rain of the early morning, someone was waving a red lantern. The engineer knew he had to stop. He assumed a lineman or a farmer had discovered a broken rail and was trying to save the train from wrecking.

As the train stopped, Fant slid down from the engine and asked if the track was being fixed. Out of the darkness, two other men suddenly appeared, brandishing revolvers. They announced the obvious. Southern Railway No. 36 was being robbed!

The three bandits, wearing masks and calling each other "captain," "number four" and "number five," ordered Fant's black fireman Rufus Johnson to "disappear." While the bandit with the lantern watched Fant, the other two robbers walked down to the express car with the intention of releasing the portion of the train from there rearward, so that the robbery could be completed without having to contend with a lot of panicky, confused passengers.

Shortly thereafter, flagman C.H. Shirley and conductor Walter T. Mooney, both of Atlanta, began walking up to the engine to find out what was happening. Seeing the man with the lantern, Mooney called out but received no response from the suspicious-looking man. The conductor later recalled that he "assumed he was dealing with a block-head," and he grabbed the man's arm and gave him a shove, demanding to know why the train had been stopped.

The man replied by sticking a revolver in Mooney's face and announcing the holdup. Thinking this was all just a bad joke, the conductor exclaimed "Cut out this foolishness! I've got to look after my train!" Only then when the masked man responded with a string of obscenities, did Mooney realize the full implication of the situation, and that he had come very close to losing his life.

Once out of the bandit's view, the conductor told Shirley to try to slip past the rear of the train and get help. The flagman did just that, running to White Sulphur Station, a small railway depot about a mile away.

Meanwhile, Walter B. Miller, in the express car, had learned of the robbery and was desperately trying to lock all of the doors to thwart the bandits' efforts. Despite his best attempts, the men entered through a door he had overlooked, and demanded the keys to the two safes. Luckily, the keys apparently were not kept on the train.

Disappointed but undeterred, Miner brought Fant and a shovel from the engine. With dirt from the outside, the bandits packed dynamite under the safes, lit the fuses, and fled the car. The resulting explosion tore holes through the roof and sides of the car, shattered the windows, and even put out the train's lights. When the smoke had cleared, only the smaller of the two safes was open.

The man replied by sticking a revolver in Mooney's face and announcing the holdup.

With time running out, "the captain" filled a bag with the loot, and then he and his two accomplices

Just as he was described by countless lawmen and victims alike, George Anderson, alias Bill Miner, never looked the part of an outlaw. He often appeared to be more of an elderly gentleman than the notorious bandit who robbed stagecoaches and trains from California to Georgia. This photo is believed to have been taken in Canada where Miner was captured following one of his many robberies. He subsequently escaped from the prison in which he was incarcerated, solidifying his nickname, "The Grey Fox." (Photo courtesy of Heritage House Publishing Company and Art Downs)

ran into the woods "disappearing as if the earth had swallowed them up," according to a subsequent newspaper report.

Fant started up his train and took it to the nearby community of Lula where he telegraphed a report of the robbery. Ten minutes prior to Fant's report, Shirley had reached the White Sulphur Station, where he hurriedly reported the news of the robbery to local authorities.

As could be expected under the circumstances, initial reports of the robbery became twisted and distorted as the news was passed from person to person. Two mythical additional bandits were included in early reports as having been passengers on the train. The gang's escape was described in various accounts as involving an automobile, a buggy, and even as involving a ride hitched on the underside of the very train they had robbed.

No complete account of the items/money stolen was ever made, but at the very least, $800 in U.S. currency, $770 in Mexican money, an unknown amount in several foreign currencies, a number of legal papers of no value to the robbers, a pair of pearl ear screws, and a watch were taken. Left behind in the safe that they had failed to blow open was $65,000 in gold and cash – an amount which would have been considered a fortune to many people in 1911.

Miner recruited his two accomplices for the Gainesville robbery – Charlie Hunter and James Handford – in Pennsylvania and Virginia respectively, in 1910. Hunter, a thirty-year-old Irishman from Michigan agreed, after some persuasion, to accompany the old bandit to a locale in the South, "to try holding up a Southern train." The pair worked for two months in a Virginia sawmill where they completed their group by recruiting thirty-three-year-old Handford from Nebraska.

The trio moved on to Georgia to prepare for what was almost unthinkable – a Wild West-style train holdup in the East. The week before they finally struck Southern Railway No. 36, Hunter pawned Miner's watch in Atlanta, using the money to buy whiskey and a lantern later used in the robbery. A track wrench later found at their camp indicated that they had considered derailing and wrecking the train.

The first reports of the incident were met with incredulity by a disbelieving Gainesville populace. According to newspaper accounts of that day, most of the townspeople dismissed the news of the robbery, thinking it was a joke. Most were dumbfounded when they learned the truth.

"The truth dawned at last," the newspaper said, "and they were confronted with the fact that here in a free, civilized, God-fearing, and law-abiding community, a train robbery was committed that would abash the most God-forsaken Wild West country to be found. That such a daring hold-up could take place right at our doors was inconceivable."

The Atlanta newspapers had a field day with the event. The *Atlanta Journal* filled the first two pages of the February 18 issue with the news. The train crew, all of whom were Atlanta residents, were interviewed and their photographs published.

When the report of the robbery reached the Hall County Police Office in the early morning hours of February 18, Sheriff W.A. Crow was at home sick with the mumps. He arose from his sick bed to organize a posse by telephone.

Assembling his deputies, Crow gave them a pep talk: "I want you to go out into the country and mountains now, and don't come back here until you bag these train robbers," he instructed. "Bring them back alive if you can . . . But if not, just bring them along anyway."

These initial efforts in locating the bandits proved futile. Deputy Sheriff Little, with the help of county officials and railroad detectives, began a search of Gainesville, to see if the robbers might have been in town all along.

The posse sent to the robbery site was delayed, waiting for the bloodhounds to be brought from Gwinnett County. By the time the dogs arrived, the rain and pepper and snuff reportedly scattered by Miner and his two accomplices had obscured the trail.

To Sheriff Crow's posse were added the Pinkertons, a deputy U.S. marshal, and detectives of the Southern Railway and

TAKING ON SUPPLIES – This primitive print shows the Merritt M. London homeplace which once stood near the intersection of Long Branch Road and Highway 60 in Lumpkin County. While fleeing lawmen in February of 1911, notorious outlaw Bill Miner reportedly stopped at the country store adjacent to this home to take on provisions. Pictured in this photo are: Merritt M. London (with white beard and hat in center of photo). His wife, Mary Neisler London stands beside the tree in the front yard. Sons Frank (in the wagon) and Bob (2nd from left) also appear. The identity of the individual in the overalls is unknown. (Photo courtesy of Annie Lou Dobbs of Toccoa, GA, daughter of Frank and Annie Kemp London)

The historic Merritt M. London homeplace at the intersection of Long Branch Road and Highway 60, was photographed in 1993, a few years prior to its unfortunate demolition. (Photo by Anne Dismukes Amerson)

Officials managing the manhunt for Bill Miner used the main room of the old Dixie Hunt Hotel (above, photographed circa 1900) as a headquarters. This structure, a portion of which still exists today on the square in Gainesville, was built in 1882 on the corner of Main and Spring streets. (Photo courtesy of Hall County Library)

Old Lumpkin County Jail – in which bandit Bill Miner was incarcerated – as it appears today. (Photo by Olin Jackson)

Express. All local law enforcement officials also went into the field, using the promise of a $1,500 reward (almost more than the bandits actually took) offered by the State of Georgia and the Southern Railway, to enlist men and boys for their posse. Despite all these efforts, the ultimate capture of the train robbers was accomplished, as the editor of the 1911 *Dahlonega Nugget* explained, "by mountaineers skilled in tracking."

Only a few days after the robbery, the search efforts were losing steam. Officials conducting the man-hunt were sitting around the main room of the old Dixie Hunt Hotel – their headquarters in Gainesville – so despondent, that they hardly noticed when the telephone began ringing. When one of the lawmen finally picked up the receiver, the caller turned out to be ex-Lumpkin County Sheriff Jim Davis calling from Dahlonega to announce that he believed he had found the train robbers in an abandoned house nearby.

Davis had learned of the men earlier, and both he and Lumpkin County Sheriff John Sergeant began having doubts about them. They claimed to be prospectors and had overnighted at Sergeant's Hotel in Dahlonega. However, between them, the three strangers had no prospecting tools other than one broken and split shovel.

When Lumpkin County resident Pete Carmichael reported the three men near his farm, Sergeant became even more suspicious. He set out for the Carmichael place where he picked up two sets of tracks. The bandits apparently had split up at this point, and Sergeant decided to follow the single set of tracks. He assembled a posse which included the aforementioned Jim Davis and Davis' two sons – Rufus and Joe.

At length, the trail led the group to the Elbert Kendall farm some 17 miles northwest of Dahlonega in the present-day Nimblewill community. The Kendalls reported that they did have a male boarder who was sleeping on a cot upstairs in a loft.

Davis and his sons reportedly mounted the stairs where they found a person who appeared to be asleep. As Davis pulled the blanket away, the stranger aimed a .45 revolver at him. Davis' salvation was found in his two sons who had a shotgun and a .22 rifle directed at the old man who in fact turned out to be George Anderson, alias Bill Miner.

Rufus Davis was still alive in 1987, and lived in Cartersville, Georgia. Though in his nineties at the time, Rufus still remembered details of this day. He also still possessed the set of handcuffs used to restrain Miner after his capture.

Jim Davis eventually collected the reward offered for the capture of the train robbers (Miner's accomplices in the robbery had been arrested earlier in the day prior to Miner's arrest.) Sheriff Sergeant unsuccessfully sued Davis for part of the reward, claiming the last capture was really his work.

Despite all the clamor of the event, the detectives, sheriffs, and other officials in the manhunt still had no idea who they had captured even after Miner was clapped in chains. The old bandit identified himself by his real name – George Anderson – and all the official Georgia police and criminal records relating to him identified him by that name. It was probably the first time in many years that he had used his actual name for identification purposes. Interestingly, when the name by which he was commonly known – "Bill Miner" – was learned by the authorities, it was assumed that that was his actual name, and that the moniker "George Anderson" was an alias.

While waiting in the Lumpkin County jail, Anderson (alias Bill Miner) talked of the great potential of Dahlonega's inactive gold mines in such a way that the *Dahlonega Nugget* published his remarks as if he were a prominent geologist, stroking local civic pride. It is ironic to note that Miner began his life of crime at the site of the second great gold rush in California and ended it at the site of the first U.S. gold rush in Dahlonega, Georgia. And even as he was captured, he was preaching the merits of the gold mining industry.

After his capture in Dahlonega, Miner was transported to Gainesville for trial. His arrival by automobile in Gainesville was greeted by crowds of hundreds of people, gathered as if to see a street parade, and caused Miner to remark "They must think I am a bear."

A special session of the Hall County Superior Court was held on March 3, 1911,

White Sulphur Road at the old Southern Railway intersection in Hall County was photographed above in 1987. In 1911, Southern Railway's White Sulphur Depot stood in the vicinity of the warning signal pictured here, and it was to this point that flagman C.H. Shirley ran to report the robbery of Train #36. (Photo by Olin Jackson)

HISTORIC CROSSING – The late Ray Shaw of Gainesville was an employee of the U.S. Postal Service in Hall County for many years, and as such, was intimately familiar with the history and terrain of the area. He was photographed above in 1987, at the spot at which Southern Railway's Train #36 was robbed by old West outlaw Bill Miner and his accomplices near White Sulphur, Georgia, on a cold February morning in 1911. (Photo by Olin Jackson)

Photographed in front of the old Lumpkin County Jail (which still stands today in Dahlonega), are: (left to right) Sheriff James M. "Jim" Davis, Gordon Davis, Joe Davis, William S. "Bill" Davis, Charles C. Davis, and Rufus Tilman "R.T." Davis. Bill Miner was captured by Sheriff John Sergeant, Jim Davis, and Davis' two sons - Rufus and Joe. Following his capture, Miner was incarcerated in this jail. (Photo courtesy of C.C. Davis, Jr.)

to try the train robbers. Charlie Hunter confessed his role in the robbery, and became the state's chief witness against Miner. Hunter received a sentence of fifteen years, but escaped within a year, and surprisingly, no effort was made to recapture him. James Handford also pleaded guilty, received the same sentence, and was granted a parole in 1918.

Miner however, insisted upon a trial. He sat impassively as the state paraded witness after witness before him. Miner's almost flawlessly polite manners, some observers believed, would carry weight with the jury, but in fact, the Hall Countians quickly returned with a verdict of "Guilty." Miner's only show of emotion came when Howard Thompson, special attorney for the express company, spoke of the dynamite used in the express car potentially "blowing into eternity sleeping women and children on the train." A reporter witnessed Miner answered that charge "with a most vengeful, glaring, and hateful glance."

When Judge Sims sentenced Miner to twenty years in prison, the old gentleman bandit reportedly thanked him, stood up and turned to a group of college girls and ladies and proceeded to provide a moral for the story they had witnessed unfolding before them:

"When one breaks the law, one must expect to pay the penalty. I am old, but during all my life, I have found the golden rule the best guide to man in this world," he said. He then smiled and sat down.

Though one of the most cold-blooded and notorious thugs in the colorful history of train robberies in the U.S., Miner is routinely described as "looking less like a criminal than almost any man one might imagine." Yet, this kindly-looking old man reportedly methodically shot virtually all of a group of possemen pursuing him from the scene of a stagecoach robbery in 1881 in California, and was identified as associated with numerous other crimes throughout his life.

Though this final event in Georgia ended forever Miner's stagecoach/train robbing days, it did not bring to a close the ability of the Grey Fox as he was called, to galvanize public attention. Above and beyond his notoriety as a train robber, Miner was also a legend as an escape artist. He had escaped from prisons in Canada and elsewhere and often boasted that no prison could hold him indefinitely.

William Pinkerton, head of the well-known detective agency of the same name, was a spectator at the trial, and warned the press that he doubted that any Georgia prison could hold the old man. His comments proved prophetic. Miner escaped not once, but twice from prison in Milledgeville, Georgia after his incarceration there. Had it not been for his aging condition and lack of resistance to exposure and the elements after his escapes, he might not have been recaptured.

Following the trial in Gainesville, the convicted trio was sent to Georgia's huge prison camp in Newton County. Life in the camp did not suit Miner, however. A personal appeal to Robert E. Davison, then chairman of the State Prison Board, finally earned him a transfer to the state prison farm for the infirm in Milledgeville.

Above and beyond his notoriety as a train robber, Miner was also a legend as an escape artist.

While at the farm, Miner recruited the services of convicted murderers John B. Watts and Tom H. Moore for an escape. Late one night, Watts somehow managed to remove the peep-hole apparatus out of the door of his cell, and squeeze through the opening. He took the keys and a pistol from a sleeping guard, and released Miner and Moore. The trio made a clean getaway.

Following his escape, Miner was brazen enough to mail a letter to Robert Davison, thanking him for giving him his opportunity for escape. "My dear sir," he wrote, "I want to thank you for your kindness in putting me at Milledgeville. My dear sir, don't trust a prisoner, don't matter how sick he is or makes out he is. Yours truly, B. Miner"

The chairman's embarrassment was also the embarrassment of the state of Georgia and the newspapers and citizens who had urged that the "sick old man be allowed to die in peace" at the lightly-guarded prison farm. The *Atlanta Journal* proclaimed that "wherever Bill Miner is, he is probably grinning and the joke is on Georgia."

It wasn't long however, before Miner was recaptured. He and Moore had headed for Augusta, Georgia. At a tiny community nearby called Keysville, a J.W. Whittle overheard a brakeman talking to two "bums" in a boxcar. When it was realized that the two matched a description of two escaped convicts, Whittle summoned help.

The boxcar was surrounded shortly thereafter by a posse, and Miner recaptured. Moore, however, chose not to return – at least not alive. He reportedly fired a single shot in the vicinity of the posse, and then in turn was killed by a single shot to the face. Inside the boxcar, members of the posse found dynamite and fuses which Miner explained "were good for catching fish." Old Bill had been a breath away from another train robbery.

Returned to his prison cell in Milledgeville, Miner boasted that he would escape again at the first opportunity. His guards, understandably, took no chances against any future embarrassment. One can only imagine their total humiliation, when on the morning of June 27, 1912, they found the Grey Fox gone again, his ankle and arm bracelets locked to his bunk, the window bars sawed out, and the bedding made into a rope which he had used to climb to the ground. It was literally the stuff from which legends are made.

Accompanied by convicts W.J. Windencamp and W.M. Wiggins, Miner was loose once again. The trio took a boat into the Oconee River this time, with the plan of reaching a port where they could ship out as deck hands. The boat capsized however, drowning Windencamp.

For three days afterwards, Miner and Wiggins were lost in a swamp near Oconee, Georgia, living on blackberries and unable to find safe drinking water. When they finally came out near Toombsboro, they offered no resistance to a posse which found them at a home begging for breakfast. Miner's escape this time had lasted only five days.

The reception the old outlaw received upon his return to Milledgeville this time even exceeded Bill's wildest imaginings. Driven in an open, heavily-guarded automobile and shackled securely, Bill was met in the downtown area by an extremely large crowd of admiring townspeople who reportedly literally applauded him and passed him money and cigars.

Always gracious, Miner stood up in the car and waved his hat to his fans. The *Union Recorder* claimed that "for a short time, it looked like a hero had come to the city instead of a man who had wrecked and robbed trains." This, however, was the last adventure for the grizzled old man who had robbed trains from coast to coast. The exact circumstances of his last days are unknown today, but it is believed the hunger, exposure to the weather, and contaminated water he consumed during his escape, apparently took their toll on him, causing him to lapse into illness.

The *Atlanta Journal*, learning that Miner was near death in September of 1913, interviewed him one last time. Before they could get the story printed, the Angel of Death visited the cell of the Grey Fox, and gave him permanent freedom at last.

Though accounts of his actual burial site vary today, the final resting place of Bill Miner is in the old city cemetery known as Memory Hill in Milledgeville. His grave is marked with a simple headstone, and is found on the southeast side of Memory Hill where the cemetery slopes toward Fishing Creek, a place where many convicts were buried when the penitentiary was located at Milledgeville. His headstone bears his pseudonym Bill Miner, since no one was certain of his true name.

Treasure-hunters still ply the railroads and other sites suspected of holding the loot Miner supposedly left behind somewhere in Hall or Lumpkin counties in north Georgia. Interestingly, almost all of the money and valuables stolen by Miner and his henchmen in the robbery in Gainesville were recovered. Miner had personally provided Sheriff Crow (of Hall County) with directions to two caches of loot. Several other caches turned up later, satisfying most recovery efforts.

The site of the famed train robbery now bears mute testimony to the events of February 18, 1911. Today, the crossing at White Sulphur is known as "Bill Miner Crossing."

The Trial Of George Corn Tassels

The execution of this north Georgia Indian became the catalyst for the determination of several important Supreme Court cases for Native Americans. Following his burial in the middle of what later became a major street in Gainesville, Georgia, the details of the crime Tassels had committed were literally forgotten – or were they intentionally destroyed?

One of the most significant crimes in the history of north Georgia remains a matter of mystery and controversy today. The identity of the murderer has never been argued. However, most other details concerning the crime committed by Cherokee Indian George Corn Tassels and his subsequent trial in 1830 have been lost in the mists of time.

The official records of the criminal proceedings involving Tassels literally disappeared within the politics of the nationally-important court cases which arose from the incident. Tassels' case would become the catalyst for subsequent litigation which reached all the way to the U.S. Supreme Court.

The amazing story of George Corn Tassels had its beginnings in the American Revolution when the Cherokee Indians were forced to move westward from the Carolinas to escape the decimation being caused by armies of white soldiers. The once-powerful Cherokees faced extinction – due in part to their alleged support of the British troops – if they remained in the midst of the warfare.

The Cherokees moved into what today is northwest Georgia. The lands there were claimed in part by the neighboring Creek Indians, but the Cherokees had little choice.

In 1802, the United States government and the state of Georgia reached an agreement for the removal of the remaining Indian nations – the Creeks and the Cherokees – from within the boundaries of Georgia. In exchange for the removal of the Indians, the state of Georgia agreed to relinquish its claims to the lands to the west which ultimately became the states of Alabama and Mississippi.

More importantly, by the 1830s, Southern and Western states had raised serious issues concerning the control of matters – including Indian affairs – within their own borders. Throughout the South, the opposition to the *"Tariff of Abominations"* of 1828 had led to claims that a state had the right to "nullify" – or claim "State's Rights" – regarding any federal laws that the state considered unconstitutional. This movement would grow to the extent of

Georgia Governor George R. Gilmer fought for the removal of the Cherokees but he lost his political support (and his office) for promoting state ownership of gold mines as a means of reducing property taxes for wealthy Georgia planters. (From Gilmer, Annals.)

Augustin Smith Clayton ultimately lost his judgeship for ruling that the state of Georgia could not constitutionally arrest a Cherokee for mining gold on the Indian's own land. Clayton later apologized to Cherokee Chief John Ross for his part in the Tassel case and other actions against the Cherokees. (Painting courtesy of Hargrett Rare Books & Manuscripts Library, University of Georgia Libraries)

threatening secession in what came to be known as "the Nullification Crisis."

Debate on the institution of slavery had also become a state's rights issue. The conflict between Georgia and the federal government over the Indian removal issue carried much of the same states rights rhetoric that would later accompany the Southern arguments in support of slavery.

Following the establishment by the Cherokees of their own formal government in 1827, Georgia began combining the issues of Indian removal and states rights. By an act of the state legislature on December 26, 1827, the Georgia General Assembly expanded the legal jurisdictions of Carroll and DeKalb counties to include the adjoining Cherokee Indian lands. Two years later, the state also extended the legal boundaries of Gwinnett, Habersham, Hall and Rabun counties into the neighboring lands of the Cherokees.

The new law, as written, also declared all actions of the Cherokee government to be null and void. In the fifteenth and last paragraph, Georgia banned any testimony by an Indian in a court suit involving a white man, unless the white man resided in the Indian territories. This law, amazingly, remained officially in force until the success of the Civil Rights movement in the United States in the 1960s.

By 1830, these acts and other issues had heightened tensions between Georgia and Cherokee officials. Because gold had been discovered on Cherokee lands in 1828, hundreds of whites had moved into the territory in search of the precious yellow metal. Georgia Governor George R. Gilmer asked for and received federal assistance in the form of troops which were used to arrest anyone of any race found mining on the Indian lands.

Later that same year, public protest of the arrests of white men by the federal troops compelled Gilmer to have the troops replaced with soldiers employed by Georgia – the "Georgia Guard." Despite this military presence, gangs of Georgians robbed, killed, burned out, evicted and otherwise abused the Indians with the knowledge that Georgia law prevented any Indian from acting as a witness against a white man.

The Cherokee leadership – described by critics as far more white than Indian and advised by missionaries from the North in schemes to control a quarter of Georgia's territory – fought back in the courts. Locally, they hired former Western Circuit Judge William H. Underwood and his partner Thomas H. Harris, as well as William Y. Hansel and Samuel Rockwell, to represent any Cherokees brought before a Georgia court. These attorneys served as legal representatives for their Native American clients in dozens of court cases over several years, sometimes under the threat of violence from white Georgians.

The Cherokees also hired former United States Attorney General William Wirt of Baltimore, Maryland, to represent their interests in Washington. As attorney general, Wirt had twice offered the opinion that the Indian nations existed as independent nations beyond the authority of the states. A nationally-recognized author, historian, and expert on Indian affairs, Wirt had such a reputation as an attorney that Georgia Judge Augustin Smith Clayton had named a son after him.

Wirt, Underwood and the Cherokees searched earnestly for strong court cases to use to test the Georgia law before the United States Supreme Court, but could not find the right case – that is, not until George Corn Tassels made the mistake of murdering another Indian on Indian lands in 1830. Wirt learned at almost the last moment that Georgia authorities had arrested Tassels and he knew he had finally found the legal case for which he had long been searching. In January of 1831, the case for Tassels' defense became part of the nationally-known *Cherokee Nation vs. the State of Georgia.*

Tassels had been jailed and indicted for murder in Gainesville, Georgia (Hall County). In September of 1830, Judge

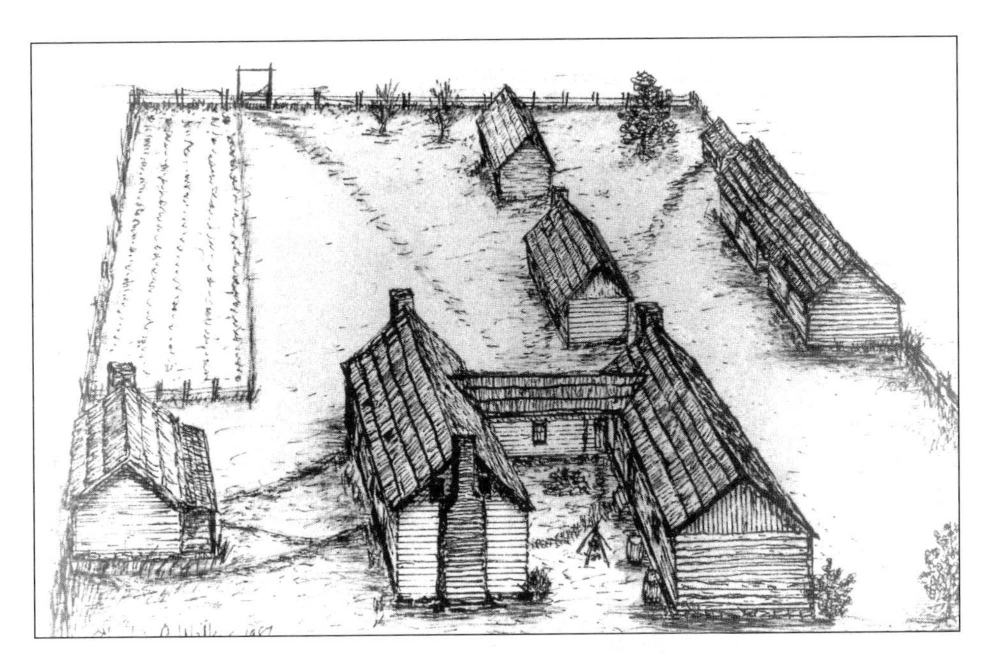

Charles O. Walker of north Georgia's Pickens County sketched this drawing of the Taloney / Mt. Carmel Indian Mission which once existed in the present-day community of Blaine.

William Wirt, as United States Attorney General, made some decisions which favored Cherokee Indian sovereignty, and others which did not. As attorney for the Cherokee Nation, however, he fought for George Corn Tassels and for the right of the Cherokees to keep their nation in Georgia. (Painting courtesy of Hargrett Rare Book and Manuscripts Library, University of Georgia Libraries)

Augustin Smith Clayton delayed the trial until he could obtain the opinion of a convention of Georgia judges at the state capital at Milledgeville, regarding Georgia's authority to try Tassels under state law. The judges – without commenting on the circumstances of the crime – unanimously recognized the force of Georgia's laws over the Cherokee Nation. The judges' non-binding opinion was cited thereafter as *State vs. George Tassels.*

The often-cited summary of this case interestingly includes only the legal decision. For reasons unknown today, the specific incidents that led to that decision have not been handed down through history. The only information on the details of the crime subsequently discovered by scholars has been a story reported by Belle K. Abbott in 1889.

Ms. Abbott was a local historian who was a correspondent for the Atlanta press. She wrote only that Tassels murdered an Indian by the name of Sanders at Talking Rock, near Taloney, in what later came to be known as the Blaine community of presentday Pickens County, Georgia.

The most obvious source for primary information on the case involving Tassels no longer exists. The Georgia State Superior Court records for the year of 1830 in Hall and Gwinnett counties have been lost. The same records for Baldwin County (Milledgeville), where the convention of judges heard the case, also have disappeared. No copy of any of the proceedings has been found in the official records of the State of Georgia, at the Georgia Department of Archives & History in Atlanta, or at the University of Georgia's Hargrett Rare Books and Manuscripts Library.

This, however, does not mean that all details of the incident have been lost. Following Tassels' execution, a Milledgeville, Georgia newspaper, the *Georgia Journal*, published a summary of the testimony in Tassels' trial which had been overlooked by researchers until just recently. The article appeared on a page otherwise filled with a legislative debate on State's Rights and a defense of slavery during the Nullification Crisis.

The summary of the testimony in Tassels' case clearly shows that the prosecution had a powerful case. Tassels never denied that he committed the crime. Letty Proctor who was present during the incident testified that Indians George Corn Tassels and Cornelius Dougherty were drunk in her home on the morning of July 15, 1830. She said the two men seemed amicable enough initially, although Tassels at some point suddenly announced that he was going to shoot Dougherty. Dougherty, however, merely took the statement as a joke.

Ms. Proctor said she felt safe in leaving

the men to go to an outhouse. She said that while she was absent, she heard a gunshot at ten o'clock and rushed back to the house as a wounded Dougherty staggered through the front doorway announcing that George had shot him in the right side.

Ms. Proctor immediately sent for the nearest constable – Mark Castleberry. John Dougherty (relation to Cornelius unknown) arrived and took care of the victim who subsequently died two days later.

John Dougherty later stated, before Constable Castleberry, that he had heard Tassels state that he had no grudge against Cornelius but only wanted to guarantee that he and his friend from boyhood would "share the same grave." George Corn Tassels apparently hoped that his own people would execute him by firing squad.

A member of the Georgia Guard later testified that Tassels spoke in English and admitted that he and Cornelius had been arguing. Castleberry reported that George stated that there had been a previous quarrel over a woman.

Historian James C. Flanigan published an account of George Corn Tassels and his victim having a dispute over a woman who later appeared in court to tearfully plead for "her lover." Whether or not he was referring to Letty Proctor is unknown today.

The actual site of the Cornelius Dougherty murder is a matter of controversy today. Reverend Isaac Proctor headed the Taloney or Carmel Mission at Talking Rock where Belle Abbott supposedly heard – more than 50 years later – that the murder had occurred. There are, however, pieces to this puzzle which simply do not fit.

It is a matter of record that the Indian community of Taloney had a reputation for violence, drunkenness, and even paganism. However, no record of a resident named Letty Proctor has been found. Also, the missionaries at Carmel did not make note of George Corn Tassels or his murder of Cornelius Dougherty in any of their writings, which is highly unusual.

As a result, the incident quite likely

For many years, scholars have believed that George Corn Tassels committed his murder at the Taloney / Mt. Carmel Indian Mission which was once located in the present-day mountain community of Blaine in Pickens County. In the early 1900s, one of the mission buildings was photographed above shortly before the site fell into complete ruin. (Photo courtesy of Charles O. Walker)

occurred someplace other than Taloney. In the 1830s at what was known as "Big Savannah" in the present-day adjoining county of Dawson, there existed a Cherokee community by the name of Dougherty. The large household of James Dougherty, Sr. lived at this site. This family quite probably was descended from a white man named Cornelius Dougherty who lived among the Indians before Oglethorpe founded Georgia in 1733. Even more coincidental is the fact that these Doughertys of Big Savannah were neighbors to a household headed by one John Proctor.

Also living nearby were the Cherokee families that used their native names of which "Corn Tassels" could serve as an example. It is also a matter of historic record that George Corn Tassels told a guard that he would prefer to face trial at "Savannah" before the Cherokees. He subsequently appeared before Mark Castleberry of Hall County, who was the nearest constable, and who, incidentally, also lived much closer to Big Savannah than to the far-off Carmel Mission at Taloney.

In late November of 1830, following the convention of judges' decision in

Milledgeville, the Tassels trial finally was held. Historian Flanigan wrote that a change of venue caused the trial to be moved to Lawrenceville in Gwinnett County, but no contemporary source supports that claim.

William H. Underwood served as defense counsel while Turner H. Trippe represented the state. On November 22, 1830, a Georgia court found Tassels "Guilty" of murder and sentenced him to death.

Judge Clayton not only delivered the jury's verdict, but also seized the opportunity for a long public discourse on "State's Rights" and the need for the removal of the Cherokees. In a later letter to Governor Gilmer, Clayton denied that he sought a confrontation with the federal government over States Rights. He had specifically promised to expedite any verdict from any case that might be used as a test case before the federal courts.

Clayton's record, however, made his assurances suspect. He had become a strong advocate of States Rights in Georgia. In the Summer of 1830, federal soldiers arrested nine white men for mining gold on the Cherokee lands and marched them at bayonet point through the streets of Athens en route to the federal court in Savannah. Clayton obtained a *Writ of Habeas Corpus* and had the men released. He provided such an adamant argument for State's Rights – the authority of the Georgia laws over both that of the Cherokees and the federal government in the Indian lands – before the Clarke County Grand Jury that his words received widespread publicity and became part of Wirt's bill that led to *Cherokee Nation vs. Georgia.*

Clayton likely also acted as a result of other motives too. He had been judge of the Western Circuit before his Troupite Party lost control of the legislature and he lost his job to Clarkite Party member William H. Underwood. A swing of public support back to the Troupites restored his judgeship, however, and allowed him to now sit in judgement as Underwood tried to defend George Corn Tassels and his other Cherokee clients.

Georgia newspapers reported that the Tassels trial would likely go to the United States Supreme Court. On December 22, a *Writ of Error* arrived for Gilmer from United States Chief Justice John Marshall. It was dated December 12. This document announced that the authority of Georgia in the case of Tassels and other matters in Wirt's petition would be heard before the high court.

Governor Gilmer found himself between a rock and a hard place. He had fought to avoid a federal challenge to the Georgia laws as he feared such action only helped the Cherokees. Wirt had a tremendous reputation as a legal power. He also had, as close friends, some of Gilmer's Virginia cousins. The governor took the matter of the writ before the Georgia State Legislature which was then in special session.

According to a critic, Gilmer reached the state house out of breath and in a panic. He urged defiance of the court. The Georgia House and Senate both quickly passed a resolution ordering Sheriff Jacob Eberhart of Hall County to carry out the sentence. Gilmer's letter to Eberhart, dated that same December 22, 1830, traveled the 120 miles to Gainesville and reached the sheriff before December 24.

On that cold day, as sleet fell, George Corn Tassels rode in his coffin to a scaffold in a large open field near presentday's Cotton Avenue in Gainesville. As with all public hangings, a substantial posse stood by, making certain the sentence was carried out without interruption. Crowds of men, women and children clogged the roads to reach the site of the hanging which had become a big public event.

When Tassels and his guards reached the site of the execution, Eberhart ordered the prisoner to stand up. He then tied the Cherokee's hands and pulled a cap over his face before securing the rope around his neck. Though it is not known for certain today, Tassels was probably hung from the branch of a tree after having a wagon or cart pulled from beneath him. Whatever the circumstances, Tassels was hung by the neck – for approximately 20 minutes – until he ceased movement. At that point, doctors pronounced him dead.

Often repeated accounts maintain that hundreds of Cherokees silently witnessed the hanging. However, a correspondent to *The Athenian* newspaper of Athens only reported eighteen to twenty Indians present.

The Cherokees, interestingly, buried Tassels in the middle of what later became South Broad Street in Gainesville. The former site of his burial is unknown today. William Jasper Cotter, according to records, witnessed the exhumation of the body some twenty years later. In his writings, Cotter noted that coagulated blood was still visible around Tassels' neck.

The execution had widespread implications. John Ross and the Cherokee leadership reported the hanging to the U.S. Congress, where their friends used it to adamantly denounce Georgia's actions in extending its authority over the Cherokees and executing an Indian in defiance of existing treaties. The case that brought George Corn Tassels to his end – *State vs George Corn Tassels* – became the primary court citation for state authority over Native Americans until 1931.

In the year following Tassels' death, the United States Supreme Court heard *Cherokee Nation vs. Georgia.* Wirt represented the Cherokees but the State of Georgia ignored the case and provided no representation.

The U.S. Supreme Court, as a result, handed down a divided and somewhat confusing, ruling. Chief Justice John Marshall and one other justice ruled that the Cherokees were not a foreign nation – as stated in Wirt's petition – and as such, could not sue in the Supreme Court. Two other justices agreed with Wirt's petition, and the remaining two justices argued that the Cherokees were neither a domestic nor a foreign nation, but a conquered people

U.S. Supreme Court Chief Justice John Marshall argued in favor of the sovereign rights of the Cherokees regarding the state of Georgia in "Cherokee Nation vs. Georgia" (the George Corn Tassels case) and in "Worcester vs. Georgia." Marshall, according to some sources, did so to help President Andrew Jackson's efforts to stop state secessionism in the Nullification Crisis, and he reportedly did it in a manner which would spare the president from being forced to uphold federal laws in favor of the Indians. (Photo courtesy of Hargrett Rare Books & Manuscripts Library, University of Georgia Libraries)

President Andrew Jackson refused to enforce the decisions of the U.S. Supreme Court regarding the protection of the rights of the Cherokee Indians. In this manner, he was able to stave off the secessionist tendencies arising within the Southern states.

without rights. Four of the justices did agree, however, that Georgia had no authority over the Cherokee lands, laying the groundwork for another suit. In that case (*Worcester vs Georgia*, 1832), concerning Judge Clayton's trials of white northern missionaries arrested for resisting Georgia's laws, the Court declared that the State of Georgia had no legal authority in the Cherokee lands.

Today, legend maintains that following this decision, U.S. President Andrew Jackson cynically stated that "Marshall has his decision. Now let him enforce it." Jackson probably never made such a statement, but his administration nevertheless took no actions that threatened the Georgia laws, and instead, continued to encourage Indian removals to the West. Federal soldiers, in fact, enforced the final removals of the last organized Native American peoples in the southern and mid-western states east of the Mississippi River in the late 1830s.

With no federal intervention in support of the Cherokees' sovereignty (despite their success at the U.S. Supreme Court) their situation steadily declined. So also followed the fortunes of other Native American societies. In 1833, the State of Georgia divided the lands of the Cherokee Nation into eleven new Georgia counties. State authorities completely ignored the existence of the Cherokee judicial system and the rulings of the United States Supreme Court.

The same summer (1830) that Tassels had committed murder, the Cherokees' own court at Coosawattee tried Cherokee Indian James Graves after he boasted, while drunk, of murdering an unknown white man. The Cherokee court found Graves "Not Guilty" due to a lack of evidence, and therefore not liable, according to treaty, for surrender to the federal Indian agent.

The State of Georgia, however, tried Graves again for the presumed murder in the newly-created county of Murray in northwest Georgia. There, a white jury found Graves "Guilty."

Judge John W. Hooper postponed the execution of Graves in a vain hope for federal intervention. The Georgia Legislature, however, again in defiance of the U.S. Supreme Court, passed yet another resolution ordering the execution proceedings to continue without delay. On November 21, 1834, Graves met the same fate as had Tassels.

In a similar set of circumstances, Cherokee John Hogg Smith was hanged in Walker County in 1834, supposedly for murdering two Indians. Following his arrest for the murders of everyone in the James L. Bowman family at Salacoa in 1832, Cherokee George Tooke (known to the Cherokees as Une'ga-tehee or "White Man Killer") escaped from the DeKalb County, Georgia jail. A white Cherokee County posse wounded and captured him in 1835 and a Cass (present-day Bartow) County jury found him "Guilty." He too was hanged. By then, an act of November 12, 1834, provided state funds to counties for the prosecution and punishment of Cherokees.

In a bit of irony, Georgia's advocates for "State's Rights" won such battles in the 1830s, only to literally lose the war for the same cause in 1861-1865 during the U.S. Civil War.

As a result of the incendiary political climate of the 1830s, the details of George Corn Tassels' ordeal had begun to vanish even while he yet lived. They were literally buried beneath the overwhelming issues of "State's Rights" and Indian removal politics.

Though his crime was murder, Tassels' trial became an important lynch-pin in the quest of Native Americans for treatment as a sovereign nation within a nation – conquered or not. It would be many years in the future, however, before the rights of Native Americans would be accepted by all Americans. In the interim, there was much suffering and despair.

Tallapoosa Law Enforcement Tragedies

Just as do many Georgia counties, Haralson County in west Georgia has a long and colorful history. One of the darker chapters in this vicinity, however, deals with the death rate of the city of Tallapoosa's law enforcement officers, one of the highest police officer death rates for this size municipality in the entire United States.

President George W. Bush once said that ". . . for too long, America's lawmen and women have been forgotten heroes. . . forgotten until there is trouble; until we are stranded on the roadside or frantically dialing 911 at home. . ." These words certainly seem to be true. The local monument to police officers killed in the line of duty is hidden in an alcove in front of Tallapoosa's City Hall. Almost without exception, it goes unnoticed as the people of our community hurry about with their day-to-day activities.

To date, more than 14,500 law enforcement officers have been killed in the United States. The first reported death of a law enforcement officer was that of United States Marshal Robert Forsyth, who was killed in Georgia in 1794.

The city of Tallapoosa was incorporated in 1860. Over the past 140 years, four police officers have been killed in the line of duty in this community. Each was killed by gunfire and died a violent death.

The names of these men have been added to the Georgia Public Safety Memorial at the Georgia Public Safety Training Center in Forsyth, Georgia. Tallapoosa and Swainsboro, among small cities, share the dubious record for the highest number of police officers killed in this size municipality. This is the story of those who made the supreme sacrifice in the city of Tallapoosa.

Marshal William H. Maegar

On Sunday February 13, 1910, William H. Maegar, marshal of Tallapoosa, was killed outside the city jail (located at that time under the old City Hall) following the arrest of "Boss" Cason.

According to The *Haralson County Tribune* newspaper, ". . . upon arriving at the calaboose, Cason, without a moment's warning, suddenly drew his pistol and fired point-blank at the unsuspecting officer, the bullet taking effect in his left side near the heart."

It was reported in the *Tribune* that Maegar said, shortly before his death, that "Boss Cason shot me. I'm done for," and he expired shortly thereafter.

Cason was later re-arrested by Sheriff Robert Parker after he was found hiding in the bedroom of his home. "He had a neat hiding place," the *Tribune* explained. "He had removed the straw from the center of

This solid-iron doorway to the old Tallapoosa Jail is located beneath the old City Hall building in Tallapoosa. It was at this site that two police officers lost their lives after being shot by assailants. The exact age of the old calaboose is unknown today, but as of this writing, it is believed to be at least 100 years old. (Photo by David Godfrey)

The heavy steel lock-up at the old Tallapoosa Jail. (Photo by David Godfrey)

the mattress and crawled in the hollowed place, and with the assistance of someone, had been covered up. . . ."

Tom Maegar, the father of William H. Maegar, was also a marshal in Tallapoosa. Due to the similarity of their names (and occupation), the elder Maegar's name is incorrectly displayed on the Georgia Public Safety Memorial.

Policeman Oscar Tolbert

On Friday, May 23, 1919, Officer Oscar Tolbert was shot and killed in front of J.B. Little's store in Tallapoosa. According to The *Haralson County Tribune* of that day, "Grover Little, his father, J.B. Little, Walter Amos, Lawrence Brown, George Gable and Joe Stepenson, all of Tallapoosa, are in jail here charged with complicity in the crime."

According to details of the incident, "The bullet which ended the life of Policeman Tolbert was a very large one, and was apparently fired from a large army rifle. Tolbert was standing just outside the doorway – on the walk – and the fatal bullet came from inside the store several feet away, plowing its way through the heavy panel of the store doors. . .

"From what we can glean, it seems that the policeman had suspected Little of having liquor, and had secreted himself up the street a ways for the purpose of observation."

It is widely believed today that J.B. Little's store stood on Head Avenue near where Ron's Barber and Style Shop stands today.

Policeman Henry C. Pope

On Thursday, September 3, 1931, Henry C. Pope was killed at the Tallapoosa Police Department which was then located in the old City Hall.

It was reported in *The Haralson County Tribune* that "Mr. and Mrs. C.W. Ledlow, of Tallapoosa, are dead and City Policeman Henry Pope, of Tallapoosa, is lying in an Anniston hospital, perhaps fatally wounded as a result of a pistol duel. . .

"According to the best information we can glean, it appears that Policeman Pope had arrested a nephew of Mrs. Ledlow earlier in the evening and just prior to the triple tragedy, Mr. and Mrs. Ledlow had gone to him with the request that they be allowed to make bond for the young man, which Pope agreed to do.

"As he was writing out the bond, so it is said, a remark was made about a former transaction which Mr. Pope said had no bearing on the case. Hot words passed and it is said Mrs. Ledlow drew a pistol and fired point blank at Pope. Fatally-wounded, he drew his gun and fired at Mrs. Ledlow, the bullet entering her mouth and killing her instantly.

"At this juncture, Mr. Ledlow attempted to obtain the pistol his wife had used and as he was lunging for it, Mr. Pope shot him, the bullet penetrating his forehead between the eyes."

Most of the residents of Tallapoosa today don't realize that the original jail at which both Maegar and Pope were killed still stands today. It is tucked beneath the old City Hall which, at one time, housed the city government, police department, and fire department. The single room of the old jail, guarded by a heavy steel door, is dark and damp, and it's walls are covered with graffiti from years gone by.

The walls inside the cell in the old city jail in Tallapoosa are covered with graffiti inscribed by inmates who had plenty of time on their hands over the years. (Photo by David Godfrey)

The barred windows of the old jail apparently had to be repaired and reinforced over the years, no doubt as a result of the constant abuse and attempts at jail-breaks by inmates. The room today, as can be seen, is used for storage. (Photo by David Godfrey)

Lt. William "Billy" Manning

On Sunday, February 11, 1973, Lieutenant William "Billy" Manning was shot and killed and his partner, Sergeant Ed Elliott, was severely wounded on U.S. Highway 78.

According to *The Tallapoosa Journal*, "Manning and Elliott were on a routine patrol early Sunday. The two, riding together, spotted a 1972 Chevrolet truck speeding and weaving through town. They stopped the truck on Highway 78, near the west city limits of Tallapoosa.

"The officers stopped behind the truck, and a young man got out and walked back toward them. When Manning asked to see his driver's license, the man pulled a pistol, believed to be a 38 caliber snub-nose, and opened fire on the officers.

"In the first exchange of gunfire, Manning and Elliott were hit once each and fell to the ground. The gunman then shot Manning twice more and Elliott once more while they were returning the fire."

Two separate suspects have been identified as the person responsible for the death of Lt. Billy Manning, but neither was successfully prosecuted. The death of Lt. Manning remains unsolved and continues to be an active case under investigation today.

West Georgia 'Law And Order' And Old Heard County Jail

The stark Romanesque Revival structure on the old town square in Franklin, Georgia, has weathered at least one lynch-mob, a jail-break and murderers. Today, it is the oldest public building in Heard County, and has been preserved as a historic window into the area's past.

Some long-time residents of Heard County can still recall occasions when their ancestors talked of how "rough" the area in west Georgia was in the late 1800s. Back then, just as today, crime was prevalent in certain locales. And also just as today, the local jail house was an important deterrent to crime.

God-fearing Heard Countians must have felt relieved when their "new" jail house was completed in 1880. It was designed to take care of the cattle thieves, murderers, carousers and public drunks which were frequenting the area. And over the years, this solid facility which still stands on the old town square in Franklin, witnessed its share of events – both within and outside the limits of the law.

The jail was built beside the swift, muddy waters of the Chattahoochee River. When the penalty for a crime called for a punishment greater than incarceration, public hangings were held near the river bank where a sturdy tree limb provided ample accommodation.

Ironically, though many jails in the 19th and early in the 20th centuries were equipped with indoor gallows, they were seldom used. Public executions were considered a moral lesson, and were therefore conducted outdoors more often than not, so more people – including children – could watch. Such was the case in Heard County.

Ironically, though many jails in the 19th and early in the 20th centuries were equipped with indoor gallows, they seldom were used.

In the 1880s, hangings were social events. Local farmers and merchants dressed in their finest clothing, loaded their wives and children into wagons, and crowded around the old town square to watch the horrible event.

Thomas Lipford remembers his father, Tom H. Lipford, describing a public hanging he once witnessed.

"My granddaddy

(R.M. 'Mac' Lipford) was sheriff and my father was about six years old then, I think," Lipford explained in an interview in the early 1990s. "My granddaddy told my father he could watch. Dad said he went there and saw someone with a rope around his neck – the fella hadn't yet been hung – and it made him deathly sick. He couldn't bear to watch.

"My father said the town was filled with more people than he'd ever seen," Lipford continued. "People climbed up into trees all around the courthouse (which was located at that time in the center of the Franklin town square) to watch, and when that fella dropped (through the trap door in the gallows), people got so excited they fell out of the trees."

According to records, more than one condemned prisoner spent his last days in the old Heard County Jail. The late Marvin Fincher, a Bowdon, Georgia businessman and veteran newspaperman, related the story of a traveler who rode through Franklin one evening in the early 1900s and witnessed such an event.

"The fella glanced toward the old jail and saw a man hanging by the river bank," Fincher explained. "That man later told me he hollered 'giddy-up!' to his mule and never looked back."

The body the traveler witnessed quite possibly was the sad result of a lynching. On May 16, 1913, the county's newspaper The *News And Banner* carried the following headline: *"Negro Kills White Man And Lynched Same Night."*

The initial death to which the headline refers occurred three miles south of Franklin, according to the article. Sheriff Henry Lee Taylor (sheriff from 1907-1914) and a number of citizens reportedly rushed to the scene. They discovered the victim *with "a bullet hole through his breast and penetrating his heart."*

The accused killer was discovered at home "with a pocketful of cartridges, but made no resistance." According to the newspaper account, friends of the victim attempted to intercept the sheriff and his prisoner, but were unsuccessful.

"He was lodged in jail safely, and the building was carefully watched all day," the article continued. *"About 10:00 p.m. however, some 50 or a hundred masked men quickly marched to the jail, covered the sheriff and his assistants – Lube Lipham and John Hodnett – leaving them no alternative but to surrender the keys."*

At gunpoint, the sheriff and his assistants were ordered by the abductors to remain inside the building. The lynch-mob then *"quietly marched to the river bridge. . ."*

They hung the accused man from *"a huge oak standing near."* Then his body was *"riddled with shot."*

The following morning, the coroner arrived to investigate the incident. A jury was empaneled and *"repaired to the swinging body which was taken down and the investigation made."*

Although the sheriff and his two assistants were closely questioned according to the article, *"it was impossible to get any evidence whatsoever for the identification of any in the large crowd that had precipitated the event."*

The official verdict which eventually was rendered might almost be considered comical if the crime had not been so horrible. .

". . . the accused came to death by strangulation and gunshot wounds inflicted by parties unknown. The body was turned over to relatives," the verdict intoned.

Today, the "old jail" which exists upon the site once occupied by the 1880 Heard County Jail, was built in 1912. The 1880 structure was found to be *"in a very unsanitary condition"* by jurors of the Heard County Superior Court (March term, 1911). In September, 1911, (according to Heard County Superior Court minutes) jurors recommended the county board *"proceed at once to build a new jail as the present one is not fit to confine a prisoner in. . ."*

According to other articles in the *News And Banner* (1912), the old jail was torn down in March of that year. Some of the

Historic Heard County Jail on the town square in Franklin, Georgia, is a museum today, displaying the area's law enforcement elements of years past. (Photo by Glovis Gore South)

Virgil Bledsoe was sheriff of Heard County from 1949 to 1980, and was the last law enforcement official to reside in the old Heard County Jail. Though the jail was equipped with a gallows, it was never used. As recently as the early 20th century, executions were considered a moral lesson, and were conducted outdoors where the public could witness the punishment first-hand. (Photo by Glovis Gore South)

materials from the 1880 structure were used in the present building: *"Work on the jail is still progressing. They have rolled the old cells out on the streets and are making ready for the new jail."*

Some measure of controversy has arisen in recent years concerning the original date of construction of the 1912 structure. Preservationists argue that newspaper accounts prove the present structure was built in 1912. Nay-sayers argue the present structure is actually the 1880 building. Legal notices of the period in the paper however, actually attest to the former.

Much of the confusion surrounding the construction date involves a fire which occurred around Thanksgiving in 1912. According to the *News And Banner* (November 22, 1912), *"Quite a little furor was caused in the city Sunday morning just after the breakfast hour by the discovery of fire in the roof of the new jail. The building had been in use only a few weeks. Heaters had not yet been installed by the board and the fire was caused by the negligence of allowing the prisoners to make fires in the flues used to ventilate the roof. The sparks went right into the roof above and a destructive fire was the result. . ."*

According to records and the newspaper accounts, there was no damage to the building other than the roof, because the building *"was fire-proof."* Some researchers contend that, since only the roof was replaced in 1912, no new jail was ever built.

While the old jail was in use, the sheriff and his family lived on the first floor and prisoners were kept in cells on the second floor, as was customary in those days. The sheriff and his family ate, slept and took care of ordinary chores downstairs.

The sheriff's wife prepared meals for the prisoners. The sheriff, or a member of his family would serve the meals and clean the jail.

Corner fireplaces downstairs kept the sheriff's family warm. Behind the hallway, there is a small kitchen with a window view of the river area.

A metal stairway leads upstairs to the

jail, and prisoners no doubt could hear the clank-clank of the sheriff's footsteps as he ascended to check on his charges each day.

The jail area itself consists of two small rooms and one large one. The larger room has two cells (with eight beds and a toilet).

The "death cell" was at the top of the stairs and was used to house prisoners who were sentenced to die. As of this writing, that cell has been removed and a historical exhibit has taken its place.

The gallows and trap-door still exist at the top of the stairs in the old jail. The release for the trap is still mounted on the rail, but with the popularity and custom of open-air executions of earlier days, the indoor gallows was never used.

Franklin native Virgil Bledsoe was the last sheriff to live with his family in the jail. He also enjoys the distinction of having resided at the old jail the longest span of time.

"Mr. Virgil" is well-acquainted with the old jail walls. . .the wooden floors. . . the jail cells upstairs. He spent 10 years of his childhood growing up there while his father – Charlie Bledsoe – was sheriff (1922-42). Virgil himself became sheriff in 1949 and maintained law and order in Heard County until 1980.

In an interview in the early 1990s, Virgil said he would never forget some of his remembrances and experiences in the old jail. "Sometimes we'd have a lot of noise from the prisoners and we couldn't sleep," he explained, sitting once again at the kitchen table of the jail during this interview. "I'd have to go upstairs and try to calm them down."

Both Bledsoe and Lipford, who were childhood friends, remember a scare they shared one night when there was talk of another lynching.

"I spent that night with Virgil and they had a prisoner who had killed a man. Mr. Charlie (Sheriff Charlie Bledsoe) thought they might try to lynch the man that night. He had his gun. . . It was a bad night for me to be there. . ." Lipford remembered, laughing and shaking his head.

Despite its seemingly impenetrable confines, a breakout did occur at the Heard County Jail. In the 1930s, two prisoners were able to saw through the steel bars on one of the windows. The escapees had fashioned a rope from bedsheets and blankets, and made good on the only escape ever accomplished from the lock-up. Rather than pay for new bars in the window during those hard times, the sheriff merely bolted plowshares over the hole. Though it was a crude deterrent, the defense proved effective, and was never removed. (Photo by Glovis Gore South)

FIRE! – Originally published in the Heard County *News & Banner* newspaper in 1912, this photo shows the Heard County Jail building as it burns. A crowd gathered just after breakfast after smoke and fire were seen billowing from the upper portion of the jail. The roof, as is visible in the photo, was destroyed, but the jail itself was saved. (Photo courtesy of Heard County Historical Society and the News & Banner)

"I was scared that they were coming too," Bledsoe added. "My daddy would have died if they came in here. We stayed in the front room and he sat up all night. He sat right there (pointing to a spot near the hallway) and if they had come in that front door he said he'd be ready for 'em."

Perhaps people in those parts knew "Mr. Charlie" well enough to know better than to try and take a prisoner from him. Regardless of the circumstances, no one ever challenged Sheriff Bledsoe that night. The accused prisoner was later sent to the state penitentiary.

On another occasion, however, Virgil Bledsoe remembers his father was challenged. Georgia state troopers released a drunken prisoner into "Mr. Charlie's" custody in what seemed like a routine lock-up.

"The jail keys used to hang right up there," Virgil explains, glancing at a spot near the kitchen door. "Dad put the man in the room by the kitchen, but somehow he got a rake and reached in here and got the keys.

In order to avoid a fight with the intoxicated prisoner, and to protect his family sleeping in the front rooms, Mr. Charlie stood guard over his charge all night. "Dad sat by that door the entire night, and the next morning, the man was sober and he gave Dad the keys."

As for his own personal experiences as sheriff, Virgil Bledsoe says he was scared for his family only once.

"I caught these two 14-year-old runaways," he recalled. "I apprehended them on Roosterville Road just before you get to Antioch Church. I brought them back here and they ate supper with us. Since they were just a couple of runaways and young boys, I didn't lock 'em upstairs in the cells."

Bledsoe's compassion for the two boys, however, almost proved fatal. Because he didn't consider them to be dangerous or threatening, he had not searched them thoroughly. One of the boys had hidden a gun between his legs, and Virgil had overlooked it.

"He pulled the gun on me while I was reading the *Atlanta Journal*," Bledsoe related. "He threatened Jan who was just a baby at the time and didn't understand what was happening. She was running around and he told her to sit down or he'd shoot her. . I told him, 'Don't you hurt my daughter, son. . . She don't know what's going on.'

"He wanted the car keys," Bledsoe continued. "The other boy got scared and ran to hide under a bed. I said 'I keep the keys in it, son.' Then, I watched until he went by that window (the front left one). I told Mildred I wasn't going to let him take my car. He'd have to shoot me first."

The plucky sheriff then ran outside, jerked open the car door and jumped on top of the boy. He wrestled the gun away from him, then took him back inside. This time, however, he locked him up in a cell upstairs.

In 1964, the Bledsoes moved out and the new jailer (Lloyd Waldrop) moved in. In 1965, prisoners were no longer kept in the old jail. A new jail had been built across the town square. The old jail was officially closed when the new county courthouse – containing the new jail – was built.

In the twentieth century, eight different sheriffs held office and resided in the old jail: Henry Lee Taylor, 1907-1914; W.S. Green, 1915-1916; Henry Lee Taylor, 1917-1920; S. Young Miller, 1920-1931; Charlie Bledsoe, 1932-1942; Hugh Goodson, 1942; L.L. Adams, January, 1943; James E. Gladney, 1943-1948; and Virgil Bledsoe, 1949-1964. (Retired, 1980)

In 1981, the old jail was added to the *National Register of Historic Places* by the U.S. Department of Interior. And in 1987, the Heard County Historical Society made the jail into a museum.

"It was not only important to Heard County, but to all of Georgia that the old jail be saved," explained Dock Heard Davis, a Franklin attorney who headed up the restoration committee at its inception. "We have a unique opportunity to save something from a way of life that's disappeared. We wanted to restore it as an authentic incarceration facility."

Night Of Terror At Merrill's Mill

With the south Georgia floods of 1994 still prominent in the memories of many Georgians, it may come as no surprise that a slightly smaller, though quite similar disaster descended upon west Georgia approximately 125 years ago.

It was a fearsome night for the families inhabiting the small mill village just outside of Franklin, Georgia. The Merrill and Roop families operated a gristmill there powered by the cold, usually quiet waters of Hillabatchee Creek. Under normal circumstances, the individuals of this little fiefdom led the tranquil lives that would be expected of a rural agrarian family. All of that, however, changed abruptly on the night of April 23, 1883.

The weather that night was a precursor of the wrath about to descend from the heavens. At the time, however, the citizenry around Merrill's Mill were oblivious to their impending doom.

Records indicate the sky over west Georgia on that Sunday was dark and threatening, composed of deep hues of red, orange and blue during the day, and a seething black when the sun dipped below the horizon that evening.

Rain began to fall lightly at first, then harder as the storm cell moved into the area. Mixed with hail, the water beat a cacophony reminiscent of bullets upon the tin roofs of homes. Thunder played like the bass notes of a Sunday organ. Dirt roads quickly became rivers of mud and goo, creating ever-widening rushing streams of dirty, red water.

The residents of Heard County didn't know it at the time, but vicious tornadoes from this storm were tearing up the countryside all across the Southeast, and the destruction was headed straight for this rural west Georgia community.

With the torrential down-pour, Hillabatchee Creek began to swell. Lightning flashed dramatically across the darkened sky. As was their custom, the families in the vicinity of Merrill's Mill began huddling together to wait out the display of Mother Nature's might.

Sometime around midnight, according to newspaper accounts of the incident, there was a lull in the storm. At this point, many of the families undoubtedly relaxed somewhat and went to bed. It was a decision which would shortly prove to be deadly.

According to news reports, the Roop and Merrill families were central characters in the disaster in the Merrill's Mill area.

The Families

Benjamin Jocephus (Ceph) Roop, 31, had moved to this mill village after marrying Georgia Merrill whose father (Robert) owned the gristmill and substantial property there. Ceph's father – Martin Roop – had been the founder of Roopville, Georgia. Census records from that time, interestingly, list Ceph's occupation as "huckster."

Ceph's house was located on the low side of the creek, just below the dam. It was a factor which would shortly prove devastating to his family. Of his household, he would be the only survivor of the impending disaster.

According to one newspaper report of the incident, Georgia Merrill Roop, (Ceph's wife) was not feeling well the night of the disaster.

Bula Roop, 5, was the oldest child of Ceph and Georgia.

H.D.R. (Homer), 3, was the middle child of Ceph and Georgia. Today, his worn tombstone lies broken – his initials on one portion and his surname on the other.

Ella Roop, 1, was the youngest child of Ceph and Georgia.

Thomas Roop was Ceph's brother, and was overnighting at Ceph's home the evening of the disaster. His home was in Roopville where he was the town's first postmaster. He also helped his brother at the mill and store.

A black female provided services as a house servant and nurse in the Roop home. Though unnamed in any newspaper accounts of the incident, she is remembered by some residents as the daughter of Harmon Ridley, 48, a black farmer with a large family who lived nearby.

Robert Merrill, 52, was Georgia's father. Robert and his wife, Sara, both survived the flood, and undoubtedly watched the terrible incident as the events unfolded that night. Their home, which was on high ground, was across the creek from the Roop home.

Henry Albert (Bit) Merrill was Georgia's brother, and Lula Miller Merrill was his wife. Lula went into labor and gave birth to their first child, Carrie Lee Merrill (Cook), sometime during the storm. Family members maintain that when water began rising in their home, Lula and Henry sought refuge with relatives (probably her parents who lived farther away from the creek).

Henry's house was also destroyed. No one in this household died that night, but all were fortunate they departed the premises. Only one piece of furniture – a three-drawer chest with oval frame – was salvaged. Carrie Merrill Cook later gave this chest and frame to her youngest daughter, Vilwon Cook Gore.

The Storm

News reports place the time of the most destructive portion of the storm between midnight and 2:00 a.m. Reporters described heavy rain, hail and immense thunder at this time.

According to an eyewitness account in the April 27, 1883 issue of the *Carroll County Times*, the lightning was so constant that for 80 minutes, it was as light as day. *"It was the grandest display of electricity I ever saw. Several responsible persons inform me that hailstones fell from the size of hen eggs to as large as*

According to this newspaper account, Ceph Roop caught a floating mattress and was carried downstream.

a man's fist. . . ."

A writer in the Thursday morning (April 26, 1883) edition of the *Atlanta Constitution*, written with a Hogansville dateline said *"Sunday night's storm was fearful around this place, but what we suffered was insignificant compared to the damage in Heard County. Every creek overflowed there and the bottomlands are almost ruined for the present year. . .*

"An awful story comes from a settlement six miles beyond Franklin," the article continued. *"Mr. B.J. Roop is one of the best-known citizens of Heard County. About midnight, the tempest lulled a little and the family was able to sleep. The rain seems to have continued up the creek (however), for the water kept on rising until it had swept beyond the highest mark it ever before had reached. The Roop family slept on unconscious of the awful doom that was creeping on.*

Between 1:00 and 2:00 o'clock, the water had risen under the house high enough to lift it from its sills. It swayed to and fro in the awful tide. The motion aroused Mrs. Roop, who was trying to wake her husband when the torrent rushed in the doors and the house began to float down the stream.

. . . The scene of terror must have been appalling. The children were screaming and the poor woman was almost frantic with grief. Roop, though almost a giant in form, stood helpless in the awful storm . . .

. . . The house, turning and reeling, reached the current of the creek and dashed swiftly down the foaming water. After going a hundred yards or so, it struck a tree with such violence that the shock shivered it to a mass of floating ruins.

A Victim Survives

According to this newspaper account, Ceph Roop caught a floating mattress and was carried downstream. His wife, children and the servant girl struggled in vain for their lives. As Ceph Roop held desperately to the mattress, his family disappeared under the black tide as strobed lightning flashed on the nightmarish scene.

According to the *Atlanta Constitution* correspondent from Hogansville, Ceph Roop eventually climbed into a small tree as the mattress lodged against it momentarily.

"He climbed high enough to escape the current and was saved," the article stated. *"Though an expert swimmer, he could never have gotten out of the rushing current from which the tree saved him. Holding on to a limb all night long, he suffered untold agony for he realized that his loved ones must all have been lost."*

At daybreak, Ceph reportedly determined his whereabouts. He was three-quarters of a mile from home and 150 feet from "shore," according to the news account.

In the Friday morning (April 27, 1883) edition of the *Atlanta Constitution*, correspondent R.J. Gaines of Carrollton wrote:

". . . The last words Mr. B.J. Roop recollects of speaking to his brother, Thomas, was while they were standing in the yard, in front of the house. He told his brother to take care of himself and he would try and save his family.

"He then hurried to the window and the water was, by this time, waist deep, and did all he could to extricate his wife and children from the impending danger. But with that unselfish love that only a mother can feel, (Mrs. Roop) refused to go unless her precious little ones could be taken at the same time, preferring to perish with them rather than leave them alone to the merciless fury of the raging waters.

"A few minutes more persuasion with his poor sick wife, who was not able to help herself, and all was lost. The dam above the house gave way and its tremendous volume of water came with all the force and terror of a mighty avalanche, sweeping everything before it . . .

No vestige of dwelling, store or outbuildings was left to mark the spot where once dwelt this happy family."

The home of Henry Albert Merrill (the

great-grandfather of this writer), was also destroyed, according to the article in the *Constitution. "He and his wife would have been lost had they not gone to spend the night with some of her relatives,"* the article explained.

A Search For Victims

Neighbors and relatives began the search for the missing individuals the next morning. The bodies of two of the children were the first to be found – about a mile away. One source said Ceph Roop found the bodies.

Volunteers searched all Monday and Tuesday for Mrs. Roop, Thomas Roop, the third child and Harmon Ridley's daughter. News accounts (*Carroll County Times*, April 27, 1883) indicate that later, the body of Thomas Roop was found about a mile below the mill site. Mrs. Roop and the servant girl were also found. Some reports maintain the bodies were in trees and under debris left by the torrent.

The third child, according to the May 11, 1883 issue of the *Carroll County Times*, was the last unrecovered body, and was finally found Wednesday, May 2, *"the buzzards indicating its locality. When found, the body was covered by the debris sufficiently to keep the buzzards from it. It was decently buried by the side of its mother."*

Jocephus Roop left Heard County that fall (1883) with several men (William Garrison, Frank McWhorter, and J.H. Parham) for Bell County, Texas, according to a news item in the November 1, 1883 issue of *The LaGrange Reporter*. Ceph reportedly remarried and reared another family there.

As explained earlier in this article, Carrie Lee Merrill (Cook) was born sometime just before or during the storm. Because many records were destroyed when the Heard County Courthouse burned in the late 1880s, Carrie later had to prove her birthdate to qualify for a pension.

To accomplish this, Carrie asked a neighbor, the late Byrd Wood of Ephesus, if he remembered her birthdate.

"He said he sure did," related Carrie's daughter, Verna Cook Smith in a later interview. "He told her it was the night of the freshet. She took him to Franklin and he told the people in the courthouse and she went to drawin' (her pension)."

Eighty years after the terrible storm, Carrie finally expired from natural causes on February 2, 1963. The petite God-fearing mother and grandmother – with the help of her husband, Lucious Riley Cook – had raised 12 children.

Merrill-Roop Cemetery

The following individuals are buried in the Merrill-Roop Cemetery, near the original mill village site adjacent to Hillabatchee Creek:

Sarah J. Merrill (May 4, 1827 – Dec. 1, 1886)

Georgia A. Merrill Roop (Oct. 15, 1856 – April 23, 1883)

Little Ella (Jan. 2, 1882 – April 23, 1883)

Bula Roop (Nov. 1, 1878 – April 23, 1883)

Homer D. Roop (broken headstone with initials H.D.R.) (April 15, 1880 – April 23, 1883)

The gristmill on the Hillabatchee was rebuilt after the flood, but the spirit of the community had been broken. The Merrills, devastated by the tragedy, moved to another mill town in nearby Alabama.

Today, very little – aside from the tiny abandoned cemetery – remains to mark the mill village which once existed on this site. With the rush of the Hillabatchee just a short distance away, Mother Earth wraps her great arms around the remains of those buried quietly here in this final repository among the tall trees and briary weeds in the low hill country of Heard County.

Fateful Day At Griswoldville: The Georgia Militia's Last Hurrah

Numerous articles have been written over the years about many different battles in the U.S. Civil War. One obscure – but very bloody – engagement of this terrible conflict demonstrated the courageous – if misguided – efforts of a remnant of the once-mighty Confederate army which, by war's end, had been reduced to mostly old men and young boys.

Because most of the state of Georgia's reserve militia were shielded from conscription into the Confederate army through special exemptions granted by Governor Joseph E. Brown, the members of the militia were often mockingly referred to as "Joe Brown's Pets" by the regular conscripts. Time and time again, the militia was granted furloughs and other opportunities to avoid the hell being endured by the line soldiers in the Southern forces, but by 1864, the South was running out of men.

Militia Brigadier General Robert Toombs who was the inspector-general and chief of staff of the Georgia Militia, was disappointed at the poor state of training he found while inspecting the battle-readiness of his organization in 1864. He described them as "a mixed crowd" composed of "a large number of earnest, brave, true men; then all the shirkers and skulks in Georgia trying to get out from under bullets."

Late in the war, the militia was finally called to active duty and served under Confederate command in the trenches during the Atlanta campaign. However, after the city fell, much to the dismay of most Georgians, Governor Brown withdrew his militia from the Army of Tennessee and, amazingly, granted them a 30-day agricultural furlough from the war.

Predictably, the militia was lampooned as a laughingstock in the newspapers for going home on "agricultural leave" while Georgia was being invaded by Sherman's army. They were even satirized by the lyrics of a popular song of the day which read:

"Just before the battle, the general hears a row;
"He says 'the Yankees are coming, I hear their rifles now.'
"He turns around in wonder, and what do you think he sees?
"The Georgia Militia, eating goober peas!" [1]

As a result of the jeers and sneers of the

A Georgia State Parks & Historic Sites marker at the entrance to the Griswoldville battlefield site details the troop movements and action of the infamous engagement which occurred in the closing months of the war in November of 1864. The battlefield stretches into the distance at left. (Photo by Joe Griffith)

general public – particularly from the Southern women who were among the fieriest proponents of the war, and the stinging remarks of their soldier counterparts in the Confederate Army, the militiamen were now under enormous pressure to prove their worth as soldiers. They were determined to show they were as willing as any man to fight for their country.[2]

A Vow To "Make Georgia Howl"

In early November of 1864, Union Major General William Tecumseh Sherman telegraphed General-in-Chief of the Armies of the United States Ulysses S. Grant, urging that he be allowed to cut loose from his base at Atlanta to march through the heartland of Georgia, living off the land, and destroying all things not needed by his army until he reached the sea. Sherman asserted: "I can make the march and make Georgia howl!"[3]

TO THE CITIZENS OF MACON.

HEAD QUARTERS,

Macon, July 30, 1864.

The enemy is now in sight of your houses. We lack force. I appeal to every man, Citizen or Refugee, who has a gun of any kind, or can get one, to report at the Court House with the least possible delay, that you may be thrown into Companies and aid in the defense of the city. A prompt response is expected from every patriot.

JOSEPH E. BROWN.

☞ Report to Col. Cary W. Styles, who will forward an organization as rapidly as possible.

One of the last stirring appeals for militia recruits was issued by Governor Joseph E. Brown in 1864, and was posted throughout Macon. (Courtesy of Middle Georgia Archives, Washington Memorial Library, Macon)

Grant agreed and on the morning of November 16, 1864, Sherman's Union army of 62,000 men, divided into two divergent columns, departed Atlanta – which was left devastated in smoking ruins – to begin their "march to the sea."

As they moved out along the Macon & Western Railroad line, one of the columns was commanded by General Oliver O. Howard. He appeared to be headed for Macon.

The other column – commanded by General Henry W. Slocum – followed the Georgia Railroad line and appeared to be headed due east toward Augusta.[4]

Along the way, both columns of Sherman's army were busy ripping up railroad tracks and consuming harvested crops as they "foraged liberally" for food on what one Union veteran described as a "gigantic pleasure excursion." Sherman's goal was to create a giant swath of destruction and horrendous devastation along his path in order to convince Georgians "that it is in their interest not to impede our movements."

Thus, with no significant military opposition from the Confederate army, Sherman waged his war against the helpless old men, women, and children remaining on their land in rural Georgia.[5]

Union soldiers feasted upon "confiscated" corn, beans, peanuts, sorghum molasses, sweet potatoes, pigs, turkeys, and chickens roasted on their campfires fueled with a Georgia farmer's fence rails. In addition, Sherman had a corps of foragers, fittingly called "bummers," detailed to operate along the fringes of the marching columns to raid the isolated farms, taking not only food, but anything of value, such as the family silverware and jewelry. They claimed the right to liberate such items as the spoils of war.[6]

Families whose husbands, sons, and fathers were away to war in Tennessee or Virginia watched from their front porches in horror as parties of the Northern invaders swarmed over their property committing acts of pillage, robbery, and violence. These bummers usually did not harm the individuals in the homes, but they took away whatever was possible to carry, and then destroyed the rest.

Sherman, no doubt, was successful in humiliating Georgians as he intended, but he also created a raging hatred for him and his brethren among the people of Georgia. In later years, they demanded revenge at any opportunity and – in many instances – at any cost.[7]

The Militia Recalled

By November of 1864, the only troops available to confront Sherman's army were the Georgia Militia who were called back into service following their 30-day "agricultural leave" to defend the heartland against the invaders.[8]

Hurriedly, the returning militiamen – along with some new recruits from other sources – were organized into the First Division, Georgia Militia,

The adolescent, almost resigned visage of Private S.J. Baldwin of the First Georgia State Line shows the youthfulness characterized by much of the militia troops by 1864. Baldwin was barely 16 years of age when this photo was taken. (Photo courtesy of Kennesaw Mtn Battlefield National Park)

A lonely headstone in Providence Canyon Cemetery identifies the final resting place of Williamson E. Perkins who was one of the many unfortunate souls who perished at the battle of Griswoldville. (Photo by Gary Elam)

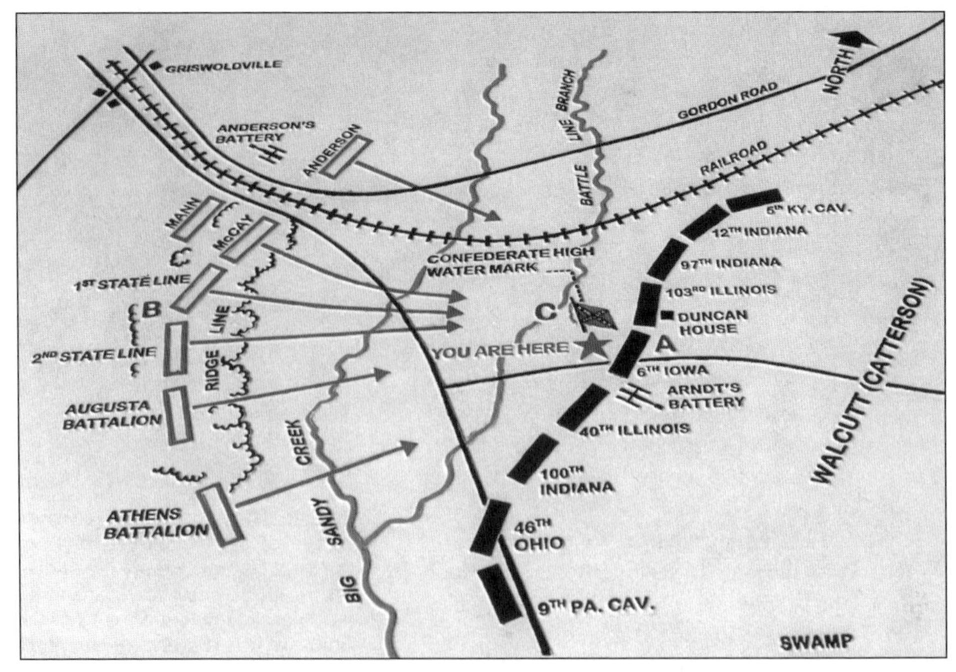

This sketch map of the Griswoldville battle action is displayed on the Georgia State Parks & Historic Sites interpretive marker. The Confederate units are shown approaching "Battle Line Branch" where they launched the final assaults upon the entrenched Union troops on the ridge. It was in the bloody branch and on the slope above it that repeated frontal attacks stalled and hundreds of dead and wounded Georgians were left abandoned on the battlefield. (Photo by Joe Griffith)

and then divided into four makeshift brigades, each about the size of a standard regiment of one-thousand men. On the morning of November 21, the commander of the Department of Georgia, Florida, and South Carolina – Lieutenant General William J. Hardee – realized that Sherman's move toward Macon was only a feint and he, incorrectly as it turned out, assumed that he was instead headed for Augusta to destroy its munitions factories. He therefore, ordered the militia division, under the command of Major General Gustavus W. Smith, to go north to defend Augusta.[9]

On Tuesday morning of November 22, three brigades of the division – along with two regiments of the Georgia State Line and Anderson's Battery of Light Artillery – marched east from Macon along the railroad tracks of the Central of Georgia Railroad on their way to defend Augusta. The division was under the command of the senior militia brigadier general, Pleasant J. Phillips, because General Smith had remained behind at Macon to make arrangements for needed supplies.

Because the tracks east of Macon had been ripped up by the Federals and as such were useless, Smith ordered Phillips to march his troops along the tracks 10 miles to Griswoldville in Jones County, and wait there for further orders. Smith was to rejoin the division there later in the day. Then, Smith planned to march his men beyond the damaged tracks to a secure area where they could be transported by rail to Augusta.[10]

Through the freezing cold weather and

the light snow flurries of the day, the militia division marched along the railroad tracks anticipating an opportunity to get into the fight against the hated Yankees. However, it would be safe to say that none among them would have guessed the price they were about to pay when they were ultimately confronted by the enemy only a half day's march away to the east at a small industrial community known as Griswoldville.[11]

The Federal Defense At Duncan's Farm

Unbeknownst to the advancing militia, on the road ahead to the east were the smoldering ruins of the industrial village of Griswoldville where there had been a cavalry skirmish that morning. Located 10 miles east of Macon, Griswoldville was a settlement along the Georgia Central Railroad in southeastern Jones County. In the 1840s, the village had grown up around a pistol factory and other industries established by Connecticut-born ironmaster, Samuel H. Griswold.[12]

On the morning of November 21, 1864, Murray's brigade of Kilpatrick's Union cavalry had avoided the Confederate cavalry which had been picketing the road leading to Griswoldville, and had approached the village through the woods where they drove off the Confederate cavalry. Murray's men then destroyed the railroad station, water tank, a locomotive with 13 cars, twenty tons of wrought iron, the pistol factory, a candle factory, four hundred boxes of soap, twelve wagons and carts, and a shoe-blackening factory. After that was completed, they set fire to the entire village except for Sam Griswold's house, the slave quarters, and one of the worker's houses. Then, the Federals had set up camp for the night on the east fork of the Little Sandy Creek about two miles east of Griswoldville.[13]

The next morning, the Federal camp was attacked at dawn by elements of Joe Wheeler's Confederate cavalry. Fighting in the vicinity continued until mid-morning when Walcutt's Union brigade arrived to reinforce Murray and enabled him to drive Wheeler back through Griswoldville toward Macon. Walcutt then withdrew his brigade to a place about a mile and a half east of Griswoldville where he and his men took up defensive positions.[14]

Although Wheeler's cavalry had been repelled from the Griswoldville area, it was anticipated that he would return to strike again. Therefore, Walcutt's battle-hardened brigade of 1,513 men was now positioned to the east of the smoldering village to guard the flank of the main columns of Sherman's army against any further interference from the troublesome Confederate cavalry.[15]

About one and a half miles east of Griswoldville along the Central of Georgia Railroad, an old abandoned farm house stood on a ridge to the southeast. Though the farm had been sold to Samuel Griswold, it was still known as "the Duncan farm." Mr. Duncan had moved to Macon County and no one lived in the house or worked the farm. On the ridge on the old farm property, General Frank Walcutt, the Federal brigade commander, formed his line of defense.[16]

The next morning, the Federal camp was attacked at dawn by elements of Joe Wheeler's Confederate cavalry.

Walcutt's troops

were spread out for approximately one mile along the ridge. His artillery battery of four three-inch ordnance rifles was positioned on the road near the old farm house.

On both flanks, there were natural barriers. A swamp existed on the brigade's left, and a deep cut at the railroad tracks existed on the right, protecting the Federals against an enemy attack from either flank. Their defensive position on the ridge afforded the brigade a perfect view and sweep of the open field leading up to the ridge from Griswoldville.[17]

Approximately 100 acres in an open field before Walcutt's troops was soon to become a bloody battlefield. Since it was formerly a cultivated field, it was bare of any trees or bushes behind which an approaching enemy might hide or take cover.

From the timber line, the field ran comparatively level, sloping gradually from the edge of the woods northeast across Big Sandy Creek and then across a small tributary of the Big Sandy, later to be called "Battle Line Branch." This branch had a swampy area centered on its stream bed some twenty yards wide at places, and was filled with gallberry, box tree briars, and other piney woods growth.[18]

By noon on the 22nd of November, the Federal brigade was fortified on the high ground of the ridge and ready to fend off any attempt by the anticipated Confederate cavalry to travel cross-country to the east on the roads through Duncan's farm.[19]

A Surprise Encounter

All the time that Walcutt was preparing his defenses at Duncan's farm – anticipating a cavalry attack – the militia division column from Macon was marching blindly into the trap. As they trudged along the railroad headed east, the militia gave the appearance of almost anything other than that of an army.

In his memoirs of the war, Sam R. Watkins, a regular Confederate army soldier who had fought from Shiloh to Nashville, gave his acerbic impression of what he called "Old Joe Brown's Pets" when they were first called up to defend Atlanta as follows:

> *"By way of grim jest, and a fitting burlesque to tragic scenes, or, rather to the thing called "glorious war," old Joe Brown, then Governor of Georgia, sent his militia. It was the richest picture of an army I ever saw. It beat Forepaugh's double-ringed circus. Every one was dressed in citizen's clothes, and the very best they had at the time. A few had double-barreled shotguns, but the majority had umbrellas and walking sticks, and nearly every one had on a duster, a flat-bosomed "biled" shirt, and a plug hat; and, to make the thing more ridicules (sic), the dwarf and the giant were marching side by side. . . ."*[20]

With no clue as to the horrors they soon would face, this motley crew of "soldiers" marched unknowingly into the terrible killing machine awaiting them up ahead on the ridge at Duncan's farm.

The men of the Battery were highly respected as artillerists by the Confederates, and feared by the Federals.

Attached to the militia for their movement to Augusta, however, were two experienced groups of soldiers. One was the Georgia State Line, composed of two very under-strength regiments which originally had included 1,000 men each.

The State Line had been organized into state service to be used primarily as bridge guards for the Western & Atlantic Railroad in the wake of the Union railroad raid at Big Shanty in 1862. However, by 1864, the State Line troops had seen considerable combat service in the trenches during the Atlanta Campaign. Now, with a total of only 400 men left in their ranks, the two regiments were marching with the militia under the command of Lieutenant Colonel Beverly D. Evans.[21]

The other experience unit attached to the militia was the 14th Georgia Light Artillery Battery under the command of Captain Ruel W. Anderson. The most seasoned of the Confederates, Anderson's battery had fought in Tennessee and Virginia, as well as in Georgia during the Atlanta Campaign.

The men of the Battery were highly respected as artillerists by the Confederates, and feared by the Federals. Anderson's four powerful Napoleon 12-pounders could rain havoc upon an enemy and definitely influence the outcome of any conflict in which they were involved. On the morning of their departure from Macon, Anderson's Battery was attached to the militia division to provide artillery support for the campaign.[22]

The Slaughter At Battleline Branch

At a point approximately one mile west of Griswoldville, at about 1:00 p.m. in the afternoon, the militia force overtook elements of the Confederate reserve that had departed Macon ahead of the militia. The Confederate reserve was composed of two battalions of workers from the Cook Armory at Athens, Georgia and the Augusta powder works at Augusta. Both battalions, at a combined strength of only 400 men,

Pictured here is the view the Confederate troops had as they moved out of the gullies of "Battle Branch Line" and charged up the slope toward the entrenched Federals at the woodline on the ridgetop in the distance. Visible right-center is the road which leads up to the old Duncan farm site. It was along this road that the Federals deployed their artillery in order to sweep the field with deadly shrapnel. (Photo by Joe Griffith)

The entrance to Griswoldville Battlefield State Park. To the left is a historical marker and information board. The interpretive marker below Old Glory stands at the approximate center of the Federals' defensive line on Duncan's farm. In the field beyond the interpretive marker is a Confederate flag which indicates the nearest point to which the Confederates were able to advance before being cut to pieces by the Union cannon and rifle fire. (Photo by Joe Griffith)

were under the overall command of Major F.W.C. Cook, an Englishman, who owned the armory at Athens.[23]

Although all the units were headed for Augusta, Cook did not wish to be associated with the disreputable militia, and had left Macon in advance of the main body of the division. Cook's battalions were mostly men of conscription age and were armed with excellent rifles of the Enfield pattern made at the Athens armory. The men had some combat experience earned during the Atlanta Campaign.

Cook now was stopped, his battalions deployed in a line straddling the railroad, facing to the east toward the smoldering ruins of Griswoldville. He was awaiting orders as to how to proceed when General Phillips arrived on the scene and assumed overall command of Cook's battalions as an attachment to the militia division, no doubt much to Cook's chagrin.[24]

Phillips believed he faced a Union force at Duncan's farm of from eight to twelve hundred men, and that his force of 5,000 men outnumbered them at least four to one. He planned to attack the flanks and then the center of the Federal line.

Phillips' men, however, contrary to this strategy, formed up into three successive lines and, supported by Anderson's artillery battery, conducted a series of uncoordinated frontal assaults on the entrenched Federals on the ridge.[25]

With bayonets fixed, noisy Rebel yells in their throats and flags fluttering, Phillips' men moved across the open field. There was an eerie calm at first as the Confederates advanced across the open field. Then, all hell broke loose.

The Federal artillery opened up and inflicted some casualties on the Confederates as the shells burst. Men dropped in their tracks as the shrapnel mowed them down.

Anderson's Confederate battery answered with its own accurate fire. The first shell destroyed a Federal caisson and subsequent rounds killed six horses. Several artillerists were also wounded, and one gun was destroyed. Fearing total destruction, the Federals pulled their remaining guns back from the line and out of action.[26]

The Federal troops on the ridge held their small arms fire until the enemy came to within range – about 250 yards – and then poured a steady fire into the Confederates as they ran forward to take cover in the gullies of Battleline Branch less than 100 yards from the Federals on the ridge.

At this point, the Confederate attack plan broke down completely. Major Cook, who was with his men to the right of Evans' men and supposed to make the initial charge in the first line of skirmishers, did not receive the order to charge until Evans' men had already made their way across the field toward Battleline Branch.

Men dropped in their tracks as the shrapnel mowed them down.

Just short of the branch, Evans' men delivered a heavy volley of fire at the entrenched Federals on the ridge, and then resumed their advance across the swampy branch and up the slope toward the Federal line. At the bottom of the slope, however, Evans' men halted once again and fired another quick volley. Due to their position in the gully at the foot of the ridge (and the resulting convex curve of the slope to the ridge), the fire from Evans' men passed high over the heads of the Federals. Of course, that same terrain feature protected the Confederates from the Federal fire also as long as they remained in the gullies.[27]

At this point in the battle, while reconnoitering the front, the Federal brigade commander, General Walcutt, was wounded in the leg by shrapnel from an artillery burst, and was evacuated to the rear leaving Colonel Robert F. Catterson in command of the brigade to finish the fight.[28]

Once again, the Federals held their small arms fire until the Confederates came up out of the branch onto the slope in front of the ridge. When the charging troops were in full view and filling the sights of the Federals' weapons, Catterson gave the order to open fire which was echoed down the line by the regimental commanders.

The line immediately erupted with a thunderous roar of fire from the Federal Springfield muskets and seven-shot Spencer repeating rifles. In the process, a literal sheet of lead which cut down the Confederate troops as effectively as a scythe cleanly harvests wheat, felled wave after wave of Southern fighting men.

As Evans' ranks crumbled beneath the horrendous hail of bullets from the fortified heights, the dazed Southerners were hurled back down the slope where they sought cover in the briars and thickets of the gullies of the branch they had just crossed with such confidence only moments earlier.[29]

And then, inexplicably, Evans' men began taking fire from the rear as well as from the entrenched troops on the ridge. The second line of the inexperienced militia had come up from behind, and as a result of the confusion amid the noise and smoke from the ridge, had begun firing into Evans' men, mistaking them for the enemy as they scrambled back down the slope seeking cover in the branch. Soon, the entire Confederate force – which for some inexplicable reason included the reserve brigade as well – had sought refuge in the overgrown branch gullies which were now crowded with a mass of desperately confused, dying, and dead Southern soldiers.[30]

Even with all the misery of these poor men, in their minds, retreat was not an option. They had suffered too much at the hands of their detractors and tormentors in the past. They would not turn tail and run this time.

For about two hours more, assault after assault was mounted from the gullies of the branch as the men desperately attempted to fight their way up the slope to the Federal line. Some reports today maintain there were three assaults, but others claim there were as many as seven unsuccessful attempts to reach the Federals.

On each assault, the result was the same. The Confederate soldiers were cut down and hurled back down the slope into the bloody branch. Not once did the charging Southerners reach the Federal line. In fact, their best effort fell more than 45 yards short of the Yankees.[31]

Then, as if God would no longer stand witness to such wanton killing, the sun began to go down at five o'clock, and under the cover of darkness, the surviving Confederates left the battlefield and moved back to Griswoldville. The Federals, their blood lust apparently sated, made no attempt to pursue them.

Later reports of this incident maintained that Phillips intended to camp near Griswoldville and bring off his dead and wounded from the battlefield, but this never occurred. Instead, the Georgia militia and its attachments apparently had seen enough of the horrors of war. They immediately departed the area to return to Macon.[32]

The Harvest Of Death

Behind him on the frozen ground of the battlefield, Phillips shamefully left the wounded and dying, along with all of the dead. When the Federal skirmishers moved down the slope from their defensive positions after dark to see what had happened to the Confederates, they discovered large numbers of wounded, dying and dead Confederates in the thickets of the branch and in the field beyond. Young boys and old men lay dead or writhing in agony, begging for a drink of water.[33]

The casualty reports of the engagement were inconsistent. The Confederates reported 422 wounded, but oddly, only 51 dead. In contrast, the Federals estimated that over 300 dead and from 700 to 1,200 wounded Confederates were left on the field of action.

The Federals reported their own losses at 13 killed and 79 wounded. Most of the Federal casualties were inflicted by the shrapnel from Anderson's effective artillery fire. The *Macon Telegraph* newspaper, in reporting the battle casualties, estimated the Confederate losses at 1,500 killed and wounded.[34]

The Federals took from the field 42 wounded Confederates that could be moved as prisoners and sent them to the rear. Those that could not be moved were mercifully provided with the canteens and blankets of the dead for their comfort, but, again, were shamefully left on the field where they fell.[35]

At 9:00 p.m. that night, Catterson moved Walcutt's brigade from Duncan's farm, and rejoined Wood's division to resume their eastward march taking along their wounded and the Confederate prisoners. The Federal dead were wrapped in their blankets and buried on the ridge where they were killed.

The dead and dying Confederates scattered on the field of action in the darkness were left to their misery, exposed to the windy cold of the night. Perhaps the next morning, a relative or friend learned of their fate and came searching for them at Duncan's farm.[36]

Ironically, Colonel Thomas Hardeman, General G.W. Smith's adjutant, sent General Phillips a message from General Smith stating: "The general [Smith] is gratified at your success in driving before you the enemies of your country."

Privately, General Smith later wrote: "He [Phillips] was instructed not to engage the enemy, but, if pressed, to fall back to the fortifications of East Macon; or, if necessary, toward the south in the direction already taken by Wheeler's cavalry. Contrary to my instructions the militia became engaged about one mile beyond Griswoldville and were badly cut up."[37]

Epitaph To The Vanquished

Since the infamous battle, numerous historians have tried to explain why the Georgia militia made such a furious – and unwise – attack on the Federals at Duncan's farm. Georgia historian Charles C. Jones, Jr., who was a Confederate officer during the Savannah Campaign, concluded that "The battle of Griswoldville will be remembered as an unfortunate accident. . . [which was] unnecessary, unexpected, and utterly unproductive of any good."

No doubt, from the Confederate point of view, the battle was unfortunate in its outcome, but it was no accident that it occurred. The militia clearly had chosen to fight at Griswoldville – to the death if necessary – to rid their homeland of the hated northern invaders. They were gallant soldiers defeated on the field of battle.

Perhaps Major General Howell Cobb, commander of Georgia's Confederate Reserve Force, best described the aggressive mood of "Joe Brown's Pets" at Griswoldville when he surmised, "They dread the jeers and sneers which they must encounter. . . more than they do the bullets of the Yankees."[38]

ENDNOTES

1/ Richard Barksdale Harwell, ed., *Songs of the Confederacy* (New York, 1951), 100-101; Steven A. Channing, Confederate Ordeal: The Southern Home Front (Alexandria, VA: Time-Life Books, 1984), 155; Joseph H. Parks, Joseph E. Brown (Baton Rouge, LA: Louisiana State University Press, 1977), 282-288; Pleasant A. Stovall, Robert Tombs (New York, 1892), 278.

2/ William Harris Bragg, *Griswoldville* (Macon, GA: Mercer University Press, 2000), 144.

3/ Burke Davis, *Sherman's March* (New York: Random House, 1988), 23; Charles Colcock Jones, Jr., *Siege of Savannah in December, 1864* (Albany, NY: J. Munsell, 1874), 3.

4/ Stanley P. Hirshson, *The White Tecumseh* (New York: John Wiley & Sons, Inc., 1997), 252-253.

5/ Davis, *Sherman's March*, 28-31; Hirshson, *The White Tecumseh*, 256; War of the Rebellion: *Official Records of the Union and Confederate Armies*, 70 vols. In 128 pts. (Washington, D.C.: Government Printing House, 1880-1901), vol. 44: 13, 152 (hereafter referred to as OR 44:13, 152).

6/ John T. Billings, *Hard Tack and Coffee* (Boston: George M. Smith & Co., 1887), 239-241; Davis, *Sherman's March*, 33-36; Hirshson, *The White Tecumseh*, 253; Jones, Siege of Savannah, 168.

7/ Billings, *Hard Tack and Coffee*, 249; Davis, *Sherman's March*, 39-41; OR 44:13.

8/ Davis, Sherman's March, 25, 29.

9/ Ibid, 53.

10/ OR 53:41.

11/ Morton R. McInvale, "All That Devils Could Wish For: The Griswoldville Campaign," *Georgia Historical Quarterly*, (Summer, 1976): 123-130.

12/ Carolyn White Williams, *History of Jones County* (Round Oak, GA: W.H. Wolfe Associates, 1992), 155.

13/ OR 44:384.

14/ Ibid, 44:82-83.

15/ Ibid, 44:82-83, 97.

16/ Ibid, 44:83.

17/ McInvale, "All That Devils Could Wish For," 125; OR 44:97-98.

18/ Williams, *History of Jones County*, 156.

19/ OR 44:97-98, 53:44.

20/ Bragg, *Griswoldville*, 122; Sam R. Watkins, Co. Aytch (New York: Simon & Schuster, 1997), 197.

21/ Scaife, *The March To The Sea*, 52.

22/ Ibid.

23/ OR 53:41.

24/ Ibid.

25/ OR 53:40-43; H.H. Orendorf, et al., compilers, *Reminiscences of the Civil War From Diaries of Members of the 103rd Illinois Volunteer Infantry* (Chicago, IL: J.F. Leaming, 1904), 151-152; Williams, History of Jones County, 161.

26/ OR 53:28, 42; Orendorf, *103rd Illinois Volunteer Infantry*, 151-152, 154; Williams, History of Jones County, 157, 161; Henry H. Wright, *A History of the Sixth Iowa Infantry* (Iowa City, IA: State Historical Society of Iowa, 1923), 366-367.

27/ OR 44:97-98, 105-107; 53:39-44; Orendorf, *103rd Illinois Volunteer Infantry*, 152.

28/ OR 44:105.

29/ OR 44:97-98, 105-107, 53:39-44; Orendorf, *103rd Illinois Volunteer Infantry*, 152, 154-155.

30/ OR 44:41-45, 97-98, 105-107, 53:28-29, 39-44; Orendorf, *103rd Illinois Volunteer Infantry*, 152.

31/ OR 44:81, 97, 53:28-29; Orendorf, *103rd Illinois Volunteer Infantry*, 152; Wright, *Sixth Iowa Infantry*, 366-367.

32/ *Macon Telegraph*, 23-24 November, 1864; OR 44:81, 97-98, 53:28-29, 40-43, 35; 53:39; Orendorf, *103rd Illinois Volunteer Infantry*, 153.

33/ OR 53:28-29; Orendorf, *103rd Illinois Volunteer Infantry*, 153.

34/ *Macon Telegraph*, 24 November 1864; Williams, *History of Jones County*, 162.

35/ OR 53:28-29, 39.

36/ Bragg, *Griswoldville*, 143; McInvale, "All That Devils Could Wish For," 128; Wright, *Sixth Iowa Infantry*, 367, 369, 371.

37/ OR 44:97-98, 143, 53:39.

38/ Jones, *Siege of Savannah*, 27; *Macon Telegraph*, 24 November 1864; OR 44:143, 45:41.

The Griswoldville Battlefield Today

Incredibly, the battlefield at Griswoldville is virtually unchanged today from its appearance as described in 1864. In June of 1977, a group of concerned preservationists purchased 17.3 acres of the former battlefield and established a small state park on the site of Duncan's farm. On November 21, 1998, an interpretive marker was dedicated at a ceremony at the park.

While positioned at the historic marker, one is standing at the center of the Federal army's defensive line and looking out over the battlefield toward "Battleline Branch," where the Confederates mounted their desperate assaults at the Union forces. Details of the action are described and illustrated to the viewer.

The present-day Confederate flag in the open field in front of the marker designates the nearest point to the Federal line reached by the Confederates during their assaults. The flag is a blood red reminder of the dead and dying Rebel soldiers – mostly militia and state troops – who ended their final charge there on November 22, 1864.

Because the individual militia and state troop units were normally recruited from a particular county, the units were filled with multiple members of various and local families, as well as close friends from the same neighborhoods. Therefore, when such a unit made a charge on the field of battle, they were proud to be aligned shoulder to shoulder with both relatives and friends – and doubly saddened at the loss of these close brethren.

When the skirmish line was mutilated on the slope at Duncan's farm, the men fell together in crumpled heaps, with family members and friends intertwined in death. According to a report, when the Federals moved down the slope after darkness had fallen and the mobile Confederates had withdrawn, they found among the dying and dead a fourteen-year-old boy still alive with a bullet shattered arm and leg. In the pile of dead around him were his father, two of his brothers, and his uncle. Such was the tragedy of the battle of Griswoldville.

Little-known today, this sanguinary battle in Jones County was the only significant engagement fought between Confederate and Federal forces as Sherman moved from Atlanta in his "March To The Sea." The Griswoldville Battlefield State Park is located ten miles east of Macon, northeast of State Highway 57.

There is no admission charge to visit the park. For more information, contact the Georgia State Parks & Historic Sites offices at (800) 864-7275 or (770) 389-7275.

In Search Of Doc Holliday In Valdosta, Georgia

His legacy as a gambler and fearsome gunfighter in the Old West are secure. Less known, however are the details of the life John Henry "Doc" Holliday lived during his adolescence in Valdosta, Georgia.

If there is one sure thing that can be said of the legacy of John Henry "Doc" Holliday, it is that there is virtually no agreement whatsoever about much of the story of his life.

No one knows this better than Susan McKey Thomas of Valdosta, Georgia, the legendary gunfighter's 82-year-old first cousin once removed, who has spent the better part of three decades trying to sort through competing popular mythologies for the truth.

"I have no ax to grind, and I have no one to protect," says Thomas, whose sharp wit and elegantly groomed appearance give little hint of her age. "I'm just trying to get to the truth."

Thomas's historical odyssey began in 1972, when members of the Lowndes County Historical Society were asked to submit summaries of their family backgrounds for inclusion in the society's records.

Wading into waters fraught with hearsay and legend, Thomas and Albert Pendleton, secretary of the society's newsletter, discovered what Thomas called "many shocking inaccuracies" about her famous relative.

"One of the first things we found out was that Wyatt Earp was a pimp," offers the 77-year-old Pendleton. Indeed, historians support the claim that several of the Earp brothers and their wives – some of whom were prostitutes themselves – ran brothels across the Old West.

The story of Doc Holliday in the West, however accurate it may or may not be, is reasonably well-known. Less known, however, is the story of the Holliday family in Valdosta, where John Henry spent much of his adolescence and young adult life.

Even here, Thomas and Pendleton ran into a myriad of conflicting stories, enough so that it took 18 months of painstaking research before Thomas felt she could submit her family story to the historical society.

The work of Thomas and Pendleton, in fact, turned up so much information that Thomas's contribution took the form of a book, "*In Search of the Hollidays,*" published in 1973 by Little River Press.

"We found out so many things that it just seemed like we needed to write them

John Henry Holliday was photographed here shortly after his graduation from the Pennsylvania College of Dental Surgery. He lived a scant 15 years after this photo was taken, the last few months of which were spent in Leadville and Glenwood Springs, Colorado. (Photo by O.B. DeMorat)

The Major Henry B. Holliday headstone in Valdosta. Just as with his famous son, Major Holliday has a headstone, but the exact location of his last remains is a total mystery today. (Photo by Martin Register)

down," Pendleton said.

The book turned out to be something of a local sensation, and in the years that followed, copies were sold to history buffs from almost every state and several foreign countries. From that effort, the desire to know more about her famous forebear has driven Thomas to an ongoing investigation about most of the Holliday mystique, including the eight years in which John Henry lived in Valdosta.

The story of John Holliday in Valdosta begins early in 1864, when his father, Major Henry B. Holliday, brought his family to a settlement of about 1,500 people in what then was a virtual wilderness in extreme south Georgia. It was far from the Holliday family home in Griffin, Georgia, but it was a safe haven from the looming Federal siege of Atlanta and surrounding regions.

Major Holliday, a veteran of the Indian wars, the Mexican War and the Civil War, had retired from military service and found refuge in a large tract of land northeast of Valdosta, near a tiny community known as Bemiss.

By that time, the Hollidays had already reared to manhood a young orphan – Francisco Hidalgo – brought home by Major Holliday in 1849 after the Mexican War.

In earlier years when he had lived in Griffin, Georgia, Major Holliday – as he was formally known – had worked as a druggist. In the largely unsettled south Georgia countryside, however, he became an entrepreneur, opening a plant nursery, planting vineyards and promoting the production of pecans, a profession which has grown into a major agricultural industry today stretching from Valdosta westward across the clay hills of southwest Georgia.

Ms. Thomas said the young John Holliday, 12 years old when he arrived in Valdosta, was remembered by area residents as being nice looking, slightly built, with piercing blue eyes and blonde hair.

Later biographies recorded Doc Holliday's gracious manners as well as his unpredictable temperament, but Valdostans remembered only a well-mannered adolescent who dressed neatly and grew into a young man known for his dancing ability amidst the musical talent of his McKey relatives.

History correctly records that young John Henry was well-educated. He was schooled at the private Valdosta Institute which, as reported by Louis Pendleton in his *Echo of Drums,* stressed classics and taught "advanced branches." Headmaster Samuel McWhir Varnedoe set up a challenging curriculum including Greek, Latin, French, advanced English, mathematics and history.

Following the end of the Civil War, the Holliday/McKey family clung to at least an appearance of affluence. The young Holliday's three McKey uncles, James, William and Thomas, bought a large tract of land in the lakes area along the Georgia-Florida border south of Valdosta in an area known as Bellview.

The McKey property, known as Banner Plantation, is said to have been a favorite haunt of John Henry, who reportedly spent much of his adolescent years hunting and fishing on the property. His favorite uncle, Tom, who was only 10 years older than John, often accompanied him.

Years later and a world away in the Kansas cow town of Dodge City, John Henry assumed the alias Thomas Mackey (as the family surname was then spelled) for a short time, presumably because he had encountered some type of trouble and needed to disguise his identity.

"I don't know why he did that," Thomas says. "He wasn't famous, really, until the OK Corral."

The Major Henry B. Holliday house in Valdosta in which a young John Henry Holliday lived for approximately four years following his mother's death in 1866. (Photo courtesy of Lowndes County Historical Society)

The Major Henry B. Holliday house as it appears today in Valdosta near the Withlacoochee River. The 140-plus year old structure still contains the original wood shingles across the front of the house. (Photo by Martin Register)

Researchers and historians often point with amusement to the many mistakes made by the engraver of Doc Holliday's headstone in Glenwood Springs, Colorado. Interestingly, even some Valdostans seem disinterested in getting the details involving the Holliday family correct today. Pictured here is the street named in honor of Major Henry Burroughs Holliday, Doc's father, in Valdosta. (Photo by Martin Register)

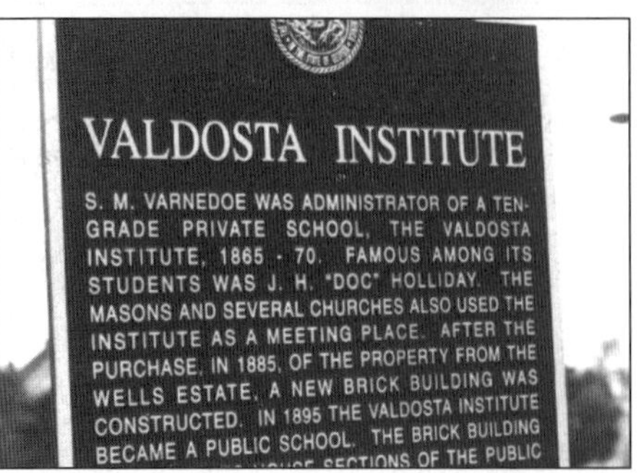

A historic marker indicates the site upon which Valdosta Institute (top photo) once stood. John Henry Holliday was graduated from this school in 1870. (Photo by Martin Register)

Many historians would reply, however, that despite the fact that he hadn't yet been involved in the famous gunfight in Tombstone, John Henry was, nevertheless, becoming known as a testy gunfighter by the time he reached Dodge.

Whatever the case, what seems to have been an idyllic childhood for John Holliday was shattered by tragedy in the form of the unexpected serious illness of his mother, who gradually lost her strength and endured a lingering and torturous state of health until on September 16, 1866, Alice Jane McKey Holliday died.

Ms. Thomas has written that Alice Holliday's death had a devastating impact on John Henry. Family stories, however, maintain that he was shaken worse by the remarriage of his father a mere three months after his mother's death. Major Holliday married Rachel Martin, 23, a young lady who was less than half his age and only nine years older than John Henry.

Other outside factors also impacted the Holliday family. The turbulent years of Reconstruction took a serious toll on the Holliday family's financial fortunes.

Rachel Martin's family owned farmland which adjoined the Holliday property. Records indicate that the Martins purchased the Holliday tract, and that Major Holliday's father-in-law gave to his daughter a house in Valdosta at 405 Savannah Avenue. The Holliday family – including young John Henry – soon relocated to this address.

Never one to take defeat easily, Major Holliday immediately began working to recover the family fortune. He opened several businesses, including a furniture store. The 1870 Census lists him broadly as "general agent." Eventually, Thomas says, Holliday regained all of his former properties.

Major Holliday also gained some acclaim in the political arena of his area. He served four terms as Valdosta's mayor.

However, while his father was prospering, the younger Holliday began pursuing the behavior for which he would become more widely known later in life. Local tradition maintains that he eventually fled town after running afoul of law enforcement officials, although the specifics of his misdeeds are not clear today.

Clues can be found in what has been called a racially-motivated shooting incident in which the teenaged Holliday reportedly was involved. He was also accused of being associated with – and indeed may even have been the mastermind of – a plot to destroy with explosives the federally-operated Lowndes County Courthouse.

Ms. Thomas says she can confirm that the young Holliday was indeed involved in a shooting incident reportedly prompted by his discovery of either a black man or a group of blacks bathing in a swimming hole used by whites near the confluence of the Withlacoochee and Little rivers at the old settlement of Troupville. This incident occurred just a short time after the close of the War Between the States during Reconstruction when racial tensions were high. At that time, many blacks reveled in their new-found status, often inflaming the situation by intentionally flaunting their ability to violate long-standing Southern social mores.

Ms. Thomas says the story involving John Henry was confirmed by none other than Thomas McKey, John's uncle and source of the alias John Henry later used in Dodge City. In the late 1920s, Thomas says McKey related the incident involving John Henry to writer Stuart Lake who was working on what later would become a controversial book about Wyatt Earp.

"He told the story of (McKey and Holliday) going to a swimming hole where whites swam, and they found some blacks in the water," Ms. Thomas related. "[John Henry] first cracked his whip and ordered the blacks out, and then he turned to get his pistol. . . . but one of the blacks got out a gun when he saw that Doc had turned to get his gun."

According to local tradition, a black federal officer was killed in the incident, but in the interview with writer Stuart Lake, Thomas McKey firmly denied anyone was even wounded by a bullet.

Today, there is no microfilm available for *The Valdosta Times* newspaper during the period in question, but McKey's assertion of John Henry's innocence is given some credence by the fact that there is no evidence of such an incident in the records of the superior court for the years 1866 through 1873.

A newspaper account of the plan to destroy the courthouse has been discovered, but it does not implicate John Henry. It does, however, give the name of five other individuals who were accused of the crime.

Major Holliday was one of five men appointed by the Valdosta City Council to draw up a plan to deal with the unrest in the area according to Ms. Thomas. One could surmise that John Henry's family connections could have protected him from prosecution in the courthouse incident, but any such conclusion, like so many others involving Doc Holliday, would be pure conjecture at this late date.

Enter Thomas's statement about her determination to "get to the truth" of the story involving John Henry Holliday.

Whatever trouble John Henry may have initiated as a teen, he went on to graduate from the Valdosta Institute in 1870. Later that year, he applied and was admitted to the Pennsylvania College of Dental Surgery from which he was graduated during the 16th annual graduation ceremonies on March 1, 1872.

During his studies in Pennsylvania, John Henry occasionally returned to work his required "preceptership" with Valdosta dentist Lucian Frederick Frink. Ms. Thomas says there is some evidence that Holliday performed dental work in Valdosta in October of 1871, and it is believed he returned home for a brief visit after his graduation, but a short time later, he struck out for Atlanta to open a dental practice. He did not know it at the time, but he was actually embarking upon a career so far beyond the pale that no one could have seen it coming.

Even as he left Valdosta, the newly anointed "Dr." Holliday was already a doomed man. Within a year, he would be diagnosed with tuberculosis, a disease for which there was no treatment until the mid-20th century.

This diagnosis was a fate that would send John Henry to the drier climate of the West for health reasons, and, within the space of four more years, find him – depending upon whom one believes – becoming a playfully subversive gambler who quite often found himself involved in physical affrays, or simply a cold-blooded killer. Ms. Thomas, in the sincere opinion of one who has sought the truth for so very long, puts Holliday somewhere in the middle of these two extremes.

Historians and researchers today maintain that John Henry almost certainly had been infected with the tuberculosis bacterium for years prior to the diagnosis of his disease. His mother's death in 1866 may well have been from TB, although Thomas says there is no proof of that today.

Interestingly, Francisco Hidalgo, the Mexican youth raised by the Hollidays is known to have died of the dreaded disease himself in 1873, providing strong evidence that the seeds of Doc Holliday's eventual demise in a Colorado hotel in 1887 were sown long before that time, either in Griffin or in Valdosta.

Once he left Valdosta, Doc Holliday apparently considered his break with south Georgia to be permanent. There is no evidence that he ever returned to visit. Indeed, for whatever reason, Doc Holliday never even wrote to his father.

A legend within the family claims that Major Holliday arranged a meeting with his son while in New Orleans at a Confederate veterans' convention in 1885, and begged the ailing Doc to come home to his family.

Whether the meeting ever took place or not is, predictably, unprovable today. What can be said with certainty, however, is that if the estranged father and son had such a meeting, it was their last. Doc Holliday did not return to Georgia, and by 1885, he was so sick that he could barely manage to support himself in the gambling profession any longer.

During her research of John Henry Holliday, Susan Thomas did make one very interesting – and very unexpected – discovery. The orphan – Francisco Hidalgo – left behind a legacy of his own in neighboring Berrien County in the form of the "Edalgo" family, of which he was the progenitor.

After more than a century, that piece of information came as a complete and total surprise to the Edalgos who continue to live there today, and who had been unable to trace their ancestry beyond their local community.

Today, the Holliday legacy is alive and well in Valdosta, even if the Major and Doc are long gone and the Holliday name itself has all but disappeared in the community.

Major Holliday, in addition to serving as mayor of the city, rose to additional prominence in Valdosta. He served as secretary of the Lowndes County Agricultural Society, secretary of the Confederate Veterans of Camp Troup, census enumerator, and superintendent of local elections. He even had a street named for him near the original site of the Holliday house off Savannah Avenue.

The Holliday house, itself, lives on as well. In the 1970s, the aged structure was purchased by Valdosta businessman Dick Davis and moved to a new location off U.S. Highway 41 South. A few years later, the home was given a new lease on life when it was purchased by a local couple and moved to one of the new subdivisions which sprawl far to the northwest of town.

After its relocation, the house was extensively renovated, although many of its original aspects were preserved and incorporated into the new additions to the structure. Today, it is owned and occupied by Dr. David Johnson and his wife, Susan, at 2605 Pebblewood Drive in Valdosta.

Susan McKey Thomas On The Acquaintances Of Doc Holliday

What do we know today that can be confirmed as factual information regarding the life and acquaintances of John Henry Holliday?

For more than a century, the Southern gentleman and Wild West gunman known as Doc Holliday has acquired a reputation as difficult to dissect as the gunfight at O.K. Corral which holds the dubious distinction of having been termed "the most confusing 15 seconds in American history." Even more conflicting, however, are the various modern descriptions of the relationships Doc had with his acquaintances in the Old West.

Fanned by dime novels, rumor, innumerable erroneous articles, books and movies, the brushfire that supposedly represents the real Doc Holliday continues to burn unabated.

Susan McKey Thomas, Holliday's first cousin once-removed, began her pursuit of the truth about her famous forebear years ago when she began trying to piece together her family history for the Lowndes County Historic Society. Perhaps then, it is appropriate that her educated, scrupulously studied opinions of Doc become, if not the last word, at least a part of the final sentence.

Kate Elder

Aside from the famous incident at the O.K. Corral in Tombstone, Arizona, in October of 1881, one of the few things about which most historians agree regarding Holliday was his intimate relationship with Mary Katherine Harony (Haroney), a.k.a. Kate Elder, a prostitute who was known by at least seven different identities during her life. She appears to have been the gunfighter's only romantic interest of consequence.

Though she passes no judgement on the Holliday-Elder coupling, Ms. Thomas says with no reservation that no marriage ever took place regarding the pair, in spite of the fact that many sources accept the marriage as fact and Elder herself was vehement in her assertions that she was Doc's widow.

Ms. Thomas maintains a long list of evidence to back up her assertion to the contrary.

"There are so many reasons not to believe he was ever married to Katie Elder," Ms. Thomas explains. "When she told the story, she said they were married in Valdosta, supposedly on a visit in 1880, and she gave a date. Well, the marriages of that period are available on record, and there is no record of it [the marriage]."

Susan McKey Thomas, researcher and cousin of John Henry "Doc" Holliday in Valdosta. (Photo by Martin Register)

Though she was called "Big Nose" Kate Elder during her years with Holliday, Mary Katherine Harony was a somewhat attractive female in her younger years. According to Karen Holliday Tanner, a cousin of Doc Holliday's, Kate nursed the ailing gunfighter in his last days, using her meager savings to sustain the couple until he died. Though Kate insisted she and Doc were married, Susan McKey Thomas, nevertheless, disputes this claim.

Thomas's argument is augmented by the fact that Doc Holliday almost certainly never returned to Georgia after traveling to the West, nor did he ever write to any of his immediate family. Thomas says most of what they knew of the prodigal son was gleaned from The *Valdosta Daily Times* newspaper.

Then there is the family *Bible.*

"I have an authentic copy of the records in the family Bible," Ms. Thomas continues. "Now his father was a meticulous man, and in that Bible are entries of births, deaths – anything that pertained to the family. The major would have almost certainly entered the marriage – whether he approved of it or not – and he did not enter anything about such a marriage."

Although Doc Holliday did not correspond with his Valdosta relatives, it is a matter of record that he did write regularly to his first cousin, Sister Mary Melanie Holliday, a member of the Sisters of Mercy convent who lived in Augusta and Atlanta. There is a great probability that Sister Mary would have passed along the news of such a marriage, unless Doc specifically instructed her to the contrary, which is always possible too.

But Ms. Thomas says there is even more evidence of the absence of such a marriage. "Katie told an interviewer about their relationship, and not only did she not know the names of Doc's family, but she got Doc's birthdate wrong – by about 10 years!"

Further evidence rests in the fact that census records from 1880 show Doc Holliday residing in Prescott, Arizona with two other men, one of whom was John Gosper, acting governor of the Arizona Territory.

The Earp Family

As far as Doc Holliday's relationship with the Earp family is concerned, it seems a little hazy too, which is not surprising under the circumstances. After an alliance with the Earps which lasted at least four years,

Holliday seems to have parted ways with Wyatt and his brother on questionable terms.

"I can't really say if they parted as friends or as friendly enemies," Thomas says. "I'm not certain, but from everything I can gather, my impression is that they just reached a parting of the ways. Sometimes friendships just reach a point where everything that can be said has been said, and people just go their separate ways. I really think that's probably what happened. Maybe there was no reason to continue their partnership after what happened [in the gunfight and its aftermath in Tombstone]."

Thomas suggests the bond between Holliday and the Earps may well have been little more than a friendship of necessity in what then was virtually a lawless environment, making a parting of the ways less than surprising.

Ms. Thomas says some insight may be gained into Holliday's life and personality, as well as his relationship with the Earps, from a letter Thomas says she received from a very elderly George Earp, dated December 21, 1958.

Responding to a letter from the McKey family written after an appearance on The $64,000 Question quiz show, Earp wrote Thomas that he had known Holliday for a very brief period in Dodge City.

"When I knew him, he was always a gentlemanly fellow," Earp wrote. "He was always wanting to die and apparently wanted to be killed. That is why he always wanted to join Wyatt Earp in those gun battles."

Bat Masterson

Ms. Thomas has a much more definite opinion about Bat Masterson, who, like the Earps, was allied with Holliday during the heady days of Dodge City, Kansas, where Masterson served as city marshal.

"For some reason, Bat Masterson didn't like Doc," Thomas asserts. "He seemed to like the Earps, but he definite-

John Henry Holliday as he appeared in the later years of his life. Gone was the vitality of youth even though he was only in his thirties, age-wise. (Photo courtesy of the Colorado Historical Society)

Bartholomew "Bat" Masterson, as he was originally named, later changed his name to William Barclay Masterson. Photographed (above) in his later years when he was a writer for the *New York Morning Telegraph,* he often spoke and wrote disparagingly of John Henry "Doc" Holliday, whom he had known as a young man in Kansas, Arizona and Denver.

ly didn't like Doc."

Ms. Thomas says she also blames much of the Holliday bad press on Masterson, who went on to write about the period known as the Wild West in respected publications such as *The New York Times.*

"Bat Masterson never wrote anything complimentary about Doc," Thomas adds. "He made some very disparaging remarks about Doc."

Though Ms. Thomas does her best to maintain a position as an impartial historian, she says she clearly sees Masterson as a self-serving opportunist eager to secure a place as one of the heroes of the period when in fact, some sources describe Masterson's law enforcement skills as lax or worse.

"Bat defended himself [in the newspaper] and he had a big audience. Poor old Doc just died young and had no one to defend him."

Movie Portrayals & Doc's Final Days

As far as the movie portrayals of Doc Holliday are concerned, Ms. Thomas says she believes actor Val Kilmer – who researched Holliday extensively for his role in the major motion picture *Tombstone* – may have provided the most accurate portrayal of the man.

"It's obvious that Val thoroughly enjoyed the characterization," Thomas says. "Of course, some of what he portrayed was valid and some was not so valid. But it was obvious he had done his homework."

Thomas says in general, she regards almost all the movie portrayals of Holliday to be wildly inaccurate as well as simply poor cinema. She critiques actor Dennis Quaid's take on Holliday in the movie Wyatt Earp as "horrible, just horrible. . . an absolute waste of time."

Another aspect of Holliday's life upon which history buffs disagree wildly are the circumstances of his death. Thomas says a letter, dated June 12, 1973, addressed to her, nails down with probable finality that information.

The letter quotes A.E. Axtell, city manager of Glenwood Springs, Colorado, where Holliday died on November 8, 1887, after spending two months in and out of consciousness at the Glenwood Hotel. Axtell tells of former Glenwood Springs Mayor Art Kendricks, who worked as a busboy at the hotel during the time of Holliday's death.

Axtell said Kendricks told of carrying bottles of whiskey to Holliday's room and each time being tipped a dime. According to Kendricks, when Holliday finally died, only the busboy and two others attended the funeral.

This seems to cement Ms. Thomas's argument against Katie Elder, who claimed she was with Holliday for the last two months of his life. Still, many sources state unequivocably that Elder was present, attending to Holliday and spending what little savings she had to pay the hotel bill, and finally, after his death, gathering Holliday's belongings and shipping them home to his relatives in Georgia.

And what about the long-standing claim that at the end of his life, Doc regained consciousness just long enough to look at his bare feet and utter the words "This is funny" then take one last breath and die?

Ms. Thomas won't even wait for the question about that incident to be finished.

"The man was in a coma!" she exclaims. "Really, I don't think he regained consciousness for those few seconds just to say that." She shakes her head in disbelief at what she clearly considers an absurdity.

Maybe that piece of folklore isn't really true, but as far as the story of Doc Holliday is concerned, no one really knows what the truth is anymore regarding many aspects of this unusual man's life. And what's more, we probably never will know either. Even the actual location of his grave is a mystery today.

The Great Dahlonega Bank Robbery Of 1913

Father Time has thinned their numbers to the point that there are only a few people remaining who can remember the blazing gunfight in the attempted robbery of the Bank of Lumpkin County on a cold winter's night in 1913.

To most eyes, the streets of sleepy Dahlonega, Georgia, were perfectly normal on the night of February 12, 1913. Theodocia Jones, however, was awakened by the sound of footsteps on the street outside her home on the west side of the public square. Since everyone in this small north Georgia mountain community of little more than 200 households normally "went to bed with the chickens," Theodocia knew instinctively that something out of the ordinary was afoot.

Shivering with dread and cold, she reached for her robe and drew back the curtain just enough to peer out the window into the street. She was alarmed by the sight of four men who were moving back and forth in front of her house. What were they up to?

While she was trying to decide what to do, the men disappeared. Still concerned, Theodocia fell back into a troubled sleep.

The next morning, she was still concerned enough to go next door to the drugstore. There, she made it a point to inform the coffee-drinking men gathered around the pot-bellied stove that "You had better get prepared, because some strangers are hanging around town."

Her warning, however, seemed to fall on deaf ears. The men didn't think Theodocia's warning was anything more than neurotic alarmism. Her husband, Dr. C.H. Jones, had died that past year, and everyone just assumed the widow Jones was nervous from being alone.

Theodocia was concerned enough to go one step further. She sent her eight-year-old daughter, Wanda, to ask a friend to come and spend the next night at their house.

Dynamiting The Safe

Shortly after midnight on February 13, the Jones family was awakened by the sound of a muffled explosion nearby. Wanda and her 10-year-old brother, Charles Harry, started to rush to the windows to see what was happening, but Theodocia grabbed her infant daughter, Frances, from the crib and then hustled her family to the dining room where they all hid behind the chimney.

Other nearby residents were also awakened by the blast, but not everyone was concerned. Mischievous cadets at nearby North Georgia College were fond of slipping out of their dormitories during the wee hours and firing one of the college can-

The house of C.H. and Theodocia Jones on the west-northwest corner of the Dahlonega town square as it looked on the night of February 13, 1913. The previous day, Theodocia had gone to the drugstore next door to warn the men there that there were strangers "hanging around town."

The Jones house, used today as a commercial shop on the Dahlonega town square, was photographed in 1997.

Wanda Jones was only eight years of age when her mother noticed strange men milling around the bank one night in February of 1913.

nons for fun. Windows had already been rattled several times since Christmas, and most people had learned to turn over and go back to sleep.

The noise in the early morning of February 13, however, was so loud and close, that Cleveland Duncan a student rooming in the Hall House on the north side of the Dahlonega town square, stepped out on the second-story porch to see what had happened. From this vantage point he was shocked to see a man with a gun standing directly below him in front of the Bank of Lumpkin County.

The stranger saw Cleveland too, and ordered him back inside, emphasizing his command by firing a round from his pistol. Duncan quickly ducked back inside but had the presence of mind to go straight for the telephone. Looking across the square, he saw that the telephone exchange was dark and closed for the night, but he knew his call would sound a buzzer downstairs in the Meaders' bedroom and summon "Central" (the person operating the switchboard) to the telephone.

Mr. R.C. "Mr. Bob" Meaders was not only the owner and operator of the telephone company, he was also president of the Lumpkin County Bank. Already awakened by the explosion, Mr. Bob was on his way upstairs to the switchboard when the buzzer sounded. When Duncan's excited voice informed him what was happening, Mr. Bob quickly sprang into action. Running back downstairs, he grabbed his clothes and alerted his wife, Maggie.

"Call the sheriff and tell him the bank is being robbed," he barked at her tersely, as he struggled with his pants and coat. "Call all the able-bodied men you can think of too, and find me my pistol!"

A Running Gun Battle

After locating his weapon, Mr. Bob slipped out the back door into the frigid air. He quietly made his way behind Will Jones's store and the Sergeant Building, and thence through the vacant lot to the east end of the apartment building known as the Hall House. He was unobserved by the bank robbers despite the white vapor made by his breath as he exhaled into the frigid morning air.

Meanwhile, "Miss Maggie" left her older daughter in charge of the two younger children and crept upstairs to the telephone exchange to ring Sheriff Tom Ray, even though she was not yet fully acquainted with the operation of the new telephone switchboard. When her image appeared in the large central window by the switchboard, the two bandits posted as lookouts at the courthouse down below knew what she was up to, and immediately opened fire on her.

With glass shattering all around her from the buzzing bullets, a trembling Miss Maggie crouched on the floor out of sight. Although she could scarcely see what she was doing, she reached up and plugged wires into the switchboard to alert the sheriff and almost everyone else in town who had a telephone.

When the sleepy sheriff picked up the receiver, he could hear only a ringing in his ear, but knew something was amiss, because he recognized the sound of gunfire coming from the direction of the town square. While he was dressing and running to investigate, Mr. Bob had already become engaged in a noisy gun battle with the hidden lookouts shooting at Miss Maggie, firing at the muzzle-flashes from their guns.

As Sheriff Ray rounded the corner, Mr. Bob called out, warning him to take cover. At the same moment, a bullet shattered the store window behind the sheriff.

Bewildered as to the nature of the events unfolding around him, Sheriff Ray ran toward the familiar voice asking, "Who are they shooting at, Bob?" He gulped when the response was, "You, nut! They've been shooting at you ever since you turned the corner!"

When Sheriff Ray realized the bank was being robbed, he gave Meaders another gun, and the two of them went down the sidewalk firing with both hands like a scene

Meaders Corner was the scene of high action in the wee hours of February 13, 1913. This dwelling (photographed here in the 1950s) was the home of Bob Meaders and his family. "Mr. Bob" operated a telephone company in the front room of the upstairs portion of this building.

The Hall House on the east-northwest corner of the town square offered rooms to students and travelers in the early 1900s. The little brick building to the left in this photo with the bars on the windows, was the Bank of Lumpkin County in 1913. These buildings still stand today on the town square.

"Hall's Block" on the west-northwest corner of the square was photographed in 1997. Beside it, painted white, is the little building which once housed the Bank of Lumpkin County which was robbed in 1913.

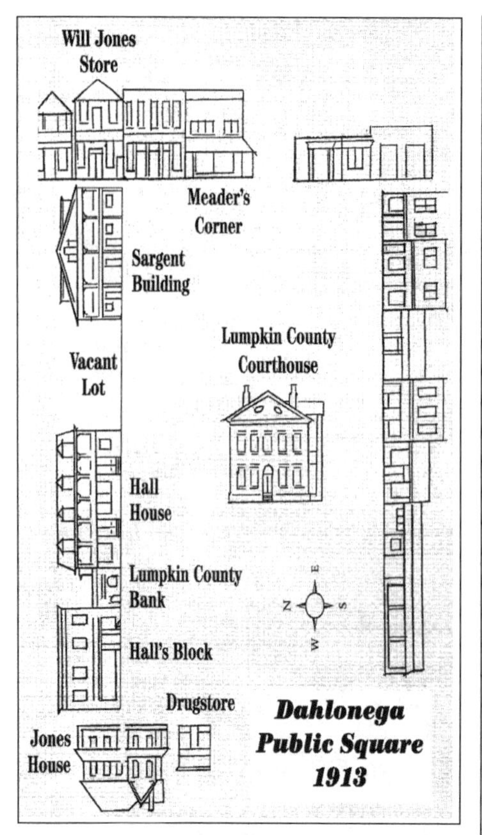

The Dahlonega Town Square is illustrated above as it appeared in 1913.

out of an old West movie. According to accounts of the incident, one of the outlaws was wounded.

Because of the unexpected offensive from the sheriff and Mr. Bob, the robbers apparently decided discretion was the better part of valor, and took to their heels. They ran for an automobile parked just off the square, and drove quickly off into the darkness.

Assessing The Damage

Daylight was just beginning to break over the horizon as a posse of two dozen horsemen set out in search of the outlaws. The bandits were discovered later that afternoon sleeping in a ditch northwest of town (some sources maintain near Ellijay). By eight o'clock that night, they were safely behind bars at the Lumpkin County Jail under the watchful eye of Sheriff Ray.

Wearing his other hat as president of the Lumpkin County Bank, Mr. Bob discovered to his relief that the only things missing from the bank were two pistols. Even though it was discovered at their trial that the bandits were professionals, they apparently had been unfamiliar with the type of safe which had two front doors, according to Mr. Bob's son, Robert, age 87 as of this writing, a retired metallurgist living in Camarillo, California.

"After drilling through the outer door, they attempted to blast through the second door, but the explosion actually sealed the door into the safe to produce what amounted to a solid steel box," Robert explained in later years. "The safe later had to be placed on the sidewalk and (cut open with a blowtorch). I remember Father taking a fine wire and scraping three or four coins out from under the door. That was the only money removed from the safe until it was torched open."

Robert's sister, Margaret, grew up to be a well-known writer who composed numerous articles about growing up in Dahlonega, including one published in the June-July, 1970 issue of *Georgia Magazine* entitled "Dahlonega's Famous Bank Robbery, As Told By One Who Was There." In that article, she described how terrified she had been as a six-year-old at the time. "I was sure that my father and my mother were both being killed and that thirty or forty cutthroats were climbing our back fence," she wrote.

Margaret Meaders wasn't the only child who grew up with vivid memories of the terror of the attempted bank robbery on February 13, 1913. Alma McGuire, who lived on the corner of North Chestatee and Hawkins Street a short distance from the square, was also awakened by the blast. At first, she thought cadets at the college just up the street were firing the cannon for mischief. But when she heard the clatter of horses' hooves and voices calling "Mr. Mac, get up! The bank has been blowed open!," she knew differently.

Her father, George Henry McGuire, quickly dressed and joined the posse in pursuit of the outlaws. "We children couldn't sleep the rest of the night for fear the robbers would come back and get us," Miss Alma recalled shortly before her death in 1991 at the age of 90. "Daddy found a flashlight they had dropped in their haste to get away, and he kept it for years."

Sheriff Ray's daughter, Pearl, also described being awakened by the explosion and how frightened they had been, "especially for Papa, who had gone to investigate." They embraced him tightly when he returned and fingered a bullet hole in his black hat with awe.

The Outlaws

Since the sheriff and his family lived downstairs in the county jail, Pearl got to know the outlaws while they were being held in the upstairs cells. "They would frequently ask one of us children to get them a drink of water or a candy bar from town," she reminisced when interviewed shortly before her death. "They were always nice and polite, and when their wives came to visit, they brought gifts to us children. I missed them after they were sent away to prison."

In her article published in *Georgia Magazine*, Margaret Meaders wrote that the outlaws "gave assumed names throughout most of their trial, but eventually were identified as professional thieves on their way to Knoxville from Atlanta. Hearing about the two little banks in Dahlonega, they had decided to 'knock off' one or both on their way north and pick up a little easy money."

According to an article published in the February 28, 1913 issue of *The Dahlonega Nugget*:

"The parties who gave their names as Charles Miller, John M. Harris, William Thornton and W.M. Flynn, charged with entering the bank of Lumpkin County and

The aged building which once housed the Lumpkin County Jail still stands as of this writing. The bandits who robbed the Bank of Lumpkin County in 1913 were lodged here following their capture.

The second floor portico of the old Lumpkin County Courthouse (present-day Dahlonega Gold Museum) served as a lookout point for the bandits during the robbery.

Robert "Mista Bob" and Margaret "Miss Maggie" Meaders were photographed in their home in Dahlonega in the 1950s.

blowing open the outer door of its safe on the morning of the 14th inst., at about one o'clock, were here last Monday before Justice of the Peace, W.B. Townsend, and all bound over to the next term of Lumpkin Superior Court on the charge of burglary, bond of each being fixed at ten thousand dollars, who have been sent to Fulton County jail by Judge Jones for safe keeping.

"The parties who entered the bank got nothing but a couple of pistols, but they secceeded (sic) in wrecking the front of the safe before they were run off by Sheriff T.M. Ray and R.C. Meaders, president of the bank. The insurance company had to replace the safe with a new one. Neither was there any positive or direct evidence that either of these men did enter this bank, but the circumstantial proof was strong against them, all of whom beyond a doubt were traveling under false colors by using assumed names.

"The quartette (sic) was convicted of burglary, by the Superior Court of Lumpkin County, and were sent to the penitentiary; but were soon pardoned out by the Governor."

The February 21 issue of *The Dahlonega Nugget* contained seven separate items concerning the attempted robbery. One of the articles noted *"A representative of the insurance company has been up this week to examine the damages done to the Bank of Lumpkin County by the safe blowers. The bank gets a new safe and all other damages, which is due by the insurance company."*

Another interesting notice, apparently designed to calm any fears harbored by depositors, subsequently appeared in the *Nugget.* It stated:

"Your money in the Bank of Lumpkin County is protected against all loss. Deposits are being received and checks cashed just as if no robbers had been to see us. We are backed by a one million dollar company who wired (to us) in less than ten hours after the robbers had left, asking our president how much money he wanted sent up that day. . . His reply was, 'We have all we need.'"

The fledgling telephone company established in Dahlonega in 1910 by R.C. Meaders less than three years before the attempted bank robbery undoubtedly benefited greatly from the event. Another item in the February 21 issue of the *Nugget* noted:

"Every citizen who wishes to keep posted about what is going on in Dahlonega both day and night should have them a phone. It was nearly 12 o'clock the next day after the safe blowers paid the Bank of Lumpkin County a visit before some of our citizens knew anything about it. The phone system kept these robbers from completing their job and carrying off a lot of money belonging to residents of both the town and country."

Historic Buildings On The Square

Interestingly, as of this writing, the present-day Dahlonega town square looks much the same as it did to the would-be bank robbers in 1913, thanks to the efforts of preservation-minded Dahlonega city council members and citizens. The old Meaders Building containing Dahlonega's first telephone exchange is gone, but the other buildings identified in the story above are all still in use as of this writing.

Today, Will Jones' store houses a whitewater rafting and outfitting business. The rehabilitated Sargent Building is the home of several shops and offices. The empty lot next door is no longer vacant, but has a building standing on its premises today. The Hall House, built in the early 1880s (and known as the Robert M. Moore Building as of this writing) still offers apartment accommodations in its upstairs section.

After Hall's death, the sturdy little brick building became the Lumpkin County Bank.

Downstairs, a selection of interesting shops beckon to travelers and sightseers.

The small brick one-story Lumpkin County Bank building where the attempted bank robbery took place was built in 1881, and originally served as the office of Captain Frank W. Hall, a mining and real estate entrepreneur who became the richest man in Lumpkin County in his day. After Hall's death, the sturdy little brick building became the Lumpkin County Bank.

The former bank building still exists today, and is located between the Hall House (present-day Robert M. Moore building) and the large brick structure called "Halls Block" which also still stands today on the northwest corner of the town square. Hall's little brick office building (since its days as the bank) has housed a number of other businesses over the years. An old safe, left over from the days of the bank, has been painted blue and is in use as a display case today.

Capt. Hall was also responsible for erecting the brick jail where the outlaws were imprisoned a short distance from the town square. This old building, which also still stands today, has not been used as a jail for a number of years. In recent years, it has housed county offices, and is a preserved historic site today, having also served as a temporary prison for the notorious Old West bandit Bill Miner who was captured a short distance from Dahlonega in Nimblewill.

The Bank of Lumpkin County eventually merged with the Bank of Dahlonega in 1931, and its name went out of existence. The combined banks moved to the southeast corner of the square where the business existed for many years.

The old Jones home, built circa 1885, is known as the Conner House today, and houses several shops. Big rocking chairs still adorn the front porch, inviting guests to sit and rock a spell while watching the activity on the town square, just as Theodocia Jones and her daughter Wanda were doing when they lived there. At age 93, "Miss Wanda" (as of this writing) still remembers the events of February 13, 1913, as clearly as if they had happened only yesterday.

The historic original Lumpkin County Courthouse, built in 1836, houses the Dahlonega Gold Museum today, and visitors come from all over the world to learn about Lumpkin County's rich gold mining history by visiting this popular site and viewing its many displays, multimedia program and items of historic significance from yesteryear. In one of the upstairs displays, a Smith & Wesson revolver offers mute testimony to the events on that night of so long ago. It is the gun which Sheriff Ray took from one of the would-be bank robbers when they were captured by his posse. The weapon remained in the Ray family until his daughter, Pearl Ray Fitts, donated it to the Gold Museum in 1990.

Another item on display at the Gold Museum is a bullet found embedded in one of the columns that were an original part of the interior of the old courthouse. Wondering if the bullet could have been fired in the gun battle between the bank robbers and Mr. Bob Meaders, Museum Director Sharon Johnson took the pistol and slug to the Georgia Bureau of Investigation Crime Lab in Atlanta for ballistics testing. There, she was told that the bullet did not come from the Smith & Wesson revolver, but that the pistol was still in perfect working order. It is possible the bullet came from Bob Meaders's pistol as he was firing toward the lookouts stationed at the courthouse.

There are only a few people still alive today who remember when the tranquility of their small north Georgia town was interrupted by the attempted bank robbery, but the story undoubtedly will continue to be passed down for many generations to come. And thanks to the pistol and printed display at the Dahlonega Gold Museum, visitors can share in the excitement that once was visited upon a sleepy Dahlonega on a cold winter night in February so many years ago.

The Branch Mint Building Fire And Price Memorial Hall

Built in 1837, the massive building housed machinery which minted gold coins until operations were ceased in 1861. The structure was donated to the state of Georgia in 1871, becoming a branch of the University of Georgia. On a cold winter night in 1878, it was destroyed by a horrific fire, and that same year, construction was begun on a new building at the site which still impresses visitors today.

Shortly after midnight on the morning of December 20, 1878, residents at North Georgia Agricultural College in Dahlonega were awakened by the smell of smoke and the terrible cries of "Fire!" "Fire!" Flames were already lighting up the night sky as faculty members and students living in the 27-room brick building hurriedly grabbed what they could and groped their way to safety.

The college's president, David W. Lewis, and his family narrowly escaped being trapped by the flames, lingering as long as they dared trying to save books from his personal library by throwing them out the second-story windows. Although rescued from the fire, the volumes were badly damaged in the process.

By daylight the following morning, the building lay in ruins. There was no loss of life, but the college's only building – including its library, instruments, and other equipment – as well as the personal possessions of those who lived in the structure, had all been destroyed.

The headline of an article which appeared in the December 24, 1878 issue of Atlanta's newspaper, *The Daily Constitution*, called the Dahlonega fire *"North Georgia's Great Calamity."* The article went on to note, *"The recent burning of the North Georgia Agricultural College is justly considered a misfortune to the whole state. It affects northeast Georgia as a peculiar calamity. Full accounts of the burning which come from Dahlonega state that the destruction was almost total, and that the remains of the well-equipped institution are blackened walls and smoldering ruins."*

A Vow To Re-Build

The cause of the fire could not be precisely determined, but it was generally believed that it originated from a beam of timber supporting the second floor located in the extreme end of the south wing of the T-shaped building. On one end, the beam rested in a groove in the brick chimney and may have been set so deeply inside the chimney that it eventually was ignited by flames from the hearth. It probably had smoldered for hours – perhaps even much longer – before actually igniting and setting fire to the rest of the building. Since the south wing was used for classrooms and was unoccupied at night, the fire was not discovered until a substantial portion of the building was ablaze.

Before the ashes were even cold, however, trustees, professors, and students of the college – supported by many local citizens – resolved that the college must not die. A mass meeting was held in the courthouse (present-day Gold Museum on the town square) three days later to plan for the reconstruction of the important building.

Immediate arrangements were made for classes to be held in the courthouse, the old Academy, and the Baptist Church (then located on what is now the college's front campus).

"We are glad to see that the faculty of the college have preserved their pluck in spite of disaster," the article in *The Daily Constitution* continued. *"The work of rebuilding will, we learn, be commenced at once."*

History Of The Old Mint

Among those taking an active part in the administration of the reconstruction was Col. William Pierce Price. This congressman from Dahlonega worked tirelessly to promote education in north Georgia when the area was still a remote backwoods region. He therefore was no stranger to adversity.

Back in 1871, Representative Price had been the individual responsible for the introduction of a resolution in Congress

A rare photo of the Dahlonega Branch Mint building prior to its destruction by fire on a cold winter night in 1878.

The cadets, administrators and faculty of North Georgia College posed for this photograph taken circa 1900 after Price Memorial Hall had been built on the foundation of the destroyed Branch Mint building.

authorizing the Secretary of the Treasury to donate the old United States Branch Mint building in Dahlonega *"for educational purposes."*

The Dahlonega Mint had operated from 1838 until shortly after Georgia seceded from the Union in 1861 at the onset of the U.S. Civil War. Following Lee's surrender at Appomattox, federal troops were quartered in the abandoned Mint building, and an inspector from the U.S. Mint in Philadelphia was sent to assess wartime damage to the structure and its equipment. The machinery was found to be rusty but salvageable and was shipped to the

The front campus of North Georgia Agricultural College was photographed circa 1910. Price Memorial Hall, with its majestic steeple, soared above all the other buildings. To the left in this photo, Bostwick Hall is visible. Built in 1899, it was also destroyed by a fire in 1912. Its construction was originally funded by an endowment from the sale of the old Calhoun and Benning gold mines once owned by Capt. J.A. Bostwick of New York. (Photo courtesy of GA Dept. of Archives & History)

A student assembly in the second floor auditorium of Price Memorial Hall was photographed circa 1914. This fine room, closed off for many years, was recently reopened (following preservation renovations) for use once again.

Philadelphia Mint.

The U.S. Treasury Department put the Dahlonega Mint building up for sale but declined selling it when the highest offer was only $1,525. Thus Col. Price's resolution authorizing the Secretary of the Treasury to donate the $70,000 building (which had become something of a "white elephant") for educational purposes fell upon receptive ears. The new facility was named North Georgia Agricultural College (NGAC).

Although the trustees of the newly-established college (present-day North Georgia College & State University) were custodians of a fine building, they had no funds for repairing or furnishing it or for the hiring of teachers to teach there. The trustees subsequently agreed for the college to become a part of the University of Georgia in order to receive the necessary financial support.

Soon, rooms which formerly had housed crucibles and dies for the conversion of bullion into gold coins were filled with blackboards and desks. Upstairs rooms which had served as quarters for the Mint officers and their families became the living quarters of President David Lewis and his family.

Early Students

When NGAC opened its doors on January 6, 1873, with the invitation of *"Whosoever will may come,"* it became the third public college in the state and the first to admit female students. *(Editor's Note: The University of Georgia didn't admit female students until nearly fifty years later.)* More than 200 students attended the college that first year, of which nearly half were coeds, including President Lewis's daughter, Willie, who would later be the only female in NGAC's first graduating class.

Notices in the locale newspaper advertised *"Free Education!"* at NGAC, with only a $5.00 entrance fee per 5-month session. Ads also advised that *"the healthfulness of the climate and cheapness of board make N.G.A.C. a desirable school for young men and women from those sections of the state visited with chills and fever."* They also pointed out *"the entire absence of temptations to vice which its location affords."*

The fledgling college had only two faculty members initially, but two students were soon hired to teach the preparatory department. A "sub-freshman class" was a necessity, since there were no public high schools in Georgia at that time. Other students gained valuable teaching experience by providing summer school instruction to hundreds of children living in rural areas.

NGAC was unique in being both a coeducational and a military institution. The first commandant of cadets was Lieutenant Joseph Garrard. An item from the April 3, 1873 *Dahlonega Signal* newspaper noted, *"The Secretary of War, General Belnap, recently assured the President of the Board of Trustees that he would supply the college with all the necessary guns, accoutrements, and the like as soon as the number of male students reached one hundred and fifty."*

On December 15, 1876, the newspaper reported that 150 Springfield Cadet Rifles and other military equipment would soon be shipped to NGAC. Since there was space for only a small percentage of NGAC's students to reside in the old Mint building, the great majority boarded with families in town. When the building burned in 1878, some rifles and munitions were destroyed, but most of the military equipment was safe because it had been issued to cadets and was kept with them in their various boarding houses.

Less than two months after the fire, the editor of the *Signal* wrote, *"The flocking of such a large number of students to the North Georgia College presents a strange phenomenon. They come every day just like the grand old building had never been wrapped in flames . . . It was feared that the students would go away and not return. But nothing of the sort has happened. . . it really looks as if two new students had already taken the place of every one who had gone away."*

Construction Of Price Memorial

Four months after the fire, plans had been drawn for a new building and bids from contractors were coming in. On June 13, 1879, the *Signal* reported: *"At this writing the old walls are being torn down to the foundation upon which will be erected according to the plans and specifications of Messrs. Parkins and Bruce, architects of Atlanta, the new building. Work will be pushed vigorously forward until instead of a mass of blackened ruins scattered around there will be a commodious and handsome edifice; a building worthy (of) the name of the North Georgia Agricultural College."*

The cornerstone of the new structure was laid with Masonic ceremonies on June 25, 1879. Col. Price, president of the college's board of trustees, donated generously to the college from his own personal assets, and the new building that rose on the foundation of the old Mint was eventually named Price Memorial Hall in his honor.

Although erected on the Mint's original T-shaped, hand-hewn granite foundation, Price Memorial's appearance was considerably different from that of the Mint, due largely to the addition of a lofty steeple which towered above the building and the town. It was a magnificent addition, but its construction was not problem-free.

NGAC was unique in being both a coeducational and a military institution.

While carpenters were raising one of the tower trusses in the steeple in August of

1880, lightning struck the building. Three workmen who were operating a large hoist were reportedly "knocked senseless." Another workman who was on the roof of the building fell to the ground but miraculously survived both the shock of the lightning bolt as well as the long fall to the ground.

The brick walls of the new structure were not stuccoed over as had been done on the old Mint building, and the second story rose to twice the height of the 12-foot ceiling in the Mint. In the center portion of the building, the Mint's plain rectangular windows were replaced with five tall Gothic arched windows, the tallest one in the center pointing upward to the bell tower.

On November 22, 1880, the *Dahlonega Signal* reported, *"Our new college building when completed, will be one of the most commodious and imposing edifices in North Georgia. Four rooms are ready for use, which were occupied by the school on Monday last. We sent up our hats, and three cheers for Colonel Price."*

Changes Over The Years

In time, as the college continued to grow, other buildings were erected on the campus, but Price Memorial continued to dominate the college and town over the years both with its tall spire and historic presence. The steeple became even more eye-catching and impressive approximately 100 years later in 1973, when it was covered with gold leaf in time for North Georgia College's centennial celebration.

Other exterior changes made to Price Memorial include a large front porch with tall columns thrusting up to support its second-story roof. Ralph Fitts, a former custodian, recalls when there were two porches – one for each floor.

"At that time the steps were on either side of the lower porch (instead of in front of the building today)," Ralph recalls, "and the military cannons were rolled under the center of the porch and into the basement for storage."

Numerous changes have been made to the interior of Price Memorial over the years to adapt it to current needs. Fireplaces were closed off when steam heaters were installed, and the extraordinarily-high ceilings were lowered twice to make the rooms more economical to heat. Unfortunately, the lowered ceilings concealed the tops of the great arched windows on the second floor. In time, other arched windows and doors were sealed up to create new office configurations, and walls were added to conceal plumbing pipes.

Over the years, Price Memorial has housed not only classrooms, but also administrative offices, a military armory, the college library, bookstore, planetarium, Y.M.C.A. room, campus post office and "canteen," and much more. The second story was originally an auditorium with a slanted floor where students and faculty gathered weekly for an assembly called "Chapel."

Virginia Ash MacAllister, whose father taught at North Georgia College from 1911 to 1929, recalls that the college allowed the local high school to hold its graduations in the Price Memorial auditorium in the years prior to the construction of the auditorium at Lumpkin County High School. Virginia says she also remembers a kind of preschool being taught by teachers from NGC's Education Department in the whitewashed basement of Price Memorial during the early 1930s.

"Being underground, it was always pleasantly cool there, even on the hottest summer days," she reminisces. The basement floor reportedly was still hard-packed dirt at that time and "as dry as snuff," according to Ralph Fitts.

Early Events & "Tales"

Erskine Rice, who followed in his father's footsteps to become a cadet at North Georgia College in 1937, relates a story his father, George Erskine Rice, Sr., told him about "Chapel" when he was a student there shortly after the turn of the century.

According to the tale, Erskine says the dignified old president of the college mounted the steps to the stage to speak to the assembled student body one morning, when suddenly, the curtains behind him opened to reveal his horse and buggy – all hitched up there on the stage – to the amazement and titillation of all in the audience. "How the pranksters managed to get the horse up those steep high steps to the second floor remains a mystery to this day," Rice smiles.

Ralph Fitts recalls when school boxing competitions and debating meets were held on the stage in the auditorium. Ralph was 10 years old in 1923 when his father, Arthur L. Fitts, became NGAC's custodian. He says he remembers helping his father to build fires in Price Memorial's numerous fireplaces and wood-stoves during the winter months.

"We started building fires at six o'clock in the morning so the rooms would be good and warm by the time students arrived," Fitts says. "In the afternoons, I cleaned out the ashes and filled the wood boxes for the next day. There was an old 1920 Ford tractor we used to generate electricity both to saw wood and to run (a projector for) silent picture shows in the auditorium."

During the 56 years that Ralph worked as custodian at the college, he did whatever needed doing around Price Memorial. Sometimes the bell rope broke, and then he would have to climb up a series of ladders to the tower and ring the bell by hand. Within the tower, there was no light except what fil-

Lieutenant Joseph Jarrard (a major by the time this photo was taken) was the first commandant of cadets at North Georgia Agricultural College, arriving at the school early in 1877 to set up the program.

The faculty of North Georgia Agricultural College were photographed in July of 1876. Pictured (left to right) are: Standing: H.H. Perry, B.P. Gaillard, Eugene Beck, R.M. Hall, and Robert Walker. Seated: Mrs. Mattie Boyd, President David W. Lewis, and Mrs. L.B. Ramsaur.

tered in through lattices, so he had to feel his way from one hand-hold to the next.

"Sometimes when the wind was blowing hard, the steeple would rock back and forth just like a ship in a storm," he recalls.

Ralph says he also remembers helping to replace the bell sometime in the 1930s when the old one developed a crack. "A bunch of us lowered the old one to the ground with ropes and then hauled the new one up to the tower," he says, describing the process. "I mean to tell you that took some doing because that bell must have weighed a thousand pounds."

Ralph says he doesn't know if the cracked bell was the original bell (which Andrew Cain's *History of Lumpkin County* describes as having been found lodged on an arch of one of the middle walls following the 1878 fire) or not. Following its removal from the steeple, the cracked bell – which may in fact be the original bell – was used as the base for a megaphone just a few steps from Price Memorial Hall. The megaphone and its historic base may still be viewed today behind Young Hall.

"One time, also in the 1930s, somebody stole the clapper out of the bell," Ralph continues, recalling another story. "It had been missing for several months when I saw one of the cadets carrying it wrapped up in newspapers. I knew what it was by its shape and reported him, so it was soon put back in place."

George Elliott, father of NASCAR racing driver Bill Elliott of Dawsonville, remembered that when he was a student at NGC in the early 1940s, a story was circulating around campus about the time mischievous cadets reportedly removed the bell from inside the belfry and balanced it on the very peak of the steeple.

Dr. John Owen, president of North Georgia College from 1970 to 1992, reported that he once had to ask construction crews working on the roof of Price Memorial to take their ladders home with them at the end of the day because some students were climbing up to the bell tower. "How they got all the way up to the top, I'll never know," Owen commented wryly, "but we knew they had been there because of the signs they left hanging on the steeple."

Modern Innovations

Until the 1960s, the cadet "Officer of the Day" was responsible for ringing the bell ten minutes before the hour and on the hour to signal the end and beginning of classes. A long rope ran from the bell to the main floor, and it required considerable effort to pull it with enough force to cause the bell to sound. In more recent years, a recording of the bell has been played over a loudspeaker.

The upper floor of Price Memorial was closed by the Georgia State Fire Marshall's office in the early 1980s because it was thought to be a fire hazard. The entire building was vacated in 1994 in preparation for a complete restoration. Prior to the renovation work in the late autumn of 1997, college workmen removed all paneling and interior alterations which had been added over the years, exposing the original floors, walls, and ceilings for the first time in many decades. It proved to be a dazzling revelation.

President Sherman Day was so impressed with the unique features and historic significance of the exposed original construction, that he invited faculty, students, and interested members of the community to visit and view the re-exposed interior of the aged building. It became a literal archaeological foray into the history of the old college structure and even the original Mint building.

Dr. Day particularly enjoyed pointing out a French lesson written on one of the slate blackboards built into the wall of a former classroom which was later paneled over to become the office of the President's receptionist. There on the old slate, printed in bold letters to one side, was the admonition, "DO NOT ERASE."

In the adjoining president's office, Day called attention to a window sill obviously hand-hewn with an ax, and revealed a square hand-forged iron nail that he personally had found lying on the floor.

President Day noted that Price Memorial is "elegant for all of its graceful arches" and pointed out some that had been covered up for many years, including the tops of the great upstairs windows. "There are people who have worked at the college for thirty years who until recently, had never seen some of these arches or the original ceilings," he remarked, noting that remodeling plans call for some of the closed arches to be reopened.

In the large room to the rear of the building, he called attention to three round cast-iron columns with Corinthian detailing at the tops. Upstairs, he pointed out enormously high doors that, when measured, were found to be eleven feet tall. Although the bell tower was not open to the public, Dr. Day described how the massive beams were numbered, notched and pegged together. He also noted proudly that engineering inspectors had pronounced the structure as sound as the day it was erected.

Relics In The Basement

For all of Price Memorial's interesting and elegant features, it was the basement that held the greatest fascination for most of those touring the building. With all paneling and other additions removed to expose the interior of the original 1837 foundation walls, those present felt themselves transported back in time.

"I feel like I am actually in the old Mint building," one person remarked in hushed tones. When another commented that it seemed a shame to cover up so much history with modern paneling, Dr. Day described plans to cover a section of the old foundation with plexiglass so that it will remain permanently visible.

Continuing the tour of the basement, Dr. Day pointed out a recently rediscovered door leading to a sloping ramp to the outside. Bordered on each side by original stone walls, this entranceway is believed to have been an access for large machinery, including a steam engine which was once used in the Mint. Although long since covered over, a 52-foot-deep well was dug in the rear section of the basement of the old Mint to supply water for the steam engine.

When bids were let for the project of remodeling Price Memorial Hall, numerous firms were interested in adding the historic old building to their resumes. The renovation and re-opening of the original Price Memorial Hall facilities was accomplished by Warren Epstein & Associates, Architects, Inc. of Atlanta. The completed project once again houses the offices of the president and other administrative offices.

Today, North Georgia College & State University in historic Dahlonega, Georgia has been recognized in many quarters as a superb educational institution. Many students have profited and many more hopefully will continue to profit from the grit and determination of a mountain congressman and his band of college and civic leaders following the terrible fire of 1878.

Note: *The name of North Georgia Agricultural College was changed to North Georgia College in 1930. The name was changed once again in 1996 to North Georgia College & State University (NGCSU). Although the school has experienced substantial growth and changes over the years, it remains the only state-supported, coeducational, liberal arts military college in the world. Coeds have participated in the military program since 1974.*

Grandpa Was An Outlaw

Jeff Anderson was the leader of a notorious band of outlaws who terrorized Lumpkin County during the U.S. Civil War. After escaping from prison in the second of several jail-breaks, he hid for the next few years in Dalton, Georgia, before heading west in 1901. Anderson family history records indicate Jeff never returned to Georgia, and never married. New evidence, however, has revealed the former outlaw lived his final years near Chattanooga, Tennessee . . . and even more interestingly, that he had a wife and children there.

Travelers still routinely come to the small but growing town of Dahlonega, Georgia, in the foothills of the Blue Ridge Mountains, seeking information about their ancestors from that area. Invariably, most of them will eventually find their way to Dahlonega Postmaster Jimmy Anderson. There is a reason for this . . . Jimmy is known in the area for his genealogy research, and in the process, he has accumulated a lot of information on the county's history over the years. Interestingly, his family roots intertwine with many of the families of the area too, but he wasn't quite prepared for what he learned from one recent visitor.

William E. Smyth traveled from Flintstone, Georgia (near Chattanooga) recently to confer with Postmaster Anderson about Smyth's grandfather, Thomas Jefferson Anderson. Although he was not related to the Thomas Jefferson Anderson family, Jimmy was acquainted with Jeff Anderson's lawless activities during the U.S. Civil War in the 1860s. What Postmaster Anderson did not know until meeting Smyth, was that Jeff had married and left descendants.

"My grandfather died before I was born, so I never knew much of anything about him until I was grown," Smyth explained in relating the story of his forebear. "Once, when I was a boy, my mother started to tell me something about Grandpa, but Daddy quickly told her to hush.

"'Those boys are going to be bad enough as it is,'" Smyth says his father admonished. "He was talking about me and my brothers," he smiled again.

"A lot of things make sense now that I have found out more about my grandpa," Smyth continued, "like the time when one of my friends got 'Sunday-punched' on the bus. I defended him and got into a fight with the troublemaker. Later, the boy's father complained to my father that he had never taught his boys to fight.

"I've never forgotten Dad's response to that comment. In sort of an embarrassed way, he said, 'Well, I never taught my boys to fight either, but I can't help what they inherited.'"

Thomas Jefferson Anderson apparently came from a respectable family. His father, William H. Anderson, and uncle, John Anderson, moved to Dahlonega from Habersham County in time to be listed in the 1834 census not long after Dahlonega and Lumpkin County were established.

This family of Andersons lived in Crumby District, east of Dahlonega in the Philippi Community (Cavender Creek vicinity).

"John and William must have been prosperous due to the numerous records one may still find documenting their activities at the Dahlonega Clerk of Court's Office," wrote family researchers who provided information about the pioneer brothers in the *Heritage of Lumpkin County, Georgia, 1832-1996.* John and William farmed, bought and sold land, and owned stock in the Spring Place Mining Company in Fannin County.

William H. and Margaret Anderson had seven sons and two daughters. Thomas Jefferson was their sixth child, born in 1839. There is no way of knowing whether Jeff showed violent tendencies in his earlier years or if his renegade activities were a product of family divisiveness created by the Civil War.

Census records reveal that William H. Anderson owned one slave. Military records show that Jeff's brothers, William M., Isaac, Henry, and Benjamin, fought for the Confederacy. However, the records also show their brother, Thomas Abraham, did not believe in slavery and enlisted in the Union Army.

Jeff initially enlisted in the First Georgia Volunteer Infantry, but soon deserted, perhaps because of the influence of his older brother Abraham's anti-slavery stance. However, there is nothing to explain why Jeff also turned into the leader of a band of outlaws known as "the bridge burners," who terrorized local folks and used guerrilla tactics to harass local Confederate units.

According to research conducted by Dahlonega historian Bill Kinsland *(Readers please see "The Civil War Comes To Lumpkin County," Volume I , A North Georgia Journal of History),* Jeff Anderson was arrested by Lumpkin County Sheriff John Early in February of 1862, and tried for *Assault and Battery, Assault and Battery With Intent To Rape,* and *Misdemeanor.* He was also arrested under an order from Captain William Martin and charged with desertion from the First Georgia Volunteer Infantry. Considered dangerous, he was confined to the "common jail" in Dahlonega with his legs fastened to the wall with a logging chain.

Early on March 9, the day that Jeff Anderson was due to be picked up by military authorities to be returned to his unit, his brothers Henry and Benjamin "Dock" Anderson – along with a friend named Bart Edge – rode into town and tied their horses in front of the jail.

This jail quite probably was the one which once existed on the east side of Chestatee Street one block south of the old Baptist Church building in Dahlonega. In this facility, the main cell was accessed from the upper story of the jail through a trap door. Prisoners entered the cell by walking down a ladder.

When Jailer John McCoskey arrived to bring the prisoner his breakfast, Bart Edge reportedly approached McCoskey and asked to visit the prisoner. The jailer obligingly led Edge and one of the Andersons into the jail and opened the dungeon door.

Jeff immediately complained that he was "powerful sick" and begged for "Doc" Howard to come attend to him. Caught completely off guard, McCoskey went to the front door to send someone for Dr. Howard, but before he could take a step back, Jeff Anderson was "halfway out of the dungeon, coat and boots off."

McCoskey later testified in court that Anderson "pitched through the jail door, I after him, and down the steps." The jailer's

An uneasy Jeff Anderson, possibly still sought by the authorities, was photographed here, probably in his late 20s or early 30s in a long frock coat. This might even have been a prison photo, due to the position of the hands which is strangely reminiscent of the position required when one is wearing handcuffs and attempting to hide that fact. (Photo courtesy of George Anderson)

Bill Smyth, grandson of Thomas Jefferson Anderson. (Photo courtesy of Anne Amerson)

nephew Walter McCoskey gave testimony that the escaped prisoner hit him in the head as he ran by and that he saw one of the men step in front of his uncle to delay his pursuit.

Whatever the circumstances, by the time Jailer McCoskey could maneuver around the obstructing relative, Jeff, reportedly, was already out of sight. According to an account of the incident, he ran "across the square, past the Mustering Grounds and down Wimpy Mill Road."

Bart Edge, Dock and Henry Anderson were later arrested and charged with the crime of *Rescue*. Sheriff Early testified that Anderson had used a rasp to cut himself loose from the log chain. Edge and the Anderson brothers testified that they had not helped Jeff to escape and "would have caught him if they could." Despite the obvious prison-break and other charges, there is no record of the case ever coming to trial.

Henry Anderson, who was two years younger than Jeff, was 21 at the time. He enlisted in Smith's Legion of the Georgia Volunteers two months later. He was transferred to Company C, 65th Regiment, Georgia Infantry a year later. He subsequently died in the Loudon, Tennessee hospital on March 29, 1863.

"Dock," whose real name was Benjamin F. Anderson, was Jeff's youngest brother and only 17 years of age at the time. He served in Company C of the 52nd Regiment of the Georgia Volunteers, Barton's Brigade. Bart Edge had enlisted in the same unit, and was captured at the Battle of Vicksburg in July of 1863.

Jeff Anderson was captured a few months after his escape in Dahlonega. An article in the October 4, 1862 *Atlanta Southern Confederacy* noted, "Yesterday a mounted escort, detailed from Captain Tillet's Artillery Company, arrived here in charge of a large amount of Gold from the Mint at Dahlonega, belonging to the Confederate government. They also brought with them in chains a desperado named Anderson, whose outrages in Lumpkin County and the vicinity have been intolerable for some time. He is a deserter from the 1st Georgia Regulars, and has been hiding himself in the caves and dens of the mountains for the last five or six months, harboring runaway negroes, stealing, robbing widows and helpless women and children whose husbands and fathers are in the war, and had become a terror to the whole country. He will be properly cared for."

Author Harold E. O'Kelley relates in his book, *Dahlonega's Blue Ridge Rangers In The Civil War*, that Jeff Anderson was imprisoned in the Atlanta jail along with "fellow Bridge Burners, Yankee POWs, and some 'Engine Thieves' who were captured during the failed Andrews' Raid." *(The story of how Union spies stole a train and attempted to destroy the Confederate rail line between Atlanta and Chattanooga was portrayed in the Walt Disney major motion picture* The Great Locomotive Chase *filmed in northeast Georgia in the 1950s. Readers please see* A North Georgia Journal Of History, Volume III, *"When Hollywood Came Filming In The Fifties.")*

According to O'Kelley, the "Engine Thieves" and "Bridge Burners" subsequently made a daring escape from prison. Some of Andrews' men later described one of their party as a "Rebel Deserter" who stayed with their group for a few days before leaving them somewhere north of Atlanta. This may well have been Jeff Anderson, who was known to have returned to the mountains of north Georgia where he continued his guerilla war tactics.

After the war was over in 1865, Jeff, who was still a "Wanted" man, reportedly hid out on his older brother Abraham's farm in Whitfield County near Dalton for a number of years. Abraham, the Union sympathizer, was described as "religious and kindhearted" and perhaps thought that his wayward brother could be reformed by providing him with a safe haven and kindness. Jeff remained with his brother for two decades but then departed for parts unknown sometime in the mid-1880s, apparently as a result of a serious family rift.

Until Smyth appeared in Dahlonega Postmaster Jimmy Anderson's office recently, the details of Jeff Anderson's life from the mid-1880s to the turn of the century were a mystery. Bill, however, explained that his grandfather had married Mary "Mollie" Rebecca Dilbeck from the Jack's River area in Fannin County in 1886 when he was 47 and she was 22. They had eight children, four boys and four girls.

The first child was Bill's mother, Mary Georgia Ann Anderson, who was born in Rockmart, Georgia, January 29, 1887. Mary Georgia Ann's parents must have been among the first settlers in Rockmart, since that town was founded circa 1887.

The other Anderson children were Maud Josephine (b. 1889), Mattie (b. 1891; married Oscar Hunter, a policeman), Charles Martin (b. 1893), William Arthur (b. 1896; known as "Clint"), Henry Franklin (b. 1899), Benjamin Harrison (born 1901) and Viola (born 1904). It is interesting to note that William, Henry and Benjamin bear the same names as three of Jeff's brothers.

"Mama told me about moving to McLemore Cove between Pigeon Mountain and Lookout Mountain when she was six years old," Bill recounted. "They moved in three covered wagons, and Mama slept in the one that held the barrels of Grandpa's whiskey. When she woke up, she couldn't walk from breathing the fumes!

"Mama said they came to Dahlonega one time when she was young," Bill continued. "She always wanted to come back to Dahlonega after that, but she said there was no good way to come because there were no bridges or even a real road back then."

Another reason Bill's mother may not have returned with her family, was that her father was persona non grata in Lumpkin County. There is, however, evidence to indicate Jeff Anderson did return to Dahlonega in the 1880s when his mother died.

Smyth's mother described the house in which she grew up as being on stilts and having a metal roof. She remembered how frightened they were when they heard mountain panthers jump on the tin roof. When that happened, a hot fire would be built in the fireplace to keep the wild cats from coming down the chimney.

Mary Georgia Ann married Robert Henry Smyth in 1905, and they had six boys, one of whom died in childbirth. Lewis was born in 1906, Chester (known as "Chub") in 1908, Jack in 1916, Robert Lee ("Bud") in 1919, and William ("Bill") in 1927.

Jeff's wife, Mary "Mollie" Rebecca Anderson, lived until 1952 when she was in her 90s. According to her grandson Bill, she was still working in her garden and cooking at that time, even though she weighed only 76 pounds. She also didn't have a gray hair on her head, probably because her mother reportedly was a full-blood Indian.

"Grandma was the sweetest person you'd ever meet," Bill describes her. "Mama was just like her too. She and her sisters were very hard-working and religious. You'd never suspect that their father was an outlaw. The boys were hard-working too, but I've heard tell they were about as rough as their father."

Bill remembers his mother describing her father as having red hair and pale blue eyes that "looked like they were looking right through you."

"I've been told Grandpa was quite a fiddle player," Bill smiles. "His son, William Arthur whom I called 'Uncle Clint,' learned to play by watching Grandpa. When Grandpa would call the steps for people to dance, they said you could hear him a mile away."

According to information about Jeff Anderson in the *Heritage of Lumpkin County 1832-1996*, he went to Bonham, Texas (near Dallas) in the autumn of 1901. Anderson descendants of Thomas Abraham wrote, "We are certain Jeff was in Texas during this period because his nephew, Henry and his wife Cordelia, went to Texas to find Jeff. While they were in Texas, their third son William was born on October 19, 1901.

"Jeff later went to Oklahoma because there was no law there in order to avoid being captured. Oklahoma was Indian territory at this time . . . We are certain Jeff was in Durant, Oklahoma around April 1905, because Henry and Henry's wife Cordelia went on a second trip in a covered wagon to find Jeff. While they were there, their fourth son, Clint was born on April 29, 1905. Henry and Cordelia spotted Jeff at a distance with several other men on horseback, but he left with some men on horseback; they never caught him. The family received messages from Jeff on two occasions, once from Durant and another time from Hugo. Jeff never returned."

That information about the outlaw Jeff Anderson was submitted by George Anderson of Maryville, Tennessee, the grandson of Abraham's son, Henry Clay Anderson, and his wife Cordelia, who went to Texas and Oklahoma looking for Jeff. George was astonished to learn that Jeff had married and fathered a number of children.

"I'm not sure we're talking about the same man," George puzzles, even after speaking by phone with Bill Smyth, possibly a cousin of whom he had known nothing until recently. "There are lots of Andersons, and there may have been two Jeff Andersons. Some of the dates just don't seem to correspond."

Were there, in fact, two different Jeff Andersons who were Civil War outlaws, and if so, how is it possible to sort out which was which? If Bill Smyth's grandfather was the same man as George Anderson's great-great uncle, why did he keep his marriage a secret from his family and not inform them of his whereabouts? A possible explanation may lie in the fact that the alienation between the brothers at the time Jeff left Abraham's household may have been so bitter that Jeff chose to permanently cut all ties and disappear.

If the man believed to be in Texas and Oklahoma for several years following the turn of the century was in fact Bill Smyth's grandfather, he must have traveled back to Georgia on occasion, as he had children born there in 1901 and 1904. It is interesting to note that Jeff Anderson made his home near the Tennessee border, less than forty miles northwest of Abraham Anderson's farm near Dalton. They apparently never encountered one another, possibly due to the mountainous terrain separating them.

According to stories Bill has heard about his grandpa Jeff Anderson, the outlaw apparently mellowed at least to some extent with age and a family, but remained feisty even in his later years.

"(I've been told) Grandpa's dog went missing one time," he laughed again. "When he heard a dog barking that sounded like his, he followed the sound until he came to a fenced-in yard. He opened the gate and walked in and started to untie his dog. When a man appeared and demanded to know what he was doing, Grandpa calmly ignored him.

"Don't you know you can get into trouble coming into a man's yard and stealing his dog?" the fellow demanded.

"Grandpa – according to the story – pulled out his gun and replied, 'Well, son, don't you know it works both ways?' He then turned around and walked back out the gate leading his dog."

Bill Smyth says he has information showing that his grandfather died in 1913, and remembers his mother showing him the outlaw's unmarked grave at Strawhill Cemetery, "down the Dalton pike" from Cleveland, Tennessee. His grandmother lived a number of years longer (until 1952) and was buried at Red Hill Cemetery just outside Cleveland. She did not want to be buried beside Jeff because she thought that cemetery was too far from where she was living near some of her children.

Bill added that he has heard that his grandfather died from being bled, once a popular medical treatment for numerous ailments. It seems ironic that in an age when maverick behavior was often blamed on "bad blood," the notorious "black sheep" of the family should meet his end by a treatment thought to rid the body of "bad blood" even though he apparently went "straight" later in his life.

Outlaw Thomas Jefferson Anderson flees the authorities following his escape from the Dahlonega City Jail in Dahlonega, Georgia. The Lumpkin County Courthouse on the town square is visible in the rear. (Illustration by John Kollock. All Rights Reserved. Reprinted With Permission)

Mary "Mollie" Rebecca Dilbeck Anderson (1862-1952), wife of Civil War outlaw Jeff Anderson, lived to a ripe 90 years.

Axe Murders In North Georgia: The Baxter Family Slayings

On a warm September evening in 1838, a horrendous triple-murder took place just across the Georgia state line in South Carolina. Though a slave was convicted of and executed for the commission of the murders, a prominent Lumpkin County, Georgia resident was also implicated in the crime. He, however, was never brought to trial.

On the south side of the Dahlonega town square, one of the most historic buildings in all of north Georgia stood for over a century. Built in the 1830s, the Eagle Hotel was the site of a number of gun battles in pioneer days, and its walls were pockmarked by bullet holes. When it burned on January 9, 1943, one of the last vestiges of the days of fiery Harrison W. Riley, the owner, disappeared forever.

In his day, Harrison Riley was known as a man with a volatile temper, ruthless in his pursuit of wealth. He once fought a running gun battle with Civil War bushwhackers from the front porch of the Eagle Hotel. In the course of this shoot-out, Riley was not wounded, but his beloved dog, Oceola, was killed in the affray.

In another incident involving Riley's quest for power and wealth, he was wounded in the shoulder by a political enemy. According to Andrew W. Cain's *The History of Lumpkin County* (1932), Riley smoked a pipe, and was leaning down to light it from the hearth of his fire (presumably at the Eagle Hotel in Dahlonega), when he was fired upon by an assailant. "Just as he stooped to light his pipe preparatory to celebrating one of his political victories, an enemy who is said to have sworn that Riley would never again go to the Legislature, shot him; but the wound was not serious."

Riley's thirst for riches apparently was so great that he once even considered robbing the United States government. According to Cain's *History*, in this instance, shortly after Georgia seceded from the Union on January 19, 1861, Riley publicly threatened to storm the U.S. Branch Mint in Dahlonega and take the gold therein. Cain's description of the incident includes an article written by the mint assayer at the time to wit: "There were some rough characters in the mountains in those early days, and when the state seceded, one of them by the name of Harrison Riley threatened to organize a crowd and make a raid on the mint, as he declared that the money belonged to nobody in particular, and that he was as much entitled to it as anybody. We heard of the threatened raid and armed ourselves, closing the vaults and putting the keys in a place of safety. Riley evidently thought better of the matter, for he never put in an appearance."

Riley's confrontations were so numerous and incendiary that they ultimately became legendary. According to Cain's *History*, "An itinerant gambler with a fat roll chanced to sojourn in the village. Riley thought that a stranger with so much money ought not to feel lonely. A game was arranged and the stakes piled on the table. In order to give a touch of solemnity to the occasion, Riley drew forth his pocket artillery and placed it on the table with a bang, at the same time saying: 'Hark from the tomb, a doleful sound.' The visitor promptly drew from his holster a 'young cannon' and slammed it down on the table with the refrain: 'My ears attend the cry!' The story goes that (in this instance), the gambler (and not Riley) went away richer than he came."

Ironically, despite this craving for riches, Riley, interestingly, was already one of the wealthiest men in north Georgia in his day. It was this lust for financial gain which *may* have caused him to be involved in a notorious murder on the night of September 30, 1838.

Witnesses To The Incident

On July 12th and 13th, 1839, the English travelers James Silk Buckingham and his wife had enjoyed the "commodious" accommodations of Devereaux Jarrett's tavern, Traveler's Rest (a Georgia state historic site today), near the banks of the Tugaloo River in what today is the eastern extremity of Stephens County not far from Toccoa, Georgia. The couple left the tavern on the morning of July 13, crossed the 454-foot-long toll bridge also operated by Jarrett, and thus passed into South Carolina.

"At a distance of a few miles only beyond the river," wrote Buckingham in the second volume of his *The Slave States Of*

Traveler's Rest outside Toccoa, Georgia, was photographed in 1953 prior to its restoration. Rather than overnight here, the Baxters decided to go ahead and cross Jarrett Toll Bridge and camp on the opposite side of the Tugaloo River in South Carolina. (Photo courtesy of the Georgia Dept. of Natural Resources)

A view down Jarrett Bridge Road in the general vicinity of the spot at which the Baxters were murdered on a late autumn evening in 1838. (Photo by J. Timothy Cole)

This structure, believed to be Jarrett's Toll Bridge, was photographed circa 1900. It was toward this crossing point that Carolina Baxter (13) possibly fled as she saw her uncle and nephew being murdered. She, however, was only able to run a short distance before being overtaken and also murdered by her assailant. (Photo courtesy of GA Dept. of Natural Resources)

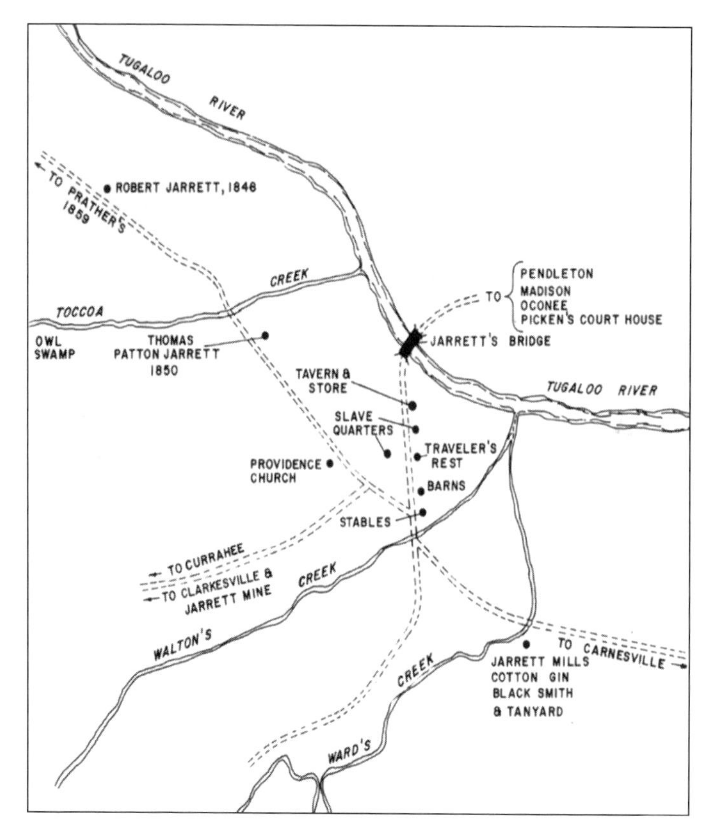

Traveler's Rest and the enterprises of Devereaux Jarrett as they existed in 1850.

America (1842), "we were overtaken by a man on horseback, of very common manners and appearance . . . , but who, nevertheless, was the Sheriff of the County [Pickens] in which we were traveling. This fact we learnt from himself, as he pointed out to us, while he rode along by our carriage, a rude gallows, formed by a horizontal beam, resting on the branches of two large adjoining trees, close by the road-side, on which, but a few months since, he had hung, with his own hands, a Negro convicted of the murder of three white persons at a bridge in the neighborhood of the place of execution."

Though the Englishman's account does not identify the victims by name (only as "planter from Carolina, his son and daughter"), we know today these individuals were of the Baxter family of Rutherford County, North Carolina. The "planter" was a forty-two-year-old slave trader and farmer named William Baxter, Jr., and the murdered children were his son, James Newton Baxter, 12, and niece (not daughter as written in Buckingham's account), Carolina Baxter, 13.

The Circumstances

The murders had taken place just over nine months earlier. They had been grisly, horrifying axe murders, and the motive had been greed – the theft of perhaps as much as $8,000 which Baxter amazingly had on his person at the time of the murders.

For several years, the Baxters were buried near the site of the murders in South Carolina, before being exhumed and removed to the family burying ground in old Rutherford. For over a century and a half, their remains have rested in silent repose on a lonely hill on the original Baxter lands not far from the small town of Caroleen. Each of the weathered marble gravestones which mark the resting places of the deceased reads *Murdered on the 30th Night of Sept. 1838.*

The following account of the Baxter murders has been drawn from public records – newspaper accounts and other sources – in five different states. Many unanswered questions still linger today, yet the records which survive tell a fascinating tale of slavery, greed, and violence. It is part of the legacy of frontier northern Georgia, during the days when Native Americans still inhabited the region. It includes a portion of the legacy of Harrison W. Riley (1804-1874), one of Lumpkin County's most memorable characters, who was implicated in this crime by the testimony of a slave, though never tried, much less convicted.

Riley was a successful merchant, innkeeper and politician who accumulated a vast fortune during the days of the Georgia gold rush. He also had a dark side to his personality, causing him to be known far and wide as a reckless gambler and a man of a notoriously violent temper who had little regard for the "laws of God and man."

Did this mean Harrison W. Riley was also a killer? Could he somehow have engineered the gruesome heinous axe murders of William Baxter, Jr. and two children? Could the money stolen that night from Baxter have helped stake the fortune that Riley ultimately accumulated, or be part of the basis for the tales of treasure and lost gold which have followed Riley's name since his death?

Were other men of Lumpkin County – perhaps in Riley's employ – also involved in the murders? Has Riley's most infamous deed of all been lost to the ravages of time and memory?

The Baxters of Rutherford

William Baxter, Jr. (1796-1838) was the third son and namesake of William Baxter, Sr. (1759-1852), a strong-willed, native Irishman, said to have been born in Bainbridge, County Down, Ireland, the son of David and Ester McDowell Baxter. William, Sr. was a very contentious individual, involved in numerous lawsuits during his lifetime, most of which he won according to records.

William Baxter, Jr., was a product of his father's first marriage to Sarah Berryhill. The older boys from this union stuck to farming and slave-trading. William, Sr.'s three sons by his second marriage, however, became attorneys – valuable assets to their father, who was so regularly involved in litigation of one sort or another.

Born on July 7th, 1796, William Jr. left virtually no record of himself prior to his marriage in 1821. He took as his wife Nancy Suttle (1801-1882?), daughter of George Suttle (1766-1816), a prominent planter of the Floyd's Creek community in Rutherford. The Suttles ranked among the most substantial slave holders of the county, and in their home – later known as the Carpenter Brick House, one of the finest homes in Rutherford County – young Nancy must have grown up privileged and carefree.

In 1822, William Jr. purchased a small tract of land in Rutherford, perhaps with the intention of remaining there, but, about 1825, he removed with his young wife to Lincoln County, Tennessee, where an older brother, James P. Baxter (1792-1859), already resided. There, in 1825 and 1826, William Jr. applied for grants of land totaling in excess of 1,000 acres.

Perhaps young William planned to farm cotton. However, court records and later correspondence also indicate he was trading slaves while in Lincoln, probably journeying to markets as far away as Natchez, Mississippi.

Money & The Slave Trade

The story of the Baxter murders actually begins in the autumn and winter of 1835-36, when William Jr., with the help of his younger brother John, transported 30 Negroes from Rutherford to Perry County, Alabama, apparently with the hope of selling them at a premium to farmers of the more productive soils of that region where cotton proliferated and "prime field hands" were in high demand.

Sixteen of the Negroes being taken to market by young William belonged to his father, William Baxter, Sr., and probably represented a majority of the elder Baxter's holdings at the time. Why William Sr. decided to sell so many of his slaves is unknown today, but William Jr. acceded to his father's wishes and transported, cared for and sold the slaves for him in exchange for the use of a wagon, three horses and the labor of his sixteen-year-old brother.

What began as a simple matter of slave trading soon became a problem for young William. His father had explicitly instructed him to accept only cash in payment for his slaves, but William Jr. apparently was unable to find buyers willing to trade on a cash basis. He ultimately was forced to take approximately $10,000 in twelve-month promissory notes. He also had the notes made payable to himself instead of to his father.

When young William returned home to Rutherford County in 1836 and presented his father with the notes, William Baxter, Sr., understandably was very displeased and refused to accept them as payment. As a result, the first of the promissory notes came due by early 1837, and William Baxter, Jr. returned to Alabama to cash them in. He then made a cash payment of $890 to his father in February of 1837, and a second payment of $2,000 that summer.

Finally, by the summer of 1838, William Jr. had succeeded in exchanging most of the promissory notes for cash, but he then encountered yet another set of problems. He had accepted payment in Alabama currency or bank bills. In May of 1837, the country had suffered a financial panic, which in turn led to the origin of a hodgepodge of state-chartered banks which issued their own currency. Thus, notes of the same denomination from different banks in different states frequently had different exchange rates. In North Carolina, for instance, Alabama currency was worth only eighty percent of its face value.

Riley, however, was perhaps best known for his notoriously violent temper.

Fateful Last Trip

Today, it is unclear what actually transpired when William Jr. offered to repay his father with Alabama bills in August of 1838. The records do seem to indicate that William Sr. took at least a partial payment in the Alabama currency (around $3,300) which he later exchanged in Augusta – at a loss – for North Carolina and South Carolina bank notes. There is also some indication that William Sr. was again very upset stating he would "as soon have oak leaves as Alabama money," and thus forced William Jr. to make yet another trip to exchange the Alabama bills for North and South Carolina currency.

As a result, William Jr. set out once again across the wilds of north Georgia, Tennessee and Alabama, carrying with him large sums of money. This time, however, he would not return alive.

In August of 1838, William Baxter, Jr. and his son, James Newton, left from Rutherford by carriage for the Cherokee Indian country of Georgia and Tennessee. The exact route he took is unknown today, but in all likelihood, he proceeded south to Spartanburg, South Carolina, then westward to Pickens Courthouse and into northern Georgia. In Murray County, Georgia, Baxter almost certainly visited his brother, Andrew (1800-1845), who resided there on land that William Jr. had purchased for Andrew's family.

It was at this juncture that Carolina Baxter (who is believed to have been Andrew Baxter's daughter) is thought to have joined the party. They then proceeded to Lincoln County, Tennessee, where William, Jr. presented his brother, James P. with a loan of $250 (one-half of a $500 Alabama bank note) from their father.

From Lincoln County, the party then began its return trip. However, rather than turn south and re-enter Georgia, William Jr. proceeded eastward toward Calhoun, Tennessee, and the Cherokee lands, perhaps because he had still not effected the currency exchange sought by William Sr. Whether or not this was the real reason for the change of direction toward Calhoun is pure supposition today.

Between May and October of 1838, the Cherokee removal was in progress and Calhoun, located in McMinn County, served as a headquarters for the Cherokee Agency. Thousands of troops and Native Americans were located there at this time, and much currency was changing hands from the sale of stores and supplies.

Meeting Harrison W. Riley

Perhaps William Jr. thought he could find someone in Calhoun, Tennessee, with whom to exchange the Alabama bank bills. This also could have led to his acquaintanceship with Harrison W. Riley of Dahlonega, Georgia, who, according to records, was then "transacting mercantile business" at the Cherokee Agency.

Riley has been described in other documents *(Readers please see "The Life And Times Of Gen. Harrison W. Riley," North Georgia Journal of History, Volume I)* as "the most famous (or infamous) character that north Georgia's gold rush has produced." He was one of Dahlonega's first settlers and is known to have erected the first store there. He rapidly accumulated land and wealth as a businessman, tavern keeper and gambler during the gold rush, and was believed at his death to have been one of the richest men in north Georgia.

In the early 1840s, Riley built a large, rambling inn – known as the Eagle Hotel – on the south side of the town square in Dahlonega. In his later years, he served in numerous political offices, even acquiring the honorary title of "General." He is believed to have fathered numerous illegitimate children – as many as one hundred according to one possibly exaggerated estimate.

Harrison Riley as he appeared several years prior to his death in 1874.

The old Eagle Hotel on the south side of the Dahlonega town square had been renamed the "Besser" Hotel by the time this photo was taken circa 1880s. The Eagle was built and owned by Harrison W. Riley, and served as his headquarters during many tumultuous years in the Lumpkin County area. It was at this site that he engaged in several gunfights and no doubt planned many of the incidents which gained him a place in Lumpkin County folklore.

Riley, however, was perhaps best known for his notoriously violent temper. Lumpkin County records are replete with accounts of law suits in which Riley was involved in assault and battery cases, especially around the time of the Baxter murders.

One account penned by Dahlonega Postmaster Jimmy Anderson states that "[almost] from the day he arrived in the gold fields, Riley was involved in one scrape after another." In March, 1838, for example, a man sued him for "furiously and violently assault[ing] your petitioner. . . a great many violent blows on the head and diverse parts of the body . . ."

According to other records, Riley showed no restraint when confronted by the fairer sex either. In 1853, a similar suit was brought by a woman.

To his credit, the record does indicate that Riley – more often than not – won these suits, indicating that many of them may have been frivolous in nature. Riley, however, also wielded considerable power and influence in Lumpkin County at that time, and seems to have been rather contemptuous of the law in general, as evidenced by his introduction of whiskey into a jury room in 1839.

Though it is unclear if William Jr. ever actually exchanged the currency he had in his possession, it is known today that in Calhoun, he purchased from Harrison Riley a slave named Isaac. Could Riley have become aware of the large sum in William Jr.'s possession at this time?

As Buckingham recorded, "The person selling the Negro happened to know the gentleman purchasing him had a large sum of money with him . . ." Might Riley have then conceived the plan to sell William Jr. a slave with orders to kill and rob him? Alternatively, could William Jr. – as an experienced slave trader himself – have "cheated" Riley by buying a slave with inflated Alabama bills, thus offending the honor of the proud man from Dahlonega? Might the murders of the Baxters have been motivated as much by revenge as by greed? No one knows today.

The Final Days

Following the purchase of the slave Isaac, the Baxter party must have proceeded west from Calhoun, eventually picking up the Unicoi Turnpike which they would have taken into North Carolina. Crossing the Blue Ridge at Unicoi Gap, they then would have dipped southward into Georgia before continuing on through the Nacoochee Valley.

Perhaps a week after leaving Calhoun, late on the afternoon of September 30th, the party passed the tavern called Traveler's Rest, crossed the Jarrett toll bridge at Walton's Ford on the Tugaloo River, and made their way into the Pickens District (Oconee County today) of South Carolina. Just a few miles beyond the river, they set up camp, perhaps near a branch of Chauga Creek (since the party would have preferred to camp near water if possible).

Even today, this vicinity remains a wild and remote spot, and it is curious that William Jr. chose to camp here instead of overnighting at the more comfortable tavern, especially since they reportedly crossed Devereaux Jarrett's toll bridge near dark.

The Baxter party's carriage, driven by the Negro Isaac, was noticed and remembered at the toll bridge. *The Greenville Mountaineer* of October 12, 1838, reported that a short time after they crossed, "two men on horseback inquired for him (William Baxter, Jr.) at the same bridge, and then passed on. The next morning, the Negro re-crossed the bridge in the carriage, and was asked where the white persons were, when he answered that he was removing them to some place in the neighborhood, and had left them. In a short time, the two men mentioned above passed the bridge, but in such a hurry that no questions were asked of them."

Who were these "persons unknown," these two men (presumably white) who were apparently following the Baxter party and noted at the bridge? Might one of them have been Harrison Riley? Or, might the two unknown men have been in his employ?

Whether or not there was a conspiracy, most sources are in agreement today that sometime in the night, after the Baxters had crossed the toll bridge, Isaac, the Negro slave whom William Jr. had just purchased from Riley, did the actual killing.

It is believed the slave somehow obtained a small axe, perhaps one which he himself used to cut firewood. After William Jr. and the children fell asleep, Isaac probably fell upon the father first.

According to an account in the *Rutherfordton Gazette*, "the head of the father, when found, [was] nearly split in two." Believing William Jr. to be dead, Isaac then "instantly" dispatched Baxter's son, James Newton. But William Jr. "exhibit[ed] further signs of life," and the slave again assaulted him and "put an end to his existence."

In that isolated place, the screams and muffled moans of the victims would have been heard by no one – save the niece Carolina, who may have attempted to flee prior to her murder. A 1903 account in the *Rutherfordton Sun* recounted that she possibly was aroused by the cries of her uncle and cousin and "ran some distance before the Negro overtook her, and she too, was knocked in the head with the axe and killed." The bodies were dragged into a ditch.

Pursuit Of The Criminals

The behavior of the Negro at the bridge the following day aroused suspicion and within hours, a trail of blood on the road led to the discovery of the bodies. A few days later, the Baxters in Rutherford County learned of the murders, and a party of four – consisting of William Jr.'s older brother, Joseph Baxter (1794-1870), and three other Baxter relatives – soon thereafter proceeded to Georgia in pursuit of the murderer(s).

Isaac managed to make his way back to Dahlonega where he was captured – with the assistance of Riley, a man named David Thompson, and other members of the community – probably no more than two weeks after the murders. Joseph Baxter stated the family recovered three horses, the carriage, about $1,300 and "three Negroes which . . . Thompson gave up to the Estate for money he had expended belonging to my Brother William Jr."

Curiously, $1,100 of William Jr.'s money (the bulk of that recovered) was said to have been found in the possession of a Negro woman who belonged to Thompson. Those who had assisted with the capture of Isaac were allowed to keep an additional $200 found in the murderer's possession.

That Isaac chose to return to Dahlonega is, of itself, perhaps suggestive of Riley's complicity. Could he have thought to obtain "safe harbor" with his former master?

Moreover, what of the individual David Thompson? It is known today that his name appears in the 1838 Georgia state census for Lumpkin County and that he owned a few slaves. But could he also have been an accomplice to the crime? If not, how did he come to possess William Jr.'s money?

Further, why did a Negro woman owned by Thompson have so much of the recovered money? Could this have been a ruse to mislead the authorities and thus protect the white conspirators?

The slave Isaac was returned to Pickens District to be tried for the murders, and though the records of the trial have not survived, one can still surmise the outcome. Slave law in South Carolina was administered by the county courts of magistrates and freeholders, which were composed of two magistrates and three to five freeholders. Conviction was by majority vote. For the capital offense of murdering a white person, the penalty was certain death.

The trial and execution took place sometime between the 17th and 19th of October, near the spot where the crime was committed, as was customary. One account states the Negro was brought to the place of execution "chained to an iron bar, and burned . . ." In fact, if Isaac was merely hanged, he was fortunate, as South Carolina historian David Duncan Wallace wrote that "execution by burning . . . was still practiced in punishing particularly heinous [slave] crimes" as late as the mid-1820s.

Gallows Confession

Before Isaac was hanged, however, he made, upon the gallows, a confession that implicated Harrison W. Riley as the instigator of the horrible murders that he had committed. Though as noted above, the records of the court have been lost, several contemporary sources recorded the gist of the slave's confession.

As the *Rutherfordton Gazette* of October 24th, 1838, reported, "he confessed his guilt upon the scaffold, and stated that he was instigated to it [the murders] by the individual from whom Baxter purchased him."

Buckingham provides more detail. He states that Isaac's former master "conceived the diabolical plan of hiring the slave to murder his new master, and seize his wealth, on condition that the Negro should share of the plunder, and receive his freedom besides!"

Isaac's confession may have done little for him, but he did succeed in casting suspicion upon Harrison Riley. On October 23rd, less than a week after the former's execution, Riley drew up a "card" or public notice for publication in various major Georgia newspapers denying any involvement in the murders and proclaiming his innocence. This notice bore the signatures of eighty-three residents of Lumpkin County and was certified by Lumpkin's clerk of the Superior Court.

Riley's public notice included the statement that "[the] Negro was apprehended through the vigilance of the citizens of this vicinity, and no man was more prompt or untiring than Mr. H.W. Riley, either in procuring the arrest of the Negro, or in securing the money of the deceased."

Regardless of this claim, of the money stolen from William Jr., only about $1,300 was reported to have been recovered by the family. All sources are in agreement that William Jr. had more than this on his person – substantially more. Estimates vary, but it is believed today that William Jr. was carrying between $2,500 and $8,000, a considerable sum in the 1830s. (This sum would be the approximate equivalent of between $40,000 to $125,000 in today's dollars.) Could this discrepancy be accounted for by the money, belonging to William Jr., which reportedly was spent by David Thompson, and for which Thompson gave three slaves in exchange?

Riley's Buried Treasure?

It is interesting that Harrison Riley's name has long been associated with buried treasure. Today, the landscape in the immediate vicinity around Riley's old homesite in White County is pockmarked with pits and excavated depressions made by treasure hunters feverishly searching for Riley's "lost gold."

Perhaps it is a long shot, but might William Jr.'s unrecovered money have something to do with these tales? Riley died in his White County home between Dahlonega and Cleveland, Georgia, in 1874, but a report in the *Mountain Signal* newspaper in Dahlonega in 1898 and reprinted in Andrew Cain's *History Of Lumpkin County* (1932) is of interest with respect to the Baxter murders. In this article, a Judge Brittain described $2,000 in gold belonging to "General" Riley. Brittain claimed he knew where the gold was buried, but that "he [was] not going to tell it so as to create a lawsuit."

A "lawsuit?" Though this is only supposition today, such a "lawsuit" might suggest that others outside of the Riley family could lay claim to this money. Could some vague memory of the murders, William Baxter Sr.'s propensity for lawsuits and his family of lawyer-sons lie behind the judge's caution?

Of further interest is the fact that in February of 1839, after Isaac the slave's confession had been followed by a published confession by David Thompson (said confession believed to have been to the effect that Thompson had spent at least a portion of William Jr.'s money), a new notice signed by 18 of the signers of Riley's original claim of innocence was published in area newspapers. This new notice by the original signers stated that they were *"withdrawing the opinion given in our card of the 23rd Oct. 1838,"* and asked that they *"be considered as neither avering the innocence or guilt of Mr. Riley . . ."*

The court of public opinion and the court of public law, however, are two entirely different entities. Ultimately, Riley's alleged responsibility for the murder of the Baxters on the Tugaloo River seems to have come down to his word versus that of a slave.

And as Buckingham recorded, "by the laws of this and other Slave States, the testimony of a Negro cannot be received in any case against a white man; and therefore, though the general opinion was that the Negro was speaking the truth – as the bad character of his former master rendered it more probable that he should be the instigator of the murder for the sake of the plunder . . . the instigator [however] escaped all punishment, while the Negro was hanged for executing his former master's wishes."

Today, it is highly unlikely that an answer will be forthcoming to the question of whether or not Dahlonega's Harrison W. Riley instigated a slave to commit the horrendous triple-murder of the Baxters in a remote corner of the state near the Tugaloo River in September of 1838. This secret was buried with Riley himself in Mt. Hope Cemetery in Dahlonega in 1874. Some may be willing to accept the epitaph on the obelisk marking Riley's grave which reads *"Let his faults be buried with his bones."* Others, however, may not.

REFERENCES

Adams, Marilyn L., ed., *Censuses for Georgia Counties Taliaferro 1827 Lumpkin 1838 Chatham 1845. Census Series, Number Four.* Atlanta, GA: R.J. Taylor, Jr., Foundation, 1979.

Anderson, Jimmy E., "The Life and Times Of Gen. Harrison W. Riley," *A North Georgia Journal Of History, Volume I,* Olin Jackson, ed., Woodstock, GA: Legacy Communications, Inc., 1989.

Anthony, Madeleine K., Collection, Box No. III-23, Folder No. 9, Lumpkin County Public Library, Dahlonega, Georgia.

Buckingham, J.S., Esq. *The Slave States Of America. Vol. II.* London: Fisher, Son & Co., 1842. (pp. 167-169)

Bouwman, Robert Eldridge. *Traveler's Rest and the Tugaloo Crossroads.* N.p.: State of Georgia, Historic Preservation Section, 1992, 3rd ed.

Cain, Andrew W., *History of Lumpkin County for the First Hundred Years, 1832-1932.* Spartanburg, SC: The Reprint Company, Publishers, 1978.

Duncan, Constance Jolley. *Through Tinted Lenses: A True Historical Narrative Of The Willis Alexander Jolley Family Of Rutherford County, North Carolina.* Asheville, NC: Gilbert Printing Co., 1959.

Evans, Tad, comp. Macon, GA, Newspaper Clippings (*Messenger*), Volume III, 1838-1842. Savannah, GA: The writer, 1997.

Evans, Tad, comp. Milledgeville, Georgia Newspaper Clippings (*Southern Recorder*), Volume V, 1839-1841. Savannah, GA: The writer, 1996.

Greenville (SC) *Mountaineer*, 12 October 1838, p. 2.

North Carolina Supreme Court, case file #6863, William Costin (sic) et al. vs. William Baxter, Sr. (1849), NC State Archives, Raleigh, NC.

North Carolina Supreme Court, case file #6862, William Costin (sic) vs. William Baxter (1846), NC State Archives Raleigh, NC.

Pendleton (SC) *Messenger*, 26 October, 1838, p. 2.

Pendleton (SC) *Messenger*, 19 October, 1838, p. 2.

Rutherfordton (NC) *Gazette* article of October 24, 1838 reprinted in the *Raleigh Register* and *North Carolina Gazette*, 5 November, 1838, p. 3.

Rutherfordton (NC) *Gazette* article (no date) reprinted in the Greenville (SC) Mountaineer, 19 October, 1838, p. 2.

The Sun (Rutherfordton, NC), 4 June, 1903, p. 6.

Wallace, David Duncan. *South Carolina: A Short History, 1520-1948.* Columbia, SC: University of South Carolina Press, 1951.

Tri-Weekly Chronicle & Sentinel (Augusta, GA), 29 November 1838, p. 4.

Southern Recorder (Milledgeville, GA), 19 February 1839, p. 3.

The Life & Times Of John A. Murrell

Some of north Georgia's treasured covered bridges were once the realm of a nasty band of outlaws, and the outlaw leader was known as "Reverend Devil."

Bandits, banditos, train robbers, and highwaymen. When we think of them, we usually think of the old West, but in point of fact, the South has had its share of outlaws too, particularly during the days of the pioneers and early settlers. One such group was the Murrells.

The Murrells roamed the north Georgia area in the early 1800s. Because of the nature of their "enterprises," the group plundered a wide territory, ranging as far west as Texas, Arkansas, and the Choctaw Indian Nation.

Ironically, they might not have pillaged northeast Georgia at all, had it not been for a unique aspect of architecture – the covered bridge – which greatly facilitated their evil ways. From the dark rafters of these innovative structures, a surprise attack could easily be launched upon unsuspecting travelers, businessmen, gold miners, stagecoaches, etc. At that time, covered bridges were numerous in northeast Georgia, creating an environment in which even seasoned travelers and former victims never knew when to suspect the next attack.

It was the Bolding house which once existed near the Chestatee River in Hall County, Georgia, that became a hideout of sorts for the Murrells shortly after the discovery of gold in the area. And nearby, Bolding Bridge likewise became a frequent site at which gang members reportedly waylaid travelers.

In the early days in north Georgia, there were few roads. People rode on horseback, or walked over trails which had been traversed by animals and Indians since time immemorial. These trails eventually began to widen, to accommodate the cart and wagon traffic that increased as more pioneers moved westward.

There were no bridges in these early years, and the task of crossing a stream with a loaded cart or wagon was often treacherous and very difficult. Good river and creek fords normally were only available at shoals and low spots in the streams, usually during the dry season. Stream crossings were particularly dangerous during heavy rains.

Thus, the era of bridge construction was born, to insure year-round travel. And shortly thereafter, the wooden structures were covered with roofs and sides. Some have said this was to keep the horses, mules and oxen from becoming frightened when seeing the water below. In truth, however, the wooden covers were designed to preserve the bridges, which were expensive and difficult to build. And protect the bridges they did, but they at the same time exposed travelers to a new danger – the outlaw.

The Murrells came to north Georgia in the 1820s or '30s. The group, at best, was a strange family. John A. Murrell – the acknowledged leader of the group – was the son of a preacher. The Reverend William Murrell doubtless had some influence in the pulpit, but at home, "the old lady" ruled the roost.

John A. Murrell was born about 1800, and the exact site of his birth is not known today. When quite young, the family lived about 25 miles south of Nashville, Tennessee, near the village of Bethesda, a serene little community surrounded and half-hidden by the Cumberland Mountains. If Murrell was charmed by this picturesque setting, he never spoke of it.

From his earliest days, John Murrell was more interested in "speculations." He watched the traffic go by over the Natchez Trace and talked with travelers who roomed at a tavern operated by his mother. He listened to breath-taking stories of robberies and looting and dreamed of the day when he too would ride away to seek adventure and fortune.

Down through the years, the bandit repeatedly maintained that it was his mother who began his life of crime. "My mother was one of the true grit," he reportedly once stated. "She learned me and all her children to steal as soon as we could walk. Whatever we stole, she hid for us, and dared my father to touch us for it. She made us hate the proud ones and go after those who had more than we did."

At age 16, a young John swindled a storekeeper. Neighbors and acquaintances however, became suspicious and began watching him too closely. John decided his rural neighborhood was just too small. He abandoned his Tennessee home to pursue his "speculations" on a grander scale in new places.

With a few accomplices, Murrell eventually traveled over much of the Southern states, stealing horses and robbing unsuspecting travelers wherever he went. He later returned to his home in Tennessee for a period of bragging, free-spending, and general carousing, but soon had spent all his ill-gotten gains.

To recoup his fortune, John set out to steal several horses nearby, but this time, he was caught in the act. After a speedy trial, the court's sentence was handed down:

"John A. Murrell shall receive on his bare back at the public whipping post in Davidson County thirty lashes, set in the pillory two hours on Monday, two hours on Thursday, and two hours on Wednesday, next, that he be branded on the left thumb with the letters H.T. (horse thief) in the presence of the court; that he be imprisoned twelve months from this day and be rendered infamous."

From that horrible day forward, John Murrell was an embittered and unrepentant man with a passion for violence and revenge.

To recoup his fortune, John set out to steal several horses nearby, but this time, he was caught in the act.

OLD BOLDING COVERED BRIDGE – Located at one time on the old Dawsonville Highway near Gainesville, this bridge linked Hall & Forsyth counties. It spanned the Chestatee River, and reportedly was a favorite of bandits who robbed travelers. A farmhouse owned by a family by the name of Bolding was also located in this vicinity, and it was from this home that a group of outlaws known loosely as "the Murrell gang" operated. This area is covered today by the waters of Lake Lanier. (Photo courtesy of Chestatee Regional Library, Gainesville)

OLD BOLDING HOUSE – Located near the Chestatee River on the old Dawsonville Highway in Hall County, this structure, according to folklore, was a hideout for a group of outlaws known as "Murrell's Gang." The house was demolished during the construction of Lake Lanier. (Photo courtesy of Chestatee Regional Library, Gainesville)

In his prison cell however, he kept a stack of old books – the *Bible* and law books – but not with good intentions. He poured over these books day after day, learning each and every opportunity in which he might use the knowledge from the books to take advantage of an unsuspecting soul.

Young Murrell later said that his study of criminal law and fundamental theology made him prepared for anything. His brother, William Jr., met him when he stepped out the prison door as a free man, and another life of criminal activity began immediately. The two men rode off on two fine, freshly-stolen horses.

Making further use of his studies, John turned to religion as a guise for his evil deeds. He often related to his cronies that as a child, he had been amused at the blind confidence a minister of the gospel could inspire, even a sorry minister like his father. As a sideline profession, John subsequently adopted the device of preaching, undoubtedly dipping into untold sums of money contributed as tithes to the churches at which he preached along the way.

His preoccupation with crime no doubt eventually forced his migration to Georgia. Men of unsavory reputations from all walks of life joined his band.

In that day, long coats and high-top

hats were symbols of superiority, honor and intelligence. The arrival of an itinerant preacher was an event that brought settlers from miles around. Revival and camp meetings became regular devices for John. His gang members, needless to say, were very busy.

"Reverend" Murrell had found that these revival meetings furnished an excellent atmosphere for his work. During the campaigns, Murrell was quietly directing his lieutenants in horse-stealing, as well as various and sundry other criminal activities.

Despite the realm to which Murrell's operations had spread however, his intended goal in fact was much larger. The hatred and bitterness in him was welling more to the surface with each passing day. His vendetta was against the whole of established society in the South, and he was intent upon the destruction of as much of it as possible.

His plot, later uncovered and thwarted, was fabricated around the idea of a slave uprising (slaves in many parts of the South at that time usually outnumbered whites 40 to 1). The blacks were being organized for just such an event on a certain day. According to Murrell's plans, all white people would be killed with the exception of some of the beautiful white women. Murrell promised the slaves (which he had been stealing now for many months and hiding away) their freedom, their own homes and money from the plantations they would plunder.

John Murrell's boldness, ruthlessness and lavish distribution of spoils attracted scores of followers. His operations, which extended over a number of states, included the robbery of mails, banks, stores, the piracy of riverboats, and slave-kidnapping. Legend also attributes hundreds of murders to Murrell and his unholy crew.

John A. Murrell's career, however, was cut short by his capture in Tennessee in 1834. He escaped the gallows for his crimes, but spent ten years in prison. He died mysteriously shortly after his release, and has been known in folklore in northeast Georgia from that day forward as "Reverend Devil."

Today, the reputed hideouts, as well as most, if not all of the covered bridges from which John Murrell began his career of crime, have vanished from north Georgia – victims of progress, time and the elements. The romantic aura and historic significance of the covered bridges, however, live on.

SIGNAL DEVICE – Circled above the porch is what has been described as a "lantern hole" through which signals reportedly were flashed by members of the Murrell Gang to one another. (Photo courtesy of Chestatee Regional Library, Gainesville)

The North Georgia Moonshine War Of 1876-77

In contrast to various other countries of the world, the United States, by and large, has been very reluctant to use regular army troops against its own civilian population. There have, however, been some rare exceptions, and considering the mixed results of even these few adventures, a strong argument could be made for the confinement of the Army's duties henceforth solely to the defense of the country from external enemies.

A good example of one of these failures was the misuse of the army in an abortive attempt by U.S. agents to enforce taxation laws involving alcohol and tobacco in the north Georgia mountains in the 1870s.

The federal revenue laws that taxed alcohol and tobacco manufacturing through licenses were first passed during the U.S. Civil War, and imposed a tremendous hardship on Appalachian families, many of whom depended upon their production of spirituous liquors as their main cash crop. It was many of these same mountain families who ironically had defied the Confederacy during the Civil War to support the federal government.

Suffering from an extremely poor transportation system in the mountains and a lack of extensive productive farmland, mountain families turned to the production of whiskey and tobacco, since these items were virtually the only marketable commodities produceable. Also, the federal revenue laws did not (and still do not to this day) distinguish between alcohol and tobacco used for home needs (as in medicinal remedies) and that used for sale on the public market.

The licenses required for the legal sale of these commodities were usually more than the average farmer could afford to pay, and therefore, thousands of otherwise honest citizens were driven into criminal activity. By 1876, cases involving the prosecution of revenue law violators virtually monopolized the docket of the Federal District Court in Atlanta, Georgia.

The system for enforcing the revenue laws made matters infinitely worse too. Revenue agents and deputy U.S. marshals, unlike the more highly regarded Justice Department commissioners, were paid on a fee basis at that time. Payment was based upon the number of illegal distilleries or "stills" captured and the number of arrests made. The agents were often accused of making fraudulent arrests to pad their fees, and their incomes reportedly were also supplemented by bribes, blackmail, and profiteering from the illegal sale of captured stills.

And as time passed, the situation began to feed upon itself in worse ways too. Residents of the areas under surveillance were hired to spy upon and testify against their neighbors. Personal and political vendettas from the Civil War and even earlier often became motives for "reporting."

The revenue agents also enjoyed a reputation for being brutal, profane and heartless. When an individual was arrested for violating the revenue laws, he or she was taken to Atlanta for confinement and trial. The family could lose everything in an attempt to pay the accused's legal fees, even if he or she was found to be innocent.

The politics of the day also inflamed an already explosive situation. With the harsh memories of Reconstruction still vivid in the minds of many involved, the fact that the revenue laws were created during and enforced by Republican administrations, did not help matters. Consequently, the revenue agents found few friends in Georgia's Democratic press, courthouses, or state capitol.

A strange twist to this situation was also discovered in the charge that some of the revenue agents who, although working for those Republican administrations, were in fact Democrats who were using the law to persecute the mountaineers who had turned their backs on the Confederacy in earlier years.

As efforts to eliminate the illegal liquor increased, the mountain men organized to fight back. The north Georgia counties were the most violent of the Southern Appalachian mountain region, with more than twice the number of alleged revenue agent casualties as those reported in second-place Tennessee between 1875 and 1881. The U.S. government in turn responded by using federal troops to protect its agents during raids as early as 1872.

In what may have been a singular incident that year, U.S. Deputy Marshal Charles B. Blacker, accompanied by a Lieutenant Wolf of the 2nd U.S. Infantry, was fired upon in the Fightingtown (Boardtown) area of Fannin County. In 1876, citing the loss of $500,000 annually in federal taxes and the reports of bands of moonshiners firing upon revenue agents, the Republican administration of then-President Ulysses S. Grant ordered increased use of U.S. Army troops for the support and protection of revenue officials.

One such patrol led by Deputy Marshal Blacker at Santa Luca in Gilmer County, visited the home of the elderly John Emory (formerly of Pickens County) on the night of January 14, 1876, and arrested, without warrants, four men who were waiting for daylight at Emory's still house. When Emory emerged from his house to investigate the cause of the commotion outside, he was shot (almost between the eyes) and killed instantly without warning by Private William O'Grady, a federal soldier.

With two other soldiers – Edward P. Wells and Frederick E. Newman – Private O'Grady concealed Emory's corpse in a nearby creek where Emory's grief-stricken widow discovered it the next morning.

On February 13, United States Deputy Marshal James A. Findley and his men fired upon Lafayette Southern seven times on a raid in the nearby Cartecay District. They captured two of Southern's stills, a wagon and a team, and 120 gallons of whiskey. Findley and his crew then arrested and carried off one

They captured two of Southern's stills, a wagon and a team, and 120 gallons of whiskey.

James Sitton who was in bed in ill health nearby.

Gilmer Countians immediately organized a written protest to the Governor of Georgia. The Georgia State Legislature was in session at that time and William Robert Rankin of Gordon County introduced resolutions in the Georgia House which culminated in a resolution requesting that Governor Smith authorize a full investigation of the outrages committed by revenue agents in north Georgia.

A warrant was issued almost immediately by Gilmer County Justice of the Peace M.A. Berry for the soldiers responsible for John Emory's death. O'Grady and his colleagues were arrested in Atlanta, but before they could be tried in Gilmer County, a *Writ of Habeas Corpus* from the President of the United States himself authorized a transferal of the trial to the U.S. Federal Circuit Court in Atlanta.

The federal government attempted to hire Blue Ridge District Solicitor General Charles D. Phillips to defend the soldiers. Phillips, however, declined the opportunity, choosing instead to be the prosecutor, and taking as his fee no income other than "Mrs. Emory's tears." However, a largely black, and allegedly politically pressured jury found O'Grady and the other two soldiers "Not Guilty."

Adding still more fuel to the growing inferno was the fact that revenue agents in the area used this incident to reinforce their calls for more federal troops, contending that Emory's death encouraged organized resistance and even revenge against federal officials. Surprisingly, had the agents known just how well-founded their fears had been, they may have been even more vocal, for the events leading up to the night of February 10, 1877, had already been set in motion.

Federal troops from McPherson Barracks in Atlanta and revenue agents left Cartersville, Georgia, on February 1, 1877. They made camp at Ellijay, Georgia, the county seat of Gilmer County. From there, they dispatched detachments with instructions to raid moonshiners and illegal tobacco manufacturers in Gilmer, Pickens, and Fannin counties.

Deputy Marshal Blacker, with a party of revenue agents and soldiers, left Ellijay at noon on February 9. They arrived at the home of a Mr. Ayers Jones at 2:45 A.M. the next morning. They were in the Frog Mountain region of western Fannin County (although they were close enough to the county line to believe they were in Gilmer County) on the headwaters of Conasauga Creek.

Having seen the light from Jones' cabin, the men initially suspected that they had chanced upon a distillery. Upon closer inspection however, they discovered the cabin contained only Mrs. Jones and seven children huddled around a fire, trying desperately to stay warm.

According to Mrs. Jones' later deposition, the men burst into the cabin unannounced, with Blacker holding a cocked pistol. They questioned her at length, and when she could not, or would not tell them where her husband was or the location of his stillhouse, Blacker became very profane.

According to her later testimony, Mrs. Jones repeatedly asked the men to leave her cabin, and one of the soldiers even supported her, urging that he and his fellow troops withdraw. But Blacker, continuing with his swearing, announced that he would stay as long as he pleased. Mrs. Jones and the children, some of whom were sick, remained in the cabin with Blacker, Corporal Calloway, two guides, and Lieutenant Augustine McIntyre, while the remainder of the party left to search for the stillhouse.

According to reports of the incident, approximately fifteen minutes had passed since Blacker and his men had arrived, when footsteps were heard outside by the men inside the cabin. It was assumed by the men inside that the sounds they were hearing were from the return of the other soldiers and agents dispatched to search for the stillhouse.

Imagine the surprise of the men inside the cabin, opening the front door to what they thought were their own men outside, when they suddenly were confronted instead by a fearsome group of strangers. A stout, dark-haired man with whiskers, nearly six feet tall, stood in the doorway with a large pistol. Shouting "Stand, God damn you. . . You're in the wrong place tonight!," the stranger fired his pistol, sending the men inside the cabin scurrying for cover. Corporal Callaway, standing by the cabin hearth, fired his carbine and then put out the lamp on the hearth. A pine knot still burned in the fireplace, but reportedly did not shed enough illumination to give the attackers any view of the inside of the cabin.

Shortly thereafter, Ralston and Anglin, the guides, fled out the back of the cabin, closing the door behind them, leaving Callaway, Blacker, and McIntyre to face the music alone. The mountain men stormed the house four times, firing shotguns, pistols, and rifles. Both sides emptied their guns through the doorway. Blacker reportedly told McIntyre repeatedly to take cover behind the bedstead, but he refused, fearing that the children might be hit by a stray bullet.

On the fourth volley from the attackers outside, Lt. McIntyre was wounded. He reportedly cried out: "Blacker, I'm shot through the heart."

With their ammunition running out, the lieutenant, corporal, and Blacker fled out the rear door. McIntyre, now weak from his wound, stumbled and fell off the rear steps of the cabin. When Blacker attempted to help him, the lieutenant, apparently realizing his wound was mortal, urged the deputy marshal to save himself.

Shortly thereafter, Blacker retreated, leaving McIntyre behind. Shouts in the distance were soon heard to the effect of: "Oh yes, we've got one of the damned son of a bitches," and ". . . We'll fix you!"

The next morning, Blacker and five men returned to the cabin. McIntyre's body still lay grotesquely where he had fallen earlier that morning. Blacker found Mrs. Jones and her children still in the cabin in bed. When the men questioned Mrs. Jones about the attackers, she pleaded ignorance. The men began cursing her. Blacker reportedly warned her that they were out for revenge, and would in three weeks burn all the cabins in the area.

During Blacker's tirade, one of the men suddenly exclaimed "Look out!" Stepping outside, Blacker saw before his eyes a forest filled with armed men, some behind rocks no more than 300 feet away. He ordered his men to withdraw immediately, surprisingly leaving McIntyre's body behind once again.

At 3:00 P.M. that afternoon, twenty-two soldiers under Lieutenant James Ulio finally recovered McIntyre's corpse, carrying it out on a horse, since the terrain was far too rugged for a wheeled wagon or cart. This group was also fired upon by a party of men from a ravine 200 yards away.

According to an article entitled *"Gilmer's Guerrillas,"* published in the February 13, 1877 issue of *The Atlanta Constitution*, three of the mountaineers were killed in the recovery of Lt. McIntyre's body. McIntyre's corpse had been robbed, and a hob-nail boot print was found on his forehead.

Federal retaliation was swift and decisive. On February 23, revenue agents, accompanied by soldiers, arrested seventy to eighty individuals, both men and women, all of whom were within fifteen to twenty miles of Frog Mountain. They were carried to Cartersville, using old arrest warrants or no warrants at all. Many of the persons arrested were seized in the middle of the night while asleep in bed, and subsequently subjected to conditions of hunger and exposure from which some were not expected to recover.

For some of the prisoners, their odyssey did not end until they were set free in Atlanta, forcing them to make their way back home on foot, a distance of more than 130 miles. On March 13, 1877, *The Atlanta Constitution* reported that on March 12, sixty-nine of the persons arrested for revenue violations were released in Atlanta after pleading guilty and receiving suspended sentences. And in the week just prior, 247 prisoners had been similarly sent home. With other arrests, the total number eventually exceeded 500 persons.

The Frog Mountain area was gradually abandoned by its families, as men who had escaped the dragnet hid out or fled to neighboring states.

Some residents remained however. *The Atlanta Constitution* reported that the local people were stockpiling powder and shot for self defense against another raid.

The quest for justice in the murder of Lt. McIntyre did not die easily either. Rewards were offered by the Governor of Georgia as well as by the federal government for the killers. James Holt and his three sons were arrested in Nashville, Tennessee for McIntyre's death, but were released when it was revealed that the only evidence against them was the fact that they were former Frog Mountain residents preparing to move to Texas.

Embarrassed by this mistake, federal authorities quietly and cautiously spirited their next group of suspects – John Davenport and five of his neighbors – into Atlanta. The only evidence against these individuals was reported to have been the testimony of a female. Following a hearing, Davenport and his friends were released.

The U.S. Army believed that the man who had appeared in the doorway of the Jones cabin had been Ayers Jones himself, and even claimed that the whole incident, including the light from the cabin and the women and children, had all been an elaborate plot to lure McIntyre and his party into an ambush – and to their deaths. The army claimed that the Jones family members were part Indian and had moved to Frog Mountain after fleeing justice in the mountains of western North Carolina.

Ayers Jones' wife and son were later arrested, but subsequently released. Ayers Jones himself, and his brother Tom, were not caught until 1879. They were not tried for murder, but were indicted for conspiracy to avoid the service of a warrant by Blacker. They were eventually tried and found "Not Guilty."

Papers in their case file in the National Archives, Atlanta Branch, shed some interesting sidelights on the death of McIntyre and details of the incident.

Informants in the incident apparently claimed that an Elijah Johnson had been in the Army's camp. Acting as a spy, Johnson had sent three men to Frog Mountain to warn the mountaineers of the impending raid. The Jones family and their neighbors subsequently armed themselves and banded together.

The Jones family and their neighbors subsequently armed themselves and banded together.

Prior to the raid by the agents and soldiers on Jones' cabin, the mountaineers apparently were actually attempting to avoid confrontation, but decided instead to storm the cabin after over-hearing the abuse being heaped upon Mrs. Jones by Blacker.

The National Archives papers further indicate that one witness testified that a W.H. Green who was related to the Jones family, was in possession of McIntyre's pistol and knew where his watch could be found. And later, during a daring rescue of a fellow moonshiner, Ayers Jones allegedly boasted that his pistol had killed McIntyre.

Ayers Jones however, was also described as "as pure a specimen of a child of nature as can be imagined," so illiterate and backward that he had never even seen a railroad. He was however, a large landowner, owning some 700 acres in the 980th District of Fannin County. He, ironically, was himself later murdered by his son – John – in Chattooga County on September 11, 1893.

In 1877, mass meetings were being held in Gilmer and Fannin counties (more than 100 persons attended the Fannin meeting) where declarations were signed and sent to newly-elected Governor Alfred Colquitt. The resolutions condemned the killing of Lt. McIntyre and the persons violating the revenue laws. However, they also charged that the revenue agents were, in actuality, the root of the current crisis. The declaration called the agents *"men without any social standing, without honor, or integrity, and who themselves have been, up to the present time, without a single exception, the most persistent violators of the law in our midst."* *The Atlanta Constitution* also blamed McIntyre's death on the revenue agents, *"a hungry pack of remorseless and heartless spies and vampires."*

When the Georgia State Legislature was again in session, Rep. B.C. Duggar of Gilmer County and Lemuel J. Allred of Pickens introduced new resolutions which were passed, requesting that Governor Colquitt investigate the situation in north Georgia. The House also passed resolutions condemning the internal revenue laws on alcohol production and the system designed to enforce those laws.

Colonel Samuel C. Williams was sent to north Georgia by Governor Colquitt to conduct the investigation. He arrived in Ellijay on February 28. Traveling through Pickens, Gilmer, and Fannin counties, he collected more than 130 depositions, many of which were later published in *The Atlanta Constitution* of May 8, 1877.

Not satisfied with only "looking into the matter at hand," Williams recorded information on the events and persons going back to 1872. He personally visited the places involved, including Frog Mountain and the Jones cabin. Everywhere, he received "not only a willingness, but a desire to help," as men even left their work to aid him in his investigation.

Williams' report was a lengthy condemnation of the entire revenue enforcement system in north Georgia, and of the men who ran it. He collected dozens of depositions of people arrested without warrants who were compelled to hire lawyers to clear themselves of nonexistent charges, and of brutal revenue agents who extorted blackmail, took bribes, and sold liquor distilleries captured in raids. Army officers interviewed were no less negative about the revenue agents, and expressed their regrets in being forced to help these men.

Col. Williams' investigation of the death of Lt. McIntyre was no less revealing. He discovered that had the "guerrillas" actually wished to wipe out the entire party of agents and soldiers, a successful ambush could have been easily carried out by two men at any of several places on the narrow trail to the cabin.

And the Jones' cabin was an oak log

pen, 12 by 14 feet in size, neither "chinked nor daubed". The attackers would have needed to do little more than to fire through the three to five-inch cracks between the logs to have killed Blacker and his entire party as they stood in the cabin.

Clearly, Williams concluded, the attackers had not intended to massacre the raiding party or to harm the soldiers. As for the mass arrests, Williams reported that McIntyre's commander believed that the attackers were not thirty men, but only four or five.

In the interim following this incident, Deputy Marshals Blacker and Findley, accompanied by troops, were still actively inciting ill will with their tactics in north Georgia.

Starting from Dawson County, they and a posse arrested a Harrison Barker of Forsyth County at his home in March, 1877. In their account of the daring and dangerous capture, Blacker and Findley described Harrison Barker as a legendary north Georgia moonshining "Jesse James" of many a daring escape and blazing gun battle.

Barker, who was subsequently captured and tried, turned out to be little more than a wiry man of average height who claimed never to have been convicted of moonshining or charged with any "mean thing." He speculated that his notoriety as a legitimate tavern keeper in Cumming may have led to his being singled out by Blacker and Findley.

Whatever the circumstances, Barker took flight after wounding Blacker in one arrest attempt. Blacker and Findley later pursued him to Kentucky, and eventually captured him, bringing him back to Atlanta for trial.

Living up to his reputation however, Barker escaped from the prison in which he was being held, but remained peacefully at home, until dragged out of his bed by Findley early one morning in 1877. Barker eventually plead "Guilty" to selling untaxed liquor ("moonshining") and was given a suspended sentence. He had also been indicted for shooting Blacker in 1873, but was never tried on this charge.

On April 10, 1877, the U.S. Army finally left Ellijay and Gilmer County. In 1879, an act of Congress prohibited the use of troops to aid civilian authorities in making arrests.

So ended what came to be known as "the North Georgia Moonshine War of 1876-1877." The official score stood at one civilian and one officer killed, with an untold number of casualties among the moonshiners and revenue agents.

Contrary to the hopes of the mountain people, the revenue laws, the revenue agents, and the local resistance all continued through to the days of the "whitecaps," also known as "the night riders," and on to the more recent days of "Thunder Road."

Some headway was made against moonshiners by such federal agents as Commissioner of Internal Revenue Green B. Raum, who, in the 1880s, used what Dr. Wilbur R. Miller has called "a systematic strategy combining force and restraint," built both on persistence and on winning local support. That moonshining has largely died away however, is due largely to the rising cost of sugar; new economic opportunities in north Georgia; and affordable, taxed, alcohol – not to the revenue agents of the 1870s, or their reluctant bodyguards, the United States Army.

Acknowledgement: *For the history of moonshiners and revenuers in the late 1800s, see Wilbur S. Miller: "The Revenue: Federal Law Enforcement in the Mountain South, 1870-1900", Journal Of Southern History, 55, (1989): 195-216. The author would also like to acknowledge the kind help provided by Charlie Reeves and Mary Ann Hawkins of the National Archives, Atlanta Branch.*

A Former 'Moonshiner' In The Mountains

In the 1930s, '40s and on into the 1950s, moonshining was an accepted way of life in the north Georgia mountains. Many individuals participated. It could be a harsh life, replete with harsh penalties, but it had its colorful characters and colorful moments.

Curtis Underwood, 81 years of age as of this writing, says he spent about 35 years of his life turning cornmeal into whiskey – or "shine" as he likes to call it. "It was hard work, but we had a lot of fun doing it," he says, reminiscing about bygone times. "In those days," he added, "we had to make whiskey to sell, because you couldn't find any other work in the north Georgia mountains."

Relating this story of his occupational history in his youthful years, Underwood, sitting comfortably in his rocking chair in his rock house near Resaca, Georgia, talked for over an hour about his exploits making moonshine in the wilds of the northern section of the state. He can still sketch out a full diagram of a still and all its working parts.

He can still sketch out a full diagram of a still and all its working parts.

"Most of my old whiskey-making buddies are gone now," he says somewhat sadly, "and most of the lawmen who tried so hard to arrest us are dead too now." He explained proudly that he himself had been arrested for moonshining only twice in his life, ". . . and on one of the arrests, I wasn't even guilty," he declared, self-righteously.

After spending a childhood that sounds like it came straight out of a Charles Dickens' novel (He was abandoned by his father and forced to live in poverty as a child), Underwood wound up living with his grandmother in Lumpkin County in the summer of 1937.

There were a number of federal revenue officers who worked the north Georgia area full-time in those days. One of the most dreaded was

Ramsey Southers who literally filled the Montgomery, Alabama prison full of individuals who had been caught making illegal whiskey. Southers' territory included Union, White, and Dawson counties.

Curtis said that when he learned that Southers had passed away, he was jubilant. To him, that meant it was safe to make 'shine again.

"County officers of the law liked moonshine so much, they usually didn't bother us much," Curtis smiled in remembrance. "If they caught you, you could usually just pay out with a fine.

"But if a federal officer caught you, you'd be charged in federal court," Curtis added, "and that was a whole different ball game."

Curtis' Uncle Claude Tipton and a friend – Big Boy ("Big 'Un") Tanner – had each served four months in prison, courtesy of Southers' efforts. Not only did the agent arrest men, but he chopped up their stills, sold the copper for junk, and burned the wood, leaving only a pile of ashes for many weeks of hard work. He had so many contacts that the moonshiners all knew that "you couldn't buy a postage stamp without Randy Southers finding out about it."

After hearing the news of Southers' death, Tipton, Big 'Un and Curtis set out to set up another moonshining business. It involved a formula they all knew well.

First, the men contracted with Curtis' grandmother to buy 50 or 60 white oak trees off her farm to cut and hew into railroad cross-ties which they then intended to sell to Southern Wood in Gainesville, Georgia. "At $.65 each, we knew we'd have to hew at least 52 cross-ties," Curtis said, "in order to generate enough money to finance the project."

The men also bought four sheets of copper – eight by two and one-half feet each – and a box of one-quarter inch copper rivets and a roll of lead solder from Gainesville Metal Works. "It took 25 square feet of copper to make a still," Underwood recalled.

A tinsmith – with whom they had hunted and fished for years – agreed to shape the 50-gallon still for them on credit. They'd repay him with the first batch of liquor they made. This fellow followed the code of the moonshiner to the letter too, adding that the men wouldn't owe him anything if the still got chopped up by "revenuers."

The next day, Curtis said they walked about 10 miles up into Lumpkin County to another man's home to contract with him to buy 50 bushels of meal, the basic raw ingredient of moonshine. "Corn cost $1.00 a bushel then," Underwood explained., "and he agreed to sell us the corn on credit too – one bushel of meal for one gallon of 'corn likker.'"

Still on foot, the men next went to a sawmill where the owner agreed to let them have 500 feet of lumber with which to make ten three-foot square still boxes. "We decided to come back another evening – after the mill hands had left for the day – to pick up the lumber, so that there wouldn't be no witnesses to the pick-up," he explained.

Big 'Un said he knew where they could get a set of grate irons – the heavy iron pieces needed to make a rack for the cooking pieces – at a still Southers had chopped up about six months earlier. The men hitched up two mules to Granny's wagon to haul the irons.

Curtis said they next began scouting around the backwoods for a suitable still site. They needed a protected and hidden place on a small stream or at a spring, where they could set up the furnace. Fresh water is an essential ingredient in the making of moonshine too.

"We eventually found a spot where two

creeks came together. It had plenty of rocks for use in the building of the furnace and plenty of wood to fire it," Curtis added. "There was no road or access down into the 'holler,' so we couldn't get the wagon and mules down to the site. We had to haul the irons downhill on our backs."

The men built the furnace, using rocks for a foundation, and laying the irons for the still to sit on. They made a return trip to the sawmill where they picked up their lumber, loaded it on the wagon and hauled it to a nearby ridge.

"It was about that time that we got word from the tinsmith that our still was ready," Curtis related. We had to take a roundabout route – 12 to 15 miles through the woods – to reach our still site, since we obviously couldn't just load the still up on the wagon and haul it on the road. It was too risky."

Next, it was time to build the mash boxes, which the men accomplished on the ridge above the still site. They then rolled the boxes down the hill to the site.

"It then was time to pick up the corn meal," Curtis smiled again in painful remembrance. "We took the wagon just at dark to haul the 100-pound sacks. We had to make two trips, the second one at the end of the following day. We hauled the meal, sugar and malt on our backs in burlap bags (covered with waterproof paper in case it rained) more than half a mile across the mountains, and that was a back-breaker.

Finally, the men impounded the creek at the still site to pool up the water they needed. They cut the wood they needed for the furnace. They were now ready to start making whiskey.

"We had a 50-gallon still." Underwood smiled again. "We filled it with 45 gallons of water and a bushel and a quarter of raw meal to produce the mash. We cooked off the meal with 200 pounds of sugar, just like

Though largely replaced today by the production of other illegal substances such as marijuana, moonshine operations are still occasionally discovered in the rural Appalachian Mountains, just as was this one recently, which was fired by a clean-burning fuel such as propane. (Photo courtesy of Joseph E. Dabney)

Curtis Underwood, an ex-moonshiner, enjoys describing the days when he made his share of "lightning" in the wilds of north Georgia in the 1930s, '40s and '50s. (Photo by Sara Hines Martin)

The five-gallon jug in this photo held five stillfuls of whiskey. Ever the wit, Mr. Underwood has labeled the small jug to read: Dr. Underwood's Cure-All. One shot cures cancer. Two shots cure snake-bite. Three shots – No pain. Four shots – Out like a light. (Photo by Sara Hines Martin)

With his wife, Dora, beside him as always, Mr. Underwood displays some of the paraphernalia he once used when making moonshine whiskey. (Photo by Sara Hines Martin)

cooking oatmeal, and we had to stir it regularly to keep the meal from scorching on the bottom."

The mash went out through what was known as a "slop arm," then through a wooden trough into a box. After that batch had left the cooker, the men poured in fresh water and raw meal and started over again. They kept the process going all day.

Each evening, the men left five boxes of hot mash to cool and distill overnight. The next morning, they shoveled out a hole in the thick mash (which was two feet deep in a three foot box) with mash sticks, pouring in water to break up the congealed meal. The mash had the consistence of cold cooked oatmeal.

"Even though working during the day was riskier, we decided to do it," Curtis continued. "We started the fire up before daylight so that the smoke could blow away before it could be seen."

The men worked at night too. "(Kerosene) lanterns didn't give enough light at night, so we made flambeaus out of empty pork 'n beans cans packed with kerosene poured over a burlap sack," Curtis said. "We tacked these up on trees around the still."

One day, the men ran off 17 stills of beer in daylight and three stillfuls after dark. "We went through 50 bushels of meal in one day," he remembered. "Twenty stillfuls was a good day's run, and we had 20 to run the next day. We didn't have a watch, but even without one, we ran one stillful every 40 minutes," he sighed. "Boy, I'm still tired 60 years later, too.

"That was the hardest work I've ever done," he added. "I was soft as a biscuit when I started, but after lugging those 100-pound sacks of cornmeal all summer, I was hard as nails. I could shoulder a keg of whiskey and walk for a couple of miles with it if I had to."

Curtis said that they went to the Rexall Drugstore in Dahlonega to get containers for the whiskey. The gentleman who owned the store – described by Curtis only as "Doc," – had a cold drink fountain there, and the Coca-Cola syrup was delivered in 10-gallon wooden kegs.

"Doc loved his moonshine, so he sold us 10 kegs on credit and even delivered them out to the house for us," Curtis said, beaming in pleasure. "All the other people furnished their own vessels for their own liquor.

"If you're wondering about all the credit we were extended, that's just the way it was in the mountains in those days," Curtis explained. "Everyone trusted us to keep our word. The only thing we had was our honesty. I've never met a moonshiner who went back on his word, and we didn't either. If your word wasn't respected, you couldn't even make *moonshine* to make a living."

The men used all the liquor they made in the first batch to settle their debts. Each bushel of meal yielded one gallon and a quart of whiskey. It took 50 gallons of whiskey to pay for the meal, one and one-half gallons to pay for the lumber, two gallons to pay for the barley malt and 100 gallons for the sugar.

"We also took a gallon of beer to Granny's to go in the cornbread instead of milk or water. That bread sure was good too," Underwood recalled with a smile.

After settling their debts, the men started immediately on the second batch of shine. Curtis said he and Big 'Un walked down into Dawson County to a fellow they knew there to get one ton of brown sugar (20 two-hundred-pound sacks) this time. Moonshiners had to vary the locations of large purchases of sugar. Otherwise, it was too obvious what you were doing, and too easy to get caught.

"We simply couldn't buy it at all in Dahlonega, because there were too many people who would report us to the Feds there," he smiled again. "Sugar cost $3 a 100-pound sack, and the Dawson County sugar source agreed to swap one sack of sugar for five gallons of shine. He gave us one-gallon tin cans for his own whiskey, and sold us 150 cans on credit. He delivered the sugar to my grandmother's house, and then we hauled it – again on our backs – 12 miles over the mountains.

"We sold this second batch to whiskey haulers who picked it up at our house and then took it to Atlanta to sell," Curtis explained. "Whiskey brought a dollar a gallon in 1937, and word soon got around that we had it available. Later, when so many people were making whiskey, they only got $.90, then $.85 and finally $.79 a gallon. At $.79 a gallon, you were barely making a profit.

Curtis says that over the next few years, he, his uncle and Big 'Un made a lot of whiskey. And when the untaxed liquor became plentiful, so also did the revenue agents in the area.

"It was in June of 1940 that I finally got caught," he explained. "By that time, I was making 'hog likker' using big 500-gallon stills that measured four feet by four feet."

Underwood says he was by himself in the stillhouse, down on his knees cutting onion sacks open. He says he just looked up and saw a revenue agent standing a few feet away.

"There wasn't any chance to run," he laughed. "Three other officers soon walked up. After cutting down the stills and pouring out 60 gallons of whiskey, they walked me out to the road."

A neighbor made Underwood's bond, and in federal court in Gainesville in November, he pled guilty to a misdemeanor charge. He received a sentence of five years probation.

"I went right back to making whiskey,"

Photographed in Lumpkin County in 1899, this moonshine "still" was located in the vicinity of the Porter Springs community in north Georgia's Lumpkin County. The individuals in this photograph possibly were with the Lumpkin County Sheriff's Office, preparing to destroy the site. Notice the thick undergrowth providing the moonshiners with ample cover, and the heavy casks which undoubtedly had to be moved to the site at least in part by manual labor. (Photo courtesy of the GA Dept. of Archives & History).

he stated emphatically, "and I kept on making it all those years, too."

Soon after that, Underwood was called up for service in the army. It wasn't long, however, before he received a medical discharge which sent him back home to the north Georgia mountains.

Shortly after that, he says he proposed to a "pretty little thing" named Dora Tipton, and they were married on September 18, 1941.

The couple lived briefly in Ohio, but Dora wasn't happy there, so they returned to the north Georgia mountains. Underwood, still on probation but unable to find other work, drifted back into moonshining.

"The war brought on a sugar shortage, so moonshiners had to turn to sorghum syrup for fermentation," Curtis explained. "A grocery store in Ellijay brought syrup in by the tractor trailer load from South Georgia. It was sold in three-quart cans that looked like paint buckets. A gallon of syrup yielded a gallon of moonshine."

Eventually, the woods and hollows around Lumpkin and Dawson counties became thick with revenue agents. To get away from the agents, Curtis says he moved to Whiskey Bill Mountain at the edge of Fannin County.

He and his uncle were soon back into the moonshine business, due again to the lack of work available in the area. Due to the low population in the Fannin County area, there was little market for shine, so the men began driving the whiskey ("tripping") to Dahlonega, Dawsonville and even as far away as Winder in Barrow County and Social Circle in Walton County, bootlegging the product.

Since trucks were more suspect than automobiles, the moonshiners used cars only to haul their illicit product. Curtis says he bought a 1957 Ford Galaxy, beefed up the suspension with extra springs, took out the front and back seats and installed a bucket seat on the driver side. He says he loaded the car up to the window level with moonshine and then spread out a quilt on top of the whiskey.

"I could carry 120 gallons in that car at one time," he says, grinning again. "It was so heavy that even with the extra springs, that Ford would drop down two inches lower when I had her full of shine. We souped up the engine too – we souped up all our trip cars – not to outrun the law, but to carry the more heavy loads."

Curtis says he had several close calls on those trips, mostly at night, but says he never got caught.

"We traveled on dirt roads at night, rather than on the highways," he remembered. "It eventually got to the point that the sheriffs and deputies were making it unprofitable for us. They wanted the souped up cars. We could usually pay our way out of the county cases, but we lost our cars in the process. We finally quit tripping after that."

Underwood says he and his wife eventually had five children – all of them graduates of high school – a fact about which both parents are still proud. He also says he never taught any of his boys the moonshine business.

"By that time, I had stopped using barley malt for making whiskey, because corn malt was so much better," Underwood continued. "I planted eight acres in the creek "bottom" with corn, doing the plowing myself because the boys were in school.

"My wife made most of the corn malt that I used in moonshining. She and I would put four or five bushels of shelled corn in burlap sacks and throw them in the creek that ran through our property. After two days of soaking, we would drag them out of the water and drain them on the banks of the creek."

Curtis says that after being submerged in the water, the corn would have sprouts approximately one-half inch long. "Some people let the sprouts grow two or three inches long, but the shorter sprouts have the best flavor," he said.

"Dora would spread the sprouted corn on top of a chicken house tin roof where it would dry in the heat. Then she'd rake the dried sprouts into a washtub."

Curtis says he would then take the sprouts to a mill in Blue Ridge where he had all of his corn ground into meal for mashing. After that, he'd go back to the still site and distill more liquor. And so it went for years and years.

Underwood makes no apologies for his illicit profession in the 1940s and '50s. To him, it was simply a way of life.

"I just want for people to understand the desperation that drove us to making moonshine," Underwood says today. "It was to support my family. It was to raise our children."

Eventually he says, the moonshine business did well enough that he was able to branch out into legal pursuits, including home construction and running a small restaurant. In 1960, he says he moved off the mountain into a house in Fannin County which he built himself.

In 1966, Curtis says he and his brother built the Old Fountain Drive-In Restaurant in Blue Ridge, and ran it for 10 years. Then he built the Pit Stop Grocery in Resaca that he ran for 10 years before retiring in 1986.

"All I have now are my memories and my family," he says with a final smile. "I drink a little Jack Daniels 'sipping whiskey,' but not much. I haven't had any good moonshine since 1965."

Guerrilla Fighter John Gatewood And A Notorious Livestock Theft

The U.S. Civil War produced a number of noted individuals who took advantage of the lack of law enforcement during the era. One of the more prominent in the Southeast was John P. Gatewood, and one of his most revered incidents involved 2,000 head of livestock which he stole from both Union and Confederate forces to feed starving families in northeast Alabama during the closing days of the war.

The American Civil War produced a number of interesting tales, many of them occurring as the war was grinding to a close in 1864 and '65. On August 19, 1865, the war – on paper – was officially ended, but in reality, the conflict continued – albeit on a much lesser scale – for years thereafter, perpetuating a lawless environment.

August of 1865 found 1st Lieutenant Archibald H. Thomson of Company D, 12th Ohio Volunteer Cavalry, taking a much-needed rest at Sweetwater, Tennessee. He had served in countless raids against the Confederates and had seen action in numerous engagements throughout the war. On this day, he was certain the harsh days of the terrible experience were behind him forever. . . but he was in for a surprise.

When he received new orders on that hot August day in 1865, Lieutenant Thomson assumed that he and his men were being relieved as General Alvan Cullem Gillem's escort, and that they all were finally going home. But when he read the new orders, he discovered to his chagrin that instead, he had been ordered to take thirty-five men from Chattanooga to recover cattle and horses in Cherokee County, Alabama, which had been stolen by the notorious bandit John P. Gatewood.

Gatewood had become a legend in north Georgia. Federal authorities believed that he had deserted from the 4th Kentucky Volunteer Infantry Regiment of the United States Army. He stood accused also of treason as the leader of a band of federal deserters who had become prominent in raids against Union depots, trains, and army outposts. No one knew the actual circumstances of his notoriety. . . only that he was a raider of Union army supplies and munitions.

Pro-Union families in northern Alabama and Georgia reportedly also were Gatewood's victims. Federal soldiers taken by Gatewood and his men reportedly were seldom seen alive again. Most, reportedly, were found with their throats slit. At least that's how Gatewood was known in the rumor-mill.

Sometimes, Gatewood and his men dressed themselves in the blue uniforms of the Union army prior to robbing and pillaging the homes and businesses of civilians, in order that the federal government would be blamed for the incident. By the end of the war, the Confederate press – what little remained of it – talked freely of how Gatewood and his band of outlaws had almost single-handedly forced the Union troops at Dalton to cower within the safety of their blockhouses.

Interestingly, John Gatewood, in fact, had actually deserted in 1863 from the 4th Tennessee (Murray's) Confederate Cavalry Regiment. He was born circa 1846 in Fentress County, Tennessee, he and his father's large family were living in Sparta, in neighboring White County, when the war began.

Thought it is unknown for certain today, some sources believed that Gatewood – through his daring exploits against the Union army – was seeking revenge for the murder of his sister by Union troops. As a result of his actions, he was regarded as a Confederate "Robin Hood," who, in addition to his other efforts on the behalf of impoverished Southern citizens, warned Southern sympathizers of approaching federal foraging parties, so that the families would have time to hide their pitiful remaining stocks of food.

The red-haired Gatewood became a "Wanted" man in short order by federal authorities, but that didn't slow him down one bit. There were just too many terrible conflicts and desperate situations for any law enforcement officials to focus upon one bandit. And Gatewood was too mobile and too shrewd to be captured.

Gatewood's brother served under him as a bookkeeper for the outlaws. Gatewood also reportedly had an Indian as a servant.

On the one occasion when he did fall into a trap, Gatewood was captured by General Joseph Wheeler's cavalry, but sympathetic north Georgians reportedly persuaded Wheeler – who no doubt could also see some value in the raider as a deterrent to Union army efforts – to release the bandit. Gatewood and his men – in addition to their raids on Union army outposts – also reportedly were constantly skirmishing against a gang of Confederate deserters who were conducting raids in the area under the outlaw Jack Colquitt.

Gatewood made Gaylesville, Alabama, the hub of his activities. He had married a woman – Miss Sarah C. Cain – from the area. Gaylesville had long enjoyed a reputation as a lair of desperadoes. In years past, it had become notorious as the headquarters of "The Slicks," a group

Gaylesville had long enjoyed a reputation as a lair of desperadoes. In years past, it had become notorious as the headquarters of "The Slicks."

During the U.S. Civil War, the Union armies in Georgia and Alabama were continuously assaulted by guerrillas such as John P. Gatewood's band of outlaws. This post-war engraving illustrates one such incident.

Guerrilla fighters usually were bloodthirsty and savage outlaws, and as a result, when they were captured, justice was usually quickly found at the end of a rope.

of outlaws prominent in the 1830s.

One of John Gatewood's more widely-known achievements during the closing days of the war was the theft of some 2,000 horses and cattle from the Union army. He had herded the animals back to Gaylesville and then had divied them up among the local residents, many of whom were literally starving as a result of the deprivations of the war.

Shortly after Lee surrendered at Appomattox Courthouse, General George Henry Thomas sent two civilians to Gaylesville to recover the stolen government livestock. To the surprise of the two men (but to no one else in the vicinity), the two were arrested as soon as they began making inquiries about the livestock. A short time later, the men were released on a $2,000 bond, and were then told that if they ever returned to Gaylesville, they would be lynched. Such was the support for John Gatewood in the community.

General Thomas next sent Lieutenant Archibald Thomson and his Company D troops to recover the stolen livestock. Lieutenant Thomson and his command met civilian scout Leab Grinsmith at Summerville, Georgia, who was to assist them in the mission.

At some point enroute, Thomson and his troops were intercepted by a large man named Hamilton who presented the lieutenant with a letter from General Thomas instructing that Hamilton be allowed to help in the livestock recovery. It seems that though this Hamilton was a pro-Union man, he had a brother who supported the Confederacy and who coincidentally was a deputy sheriff of Cherokee County in which Gaylesville was located. General Thomas apparently thought the assistance of the pro-Union Hamilton might "smooth the waters" in Cherokee County where the men had been instructed to recover the stolen livestock.

Instead of traveling into Gaylesville "en mass," it was decided that the main body of Thomson's Company D would remain outside the town, and that Hamilton would set out with a detail of five men to recover the cattle. Hamilton, however, had not been gone more than two hours (according to Thomson's report), before he reappeared to report that the Rebels had captured the five federal troopers. Hamilton said that he himself had even been shot at by his own brother – the deputy sheriff – who it seems had used a ruse to capture the men.

According to the story, the five men and Hamilton had been joined by a group of squirrel hunters who reportedly were admiring the soldiers' Spencer rifles. The "squirrel hunters," after they had been handed the weapons to admire, then turned them on the five men. Hamilton, however, said he had managed to escape the men.

A short time after this, Deputy Sheriff Hamilton arrived with a posse and demanded to know by whose authority the remainder of the federal detachment had invaded "his" county. Lieutenant Thomson reportedly responded with his drawn Colt revolver, and was quickly backed up by his men and some twenty Spencer rifles. The deputy sheriff and his men were handcuffed to trees, where they remained until they were released the following morning.

Thomson, meanwhile, had divided his command into small parties of some five men each to set out in different directions to look for the stolen stock. All of the patrols were soon attacked. Thomson and his men captured three men and killed a fourth who had tried to escape.

One of the prisoners informed the lieutenant that the local sheriff – a Mr. Daniels – had called for a posse of 100 men to rendezvous at Thomson's camp to arrest the Yankees. Upon hearing this, Lieutenant Thomson and his men hurried back to camp where they found one of their comrades, Edward J. Latson, dead and three others wounded. The posse had wrecked the camp, killing one or two horses and leaving only a frying pan and a saber.

Terrorism was prevalent during the later years of the War Between The States and immediately thereafter. Homes of loyalists - on both sides of the issue - were burned and their property looted in a bloodthirsty quest for revenge.

One of John Gatewood's more widely-known achievements...was the theft of some 2,000 horses and cattle from the Union army.

Thomson made certain the injured were attended to (They were left at a farmhouse in the care of a doctor), then he and the remainder of his men set out in the direction of Summerville in pursuit of their attackers. They had proceeded scarcely a mile when they encountered – and subsequently rescued – five more of their comrades who had been searching for the stolen cattle.

The leader of the outlaws holding the search party reportedly rushed Lieutenant Thomson. He came within inches of killing the officer before Grinsmith – the guide – chopped the attacker with the butt of his shotgun. The man fell from his horse and was then gunned down as he tried to flee. The other three outlaws gave up without further incident.

Now with ten men, Thomson continued on and encountered nine or ten more of the enemy. They were holding trooper J.C. McClintock as a prisoner.

When they realized they were outgunned (the soldiers all had the deadly Spencer repeaters), the abductors fled without inflicting any harm to McClintock.

Half a mile further on, however, Thomson's command encountered twenty-five more of the culprits. Picking out the leader, Thomson reportedly rode straight at him, pointing a revolver between the eyes of the raider, demanding his surrender. The rest of his command did likewise and Thomson now found himself guarding twenty-seven men with only a dozen troopers – including himself.

At this point, Lieutenant Thomson reportedly decided discretion was the better part of valor, and he set out toward Chattanooga where he knew he could get reinforcements. He suspected he wouldn't be safe until he reached the city, and his intuition proved correct. After passing through Summerville and camping at a farmhouse, the Yankees had to use their superior firepower – the Spencer rifles – to drive off an outlaw rescue party of forty-five to sixty men.

After they had arrived back in Chattanooga, General Gillem wanted to know why Thomson had not solved his prisoner problem by simply hanging the raiders as he captured them. Blood lust, as is well-known today, existed on both sides of the terrible war. Thomson, however, would have none of that. He had seen enough blood during the past four years.

All of the federal troopers being held back in Cherokee County, Alabama – including the wounded – were safely recovered shortly thereafter. No harm had come to them from the citizenry of the countryside.

The men captured by Thomson's Company D explained that the horses and cattle the federals had sought had been stolen from both Union and Confederate armies by Gatewood and his friends Joseph Killett and Brooks Giffett. They added that the livestock was desperately needed for the starving and impoverished families in Cherokee County.

General Thomas surprisingly, ultimately accepted Lieutenant Thomson's request to release the captive raiders. He also agreed that the livestock in Cherokee County best served the nation there in helping the local residents rebuilt their lives.

The prisoners, Samuel McSpadden, George S. Clifton, Leon A. Clifton, Edward Bradley, Joseph Hardwich, J.M.P. McCoker, Thomas Y. Wilder, Wm. D. Wilder, William G. Shook, Thomas G. James, James Hill, James Newman, John Yeargin, and Simeon Jordan were all sent home.

The federal scout, Grinsmith, and John Gatewood, both moved to Texas after the war. They both died there decades later.

As a result of his outstanding service, Lieutenant Archibald H. Thomson was offered a commission in the regular army by General Gillem. He (Thomson) however, declined the offer and returned to his home, convinced he had witnessed enough bloodshed to last him the rest of his life. He died in 1920.

Much of the information for the article above was obtained from the September 1, 1865 issue of the Macon, Georgia Daily Telegraph. *Lieutenant Thomson's memoirs appear in* Military Order Of The Loyal Legion Of The United States, *Volume 6, pp. 63-70.*

Forgotten Union Guerrillas Of The North Georgia Mountains

Though it has received less attention over the years, opposition to secession was very real among the people of extreme north Georgia during the Civil War, despite the fact that support for the Southern cause was also very strong.

The major resistance to the Confederacy centered among the hardy, independent, isolated, north Georgians who simply opposed the intrusion of elements of the war which brought unwanted hardships. Life was difficult enough in the mountains as it was.

The lack of economic necessities coupled with a period of severe climatic droughts that plagued the region during the war years, made the hiding of livestock and foodstuffs from Confederate impressment officers a matter of survival for many mountain families. The additional hardships such as taxes, impressment of private property, and the war's draft, only added fuel to a smoldering resentment.

Life was difficult enough in the mountains as it was.

Problems such as these existed everywhere in the South, but the vastness of the Blue Ridge and Great Smoky Mountains substantially increased the ability of the mountaineers to avoid the unwanted impressment brought on by the war effort.

The most common resistance to the Confederacy in north Georgia and elsewhere in the South, was draft evasion and desertion from the Confederate forces. In mountainous terrain and among sympathetic mountain families, "hiding out" was accomplished more easily than in other parts of the Confederacy. The state of Georgia was occasionally forced to make massive roundups of these deserters.

The bloody Confederate victory at Chickamauga in northwest Georgia in 1863 was the final straw for many war-weary rebels. Of the north Georgians at Chickamauga, many simply quietly returned home without orders. They soon learned that a loosely organized "underground railroad" was already in existence to guide them to the Union lines in Tennessee, should they desire to flee from the South. Once out of Confederate-held territory, deserters and draft evaders could join the Union Army or Navy or even travel north of the Ohio River to work for the U.S. government as cowboys and civilian contractors.

The state of Georgia fought back against deserters by forming what came to be known as Confederate "Home Guard" units from the state militia. These men were authorized to obtain draft animals and supplies for the Confederacy and to deal with draft evasions and desertions.

Tactics used by the Home Guards included torture, executions without trials, and retaliations against families and friends of the resisters. The folklore of north Georgia includes numerous accounts of corpses found after the Home Guards had departed, and of men having their Achilles' tendons cut on their feet and being made to walk or crawl for miles before finally being hanged.

Many north Georgians claimed that the Home Guards were nothing more than officially sanctioned murderers and horse-thieves. In many instances, even pro-Confederate families were made to suffer as well. Some men deserted the Confederate Army in order to return home to protect their families from the Confederate Home Guard! In short, in many instances, the men who had been organized (via the Home Guard) to provide a semblance of law and order in the mountains virtually became outlaws themselves. In fairness, however, the entire region was virtually lawless at this time, with depredations, unlawful executions and general persecution being meted out by guerrillas and regular army units on both sides – both Northern and Southern.

When General Sherman's Union Army invaded north Georgia in 1864, they found that the same people who had been helping men to evade the Confederate draft or desert, were willing to act as spies and guides for the Union, including helping Sherman's foragers seize property from the pro-Confederate families.

The Confederate Home Guards responded by increasing their raids and executions. Sherman, in turn, answered by sending Union troops to Pickens County and elsewhere to rescue the families opposing the Confederacy, and to suppress the Home Guards. Union forces burned Canton, Georgia, in retaliation for atrocities committed against north Georgia families.

Federal officials believed that resistance to the Confederacy and the Home Guards could be channeled into practical support for the Union. On November 18, 1863, twenty-four-year-old Major Dewitt C. Howard of the 103rd Ohio Infantry was ordered to form Georgia units for the Union Army. Howard was a Georgian, and, judging from the streams of refugees he witnessed daily coming into Federal camps in Chattanooga, he was convinced that he could raise an entire brigade. After several months of detached duty however, he failed to enlist more than a handful of men.

The attempt to recruit a Georgia unit for the Federal forces was revived in 1864 by James G. Brown, civilian chief of scouts for Union General George H. Thomas. Brown had organized a spy ring in north Georgia and often would conduct his own personal reconnaissance missions, sometimes disguised as a member of the Confederate Home Guards!

On August 9, 1964, Brown was ordered by General James B. Steedman to enlist as many men as possible for use in the protection of General Sherman's supply lines in north Georgia. In response, Brown arranged for six companies of north Georgians to gather near their homes in Pickens, Dawson and Union counties on or about July 1. They included men brought to Cleveland, Tennessee on July 10 by Dr. John A. Ashworth of Dawson County and a Union Home Guards company organized in Pickens County by Federal troops.

At the request of Ashworth, his brother-in-law Iley T. Stuart raised a company, and in Morganton, William A. Twigg rallied enlistees with a stirring speech calling for the removal of the Confederates out of north Georgia.

By the end of August, 1864, James G. Brown had approximately 300 enlistees, but far from the 800 to 1,000 men he needed for a regiment. As a result, one of the companies raised by Stewart went to Tennessee and became Company C of the 5th Tennessee Mounted Infantry Regiment, U.S. Army, on September 23,1864. Others who had answered Brown's call served in an independent company in Fannin County under William A. Twiggs that on February 1, 1865, became Company H of the 5th Tennessee.

Brown organized his remaining four companies as the 1st Georgia State Troops Volunteers, with himself as colonel, Ashworth as lieutenant colonel, and Henry L. Carroll of Union County as acting major. The men were promised a bounty of $300, army pay, and clothing, in exchange for enlisting for three years to serve exclusively as guards for the railroads in Georgia. They were provided food, ammunition, and probably weapons, but apparently were compelled to take horses and mules from pro-Confederate families.

Despite the circumstances, Brown's unit was never actually accepted into the U.S. Army. The official reason was a precondition of the unit's existence – that being that the unit would only serve in Georgia. However, a more likely reason for this non-recognition was the unsavory reputation these men earned for themselves in the months between the time when Brown first recruited them, and when they were finally released from their duties.

Col. L. Johnston, commanding the largely black garrison at Dalton, later blamed his surrender to General Hood's Confederate Army on October 13, 1864, upon the men of Brown's 1st Georgia State Troops. Johnston claimed that the men of the 1st Georgia failed to do their duty as scouts, and when Hood's Army approached, they fled to the mountains, as they had done upon the approach of Wheeler's Confederate Cavalry on October 2.

The Confederate Home Guards responded by increasing their raids and executions.

On November 5, while on a raid to obtain horses and mules, Lt. Col. Ashworth, Capt. McCrary, and nineteen other members of Brown's command were captured by Col. James J. Findley and his 1st Georgia State Cavalry Home Guards in Bucktown in Gil-

William Washington Burlison of Pickens County served in the 1st Georgia Infantry Battalion, United States Army, during the War Between The States. **(Photo courtesy of Dixie Blackledge)**

mer County. Three others of Brown's command were wounded and four were killed. Captured with these men were papers that gave the names of their local supporters, including such prominent men as Dawson County Sheriff George R. Robinson, justices Cleveland Andrews and John Fouts, Lindsey Vaughters, and Hiram Brooks.

As Findley took his command through Dawsonville, these civilians were arrested. A dozen of the men captured turned out to also be deserters from Confederate units. They were executed at Gainesville on November 7,1864.

Their bodies were transferred to the National Cemetery at Marietta, Georgia in July, 1867. They are today buried in Section E, Numbers 6012-6023

Col. John Azor Kellogg, a Union escapee from a Confederate prison in South Carolina, had more positive experiences with Brown's men. A group of the 1st Georgia found Kellogg and his companions in Pickens County and, under Capt. McCrary, escorted them safely to the Union lines. Kellogg would remember these men as "generous, hospitable, brave and Union men to the core." He described them as effective guerrillas, providing armed protection for local farmers against the Confederate Home Guards.

However, if Kellogg's report to his superiors was as accurate as his memoirs, he must have also added that Brown's men were hiding a Union deserter, conducting raids to plunder pro-Confederate plantations in other counties, and refusing to accept offers of a truce by Capt. Benjamin F. Jordan's Cherokee County Home Guards. Hit and run ambushes between Brown's men and the Confederate Home Guards were apparently happening almost daily.

Col. Kellogg was sympathetic to Brown's men, but it is doubtful that his feelings were shared by the Union officials camped safely behind their own armies. Brown's men were not trained, equipped, or led as regular soldiers. They could not be scouts or guides at Dalton while their own families were left unprotected, nor could they allow themselves to be captured at Dalton (or anywhere else), since many of them were also Confederate deserters.

The men of the 1st Georgia however, regardless of the circumstances, could not be prevented from seeking revenge upon the Home Guards, now that they too were armed and organized. They were fighting a merciless guerrilla war against men who had abused them and their families and friends for several years now, and it had almost become a way of life for many of them.

After the Secretary of War and General

Sherman finally decided not to allow the 1st Georgia to be admitted into the United States Army, Brown's men were ordered dismissed on November 2, 1864, and they formally disbanded on December 15, 1864. They received no pay, bounties, or compensation for their months of service, sufferings and fighting.

Shortly thereafter, Brown again contacted his commanding officer – General Thomas – informing him that 600 or 700 north Georgians could still be raised for the Union Army. Thomas offered to allow them to be formed as an independent battalion or regiment with Brown in command, if they reported to Chattanooga. However, nothing ever came of this idea.

Many of Brown's men did enlist in the previously mentioned 5th Tennessee United States Mounted Infantry, particularly in Capt. William Twiggs' Company H and Capt. Martin V. Woods' Company K, and other Tennessee units. Several of the men of the now-defunct 1st Georgia who were captured at Bucktown and elsewhere, were subsequently paroled by Brigadier General William T. Wofford, Confederate commander for north Georgia.

A few of Brown's men however, joined a new 1st Georgia. Dewitt C. Howard created his own 1st Georgia Infantry Battalion (at least on paper), at Marietta on October 31, 1864. Some of the men from Dawson County enlisted in Company A. and some from Pickens County joined Company B. The two companies were filled out with men recruited from Confederate POWs in Atlanta, after the city fell to Sherman. They guarded Sherman's rail lines in the northern part of the state until disbanded on July 19, 1865.

The problems of Brown's men did not end with the war. Civil War related revenge killings continued long after Appomattox. For forty years, the families

This illustration of Southerners welcoming the arrival of federal troops in 1865, was drawn to accompany a publication of the post-war song, "Marching To The Sea Through Georgia." (Courtesy of Library of Congress)

of Brown's 1st Georgia unsuccessfully petitioned Congress for financial compensation to which they felt they were entitled as a result of their affiliation with the Union cause. These efforts were largely unsuccessful due to the fact that so few of the leaders of these families had survived to help with the petition.

James G. Brown remained a scout for General Thomas to the end of the war, and died in late 1866. Dr. John A. Ashworth died in Raleigh, NC ("by reason of starvation and ill treatment whilst a prisoner of war in the hands of rebel authorities"), shortly after General Sherman's army released him from the Confederates. Capt.

George W. McCrary was killed by Confederate guerrillas on November 10, 1864. Ironically, he was not serving in Georgia at that time, contrary to the terms of his enlistment, but was in Tennessee.

Transcribed on the pages which follow are the rosters of Col. James G. Brown's 1st Georgia State Troop Volunteers, reproduced from memory by men from Brown's command. (Obtained from the National Archives, Washington D.C., R 882, V.5., Box 842, Record Group 94). Microfilm of these records has been donated to the Georgia Department of Archives and History. The original rosters and papers of this unit were destroyed in Hood's attack on Dalton in October, 1864. The names of Dewitt C. Howard's 1st Georgia Infantry are published in Robert S. Davis, Jr.'s *A Researcher's Library Of Georgia*, (1987). Their complied service records are available from the National Archives and on microfilm reel 279-34 at the Georgia Archives. Members of the 5th Tennessee and other Tennessee units are listed in Pt. II of *Tennesseans In The Civil War*, (Nashville, 1964)

(Information in brackets was added by the authors).

COMPANY A (Union County)

(Roll prepared from memory January 10, 1870)

George W. McCrary, captain, killed in battle by guerrillas, November, 1864

Henry L. Carroll, 1st lieutenant, (Later in company B of Howard's 1st Georgia U.S. Infantry).

Leander McCrarey; 2nd lieutenant; dead since service.

1/ Milton Nix, 1st sergeant, killed at Gainesville; prisoner of war; (Also called A.M. Nix; had been in Co. C, 52nd Georgia Confederate Infantry; buried at National Cemetery in Marietta, GA).

2/ Harper McCrarey, 2nd sergeant.

3/ Jesse Allen, 3rd sergeant; (later in Co. C, 5th Tennessee U. S. Mounted Infantry?).

4/ Henry Ducket, 4th sergeant.

5/ Willis McCrarey, 1st corporal; killed by rebels in battle, November 1864.

6/ Robert Bennett, Jr., 2nd corporal.

7/ William Elkin, 3rd corporal.

8/ Jacob Denson, 4th corporal (later in Co. H, 5th Tennessee U.S. Mounted infantry).

Privates:

9/ Allen, David

10/ Anderson, John W.

11/ Ash, Henry

12/ Blackwell, Daniel, killed at Gainesville, GA while a prisoner of war, November 1864. (Had been in Company C, 65th Georgia Confederate Infantry; buried in the National Cemetery, Marietta, GA.)

13/ Braidy, Lewis; (had been in Company D, 52nd Georgia Confederate Infantry; later in Co. H, 5th Tennessee U. S. Mounted Infantry).

14/ Braidy, Braxton; (Later in Company H, 5th Tennessee U. S. Mounted Infantry).

15/ Blackwell, Sidney

16/ Bramblet, Jesse

17/ Barrett, Thomas

18/ Brown, Joseph N.

19/ Brown, William (Later in Company B, Howard's 1st Georgia U.S. Infantry).

20/ Bramblet, Reuben E.

21/ Colbert, James

22/ Cockran, James (Later in Company H, 5th Tennessee U. S. Mounted Infantry).

23/ Dotson, William (Later in Company H, 5th Tennessee U.S. Mounted Infantry).

24/ Davis, Benjamin

25/ Dowdy, James R. (Had been in Company D, 52nd Georgia Confederate Infantry; later in Company H, 5th Tennessee U. S. Mounted Infantry).

26/ Daniel, Albert

27/ Edmonson, Thomas; killed by rebels

while prisoner of war at Gainesville, GA, November, 1864. (Had been in Company D, 52nd Georgia Confederate Infantry?)
28/ Edmonson, William: (Had been in Company D, 52nd Georgia Confederate Infantry; had been in Company E, 30th Georgia Confederate Cavalry?)
29/ Eavens, George
30/ Fowler, Johnson
31/ Ford, John; (Later in Company F, 5th Tennessee U. S. Mounted Infantry).
32/ Free, Ebenezer
33/ Gladen, William; (Had been in Company D, 1st Georgia State Line Regiment; later in Company H., Tennessee U. S. Mounted Infantry).
34/ Gilrith, John
35/ Garrett, Martin L.
36/ Griffith, John
37/ Garrett, Joseph
38/ Griffith, William
39/ Garrett, Robert
40/ Hix, James
41/ Hopper, Charley
42/ Ingram, John
43/ Kerby, William; killed in battle, October, 1864
44/ Lacky, Wm.
45/ Long, James M; (Had been in Company B, 52nd Georgia Confederate Infantry).
46/ Long, Joseph
47/ Long, John
48/ Long, James, Sr.
49/ Long, Connord
50/ Long, Henry
51/ Long, Jasper; (Had been in Company B, 43rd Georgia Confederate Infantry).
52/ Long, William; (Later in Company H, 5th Tennessee U. S. Mounted Infantry).
53/ Long, Nathaniel B.
54/ Long, James, Jr.
55/ Lovengood, William; killed in battle, October, 1864.
56/ Moore, Joseph
57/ McCloud, William M.
58/ Newberry, Jackson
59/ Payne, John; (Later in Company B of Howard's 1st Georgia U. S. Infantry?)
60/ Payne, George W.
61/ Rogers, Joseph
62/ Ray, Joseph (Later in Company H, 5th Tennessee U. S. Mounted Infantry).
63/ Ray, Archable; (Had been in Company D, 52nd Georgia Confederate Infantry; later in Company H, 5th Tennessee U. S. Mounted Infantry).
64/ Ray, John D. (Later in Company H, 5th Tennessee U. S. Mounted Infantry).
65/ Ray, Martin; (Later in Company H, 5th Tennessee U. S. Mounted Infantry).
66/ Stanley, William, Sr.
67/ Stanley, William, Jr.
68/ Stanley, Braxton
69/ Stanley, Reculious
70/ Stanley, Samuel
71/ Stanley, Elisha
72/ Tuner (Turner?), William: (Later in Company F, 5th Tennessee U. S. Mounted Infantry).
73/ Thompson, James; (Later in Company H, 5th Tennessee U. S. Mounted Infantry).
74/ Woody, Robert; (Later in Company H, 5th Tennessee U. S. Mounted Infantry).

Roll certified by Henry L. Carroll, January 10, 1870.

COMPANY B (Dawson County)

Roll prepared from memory January 10, 1870.

Alvin W. Prince, captain; wounded in battle.
Henry B. Chatlin, 1st lieutenant.
James M. Reece, 2nd lieutenant.
Martin P. Berry, 1st sergeant; killed by guerrillas; (Had been in Company 1, 52nd Georgia Confederate Infantry; later in Company H, 5th Tennessee U. S. Mounted Infantry).
Thomas N. Mathews, 2nd sergeant.
Thomas Chatlin, 3rd sergeant.
William A. Aarnhart, 4th sergeant.

Nelson Bearden, 5th sergeant.
John T. Spriggs, 1st corporal.
James L. Griggs, 2nd corporal; (Had been in Company D 52nd Georgia Confederate Infantry).
Jeptha Cochran, 3rd corporal; (Had been in Company D, 52nd Georgia Confederate Infantry; later in Company H, 5th Tennessee U. S. Mounted Infantry).
John Reed, 4th corporal; killed at Gainesville, GA, November, 1864; (John A. Reid; had been in Company D, 1st Georgia Confederate Sharpshooters; buried in National Cemetery, Marietta, GA,)
Joseph Rider, 5th corporal.
W. P. Turner, 6th corporal; (Later in Company F, 5th Tennessee U. S. Mounted Infantry).

Privates:
1/ Ayers, Elijah
2/ Clayton, Elias
3/ Burlison, William (Later in company A of Howard's 1st Georgia U. S. Infantry).
4/ Beardon, R. M.
5/ Cochran, Francis M.
6/ Cantrell, Andrew J. (Later in Company E, 7th Tennessee U. S. Cavalry).
7/ Dempsey, E. F.
8/ Denny, Elisher
9/ Dotson, William (Later in Company H, 5th Tennessee U. S. Mounted Infantry).
10/ Evans, John (Later in Company H, 5th Tennessee U. S. Mounted Infantry).
11/ Ewards, Thomas
12/ Frix, Pleasant (later in company H, 5th Tennessee U.S. Mounted Infantry).
13/ Craine, Yerba
14/ Garman, James (Had been in Company I, 52nd Georgia Confederate Infantry, later in Company I, 12th Tennessee U. S. Cavalry).
15/ Gladden, William (Had been in Company D, 1st Georgia State Line Regiment; later in Company H, 5th Tennessee U. S. Mounted Infantry).
16/ Lingefelt, John
17/ Lively, John (Later in Company A of Howard's 1st Georgia U.S. Infantry? Jobry Lively?)
18/ Mincy, James; (Reported to have been in Company E, 30th Georgia Cavalry; captured at Bucktown, Gilmer County).
19/ McDugle (McCugle?), John C.
20/ Morgan, Cunningham; died in service.
21/ Prince, Martin; (Later in Company K, 12th Tennessee U. S. Cavalry).
22/ Reed, Robert G.; killed in service.
23/ Ray, Joseph;(Later in Company H, 5th Tennessee U. S. Mounted Infantry)
24/ Ray, Archibald; (Had been in Company D, 52nd Georgia Confederate Infantry; later in Company H, 5th Tennessee U. S. Mounted Infantry).
25/ Reece, A. J.
26/ Reece, (?) Jackson T.
27/ Rider, Henry
28/ Swaney, James C.
29/ Scoogins, Mathew
30/ Turner, O. P.
31/ Williams, Wm. W.; (Later in Company A, 13th Tennessee U. S. Cavalry).
32/ Prince, Archibald A.
33/ Reece, William
34/ Newberry, Hegga

Roll certified by Alvin W. Prince, January 10, 1870

COMPANY C (Dawson County)

Rolls prepared from memory January 4, 1870.

Elias Darnel, captain; (Had been in Company I, 38th Georgia Confederate Infantry).
Calvin J. Lawless, 1st lieutenant
John Kelly, 2nd lieutenant
Virgil D. Monroe, 1st sergeant; (Had been in Company I, 52nd Georgia Confederate Infantry; later in Company H, 5th Tennessee U. S. Mounted Infantry. In 1889, he wrote to the National Cemetery in Marietta enclosing the names of the men of Brown's 1st Georgia

unit buried there as "one of their old comrades.")

William A. Chumbly, 2nd sergeant; (Later in Company A of Howard's 1st Georgia U. S. Infantry).

John Tatum, 3rd sergeant; paroled under Gen. Wofford.

Thomas Darnell, 4th sergeant.

Joseph M. Chamber, 1st corporal; paroled under Gen. Wofford.

Josiah W. Haithcock, 2nd corporal.

Pollard Kelly, 3rd corporal.

Jordon Anderson, 4th corporal

Privates:

1/ Anderson, William, Jr.; died since the surrender.
2/ Anderson, William, Sr.; died since the surrender.
3/ Bennett, Jackson
4/ Bennett, Robert
5/ Bennett, William
6/ Beck, John; paroled under Gen. Wofford.
7/ Brooks, Aaron T.; killed at Gainesville, GA in service, November, 1864. (Aaron Thacker "Zack" Brooks; had been in Company G, 8th Georgia Confederate Battalion, buried in the National Cemetery, Marietta, GA).
8/ Baird, James L.
9/ Blackburn, Jesse W. (Later in Company H, 5th Tennessee U. S. Mounted Infantry)
10/ Braden, Elias W.
11/ Carlisle, John
12/ Chambers, Phillip; paroled under Gen. Wofford.
13/ Carnes (?), Marshall; paroled under Gen. Wofford.
14/ Carnes, Tandy W.; paroled under Gen. Wofford.
15/ Chambers, Barak; paroled under Gen. Wofford.
16/ Carney, Absolem
17/ Chumbley, Thompson
18/ Denson, Joseph; (Later in Company H, 5th Tennessee U. S. Mounted Infantry).
19/ Denson, George W.; (Later in Company H, 5th Tennessee U. S. Mounted Infantry).
20/ Denson, Jethro
21/ Elkins, William
22/ Elkins, Jordon; died in service.
23/ Evans, Nehe M.
24/ Evans, John (Later in Company H, 5th Tennessee U. S. Mounted Infantry).
25/ Fouts, John
26/ Hyde, Asa A.; paroled under Gen. Wofford.
27/ Henry, Alexander; paroled under Gen. Wofford.
28/ Hix, John
29/ Kelley, Pollard
30/ Kelley, William
31/ Ledbetter, Joseph; paroled under Gen. Wofford.
32/ Monroe, Daniel P.
33/ Monroe, Samuel L.; paroled under Gen. Wofford.
34/ Millsips, Solomon; (Later in Company H, 5th Tennessee U. S. Mounted Infantry).
35/ Monroe, Vanburen H.; paroled under Gen. Wofford.
36/ Martin, Morgan
37/ McCrary, Julius
38/ Millsaps, Stephen S.; (Later in Company H, 5th Tennessee U. S. Mounted Infantry).
39/ Nelson, Henry
40/ Pinyan, Jeptha; paroled under Gen. Wofford.
41/ Pinyan, Abraham D.
42/ Payne, Ambrose
43/ Payne, Thomas; killed at Gainesville, GA, by rebels November, 1864, while in service. (Thomas W. Payne; had been in Company K, 52nd Georgia Confederate Infantry and Company G, 30th Georgia Confederate Cavalry; buried at the National Cemetery, Marietta, GA.)
44/ Robinson, Andrew J.; killed at Gainesville, GA by rebels November, 1864,

while in service. (Had been in Company C, 7th Tennessee U. S. Cavalry?)

45/ Robinson, George R.; (Had been in Company I, 38th Georgia Confederate Infantry)

46/ Smith, Collins

47/ Simmermon, Jacob

48/ Simmermon, James; (Later in Company A of Howard's 1st Georgia U. S. Infantry)

49/ Stone, Jordon; killed at Gainesville, GA, by rebels while a prisoner of war. (Had been in Company D, 52nd Georgia Confederate Infantry; buried at the National Cemetery, Marietta, GA.)

50/ Stone, Jeptha

51/ Sutton, Amos

52/ Tesseneer, James

53/ Tatom, Horatio

54/ Turner, Tandy W.

55/ Vaughters, Linza; died since service

56/ Whitmore, Henry

57/ Whitmore, William; (Had been in Company I, 22nd Georgia Confederate Infantry.)

58/ Whitmore, Charles; killed at Gainesville, GA, November, 1864, while in service. (Buried in the National Cemetery, Marietta, GA.)

59/ Willey, John; paroled under Gen. Wofford. (Later in Company H, 5th Tennessee U. S. Mounted Infantry.)

60/ Whitmore, Henry T.; hanged by General (?) ACock (?) In November, 1864

Certified by Elias Darnell, January 4, 1870

COMPANY D (Pickens County)

Roll prepared from memory January 14, 1870

George H. Turner, captain. (Had been in Company E, 23rd Georgia Confederate Infantry.)

Robert B. McCutchen, 1st lieutenant. (Later in company B of Howard's 1st Georgia U.S. Infantry.)

Hezekiah M. Paris, 2nd lieutenant.

Thomas Taylor, 1st sergeant; killed in battle.

William G. Brown, 2nd sergeant. (William T. Brown later in Company B of Howard's 1st Georgia U. S. Infantry?)

Joseph Morris, 3rd sergeant.

Samuel Brown, 1st corporal. (Later in company H, 5th Tennessee U.S. Infantry.)

Privates:

1/ Anderson, Woodville B.

2/ Allred, Elias R.; paroled by Gen. Wofford.

3/ Berry, William A.; captured and killed. (William J. Berry; buried in the National Cemetery, Marietta, GA; had been in Company E, 23rd Georgia Confederate Infantry.)

4/ Berry, Milas D.

5/ Bearden, Ancil

6/ Bearden, William M.

7/ Bennette, Hiram

8/ Brooks, Isham A.

9/ Brown, Robert S.

10/ Brooks, Alexander (Later in Company K, 5th Tennessee U.S. Mounted Infantry.)

11/ Brock, John J.

12/ Bruce, Madison

13/ Bozeman, Henry B.

14/ Bozeman, William A.

15/ Brown, Thomas C.

16/ Cowart, Thomas A.

17/ Cowart, Frances M. (Later in company K, 5th Tennessee U. S. Mounted Infantry.)

18/ Carney, L. B.; paroled by Gen. Wofford

19/ Coffey, Martin V.

20/ Carney, Edmond; paroled by Gen. Wofford

21/ Carney, S.; paroled by Gen. Wofford.

22/ Cunningham, Robert (Later in Company K, 5th Tennessee U. S. Mounted Infantry.)

23/ Cook, Lemuel

24/ Chapman, John (Later in Company K, 5th Tennessee U.S. Mounted Infantry.)

25/ Chambers, James

26/ Chambers, William B. (Later in Company B, 6th Tennessee U. S.

Infantry.)
27/ Dearing, Reubin
28/ Darnel, Joshua; since died. (Later in Company K, 5th Tennessee U. S. Mounted Infantry.)
29/ Darnel, Sion A. Sen. (Later in Company K, 5th Tennessee U.S. Mounted Infantry.)
30/ Darnel, William J. (Later in Company K, 5th Tennessee U. S. Infantry.)
31/ Evans, G. M.
32/ Evans, Mirey
33/ Goode, M. H.
34/ Goode, Abram
35/ Griffeth, Robert; captured and killed.
36/ George, James
37/ Green, Garland S. D.
38/ Goode, Silome (Later in Company K, 5th U. S. mounted Infantry.)
39/ Hood, Tate
40/ Honea, George M.
41/ Heath, Griffin; died. (Later in Company K, 5th Tennessee U. S. Mounted Infantry.)
42/ Hendrix, John (Later in Company K, 5th Tennessee U. S. Mounted Infantry.)
43/ Hyde, A. A.
44/ Howell, Russell
45/ Howard, Samuel
46/ Hood, Samuel
47/ Howard, John L.
48/ Jordan, John G. (Later in Company A of Howard's 1st Georgia U. S. Infantry.)
49/ Lovin, Reubin; killed by the enemy.
50/ Loveless, C. C.
51/ Loveless, Abner T.
52/ Manly, Lewis F.
53/ Moss, John (Had been in Company I, 52nd Georgia Confederate Infantry.)
54/ Martin, William P. (Later in Company B, 5th Tennessee U. S. Mounted Infantry.)
55/ McHan, W. M. (Later in Company K, 5th Tennessee U. S. Mounted Infantry.)
56/ Manley, Julius C.
57/ Mann, Emsly O.
58/ Mosley, Albert (Later in Company B of Howard's 1st Georgia U. S. Infantry.)
59/ Mullins, James P. (Later in Company B of Howard's 1st Georgia U. S. Infantry.)
60/ Mullins, Martin B. (Later in Company B of Howard's 1st Georgia U. S. Infantry.)
61/ Mullins, Green D. (Later in Company B of Howard's 1st Georgia U. S. Infantry.)
62/ McHan, Wilkie
63/ McHan, Alfred
64/ Mullins, George R. (Later in Company B of Howard's 1st Georgia U. S. Infantry.)
65/ McCravey, William
66/ McHan, Henry
67/ McCravey, D. S.
68/ Nelson (?), William J. (Written over Joseph Morris?); captured and killed.
69/ Newman, James
70/ Patterson, E.D. (Later in Company K, 5th Tennessee U. S. Mounted Infantry.)
71/ Pinyan, James H.
72/ Pinyan, Jacob
73/ Padget, Isaac (Later in Company B of Howard's 1st Georgia U. S. Infantry.)
74/ Payne, John W. (Later in Company B of Howard's 1st Georgia U. S. Infantry.)
75/ Patterson, Hix (Later in Company K, 5th Tennessee U. S. Mounted Infantry.)
76/ Patterson, Edward (Later in Company K, 5th Tennessee U. S. Mounted Infantry.)
77/ Patterson, Asa (Later in Company K, 5th Tennessee U. S. Mounted Infantry.)
78/ Pool, William (Later in Company K, Tennessee U. S. Mounted Infantry.)
79/ Presley, J. Marion
80/ Padget, Alfred L.
81/ Padget, William J. (Had been in Company I, 52nd Georgia Confederate Infantry, later in Company B of Howard's 1st Georgia U. S. Infantry.)
82/ Padget, John
83/ Roe, Ancil C.; captured and killed
84/ Russell, John
85/ Ray, Thomas
86/ Sizemore, A
87/ Stone, James J.
88/ Shirly, Nathan (Later in Company B of Howard's 1st Georgia U.S. Infantry.)
89/ Swoffered, William M.

90/ Turner, James (Had been in company I, 52nd Georgia Confederate Infantry.)
91/ Turner, Martin
92/ Taylor, William (Later in Company K, 5th Tennessee U. S. Mounted Infantry.)
93/ Taylor, Cicero
94/ Taylor, Lewis
95/ Turner, David; has since died
96/ Tally, John
97/ Turner, Fielden
98/ Turner, H. Green B.
99/ Turner, Memory
100/ Townsend, David
101/ Wigington, James S.
102/West, Columbus J.; paroled under Gen. Wofford
103/ Warren, Jeremiah
104/ Watkins, Elias
105/ Yancy, Obadiah
Certified by George H. Turner, January 14, 1870

OTHERS:

The compilers of these rosters admitted that omissions and errors had occurred. A newspaper account of the fighting at Bucktown, for example, mentions that James M. Weaver, a deserter from Company G of the 39th Georgia Confederate Infantry, was among the members of Brown's 1st Georgia taken prisoner. Weaver's name does not appear on the above rosters or the lists of the men buried at the Marietta National Cemetery. Similarly, a Lewis Lively of Company B appears on Virgil D. Monroe's list of the members of the 1st Georgia executed at Gainesville and on early burial records at the National Cemetery, but not in the rosters.

The persons listed below are found at the end of the microfilm of the compiled service records of Howard's 1st Georgia U.S. Infantry under the title *of "Cards Bearing Names That Do Not Appear on Rolls of the 1st Battalion Georgia Infantry."* A copy of this microfilm is reel 279-34 at the Georgia Department of Archives and History. Some of these men were members of James G. Brown's 1st Georgia State Troops Volunteers and others were probably men recruited by Dewitt C. Howard in late 1863 and 1864.

1/ Young, Wilson Abercrombie
2/ Jesse C. Cox; deserted May 4, 1865
3/ John Fitzgerald; deserted May 5, 1865
4/ Sargent M. Holcomb; deserted May 24, 1865
5/ John Jordon; deserted April 25, 1865
6/ Henry H. Masis; deserted April, 1865
7/ Richard Robison; deserted May 16, 1865
8/ Andrew B. Stewart; deserted June 18, 1865
9/ Leander J. Thompson; private; Company B, 1st Georgia Cavalry
10/ Francis Wisdom
11/ Col. J. H. Ashworth; prisoner-of-war.
12/ Capt. Wm. F. Curry (or Carry); Company A; wounded in the thigh, January 16, 1864.
13/ James Davis, died of typhoid, March 5, 1864
14/ James B. Fowler; Company A 1st Georgia Cavalry; died December 12, 1864, of diarrhea; buried at Sharptop, Cherokee County, GA.
15/ William A. Prewitt; died March 13, 1864; age 18.
16/ Meager Russell; Company B (A?); 1st Georgia Cavalry; died March 18, 1865.
17/ C. C. Spurlin; 1st Georgia Cavalry; died 1863
18/ E. P. (J. B.?) Thompson
19/ Tablah Vineyard; died August 21, 1864, of diarrhea.
20/ William Walden; died January 23, 1864, of measles.

The author gratefully acknowledges assistance provided by Michael Musick and Tod Butler of the National Archives in Washington, D. C., in the research necessary for this article.

Early Northwest Georgia Railroad Disasters

In the early 1900s when rail transportation was beginning to blossom across the United States, the timetables for the trains became increasingly important. As a result, in the interest of maintaining the timetables, proper caution sometimes was not observed by the engineers at the helm of the huge locomotives. The resulting accidents and derailments often were disastrous, and a route through northwest Georgia's Paulding County was the scene of a number of these mishaps.

"They were goin' down grade making ninety miles an hour,
When the whistle broke into a scream -
He was found in the wreck with his hand on the throttle,
Scalded to death by the steam."
– From "The Wreck Of Old 97"

"*Train Number 81, southbound on the Southern Railway, had a few minutes to get in the clear at Dallas for Number 18 northbound vestibule Sunday morning,*" according to a news report in a 1903 issue of the *Dallas New Era*. The men on board did not know it at the time, but a sizeable disaster was only a few moments away. . .

The article continued by explaining "*Engineer Jim Nichols opened the throttle of his monster engine on the summit one mile south of McPherson. Engine 345 never acted better, the big machine moved forward at a terrific rate with twenty-five cars behind. The engineer looked at his watch and knew that time was precious.*"

What happened in the next few minutes on that autumn day of October 23, 1903, is not remembered by many people today, for obvious reasons. Most of those

The disaster broke the stillness of a quiet Sunday morning approximately one mile north of Dallas with a horrendous crash.

witnesses have long since passed on into eternity.

Pumpkinvine Creek Trestle

The disaster broke the stillness of a quiet Sunday morning approximately one mile north of Dallas with a horrendous crash. It was the type of accident that, unfortunately, was not unusual on lonely mountain trestles in the early days of railroading. It was also the type of accident which immortalized the trainmen who traveled dangerous routes – often at excessive speeds – day after day until fate finally overtook them.

Train Number 81 was a very heavy train. It included some twenty-five cars, and was hurtling down the track at close to 60 miles an hour when the huge locomotive rolled onto the high steel bridge over Pumpkinvine Creek. The engineer later said he felt the trestle lurch from the weight, and he quickly throttled back, but it was too late. Behind him, six spans of heavy steel trestlework began collapsing with a thunderous roar into the creek-bed seventy-seven feet below, taking thirteen freight cars, the engine tender, and the fireman into eternity.

Then, just as suddenly as the horrifying accident had begun, it ended, bringing a deathly silence to the spot. As he brought his locomotive to a screeching stop, Nichols reportedly turned and looked desperately for his faithful fireman, John Fagala (also reported as *"J.M. Flagler"* in the news article), who had been standing on the tender when the collapse began. After a quick but futile search around the locomotive, Nichols next went back to the edge of the high broken trestle where his eyes landed upon the sight he feared he would find in the ravine below.

The tender had been ripped from the engine coupling as the track collapsed beneath it. It was lying far below in a tangle of trestle steel and freight cars. John Fagala (Flagler?) probably never had a chance. He may have jumped free, hoping for the best, or maybe he had simply been tossed off the precipice as the tender was snatched from the engine. Whatever the circumstances, his body was found in the wreckage, his neck and leg broken. He had been killed instantly.

Miraculously, the last cars of the train had remained on the track on the opposite side. Consequently, the conductor and flagman in the caboose survived the devastation without a scratch.

The 360-foot bridge across Pumpkinvine Creek was one of the longest and highest in northwest Georgia. It had safely carried hundreds of fast trains in the late 1800s. Today, no one knows what caused the bridge to collapse, but many individuals knowledgeable of rail accidents have speculated on the cause. One report indicated the large locomotive had simply been traveling too fast and had jumped the rails on the curved trestle, leading the cars behind it to devastation.

"The first time I heard of the Pumpkinvine trestle collapsing was from Mr. Paul McDonald, Southern Railway's third trick operator at Rockmart," explained the late Duane "Cowboy" Mintz, a former conductor on Southern (present-day Norfolk-Southern) Railway, who says he passed back and forth across the Pumpkinvine Creek trestle continuously during his career. "Later, after I went to work for Southern, I mentioned the incident while dead-heading to Chattanooga on (Train) Number 32, Rockmart's four o'clock train in the afternoon. I was rebuffed by some of the veteran railroaders for passing on tales they had never heard of. The old head conductor, Mr. E.E. (Emmett) Whittle, however, came to my rescue. 'The boy's right,' he told them. 'It happened not long after I went to work (for Southern). I almost quit the railroad on account of it.'"

The Pumpkinvine Creek trestle is located on the line between Atlanta, Georgia and Chattanooga, Tennessee on the route known as the "Georgia Division" of Southern Railway. Even today, trains pass over a steel trestle (one of the longest and highest on the division) at this same site above the creek many times a day. "I, as well as a lot of others, never did like crossing it," Mintz adds. "I personally don't like any trestle that is built as part of a curve like that one is."

The Dallas to Rockmart portion of the Georgia Division has long been a dangerous one. As a part of the Atlanta to Chattanooga line in Southern Railway's network it was completed on July 1, 1882. There have been at least four major disasters on the Dallas to Rockmart segment alone in the past 90 years, and possibly numerous others.

Break-neck speed and a tight railroad time-table undoubtedly were major factors in several of the incidents. In 1902, Southern Railway obtained a contract to haul the mail between Washington, D.C. and Atlanta, Georgia, on the New York to New Orleans line. The U.S. government wanted the best means possible for quick transport of the mails, and fast locomotives were the answer. In return, Southern Railway earned $140,000 a year for this service. In those days, that was big money.

But it was a double-edged sword. If Southern Railway couldn't keep up with the schedule, it was penalized $100 for every thirty minutes the mail was late at every destination. That was more than enough incentive for rail management to put heavy pressure on trainmen to maintain schedules. This often meant exceeding the speed limit by many miles an hour more than the

Pumpkinvine Creek Trestle suddenly collapsed beneath train Number 81 of Southern Railway on October 23, 1903. The disaster killed the fireman of the train, John Fagala (Flagler?). Engineer Jim Nichols was fortunate to get his locomotive - Engine No. 345 - to a stable portion of the bridge.

The trestle at Pumpkinvine Creek in Paulding County was photographed in 1997. At the time of this writing, trains still passed over the creek gorge at this spot daily. (Photo by Gordon Sargent)

The Southern Railway Depot in Rockmart, Georgia, as it appeared in the early 1900s. Rockmart was the next major stop on the Southern after Dallas, Georgia.

On December 23, 1926, a horrendous collision between the *Ponce de Leon* and the *Royal Palm* passenger trains resulted in one of the worst rail disasters in U.S. history. This accident in Rockmart, Georgia, occurred not far from the Pumpkinvine Creek disaster site, and was responsible for the death of at least nineteen individuals (the exact number is still unknown today). (Photo courtesy of Atlanta History Center)

speed for which a stretch of rails and their supporting components (such as trestles) were designed. And the fact that some trains were traveling on dangerous stretches of track to begin with, only added to the propensity for disaster.

One such example is the stretch of tracks between Dallas, Georgia and Rockmart. On the evening of December 23, 1926, on the outskirts of Rockmart, the Ponce de Leon passenger train, traveling in excess of 50 miles per hour, collided head-on with the *Royal Palm* passenger with devastating results. There were at least 19 and possibly 20 or more fatalities (the exact number is unknown today). At least 113 passengers, 4 Southern Railway employees and 6 Pullman employees were injured. This wreck remains as one of the worst disasters in the history of the railroad in the United States.

Big Raccoon Creek Trestle

Another accident (on that same dangerous stretch between Dallas and Rockmart) which caused the death of several individuals occurred nearby at Big Raccoon Creek trestle in February of 1883. The bridgework at this site was practically new at that time, and railroad historians have long pondered the reason for its collapse. "It's just another of the many puzzling events in the annals of railroading in the early days," Mintz added matter-of-factly.

The 44-year veteran of the rails served on the Georgia Division Safety Committee of Southern Railway for ten years. "I wrote, printed and distributed a safety newsletter, and one of the articles I carried in the newsletter was a description of the Big Raccoon Creek accident," he smiled.

The trestle at Big Raccoon Creek is seven miles north of Dallas. The creek is comparatively small but the creek-bed is significantly deep with high bluffs on either side. At the time of the accident, the trestle was a three-deck trestle, spanning 1,480 feet from bluff to bluff and rising 94 feet from the creek-bed.

Mr. Mintz's newsletter article of this disaster, reprinted from a news report in the February 22, 1883 issue of the *Dallas New Era* newspaper, described the accident as follows: *"Last Saturday morning, about*

10:30 a.m., as Train Number 59, a through-freight of the E.T.V. & G. R.R. (East Tennessee, Virginia & Georgia Railroad) was leaving the switch at the tunnel, south-bound, Conductor Bob Shoemaker boarded the engine, as it was convenient for him at the time, and (he) remarked to his engineer that he would ride with him down to Dallas rather than drop back to his caboose.

"All went well until the train, running at the rate of 7 or 8 miles an hour, ran upon Big Raccoon Trestle. . . Having passed across to within a few yards of the south side with his engine, Mr. Neeley gave her a little more steam in order to pull over the grade immediately in front. Almost immediately, a severe shock being felt, Mr. Shoemaker, apprehending the cause and looking back, shouted, 'Pull her open! Pull her open! The bridge is going!' . . . The terrible crash that followed left them standing upon the very brink of a yawning abyss – the bottom of which was covered with ruins, all within a moment of time.

"The (collapsed) section consisted of ten or eleven cars laden with merchandise, and the caboose. There were three men in the caboose and a Negro brakeman about midway of the train . . . The unfortunate brakeman was killed outright. Mr. R.P. Kidwell . . . was on board, enroute to Atlanta to visit his family. He too was so fatally injured that death came as a relief to his sufferings very soon after being removed from the debris to the car in waiting. Mr. John Cox . . . also in the caboose, sustained injuries that proved fatal to him, living until Saturday night totally unconscious all the while. Mr. Charles Camp, flagman . . . remained unconscious for several hours, then awoke to the realization of his remarkable escape . . . (He had) a scalp wound, a crushed ankle, and a dislocated elbow, (but he was alive!)."

The heavy train had passed across the trestle until the caboose was immediately over the creek. At that point, according to the news account printed in the *New Era*, section after section of the trestle began giving way somewhere near the center of the train. The general collapse of the trestle was very similar to the collapse of the trestle just six or seven miles away at Pumpkinvine Creek in 1903.

Common Cause For The Disasters?

The 360-foot trestle across Pumpkinvine had safely carried hundreds of fast trains over the years. The cause of its collapse is still unknown also, but the news account in the 1903 *New Era* speculates upon the possibilities. "*Some think train wreckers had removed a rail causing the wreck, while others believe that the high rate of speed caused the terrible disaster,*" the newspaper intoned.

Duane Mintz said he didn't think a missing rail had caused the accident at all. "If a rail had been missing, the whole engine would have gone over the side of the trestle, and it wouldn't have caused much trestle damage either," the trainman explained. "I think simple structural weakness caused both the Raccoon Creek and Pumpkinvine Creek disasters."

Mr. Shoemaker, comprehending the cause and looking back, shouted, 'Pull her open! Pull her open! The bridge is going!'

A very similar accident, which was highly publicized across the United States, had occurred on the Southern Railway just three weeks earlier. The wreck of the "Old 97" which occurred in Danville, Virginia, became the subject for a popular ballad which is still remembered by many railroad enthusiasts today:

Steve Broady, the engineer of the "Old 97," was pushing the mail train faster and faster to make up lost time. Witnesses claim the train reached ninety miles an hour as the 80-ton behemoth swept down a grade and struck the "curved" timber trestle. Reportedly, a flange on one of the wheels broke off, and the engine with its cars plunged seventy-five feet into the creek below.

Twelve of the nineteen individuals on board "Old 97" were killed. The engineer and fireman were found with the skin flayed from their bodies by the super-heated steam from the crushed boiler. It was a fate from which the engineer at Pumpkinvine Creek had mercifully been spared, but there's no arguing that the Danville, Virginia and Pumpkinvine Creek, Georgia disasters were strangely similar in nature.

Whatever the cause of the wreck at Pumpkinvine, rail officials were determined not to allow the accident to keep the line out of service any longer than absolutely necessary. Service between Chattanooga and Atlanta was temporarily rerouted through Rome, while a huge work crew labored feverishly to repair the damage. Every hour the line remained out of service represented a great financial loss for Southern.

"Two wrecking crews reached the scene about 12:00 p.m., six hours after the occurrence, and more than two hundred men were clearing away the debris," the *Dallas New Era* explained.

Even this amount of man-power, however, apparently was not enough, and still more men were dispatched to the site to help. Working around the clock, the men had the track and trestle repaired three days after the disaster. By Wednesday morning, the first train steamed safely over the repaired bridge, heading north to Chattanooga.

Once the wreckage had been cleared away and the repairs had been made, the scene at Pumpkinvine Creek quickly returned to normal too. Previously on that fateful Sunday, sightseers had streamed out of Dallas to view the site of the disaster. And with the crowds came scavengers who dug through the wreckage in search of booty.

The atmosphere, no doubt, was like a country carnival. The crushed freight cars had spilled their cargoes of corn, oats, cotton, and apples, and according to one wag, a load of Bull Durham tobacco. It was reported with some mirth, that virtually every boy in Paulding County learned to smoke as a result of this wreck.

Meanwhile, in a community northward, the festivities were not quite so lively . . . A railroader – the poor fireman at the Pumpkinvine Creek accident – had been killed, and in sleepy Varnell, Georgia, near the Tennessee state line, a grieving wife and two small children received their loved one home from the railroad for the last time.

Every hour the line remained out of service represented a great financial loss for Southern.

Last Days Of The Civil War In Pickens County

For several years prior to the official end of the U.S. Civil War (and indeed for a number of years thereafter), much of north Georgia as well as other parts of the South were subjected to a period of extreme lawlessness. Politics and class warfare were catalysts in the murder, robbery and general mayhem which occurred on a regular basis. The incident at Scarecorn Campground was a microcosm of this arena of unrest.

In the popular mind (and indeed in many formal histories of the subject), the U.S. Civil War (or the War Between The States, depending upon one's perspective) ended when Confederate General Robert E. Lee surrendered to Union General Ulysses S. Grant in April of 1865. In point of fact, however, some other Confederate troops did not surrender until months later, and some – such as General Nathan Bedford Forest's cavalry troops – did not surrender at all, but eventually just disbanded. Disorganization and general lawlessness were the order of the day at this time.

Two books have covered some of the turbulence of this period: Burke Davis' *The Long Surrender* (1985) and Noah Andre Trudeau's *Out Of The Storm* (1994). Despite these efforts, much remains to be told of this period in our nation's history.

During the latter portion of the decade of the 1860s, hordes of starving and desperate Confederate soldiers faced a very bleak future. Their way of life was gone; their property was being taken from them when they could not pay the taxes; their families were being turned out with no place to call home; and the men confronted with these anguishing circumstances had nowhere to turn for help. These were desperate times indeed.

Even before the Civil War had ended, gangs of armed deserters from both the Union and Confederate armies had begun roaming the South, pillaging the land and doing so just out of the reach of any organized law enforcement. Riots, espionage, arson, vandalism, robbery, and other forms of rebellion and crime were commonplace.

During the days prior to the battle of Gettysburg, President Abraham Lincoln was not certain the war could actually be won by the Union army. As a result, he had considered peace terms with the South which – as a conciliatory gesture – would allow local officials in the South to remain in their respective public offices. Such a plan, he believed, would also keep operational the machinery of civil law and order in many areas of the Confederacy which he knew was becoming more lawless with each passing day. The further the South was decimated into a classless society, the more lawlessness would prevail.

However, with the fall of Vicksburg (which divided the South) and the decisive victory at Gettysburg, Lincoln abandoned his consideration of a peace offer to the South, and the region fell further yet into lawlessness. The president's own assassination shortly after Lee's surrender at Appomattox hardened federal authorities against any continuation whatsoever of Confederate civil authority, assuring the decimation of the region.

Historian Henry C. Hyde, Jr., argues that the elimination of civil authority coupled with the decline of local influence of the wealthy planter aristocracy brought on an era of escalating acts of personal violence throughout the South which was unprecedented, and which continued into the 1890s. A class of Southern "plain folk" who were armed, accustomed to violence, and who substantially disregarded political authority, acted as vigilantes whenever and wherever they felt necessary.

One particularly bloody incident exemplifying this social upheaval took place at Scarecorn Methodist Church Campground and Tabernacle in the Pickens County community of Hinton, Georgia. Today, this sleepy little crossroads hamlet is quiet and peaceful, but on an autumn day in 1865, it became a site of slaughter.

Hinton, in particular, had gained a notorious reputation for violence which persevered into the 1920s.

The people of Hinton live in a rough hill country. In the 1850s and '60s, they lacked both a transportation system (railroad) and the productive farmland necessary to make the cash crop of that era – "King Cotton" – a viable agricultural product in their vicinity.

As a result, very few of the Pickens County residents owned slaves, and they greeted secession with mixed feelings. Strongly Methodist in religion, the residents of Hinton likely named their community after James Wooten Hinton, the well-known author and north Georgia Methodist leader. When the war arrived, Hintonians had become a people divided, with those opposed to secession forming a Methodist church separate from the original Methodist church in the community.

Hinton's problems were a microcosm of those involving not only Pickens County, but a large portion of the South in general. In the Pickens County seat of Jasper, supporters of the Union raised and protected a United States flag over the Pickens County courthouse in protest of secession during the early days of the war. Later, Pickens raised both Confederate and Union army companies while suffering cavalry invasions from both armies as well.

The war officially ended in the spring of 1865, but the hatreds and the violence continued unabated.

Pickens County native Henry Ledford had traveled north of the Ohio River to avoid the war. He eventually enlisted in the 144th Indiana Infantry. Shortly after

his return to Pickens County after the war, he was gunned down in a street in Jasper by former Confederates. He died quickly.

When a Pickens County Grand Jury later was convened (under the protection of federal troops), jury members lamented the general feeling in the community that one needed to carry firearms in order to safely walk the streets. Hinton, in particular, had gained a notorious reputation for violence which persevered into the 1920s. Many of the Civil War veterans held and maintained grudges which were long-standing in nature.

In 1862, a John H. Paxton had recruited men in eastern Gordon County and western Pickens County, including men from the vicinity of Hinton who all wanted to serve in the Union army. Guilefully, Paxton had offered to take the men safely through the Confederate lines to achieve this goal. However, instead of passing stealthily through the lines, Paxton stopped at a Confederate camp where he turned his men over to the men in grey. The recruits, including brothers Benson M. Nally, Bailey M. Nally, and Elijah Nally of Hinton,

Rev. Charles O. Walker of Jasper, Georgia, a well-known historian and illustrationist, depicts an incident in Pickens County when the federal flag was briefly raised by Unionists in 1860 in front of the Pickens County Courthouse. (Courtesy of Rev. Charles O. Walker)

Peter Cantrell was one of numerous Pickens County unionists killed by vengeful Confederates both during and after the war. (Courtesy of Robert S. Davis, Jr.)

Georgia, were forced to serve in Company F of the 1st Georgia Confederate "Volunteer" Cavalry Regiment.

As a result of his handiwork, Paxton ultimately was promoted to the rank of lieutenant and received a large bounty fee for his "recruits" before departing for

Pickens County on sick leave. Shortly thereafter, he obtained a medical discharge from the army. His "victims," however, went on to endure hard fighting in Tennessee and Kentucky, before successfully escaping in 1863 to finally join the Union army. It, understandably, was not unusual for Southerners with pro-Union sentiments to experience hardships at that time – and to cultivate hard feelings toward many of their Southern countrymen.

According to Nally family tradition, the proverbial "straw which broke the camel's back" and culminated in the Scarecorn shootings, was the theft of a simple cow. With the war over and having been discharged from the Union army, Jesse Aaron, Bailey M., and Elijah Nally of the 10th Tennessee Regiment (Union Army) returned home to Pickens County. There, they discovered their farm had been looted, their mother had become traumatized from abuses by the Confederate Home Guard, and their family cow had been stolen. These depredations were not unusual at all, and indeed had been perpetrated by Northern riff-raff and criminals just as often as by Southerners. The Nallys, however, as Union sympathizers, undoubtedly had become sensitized to the abuse.

Some accounts claim that the cow actually belonged to Edy Gravely, the mother of the Nallys' neighbor, Frank Gravely, who had served with the 1st Tennessee Artillery (Union). Whatever the circumstances, the Nally brothers, accompanied by Frank Gravely, set out for Scarecorn Campground to confront the men they believed had taken the cow.

The motivations for the violence which followed extended far beyond the simple theft of a cow. The issues ranged from "poor versus rich," "Northerner versus Southerner," "large plantation owners versus migratory mountaineers," "criminals versus non-criminals," and "slave owners versus non-slave owners." These all were smoldering embers which were flaring up all across the South as a classless society became more prevalent and civil disorder commonplace.

According to a newspaper account which appeared in the *Rome Weekly Courier* on September 7, 1865, *"a man named Nally and a man named Gravely on Sunday, August 27, 1865, entered a church in Pickens County during preaching and called out for two men against whom they had a long-standing grudge. When the men refused to comply, Nally and Gravely went in and killed one while mortally wounding the other. A woman was accidentally wounded, but later recovered.*

"The following Wednesday, Lieutenant Harper of the 29th Indiana Infantry arrived with three soldiers and three Cartersville civilians – Thomas Hancock, Bell Collins and Ben Smith – at the Gravely home. In the fray that followed, Collins, Smith, old man Gravely, Gravely's three sons, and Nally were killed or mortally wounded, with no injury to the federal troops or to the two women present in the cabin."

The Collins brothers reportedly pulled knives while the Nallys and Gravely drew firearms.

A different version of the incident (presented by a Collins relative) appeared in the *Cartersville Courant* on July 2, 1885. The Collins family had moved to north Georgia in the 1840s from Cleveland

County, North Carolina. Many of them had served in the Confederate army, including Captain Miles Collins of the 23rd Georgia Infantry, so they had strong pro-Confederate leanings.

According to the Collins version which appeared in the *Courant*, several Collins family members were attending a funeral at Scarecorn Campground when a group of men – the Nally brothers and Gravely (pro-Union) – entered the tabernacle and called for Boswell Collins (pro-Confederate) to step outside. Boswell's brother, Miller, reportedly told Boswell not to comply.

The Collins brothers reportedly pulled knives while the Nallys and Gravely drew firearms. In the shooting which followed, Berry Collins was killed outright. His brother, Boswell Collins, was mortally wounded, and reportedly left a bloody hand-print on the pulpit. A Collins relative, married just that morning, was wounded through an elbow, while another bullet passed through the hip of a small boy. And according to notes belonging to the late Luke Tate, former Pickens County historian, Bailey and Elijah Nally suffered knife wounds.

When Bell Collins of Cartersville learned what had happened to his brothers-in-law in Hinton (Bell coincidentally had the same surname), he went to a federal detachment at Cartersville for help. With a posse of federal troops and civilians, he reportedly reached the Nally cabin (misidentified in the *Rome Courier* article as *"the Gravely home,"*) between the present-day communities of Ludville and Fairmount by the following Tuesday night.

Bell Collins and Smith reportedly stormed into the cabin, yelling that if the Nallys wanted the Home Guard, they would have them now. (Collins and Smith apparently believed the Nallys and Gravely had been seeking vengeance on the Confederate Home Guard when they attacked the Collins brothers in Hinton. Whether or not they were accurate in their assumptions about the Collins brothers' involvement with the Home Guard is unknown today.)

In the gunfire which followed, Collins and Smith both were shot dead. Ironically, the federal soldiers then began firing through the gaps between the logs at their former Union sympathizers. Frank Gravely was wounded and fled the cabin. He reportedly offered to surrender, but, according to a Collins relative's account, he then tried to fire his weapon and a federal soldier bayoneted him. According to his mother's later pension claim, Gravely died the next day at her cabin.

At this point, Lieutenant Harper apparently decided discretion was the better part of valor, and made preparations to withdraw from the cabin and the site without further bloodshed. The federal soldiers loaded the bodies of Collins and Smith in their wagons and departed.

Benson Nally, head of the Nally family and the South Carolina son of an Irish immigrant, was wounded but lived and later moved to Illinois where he died in 1888.

Many years later, the brothers Jesse and Bailey Nally told their version of the incident in their federal pension claims. They, however, omitted the details of the Scarecorn Campground shooting, explaining simply that Confederate bushwhackers had stormed their home at suppertime in August of 1865, leaving their brother, Elijah, and their sister, Gracy Ann, dead.

At some point following the incident, Jesse Aaron Nally changed his name to Jesse P. McAnally, and lived at various times in Alabama, Mississippi, Tennessee and Texas before his death in Pemiscot County, Missouri on September 15, 1924. His brother, Bailey, as had his father, moved up north to Illinois, dying there in Pulaski County on January 1, 1927.

Jerry Nally, a Nally descendant living today in Pickens County, Georgia, believes that, aside from the regional prejudices inflamed by family feuds, the differences between the original account in the *Rome Courier* and the various family stories can be understood if one imagines the tragedy as seen through the eyes of Lieutenant Harper. Bell Collins (a staunch Southerner and Confederate) had – despite his political leanings – successfully persuaded Lieutenant Harper (who was serving in a provost marshal detachment at Cartersville) to intervene in what Collins no doubt described as a murderous public outrage. Instead of dealing with the crime properly, Lieutenant Harper and his men unfortunately found themselves in the middle of what they realized was nothing more than a bloody family feud.

By the time the smoke had cleared and the gunfire had ended, most of the principals in the dispute were dead. With none of his own men harmed, Harper undoubtedly decided that fortune had smiled upon him after all, and withdrew before a bad situation could become even worse.

Harper also quite likely was the source of the garbled story carried in the September 7, 1865 article in the *Rome Courier* that misidentified the Nallys as *"old man Gravely and Gravely's three sons,"* and the Nally cabin as *"the Gravely home."* He (Harper) likely used the story to convince his superiors that no further investigation was necessary. His plan may have succeeded too, for no paperwork exists today in the National Archives in Washington, D.C. regarding the Scarecorn incident beyond the pension depositions that the Nallys made decades later.

Because of the growing number of problems with which the overtaxed federal forces had to deal in the summer of 1865, Harper's superiors likely decided the incident at Scarecorn was the least of their worries. The federal army had jails in Georgia filled not only with their own unruly soldiers, but with growing numbers of civilians guilty of crimes as well. At that same time, federal troops were dealing with guerrillas in Chattanooga; men in federal uniforms committing robberies in Twiggs County, Georgia; roving gangs in Columbia, South Carolina; and lynchings in East Tennessee; just to describe a bit of the turmoil of that day.

Lieutenant Harper and his regiment were formally mustered out of the service on December 2, 1865. He moved to Douglas County, Minnesota, where he married Mary Ingersoll on June 24, 1868, and began a large family. He died at Cheppewa Lake, Medina County, Ohio on January 24, 1891.

For Harper, the U.S. Civil War never ended completely until the day he died, when no one could question him further about the incident at Scarecorn Campground back in Georgia. The Nallys, Gravelys and Collinses probably enjoyed peace no sooner.

Although the Scarecorn incident took place after the surrender of the major Confederate armies, it also occurred prior to the restoration of any civil law and order in the South. As the attorney for Edy Gravely, Frank Gravely's widowed mother argued – *"When and by whomever's hand he died, he did so because he had been a soldier of the United States army and at a time when that army owed him protection. In the region-wide confusion of the times, however, he fell at the hands of his comrades* (Union troops) *as they defended their former enemies."*

As unfortunate as the deaths were, they personify the terrible nature of war. It seldom plays favorites, often smiling upon the side which is the most terrible in the horrors it metes out.

The Last Raid Of Lee Cape

The folklore associated with the Southern Appalachian Mountains is replete with many descriptions of "moonshining" and the violence often associated with this staple of the uplands. The murder of Lee Cape, a fabled lawman in north Georgia's Pickens County, undoubtedly will be remembered as one of the more grisly chapters in this enduring saga.

Of all the information associated with Pickens County, no single episode remains as controversial as the gruesome 1927 murder of County Policeman W. Lee Cape. On a sunny afternoon on September 17 of that year, the respected lawman lost his life in one of the most heinous murders in Pickens County history.

Pro-Cape accounts (including those of the newspapers of that day and from interviews of persons who knew him well) contend that Cape was guilty of nothing more than law enforcement, an effort for which he paid the ultimate price. Other suspicions, however, maintain that he was excessive and over-zealous in the performance of his duties, and that in the final analysis, he simply became careless and fell victim to a wanton murderer.

To some, Cape was reckless; to others, he was simply relentless. Almost invariably, however, he was respected.

Born in South Carolina on June 5, 1862, during the height of the U.S. Civil War, Lee Cape was orphaned at an early age. He undoubtedly learned to be self-sufficient and independent at an early age. By 1880, he was living with his grandmother Cape in Pickens County, Georgia.

By 1927, Lee Cape had spent more than forty years in law enforcement, and was a respected citizen and policeman. Those who knew him agree he was determined in his efforts to enforce laws against the trafficking of untaxed liquor ("moonshining" and "bootlegging") which was so prevalent in the north Georgia region at this time.

The "Roaring Twenties" was a time of firearms, illegal liquor, and violence. In general, Chicago was – and remains

FINAL PHOTO – Lee Cape (1862-1927) was born during the U.S. Civil War and raised during the hard times of the Reconstruction in the South. Despite these hardships, Cape was the consummate lawman, and was highly respected in Pickens County. He was photographed above during the last years of his life.

MOONSHINING – The struggle for survival was never more intense than during the harsh years of Reconstruction in the South. Mountaineers, who had virtually no other means of support, found they could eek out a better life by taking their corn to market by the gallon than by the bushel. Pictured here is an illegal distillery (moonshine still) photographed in Pickens County circa 1875. (Photo courtesy of Georgia Dept. of Archives & History)

today – the symbol of these times, but in point of fact, the social ill was a nationwide phenomenon. Much of the illegal liquor was produced in remote mountain regions, and Pickens County was as active as any locale.

It was during these times that the counties added extra deputies and county police (such as Lee Cape) to ease public fears and to beef up rural enforcement efforts in what had become an American guerrilla war against those persons who made and transported the illegal liquor.

Lee Cape was one of the more active county policemen who pursued the illicit traffickers. As a result, he was a sharp thorn in the side of many mountaineers who depended upon the production of illegal liquor for income.

As early as 1890, Cape's name was discovered on a list of law enforcement officials targeted by Pickens County vigilantes known as "The Night Riders" (also known as "The Honest Man's Friend & Protector"), who were burning and raiding homes of law enforcement officials and others in retribution of the liquor laws and their enforcement. The Night Riders, however, were apprehended before they were able to savage Cape's home.

Despite the threats on his life and property, Lee Cape eventually advanced in service and was appointed as a deputy United States marshal. To put this in perspective, the famed gunfight at the O.K. Corral in Tombstone, Arizona, which involved another deputy United States marshal – Virgil Earp – and his deputy, Wyatt Earp, had occurred only a few years earlier in 1881.

In 1893, Lee Cape reportedly was apprehending and bringing in moonshiners almost daily. According to records, he had even been known to arrest his own sons on occasion.

Cape's sons, in fact, frequently appeared in the Pickens County court records, and were the subject of almost as much sensation as Cape's untimely death. In 1924, Levi, amazingly, was sentenced to life in prison (he was paroled in 1934) for killing his brother, Hobert, and leaving Lee Cape for dead in Hinton where the family lived. The third son, Waldo, was killed in 1942 in Hinton, during a drunken brawl.

It can only be considered ironic today, that despite his heroic effort at the elimination of illegal alcohol in the Pickens County area, much of Lee Cape's family was erased by the illicit drug – their lives snuffed out by excessive consumption, violence, and the violence of the times in which they lived.

Cape took his job of law enforcement – particularly as involved the illegal liquor trade – very seriously. Law enforcement during these times in north Georgia was an extremely dangerous occupation, yet Cape, surprisingly, never expressed any concern or gave any indication that he feared for his life. He frequently traveled unarmed, and his "deputies" in his raids, more often than not, were his wife or his young grandsons.

Despite the hazards and physical nature of such an occupation, Cape always seemed up to the task. Even as a middle-aged man, he was known to be fleet of foot, able to out-run most fleeing offenders.

To some, Cape was reckless; to others, he was simply relentless. Almost invariably, however, he was respected. As late as 1922, he was described as having never harmed anyone in the pursuit of his duties. Even in the testimony in the trial of persons accused of his murder, including that of the men later convicted of the crime, Cape was described as well-liked and even as a friend of the very individuals he often arrested.

Cape's neighbor, Tom Evans, however, remembered that Cape was once given a rude awakening late in his career. According to accounts published at the time in the *Pickens County Progress*, at 11:00 a.m. on Friday, April 7, 1922, Cape, with the sheriff and other county policemen, had been working a road-block all night, successfully arresting bootleggers at the Aiken Cemetery, three miles north of Jasper. The lawmen had just arrested thirty-three-year-old Willie Pickett McFarland of Keithsburg Community in Cherokee County. McFarland's buggy had been obviously overloaded, and upon inspection, had revealed a load of contraband whiskey. When the bootlegger had attempted to escape, he and Cape became involved in a struggle. In the midst of the fight, a pistol which Cape had confiscated from another prisoner accidentally discharged, killing McFarland.

The victim was described as an honest, hard-working, peach-grower, with a wife and two children. His mistake, according to the paper, had been an attempt to supplement his pitiful income with proceeds from illegal whiskey trafficking. The paper, however, exonerated Cape, describing him as *"fearless, truthful, and always self-possessed."* Tom Evans, however, remembered that Lee Cape was "never the same" after the McFarland shooting.

McFarland's widow subsequently moved to Alabama. Interestingly, by crossing the state line for her residence, she was able to sue Cape in federal court for the death of her husband and her loss of income. She won $1,273 of the $35,000 she sought in damages for Cape's "recklessness."

Lee Cape, however, remained relentless in his pursuit of moonshiners and bootleggers. With his usual disdain of personal safety, he departed Hinton on what would be his last raid on September 17, 1927, at 7:30 a.m. His open "touring car" was driven by his sixteen-year-old grandson, Surber

Cape, and they were accompanied by Surber's young friend, Will Evans (Tom's brother). The boys carried a shotgun; Lee Cape had a pistol.

According to later testimony, the group reached the top of nearby Henderson Mountain near the Cherokee County line approximately half an hour later. Lee Cape stepped out of the car and instructed the boys to search the western slope of the mountain. They agreed to fire shots if anyone in the group discovered anything. They were to meet at a nearby house at 3:00 p.m.

At 12:30, the boys discovered a large illegal liquor operation ("still") which had been set up for fermenting beer and producing liquor. They fired the shotgun as instructed, but Cape did not answer. They then drove to the rendezvous point. An hour later, when Cape still had not appeared, the boys drove around the mountain searching for the lawman.

According to court testimony, at approximately 3:30 p.m., the boys encountered three men – Lindsey Evans, his brother Hoyt Evans, and C.L. Smith – who were blocking the narrow road with their car. Lindsey Evans recognized the boys' car as Lee Cape's vehicle, and the men angrily charged up to the boys yelling and cursing, apparently guessing that the youngsters were helping Cape search the neighborhood for moonshine operations.

Surber, realizing he was in danger, quickly attempted to shift the vehicle into reverse, but when the stubborn machine wouldn't comply, the boy sprang from the car and ran. The by-then enraged Evans reportedly grabbed young Will Evans (no relation to Lindsey or Hoyt Evans) by the head and attacked him with a knife, cutting one of his fingers. The younger Evans broke free, however, and fled also.

Surber, shortly thereafter, arrived at the home of Dott Pharr, a local bailiff, and reported the attack. Pharr reached Cape's automobile as the Evans brothers and Smith were fleeing, having stolen the boys' shotgun.

According to courtroom testimony, the three men stopped at the home of Lindsey Evans who went inside to retrieve his own shotgun. Evans then checked his weapon – firing both barrels – then climbed back into the car.

Meanwhile, Lee Cape was oblivious to the circumstances unfolding around him. He had not heard the boys' signal shot because he had left the mountain to explore nearby Salacoa Creek. At some point after 12:00 noon, he began to walk back towards the scheduled rendezvous with the boys – a walk which would prove to be Cape's last.

R. Seab Newborn saw the county policeman as he trudged down the road, and then, thirty minutes later, on the same road, saw the car and the three men who had accosted the boys. Newborn later testified that twenty to thirty minutes later, he heard shots.

On their initial encounter on the road, the three men reportedly passed Cape without attempting to harm him, but Lindsey Evans angrily demanded that they turn around so he could confront Cape. The driver of the vehicle, Hoyt Evans, however, continued on, apparently preferring to avoid further problems.

Unbeknownst to Hoyt however, the spot he picked to eventually park the vehicle (the Evans family home on old Goshen Road, one and one-half miles below the former site of the community of Talmadge) was the very spot at which Cape was scheduled to rendezvous with his two young assistants. Lindsey Evans was later quoted in court as stating "Me or old man Lee Cape one is going to die, when he comes out the road."

As he hiked up the road that day, Lee Cape reached the men in the car and in his usual inquisitive manner, inquired as to the owner of the vehicle. Cape, familiar with the men and apparently suspecting something amiss, began searching behind the vehicle's seats – undoubtedly for illegal liquor.

At this point, Lindsey Evans reportedly warned Cape that he would have to pay for any damages to the vehicle. Had he known of the danger afoot, Cape undoubtedly would have reacted differently, but he had no reason to suspect the murderous circumstances which were slowly unfolding around him. His reply to Evans's statement reflected Cape's usual fearless (and some would say reckless) demeanor.

"Well that would be very easy done I guess," Cape was quoted as saying. "You've been tryin' to run ablazin' around all the time; nobody ain't scared of you."

Those words proved to be Cape's last. Witnesses at the scene later testified that Evans quickly took out a shotgun (specifically whose shotgun was never proven) and fired three shots point-blank into Cape, killing the famed lawman almost instantly. He fell onto the side of the roadway, dead from multiple wounds.

Hoyt Evans, at this point, grabbed the weapon from his brother and pleaded with him to stop. Eyewitnesses at the scene ran into the Evans home.

The killer, however, was unrepentant, and threatened to shoot his fleeing neighbors as well as his brother. Cape's body was stuffed into the trunk of the men's automobile and the two brothers then drove off.

Any hope of an unwitnessed disposal of the body was virtually wasted, for in their panic, the two men careened up the road from Fairmount to Adairsville at an extremely high rate of speed. Their reckless driving and open touring cars (they drove two vehicles to dispose of the body) made identification easy for the numerous individuals who later testified against them.

The Lee Cape home still stands in Hinton at the intersection of Highways 53 and 136 in Pickens County. It was from this domicile that Cape departed on the cool autumn morning of September 17, 1927, when he was brutally murdered and dismembered. (Photo by Olin Jackson)

Lee Cape and his daughter squint toward the camera as this photo was taken on a summer afternoon during the lawman's last days. They pose in front of Cape's well-known 1925 Ford Touring Car. Cape, as can be discerned from this photo, was well up into his years by the time this photo was made. He rode to the scene of his murder in this vehicle.

Grisly and varying accounts of what next transpired have been circulated for years. According to court testimony, the corpse was mutilated in a twisted hope that this would in some manner render identification of the body impossible (For reasons unknown today, the fact that the crime had been committed in full view of several wit-

CAPE BODY DUMP SITE – This lonely crossroads south of Adairsville, Georgia (Gordon County) was the site at which the corpse of Lee Cape was beheaded and dumped. The head reportedly was thrown on the right side of the road, and the torso on the left. (Photo by Robert S. Davis, Jr.)

Pickens County Policeman Lee Cape's grave in Hinton Cemetery. (Photo by Robert S. Davis, Jr.)

nesses seemed to have been lost upon the Evans brothers.).

Whatever the circumstances, at what is still (at the time of this writing) a lonely dirt crossroads five miles south of Adairsville, the body of Lee Cape was dumped. Horrifyingly, Cape's head was severed from his body and mutilated by shotgun blasts which rendered the face unrecognizable. The head was then thrown to the opposite side of the road from the remainder of the lawman's body. The body was also stripped naked before being abandoned.

News of the murder traveled swiftly. The following morning, when the brothers paused for a meal at a Fairmount roadhouse, a crowd gathered around their automobile searching for grisly signs of the murder. By that evening, a crowd of more than one hundred had gathered at the home of Lindsey Evans, hoping to cash in on the $500 reward already offered by the Pickens County commissioner's office for information leading to the identification and capture of Cape's murderers.

Coincidentally, one of the first persons at the scene when Cape's body was accidentally discovered by T.R. (Rex) Sherman two days later was C.H. Peacock of Canton. Peacock had administered to Cape years earlier when the lawman had been wounded by his drunken son. Peacock had no trouble identifying the body then and later for the court.

Lee Cape was given a hero's funeral, attended by more persons than any previous funeral in Pickens County history. The old lawman was laid out in an open casket (although his head was concealed). Marble magnate Sam Tate gave the eulogy.

Two men subsequently were appointed to fill Cape's position as county policeman, but filling his shoes was no small feat. According to an editorial in the *Pickens County Progress* newspaper, doubts existed: *"Can Pickens County get another Lee Cape? Do you know any man that will lay out all night in the cold, sleet and rain that people might enjoy full protection? . . . At public gatherings, he was usually on hand, and when he came up, everybody knew there would be no disturbance, no matter how large the crowd. . . He didn't know the meaning of the word 'fear'."*

Over the years, numerous bizarre tales have been circulated regarding the motive for Cape's murder. The most likely explanation, however, and the one supported by the trial transcript, maintains that the killer was enraged because he mistakenly suspected Cape had discovered his moonshine still, and that he (the perpetrator) was about to be arrested for the production and possession of illegal liquor (moonshining), a highly volatile issue in the mountains of north Georgia. In a rage, perhaps enhanced by alcohol intoxication, the assailant committed an unplanned act of violence.

During the trial for Cape's murder, no evidence was presented which in any way indicated any dislike whatsoever of Cape by his killer, Lindsey Evans. Surprisingly, despite being indicted for the horrifying murder, Evans managed to avoid capture by the authorities. He was never brought to trial.

Twenty years after the murder, an individual held in a Texas jail was suspected of being Lindsey Evans. However, when representatives from the Pickens County Police arrived in Texas, they were unable to make a positive visual identification, and other criminal investigation tools such as fingerprinting, etc., had not been used in Pickens County in 1927. Lindsey Evans remained at large. A Jasper, Georgia physician later claimed to have administered to Evans in the 1950s, as the wanted man lay dying.

Four other men were subsequently brought to trial for participation in the Cape murder. Despite being ably defended by Atlanta attorneys, C.L. "Seal" Smith and Hoyt Evans were convicted and given life sentences. Smith later escaped from prison and was never recaptured. The other two defendants – Carter Wilson and Carter Jones – plead "Guilty" and were given twelve-month sentences each.

An illegal liquor still near the site of Cape's death is presumed to have been the motive for his murder. The still was destroyed the day after his shooting.

The men convicted for Cape's murder were also found to be guilty of the possession and production of illegal liquor. Their sentences for this crime were added to the sentences for Cape's murder.

Little more than verbal accounts remain of the sites associated with Cape's murder today. The roads and communities associated with the murder have either been considerably changed, or have disappeared completely.

In Hinton, Lee Cape's prominent home still stands as of this writing. It has been nominated for inclusion on the National Register of Historic Places. Across the road, in Hinton Cemetery, Lee Cape's monument is easily recognizable. On his headstone, a final epitaph is chiseled: *"Through The Performance Of His Duty In The Enforcement Of Law He Sacrificed His Life."*

Lee Cape, undoubtedly, would have been proud.

News of the murder traveled swiftly. By that evening, a crowd of more than one hundred had gathered... hoping to cash in on the $500 reward.

Murder In Pickens County

Pickens County tales abound in whispered legends, told in passing by long-time residents to curious newcomers. One such piece of folklore – a sensationalized murder involving a woman – is still described by some natives even today, and in 1877, it focused national attention on the county.

The mountainous northeastern district of Pickens County had an unsavory reputation for immorality and violence during the late 1800s. Here was the home of house-burners and night riders of the 1880s who were involved in many illegal activities. And in 1884, Democrats in Jasper – the county seat – celebrated Grover Cleveland's presidential victory by exploding two anvils full of gunpowder, making a racket so loud that it caused area resident Clark McClain to comment, "*They are having this joyful noise away over at Sharp Top Mountain, where there's neither God nor law.*"

Interestingly, the area around Sharp Top, the volcano-shaped peak that can be seen so clearly from Jasper, produced its share of preachers and lawmen. However, the community there was secluded, and involved a very different culture from the hill people or "flatlanders" of nearby Jasper.

The natives of Sharp Top were the southernmost extension of the reclusive, isolated, Appalachian people that represent the stereotypical mountain clans. They usually had no greater problems than any other group, but unfortunately, it seems only the bad news about them reached the ears of outsiders.

A Deadly Party

In 1877, John Hambrick lived on land lot 111-5-2 in the Lansdown, a wooded valley in northern Pickens County near the Gilmer County line named after the area's most prominent family. The Lansdown was always isolated, and is even more so today.

Hambrick had a wife and four daughters, all nearly grown, in February, 1877, when he decided to have a party – which they called a "play," with dancing and fiddling. That he planned such a get-together is strange in view of the fact that his daughter, Kate, would later claim that it was *"the fust time I ever seed a reel (dance) run."* His part in what happened next depends very much upon which version of the account is read.

Nineteen-year-old Catherine or "Kate", was married to Robert Southern. She was angry with Narcissa "Sis" A. M. Fowler, a woman of the same age, for spreading rumors that Kate had been seeing a man named Woods in the cane swamp.

Sis Fowler had been the subject of a great deal of gossip herself. She was married to Taylor S. Cowart, by whom she had a daughter. In 1873, Sis tried to divorce Taylor for adultery, and for having held her head between his legs while he beat her. Cowart deserted her before divorce papers could be served.

Rachel Bramlet would later testify that

she had heard Kate threaten in July, 1876, to *"cut Sis' haunch out"* if her father did not sue Sis for slander, even if she had to do it at a church meeting.

At noon on Saturday, February 10, 1877, the day of the dance, Mary Mealer was at the Hambrick home. She later stated that Kate asked, to no one in particular, if Sis Fowler would be at the party, adding that if Sis showed up, she (Kate) was going to kill her. (Other persons present would later testify that these comments never occurred.)

If these threats reached Sis Fowler, she probably wasn't terribly worried. She and Kate were about the same height (5 ft., 5 in. tall), but while Sis was very stout, Kate was thin and sickly, weighing only 110 pounds, thirty pounds less than even her younger and shorter sister Amazilla Hambrick. What Sis Fowler apparently did not anticipate, however, was a fight with the whole Hambrick family.

John Haynes, Kate's brother-in-law, set out for the party with a group of his friends. "Someone" suggested that Sis Fowler be invited, supposedly to insure that enough women were at the dance, and because she was known to be "a good hand". So the wagon stopped at Sis' house and she climbed aboard.

It was only when Haynes pulled up at the Hambrick house that Sis reportedly realized that the "play" or dance was not at the Haynes' house. She expressed a reluctance to go into the house, but Kate's parents – the Hambricks – invited Sis in and Haynes told her that she might as well go ahead. Sis relented and went in to what would be her last dance. A Pickens County prosecutor would later refer to the Hambricks as *"welcoming her with hospitable hands to a bloody grave."*

The dance reportedly went on for hours to the music of fiddler William Bramlet. Witnesses guessed that from a

This illustration of Kate Southern appeared on the cover of a book which was highly supportive of her defense in the murder trial.

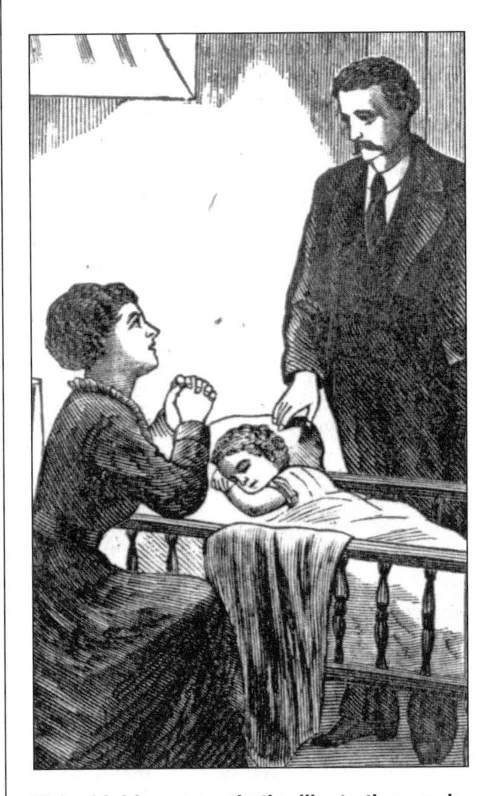

This highly sympathetic illustration, published in a number of newspapers, was intended to depict Kate and Robert Southern and their deplorable circumstances in the Pickens County Jail. Both Robert and Kate were depicted as being much more genteel than was actually the case.

dozen to twenty people were present in a room that was between 14 x 14 feet and 16 x 18 feet. Space for the square dance was at a premium, because the two beds and other furniture were still in the room. Whiskey was passed around, compliments of the host – Kate's father, John Hambrick.

Despite the close quarters, visibility was poor, for it was late at night, and the only light came from the fireplace and a small brass lamp on the mantle.

Kate was on one of the beds with her husband, Bob. She went outside and asked her father for the loan of his pocket knife, to trim her nails and to cut some "tooth brushes" (black gum twigs) for the girls. She left the house but came back a few minutes later.

Cold-Blooded Murder

As midnight approached, Sis was dancing with James Honea. He would later testify that she stumbled and then complained that for the third time that evening, Kate had tripped her. Sis, at this point, reportedly warned Kate not to trip her again. The music then stopped, and all eyes turned on the two women.

According to testimony, there was silence for a few minutes. Kate then approached Sis and said something only they could hear.

Sis challenged her to "Come ahead."

Kate replied "Oh yes, God damn you," and the fight was on.

Sis pulled Kate to the floor, and yanked her hair while hitting her over the head.

Amazilla, (Kate's sister), then joined in by grabbing Sis by the hair and hitting her over the head. At that moment, Kate pulled herself up by Sis' shirt tails and started landing some blows herself.

John Griswold later claimed that Bob Southern pulled Sis back. The struggle lasted only a few minutes. The sickly Kate and the stout Sis started at one of the beds, and then tumbled over to a corner, rolling near the fireplace, and finally to the door. No one moved to stop what appeared to be a fair fight.

The brawl suddenly stopped at the door. Sis fell over on her side, as blood poured out of her breast. Honea pulled her to her feet, but it was too late. Sis was already in her death throes.

Honea then stood in front of the door and instructed everyone to remain where they were. Kate screamed at him to get out. When he refused to move, her husband, Bob, reportedly pulled out a revolver and forced Honea to leave.

Within the confines of the dark room, there was no one who actually saw Kate use the knife on Sis, but no one doubted what had happened either. Kate had cut both of her own hands, particularly her right hand, where she had nearly severed a little finger.

Amazilla was heard to ask Kate if she was sorry for having killed Sis, to which Kate reportedly replied that she did what she wanted to do.

Investigation Of The Murder

Susan Petit, a make-shift undertaker, was called ten to eleven hours later to remove the body. She took the corpse to the house of Sis' father and dressed Sis for burial later that day. In Pickens County Superior Court, she would later serve as a coroner of sorts, a capacity in which she served well.

Petit stated that Sis was about twenty to twenty-five years of age; a very stout woman and larger than Kate. She explained that the body had six knife wounds, one on the temple, one of the jaw, one under the collar bone, one below the breast, and two others in the chest. The wounds appeared to have been made by a knife that was pushed straight into the chest. Hair which Ms. Petit said she found in Sis' hands at the Hambrick house and at the Fowler house, looked like Kate's hair.

News of the murder quickly reached Jasper. According to a traditional account told by Jasper resident Dallas Byess, when Sheriff John Lindsay arrived to search the Hambrick house, the Hambricks and Southerns were washing blood from their clothes. The lawmen failed to find Kate, reportedly because she had hidden in the arch of the chimney.

Kate, to her disservice, reportedly bragged that she was the "man" who had killed Sis Fowler. She and her husband Bob left the community almost immediately, but along with the Hambricks, were indicted for murder at the next term of the Pickens County Superior Court.

Amazilla, Kate's sister, was tried, and on May 31, 1877, was sentenced to two years in prison for her part in the murder.

A Flight From Justice

The governor offered a reward of $150 and Sis Fowler's family offered another $250 for the arrest of Kate Southern. She and Bob, however, had disappeared.

The Southerns remained at large for over a year, at which time, it was decided that more sophisticated help would be needed to locate them. Men like Walter Webb (W. W.) Finley were called "mountain trackers," although tracking, in the usual sense, had little to do with their work. They were really north Georgia detectives.

These lawmen, sometimes working as sheriffs or deputies, and at other times as freelance posses, knew the mountain roads and the mountain people. They knew who to ask for information and what to ask. With common sense, experience, and patience, they enjoyed a high success rate for the apprehension of criminals.

Ex-sheriff Walter Webb Finley of Fannin County was one of these men. He set out to collect the reward for bringing Kate Southern to justice.

An illustration of Robert Southern - depicted as a refined Southern gentleman of means and substance – also appeared in the book written in the Southerns' defense.

Narcissa Cowart Fowler as depicted in a book about her murder and the trial of her accused murderer.

In late January, 1878, Finley finally learned the Southerns were living on a farm near Franklin, North Carolina. With two other men, he arrived at the farm only minutes after the Southerns, accompanied by Bob Southern's father and two brothers, had left in an ox-drawn wagon for northern Alabama.

Finley and his associates set out in pursuit and, after riding most of the day and night, finally closed within a few minutes of their quarry at Murphy, North Carolina. Leaving his party at a hotel, Finley scouted the Southerns' camp. He decided to make his move at 4:00 a.m. the next morning.

The next morning, despite the dark and the rain, the Southerns broke camp minutes before the posse arrived. Finley, with Bob Howell of Murphy, calmly rode on up the trail past the Southerns. The mountain detective and his men then closed on the Southerns from front and back, taking them prisoners before the Southerns could use their two long-guns, two pistols, and knife.

Bob Southern's father, William, and two brothers, James and Miles, were turned over to a local bailiff for having passed through the gate at the Western North Carolina Turnpike without paying the toll, while Finley took Bob, Kate, and their recently-born baby to a nearby house for breakfast.

No sooner had everyone started to eat, than William Southern and his sons attempted a rescue. According to accounts of the incident, Finley and his men were far and away the better of the match-up however, and disarmed the attackers, taking two more pistols and a knife and avoiding any injuries. Shortly thereafter, Bob, Kate, and their baby were in the Pickens County jail.

Old man Southern and his sons would later claim that they had persuaded Bob and Kate to surrender to the authorities and were on the way back to Jasper to collect the reward to give to Kate's mother when Finley arrested them.

A Media Frenzy

The Atlanta Constitution did not report the murder in February, 1877, although it could have reprinted the account from the *Marietta Journal*. The trial and conviction of Kate's sister, Amazilla, was also missed by the *Constitution*. The first account of these events to appear in the *Constitution* was a reprint from the *Ellijay Courier* which described Finley's capture of the Southerns. A news editor at the *Constitution* apparently realized at last that somewhere in this tidbit of information, a story could be found (or made).

Almost a year to the day after the murder, the *Constitution* published a lengthy – and decidedly distorted story – of the whole affair. The article was run in the February 14th (St. Valentine's Day) issue.

Contrary to the facts of the incident, the *Constitution* story "The Fatal Dance" added some twenty-five pounds to the skinny, sickly Kate Southern, to make her *"one of the prettiest girls in the up-country,"* and the simple fiddling at the Hambrick house suddenly became a *"ball."* Here, Kate caught husband Bob *"in a cotillion"* with Narcissa Fowler, now described as a former girl friend. In a fit of jealous rage, Kate, according to the article, pulled out the knife and shouted *"You have danced enough,"* killing the very plump Narcissa with a single blow to the neck that cut all the way to the heart.

As a hedge, the *Constitution* printed the disclaimer that *"the tragedy was committed in the heart of Pickens County, beyond the reach of newspapers, and what we know of it is received through mere hearsay."* However, the newspaper's version, faulty even in describing the Pickens County geography and in ignoring the coverage by the *Ellijay Courier* and the *Marietta Journal*, would be the version that the national press, both pro-Kate and anti-Kate, would use to build their own feature stories on the incident.

Even the local tales of this murder would be based at least in part upon this romantic fiction. If the *Constitution* had failed to find the truth (and had not even looked very hard for it), it at least had apparently found a money-making story. For several issues, Kate Southern articles were featured, frequently on the front page.

A Trial For Murder

In Pickens County, however, the officials were looking for the truth. Kate Southern, her husband Bob, her father John Hambrick, her mother Sarah, and brother-in-law John Haymes had all been indicted for the murder in 1877, and were now all crowded by Sheriff Lindsay into Pickens County's rock jail (demolished in the 1960s; not the restored 1906 brick jail.).

On April 23, 1878, Kate Southern stood before the bench. Thirty-six extra jurors had been summoned to guarantee that an impartial jury could be picked.

The testimony of the witnesses in this case, in the trial of Amazilla, and in the trial of the rest of Kate's family, has survived. In none of this material did any witness suggest that Bob Southern even knew Narcissa Fowler, much less that he had danced or was having sex with her, contrary to the sensational stories being published in the *Atlanta Constitution.*

Kate's motive, given by only one witness and suggested in the questions put to the witnesses, was the gossip Narcissa reportedly had been spreading about her. The witnesses variously explained how Narcissa had been provoked into what appeared to be a fair fight, not knowing that Kate had concealed a knife. The prosecution tried to prove that the dance was *"a deliberate and willful conspiracy, that was planned"* by the Hambricks and their friends to set up the circumstances for the fight and possibly even for the murder.

Opening and closing arguments were not recorded, but nothing in the *Ellijay Courier's* report of the trial supported the love triangle or jealousy motive stated in the *Atlanta Constitution.* S.A. Darnell, J.C. Allen, and T.F. Greer represented the state, and the defense was composed of D.P. Lester, W.T. Day, Carey W. Styles, and W.H. Simmons.

Both sides would be credited with making strong cases. Seven arguments were heard, besides the opening argument. The testimony took up a day and a half, the arguments required as much time, and the jury took twenty-four hours to find Kate Southern guilty but with a recommendation of mercy, if possible.

Judge George N. Lester had seen his share of death on Civil War battlefields, but he announced that the verdict he was about to render – the only one that law allowed him to make – was the saddest moment in his life. On Saturday, April 28, he told Kate to make peace with her God, and, while he openly wept, sentenced her to be hung by the neck until dead between the hours of 10:00 a.m. and 3:00 p.m. on Friday, June 21.

Kate's lawyers announced that they would appeal for a new trial at the June term of the Gilmer County Court. However, Judge Lester met with

No sooner had everyone started to eat, than William Southern and his sons attempted a rescue.

an accident that left him incapacitated and, on May 10, the June term of court was postponed until July.

This was bad news for Kate, but for the *Atlanta Constitution*, matters could not have taken a better turn. A photographer from Canton was hired to make photographs of Kate, her husband, and her baby. The photographs were copyrighted and then printed, not for publication in the *Constitution*, but for sale to the public at the *Constitution's* offices and to other newspapers. A discount was offered if all three photographs were ordered. The *Constitution* advised that *"the history of this remarkable case cannot be thoroughly understood until these pictures have been seen."*

Further Distortions In The Media

On May 3, 1878, the *Constitution* reported the trial and its outcome in "A Woman's Sin," which was hardly more than a rehash of the earlier "Fatal Dance." Previous inaccuracies were actually expanded. The very plump Narcissa Fowler was now described as *"a beautiful young lady, one of those handsome country girls who, knowing her charms, delighted in making conquests of men."* The *"ball"* was now explained as being given to celebrate Kate's marriage to Bob Southern and described as attended by *"all the belles and beaus of the neighborhood."*

Very little of the actual trial was mentioned in the *Constitution* rehash, beyond the sentence of death by hanging. The story did add Congressman H.P. Bell to the defense team, and Kate was described as holding her baby in her arms while the sentence was read. The paper even misspelled her name as *"Sothern,"* an error that was continued in the later articles.

The *Atlanta Constitution* ended its coverage of the trial of Kate Southern by pointing out the censure that former Governor James M. Smith had received for not commuting the death sentence of Susan Eberhart and that the present *"Gov. Colquitt will have to be thoroughly convinced of the justice of the sentence before he will allow her to hang."*

As inaccurate as the stories were that appeared in the *Constitution*, even stranger was the "Atlanta Special" that appeared in the *Chicago Times* newspaper on May 12, 1878. The fatal dance was described in that account as having happened during a public Christmas ball held in Jasper in December, 1876. The former Kate *"Hambright," "acknowledged belle of what is known as the mountain counties"* was described as recently married to Bob Southern, and *"better fitted for breaking hearts than for any practical business."*

After an angry confrontation with Bob's ex-girl friend Narcissa Cowart, in the *"dressing room,"* Kate, in this version, reportedly caught Narcissa and Bob dancing. The jealous wife next entered the dance floor and, after shouting *"You have danced enough!"* plunged a knife to the hilt into Narcissa's shoulder, severing an artery. Not finished, Kate then slashed Narcissa across the breast, cutting through the heart. Finally, with an effort worthy of Jack the Ripper, she, *"like an infuriated tigress, jumped upon the dead body, ripped open the abdomen, and would have literally hacked it to pieces, had not someone attracted her attention."*

Through such publicity, Kate Southern became a national issue, and the *Atlanta Constitution* became the forum for a debate on whether she should or should not be hung, publishing letters and reprinting editorials about the sentence. However, these pieces were based upon the romantic fiction in the "Fatal Dance" and other stories published in the *Constitution*, not upon the court case testimony or the local newspaper accounts.

The *New York Herald* published an editorial that cited the Southern case as an argument for exempting women from capital punishment, while the *New York Globe,* refusing to comment on the reported circumstances of the case, argued against any *"discrimination in hanging on false and sentimental grounds."* The *Constitution* claimed that of the numerous petitions and letters that the governor had received from Georgia and elsewhere concerning Kate Southern, no one had written urging that the death sentence be carried out.

A Saviour For Kate?

In the midst of this ink war, Kate acquired an anonymous white knight. Writing under the pseudonym of *"Mortimer Pitts,"* a lengthy letter in opposition to the hanging of any woman, and particularly under the circumstances reported for Kate Southern, appeared on the front page of the *Constitution.* Pitts reported that Kate Southern's case would be heard by the Georgia State Supreme Court in August, and possibly retried before Judge Lester in Pickens County in September. At the earliest, Pitts felt Kate could be hanged in November. He argued that the people of Georgia would do all that they could to prevent that from happening.

Pitts' letter drew a number of responses and a few days later, another article he had penned appeared once again in the *Constitution.* In a story headlined *"Mrs. Sothern's (sic) Neck,"* Pitts argued that women are instinctively unable to commit murder except under the influence of whiskey or while otherwise not in full control of their senses. In Kate's case, Pitts claimed that she had suffered three epileptic fits the Monday before the murder, and was sick from her pregnancy which, with the noise of the party and the provocations from the victim, left her unbalanced.

S.A. Darnell of Atlanta, one of the prosecutors in the case, later responded that Kate Southern had been examined in Pickens County Jail by physicians who were prepared to testify on her behalf as to a plea of *"Guilty By Reason Of Insanity"* because of the epilepsy. Darnell felt that the defense, having refused to plead insanity at the trial, should not be allowed to do so now. The defense attorneys subsequently withdrew the plea, opting instead to enter a plea of *"Not Guilty."*

Kate was described by Mortimer Pitts as an active church member and as a person who had never attended a dance prior to the one held on the night of the murder. He explained that she only happened to be staying with her parents that evening because of her ill health.

Pitts also reported that Kate's attorneys had decided against any further appeals in court, and that they were going directly to the governor. He added that Kate Southern was again pregnant, and that the baby would be due in October if Kate didn't hang in June.

In a postscript, Mortimer Pitts announced the impending arrival in Atlanta of Kate's attorney – Col. Carey W. Styles – who intended to see the governor on her behalf. It is the defense of Southern by Col. Styles which remains as one of the mysteries of the trial. Styles was from extreme south Georgia, but was well-known throughout the state as a soldier, politician, and newspaperman. Among the twenty-two newspapers with which he was associated, was the *Atlanta Constitution,* which he had founded. He was a lawyer, but had practiced little or no law.

As of this writing, at least one Pickens County native still recounts the tale of Kate Southern and other legends of the mountains, as they have been handed down to him. On the day of her scheduled execution, this individual maintains Southern rode from the old rock jail behind the Pickens County Courthouse, sitting in her coffin, carried in a wagon. Beneath a tree across from the Norton Cemetery, a

"Gregorian Tree" (a gallows) had been erected. Just prior to the scheduled execution, a rider on a black horse supposedly raced the short distance from town to announce that the hanging had been canceled; the governor had commuted the sentence.

Death Sentence Commuted

Due to circumstances such as that described in the above paragraph, it is not difficult to see how some individuals believed the hanging had actually taken place. In actuality, however, Gov. Alfred Colquitt had commuted the sentence on May 22, a full month before the execution was to have happened, and the executive action was reported almost immediately in the *Marietta Journal* and the *Atlanta Constitution*, newspapers that were distributed and read in Pickens County. It is therefore highly doubtful that even something as unthinkable as a mock execution, could have been carried out in order to teach a lesson, even if these officials had been so inclined.

Gov. Colquitt had made a tough decision, despite the pressure by the news media and letters from the public on Kate's behalf. His term came near the end of what historian E. Merton Coulter characterized as *"the golden age of Georgia hangings."*

Colquitt maintained his decision was based upon additional written testimony by respected Pickens County citizens. . . testimony which was not used in the trial. He also noted a petition signed by all of the jurors which stated that they would not have found Kate guilty had they known she would be sentenced to die. Gov. Colquitt ultimately reduced the original sentence to ten years in prison.

No lesser a journalist than Henry W. Grady covered the reprieve for the *Atlanta Constitution* (the only known copy of this article, "Mrs. Sothern's Neck Feels Relieved, "is located in Grady's scrapbook at the Woodruff Library of Emory University). This piece is the nearest the *Constitution* came to a balanced account of the murder of Narcissa Fowler. Grady described the affidavits that Col. Styles presented to Gov. Colquitt in great detail, and then followed with a much briefer account of the county's case against the Hambricks. Three of the signed statements dealt with Narcissa's bad character, including one *"the details of which cannot be published."* A deposition by Kate's husband Bob, claimed that his relations with Narcissa were "criminal," and the affidavit by Bob's father stated that Fowler frequently came to the fields when Bob was working and took him away, usually for all night. Other statements implied that shortly after Bob and Kate were married, Narcissa and Bob stayed alone together late into the night after a corn shucking, a story that had reached Kate. Several depositions claimed that Narcissa had threatened Kate's character and life.

Amazilla's Destiny

A short time later, the *Atlanta Constitution* reprinted an interview with Amazilla Hambrick, Kate's sister, from the *Sandersville Courier*. Amazilla had turned sixteen and seventeen while serving her sentence for helping Kate murder Narcissa Fowler. A note beside Amazilla's name in the convict registers at the Georgia Department of Archives and History reads: *"young and pretty; ought not to be sent to the penitentiary."*

Georgia did not have a prison at that time, but sent convicts to county work camps or leased them to private individuals and companies as laborers. Amazilla had been lucky enough to be sold to Colonel Jack T. Smith's farm in Washington County. She did light work as a domestic for Smith's wife, and had learned to read and write as well as to cut and sew garments.

In her interview, Amazilla repeated the story that Narcissa had been trying to take Bob Southern back from Kate, and added that Narcissa's husband had left her because she was having sex with Bob. Narcissa was even quoted by Amazilla as having said at the dance: *"I knew Bob before you did and have as good a right to him as you."*

Amazilla added that her sister Kate did not approve of dances, did not know that the dance was even being held until the visitors started to arrive, and had been persuaded to stay. She described her family as land-owners who all worked together in the fields. Amazilla also claimed that she had pulled both Kate and Narcissa apart and had only tried to stop the fight. In the end, Amazilla ironically had no interest in being pardoned, and even indicated that she hoped she could stay with the Smiths after her sentence expired in twelve months.

Amazilla's account of the murder does not correspond with the court testimony, any more than did the stories in the *Constitution*, but coming from Amazilla Hambrick, this version suggests that the story of Narcissa's affair with Bob Southern was an invention by the Hambrick family to help Kate or to save themselves from being prosecuted as co-conspirators.

Kate Joins Amazilla At The Prison Farm

On May 28, 1878, in a front-page announcement, the *Atlanta Constitution* informed its readers that Kate Southern would arrive in Atlanta en route to confinement at Col. Smith's prison farm in Washington County. She would be carried sixty miles in an open buggy to the railroad

In a story entitled "The Woman In Black: A Greeting To The North Georgia Murderess," Henry W. Grady reported of her arrival and the near riot at the train station. A mob of the curious, *"probably the largest crowd ever assembled in Atlanta so late at night,"* pursued her to the women's saloon at the train station and appeared ready to storm the building. Men and boys climbed over each other at the windows to see her. Some of the crowd reportedly stood on top of the train cars to catch a glimpse of the woman in black as she went by.

They undoubtedly didn't see much, however, because Kate wore a dark hat and black veil. Having earlier described her as robust and beautiful, the *Constitution* shortly began reversing its estimation of her, admitting tactfully that in reality, she *"was not particularly striking, being tall and slender and with rather delicate features."*

The *Columbus Enquirer* was less kind, writing *"Kate Southern is not pretty even"* but only *"passably good looking"* and *"very ignorant, can hardly read and write,"* and speaks with *"the twang of a north Georgia cracker."*

With her was her baby and her husband. Captain J.W. Nelms, keeper of the state convicts, had secured a position of light duties for Kate cooking and washing for the prisoners at the same farm where Amazilla worked. He even arranged for Bob Southern to be employed there as a guard. A gentleman from Atlanta donated Bob's train fare. Shortly thereafter, Kate Southern and her little family pulled out of Atlanta on the train for Sandersville.

At this juncture, the *Atlanta Constitution* apparently decided that public interest in the story was exhausted. No mention was ever made in the *Constitution* of the trial in the April, 1879 term of Pickens County Court in which Bob Southern and the Hambricks were tried for their alleged part in the circumstances which led to the murder of Narcissa Fowler. A verdict of *"Not Guilty"* was handed down in this case.

The last Kate Southern story to appear

in the *Constitution* was printed on the last page of the March 26, 1882 issue, and carried an account of her pardon by Governor Colquitt. In his executive minutes, the Governor cited petitions for Kate's release from all parts of the state and her ill health, a case of nervousness brought on by another pregnancy. (She bore at least one and possibly two children during her stint at the prison farm.)

So ended what the *Constitution* proclaimed as *"one of the most noted cases ever in the courts in Georgia; one that created perhaps more interest and excitement than any ever known in the state."* After Kate reached the prison farm, the *Macon Telegraph* obtained a copy of the testimony in her trial from the Governor's Office, and printed the entire text. The *Columbus Enquirer* then reprinted the same and added in an editorial that was copied by the *New York Times: "On reading this evidence one feels utterly disgusted with the amount of sentimental twaddle that has been expended on the case. We do not believe there is a single woman, no matter how warm and sympathetic her heart may be, who, after reading this sworn testimony, will sign a petition for Kate Southern's pardon."*

The Later Years

Some mysteries to the Kate Southern story remained for a number of years. The identity of the individual who wrote under the pseudonym of *"Mortimer Pitts"* and who helped to create the sensational account which made Kate Southern's plight a national issue, is now known to have been Henry W. Grady.

Years later, when Grady won worldwide fame as the champion of the *"New South,"* he frequently made reference to a fable which he had invented about a funeral in Pickens County where the deceased was buried with tombstone, coffin, clothes, etc. purchased from outside of the South, even though all the identical raw materials for these products existed in his native Pickens County. Grady had chosen Pickens County – a place about which he knew little, and quite possibly had never even visited – as his example of all that was wrong with the thinking of his beloved South.

We cannot prove that Grady orchestrated the campaign to save Kate Southern. However, as Grady would often answer when pressed about the truth of his Pickens County funeral story, *"Why be hampered by the facts? It could be so!"*

After the trial, the Southerns announced they would never again return to Pickens County to live, but eventually, they did. The "sickly," epileptic Kate Southern lived to have at least eight children. She raised her brood among neighbors who could tell them all about her dark past.

Kate must have known a great deal of unhappiness. At least two of her children died before the age of seven. One of her daughters reportedly discovered her father's pistol under his pillow, and was killed when the weapon went off as Kate was trying to extricate it from her daughter's grasp.

In the final analysis, Kate Southern seemed never able to escape a legacy of violence and misfortune. Interestingly, one of her granddaughters remembered her as "the best grandmother anyone could have."

Postscript: *According to records, Kate and Bob Southern were living in the Lansdown after 1900, raising a large brood of children almost in sight of Long Swamp Cemetery where Narcissa Fowler is buried. Two of their children are buried at Burnt Mountain Baptist Church Cemetery near Jasper. The Southerns eventually moved to Alabama, where Kate died on February 15, 1927. Her grave can be viewed there today. Robert Southern died there on October 9, 1930.*

The Murder Of Narcissa Fowler Revisited

Recently discovered information reveals the sentence imposed upon the perpetrator of this grisly murder in the mountains of north Georgia in 1877 was far from fair.

While working on an oral history of Pickens County recently, I repeatedly learned of stories of a murder which had occurred in the mountains of that county in the late 1800s. After examining court records and newspaper accounts of the incident, I discovered a gory tale of murder, as well as accounts of a judicial system which had been completely manipulated by the media.

On the night of February 10, 1877, Hannah Catherine "Kath" or "Kate" Hambrick Southern, wife of Robert R. Southern, stabbed to death – in cold blood – Narcissa A. M. Cowart Fowler, at a dance held at the home of Kate's parents. Walter Webster Findlay, a professional bounty hunter, eventually tracked down Kate and brought her back to justice in Jasper, Georgia.

Following the trial in Jasper in April of 1878, Judge George N. Lester sentenced Kate to death by hanging. For reasons unknown today, Henry W. Grady, editor of the *Atlanta Constitution,* came quickly to Kate's defense, publishing news accounts which leaned in her defense. Remarkably, in a short period of time, the national press had picked up on the story and Kate's case – quite literally – had become a national issue.

A great debate began to center around an argument of whether or not a woman could, with a sound mind, commit murder, and whether she should then be executed. At that time, this offense by a female and her punishment by execution were almost unthinkable in America.

Fabricated tales that attempted to justify Kate's actions as righteous acts conducted to protect her marriage began appearing in print. In point of fact, however, witnesses at the trial testified that Kate had no motive other than a deep-seated anger and vengeful determination to repay Narcissa Fowler for unsavory gossip the victim reportedly had spread long before Kate's marriage.

On a recent trip to the South Carolina Department of Archives and History, I stumbled upon a bibliographical reference to a work by A.J. Wright called *Criminal Activity In The Deep South, 1700-1930,* (1989), and from that I learned, to my surprise, that a book had been published after Kate Southern's trial. It was called *Mrs. Kate Southern's Sad Case: How A Bad Woman Brought A Loving Wife To The Gallows! The Unfortunate Wife Is Now Dying In Prison!* (1878). (Even the expansive title was blatantly biased toward Kate's supposed innocence.)

The book offers an almost comical account of the murder and subsequent trial. It clearly demonstrates that sensationalism

LONELY ROAD TO AN EARLY GRAVE – On a cold February night in 1877, Narcissa Fowler followed this remote mountain trail, photographed here in the 1980s, to the cabin of the John Hambrick family for a party. There, a lover's quarrel resulted in her death, and a sensationalized trial for her murderess. (Photo courtesy of Robert S. Davis, Jr.)

Photographed quite likely on the day of Kate Southern's incarceration in the old stone Pickens County Jail, Sheriff John Lindsay and his family no doubt took advantage of a photographer who was present to record the incident. (Photo courtesy of Marble Valley Historic Society)

and a tendency toward distortion of the facts were prevalent in 1878, just as they are in some instances in the media today. For many publishers in 1878 (just as today), it was more important to sell copies of a publication than it was to print the true and accurate facts.

The story of Kate Southern, as told in the book, contains many of the inaccuracies as published in the newspapers of that day. And many of these inaccuracies undoubtedly were published in an effort to stimulate leniency for Kate in a complete disregard for the grisly facts. Kate's actions are portrayed as justified vengeance by an injured wife whose husband had precipitated the murder by having an all too public affair with the victim.

"Of course in that kind of country (Pickens County)," the author wrote, *"young women were warmly inclined"* towards the handsome and wild Robert Southern. Kate and her "Bob" are quoted at length in excellent and even flowery English rather than their backwoods slang. The author also explains how Kate, since the killing, has become a mother and that it's unthinkable for her to be facing the gallows. Then, on the last page of the book, a late-breaking announcement describes how Kate, her sentence reduced to ten years in prison, is living with her husband on a prison farm (and again pregnant), and is reported to be dying.

Narcissa, the victim, receives no mention in the book, nor any sympathy for the fact that she also was a mother, as well as a physically-abused wife. Such details, of course, would have derailed the train of illicit sympathy for Kate and the outrage being directed against Narcissa.

The book did include "documentation," in the form of a letter from Kate's lawyer and interviews conducted with Kate by a reporter for *Field and Fireside.* The latter included a description of her cell as a 10 x 6-foot cage in a stone room of 15 x 15 feet with only two barred windows. No comparison of the jail to the log "pen" where she and her large family lived in the mountains was offered.

The author also described in detail how

Kate's husband walked 150 miles from Jasper to Atlanta to deliver a petition to the governor of Georgia on Kate's behalf. It is interesting to note that Jasper is actually less than ninety road miles from Atlanta, and that, even in 1878, the Southern home was only some twenty road miles from a railroad station and easy rail access to Atlanta.

The author also wrote that there had never been such an outpouring of support for the defense of a woman, apparently implying that vigilante justice couldn't possibly be in error. This was a message that was carried in reports of this incident all across the United States.

Through these sympathetic newspapers, Kate's supporters very obviously were appealing to the stereotypes and prejudices of the national reading audience, implicitly implying that Kate's family's Republican politics had unfairly influenced Democratic county officials against her. Kate's lawyers did not overlook this opportunity for sympathy either. They very effectively used the news accounts and wide coverage to place pressure upon the state's judicial system.

Governor Alfred Colquitt of Georgia, aware of the criticism his predecessor had received in failing to commute another female's death sentence, ultimately reduced Kate's sentence to ten years in prison, and later even granted her a full pardon.

In time, several newspapers did obtain a copy of the transcript of Kate's trial, and published it in full. As a result, a national backlash denounced the *"sentimental twaddle"* that had previously been published by the national press. By then, however, it was far too late to change any of the circumstances of Kate Southern's sentence.

After serving her sentence, Kate Southern and her husband returned to Pickens County where they lived for a number of years, raising a large brood of children almost in sight of Long Swamp Cemetery where Narcissa Fowler is buried. The Southerns eventually moved to Winston County, Alabama, where Kate died on February 15, 1927. Her grave can be viewed there today. Robert Southern died there on October 9, 1930.

Before *ATLANTA CONSTITUTION* Editor Henry W. Grady became the "Champion of the New South," he championed the cause of Kate Southern during her dramatic murder trial, using the pseudonym of "Mortimer Pitts" in a number of editorials on her behalf. (Photo courtesy of Hargrett Rare Book and Manuscript Library, University of Georgia Libraries)

Kathryn "Kate" and Robert "Bob" Southern were photographed circa 1909. They had moved to Franklin County, Alabama in the early 1900s. They were buried at Posey Mill Baptist Church cemetery. (Photo courtesy of Robert S. Davis, Jr.)

Pickens County In The Civil War

Nothing concerning Pickens County has spurred more debate over the years than the circumstances of its participation in the U.S. Civil War. It has been reported variously that Pickens Countians were "all Republicans," "seceded from the Confederacy," and raised a Union flag in defiance of the Confederate authorities.

It has also been reported by historian Luke E. Tate in his seminal 1935 history of the county that somewhere between one-eighth and one-sixth of the county's population in 1860 served in the Southern forces and that the county strongly supported the Southern cause. The truth lies – as it usually does – somewhere between the two extremes.

Yes, a Union flag was flown in Pickens County after the South seceded, in protest to the secession. Lemuel Allred, the member of the Georgia Legislature who had pushed for the bill to create Pickens County in 1853, later took credit for the flag in his claim for compensation from the federal government. The flag flew from the courthouse, and in a weird bit of irony, was torn down, not by Confederates, but by a sudden thunderstorm.

Despite the storm's destruction of the emblem, Allred maintained that a local mob threatened to burn down his cabin in retribution for his "Unionist" activities. State authorities, however, were surprisingly sympathetic to his cause.

Governor Joseph Emerson Brown, formerly of Canton and one-time judge of the Superior Court in Pickens County, supported his friend Lemuel, despite the fact that Brown was a rabid secessionist. He allegedly wrote: *"Let it float. It floated over our fathers, and we all love the flag now. We have only been compelled to lay it aside by the injustice that has been practiced under its folds. If the people of Pickens desire to hang it out, and keep it there, let them so do."*

After the war, Lemuel's flag was displayed in the courthouse in a place of honor. Shortly thereafter, a community and several Pickens Countians were named after Union General William T. Sherman, whose name was despised in other parts of Georgia.

Pickens County had no shortage of Confederates or Democrats, then or since.

The *Piedmont*

Republican and some of its other Pickens County predecessors were noted as the only white Republican newspapers in Georgia. Luke Tate's calculation of one-eighth to one-sixth of the county's population serving in the Southern forces is very misleading and in need of qualifying. Many of his "Confederates" were draftees who didn't support the Southern cause and the members of the county militia were required to serve in it no matter what their political sympathies happened to be. Many boys enlisted for no other reason than to leave their mountain farms to see something of the outside world and to seek a change from what were intolerable circumstances. As in many wars, everyone was sure the fighting would be over before the leaves fell.

Luke Tate correctly quotes the Pickens County Grand Jury Presentments, that in stirring support of the South, Pickens County rivaled any county in the Confederacy. This support was not limited to the men on the grand jury either. Miss Henrietta Cunningham of Jasper, a schoolteacher, presented Company E, 23rd Georgia Volunteers, the first company raised for the Confederacy in Pickens County, with a battle flag. In September 1861, "Kate" of Jasper has a poem published in an Atlanta newspaper urging her lover to volunteer, even if he might be killed, *"Ere you return, we'll meet again in that blest world on high!"*

Pickens County had no shortage of Confederates or Democrats, then or since. In point of fact, Pickens County stands out as "Republican" in the history of the Civil War in Georgia not because of widespread opposition to secession but because it had an active pro-Union element that was often, but not always, missing in other counties. A majority of Pickens Countians quite possibly were not active supporters of either cause but would have preferred to simply have been left alone. Unfortunately, they were not to have their way.

In the popular mind, the Civil War suddenly started at Fort Sumter in April of 1861. The reality was very different. In 1832 South Carolina threatened secession in the Nullification Crisis. British traveller G. W. Featherstonhaugh (pronounced Fanshaw) found people in what later became Pickens County still hotly debating secession in their local taverns in 1837.

South Carolina failed to bring on the Civil War then, however, largely because of a lack of support by Georgia. During the crisis of 1850 South Carolina again threatened to secede and again failed largely due to Georgia's unwillingness to support them. In North Georgia at that time, political rallies were held by different groups to show support for the Union and for States Rights, respectively.

By that time, a substantial number of the hardy residents of the mountains had a reputation for being "Union men." Various reasons have been given for their lack of enthusiasm for secession. In 1860 only Samuel Tate (grandfather of the marble millionaire of the same name) was recorded in the census as having enough slaves to be counted a planter in Pickens County. It was only after the railroad later came that the county was able to take its place as the northern-most Georgia frontier of the cotton kingdom.

Not only did Pickens Countians not have many slaves but in their isolation were less dependent on Northern goods and Northern prices than were the planters in the cotton belt. Many mountain families feared that slavery might in time even be extended to include them. They had moved into the Pickens County area after 1832 from the Carolinas and Virginia, from which many had been forced to move, in some instances more than once, by the encroachments of the planters with their money and slaves. Small free farmers often could not compete against "cotton corporations" with large forces of slave labor.

In the final crisis of 1860 that brought on the Civil War, many persons elected the county's delegates to the Secession Convention on the assurance that delegates would vote "No" to the very end regarding the issue of secession. If James Simmons, former Indian trader whose home, the Simmons House still stands as of this writing, made such a promise, he kept it. The Georgia Convention had a very large pro-Union minority from across the state but in the end all but six of them voted for secession in a traditional show of unity. Among the six abstentions was Simmons, who did sign a statement to *"hereby pledge our lives, our fortunes, and our sacred honor to the defense of Georgia, if necessary, against hostile invasion from any source whatsoever."*

The war that followed was not over before the leaves fell. The Confederacy remained almost completely intact for over two years, until the disastrous defeats at Vicksburg, Gettysburg, and Chattanooga, but even during that time, the Confederacy had serious problems. Volunteers could not be enlisted fast enough to meet the army's demands and an extremely unpopular draft law was passed by the national government. Many poor families were left almost to starve while all of their men were conscripted. However, special exemptions were given planters to insure that enough white men remained to supervise the slaves.

As a result, desertions rose steadily, encouraged, as the war continued, from shortages of supplies and Confederate defeats. Soon most of the South's military-age men, draft or not, were back at their farms, with or without official sanction. The South had imported much of its food and other commodities from the North prior to the war, and when the Northern blockade of the South began taking effect, the cotton kingdom was reduced to starvation. Bread riots broke out even in the early days of the war.

Pickens County was a major supplier – interestingly through agent Lemuel Allred of all people – of alcohol to the Confederate hospitals in Atlanta and presumably to the ordinance bureau as well. To ease the food shortage, the first laws against "moonshining" were passed in the South and, consequently, the first indictments of Pickens Countians – doing what they had been practicing for centuries – quickly followed.

Salt was the most famous item of shortage in the war and many Southern families have traditions of such extreme measures as digging up smoke house floors for this precious commodity. Iron, leather, lead, coffee, and many other products also disappeared except for that which could be bought from profiteers. These shortages and problems are documented in letters to Governor Brown by such Pickens County officials as James Simmons.

*Sometime in the confusion,
the jail burned and
the locks from the courthouse
were stolen.*

Pickens Countians did actively serve in the Confederate army, and some in the Union army as well, seeing service in all of the major campaigns. They could be found on almost every battlefield and many can be found the cemeteries there today.

The fighting did

not approach their homes back in Pickens County until the Union invasion that resulted in the Battle of Chickamauga and the temporary suspension of the Pickens County Superior Court (many of the court officials including Judge Rice being called to the army) in the Spring of 1863. The following year Sherman's army began the campaign through north Georgia and the fighting came to the very doorstep of Pickens County homes.

North Georgia became a popular refuge for Confederate deserters, where hiding was easier in the mountainous terrain, and where persons could be found who supported the Union and would help deserters, as a means of helping defeat the Confederacy.

Several expeditions of state troops were sent into these mountains to arrest deserters. As Sherman's army approached, the state troops expanded their operations to include Union supporters or "Tories." In short order, depredations, robbery, vandalism, arson, assault and murder became the order of the day as the horrors of war sprang free. Lawlessness – initiated by both pro-Union and pro-Confederate forces prevailed.

Union sympathizers began leading foraging parties from Sherman's army to plunder the farms of Confederate families to feed the Union army. Since the Union sympathizers wore no uniforms, they could be treated as spies and executed. However, many critics of the state troops contended that the state troops or "Home Guard" were bandits and murderers themselves, who used the army as official sanction to plunder anyone they chose, even families that were supporting the Confederacy.

The Pickens County Grand Jury Presentments are filled with indictments against the Home Guard and specific incidents such as the "Covington Gang" have become legendary. To stop the Home Guard, Rev. Elias Allred, Lemuel's brother, obtained help from the only source available to him – the Union army of Gen. Sherman. Captain Joseph P. Cummings, commanding the 3rd Kentucky Cavalry of the Union Army, entered Pickens County in July 1864. They defeated the Confederate Home Guard near present-day Talking Rock and formed, under Elias Allred, a 125-man defense force to prevent further depredations. Cummings and his men also brought a number of families out of Pickens County to the safety of the federal forces. Under such circumstances, the gratitude of the people of Pickens County to Gen. Sherman is understandable.

The last days of the Civil War in Pickens County can only be outlined from bits of information found in the Grand Jury Presentments. Sometime in the confusion, the jail burned and the locks from the courthouse were stolen. As a result, Pickens County's official records were at first presumed to have been destroyed, only to later turn up in other counties, with local officials who had moved the records and themselves to safety.

The grand juries lamented the fact that public education had ceased to exist and called upon ministers and local churches to take on this task, remedying this shortcoming. That the citizens felt the need to carry guns as they walked the streets was also noted.

A Union flag again flew in Pickens County, that of the federal garrison of Capt. Levi M. Hess, Company I, 29th Indiana Volunteer Infantry, who helped the Grand Jury to meet. The Civil War brought division, shortages, feuds, crime, heroism, and a great deal of confusion to Pickens County. No simple answers or explanations existed then nor can they, after more than a century, be found now.

The 1923 Pickens County Jail Break

Prisons – especially small-town county jails – hold more than just warm bodies. They often are a repository of folklore and tales handed down from generation to generation. Today, all too often, these small "calabooses" from yesteryear are disappearing from the landscape as newer facilities are being built. And with the demise of these aged lockups, many of the colorful tales from north Georgia's historic past are also disappearing. On a sunny afternoon in 1923, the old Pickens County Jail (which still exists as of this writing) in Jasper, Georgia, became the site of one of these episodes.

Most accounts of legal incarceration, by nature, are tragic, but at least one chapter in the history of the old Pickens County Jail (now listed on the National Register of Historic Places) includes more than a touch of comedy, and a fair share of downright heroism.

At 5:00 p.m. on May 23, 1923, Pickens County Sheriff D.P. Poole climbed the stairs to the cells on the second floor of the jail to bring his prisoners a bucket of water and to lock them in their cells for the night. A seasoned lawman such as Sheriff Poole normally would have exercised more caution in such a situation. On this day, however, Poole apparently misjudged the criminals confined in his accommodations.

Among the "guests" on the second floor that day, was Ralph King, accused of "assault with intent to commit murder," and his accomplice, Fred Hill. The latter had escaped from this same jail hardly a month earlier via a route which surprisingly had been used by several previous prisoners. The bars in the windows of the cells apparently had not been sturdily installed. Hill merely loosened one of the bars, removed it, and then slid quietly down to the back porch roof.

As is obvious from the above, the Pickens County Jail was not the most dependable of lock-ups in the 1920s, but then, that's nothing new for this colorful rural mountain county. The first Pickens jail was built in the 1850s. It was two stories tall and made of logs. It was burned during the chaos of the War Between The States.

The second jail was made of rock and existed behind the present-day courthouse. The construction of new jails historically was not a priority for the Pickens County citizens and government. If a criminal was unfortunate enough to wind up there, then he simply had to suffer the consequences of what was known to be inhospitable circumstances.

By 1906, however, the then "old jail" had apparently absolutely reached the end of its useful life, and a new structure was built. It was described in April of 1907 as *". . . constructed with all of the modern conveniences, both to the health and good keeping of the prisoners."* However, fifteen or twenty years of wear and tear by unruly prisoners quickly takes a toll on any jail, and the 1907 facility was no exception.

On the day that Fred Hill escaped from the jail for the first time, he had been visited by his wife earlier that morning. She had mentioned to one of the guards in passing that she would be staying with her parents, so the pursuing lawmen had a hunch where they might recapture Hill.

Interestingly, despite being surprised by lawmen on the premises of his wife's parents' home, the determined fugitive nevertheless eluded his captors once again as he lit out across a swamp. He was later apprehended some 50 or 60 miles away in Rome, Georgia, and had been back in jail only a week, when he and King decided to attack Sheriff Poole.

Despite the background of these two men, Poole apparently did not consider them dangerous. He didn't even holster a handgun as he ascended the stairs to tend to them for the night.

At the top of the stairs, the two men jumped Poole. One of them had a brick which he had worked loose from the jail wall, and the other had a bottle. Poole fell to the jail floor after being struck by the men, and pretended to be unconscious.

Constructed of sturdy bricks, mortar and solid stone, the historic Pickens County Jail in Jasper appears impregnable, even in 1992 when this photo was made. It, however, was anything but secure, particularly on a summer afternoon in 1923.

Photographed at the time of the 1923 riot, the old Pickens County Jail building has not changed in appearance over the years. At the time of the escape, Oscar Champion was living in the house to the left of the jail. (Photo courtesy of GA Dept. of Archives & History)

While the men searched him for a weapon, Poole recovered and began fighting back. The prisoners attempted to drag Poole into a cell, but the determined sheriff continued to struggle. With exhaustion near at hand, the two men finally decided flight was their best option, and turned to run down the stairs to Poole's living quarters on the first floor of the jail.

Not one to be conquered so easily,

however, Sheriff Poole latched onto the two prisoners with all his might, apparently hoping to slow them down long enough for help to arrive.

By this time, Poole's wife had heard the struggle taking place upstairs, and had run to the bottom of the stairs, screaming like a banshee. Jasper resident Oscar Champion lived next door to the jail at that time (his home existed on the spot occupied (as of this writing) by the automated teller banking machine). Champion had been alerted by Mrs. Poole's screams and had run onto the back porch of the jail. Realizing that a prisoner escape was in progress, he ran into the sheriff's living quarters and found Poole's pistol.

By this time, the two prisoners had finally reached the bottom of the stairs and were only inches away from freedom. King finally broke free and leaped from the jail porch, heading towards a cotton field (a site occupied today by the Jasper Elementary School) and freedom.

Oscar Champion had never fired a weapon at anyone before (or since) in his life. However, on this day, he closed his eyes, pointed the pistol at the escapee, and ordered the fleeing man to stop.

When the man failed to halt, Poole yelled at Champion to shoot. Oscar squeezed off a round from the big pistol and the countryside around the normally peaceful mountain community resounded from the discharge. According to Mr. Champion, despite the fact that King was running at an incredible clip, he almost fell backwards in his immediate effort to halt and raise his hands. He then marched quietly back to the jail as the sheriff subdued the other man.

This, however, was not the conclusion of this tale. Things were just beginning to get interesting. . .

The sheriff, as one might imagine, assumed he would simply return his two escapees to the lock-up with the rest of the prisoners on the second floor. By this time, however, the general population of remaining prisoners had been exposed to a taste of freedom, and were reluctant to acquiesce so easily. According to reports, they rained a shower of bricks, soft drink bottles and disinfectant upon anyone who attempted to reach them, refusing to allow the sheriff access back into the facility.

His patience exhausted, Sheriff Poole answered this revolt with a gunshot. The prisoners, unimpressed, responded with still more bottles and bricks. Fifty or sixty men, most of them armed, gathered around the jail and one of them – Felix Allred – directed the prisoners to give up or die (prison revolts and negotiated settlements, all things being equal, did not exist in those days; a semblance of frontier justice still prevailed.) The disgruntled prisoners, realizing they had little choice, succumbed, but remained restless and agitated.

Ironically, the two escapees were eventually found "Not Guilty" of the original charges for which they were being held, but were each sentenced to two years in prison for the attack on Sheriff Poole.

Poole, by this time, had decided to pursue a profession other than law enforcement. He chose not to seek reelection to his position as sheriff.

As of this writing, Oscar Champion lives in Tate, Georgia, and is nearing his 100th birthday. He will talk of the Pickens County jail-break and riot of 1923 only if specifically asked. He maintains he cannot recall what he has done with the front page article from the *Atlanta Constitution* which chronicled his feats that day. The entire episode, for the most part, has faded into the mists of time.

The Cherokee Village At Long Swamp Creek

Two major events in the history of the Cherokees are said, by tradition, to have occurred at the site of an Indian village where Long Swamp Creek joins the Etowah River, a few miles from present-day Ball Ground, Georgia.

Here, supposedly, a major battle was fought between the Creeks and Cherokees around 1755, that resulted in the Cherokees gaining possession of all of present-day northwest Georgia. At the same place in 1782, General Andrew Pickens, for whom Pickens County would later be named, is credited with having forced the Indians to agree to give up their lands east of the Chattahoochee River.

The first of these events probably did happen and the second is documented, but the results of both have been greatly exaggerated to the point that the real significance of the Long Swamp village site to Cherokee history has been misunderstood.

The true Indian history of the Long Swamp area is tied to an important early Indian trail. The "War Path" was a road that on early maps is shown as the principal route between the Cherokees in what was later Tennessee and the Creeks, whose lands were in today's south Georgia and Alabama. The War Path crossed Long Swamp Creek above where the creek meets the Etowah River.

From the 1740s to 1753, the Creeks (aided by the French) and the Cherokees (with support from the British colonists) were at war. Although the specific details of this conflict are not known, the War Path undoubtedly played a major role in the campaigns of the two tribes.

During this fighting, the Battle of Taliwa supposedly occurred. The only account of this engagement that has survived is by no means reliable. It appeared in James Mooney's *Myths Of The Cherokees* (1902), pp 384-5:

"The battle of Taliwa, which decided in favor of the Cherokee the long war between themselves and the Creeks, was fought about 1755 or a few years later at a spot on Mountain Creek of Long-swamp Creek, which enters Etowah River above Canton, Georgia, near where the old trail crossed the river about Long-swamp town. All our information concerning it is traditional, obtained from James Wafford, who heard the story when a boy, about the year 1815, from an old trader named Brian Ward, who had witnessed the battle sixty years before. According to his account, it was probably the hardest battle ever fought between two tribes; about five hundred Cherokee and twice that number of Creek warriors being engaged. The Cherokee were at first overmatched and fell back, but rallied and returned to the attack, driving the Creeks from cover so that they broke and ran.

Skirmishes with the Cherokees in north Georgia were usually bloody and quite decisive affairs. In this early engraving, Gen. Andrew Williamson and Col. Andrew Pickens lead militiamen against the Cherokees in north Georgia in 1779.

The Oostanaula River (left) and the Etowah River (middle, distance; also known as "Hightower" River) combine to form the Coosa River (foreground). The span over the Etowah is the South Broad Street Bridge. Kelly's aborted crossing may have occurred near the bridge. (Photo by Daniel M. Roper)

The victory was complete and decisive, and the defeated tribe immediately afterward abandoned the whole upper portion of Georgia and the adjacent Alabama to the conquerors. . . . It was in consequence of this defeat that they (the Creeks) abandoned their town on Nottely River, below Coosa Creek, near the present Blairsville, Georgia, their old fields being at once occupied by the Cherokee, who moved over from their settlements on the head of the Savannah River."

In support of this story, Mooney claimed to have discovered several Creek Indian names in north Georgia that had been retained by the conquering Cherokees, such as Taliwa (probably Etowah, originally pronounced something close to "Itawa" or "Hightower"). However, Dr. John H. Goff, Georgia's foremost authority on place names, later found proof that Mooney's Creek Indian place names were actually Cherokee words distorted by white settlers.

Evidence of the battle of the Creeks and Cherokees at Long Swamp has survived elsewhere, however. Ball Ground was supposedly named for a story that the Creeks and Cherokees settled their claims to north Georgia lands by playing a ball game – won by the Cherokees – in the vicinity. Some writers have pointed out that the similarity between the Cherokee words for ball game and battle may have led the white settlers into misunderstanding the story and confusing the Battle of Taliwa with an Indian sporting event.

At any rate, the stories of the Creek-Cherokee conflict that led to this battle are also memorialized in the names of Slaughter and Blood mountains in Union County, near where the Creek village at Nottley supposedly once stood. Even Talley Mountain in Pickens County has been credited with being named for the Battle of Taliwa, although the mountain was probably really named for the Talley family of Pickens County.

What is accurately known about the Creek-Cherokee war at the very least refutes that it resulted in the Creeks losing north Georgia. The Cherokees actually lost the war and were forced to give up their claims to the lands around present-day Wilkes County, Georgia. Indeed, when the war ended, the Cherokees were fighting to defend their villages in Tennessee.

While a victory at Long Swamp Creek might have been won by the Cherokees, the battle was almost certainly not as large, nor did it achieve the results Mooney's source claimed. No contemporary account of such a battle has ever been found.

However, John G. William DeBraham, wrote in his report of the survey of the southern colonies that he witnessed a Cherokee army passing British Fort Loudoun, in present-day Tennessee, in 1756. Led by the famous Cherokee headmen Attacullaculla and Oconostota, the Indians said they were going to attack the French on the Mississippi. The warriors returned six weeks later claiming they had been forced to abort their campaign upon reaching the Mississippi. The Cherokee, however, may have actually conducted a raid against the Creeks and then lied about their destination to prevent British anger over the violation of the peace with the Creeks.

How did the Cherokees come to live at Long Swamp Creek and in northwest Georgia?

Angered at white encroachments upon their land, the Cherokees attacked the South Carolina frontier in 1760. British regulars and Southern militiamen responded to these raids by devastating the Cherokee villages and forcing the Indians to sue for peace.

In 1776, the Cherokees attacked the entire southern frontier and were again defeated and their villages destroyed, this time by armies of militiamen from Georgia, the Carolinas and Virginia. Although white losses in these wars probably numbered less than three hundred people, the Cherokees lost thousands as a result of the fighting, and the devastating diseases carried by the settlers and soldiers. The Indian losses were further compounded by the loss of their crops and homes which the militiamen destroyed.

As a result of these wars, many Cherokees began to move down the War Path into present-day northwest Georgia, apparently fearing trouble with the Creeks less than the danger of remaining near the white settlements. That this migration took place when it did is supported by the fact that no Cherokee villages south or west of present-day Habersham County are shown on any maps as late as 1781. The South Carolina militia which destroyed the southernmost of the Cherokee towns claimed that there were no Cherokee settlements any further south or southwest of Chote, near present-day Helen, Georgia. Even this Chote village was reported to be a Cherokee settlement on Creek lands.

The earliest references to the villages in

northwest Georgia are in 1779. British agents regularly visited these villages to incite violence against the rebelling American colonists and to curry favor among the Indians for the king of England against the colonists. By that spring, the British agents were in "Ustanaula" (Oostanaula, near present-day Calhoun) and "Celaqoue" (Silacoa, near where Pickens, Cherokee, Bartow and Gordon counties now come together), apparently taking advantage of the war path. Using this trail, the agents could send spies and emissaries to the principal Cherokee towns in Tennessee, while having an escape route to the Creeks and beyond to the safety of British Pensacola.

South Carolina General Andrew Williamson and 400 of his militiamen set out in August of 1779 to capture the British agents and to retaliate for Cherokee raids against white settlements. His troops captured Oostanaula and Silacoa, but the principal British agent, Alexander Cameron, had learned of Williamson's approach and had fled to the Cherokee settlement at Sharp Mountain, in present-day western Pickens County.

Colonel Andrew Pickens, for whom Pickens County was later named, set out with 160 men for the Sharp Mountain village, only to discover that Cameron had escaped again. Williamson's command destroyed eight villages and 50,000 bushels of corn before returning to South Carolina in September. They also forced the Cherokees to agree to abandon these settlements and return to their older villages in the north.

However, the Cherokees remained in northwest Georgia and their villages became a refuge for British sympathizers, also called "Loyalists" or "Tories," who fled from Georgia and the Carolinas to escape their "Patriot" or "Whig" neighbors. The most prominent of these Loyalists was Col. Thomas Waters, who moved to the village at the mouth of Long Swamp Creek in 1782. As a deputy British Indian superintendent, Waters had been ordered to organize the Cherokee for raids against the southern frontier, to draw Whig troops away from the siege of the British armies occupying Savannah and Charleston, during the American Revolution.

Andrew Pickens, now a brigadier general, was determined to stop the activities of Waters and his followers, although Pickens had very little with which to conduct a campaign. With the 316 of his own militiamen that he could gather, Pickens joined the Georgia militia under Lieutenant Colonel Elijah Clarke at Long Creek, the present boundary between Oglethorpe and Wilkes Counties, on September 17.

Clarke had only been able to obtain ninety-eight men for the expedition and ten of them were volunteers from neighboring Richmond County under Lieutenant Colonel Issac Jackson. Even these few Georgians refused to join the campaign without a promise from Pickens that the general would somehow find the means to pay them.

Georgia's resources by that late point in the war were so scarce that Pickens also had to supply the men with provisions for the march. Pickens' own supplies were so low that his soldiers only averaged five or six rounds of ammunition per man and a third of his command were armed only with swords.

This rag-tag army marched west along a trading path and then turned north on another path to cross the Chattahoochee River at Beaver Shoals on September 26. Detachments were sent out to destroy the villages along the Chattahoochee, while Pickens, with most of his command, crossed the Etowah River and, led by an Indian captive, approached the village of Long Swamp.

The Indian settlement was west of the creek along the banks of the Etowah. The militiamen in attacking the town from the west were unaware of the creek on the east side of the village. As a result, most of the warriors escaped, leaving fifty women and children and a few men to become Pickens' captives.

The following account of the capture of Long Swamp Village in 1782 is taken from Clyde R. Ferguson's *General Andrew Pickens*, pp.273-5, a Ph.D. dissertation at Duke University in 1960.

"Waiting for time to attack, the men held their horses by the reins, lest a stray betray the intruders. At daylight, the militia mounted; Pickens again warned them to spare old men, women and children, but ordered that all braves be killed. To save ammunition, he told his men to use their swords and ride quickly over all opposition.

"The whites then divided into two detachments, Clarke taking a position at one end of the village, Pickens at the other. They charged simultaneously. Completely surprised, many of the red men were run down by the horsemen, but others escaped by way of a creek that flowed through the town.

"According to cousin Andrew Pickens, 'one W. Greene, a very large and powerful man, had a sword of great size, would cleft upon the heads of the flying Indians like so many pumpkins.' A man named Parata chased a Cherokee into the creek and after killing the warrior, he smashed his head with his gun barrel while shouting 'god damn you!' Witnessing the incident, Pickens said that Parata was a fool.

"Later during the fight, David Pickens, a Tory cousin of the general, was captured. When the boy was brought before him after the battle, Andrew Pickens refused to speak to him, and David was herded in with the other captives. The struggle had ended in complete American victory; between 30 and 40 Cherokees were dead on the field, and approximately 50 women and children and a few Tories were taken prisoner. Unfortunately, Waters had fled before the attack.

"Pickens immediately dispatched Robert Anderson up the Chattahoochee and John White down the river, ordering them to raze the villages along the stream. Discovering that Waters had retreated towards Vann's Old Place, the general sent Clarke and the Georgians to the northwestward with orders to bring the Loyalist back to Long Swamp. Although unable to overtake the Tory, Clarke pursued him down the Coosa River and captured nine Negroes that Waters had abandoned during his flight.

"Wishing to capture all white renegades still dwelling among the aborigines and desiring to make a lasting peace with the Cherokee, Pickens sent three Indian prisoners to their people with peace terms. The general said he did not blame them for recent troubles as much as the evil whites who urged a continuance of the war. He promised to halt the destruction of the Red Man's villages if the Cherokee, within two days, delivered all Tories to Long Swamp.

"Should the Indians choose to return captured patriots, Pickens offered to free all Cherokee who had been taken during the campaign. . . . and if they refused to comply, he promised to advance as far as he was able and destroy as many of their towns and as much of their provisions as possible and if they wished to fight, they knew where to find him.

"The Cherokee sent a truce flag the following day and requested more time to consider the terms. Pickens said they must decide within three days. At the end of that period, several braves brought in six Tories, bound in ropes, and agreed to meet for peace talks on the 17th of October.

"Twelve chiefs and over 200 warriors appeared at Long Swamp on the 17th, where, after an exchange of talks, they signed a treaty, ceding a large tract of land south of the Savannah River and east of the Chattahoochee. They agreed to meet at Augusta such commissioners as the governor of Georgia should appoint to ratify a treaty. The Indians promised to remain at peace with the

Americans and permit no Tories to dwell in their nation."

In the treaty described above, Pickens was asked by the Cherokees to define the boundary between them and the whites, as a means of helping to keep the peace. The South Carolina general complied and described the border as the Chattahoochee River and a line from there to the western border of North Carolina. From this incident came the stories that Pickens made a treaty at Long Swamp wherein the Cherokee gave up the present-day northeast Georgia.

Pickens, in his copy of his talks with the Cherokees, made the earliest known reference to the village and the creek as "Long Swamp." The name has stayed with the creek since, although some of the upper branches are called Darnell Creek and Pendley Creek.

A number of people have questioned the name "Long Swamp," pointing out that the creek is not deserving of the name, being "big and deep. . . . its margins do not impress one as being particularly swampy." Dr. John H. Goff theorized that the Cherokee name for the creek was probably something close to "Gatigunahita" (from the word "igati" which meant "swamp" or "thicket," and "gunahita" which meant "long.") Goff believed that the intended meaning of the Cherokee name for the creek was actually "long thicket," a name which is supported by an early map of the region that shows the creek as Long Cane Creek.

Following Pickens' expedition, a shaky peace existed between the surviving remnants of the Cherokees and the whites. More of the Indians went down the war path and other trails to settle in today's northwest Georgia as white settlers moved onto the old lands of the Cherokees in Tennessee and North Carolina.

Not all of the travelers were Indians seeking new homes, however. Marinus Willet used the War Path to escort Creek ambassadors to New York in 1790. En route, he and his party stopped at the Long Swamp village for breakfast.

The village was shown on a map of Georgia and the Cherokee lands that was published in 1795, and in November of 1796, American Indian agent Benjamin Hawkins passed through Long Swamp en route to the Creeks. Hawkins left the following description of what he found at the village:

"Continued two miles down the river and crossed Loocunna Heat (Long Swamp), a creek 35 feet wide; turned down the creek and thro' the remains of the town of this name, there were some peach trees, cotton stalks, and corn."

What had happened between Willet's visit in 1790 and Hawkins' in 1796 to have caused the village to be abandoned?

In 1792, John Sevier and 700 militiamen from Tennessee conducted one of the last campaigns against the Cherokees. They destroyed the villages along the Etowah River and won a battle against the Cherokees and Creeks near present-day Rome. The Cherokee village of Long Swamp, founded as a result of the war path and settled by refugees from the invasions of the white settlers, apparently was destroyed in this last campaign. It was, however, later resettled and is shown on Coffee's 1829 survey of the Cherokee border.

The Cherokees continued to live in the Long Swamp area, and this community even had something of a revival after a major new road – the Federal Road – was opened after 1804. The new road crossed Long Swamp Creek near present-day Tate and a new village of Long Swamp was founded there.

The tragic story of this later settlement is tied to the history of the new Cherokee Nation by its road and, like the first Long Swamp village, with a forced Cherokee removal, this one to the west on the "Trail of Tears."

The Night Riders Of Pickens County

"Many men of many minds, Many birds of many kinds."

(Poem written in prison by one of the Night Riders who died there June 18, 1891.)

In 1889, some twenty odd men in the Sharptop Militia District of Pickens County, Georgia gathered around a blazing fire in a secluded area back in the mountains. They were vigilantes who had dubbed themselves "The Honest Man's Friend and Protector" (hereafter referred to as HMF&P), and for the next two years, they provided Pickens with a period of unwanted statewide notoriety.

Dressed in "weird and terrifying black cloaks and hoods," the men always gathered under the cover of darkness. Their existence was generated out of a self-described need "to fight the revenue laws for the good of the country and ourselves."

The men all swore to protect each other, even if it meant perjuring themselves in court. They would help each other "in bearing the business of life," and promised death to any member who divulged their secrets.

Members of HMF&P did not use their own names in signing their bylaws, but assumed the names of local law enforcement officials and the men who testified against "moonshiners" for rewards (called "reporters"). Members who failed to appear when summoned were fined fifty cents, and an absence cost twenty-five cents. Members arriving drunk at a meeting were tempered with the whip.

North Georgia has a history of such groups. Vigilantes helped remove the Cherokees in the 1830s. Before the Civil War, secret political societies such as the "Know Nothings" and related organizations also existed. Later, groups of mountain men banded together to fight for or against the Confederacy. And the Ku Klux Klan (KKK) served as a model for later secret societies in the mountains after the war.

Although identified then and since with the KKK, the members of the HMF&P were not Klansmen. The Pickens County night riders were not concerned with racial circumstances. Their one and only objective was the elimination of the revenue agents who were depriving the mountaineers from their main source of revenue – untaxed whiskey.

During the first half of the 1860s, the Confederacy had prohibited the distillation (production) of alcoholic beverages, in order to conserve foodstuffs such as the corn used to make the liquor. After the war, the federal government continued the trend, imposing licenses and taxes on the "luxury" and "vice" of alcohol. This "luxury," however, was the only real source of income available to many small farmers in the mountains, and the federal taxes quite simply were more than the farmers could afford.

Faced with the choice of losing their livelihoods or carrying on their occupations in secret by working "blockade stills," many mountain men in Pickens County and elsewhere chose the latter. They had little choice.

The United States Treasury responded with a system of paying local citizens a fee for "spying" on their moonshining neighbors. Persons later arrested were taken to Atlanta for trial, leaving their families with no alternative but the sale of family possessions for payment of legal costs. If convicted (and virtually all were convicted), a moonshiner would be sent to prison while his family struggled to survive on little more than charity.

The moonshiners therefore fought back with violence. In neighboring Murray County in 1888, and almost immediately afterwards in Pickens, Gilmer, Whitfield, and Gordon counties, this resistance became organized. The men apparently were desperate individuals, but beyond their illegal moonshining endeavors, most were not criminals. No record of previous illegal activity has been uncovered for any of the Pickens County vigilantes.

The federal commissioner of Pickens at that time testified at one point that the Pickens County vigilantes were men of good character. They included five county or former county officials.

On a Sunday night on November 10, 1889, the HMF&P had reached a fever pitch in Pickens. They gathered in the "Sea Field" to organize their first raid.

The following Tuesday, they entered the house of a man who, despite their warnings, was in Atlanta testifying against moonshiners. After robbing the man's home of food, some of which they scattered down the road, the HMF&P burned the house, sparing only a stack of hay and a cow and a calf. The owner's family was not home at the time.

The situation was different on December 3, when the HMF&P came down Sharptop Mountain, passing around a bottle en route to a rendezvous at a nearby church. From there, dressed in bizarre disguises (their captain wore "blacking" on his face, a white moustache, purple coating on his chin, and an oil skin coat), they walked to a house on Jones Mountain to pay a visit to another man testifying in Atlanta.

The wife and children of their intended victim were at home asleep when the HMF&P stormed the farm from two sides. The wife was awakened by the noise of the stable burning. Running outside into the freezing cold night, she was met with gunfire, shouts and laughing. The house was burned next, while the frightened mother gathered her children. The leader of the vigilantes mocked the baby's crying.

The HMF&P's of Pickens County eventually burned the homes of at least three men who testified in Atlanta. Folklore and local legends have exaggerated the burnings of the group over the ensuing years to "100 houses in the Marble Hill area."

Activities such as these were common in north Georgia during this period, as small, desperate but otherwise law-abiding farmers fought for what they considered to be their chief means of supporting their families. In Pickens County, however, the activities of the HMF&P were quelled after a brief two-year stint.

When the incidences of arson began on November 12, 1889, a posse of deputies were organized. Local lawmen and federal agents began a practice of rounding up the persons against whom testimony had been rendered in Atlanta. In the first instance of these arrests, the men were brought before the justice of the peace in the Sharptop District, but were strangely released. (The agents didn't know the JP himself was one of the house burners.)

Despite this fact, the posses continued to disrupt the activities of the HMF&P. Some of them fled to other states to assume new identities and lives. Other members remained, but were forced to post "lookouts" and patrols to avoid capture, a necessity which began draining their resources.

In one gun battle with a posse, one

member of the HMF&P was seriously wounded. Other members were eventually captured, and to avoid prosecution, they began informing on their comrades.

A copy of the bylaws of the organization with a black cloak and hood was recovered from a hollow tree at one point. The leader of the vigilantes was arrested with another member and confined in the Pickens County Jail in Jasper. A group of their friends helped them escape during a storm on the night of February 13, 1890, but they were soon recaptured.

The conviction of these "nightriders" proved to be much more difficult than the arrests. In May, 1890, seven men "who a year ago were put down as staunch and respectable," were tried for arson. Evidence and witnesses (principally HMF&P members who turned state's evidence) could only be obtained for a single house burning incident.

The *Atlanta Journal* reported that there *"was never such excitement over the trial of criminal cases in Georgia or the South. Hundreds of men and women thronged the courtroom and the town."*

The seven men ultimately were sentenced to life in prison. Arson, which after the Civil War had become a form of social protest that extended even to the burning of whole towns, could seldom be punished, but when it was, it was treated with a maximum penalty.

At the time of this trial, these seven men were reported as the largest single group sent to prison in the state's history. The convicted men ultimately were sent to work in the coal mines of Dade County, Georgia. Among them was the leader of the HMF&P and his son. He was killed and his son seriously wounded in the Coal City mutiny of June 21, 1891.

The son later escaped from prison on January 5, 1893, and returned to Pickens County long enough to inspire a number of stories. He subsequently moved to another region where it is assumed he changed his name and began life anew.

Ten other members of the HMF&P

A rare photograph, taken in 1889, of one of the "Night Riders" of Pickens County. (Photo from The Pickens County Picture Book, courtesy of Joe Dabney)

were tried in Atlanta for conspiracy before the Federal Circuit Court of May, 1891. Certain of a conviction, their lawyers were announcing plans for an appeal even before a verdict had been rendered by a jury. One can only imagine their surprise when a verdict of *"Not Guilty"* was announced. Despite this fact, five of the defendants were almost immediately tried for defrauding the federal government of alcoholic beverage taxes.

The persistence of federal officials eventually ended the HMF&P throughout north Georgia. Individual resistance to the revenue laws however, continues, even to this day.

A Night Of Terror:

The Whitestone Disaster Of 1938

One of the most devastating floods in Georgia history occurred in a little community in Pickens County called Whitestone.

"Their screams were heard by people, who stood and watched them go, and saw the light in their house, as it swung to and fro." (From *The Whitestone Tragedy* by Mrs. Mark Forrester)

April 7, 1938, was one of those rare days when the weather moved from the back page to the front page of many newspapers in the nation. On the morning of April 8, the *Atlanta Constitution* reported that Georgia had been fortunate in suffering no serious weather-related damage. However, the *Constitution* is a morning paper, and at that time of day, no one had been able to reach an operating telephone to report the tragedy in what then was far-off Pickens County, Georgia.

In the previous 24 hours, savage storms had raged over half of the continental United States – from blizzards in Texas to high winds in Massachusetts. On that eerie night, tornados in Alabama killed eleven people while floods drowned another fifteen. Floods in Rome, Georgia, had trapped 250 families who were later rescued; in Cornelia, Georgia, hen egg-sized hail had damaged homes and trees; in Douglasville, Georgia, houses had been leveled by high winds; and at Fairmount, Georgia, eighteen of forty-two railroad cars loaded with coal had been de-railed by the rising waters of the Coosawattee River.

The destruction was swift and devastating. Mill dams that had stood for almost a century began to collapse.

Across the country, the Red Cross estimated 150 communities suffered significant damage.

On the Pickens-Gilmer County line, the marble mining community of Whitestone had a population of approximately 200 people in 1938. It was a quiet little backwoods community where people set out fish hooks to catch their dinner from Talona Creek, and where the night-life became exciting when a game of Rook commenced.

Located in the Talona Valley and surrounded by high hills and mountains, Whitestone resembled a giant soup bowl, a geographic characteristic which proved deadly on the night of April 7, 1938. The Reverend Walter Payne lived at Whitestone, and in his memoirs, he wrote that the day began as any other overcast day. However, a heavy hail-storm and rain began at 4:00 p.m., followed by more thundershowers from 6:00 p.m. to 8:00 p.m. Then the weather turned really bizarre.

The clouds at this point, according to reports, suddenly became very thick. Rain came down so heavy that it sounded like huge barrels of water were being emptied upon the roofs of the houses from the heavens above, and the sky became a continuous electrical storm, so bright, that you could almost read by the lightning.

Talona Creek began rising above its banks, and suddenly, the whole valley began filling with water – just like a huge bowl. A loud crash was witnessed by Rev. Payne and his family, an occurrence later identified as a series of simultaneous "cloud-bursts" on the hilltops around the valley. Rev. Payne in his memoirs explained that he initially thought an entire mountainside had come crashing down.

The destruction was swift and devastating. Mill dams that had stood for almost a century began to collapse. People awakening at home realized instantly that their only hope lay in a quick retreat to higher ground. One group which had been to a singing at Talking Rock School, had to abandon their cars and trucks as the surging waters rose above the vehicles, drowning out the engines.

Will Ponder, a night watchman at the Willingham-Little Stone Company, was punching in his time card at 9:00 p.m. when he witnessed a tremendous cloudburst on the mountain above and behind his house and the combined house/drygoods grocery of Forrest Carter Conner. He sensed a disaster was approaching, and hurried to go warn the Conner family.

When he reached the Conner house on the banks of what was quickly becoming a deadly Talona Creek, the waters were already far too dangerous to cross. On this particular night, Will's two young stepdaughters were at the Conner house, spending their first night away from home. Will knew he needed to alert the family to the impending danger of the rising waters, but despite his repeated attempts to awaken them by yelling and throwing rocks at the windows, he received no response.

Will next went to his own house, and brought back Howard Lindsey and C.W. Owensby. Ignoring the dangers involved, the two boys, amazingly, swam to a railroad boxcar on a siding between them and the Conner house. From there, they literally swam to the Conner porch, such was the rapid rise of the waters of Talona Creek. They immediately banged upon the door until the family was awake.

With tension rising and the situation growing more dangerous by the moment, the young children in the house began screaming. The water quickly became knee-deep in the Conner house.

According to an account of the incident, Will tried unsuccessfully to throw a rope and chain to the porch of the home, but failed. At one point, he was pulled into the swirling waters dangerously close to the point of no return.

Meanwhile, upstream, the sudden cloud-bursts and rising waters had swept away a sawmill. Logs from the mill had jammed into a narrow gap through which the creek passed, damming up the gap as debris collected between and among the logs. As the water quickly rose behind the logs, it rushed over an adjacent embankment, suddenly releasing the lake of water onto the valley. The resulting malevolent onslaught of water quickly rose to a depth of four feet in an estimated ten minutes in the valley.

Forrest Conner, his son James, and brother-in-law Carl Lindsey (Howard's brother) were now with Howard Lindsey and C.W. Owensby on the porch. With total destruction imminent, they were about to try to swim for the rope Will Ponder had thrown, when suddenly, the deadly wall of water hit the house. The porch, reportedly, was cleanly washed away. The house was lifted off its concrete block foundation and swept down the valley, floating crazily on the terrible waters.

Howard and C.W. amazingly swam to the safety of a group of nearby railroad box-cars. Will Ponder found refuge in the nearby train station (another person reportedly escaped by climbing the station flag pole).

Forrest, James, and Carl however, had shared the fate of the rest of the family. Forrest Conner's last words above the roar of the waters were, "Whatever happens, it will happen to all of us."

Witnesses to the tragedy said that the house floated away with its lanterns still visible through the windows and swinging crazily. Others reported that the screams of the children could be heard above the noise of the water, but Mr. B.L. Green who had retreated to high ground near the swelling maelstrom, later said that no sound whatsoever emanated from the ghostly structure as it rushed past him. The house ultimately traveled a quarter of a mile before crashing into a group of trees and then breaking up into pieces into the swirling waters.

Later that night, almost as suddenly as it had begun, the raging storm ended, but it took longer for the water in the valley and the swollen creeks to subside. Rescue efforts began almost immediately, but in the dark, with mud and debris strewn across the valley, little could be accomplished before daylight.

Howard and C.W., despite being injured, wet, and exhausted, were among the first to begin searching for survivors. The task of relaying the message of the need for emergency assistance proved to be just as difficult, since roads had been washed away or were still submerged, and the steel bridges in the area had all collapsed.

As bodies were located, they were carried by hand to ambulances at the nearest passable roads. When the news of the catastrophe did reach the media in the outside world, it was carried nationally, and thousands of people came to the little valley to offer help, including

The house was lifted off its foundation and swept down the valley, floating crazily on the terrible waters.

150 Works Progress Administration (WPA) and Civilian Conservation Corps (CCC) personnel from Cartersville, Georgia.

All thirteen persons in the Conner House that night were drowned. Oleta Conner, age 6, and Claude Conner, age 8, were found at 6:00 a.m. the next day, a mile from where the house had stood. Their bodies were discovered across the creek and the railroad track, tangled in debris. Eugene Conner, age 1, was found shortly thereafter, a mile and a half from Whitestone. Forrest Conner, age 41, was found next, hanging grotesquely from the limbs of a tree where the wall of water had tossed him. In the afternoon of the same day, Mildred Conner, age 11, and Mrs. Martha Conner, age 33, were found.

On April 11, the CCC workers discovered Harold Bud Conner, age 9, in an old mill dam a mile and a half from Whitestone, and Flora Sue Conner, age 4, in a drift five miles from Whitestone. On April 15, at 9:00 a.m., the body of Carl Lindsey, age 21, was found wedged in a trestle approximately two miles from Whitestone.

Thelma Abercrombie, age 9, was found buried in the mud a mile and a half from Whitestone shortly thereafter. Her sister, Bonnie Abercrombie, age 4, was found next in a drift, and then James Conner, age 14.

Every possible effort was made to locate the final and still missing body – that of Forrest Conner, Jr., age 16 – in time for the family's mass funeral. The search, however, was unsuccessful.

The other ten members of the Conner family laid in state at the Lawson and Poole Funeral Home prior to being taken for funeral services to what, as of this writing, is the auditorium of the Jasper Elementary School. A crowd estimated at 10,000 attended the funeral, and state troopers were necessary to assist with traffic (some 2,000 vehicles) in the tiny mountain community.

The coffins were carried to nearby Philadelphia Church for burial in a mass grave thirty-three feet in length. A photograph of the grave was featured in *Life* magazine. The funeral was a military funeral, and the burial a Masonic burial, since Forrest Sr. had been both a World War I veteran and a Mason.

Thelma and Bonnie Abercrombie, Will Ponder's stepdaughters, were buried at Mt. Pisgah Cemetery in Gilmer County on the same day.

As for the body of Forrest Conner, Jr., it was Ed Chester, a local house painter in Talking Rock who ultimately solved the mystery of the location of this body. Ed explained that he had had a dream concerning the location of Conner. With his friend – Zeb Haygood – Chester went to the site he envisioned in his dream. It was an extremely deep hole in Talona Creek. There, almost completely submerged beneath sand and gravel, they found the body.

Forrest Conner, Jr. was buried beside the rest of his family that same day.

As a footnote and a final unsolved riddle in the tragedy, the heavy steel safe of Forrest Conner Sr.'s store was one of the many items tossed about by the terrible waters in the Whitestone flood. Whether the safe was ultimately buried beneath the sands of a deep recess in Talona Creek or was somehow whisked away by a resourceful looter, is unknown today. It is known, however, that since the day of the flood, the immensely heavy device has never been seen again.

The Amazing Polk County 'Pot Plane'

On a hot August night in 1975, one of the most outrageous drug-smuggling schemes ever attempted in Georgia occurred in a remote area of the northwest portion of the state.

The roar and screeching of bulldozers broke the peacefulness of a humid Sunday in August of 1975, but nobody paid much attention. . . . probably just farm tractors, or crews working overtime to down pulpwood in the sparsely-populated Fullwood Springs area south of Cedartown, Georgia. "Nobody comes by here except the mailman," explained one Georgia Bureau of Investigation (GBI) agent later.

That evening, beneath a moonless sky, several trucks intermittently turned west off Highway 100 onto what normally was an abandoned rough gravel road, their headlights slicing through the forest gloom. The vehicles were headed for the area being cleared – even in the twilight hours – by the hard-working bulldozers.

The presence of these men and their trucks also went unnoticed, for the most part. The few residents in the vicinity had already turned in for the evening, and there were no law enforcement officials patrolling that area.

Early Sightings

Toward midnight, one of the men in the clearing yanked on a recoil starter and a gas-powered electric generator chugged to life. Strings of lights suddenly lit up a stretch of raw earth the size of a football field, newly cleared from the forest and thick undergrowth.

At one end of the clearing, a flashlight bobbed and flickered as a lone smuggler shinnied to the top of a tall pine. He was to be a guiding beacon for a pilot making an incredible landing at the site. The flashlight he was holding was intended to mark the top of the trees at the end of the runway, keeping the appointed aircraft from crashing into the deadly pines.

Just before the midnight hour, a huge aircraft roared low over farms in the vicinity. And for the first time, the enterprise of the daring criminals began drawing attention. Despite this fact, had it not been for two incidental miscalculations, the smugglers might have succeeded in their huge scheme.

"Some citizens down near Esom Hill called in to the sheriff's office that night," explained Hoyt Dingler, a former detective with the Polk County Police who worked on the case. "They said that a plane had crashed; that it had almost hit their house; that they saw it go down. That's when the police got involved."

Another individual – a truck-driver on Route 100 six miles south of Cedartown – was driving along unconcerned, when suddenly he received the shock of his life. A huge four-engine aircraft suddenly appeared before him, roaring low over the forested hills. The behemoth appeared to be just seconds from crashing. The trucker immediately radioed the Haralson County sheriff's office to sound the alarm.

What the trucker and others had seen was a 30-year-old DC-4 cargo plane (C-54 military designation) delivering a shipment of marijuana and hashish from Columbia, South America. It was an unprecedented attempt at distribution of the illegal substances in Polk County. It was the largest plane ever to land in the county up to that time, and carried the largest shipment of illegal controlled substances ever brought into the county for distribution. It was also the most daring landing ever before attempted in the county.

An Amazing Landing

The pilot had homed in on the two rows of feeble runway lights, roaring in from the west where he dropped to tree-top level. His landing lights showed pine branches rapidly rising up below his craft's wings. His propellers chopped handfuls of pine needles and his lowered landing gear snagged pine branches as he maneuvered to land the huge plane on the tiny hidden airstrip.

The smuggler perched in the tree-top waved his flashlight frantically, because, according to later reports, he could see the big DC-4 was dropping down too quickly. The pilot, however, apparently had realized just how little space he had for landing the plane, and he was forced to drop down immediately at the end of the runway – much to the horror of the tree-top smuggler.

"It knocked him clean out of the tree," Dingler continued. "He was so scared though that he somehow wasn't physically injured. . . but he later told me that he "died" up in that tree. He said he looked up and saw the plane coming and knew it was going to hit."

The big four-engine aircraft normally operated on runways of 3,500 feet or longer, but the smugglers, with time running out, had only been able to clear 1,000 feet in their hastily-constructed landing strip. Amazingly, the pilot landed the huge craft in only 350 feet of space.

"The freshly pushed up dirt in that clearing let the plane wheels sink down into it, and that's what held it back," explained Dingler. "I guess 25 feet or more and the plane would have gone off into a ravine and nosed over."

In admiration of the unknown pilot, the astonished Georgia State Patrol chopper pilot, Mac Chumley, said "He just locked it down and slid in all the way. He had to be either a whole lot of good, or a whole lot nuts."

The behemoth appeared to be just seconds from crashing.

One of the arrested suspects, talking later to police, said the pilot had planned to make his getaway in the aircraft just as soon as he could dump the cargo, but with such a short strip, he was forced to abandon the plane.

According to reports of the incident, when the pilot emerged from the craft, he was anything but pleased. When the crew who had hurriedly prepared the strip greeted the pilot, they were stunned by his reaction. He was furious at their meager preparations which could have cost him his life, and equally angry because he had been forced to abandon his aircraft.

Police Pursuit

Meanwhile, other things were beginning to heat up for the bandits as well. The few individuals who had witnessed the huge plane in the area knew it was unusual for the big craft to be flying that low, and as a result, the local authorities were now out combing the area.

Had it not been for these few midnight calls from concerned area residents however, the smugglers and two tons of marijuana undoubtedly would have vanished into the night in the next hour. The 93-foot giant with a 118-foot wingspan abandoned on its make-shift landing strip a mile from the highway remained undiscovered by law enforcement authorities for the next fourteen hours.

While surprised law enforcement officers were scurrying to answer the calls about the bizarre event, the smugglers were hurriedly unloading their valuable cargo. Contingents of the Polk County Civil Defense fanned out over the area immediately in a vain attempt to find what they presumed was a downed craft. The area however, included much thick undergrowth and impenetrable forest land, impeding the search.

Sheriff's deputies from Haralson and Polk Counties were combing the backroads. Shortly after midnight, the driver of one of the patrol cars stopped to examine debris on the road. Before he and his partner could get back into the car, a Chevrolet Blazer came swiftly around a curve and almost hit the two men, speeding away without stopping. The two officers radioed for help and minutes later, the Buchanan Police Department pulled the Blazer over and arrested the driver.

The police officers who had first encountered the Blazer became even more suspicious of every vehicle on the highway that night. They next encountered a large U-Haul truck on a small secondary road and pulled it over. "We thought it was sort of strange meeting a U-Haul vehicle in that area a little after midnight," one official smiled.

The truck was muddy and it was trailing a number of honeysuckle vines, indicating it had been driven in heavy undergrowth. "It looked just like a load of moonshine headed for market," one of the officers later explained. "We thought it had been loadin' up from a still." The Fullwood Springs area had long shared a reputation with nearby Esom Hill as a site for the production of considerable amounts of untaxed alcoholic beverages (i.e. "moonshine").

Surprises In The Hills

Once the policemen – contingents of the Haralson County Sheriff's Department – had escorted the truck back to the Haralson County Jail in Buchanan, they reportedly obtained a "whiskey warrant" to authorize a search of the vehicle and its compartments for moonshine. When they opened the doors to the rear of the truck however, they found, to their surprise, three men sitting sheepishly on a large load of 60-pound bales in burlap, the contents of which turned out to be marijuana.

The large DC-4 aircraft which landed south of Cedartown in 1975. In this photo, the craft is being checked out by contingents of the Georgia Bureau of Investigation, as curious bystanders press for a closer look. Pine branches had been snagged in the landing gear, such was the extremely dangerous nature of the landing made on the small airstrip hastily constructed by smugglers. (Photo courtesy of Dennis Holland)

After they had weighed the bales of illegal weed, the officers learned the truck was carrying 3,260 pounds of marijuana and 84 "bricks" of hashish, all with an estimated street value at that time of over $750,000.

Meanwhile, in the fast-moving events unfolding back in the Fullwood Springs area, Detective Dingler was among the numerous law enforcement officials patrolling the area and searching for a sign of the wrecked aircraft. To the surprise of the lawmen, they could find nothing amiss, that is, not until the next day when the plane was finally spotted around 2:00 p.m. Dingler laughs today in remembrance of the incident.

"The next morning, the Georgia State Patrol brought in a helicopter to fly over the area, and they spotted the plane," Dingler explained. "A man by the name of Wilson Weaver was one of the people in the chopper. I was in a car on the ground in the area.

"In those choppers, you've got two buttons on the stick," Dingler added. "One is for the intercom in the chopper; the other is for the (communications) radio.

"Wilson got so excited when he saw that big plane, that instead of pressing the intercom button (to talk to his co-pilot), he pushed the radio. He said 'Geez, look at that big S.O.B.' Then he started yelling 'There's a person running! We've found the plane!' He could see me (on the ground and was shouting) 'Take a right! Take a left! There's a person running from it!'"

Later investigations revealed that the ground crew had actually created the

A side view of the DC-4 and the airstrip on Treat Mountain just south of Cedartown, Georgia. (Photo courtesy of Dennis Holland)

airstrip in the wrong place. In fact, it was in the wrong state! According to testimony, the smugglers' research had revealed that Cleburne County, Alabama, had only a sheriff and two deputies in a much less-populated area, and that was where the smugglers had planned to make the drop. Had the landing been made there, it might well have been successful.

The 30-year-old DC-4 immediately became the talk of the town. Polk County had entered the drug war on a big-time basis, and folks flocked to the scene of the now-infamous crime. Polk County suddenly started getting a lot of ink in newspapers across the state.

An Atlanta Connection

The men being held and charged with the crime included the driver of the U-Haul truck and his four accomplices. When the five men were searched, lawmen discovered keys for an Atlanta motel.

Assuming they were witnessing the attempt of a huge crime, law enforcement officials widened their drag-net for additional accomplices. Cobb County police promptly staked out the motel identified from the keys.

Their patience paid off. They eventually nabbed a suitcase full of money and additional amounts of marijuana.

"About the time we set up our surveillance, they (the suspects at the motel) got 'antsy' and took off," explained one of the Cobb County lawmen. "When we stopped them, they were really amateurish. They immediately consented to a search... We found a small amount of marijuana and the money. They claimed they didn't have any idea where the $180,000 came from."

"Most of the individuals charged were just college students," Dingler continued. "There was quite a bit of paperwork on the plane. It had had some work done on it and the receipts were all in the (aircraft), so it was real easy to trace it."

Besides the eight men and the suitcase containing bundles of cash, police also seized a blue pickup truck and a four-wheel-drive vehicle. Some of the law enforcement personnel speculated that the Atlanta men had been waiting at the motel to purchase marijuana from the five who had been captured earlier near the landing site. They also speculated that in addition to the captured marijuana, another two tons of the weed had disappeared.

"One of the men that cooperated with us gave us a lot of information," Dingler continued. "It was mostly out West that they were flying in the stuff. He said they had U-Haul trucks waiting. The plane would fly in, throw the dope off, and then fly back out. Then they would put the dope on the trucks. They (apparently) had gotten by for a long time."

What does one do with a big four-engine plane stuck in the woods?

Courageous Pilot?

Despite the arrests in the case, the pilot of the aircraft had not been found. He, however, was quickly becoming somewhat of a folk-hero for his daring midnight landing on the hastily scooped-out landing strip.

A broad red band ran the length of the white aircraft and carried the number

"N67038." The registration number led authorities to the owner, Robert Eby of Ft. Lauderdale, Florida.

According to a published report in the August 7, 1975 issue of the *Atlanta Constitution*, Eby had purchased the DC-4 at a military auction in Tucson for $16,000 and had spent several months and at least $30,000 overhauling it and obtaining a pilot's license.

The paper trail also led to more recent activities of Eby at Boca Raton, Florida. According to the August 18, 1975 issue of the *Atlanta Constitution*, Eby had been flying "touch and go" landings there for several weeks. Then the DC-4 left that airport, and some twenty hours later was seen going down in Polk County.

Two weeks after the momentous event, Robert Eby, the suspected pilot in the surprising landing, turned himself in to authorities in Polk County, accompanied by his attorney from Tucson, Arizona. The lawyer denied that Eby was either the owner of the aircraft or the pilot.

The attorney also stated that his client was an entrepreneur with many business interests, including that of the construction of a prototype patrol boat for use by the U.S. Coast Guard in the chase and capture of narcotics smugglers.

Case Dismissed!

Surprisingly, a year after the arrests in the case, federal charges against the defendants were dismissed, and the case was turned over to Polk County for prosecution on state charges. Ultimately, the defendants were never brought to trial. The largest drug bust case in the county's history was abandoned.

Despite the dismissals, state and federal authorities retained the cash seized from the arrests in Cobb County. And the DC-4 was auctioned for $20,000, with federal officials retaining those funds also.

According to Hoyt Dingler, there were several reasons the case was foiled, including a lack of "probable cause" in the arrests of the men in the U-Haul truck by Haralson County officials. The arrest technique was problematic too.

According to one of the defense attorneys involved in the case, "Under the terms of the U.S. Constitution, a warrant cannot be issued under general terms. You can't search a house or a car just because you want to get in there and see what you can find. You've got to have probable cause."

Also, when the defendants appeared for the initial hearing on their case, they brought an array of "big gun" attorneys with them. With such stumbling blocks in the prosecution's case, Polk District Attorney John Perrin decided the case would simply be too costly for the county to try.

Meanwhile, out in the Polk County piney woods, the huge plane was still drawing curious sightseers from far and wide. One individual who admitted he had nothing better to do, drove all the way from Michigan to join the throngs visiting the 93-foot aircraft parked on the mountainside.

What About The Plane?

The authorities who had inherited the plane had a perplexing problem to be sure. What does one do with a big four-engine plane stuck in the woods? The 30-year-old craft was estimated to be worth $20,000 at that time – if it could be moved intact from the forest.

Numerous schemes were suggested to recover the prize. It was suggested it could be dismantled and air-lifted in sections by giant helicopter. Weeks of bureaucratic wrangling between the Justice Department and the Department of Defense finally resulted in a decision on that idea: The federal government would not undertake the task of removing the plane.

Maybe rockets could be attached for a "JATO" (jet-assisted take-off) as the military did with their aircraft. The Federal Aviation Administration (FAA) however, advised that since the DC-4 was not designed for "JATOs," they could not approve the procedure.

Of course, the trophy could be left in place and turned into a paying tourist attraction. There was even talk of making the handsome DC-4 into a monument to marijuana smuggling. Town fathers, however, were not amused.

Since the accused pilot, Robert Eby, denied being either the pilot or the owner, federal authorities simply took possession of the craft and made plans to sell it at public auction, and that was exactly what they did.

The plane had been trapped for three months in the isolated clearing when Jim West, a state representative from Jonesboro, Georgia, made the winning bid of $20,000 for the craft. Now, all he had to do was get the aging albatross off the mountain.

A Pilot With Nerve

Of all the participants, Rep. West may well have been the most enterprising. Following the auction, he declared, "I'm going to charge $5 a ticket for people to come in there and see me fly the plane out. I do intend to fly it out myself."

West planned to further capitalize on his new acquisition by filming a movie, complete with all the action of the take-off, regardless of the circumstances.

Before any filming of the take-off could occur, the 1,000-foot airstrip would have to be extended to 3,500 feet. The FAA was firm on the length requirement, but compromised on one other. The agency declared it would not block any take-off attempt, but instead would make the pilot responsible for the violation of any rules.

West had the field lengthened, and by March of 1976, he was ready to make his movie. According to reports, he arrived at "Treat Mountain Airport" with three camera crews, two pilots, and some spark plugs in his pocket. However, there was no one was on hand to witness the take-off except for one security guard. For reasons unknown today, West claimed the movie-making required such secrecy that he didn't want to leak any of the details prior to the release of the movie.

Once everything was ready, West, with his pilot and co-pilot, climbed into the plane and started the engines. After months of forced idleness, the 30-year-old cargo plane lumbered down the runway and quickly lifted into the air, sailing off into the wild blue yonder.

West says he ultimately sold the plane to "a guy in Miami," and as far as he knows, it is still carrying freight after all these years.

In explaining his sometime movie, West said "Yeah, we did do a movie on it. We released it as "*In Hot Pursuit.*" He, however, wouldn't elaborate further on the project.

West said the movie was purchased by an individual who took it to New York, and before he could strike a deal with it there, he fell victim to an attack.

Thus ends the amazing and strange saga of the "Polk County Pot Plane," and several weeks of unusual news events in the area. Today, the site once known as "Treat Mountain Airport" has been reclaimed by nature, and newcomers to the area are blissfully unaware of the huge drug smuggling incident of 1975. Area old-timers, however, check twice these days when they hear earth-moving equipment being operated during hours of darkness.

The Wreck Of The *Royal Palm* And The *Ponce de Leon*

The sleepy northwest Georgia community of Rockmart was not widely-known in the state in 1926 – that is, not until a horrible disaster two days before Christmas in 1926.

"I heard the shrill whistle and saw the headlights ahead, but the northbound was not slowing. . . When I saw the collision was certain, I slammed on my brakes and called to my fireman to jump."

–Arthur M. Corrie
Engineer of the *Royal Palm*

The Christmas season normally is a joyous occasion, replete with celebration, home-comings of family and friends, and many happy memories. The evening of December 23, 1926, however, is still remembered with horror by a dwindling number of the citizens of Rockmart, Georgia, and most certainly by the survivors of the *Royal Palm* and the *Ponce de Leon* passenger trains which collided on this date in one of the worst railroad disasters in the history of the United States.

In 1926, with the exception of the Southern States Portland Cement Plant on one side of town and a slate quarry on the opposite side, Rockmart, for the most part, was a sparsely-settled township, known mostly as a farming community in Polk County. To the surprise of many, however, despite its small size, it had enjoyed passenger rail service since the earliest days of the railroad in the county in the 1870s. This was due in no small measure to one of the community's early residents, Seaborn Jones.

According to tradition, Jones, in return for the donation of his property for railroad rights-of-way, had stipulated that the community of 'Rock Mart' (as it was known then) always be provided with railroad passenger service. It was this passenger service, and the strict timetables followed by the railroad, which quite possibly set the stage for disaster in 1926.

On that fateful day, the *Royal Palm* and the *Ponce de Leon* – both crack passenger trains of Southern Railway – were filled near capacity with happy travelers. Both trains were renowned for their good food, accommodations – and timely schedules. December 23rd was no exception, as both trains traveled toward a date with destiny.

Leonora (Mrs. Robert Henry) Mintz was seventeen years of age on the day of the accident. As of this writing, she lives not thirty feet from the tracks of the Norfolk-Southern Railroad (formerly Southern Railroad) in Rockmart, and

Freight trains still thunder down the same line on which the *Royal Palm* and the *Ponce de Leon* collided two days before Christmas in 1926. (Photo by Olin Jackson)

Another view of the wrecked cars from the *Ponce de Leon* and *Royal Palm* trains. This photograph was taken from a cotton field at the approximate spot at which the Goodyear Mills complex stands today in Rockmart. (Photo courtesy of Rockmart Library)

The mill town of Rockmart, Georgia was photographed in the early 1900s from a hill above the community. A trestle on the Southern Railway is visible in the distance.

approximately one mile from the scene of the 1926 disaster. Though it has been over 66 years, she says she can still remember that fateful Christmas.

"We lived on our family farm (near the site of present-day East Side Elementary School) at that time," Mrs. Mintz explained in an interview in the early 1990s. "We heard the crash all the way from there. It was so loud, we thought it was thunder."

That December evening was a dark and rainy night in the foothills of north Georgia. Despite the miserable weather and gloom outside, the Pullman coaches in the *Ponce de Leon* must have been warm and alive with diners and Christmas cheer.

It was at a long side-track at Rockmart that the *Royal Palm* and the *Ponce de Leon* regularly passed each other. The Southern Railroad through Rockmart was not double-tracked, so the side-track at the Rockmart depot made it possible for these two luxury trains to continue their destinations in opposite directions.

According to records, Engineer Arthur M. Corrie on the *Royal Palm* had throttled down and was easing his locomotive southward at approximately 4 miles per hour, waiting for the north-bound *Ponce de Leon* to take the siding as scheduled. To his horror, however, Corrie suddenly realized that not only was the huge locomotive in the distance not taking the siding, it was bearing down on him at a considerable rate of speed.

As an experienced trainman, Corrie knew that he had just enough time to yell a warning to his fireman, pull on the whistle-cord as another warning to his passengers, and then to jump from the train. After he had jumped, the next thing Corrie heard was the horrendous blast from the collision, the grinding of metal, and the screeching of the rails.

According to reports, Corrie later told Interstate Commerce Commission (ICC) investigators that he turned and watched as the *Ponce de Leon*, traveling at approximately fifty miles an hour or better, crashed head-long into his beloved *Royal Palm*.

"I will never forget it," Corrie later stated. "It sounded like the heavens had split open. I don't want to ever hear anything like it again."

Despite the enveloping darkness and rain on the fateful evening, the noise of the crash immediately brought local residents running to the crash site. The provision of help to the injured and dying proved a challenge for the citizens of the tiny, poorly-equipped community, for the carnage at the wreck site was almost overwhelming.

"When the *Royal Palm* and the *Ponce de Leon* collided, we weren't allowed to go up there to see it, because it was just too horrible," Mrs. Mintz explained emphatically, still shaken by the tragedy. "A friend of mine told me she and some other friends went to the wreck, and she said they saw the best-looking gentleman in a car. All of a sudden, it seemed like his head just rolled off his shoulders. He had been decapitated.

"Rockmart was a very rural area back then," Mrs. Mintz continued. People were begging for help. We had no ambulances here at that time. Some people were carried in private automobiles to Rome (Georgia); some others were carried as far away as Atlanta. It was just chaos."

One can only imagine today the misery and pain endured by the injured as they were carried out of the wrecked train cars and huddled into automobiles for a long, bumpy ride to a hospital many miles away. It is not known today how many victims died of their injuries enroute to hospitals and doctors.

Mr. Hal Clements, a retired educator and a native of Rockmart who, as of this writing, lives in Atlanta, was a lad of 11 at the time of the disaster. He and his family resided on Bluff Street in Rockmart. He remembered traveling with his father to the wreck shortly after it occurred.

"It happened just east of the present-day Goodyear Mill complex in an area we used to call 'Barber's Woods'," Clements explained. "I was only eleven

A side-track, located at almost the identical spot of the siding which was the focal point of the 1926 collision, still existed in Rockmart as of this writing. (Photo by Olin Jackson)

The Southern Railway Depot in Rockmart as it appeared in the early 1900s. The *Ponce de Leon* and the *Royal Palm* both made stops at this depot for passengers and freight.

Photographed just a few hours after the collision, the devastation from the impact is clearly visible. Curious onlookers view the two locomotives. Two other individuals are bent over what appears to be a victim. (Photo courtesy of Atlanta Historic Society)

years old, so I don't remember a lot. I do recall, however, that the steam was still rising from the locomotives. And I remember later that they brought a lot of boxes down to Cochran's Funeral Home.

"My father drove immediately to the accident, because he wanted to help in any way he could," Clements continued. "As I remember, I held onto my father's hand the whole time. I knew there were a lot of bodies in those crushed cars."

Much of the horror of the disaster was caused by the Pullman cars of the *Ponce de Leon* which telescoped into each other when they met the immovable force of the huge locomotive which suddenly had come to a halt. The impact was horrendous – crushing and mutilating passengers as the heavy cars crashed into each other.

After the shock of the initial crash had passed, the screams of the dying and injured passengers – many of whom were trapped beneath the wreckage – horribly filled the night. The *Associated Press* reported *"The screams of women pinned beneath the wreckage were mingled with the hoarse shouts of men and the prayers of a Negro waiter when he was released, uninjured, from a hole in the side of the dining car."*

According to the Rome, Georgia *News-Tribune*, *"The scene. . . tested the strength of strong men. Bodies of victims crushed and mangled beyond description were . . . unreachable because of tons of weight upon them. The roof of the diner was rolled up like paper. The body of one man was hanging from a window, his legs pinned beneath the heavy weight."*

Most of the residents of Rockmart were unprepared for the trauma involved in a disaster of the magnitude of the 1926 wreck. Some rescuers went about their work numbly; others found themselves unable to continue.

"After the survivors had all been removed, they finally had to get some of the men about half drunk, I think," Mrs. Mintz continued, before they'd go back into the wreck. They'd try to lift a body and it would just fall apart. Even after we returned to school (Rockmart School just across the tracks from the wreck site) following the Christmas holidays, there were still body parts in some of the wreckage. It really was tragic – a terrible thing."

Most sources today agree there were approximately 20 fatalities as a result of the collision. The official Interstate Commerce Commission report, filed January 11, 1927, reported that 11 passengers, 7 Southern Railway employees, and 1 news agent were killed (a total of 19 deaths as of that date; others may have died at a later date as a result of injuries from the disaster.). The report went on to explain that 113 passengers, 4 Southern Railway employees and 6 Pullman employees were injured in the wreck.

On December 24, the front page of *The Atlanta Georgian* trumpeted "18 Dead In Wreck." Due to the confusion which reigned at the scene of the accident and the inaccuracies in news reports of that day, several variations of the death count were published.

The dead in the *Ponce de Leon* included Road Foreman of Engines, Robert M. Pierce, who had assumed the engineer's duties from the regular engineer shortly before the crash. An arm and a leg were amputated from Pierce in a futile effort to save his life, but he succumbed shortly thereafter. Also dead was the fireman in the engine with him – H.R. Moss – who was killed instantly. W.H. Brewer, the baggagemaster, died a few hours later.

Others listed as dead in the December 24, 1926 issue of *The Atlanta Georgian* were:

- Dr. P.T. Hale, 69, a professor of evangelism at Southern Baptist Seminary in Louisville, KY.
- W.L. Dynes, 56, an Atlanta real estate developer who lived at 951 Courtney Dr.
- J.E. Frost of 509 Foster St., Chattanooga, TN.
- L.B. Evans of Lebanon, KY, Kansas City and Jacksonville, FL addresses.
- Mrs. J.W. Whitaker of Chattanooga, TN.

- Goldie Williams, the infant daughter of Mrs. Alice Williams of Detroit, MI.
- J.W. Whisenhunt of Aragon, GA.
- W.I. Dowie, Jr. of Jacksonville, FL.
- A young boy, age approximately 8 years, believed to have been the son of Mrs. George Hardy of Toronto.
- A young girl, age approximately 10 years, with the initials H.M.H. on a bracelet, believed to have been the daughter of Mrs. Hardy.
- Six other individuals were unidentified: two white and four Negro.

Those listed as injured in the same article were:

- Mrs. George Hardy of Toronto.
- J.W. Dosser of Chattanooga, TN.
- F.W. Swann of Bolton, GA.
- Will Kuhn of St. Louis, MO.
- L.I. Seibert of Chattanooga, TN.
- Corporal Gus Rusts of Ft. Oglethorpe, GA.
- Dan Lobrugh of Cincinnati, OH.
- Robert Hilty of Lansing, MI.
- Edward Wiseman of Louisville, KY.
- H.E. Bullis of Lexington, KY.
- R.L. Bateman of Macon, GA.
- Mrs. J.J. Finlay of Chattanooga, TN.

As for the *Royal Palm*, the injuries were much less severe, and there were no fatalities. Much of this was due undoubtedly to the slow speed of the *Royal Palm* as its heavy engine impacted the *Ponce de Leon.*

"The hand of providence guided the destiny of the Royal Palm last night," Corrie told a reporter at his home Friday morning following the accident. *"I was barely moving, pulling my engine along about 4 miles per hour as I neared the switch at the siding. I was obeying orders to await the Ponce de Leon which was to pull up and go into the siding so I could pass. When I saw the collision was certain, I slammed on my brakes and called to my fireman to jump. I jumped to the ground and rolled down a steep embankment. I don't suppose I was 30 feet away when the two engines met. . . . I fully expected the engine and cars to topple over and roll down upon me, but they didn't."*

Though his counterpart on the *Ponce de Leon* was killed in the accident, Arthur M. Corrie, engineer of the *Royal Palm*, jumped from his train as he realized disaster was imminent. He miraculously lived to tell of the incident.

The *Royal Palm* consisted of one club car, five Pullman sleeping cars, one dining car and two Pullman sleeping cars of all-steel construction. They were pulled by Engine #1456.

The *Ponce de Leon* consisted of one combination car (half baggage & half coach), one coach, one dining car, and seven Pullman sleeping cars, all of steel construction, pulled by Engine #1219.

Following the impact, both engines were derailed, but miraculously remained upright. Engine #1219 (*Ponce de Leon*) was badly damaged and its tender was torn from its frame and thrown down the embankment on the inside of the curve. The combination car was telescoped at its forward end nearly the length of the baggage compartment. The coach immediately following it telescoped into the dining car.

The specific cause of the accident is still not known to this day, and many ques-

The terrible collision caused the railroad cars to "telescope" into one another. In this photo, the daycoach has jammed crushingly into the dining car. It was in this car that many of the passengers were killed and mutilated. (Photo courtesy of Atlanta Historic Society)

Another view of the mayhem at the tragedy. (Photo courtesy of Atlanta Historic Society)

An individual photographed in front of one of the engines in the collision.

tions linger. What about the switch controlling the entrance to the siding? Much speculation has centered around this device. It is not known today if it (the switch) was open to admit the *Ponce de Leon* to the siding, but even if it had been open, the *Ponce de Leon* was moving at a rate of speed much too great to have allowed it to negotiate the arc of the turn leading into the switch.

The mountain descent down into Rockmart can be a perilous route. As recently as 1961, another train – this time a freight – was derailed in almost the identical spot as the 1926 disaster, causing an immense catastrophe in its own right. Speed and a lack of familiarity with the incline from the Braswell Mountains into Rockmart quite possibly played a role in that accident, and are suspected as prime catalysts in the 1926 disaster as well.

Just a few moments prior to the 1926 accident, S.J. Keith, the regular engineer, was directed by Pierce to *"go back into the train."* According to Keith's later statement, Pierce was running behind time at a high rate of speed, *"dropping down off the mountain below Rockmart."*

According to the 1927 Interstate Commerce Commission report on the accident, *"When it (the Ponce de Leon) stopped at McPherson, 11.4 miles south of Rockmart, for the purpose of meeting an opposing train, Road Foreman of Engines Pearce, who had been riding in the combination car, boarded the engine and took charge of it, Engineman Keith going back to ride in the combination car.*

"Train first No. 2 (the Ponce de Leon) departed from McPherson at 6:23 p.m., 15 minutes late, passed Braswell, 6.4 miles from McPherson, at 6:35 p.m., 16 minutes late, passed the south passing track switch at Rockmart and collided with train #101 while

traveling at a speed believed to have been approximately 50 miles per hour."

Some individuals have speculated that the blinding rain, coupled with Pierce's unfamiliarity with a newly-installed switch-head, were responsible for the tragedy. Others have maintained that in the driving rain, Pierce mistook a freight engineer's signal from a siding further up the line as the *Royal Palm's* signal that all was clear. This, at the very least, might provide a measure of explanation for Pierce's obvious decision to continue on at top speed without taking the proper side track.

The Interstate Commerce Commission report, however, concluded that the wreck occurred because Road Foreman of Engines Pierce, who had relieved Engineman Keith, either failed to have a thorough understanding with the engineman as to the contents of Train Order #92 (requiring him to take the siding), or else forgot it.

The true reason for the tragedy may never be known, since this information departed with Robert M. Pierce when he succumbed to his injuries shortly after the wreck. However, as of this writing in the early 1990s, there are some long-time former employees who have developed interesting opinions and theories over the years.

Mr. H.D. "Cowboy" Mintz, a retired Southern Railways senior conductor and the son of Mrs. R.H. Mintz of Rockmart, says passenger train crews always consisted of the oldest men on the seniority list. Therefore, most of the Southern Railway employees from the *Ponce de Leon* and the *Royal Palm* who were involved in the accident were either deceased or retired by the time he was employed by Southern in the mid-1940s. A few, however, were still around, and shared their thoughts with him.

"I worked with Nath Turner, an engineer on the *Royal Palm*; Henry Sorrells, the conductor; and Harry Smith, the flagman," Mintz relates. "Harry told me he and Henry were up in the cupola on the caboose on the rear of the *Royal Palm*, and they could hear the *Ponce de Leon* 'still working steam' as it was approaching. The whole train should have been coasting down the grade by that point. He always thought Bob Pierce was attempting to make up the lost time the train was suffering from."

But Mr. Mintz also says there have been rumors over the years of a personal vendetta between Keith and Pierce. There has also been speculation regarding the possibility that this may have played a role in the disaster.

When Keith was relieved of control of the engine by Pierce at McPherson, could he (Keith) possibly have intentionally neglected to inform Pierce that the *Ponce de Leon* was to take the siding in Rockmart? Surely Keith would have known that failure to communicate these instructions to Pierce would have meant almost certain death or injury to himself.

The Interstate Commerce Commission report however, states unequivocally, that "After the accident, Mr. Copeland assisted in removing Road Foreman of Engines Pearce from his engine and he said the road foreman asked him how the accident had occurred. When told that he had failed to take the siding for train #101 (the *Royal Palm*), he replied that Engineman Keith, Fireman Moss and everyone concerned had told him that he was to hold the main track."

"Harry Smith's personal observation, Engineer Keith's statement that he explained the conditions of the orders to Pierce, and the theory of a personal vendetta between Keith and Pierce will always add to the mystery of the Rockmart wreck," Mr. Mintz added. "We'll never know the answer for certain."

Despite occasional mishaps on the railroad, it remains as one of the most viable (and safe) forms of transportation in our nation today. With any luck at all, Rockmart, with its railroad rights-of-way still intact, has a promising future, and will hopefully close the door forever on the disaster of a grim Christmas in 1926.

Frontier Gunslingers: The Asa Prior Family

Though one of the most colorful and successful families in the history of Polk County, the Priors are also remembered for being involved in one of the bloodiest feuds on record there.

After the Georgia land lottery of 1832, large numbers of white settlers began moving in and taking over the lands of the Cherokee Indians. Some of the richest farm land – Paulding County's Cedar Valley – was drawing the adventurous and ambitious to the area. Among them was a family called Prior, a name which would become synonymous with the epic history of the county during the dark days of the U.S. Civil War.

By the time that the U.S. Army had rounded up the last Cherokees in 1838 for removal west, settlements were springing up and developing into towns like Cedartown, with farms and shops, schools and churches, roads and post offices. Led by family patriarch, Asa, the Priors were one of the earliest families to arrive, and prospered greatly, not only from farming, but from buying and selling land.

The Priors were not strangers to tragedy. Five of their fourteen children had been born deaf.

In the early 1800s, traders, hunters, and hoards of prospectors had been continually scouting the Cherokee Indian Territory. About 1826, two scouts – Linton Walthall and Hampton Whatley – visited the area along Cedar Creek. Both men envisioned a bright future for this fertile valley.

After the state legislature created ten new counties from the Cherokee lands in 1832 and conducted land lotteries, Walthall and Whatley established trading posts in the vicinity of the beautiful valley they had discovered. Walthall located his post above one of the largest springs in the territory, and Whatley chose a spot near Tanyard Branch, a little creek south of the new village already beginning to take shape along Cedar Creek.[1]

The Asa Prior Family

Before Asa Prior moved to Cedar Valley, he had lived in Morgan County, Georgia, near Madison, where he had built a blacksmith shop, working long and hard hours as the village smithy. Over a 25-year period, "Sally," as Prior referred to his beloved wife, bore him 14 children. Three of these had died and one had married by the time the Priors moved to their new home in Paulding (later Polk) County.[2]

According to records, the blacksmith from Morgan County was among the very first settlers in Paulding, arriving in 1832.[3] For the first year or two, the living conditions for the newcomers undoubtedly were primitive and exhausting, in spite of the availability of slaves for the heaviest labor. The hardy settlers found abundant game, timber, and water, but farm land had to be cleared, planted and maintained. It was a long and arduous process.

A log shelter also had to be completed promptly for the family. When W.O.B. Whatley arrived about 1832, his family lived in a rude log cabin for two years until he could construct their fine home. *(Readers please see "Namesake Of Collard Valley," A North Georgia Journal of History, Volume III, published by Legacy Communications, Inc.)*

It is not known today exactly where the Priors first lived in Cedar Valley, but in 1848, Asa reportedly built a substantial structure in the center of the new community, not far from the Big Spring. That house still stands as of this writing, but Asa Prior would not recognize it.

Mrs. J.W. Pickett, a later owner of the Prior home, had the house jacked up and rotated 90 degrees, all accomplished by lowering the house onto logs lubricated liberally with grease. Instead of fronting on East Avenue as originally constructed by the

John T. Prior was photographed in 1899 in Cedartown with his mother, Ann M. Prior (far right), and his daughter, Anna Lou Davis. (Photo courtesy of Polk County Historical Society)

The old Polk County Courthouse and Jail were photographed in the early 1900s. In 1852, Asa Prior sold 19 acres – including the rights and access to the big spring on the site – to the city of Cedartown for $1,200.

This 1864 illustration by W.D. Matthews was published in *Harper's Weekly*. It depicts a raid on a Southern plantation much similar to the lawlessness of northern Georgia during this period.

Cedartown was one of many communities burned to the ground by Gen. Sherman's troops during the U.S. Civil War. However, by 1899 when this photo was taken, the town had rebounded and appeared to be a lively city once again. This view of the town shows Main Street.

It was the large spring in the vicinity of what today is downtown Cedartown which originally attracted early settlers to the area. Photographed here circa 1918, the spring water was being pumped to homes in the area. This property was once owned by Asa Prior.

Photographed in the mid-1990s, the old water plant was still being used to pump the clear spring water to area homes and businesses.

elder Prior, the house was turned to face North College Street. After still more changes by later owners, the house gained a considerably different appearance. It serves today as Gammage Funeral Home.

During his early years in Cedar Valley, Asa Prior suffered a great tragedy. His wife, Sarah – who was so dear to him – died on January 2, 1838, at age 54. The spot chosen to receive Sarah Prior's remains, some say, quite likely was near an earlier Prior home. Her gravestone, the first in that little cemetery a mile south of the center of town, still stands, but the passage of time has virtually erased the date and a touching epitaph:

Sleep on my loving wife sleep
This world shall thy memory keep
But deeper on my heart is graven
The thought that we shall meet in heaven.[4]

The Priors were not strangers to tragedy. Five of their fourteen children had been born deaf. One can only imagine the anxious parents gently tinkling a little bell or some other attention-getter near the ear of the latest newborn, waiting patiently – but in vain – for the first response from the infant.

Throughout his life, Asa Prior was deeply concerned with caring for his handicapped children. Prior's last will and testament is a tangible reminder of his angst. In this document, he provides a life-long income for each of his deaf children, painfully but firmly identifying them as "deaf and dumb."[5]

Prior Landmarks

Asa Prior appears to have been a charter member of Cedartown's Baptist church. In 1835, the Baptists rented a building located on a knoll above Tanyard Branch which served as both church and school. (The site may later have included the cemetery where Asa's wife was buried.)

After a period of ten years, the congregation decided to build a proper church. A tract of property with a beautiful grove along what would become Main Street and West Avenue was donated for the purpose. One acre for the site of the new church and graveyard was donated by Asa Prior,[6] and the adjacent acre was contributed by William E. West.[7]

The church and graveyard stood where the First National Bank of Polk County stands (as of this writing) on West Avenue near Main Street. *(Author's Note: When workmen were preparing a parking lot for the bank, they reportedly discovered old graves and had to reconsider their plans.)* A second church on a new site replaced the first in 1891, but today, both of the old churches have disappeared, replaced by a handsome modern structure.[8]

The one building most often associated with Asa Prior – a gristmill – still stands as of this writing in Cedartown. It wasn't that there was a scarcity of mills. There, in fact, were several gristmills within a short ride. Just as with today's fast food chains, however, there quite likely was simply a measure of 19th century commercial over-development.

The fact there already were several gristmills in the area did not discourage Asa Prior in the least. According to Charles K. Henderson's *Polk County Persons And Things*, written by Henderson and first published in the *Cedartown Standard* newspaper starting on May 27, 1897, "Greenwood, the Indian, owned the mill located at the junction of Big and Little Cedar," (later known as Judkin's Mill).[9] John Wilson had a mill at Hightower Falls in 1832, later owned and operated by Elias Hightower *(Readers please see "Memories Of Polk County's Hightower Falls," A North Georgia Journal of History, Volume III published by Legacy Communications, Inc.).* On upper Big Cedar Creek yet another mill was operated by George Watts.

To build his gristmill on Cedar Creek, Prior engaged Milton H. Hanie of Cave Spring about 1849. This structure somehow survived the U.S. Civil War, and for almost 100 years, Cedartown residents took their corn to this facility to be ground into meal.

This mill later changed hands and became known as Benedict Mill. Finally, in 1945, the little enterprise fell victim to progress, as were gristmills all over the country at this time. Electricity and the industrial age had ushered in a new era of modern electrically-powered facilities, and fresh meal and flour were all now offered in shops and groceries. Operations at Prior's old mill ground to a halt – no pun intended.

In 1960, the aged mill underwent a rejuvenation of sorts, when Robert L. Stevens and his wife, who had operated a restaurant in Cartersville, purchased the Prior's old mill and opened what they called "The Old Mill Restaurant." The site quickly became a popular dining spot, lasting for thirty-one years, before closing.

During his days in Cedartown, Prior reportedly accumulated six thousand acres of land and 500 to 600 slaves. By the 1840s, he had a large plantation approximately eight miles west of town. Asa's son – Haden – lived on the plantation in a fine home, and managed the plantation for his father. Asa maintained his residence in town.

When the Southern Railroad laid rails from Rome, Georgia, to Birmingham, Alabama, a railroad depot – "Prior Station" – was established on Prior plantation.

Cedartown In The Early Days

Much of the property in the central portion of what today is downtown Cedartown was once owned by Asa Prior. In 1852, the benefactor made an impressive contribution to the community. He sold, for $1,200, an area encompassing 19 acres – including rights and access to the Big Spring – to the city of Cedartown.[10]

A courthouse ultimately was built on the site. When completed, the large brick and granite structure housed offices on the first floor and a courtroom on the second. This structure, however, and most of the rest of the town, were put to the torch by Kilpatrick's cavalry of Sherman's army during the Civil War. It was therefore, rebuilt in 1869.[11]

Another courthouse was built in 1891. Today, on the same site as the original courthouse in the 1852 town plan, the Polk County Courthouse built in 1954 now stands.

Prior to the Civil War in the 1850s, Cedartown increased in importance when it became the county seat. Polk County had recently been formed (mainly by taking a portion of Paulding County), and needed a more centrally-located seat of government. Van Wert, formerly the seat of Paulding, was now in Polk, but it was near the edge of the new county, and thus was unsuitable as the new government seat.

Despite this vigorous growth in the community he had helped found, Asa Prior pulled up stakes in Georgia sometime around 1850. He moved to Sabine County, Texas, purchasing a new spread not too far from his son, Andrew, who had been bitten by wanderlust earlier, settling in nearby Rusk County.

A Changing Of The Guard

Asa's son, Haden, remained behind in Georgia to maintain the Prior plantation and land development businesses there. He, quite likely, was one of the most prosperous planters in the area. It, unfortunately, was a reputation which later would prove fateful to Haden.

Asa Prior may merely have been visiting Cedartown from Texas, when he made his last will and testament dated October 13, 1853. In this document, he left instructions for the disposition of the Prior properties both in Cedartown and Texas.

It is unknown today whether or not Asa knew of or suspected his impending death. Whatever the circumstances, a few months later, on July 2, 1854, the man who had done so much to foster the growth and development of the city of Cedartown, Georgia, passed away. He was buried in Sabine County, Texas.

The enterprises and investments of the Priors undoubtedly continued to flourish throughout the 1850s, but came grinding to a halt with the advent of the 1860s, and the divisive conflict at that time between the Northern and Southern states.

The Terrible Civil War And Its Aftermath

Asa had one son and one grandson who enlisted on the side of the Southern cause in the Civil War, joining the Confederate Army in 1862. William H.C. Prior went off in June with a Polk County company. John left Rome on April 5th with 65 other cavalrymen in a Cave Spring company,[12] but was able to return home a few months later after he hired a substitute.[13]

John reportedly was convinced there was no hope of the Confederacy winning the war, and thus did not strongly support the cause. It would not be long, however, before he would be confronted with a war of his own, one which would test his endurance.

As the Civil War drew to a close, affairs in Polk County were going from bad to worse. Sherman's troops had swept through the area on their "March To The Sea" and had burned Cedartown to the ground. Outlaw raiders, some of whom were Confederate deserters, laid waste to what little was left in the countryside.

Lawlessness prevailed during this period, mainly because virtually all men – including law enforcement personnel – and even young boys barely big enough to carry a weapon were serving in the Confederate Army. It was a situation ripe for crime. Homes were looted and residents who did not readily hand over their valuables were persecuted, maimed and murdered.[14]

Outlaws so terrorized the citizenry during the war that the state of Georgia organized what came to be known as "home guards," which were militia companies designed to provide law and order in the trouble spots. For the Cedartown district, Governor Joe Brown appointed Haden Prior to command the company.

Prior's standing in the community apparently out-shined what had been, at most, a lackluster support of the Confederate cause. By the closing days of the war, however, Haden probably had become more involved in the revolt against the North. A few months earlier, Union soldiers had burned his barns and warehouses and carried off whatever cattle and provisions were available.

Out of pure desperation, Haden and several of his sons were inexorably drawn into the vortex of these events in the last years of the war. It was a preoccupation which eventually would cost Haden his life, erupting into one of the bloodiest feuds in Polk County history.

The former site of Asa Prior's plantation leaves much to the imagination today. The only remaining remnant of the plantation is the overgrown plot to the left – old Prior Cemetery – where Haden Prior is buried.

One of the oldest homes in Polk County still stands, but its original owner, Asa Prior, undoubtedly would not recognize it. It has undergone extensive renovations, and is used (as of this writing) as a funeral home.

Prior Mill, built for Asa Prior in 1849, ground corn and other products into meal for many years. In more recent times, the historic structure has been used as a restaurant.

Plagued By Outlaws

The story of the events which follow was documented by a reporter in an 1897 Rome, Georgia newspaper following an interview with John Thomas Prior, Haden's son. Needless to say, the events precipitated by the feud are still told in old-timer circles in Cedartown to this day.

At some point in the mid-1860s, word reportedly reached Haden and his militia that an outlaw group led by an individual named Jack Colquitt was raiding local farms in Cedar Valley. The local Home Guard militia, including Haden and his son, John, promptly set out to hunt the men down, per their instructions from the governor of Georgia.

After picking up the outlaws' trail, the Home Guard soon caught five of the raiders on the road between Cave Spring and Prior Station. One of the outlaws reined in his horse, quickly turned him around and made the mistake of trying to escape. John Prior drew a bead on the fleeing horseman and fired, knocking him out of the saddle with one shot. He was the first of six men John would ultimately kill in a personal vendetta against the Colquitt gang.

Following a successful first stage in eliminating the Polk County of the lawless riffraff, the posse brought back the four men they had captured and lodged them in the Cedartown jail. Within a few weeks, however, all four surprisingly had been released – possibly for lack of evidence, but also possibly due to a breakdown in civil order. Regardless of the circumstances, the criminals were soon back terrorizing the citizens of the county.

Eight Slugs From A .44

"A fellow named Phillips was very bitter," John Prior explained in later years to the Rome reporter. *"Colquitt's gang put out the word that they would kill my father for having them arrested, but he never took it seriously."*

Determined to arrest Colquitt and bring him to trial before he and his gang could carry out their threat or inflict more suffering upon innocent farmers, John and his brother, James (who was also a member of the Home Guard), set out to search for Colquitt one night. It is not known today why the Prior brothers decided to search for the renegade at night, or if in fact they were simply availing themselves of an opportunity of which they had learned.

Whatever the circumstances, the two men appeared at a Cedartown grocery store that night where they found the outlaw in a drunken stupor, lying on the store counter. Colquitt did not know it at the time, but his final day on earth was quite near at hand.

"When we aroused him," John continued, *"he was very quarrelsome and cursed loudly. We let him rave, but when he reached for his pistol to shoot us, . . . I (put) a bullet through his heart."*

"One of them made a movement to reach for his gun."

George Battey, in his seminal *A History Of Rome and Floyd County*, added some details to John Prior's account. According to Battey, when the shooting began, both brothers fired at Colquitt, putting a total of eight bullets into him.

It seems apparent

from the description of the incident, that the brothers wanted to make certain Colquitt did not move from the spot – at least not without being carried out. John later told a friend, "I was so close when I fired my first shot that I saw smoke coming out of his mouth."

The killing of Jack Colquitt, however, did nothing to dampen what by then had become a blood-lust among his men, particularly regarding Haden Prior. It was a scene very reminiscent of the circumstances which led up to the now famous gunfight at O.K. Corral in Tombstone, Arizona some 16 years later.

The Colquitt gang, undeterred by their leader's demise, bided their time, waiting for just the right opportunity for revenge. It finally came on April 6, 1865.

As events in Cedartown were boiling over, the final curtain on the U.S. Civil War was being drawn. On that Sunday, two gentlemen, one in blue and one in grey, met at a tiny town called Appomattox Court House for an epic surrender. The following Friday, an event at Ford's Theatre in Washington City (D.C.) would further stun a nation that was already reeling.

Haden Prior Murder

In the spring of 1865, Haden Prior was visiting a Mr. Hampton about two miles from his Prior Station home. Haden was accompanied by an adolescent Negro servant.

As Haden was leaving the Hampton residence, four of the Colquitt gang-members apparently confronted him not a hundred feet from the front gate of the Hampton home. According to later accounts of this incident, Phillips, the leader of the party, exchanged a few words and then drew his pistol and shot Haden through the heart, killing him instantly. He also killed the servant.

Around noontime, Haden's son, John, learned the shocking news of his father's violent murder. He immediately saddled up and rode out to the Hampton property where he learned the details of the crime.

John Prior has been described as a typical Georgia mountaineer – about five feet and eleven inches in height, and thin and wiry. His slight stature was said to have been deceptive, however, for he reportedly had a muscular physique.

The feature, however, which most impressed those who knew him, was his eyes. They were said to have been small, gray, and glittering like jewels. Stranger still, there reportedly was no white around the glassy gray iris.

John once stated, "I never center my eyes on anybody but a person I hate, because I know their effect on people. I never stare at anybody because it would frighten them."

John Prior's anguish upon the discovery of his father's crumpled body can only be imagined today. It is known that he wasted no time in setting out with a few friends to hunt down the killers.

Deadly Pursuit

By sun-up the next day, the trackers had found first one and then another home plundered by the bandits who could be only a few hours ahead. The trail led west into Alabama and the area of Piedmont. There, however, the trail grew cold.

As John Prior later recalled, *"We rode on rapidly across the Alabama line to Ladiga* (present-day Piedmont), *for which point we thought they would make, but we could learn nothing of them. Baffled, but never despairing, I rode three miles to Cross Plains, a point lower down. Here, I could find no clue."*

Returning to Ladiga, John remembered another road leading out of town. He questioned some young boys at a school on the road and fortunately received a good description of the men they were trailing. They were able, once again to pick up the trail, and rode north for several miles.

"It was between 11 or 12 o'clock when just beyond Coloma, Alabama, I rode up in front of the Widow Lane's house and saw two men sitting under some trees and three horses tied nearby. I remember the pink and white blossoms of the peach trees. The house, situated as it was at the foot of the Wiseman Mountains, made a most inviting place.

" The men, I think, saw me about the same time I saw them and both sides were somewhat surprised. One of them made a movement to reach for his gun. I jumped off my horse, cocked my double barrel shot-gun, and fired before he raised his.

"One of them fell over riddled with buckshot, while the other ran around the house. I drew my pistol and ran after him, but just around the corner came upon his dead body where he fell."

The third man fired and fled into the woods. Prior quickly caught up with him and killed him. Later, he said, *"They were not the murderers of my father, but doubtless belonged to the same gang."*

Within twenty-four hours of his father's murder, John Prior had found and killed three of the gang. Together with the earlier shooting of Colquitt and the gang member who had tried to escape when threatened with arrest, the death toll had now reached five men. However, the actual killer of Haden Prior – Phillips – and his two henchmen who had been identified as Montgomery and Bishop, were still at large.

Four Horsemen Of The Apocalypse

"I learned that Phillips, when not on a free-booting excursion, lived on a farm down in Haralson County," John continued. "It was early July that (I with) one of my brothers and two friends started out about nightfall for Phillips' home with the determination of killing him. We surrounded his home somewhere about 3 o'clock in the morning."

Early the next morning, John cornered his quarry. Phillips had emerged from his house and walked to a nearby field, beginning a day's plowing.

John Prior later explained it was an easy matter to get close enough to surprise Phillips. John said he rode to the top of the hill above Phillips, dismounted, then eased down to the edge of the field, concealing himself in the undergrowth. He then waited until Phillips plowed to the end of a row, and then just as he was about to turn his horse, John said he stepped out of the woods and covered the man with his pistol.

"Phillips," he said, "I want you."

"Let me go to the house first to see my wife," Phillips reportedly pleaded.

"No. I want you right now," Prior replied harshly.

"Well, let me unhitch my horse from the plow."

"All right. Go ahead, but be quick about it."

John could see the bandit's women and children in the distance running out of the house. They, no doubt, had seen members of John's party and suspected the worst, running to Phillips to warn him.

"I knew that unless I killed him pretty quick, the women and children would all be crying around me very shortly," John later explained.

Probing for a confession, John asked,

"Phillips, who killed my father?"

Phillips responded with the name of a man who John knew had no connection with the murder.

"I have the best evidence that you did the killing," John replied, and with that, Phillips reportedly fell on his knees and began to beg for his life.

"You needn't expect any mercy from me," John added. "I'm going to kill you."

Desperate and realizing that his end was near at hand, Phillips reportedly broke into a run. John quickly shot him in the back.

Phillips fell on his side and then rolled over on his back. With the women and children watching a short distance away, John walked over and shot Phillips again, this time through the heart at close range.

After making certain that his quarry was too dead to even kick again, John remounted his horse and set out in search of Montgomery, another of his father's murderers. After killing six men, there were still two more to hunt down.

Montgomery had fled the district, but John Prior was relentless. After following clues for a length of time, he finally discovered the man in Arkansas, but for reasons unknown today, he relented and spared his victim this time.

Maybe John had seen enough killing. The exact circumstances have been lost through the passage of time. Montgomery died about five years later in Arkansas.

The final man, Bishop, had died of natural causes by the time John finally located him. The hunting and killing was over.

The manhunt and ultimate murders of men – without benefit of a legal trial by jury – may seem horrific to a reader in modern times. However, during the U.S. Civil War and its immediate aftermath, the southern United States was a lawless area, besieged by cutthroats and criminals of all makes and descriptions. It was a brutal and bloodthirsty time, when many men lived by the gun. Violence was a way of life.

Peace At Last

Following this series of horrendous events, John Thomas Prior enjoyed a surprisingly quiet and uneventful life. He was never charged with any crimes for the shootings and the men he had killed. It is quite possible that many residents of Polk County wanted to honor him, not prosecute him.

Six months after John Prior's story appeared in the Rome, Georgia newspaper in 1897, his son, George Prior, married and moved away, settling in Roseburg, Oregon. John and his daughter later moved there to live with him in 1906.[15]

Two years later, John's daughter married, and around 1910, the proud old avenger posed for a photograph with his new granddaughter, Georgia M. Davis.[16] That same year, John T. Prior reached the age of 70, and died peacefully at his daughter's home.

John's cause of death was attributed to "the direct infirmities attendant to old age."[17] He was buried in the old Masonic Cemetery, now Memorial Gardens in Roseburg, Oregon.

Back in Cedartown, Georgia, it wasn't too many years after the Civil War and the infamous murder of Haden Prior, that the pleasant residence of Prior Station was finally abandoned by the Priors. Through investments and good business acumen, the family possibly had become financially independent. They had all drifted off to the West, always west.

Today, descendants of Asa Prior can

still be found in Cedartown, but few with the Prior name. And as for Prior Station, all traces of the once-grand plantation have vanished.

As of this writing, a home owned by dairyman Ernie McMillan occupies the site where the Prior house once stood. The railway depot and rail line near this site disappeared years ago. Nothing remains except the small overgrown Prior family cemetery surrounded by an iron fence – with a gate facing westward.

The city built by a blacksmith, and protected by his sons and grandsons, still thrives today. And sometimes, when native sons of the community gather to reminisce about area folklore, the life and times of the Asa Prior family inevitably become a topic of conversation.

Acknowledgements: *The generous sharing of Prior family materials by the following is gratefully acknowledged: Miss Matilda West, Cedartown; Mrs. Marjorie Brown, Longview, Texas; Mrs. George O. Marshall, Jr., Athens, Georgia; and Ms. Eileen Talburt, Douglas County Genealogy Society librarian, Roseburg, Oregon.*

ENDNOTES

1/ Whatley, George Fields, "Cedartown's Big Spring," *Georgia Life*, Spring, 1978, p. 20-21.

2/ Georgia DAR Book 8, 1949-50, *Bible Records Of Revolutionary Soldiers.* William H.C. Prior family Bible. Prior file in genealogical records at the Georgia Department of Archives & History, Atlanta, GA. In the various records, the spelling of the family name changed with Haden although the records appear to be consistent otherwise. Fourteen children with their birthdays are listed for Asa Prior.

3/ Floyd County Deed Record Book C, p. 6. Deed records of Paulding County go back only to 1848, but Floyd County records show Asa Prior was a resident of Paulding County who was buying and selling numerous lots in Floyd County. His earliest recorded transaction was November 8, 1832.

4/ Brown, Marjorie Maxwell, various Prior family materials.

5/ Prior, Asa, October 13, 1853, recorded last will and testament in Record of Wills, Book A, Polk County, Georgia, pp 26-27.

6/ Paulding County Deeds, Record Book X, p. 579. It is interesting to note that the 1832 survey shows the road which would become Main Street, although it had several twists in it which have disappeared.

7/ Paulding County Deeds, Record Book X, p. 580. The surveyor noted that one forty-acre lot included Judge Witcher's yard and field and another 160 acres included Witcher's farm. By 1845, this farm was owned, at least in part, by William E. West.

8/ Johnson, Larry G., *A History Of The Polk County Missionary Baptist Association*, Nashville, TN, 1977, p. 98.

9/ Henderson, Charles K., *"Polk County Persons And Things,"* Chap. 11 from the series appearing in the *Cedartown Standard* starting on May 27, 1897. Henderson observed that the mudsills of Greenwood's mill could still be seen. The state survey of 1832 noted the Indian, Greenwood, and his mill on Lot 887 on "East Cedar Creek." This lot appears on a current Polk County map at the junction of Cedar Creek and Pumpkin Pile Creek.

10/ Polk County Deeds, Record Book A, p 191.

11/ Henderson, op. cit., Chap. 2.

12/ Kinney, Shirley Foster and James Paul Kinney, *Floyd County Confederates* (and surrounding counties), Vol. VIII, SFK Genealogy, Rome, Georgia, 1992, p. 215.

13/ Battey, George Magruder, Jr., *A History Of Rome And Floyd County, Vol. I*, Atlanta, 1922, p. 384-385. It may have been no coincidence that the company commander was Capt. M.H. Hanie – the same individual who had built the gristmill for Asa Prior.

14/ Battey, op. cit., pp. 205-208.

15/ Marshall, Mrs. George O., Jr., Athens, Georgia.

16/ U.S. Census of 1910, Deer Creek District, Douglas County, Oregon.

17/ Obituary of John Thomas Prior, *Umpqua Valley News*, November 7, 1910, Roseburg, Oregon.

Moonshine And Murder At Esom Hill

As long as most people can remember, this community in northwest Georgia has held a reputation for high crimes and high times.

A neatly-dressed stranger from an out-of-town company was examining a lot upon which his firm had contracted to build a home for a local resident. Suddenly, a man with a shotgun walked up. "Get out of Esom Hill," he rasped at the builder. "You ain't got no bizness here." After a glance at the barrel of the deadly weapon, the builder had to agree, and quickly departed.

Such has been the reputation for the little state line community in northwest Georgia's Polk County for well over half a century, an image fostered by a long record of illicit activities such as "moonshining," gambling, and even darker crimes like murder. And surprisingly, it seemed the stronger the criminal element became in the township, the less visible was law enforcement.

Despite its infamy, Esom Hill, according to many residents, is a friendly community with caring neighbors and a bad name circulated by "outsiders." Just like many situations, the truth lies somewhere in between.

Settlers in this western-most edge of what once was Cherokee Indian Territory were among the last to arrive in Paulding County, Georgia (later reorganized as a part of Polk County in 1851). The beginnings of Esom Hill occurred with the founding of Shiloh Baptist Church in 1848[1] and the first post office in 1850.[2]

Partly as a result of its close proximity to the Georgia-Alabama state line and partly due to its generally remote location, Esom Hill has long been frequented by lawlessness and controversy. Local tales describe – tongue-in-cheek – how bootleggers escaped law enforcement officers by moving their liquor from one room in a building (in Georgia) to another room in the same building (in Alabama).

Another claim even maintains the first Esom Hill post office was actually established in Alabama (1847) and then later moved to Georgia (1849).[3] This possibly could be explained by the fact that the first postmaster – Benjamin Wheeler – lived in Alabama and actually operated the post office there from his home or store. Today, no one really knows for certain.

Local folklore maintains the name of the little community sprang from an old trading post once operated by an Indian named "Esom" or "Easom," possibly prior to the removal of the Cherokees from the territory. The "Hill" apparently was added later.

Another version of the origin of the town name claims it came from an early settler now buried in Shiloh Baptist Church cemetery beneath an unmarked fieldstone. Whatever the origin, the name of the tiny township has spread far and wide over the years, always accompanied by its dark reputation.

A book entitled the *Georgia State Gazeteer*[4], published in 1881, lists Esom Hill as a community of 169 people with five general stores, three churches, a school and a saloon. The village also boasted a steam gin, a water-powered gin, and a sawmill.

Early Commerce

Four years earlier in 1877, when Amos West founded his Cherokee Iron Company in Cedartown, Esom Hill must have shared the prosperity as mining operations grew (supported by plentiful iron ore deposits in the area). Farming, of course, undoubtedly also figured prominently as a professional pursuit, as did a number of small businesses which suggest a self-sufficient little community:

- W.P. West, postmaster
- J.P.S. Brewster, general store
- Rev. V.A. Brewster, Baptist pastor
- A.A. and J.W. Camp, saw mill
- Dukes and Pearson, blacksmith
- H.A. Edmonson, notary and J.P.
- Jeremiah "Jerry" Isbell, general store
- M.E. McCormack, tax collector and teacher
- J.S. Mercer, general store
- Nobles and Adkins, blacksmith
- T.J. West, general store
- W.P. West, general store
- West and Hackney, grist and saw mill
- C.M. Wheeler and son, saloon

The production of untaxed whiskey eventually grew into big business in the hills.

Today, many of these original residents of Esom Hill rest in Shiloh Cemetery, and their descendants still live in the same community.

The general stores of Brewster and Isbell are still remembered – one in the village center and the other three miles east at Akes Station. The original building reportedly burned, and Brewster built a new store across the street in 1901, a structure which functions today as the Esom Hill Trading Post.[5]

Jeremiah Isbell's country store operated out of the front room of his home[6] and stood until a few years ago when it was demolished.

The Brewsters and Isbells were among the original families to settle in Esom Hill. In 1860, the Rev. Vann Allen Brewster left Haralson County and moved to Esom Hill with his family.[7] Jeremiah Isbell returned to Floyd County from the war in 1865 and found that his family had "refugeed" to Polk County.[8]

The Brewster and Isbell children grew up together as next-door neighbors. The families were formally linked in 1879 when a son and daughter married – Joseph Proctor Screven Brewster to Laura Jane Isbell. From this union came twelve children, contributing to the family of the proud grandfather.

Jerre Isbell boasted in his eighty-first year: "There are now living, and physically and mentally strong, not an idiot nor invalid nor a deformed one, in whose total reaches 198."[9]

The Brewster Mercantile Company became one of the first in the county to have electric power when Brewster installed a

"Delco System" to generate power for lights in his store and in his home across the road.[10] The store carried everything from toothpicks to two-horse wagons to serve the farmers in the surrounding area.

A counter and post office boxes were located behind swinging doors at the back of the store.[11] The enterprising Joseph P.S. Brewster also served as postmaster. (Later his son, Fred, would become postmaster when he and brother Gordon succeeded their father in the operation of the store.)[12]

Mail deliveries were carried over two mail routes out of Esom Hill. In 1928, when Jack Phillips began carrying the mail, he covered two routes (Routes 1 and 2) which apparently were combined into one route at about that time. According to Cora Belle Honea, Phillips drove a car to make his deliveries.

Prior to Phillips' tenure, Ben Griffith drove Route 1 and Jim Woods drove Route 2, both of them using a horse-drawn postal buggy. In the beginning, Phillips also reportedly drove a horse-and-buggy postal van. When his first horse, Maude, grew too old and slow, he bought another faster horse which he named "Dammit." The frisky beast would often trot too fast, necessitating a "Whoa, Dammit!" much to the amusement of any bystanders."[13]

As a rural mail carrier, Jack Phillips provided some services totally unavailable today. As he made his rounds, he could be persuaded to carry eggs from one farm to another, or a basket of fruit to a shut-in. This courier might even delay the swift completion of his appointed rounds by stopping to read or even write a letter for someone needing assistance. Phillips reportedly even helped one elderly lady to order a corset and some batteries for her radio from the Sears Roebuck catalogue – even installing them when they were delivered (the batteries of course, not the corset).[14]

Moonshine & Murder

It was from this bucolic setting that the illicit activities of Esom Hill eventually evolved, and the community, in many instances, did nothing to diminish its reputation either – often even reveling in it. At one point many years ago, alongside the approach road and next to the railroad crossing, the town name and population were proudly and boldly inscribed across the face of a decommissioned moonshine still.[15]

The production of untaxed whiskey eventually grew into big business in the hills and hollows between Esom Hill and Borden Springs, five miles to the west in Alabama. Brokers lined up orders for moonshine, distributing the spirits in a wholesale operation. During Prohibition (1920-1933), huge trailer trucks reportedly transported thousands of gallons of illegal whiskey from these hills northward to thirsty markets such as Chicago. Cars and small trucks could be fitted to handle loads of 100 to 150 gallons.

When law enforcement officials stepped up arrests and crack-downs on the production of untaxed whiskey in northwest Georgia in the 1950s, they began at Esom Hill. One group drove out to the Treat Mountain area south of Esom Hill, parking their car alongside the road. While they were off searching for distilleries ("stills"), the car mysteriously caught fire and burned to the axles. The insult so stung the officials that they opened a local office and dedicated it to the eradication of Polk County moonshining.[16]

Because it often involved so much money and represented the main source of income for so many rural citizens, moonshine (or its destruction) could result in violent consequences. Just like the Hatfields and McCoys, disputes between neighbors at Esom Hill frequently got out of hand and

Law enforcement officials destroy a moonshine site near Esom Hill, circa 1928. (Photo courtesy of Mrs. Brenda Bentley)

became a deadly contest.

Of the many storied shootings at Esom Hill, the day in April of 1933 that Warren Bailey fatally wounded Robert Hackney undoubtedly stands out prominently in the memories of some old-time residents.

According to the *Cedartown Standard* of that day[17], "Deputy Sheriff Stone was called to the scene early Sunday night and found the body of (Robert) Hackney alone in the Bailey home. He had been shot through the body by a Winchester rifle and death was believed to have been instantaneous.

"Investigation by Mr. Stone revealed that Hackney held a pistol in his right hand under his body and that the pistol had been recently fired twice. Alvin Bailey, son of Warren Bailey, claims to have been an eye witness to the affair and states that Hackney entered the home under the influence of liquor and shot at his father with the pistol and that the elder Bailey then grabbed the rifle and killed him. The rifle load indicated it had been fired one time."

The shooting apparently took place in the Bailey home. The "liquor" which Hackney had consumed was of the Esom Hill variety. Prohibition did not end until December 5, 1933.[18]

Warren Bailey ultimately was acquitted by a grand jury. Three years later, in another notorious incident, he was killed by his nephew, Clayton Bailey.[19]

"Bell Tree" Smith

Of all the liquor legends floating around Esom Hill, the most popular one by far involves an individual named Will Smith, better known as "Bell Tree" Smith, the moonshine king. Over the years, the legend undoubtedly has mushroomed. Will's son, William Smith, and his family maintain that much of the information in the tales simply is not true.

Despite this disclaimer, it is known that Will Smith had a unique method of selling his corn liquor – a system which somehow seemed to protect him from detection by law enforcement officials. It actually was very simple in design. Not far from his still, Smith rigged a dinner-bell in a large oak tree, attaching a rope from the bell so that it could be rung by customers. A buyer would set his empty jug and money by the tree, give the rope a tug to ring the bell, and then leave the premises. When the bell rang again, the buyer would return to the old oak tree to find his jug filled with "shine" and the proper change left, all accomplished without any sign of the proprietor.

The tree under which all this activity took place was eventually dubbed "the Bell Tree," and over the ensuing years, Will Smith became known as "Bell Tree" Smith.

Although Esom Hill today lays claim to the Bell Tree legend, the former site of the old oak was not even in Georgia. The

Bell Tree rotted away years ago, but by most accounts, it stood in Alabama near the Georgia line, in a hollow formed by a stream draining the south side of Flagpole Mountain north of Tecumseh, Alabama.

Will Smith's family today "does not recall" any ties the elder Smith might have had with Esom Hill, or even the location of the infamous old oak tree.[20] Though many of the tales concerning Bell Tree Smith may vary, his ultimate demise is known for certain. On a warm Sunday in August of 1908, the legendary Smith was killed by an individual named Will Chandler.[21]

According to a description of this incident, Smith reportedly had attended an all-day church singing in Borden Springs, Alabama. Gradually, the men had separated from their womenfolk after eating lunch, and had drifted off to a field near the Borden Springs Post Office.[22]

According to reports, Will Smith and Will Chandler – with his brother Joe Ben – got into a heated argument over payment for two yearling bulls. It has also been reported that Smith was attempting to stop the Chandler brothers from roughing up a young friend who happened to be present.

Will Smith was recognized as a community leader, accustomed to being called upon by neighbors to help keep the peace. In those days, the sheriff normally took an hour to reach these parts, and many times he would arrive too late to help.

On this fateful day, Smith stepped into the fracas and proceeded to subdue the attackers. As he left the fray and climbed into his buggy, a stone reportedly was thrown by one of the Chandlers. It struck Smith, stunning him, and before he could recover, Will Chandler reportedly shot him, killing him instantly.

An unusual twist to this story occurred when Will Chandler was tried for the crime. He ultimately was convicted, but strangely was only sentenced to one year in the Alabama State Penitentiary. And before he served even a single day of his sentence, young Will received a sudden pardon from none other than the governor of the state himself.

Joseph Proctor Screven Brewster (1856-1913) was a member of the original pioneer families in the Esom Hill community. The original Brewster General Store in town burned, and a new structure, built in 1901, still stands today. This photo appears to have been retouched. (Photo courtesy of Phillip H. Brewster)

Today, William Smith lies buried in the Salem Baptist Church Cemetery in Bluffton, next to his father, Melton. A simple but eloquent inscription on William Smith's tombstone reads: *"A light from our household is gone. He was a kind and loving son and affectionate brother."*

Frank Lott Murder

One of the most infamous crimes ever associated with the Esom Hill area occurred more recently in 1974, with the murder of prominent Polk County Sheriff Frank Lott, Sr.

Jeremiah Marion Isbell (1829-1913) operated a country store out of the front room of the family home, and was also among the original families that settled in Esom Hill. (Photo courtesy of Mrs. Sue Isbell Stone)

Much of the illicit activity at Esom Hill had been interrupted by investigations and arrests carried out by Lott in the late 1960s and early 1970s, when, as the newly-elected sheriff, Lott began cleaning up the county. As a result of his uncompromising efforts in law enforcement, Lott undoubtedly made his share of enemies in Esom Hill. Though no direct link has ever been established between his murder and a pay-back from bootleggers at Esom Hill, much public speculation about just such a connection has surrounded the incident. Lott's son, however, disagrees.

"When Dad went in (to the Esom Hill area just prior to his election as sheriff), a lot of the bootleggers asked him, 'How are you going to be if you're elected?'," explained Frank Lott, Jr. "Dad told them, 'My advice to you is if you're doing something illegal, you need to find another line of work.'

"(As a result), a good many of them did change their line of work. Some of them didn't though, and in time, Dad caught them, but he was always straightforward with them and I don't think they would have hurt him."

Frank, Jr., says that on the evening just prior to the murder, some of the family had gone with his father to Rome for dinner. Upon returning from such a trip, he says his dad always went by the jail at night to make certain everything was in order. On this particular night (June 23, 1974), Lott reportedly was making his check on the jail when a silent alarm indicated a burglary was in progress at Cedartown High School.

"There was a trustee at the jail that night," Lott, Jr. continued. "He had a drinking problem and was serving some week-end time. He went with Dad (to the burglary), and when they got to the school, Dad drove around (to the back) where they saw a man getting into a car.

"When Dad got out of his car, the (burglar) got out too. Dad asked him 'What's going on here?'

"Dad started approaching the (burglar) and got between the cars (where) the lights probably blinded him. The (burglar), while he was standing there, apparently had a gun in his hand, and he came up firing and hit Dad three times."

The burglar, according to reports, then jumped into his car and sped away.

"(Later), the boy that was with Dad was put under hypnosis," Lott added. "He was certain about the (burglar's) car – a Ford Torino. (They later found a car by that description) that was burned around Esom Hill."

The prime suspect in the crime was described as a white male with long hair and driving a car with an Alabama license plate. When asked if the individual was from Esom Hill, Frank Lott Jr. would only reply, "They thought he was a psychopath. He later killed himself. After (the killing of the sheriff), nobody would have anything to do with him. Some of them at Esom Hill that had been friends with him didn't even want anything to do with him."

Hoyt Dingler retired from the Polk County Sheriff's Department following 30 years of service. He maintains that he and others in the department knew who committed the crime, but that there simply was never enough evidence to make a case against the killer, described also by Dingler as an Alabama man.

Dingler also maintained that the murder was not a set-up – at least not as far as Sheriff Lott was concerned. "There's no way they could have known that Frank would have answered the call that night, because ordinarily, he wouldn't have," Dingler explained. "At night, it would have been the county police that answered a burglary alarm at the high school. And it was also a fenced-in area with only one gate out. A person is not going to fence himself in to commit a murder."

As a result of its netherworld activities, Esom Hill, according to Dingler, is pretty widely known. "I've been in other parts of the country, and when people want to know where I'm from, and when I reply Cedartown, Georgia, they often say they've never heard of Cedartown, but they've heard of Esom Hill."

Today, Esom Hill is like any other rural northwest Georgia crossroads community. Most folks are friendly and accommodating, and you'd be hard-pressed to find any visible sign of criminal activity. Despite this seemingly peaceful demeanor however, one can't help but sense that just below the surface in this cross-roads fiefdom, the action is still bubbling in Esom Hill.

ENDNOTES

1/ Johnson, Larry G., *A History Of Polk County Georgia (GA) Missionary Baptist Association,* Curley, Nashville, 1977, p. 7.

2/ U.S. Post Offices, Polk (and Paulding) County, U.S. Records, Microfilm Drawer 281, Box 32, Surveyor General Dept., Georgia Department of Archives and History, Atlanta, GA.

3/ Stewart, Mrs. Frank Ross, *Alabama's Cleburne County,* Centre, AL, 1982, p. 68.

4/ *Georgia State Gazeteer* (sic) *& Business Directory,* 1881-82, Atlanta.

5/ The date of construction was once inscribed in the concrete on the front step, but is no longer legible today.

6/ Hoyt Dingler interview, August 17, 1994.

7/ "A Pioneer Dead," *The Cedartown Standard,* October 28, 1897.

8/ Jeremiah Isbell served in the U.S. Civil War with his eldest son. His father, Pendleton Isbell (1806-1873), served also, as did eight of his sons and three of his grandsons. All returned home safely, except one son and one grandson, who were killed.

9/ NW Georgia Document Preservation Project, 1993. Microfilm SHC-156, Brewster/Isbell Papers.

10/ Brewster, Phil, Sr., Cedartown, Georgia, video interview, August 7, 1988.

11/ Honea, Cora Belle, Cedartown, Georgia, letter to Dennis Holland, August 31, 1992.

12/ NW Georgia Document Preservation Project, Op. Cit.

13/ "Vacancy At Esom," *The Cedartown Standard,* c. June 29, 1971.

14/ IBID

15/ Hoyt Dingler interview, August 17, 1994

16/ Hoyt Dingler interview, August 17, 1994

17/ "Warren Bailey Is Held For Murder In Hackney Death," *The Cedartown Standard,* April 20, 1933.

18/ Distilled spirits were taxed from 1862 onwards to help pay for the Civil War. Georgia voted out whiskey in 1907 and Alabama the next year. Prohibition went into effect in early 1920. Dabney, Joseph Earl, *Mountain Spirits,* Charles Scribner's Sons, New York, 1974, pp. 74, 103.

19/ "Clay Bailey Is Held For Killing Of Warren Bailey," *The Cedartown Standard,* August 1, 1935.

20/ Smith, William E., Tecumseh, Alabama, interview on July 29, 1994.

21/ "'Bill' Smith Is Killed," *Cleburne News,* August 20, 1908.

22/ Charlie Collins, Muscadine, Alabama, letter, March 4, 1994, interview, March 7, 1994.

Murder And The Aragon Mill Strikes

The tiny mill town of Aragon, Georgia, has always been a "rough and tumble" community in northwest Georgia's Polk County. In 1934 and 1951, workers at Aragon Mill went on strike. Terrorism and mob violence eventually became the order of the day, and homes were shotgunned, cars were overturned, and one individual paid with his life.

On a Thursday night, September 13, 1934 at approximately 11:00 p.m., the unthinkable happened in tiny Aragon, Georgia. Three cars of a "flying squadron" containing men with murder in their hearts, roared through the little mill-town, firing weapons into the night air. Three deputized guards were standing on a street corner near the textile mill's baseball park which still exists today. The guards, alarmed by the approaching cars, reportedly brought the cars to a halt. Then, suddenly and without warning, the men in the cars opened fire on the three deputies, mortally wounding Russell "Napp" Brown.

According to press reports of that day, Brown was shot twice by shotgun blasts from the strikers. *"One load entering his body and the other his leg, after he and a companion gave chase to the squadron cars and attempted to stop them,"* said the *Rockmart News Tribune.*

As he crumpled to the ground, Brown dropped his gun. One of the other guards, seeing Brown slump to the ground, quickly picked up the slain man's gun and returned fire at the cars, hitting the last one.[1] After shooting Brown, the cars raced away toward nearby Rockmart, Georgia.

The fatally-wounded Brown was rushed to the hospital in Rome, Georgia. A valiant attempt was made to revive him, but he died while in the hospital elevator on the way up to surgery. His wounds – probably from buckshot – had been too terrible for him to survive.

The victim left a wife and four older children. Brown's nephew – Wesley Brumbelow – still lives in Aragon as of this writing. When interviewed in February and May of 2000, he related how he had been eleven years of age at the time of the workers' strike at the mill and the fateful event on an autumn evening in 1934. He says it devastated his family.

"The reason, I think, why they killed my uncle, he was very much like a man who was one of the men at Aragon who was a leader against the union. He was short and kind of chubby-built and wore a black hat, just like the man that was leading against the strikers in Aragon at the mill. They tried some fellows (for the crime), but they (were cleared) in the court. Nobody was ever punished for it."

The three men on the Aragon street corner on that fateful night had been posted by Deputy Sheriff C.D. Stone from Cedartown to help maintain order at Aragon Mill. Many textile mills across the country – including the mills at Aragon, Cedartown and Rockmart – had been closed as the result of a nation-wide strike of textile workers. It was the greatest strike in American history up to that time.

The huge strike began on Monday, September 3, 1934. Truckloads of demonstrators cruised the highways from Virginia to Georgia looking for textile mills. "Upon arriving at a mill, they would storm the place, forcing open doors and running through the hallways tearing down the thousands of 'ends' and stopping the machinery. Then they loaded into trucks to speed down the road (to find another mill). Considerable damage was done by these so-called 'Flying Squadrons,' or mobs of (strike organizers and sympathizers) who attempted to terrorize non-striking workers."[2]

In an effort to improve working conditions at the mills, the work week had been reduced by one-fourth. This meant that the workers, of course, didn't have to work as many days, but it also meant that they would receive only three-quarters of their previous pay. This was deemed unacceptable by many of the employees.

To avoid hiring more hands, the mill managers also assigned more machines for each worker to tend. The workers also rebelled at this "stretch-out," as they called the increased workload, and complained that they were being fired for union activities.

"Just a little more than a year (earlier), on July 17th, the first NRA (National Recovery Administration) code went into effect. This was the textile code, hailed as a model for later codes and the solution of many labor problems in the textile industry. Labor conditions were vastly improved under its direction. Child labor was abolished and working hours were cut shorter than ever before; wages were increased and working conditions improved. Spokesmen for the NRA and the textile industry made speeches hailing the code as a great step forward in social and economic conditions.

"(Despite this progress) labor's indignation mounted; and the current strike, affecting nearly half a million workers, resulted, accompanied, as usual, by violence."[3]

In addition to the several hundred employees at the Aragon Mill, Goodyear Mills employed more than 2,000 workers in Polk County – workers who, interestingly, wanted to continue working during the national textile strike. This anomaly would have unusual implications for Polk County.

The violence wrought by the army of visiting picketers from other localities quickly got out of control. Local police simply could not handle the increased duties, and they appealed to the governor for National Guard troops to protect the workers, their families, and their homes. A few days later, the governor reluctantly declared martial law and sent National Guardsmen to Polk County's three cities.

Polk was occupied by troops from Macon, Georgia, and a company was posted at each textile mill. Goodyear Mill Number 3 in nearby Cartersville, Georgia (Bartow County) had

As he crumpled to the ground, Brown dropped his gun.

Aragon Mill was photographed above on May 25, 1943, for the U.S. Navy "E" Award Ceremonies. Approximately nine years earlier, the strike of 1934 occurred here, resulting in the death of one employee and the creation of fear and intimidation in numerous others.

Wesley T. Brumbelow who was eleven years old at the time of the Aragon Mill strike in 1934, remembered many events of that day. "They threw rocks and poured buckets of paint on cars," Brumbelow recalled. "At some houses, they set off a home-made bomb close to the house."

been able to hire private guards, and when the militia arrived, they found that the situation there was under control.

The National Guard unit at Cedartown, Georgia (Polk) was sent to Social Circle (in Walton County, southeast of Atlanta), obviously in an attempt to prevent any conflict of interest between strikers and the Guardsmen. When that unit was mobilized, in spite of the inclement weather, open trucks were ordered to carry the company to headquarters in Atlanta. The prevailing sentiment of Polk citizens was so opposed to the strike, that *"local citizens volunteered cars enough to carry the entire company in comfort (to) Atlanta (headquarters)."*[4]

With the arrival of the militia, the textile mills resumed operations and workers returned to their jobs. With a company of National Guard maintaining law and order, the mill at Aragon resumed operations just two weeks after the strike had begun. Not taking any chances, however, the National Guard positioned a machine gun on the roof of the mill – with the gunner somewhat hidden – in order to keep a low profile.

Aragon Mill was originally constructed circa 1898, and began textiles production in 1900. After World War II, Aragon Mill was converted from the production of cotton "duck" for wartime usage, to corduroy and laundry bagging fabrics. The mill, as far as can be determined, operated strike-free for the next fifteen years.

Trouble, however, reared its ugly head once again as the 1950s neared. The management at Aragon Mill was still receiving a large number of worker grievances which the mill management considered to be without merit. As a result, the management was not responding to the grievances. The workers' union, in turn, complained of unfair labor practices.

One manager – James C. Platt – reportedly finally lost his patience at one grievance meeting at Aragon in June of 1949. "How the hell do you expect me to run the mill if I can't put who I want to on a job?" he exploded. "If we can't put people of our choice on jobs, we will just close the plant. If you keep taking up grievances of this type we will have to close the plant; then we will see what good you can do by arbitrating."[5]

In a memo dated August 10, 1949, the home office complained to the Aragon plant manager that *"Unfortunately, conditions at Aragon have not been and still are not what they should be in keeping with the high standards we cherish."*[6]

In 1951, management at the mill advised the union that they intended to change the collective bargaining agreement. *"It is undisputed that when the present Management took over, production at the mills (Aragon and Rome), both in quantity and quality, had reached a distressingly low ebb."*[7]

On April 12, 1951, the first of several new strikes occurred. Prior to the strike, Roy E. Brasil, plant superintendent at Aragon had offered the union wage increases to the full extent allowed by the Wage Stabilization Board, but the union turned down the proposal. Plant employees subsequently walked off the job when the shifts changed at midnight. Some 750 workers were affected.

"Grievances include wage increases of an average of 13 cents an hour plus other benefits, which, according to the Southern Textile Industry, would amount to an average of 42.1 cents an hour increase."[8] This strike ended on June 15th when Aragon plant management ultimately agreed to a number of the issues important to the workers.

However, on Monday, July 29th of 1951, the union called a wildcat strike and workers walked off their jobs again at Aragon Mill. They claimed the company had failed to live up to the agreements which had ended the previous strike. "The disagreement reportedly arose at Aragon over job assignments and work loads."[9]

Within two days, the union and the company settled their differences once again, and the workers returned once again to the mill. However, just days later, the textile workers' union (UTWA) at Aragon went on strike again. This time, tensions rose quickly and the desperate strikers resorted to violence.

As a result of the strike, some supervisors were forced to cross the picket lines daily to work a shortened workday of just four hours. According to one of the strike leaders, James T. Garrison, the men threw roofing nails into the path of cars going up the street. They also attempted to turn automobiles over, successfully tipping over at least one car.

Mr. Garrison still lives today in Rockmart, Georgia, and remembers the '51 strike with dismay. "I know about one thing," Mr. Garrison said in an interview on April 28, 2000. "I don't ever want to go through another (strike). There's things happened there that I wished I had never been involved in that strike."

A few months earlier in 1951, a non-striker had been killed during a strike at the Berryton Mills in nearby Summerville, Georgia. Miss Nellie Tucker was in a car carrying four other women in a convoy attempting to drive into the plant to work. Just as Miss Tucker opened the automobile door to escape, the strikers tipped the car over, and she was crushed to death.[10]

Wesley Brumbelow recalled one tense

moment at Aragon Mill: "From where I lived, I had to come down the street in front of the mill, and they tried to block the street. They weren't going to let me by. I had a shotgun in the car, and I just stepped out with it in my hands. I came on home (because) I wasn't asking for any trouble."

Union members on the picket line at Aragon set up a loudspeaker to address non-strikers working in the mill. Brumbelow, a supervisor, says he still has vivid memories of the song they broadcast over and over again: *"Shall We Gather At The River?"* The message was intended to bring employees such as Brumbelow out of the mill to join the strikers.

"They had a bunch camped out near the mill, had tents, and when they wanted them to come, when they thought there was something was going to happen, they put that song on the loudspeaker. You could hear it from where I live now, because I'm living in the same place I was living then."

Other attempts to terrorize non-striking workers were not so benign. According to the recollections of Brumbelow, "They threw rocks and poured buckets of paint on cars. At some houses, they set off a home-made bomb close to the house."

Some of these bombed houses were in Rockmart where some supervisors lived, but apparently none were damaged. The mill itself escaped the strikers' wrath.

Ruth Williams described the terror: "We were scared to death. My nephew came out with his gun and helped us guard the property, you know, the house, because we were afraid they'd set it afire."

"It was pretty bad there for awhile," related James T. Garrison, "but people (finally) got fed up with it." The company and the union finally came to terms once again in late October, and the workers returned to their jobs.

Years after the strike, Garrison still deeply regrets being involved in the strike. "I know about one thing. . . I don't ever want to go through another strike."

The city of Aragon found itself in a fine mess. The mill had provided all the city services – water and garbage pick-up – just to name a few. At one time, Aragon was considered to be an industrial utopia – *"a mill village whose inhabitants find well-being and happiness through employment and recreation offered them by one of the original industrial enterprises of Polk County,"* according to a 1929 *Cedartown Standard* article.

In 1929, the mill owned and paid much of the school's costs. The Aragon Club, the social center of the community, included meeting rooms and a theater, which also were owned by the mill. All of this and more ceased after the strike.

Two years after the 1951 strike had been resolved, Aragon Mill was acquired by United Merchants & Manufacturers. It operated for approximately 20 years thereafter, but in 1970, it was shut down. The property was later acquired by Integrated Products, and resumed operations until it closed permanently in 1990.

Acknowledgements: *The generous assistance of the following individuals and organizations is gratefully acknowledged: Wesley Brumbelow of Aragon; Frank Shelley of Aragon; David Evans of the Sara Hightower Regional Library, Rome, Georgia; the staff at the Southern Labor Archives, Pullen Library, Georgia State University, Atlanta, Georgia.*

ENDNOTES

1/ The *Cedartown Standard*, 9/20/34

2/ Mildred Gwin Andrews, *The Men And The Mills, A History Of The Southern Textile Industry*, Mercer University Press, Macon, GA, 1987, p. 100.

3/ Ibid

4/ The *Cedartown Standard*, 10/4/34

5/ Letter, Truman T. Henderson, TWUA representative to C.A. Townes, 6/13/49.

6/ Letter, W.D. Lisk, State Director (of TWUA) to John T. Lathem, 9/13/50.

7/ Letter, Roy E. Brasil, general superintendent, to J.D. Pedigo, union business agent, 3/1/53.

8/ *Rome News Tribune*, 4/20/51.

9/ *Rome News Tribune*, 8/1/51.

10/ *Rome News Tribune*, 8/1/51 and 8/3/51.

Murder At The Old Fisher Place

The identity of the individual who fired the first shot in the Fisher house on the terrible evening of July 19, 1983, may never be known. It is known, however, that two individuals were murdered in a most horrible manner, and the only person with first-hand knowledge of the crime died himself on August 1, 1997.

The aged farmhouse – built in 1823 – at the corner of present-day U.S. 441 and Wolffolk Road in Rabun County has always fascinated people. It is a unique structure – obviously very old – and probably should be preserved as some type of historic site. For most people in Rabun, however, it is little more than a reminder of a terrible summer night back in 1983.

According to local history, a pioneer – Peter Lamar – brought logs all the way from Augusta to present-day Mountain City. Once he had reached his homesite in Rabun, Lamar planed, on-site, the wood of which the house is built.

The original structure reportedly had 10 to 12 rooms and four great chimneys built of granite. The present-day house has been pared down to four rooms downstairs (with an enclosed back porch) and two rooms upstairs. Two of the original granite chimneys also survive. The structure – still very sound even today – reportedly was the first house in the county to be painted, and the first to have glass-paned windows. It, however, is the old home's violent history which fascinates people the most.

For reasons unknown today, a local arsonist burned the barns on the property and then threw "Molotov cocktails" through a window of the house in an attempt to burn it in 1887. The cocktails ignited, but strangely, they only burned a portion of the floor and then the fire went out. The burned places remain on the floor to this day.

Then, on July 19, 1983, the house became the site of the incident which earned it a permanent spot in the annals of Rabun County history.

According to records in the Rabun County Sheriff's office and to testimony from the trial for the crime, Miss Jane Snider, 80, had been hired by the Fisher family in the 1920s to care for an invalid family member, and she had remained as a

Rabun County Sheriff Don Page who was a 35-year-old investigator with the sheriff's office at the time of the murders at the Fisher residence described the crime as "the worst case with which I've ever been involved." He photographed the Fisher house (above) a few days after the bodies were discovered. (Photo by Don Page)

resident in the home since that time. Mr. Jay Fisher, 84, had lived nearby for many years, and after Fisher family members residing in the home died, he also had moved into the structure.

According to a report published in the July 28, 1983 issue of *The Clayton Tribune* newspaper, Miss Snider had bought some groceries the afternoon of the day of the crime. She had also been to visit a brother and sister in a local nursing home. After returning to the Fisher residence, Miss Snider apparently had prepared a late snack in the kitchen.

The Reverend J. C. Quilliams had driven Miss Snider to visit her relatives at the nursing home. According to his later courtroom testimony, Rev. Quilliams had come into the Fisher home to bring in the groceries for Miss Snider. The two noticed that Mr. Fisher's bedroom door was closed on that very hot evening, a circumstance which seemed unnatural.

Although they heard no voices from the room, Quilliams later testified at the trial that he had a strange feeling there was someone in the bedroom with Fisher.

George W. Welch, 67, of Mountain City, was a self-employed farmer who also repaired machinery. He and Fisher, according to testimony, had been embroiled in a long-standing feud over land Welch had rented from Fisher. The two men had disagreed over some aspects of the rental situation, and Welch subsequently had removed all of his equipment from the site except for one item – a screen used in a rock crusher operation.

According to courtroom testimony in which Welch was represented by his attorney, Robert Oliver of Cornelia, Georgia, Fisher had told Welch to come by his home to discuss retrieval of the screen. On the day of the incident, Welch entered the home. Fisher, reportedly, was in bed and invited Welch to have a seat.

Welch, according to the testimony provided by his attorney, noticed that a quilt covered Fisher's right arm and hand. He also noticed that Fisher was in a visibly distraught state of mind and very angry. He told Fisher he had come to retrieve the screen. At this point, according to Welch's testimony, Fisher very abruptly told Welch "I'll blow your _______ head off," drew a .38-caliber revolver and cocked it.

Welch, according to the courtroom testimony, then quickly raised his hand to his head protectively at about the same time as the pistol was fired. The round from the revolver reportedly struck Welch in the forefinger, then grazed his head, causing a concussion.

Oliver said Welch remembered nothing from that point onward. Welch's courtroom testimony maintained he did not remember shooting Fisher who had five bullet wounds in his body, one of which was effected with the muzzle of the weapon placed against the top of Fisher's head. Welch's courtroom testimony also maintained he did not remember shooting Miss Snider twice (once in the shoulder and once in the face.)

Blood-typing and an investigation conducted by the Georgia Bureau of Investigation Crime Lab later revealed that Fisher had type A blood, Jane Snider type B blood, and Welch type O blood. Welch's blood type was found on Miss Snider's legs, indicating that he had stood over her body, bleeding, following her shooting. Welch also left a blood trail inside the hallway, on a doorknob inside the home, on the porch handrail, and on gravel in the driveway.

According to the account of the trial published in *The Clayton Tribune*, District Attorney V.D. Stockton attempted to prove that Welch had shot Miss Snider first, and then had shot Fisher – who supposedly had heard the shots and come to investigate. According to Rev. Quilliams' testimony, however, Welch was probably already in the bedroom when Miss Snider arrived back at the house from grocery shopping. Further, Welch's blood on Miss Snider's body possibly indicated the altercation between the two men had already taken place before Miss Snider was shot.

A number of witnesses were called to testify in the trial according to the *Tribune* article. One of these – Vernie Burrell – was an employee of Sangamo Weston in Rabun Gap. In her testimony, Ms. Burrell explained that she took a supper break each night at Don's Convenience Store across from the Fisher home. On the night of the crime, Burrell testified that she had heard "about three gunshots, screaming, and more gunshots" coming from the Fisher home at about 8:40 p.m. as she ate her meal in Don's Convenience Store.

After the shootings, Welch, again according to his courtroom testimony thru his attorney, went to D's Tavern nearby, arriving there about 9:00 p.m. According to courtroom testimony from Nancy Wilkes, a bartender at D's Tavern, Welch came in "covered with blood." Ms. Wilkes said she asked Welch what had happened to his hand, and he said he had hurt it on a garden tiller.

David Watts, another employee at D's Tavern, was also called as a witness in the trial. According to the account of the trial in the *Tribune,* Watts stated that he was a first cousin to Welch and that he took him into the men's room at D's Tavern to wash the blood off of Welch's wound. At that point, Watts said that Welch told him he had "shot them S.O.B's." Later, in the backroom of the tavern, Watts said Welch told him he had "shot the old Fisher man and the woman who lived with him." He said Welch then told him, "You had better not let me down," and "Don't tell anyone what I said today."

Watts added that Welch had said he was "in poor financial shape," and that he had gone to Fisher "to ask for some of the money." Watts said Welch explained that he and Fisher had had a "land deal" ten to fifteen years ago and that the old man owed him some money.

Welch then reportedly left the tavern and went to the home of his daughter in nearby Tiger, Georgia. She later testified at the trial that "He was bloody and acting strangely." She then cleaned him and his car and then took him home.

Wilma Bleckley, a friend of Fisher's, was also called as a witness in the trial. According to her testimony, she had been in the habit of going to the Fisher home every day, many times to take Fisher for a ride. It was she who discovered Jane Snider's body covered with blood on the morning of July 20.

According to the police report, Ms. Bleckley went immediately to Guy Rogers' fruit stand near the Fisher home to get help. Rogers went to the Fisher home and found Miss Snider's body. He reportedly followed the blood back through the dining room to Fisher's bedroom and found Fisher dead on the front porch.

Rogers then reportedly called loudly across to the convenience store instructing personnel there to call the Rabun County Sheriff's Office. Rogers later testified at the trial that when Fisher would be at the fruit stand and George Welch would pass, Fisher "would become pale and get shaky."

"That was the worst case with which I've ever been involved," says Rabun County Sheriff Don Page who was a 35-year-old investigator with the sheriff's office at the time of the crime. "A double-murder in Rabun County caused a lot of notoriety. This was the kind of community where everybody knew everybody. People were deeply shocked."

Page says he found a lot of blood both outside and inside the house. Crime scene technicians' samples indicated that some of the blood belonged to someone other than the victims. "I received a call from a 'confidential informant' who said that Welch had a gunshot wound and should be interviewed concerning the crime," Page added. "The blood found at the crime scene matched Welch's."

"Sheriff (Chester) York and I went to the Welch home in Mountain City on July 22," Page continued. When I questioned Welch about being at D's Tavern on the night of July 19 with a wounded hand, he told me that he had been hurt shoeing a horse."

Welch eventually turned himself in to his attorney on the Monday following the killings. His trial started February 2, 1984, and the courtroom was packed in Clayton on the appointed day. At times during the week, up to 30 people stood in the rear of the room to hear the testimony.

Near the end of the trial, attorney Robert Oliver gave a 60-minute final plea to the jury of 11 men and one woman. "First, Welch didn't kill these people," Oliver said, "and second, Welch didn't have the mental capacity to maintain criminal intent."

At the close of the week-long trial, the judge charged the jury as to the possible verdicts for the two counts of murder: guilty, not guilty, or voluntary manslaughter. The jury deliberated two hours before reaching its verdict. The foreman read the verdict – "Guilty of murder on both counts" to a packed courtroom.

In the sentencing phase, the judge instructed the jury that Welch could either receive mercy (which would allow life imprisonment), or the death sentence.

The jury rendered the following decision: Count 1: Life sentence for Fisher's death; Count 2: Death by the electric chair for Miss Snider's death. The execution date was set for April 2, 1984.

Interestingly, the Georgia Supreme Court later overturned Welch's conviction. In a second trial in 1986 in Union County, Welch received the same conviction but a different sentence: Life imprisonment.

Approximately 11 years later, George W. Welch died on August 1, 1997 at Georgia Medical Hospital in Augusta, Georgia. He was buried in the family cemetery on the homeplace in Mountain City, Georgia.

'Doc' Holliday's Early Life In Georgia

As of this writing, John Henry "Doc" Holliday has been dead for well over a century, but his legend is more profound and widely-known today than ever before. He was born in Griffin, Georgia, and was raised in Valdosta, Georgia. He also often visited close relatives near Atlanta. One of the homes at which he spent this time still stands in Fayetteville, Georgia.

Many Southerners have often claimed that historians – particularly Northern historians – were nothing more than myth-makers when it came to documenting factual information. When faced with yet another "accurate portrayal" of local history told from an outsider's limited perspective, the Southerner often leans back in a rocker and chides the historian saying, "Well, friend, that's your tale and I'm a'settin' on mine."

In fairness, while some historians have been known to rewrite history, Southerners have been known for embellishing it. When the two forces are combined, a myth of epic proportions is usually the end product.

Victoria Wilcox, chairman of the Holliday-Dorsey-Fife House Association of Fayetteville, Georgia, asserts that the "Doc" Holliday of Western lore represents such a myth. "I don't think John Henry (Doc) ever wanted to be a gunfighter," she asserts. "I believe what he really wanted was the kind of life his uncle lived right here in Fayetteville. He was even named after his uncle – Dr. Holliday – who was a medical doctor."

Doc's uncle was Dr. John Stiles Holliday, a Fayetteville physician. "John Stiles was the first of the Holliday family to obtain a college degree. John Henry was the second," Ms. Wilcox adds, as she quickly ticks off facts about the famed gunslinger. She has, in fact, mentally stockpiled a wealth of information since she is working on a book about John Henry.

As chairman of the Holliday-Dorsey-Fife House Association, Ms. Wilcox has made it her business not only to help restore the family home, but the family's legacy as well. And that obviously includes John Henry Holliday.

"We currently have around 200 people involved with this project as either volunteers, donors, or laborers," reports the ambitious Wilcox. "The Holliday House is the 'most intact' ante-bellum home in all of

The John Stiles Holliday home in Fayetteville, Georgia has been in existence at least since 1855, and quite possibly was built as early as 1846, when Holliday first purchased the property. Dr. John Stiles Holliday was the uncle of John Henry "Doc" Holliday, and it was at this home that young John Henry spent much of his youth. (Photo courtesy of the Holliday-Dorsey-Fife Home Association)

John Henry Holliday was photographed here shortly after his graduation from the Pennsylvania College of Dental Surgery. He lived a scant 15 years after this photo was taken, the last few months of which were spent in Leadville and Glenwood Springs, Colorado. (Photo by O.B. DeMorat)

metro-Atlanta," she notes proudly. "What I mean by intact is that when you walk in, you stand on the original Georgia heart-pine floors that have been there since the house was first built. Very little has been altered in the home since Dr. Holliday first lived here. Plumbing wasn't even added until the 1940s."

The Holliday home, as it exists today, has been around since 1855, but the original structure was probably built before that time, perhaps as early as 1846 when John Stiles Holliday first purchased the property. "The original dwelling would have been considered a vernacular I-frame home," explains Wilcox. "A formal entry flanked by two rooms, one on each side with a stairway leading to two more rooms upstairs."

Prior to moving in with his family, Dr. John Stiles Holliday remodeled the house.

Without the aid of an architect, Dr. Holliday added six massive Greek columns to the front verandah. He also added four more rooms to the rear of the home, making a total of four rooms downstairs and four upstairs. And nearby, he cultivated a vegetable garden and a small orchard to provide some of the family's foods.

The old home has other interesting roots beyond that of the Holliday family. Prior to occupation of the home by his family, Dr. Holliday agreed to allow students at the new Fayetteville Academy to use the new home to board in. Thus the Hollidays did not take up residence there until 1857.

Annie Fitzgerald, the grandmother of famed author Margaret Mitchell (*Gone With The Wind*), was one of the young girls attending Fayetteville Academy. As a result of this connection, Mitchell would later send her heroine, Scarlett O'Hara, to the "Fayetteville Girl's Academy," modeled after Fayetteville Academy.

Mitchell's family experiences did not stop with Scarlett. The writer's cousin from the Fitzgerald clan, Martha Anne "Mattie" Holliday, was the prototype for Mitchell's character of Melanie in the famed novel.

Mattie spent her childhood in Fayetteville and nearby Jonesboro. A close-knit Irish clan, family gatherings at the Holliday home were common.

It was during these and other gatherings that the strong bonds between Mattie and John Henry (Doc) Holliday were established. Only twenty months older than Doc, Mattie was his playmate and companion during these assemblies.

The secrets these two shared as children formed the basis of an intimacy that lasted throughout their lives. The depth and breadth of this relationship and its exact details are not known today. It however, has been fodder for considerable myth-making over the years. In the major motion picture *Tombstone,* starring Kurt Russell and Val Kilmer, a mythical Doc confesses to Wyatt Earp that an affair with a cousin caused her to enter a convent and him to leave his home in disgrace.

Cousin Mattie, born December 14, 1849, was raised a Catholic, and became a nun at the age of 34. She took the name "Melanie," in honor of Saint Melaine, who, after marrying a kinsman, sought to live a life of complete devotion to God. Did Mattie take the name Melanie because she was in love with her own cousin, Doc?

"Family members in the past have been reluctant to admit that any such relationship existed between John Henry and Mattie," confesses Wilcox. "But the myth that he left Georgia because of poor health is questionable. Supposedly, John Henry left for a higher and dryer climate to combat his tuberculosis. But he actually traveled to Dallas, Texas, which is a lower elevation, geographically, than even Atlanta, and is almost as humid. (Maybe he just wasn't aware of that fact.)

"In all likelihood, the Doc-Mattie relationship probably did in fact play a role in his leaving Georgia. After all, many people with advanced cases of TB were going to Florida for treatment in those days." (In fairness, however, many travel decisions made by Holliday the last few years of his life were not logical ones, but seemingly aimless wandering.)

It is entirely plausible that Doc fell in love with his favored cousin Mattie the year he turned sixteen. By 1867, Doc's family had moved away from north Georgia to Valdosta in the southern part of the state. Sometime near this period, Doc spent one summer with Mattie's family in Jonesboro.

And even long after she became "Sister Melanie," Doc maintained his friendship with her, often writing to her of secrets only the two of them shared. Who knows if they were love letters? We'll never know. Mattie burned the letters.

According to family legend, Mattie later regretted the destruction of the letters. *"Had I not destroyed most of his letters myself, the world would have known a much different man than the one of Western lore,"* she later confessed.

According to records, Doc went on to school at Pennsylvania College of Dental Surgery, graduating in 1872. He was planning for his future, totally unaware he would be gone in a scant fifteen years.

After graduation, he practiced his profession in Atlanta. It was at about this time that he was diagnosed with tuberculosis, a dreaded disease at that time for which there was no cure.

It was shortly thereafter that Doc departed for Texas, sometime around 1873. One can only imagine his pain and despair his fate must have caused him. He probably had suffered a tragic love affair from which there was no recourse, and then shortly thereafter, he learned that he had contracted a fatal disease.

After arriving in Dallas, Doc must have

needed funds, for he set up a dental practice there not long after his arrival. At this time, the West was still a wild frontier in many respects. In short order, Doc became a part of this wildness, picking up the traits of drinking, gambling, and using a revolver. He, however, also continued to practice dentistry.

According to O.K. Corral chronicler Paula Marks, Doc soon garnered a reputation as *"one of the touchiest drunks in the West."* Wyatt Earp himself declared *"Doc's fatalistic courage . . . gave (him) the edge over any out-and-out killer I ever knew."*

Doc was arrested January 1st, 1875, for shooting at a saloon-keeper in Dallas. He decided it was time to leave Dallas, and drifted on to Fort Griffin where he met another individual who would gain fame in the West – Katie Elder. He traveled with Kate, to Denver, Colorado, where he regularly dealt faro games.

By 1878, Doc had arrived in Dodge City, already preceded by his rather substantial reputation as a dangerous man. It was here that he played poker in the Long Branch Saloon, and rode in posses with Wyatt Earp and Bat Masterson.

Wyatt Earp and his brothers travelled to Tombstone, Arizona in 1879, and it wasn't long before they were followed by Doc, Kate, and Bat. Along the way, Doc had shot "a young sport" in Trinidad, Colorado, as well as an ex-army scout and a bartender in Las Vegas, New Mexico, building an ever-larger reputation.

Just as with the rest of Doc's life, controversy and conflicting information surrounds the famous shoot-out at the O.K. Corral. Some accounts maintain Doc and Wyatt shot the men there in cold blood. Others maintain they fired solely to defend themselves against the Clantons and McLaurys who were their bitter enemies.

Whatever the circumstances, when the dust had cleared and some 30 rounds had been fired, Tom and Frank McLaury and Billy Clanton had been killed. Both Virgil and Morgan Earp were wounded, but later recovered. Doc had been grazed on the hip. Ike Clanton and Billy Claiborne dashed to safety, escaping with their lives.

In the bitter feud that continued, Virgil Earp was later shot from an ambush and crippled for life. Morgan Earp was later assassinated. Wyatt and Doc tracked down several of the suspects and meted out equal punishment to them. With those acts, Earp and Holliday became "Wanted" men themselves, and were forced to leave Arizona.

The two men rode together for a period of time, wandering about the West. According to accounts of this period they eventually quarreled and Wyatt then departed for another section of Colorado and later for California.

By 1887, Doc's tuberculosis was overtaking him completely. He had traveled to Glenwood Springs, Colorado, where he had read there were warm springs with recuperative powers. He took up quarters in a hotel downtown in the mountain community.

By this point, the fabled legend of the Old West had become only a shadow of his earlier Wild West persona. In only a few months, he died in the Glenwood Springs Hotel from an advanced case of tuberculosis. He was 36 years of age.

Today, the legend of Doc Holliday lives on in infamy, or as a faded hero of the Old West, depending upon the source of the information. Whatever the circumstances, in Tombstone, Arizona today, there are four magic words when one markets a product or property in the community . . . They are "Earp," "O.K. Corral," "Tombstone," and "Holliday."

And back in Georgia, the remnants of John Henry Holliday's former existence live on, a reminder of one of the state's native sons who seems bigger than life itself today.

John Henry Holliday's Travels In The West

A native son of the Old South
– John Henry "Doc" Holliday –
earned lasting fame in the old West in the 1880s.

John Henry Holliday traveled to and took up temporary residence in many towns of the Old West. Places such as Dallas, Fort Griffin and Jacksboro, Texas; Pueblo, Leadville and Denver, Colorado; Cheyenne, Wyoming; Deadwood, South Dakota (He reportedly was there when James Butler Hickok was murdered); Dodge City and Trinidad, Kansas; Las Vegas, New Mexico; Prescott, Arizona, and numerous others all witnessed the comings and goings of Doc. However, it was the town of Tombstone that really defined him. It was the years he spent in Tombstone – while he was still reasonably healthy – that gave him lasting fame.

By the early 1990s – with the Hollywood releases of movies such as *Tombstone* (starring Val Kilmer, Kurt Russell, and Sam Elliott) – the name "Doc" Holliday had reached almost mythic proportions in the folklore of America, but it was not always so. After the initial newspaper coverage of the shoot-out at the O.K. Corral in Tombstone in 1881, much of the fame of Wyatt Earp; his brothers Virgil, Morgan and Warren; and Doc Holliday, died out over the ensuing years. After the huge water pump at the Tombstone silver mines failed and the price of silver plummeted in the late 1880s, Tombstone had withered and died, and the exploits of the Earps and Doc Holliday were almost forgotten completely.

Old Tombstone Today

By the 1890s, most of the miners had left Cochise County (which included Tombstone). Since Tombstone was located out in the middle of the desert, many people just boarded up their homes or stores and left town on horseback. Most of them never returned, and simply abandoned whatever possessions they had left behind.

As a result, the town – despite two major fires – remained much as it had been in Doc Holliday's and Wyatt Earp's days. There really wasn't any way to steal large amounts of the relics. Who would chance it across the desert. It remained this way for

John Henry Holliday was photographed, probably in Texas or Arizona, circa 1879.

Though the streets are paved today and a few new buildings have filled in spots where older buildings had rotted away, Allen (Main) Street in Tombstone is little-changed from the days of Doc Holliday and Wyatt Earp. Many of the original structures still stand.

over half a century, until the 1950s when American servicemen at Fort Huachuca began taking weekend excursions to the old historic site. Luckily, the handful of local townspeople who remained in Tombstone – which had become a virtual ghosttown – apparently realized they had a money-maker on their hands. They banded together and created a historic district out of the town, preserving it for future generations.

Many of the same structures which the Earps, Doc Holliday, Buckskin Frank Leslie, Bat Masterson, Ike Clanton, Johnny Ringo, Texas John Slaughter, the McLaury brothers and many other figures of the Old West had frequented, amazingly still stand in Tombstone. Though it burned in one of the town fires, portions of the old O.K. Corral site still exist, as do the Birdcage Theatre and the Crystal Palace Saloon in which Holliday, the Earps and all the rest spent many days.

Even the home once owned and lived in by Virgil Earp on First Street still stands in town (as of this writing), as does the Wells Fargo office, the bank, and numerous other original structures.

The Birdcage Theatre is one of the more prominent relics from this day. Built in 1881, this structure was a popular place to enjoy bawdy women, gambling, and other forms of entertainment in old Tombstone.

Holliday's Early Years

For those unacquainted with him, John Henry Holliday was born in Griffin, Georgia, in 1852. His father moved the family to Valdosta to escape the onslaught of the U.S. Civil War in the early 1860s. They struggled to survive during the war years, and later during the post-war devastation of the South.

John Henry was educated at a private academy in Valdosta. He attended dental school at the Pennsylvania College of Dental Surgery in Philadelphia, Pennsylvania. He was often challenged by bigger stronger men who thought they could take advantage of Doc's weak physical condition. That, more than anything else, is what made this Georgian larger than life itself to so many students of the history of the western United States. The frail young man from Valdosta was many things, but he certainly was no coward.

Shortly after he completed his studies in Pennsylvania, John Henry returned to Georgia to set up his dental practice. He began working in the Atlanta dental office of Dr. Arthur C. Ford. During the summer of 1872 at the age of 21, John Henry inherited a substantial office building in Griffin from his mother's estate, and according to records, he had made plans to set up his business there. It was only a short time later that he learned of his terrible illness.

John Henry, quite possibly, caught his tuberculosis from his mother who, according to records, quite possibly was also tubercular. However, he might also have contracted the disease from the many sick and unhealthy vagrants upon which the dental students of that day often practiced their trade during dental classes in Philadelphia. When his illness was diagnosed in Atlanta, Doc was informed that he had approximately six months left to live, and that a dryer climate undoubtedly would help to slow – but not cure – his illness.

Today, the old office building at the corner of Alabama and Whitehall Streets (present-day Underground Atlanta) in which Doc set up his original practice in Atlanta is long departed, torn down years later, no doubt, in the midst of urban renewal in the state's capital city. But down in Griffin, Georgia, a few miles to the south, the old Iron Front Building which John Henry had inherited from his mother and in which he

The site at which Campbell & Hatch Billiards Parlor once stood is occupied by a building of the same name today. This structure reportedly burned the 1890s. It was here that Morgan Earp was assassinated in 1882. (Photo by Olin Jackson)

Wyatt Berry Stapp Earp was born in 1848 and died in 1929. Wyatt was one of the few Old West gunfighters who was never wounded. Doc saved Wyatt's life on at least one, and possibly two occasions. As a result, Wyatt and Doc maintained a close friendship as long as Doc lived. They last saw each other in Denver, Colorado in 1886, shortly before Doc's death in 1887.

Morgan Earp was Wyatt's younger brother. Because of his playful nature, Morgan became fast friends with Holliday. The two spent many long hours drinking, gambling and enjoying attractive ladies in Tombstone. Holliday reportedly was particularly bereaved when Morgan was murdered in Tombstone in March of 1882.

On March 18, 1882 at 10:00 P.M. Saturday night, Morgan Earp was shot in the back while playing pool in Campbell and Hatch Saloon on Allen Street near the intersection of 5th Street in Tombstone. At the time that he was shot, Morgan was standing with his back to the rear of the saloon. A gunman fired thru one of the panes in the left rear door.

had planned to set up his dental practice in 1872, does still stand today. On cold wintry nights, the spirits of the dead no doubt moan a sad refrain for the departed soul of John Henry Holliday.

Most people would have folded up emotionally and simply withered away in bed at home, but not John Henry Holliday. Even when confronted with the ultimate test of one's courage – death – he was resolute. According to eyewitness reports, he was more determined than ever to experience and enjoy as much of life as possible in the short time left to him.

A Life In The West

Holliday was 21 in 1872, when he began his travels. Interestingly, though his doctors had told him he had less than one year left on earth, he, in fact, lived for 15 more years, and in the interim, he traveled throughout the last frontier in the United States, earning a well-deserved reputation as one of the deadliest gunmen to grace the dusty streets of the old West.

Doc was also accused in print and folklore of being testy and irritable, but, in retrospect, who wouldn't have been short-tempered under his circumstances. He was also known to be very gracious to those who were courteous to him, and his honor was the most valuable possession he owned. When bullied or persecuted as a result of his frail appearance, John Henry Holliday invariably proved his mettle.

He was one of the first gunmen to use a shoulder holster, and it has been documented in testimony from both Wyatt Earp and Bat Masterson that he was one of the deadliest gunmen they both had ever known.

Equally amazing, is the fact that Doc Holliday – despite the many gunfights in which he was involved – was not killed as a result of one of these conflicts. He was seriously wounded at least twice, and at the O.K. Corral gunfight, a glancing bullet bruised his hip, giving him a bad limp for several days, but he quickly recovered in every instance. Few other prominent gunmen of the old West – Earp and Masterson interestingly being two of the few exceptions – endured this life without being killed. Earp, amazingly, was never even wounded.

All four of Wyatt's brothers were seriously wounded at some point in their careers, and two of them were killed. James Butler "Wild Bill" Hickok was killed, as were Johnny Ringo, most of the Clantons and McLaurys, William "Billy the Kid" Bonney, Jesse James, Pat Garrett, Butch Cassidy and the Sundance Kid, and many others. Doc and Wyatt, however, seemed almost invulnerable to bullets, despite their lifestyles.

A Friendship With Earp

Doc and Wyatt had become fast friends in Dodge City, Kansas, while Wyatt was a deputy marshal there. Doc saved Wyatt's life on two separate occasions – once in Dodge, and later in Tombstone – and Wyatt never forgot it. The two men remained close friends to the end.

Wyatt was quoted as saying he enjoyed Doc's company because the clever dentist made him laugh. Doc was indeed known to have quite a sense of humor, as well as a love of practical jokes. According to one documented report, on one occasion when a stranger rode into Tombstone wearing a derby hat, Doc followed him throughout the town, merrily ringing a hand-held dinner bell.

There is so much history in the little town of Tombstone, that one would be well-advised to spend at least a weekend in explorations there today. Above and beyond

The Bird Cage Theatre is one of a number of original structures still standing in Tombstone. It was built in December of 1881, and still contains many of its original furnishings.

The corner site (above) was once the Oriental Saloon in which Wyatt Earp owned and operated a gambling concession, and in which Doc Holliday gambled and became embroiled in at least one gunfight in 1881. The Oriental, in fact, was the site of numerous shootings, one of which involved Tombstone Marshal Virgil Earp who was shot and crippled for life as he walked from the Oriental and crossed the street (left foreground) on the night of December 28, 1881.

This view of Allen Street at its intersection with 5th Street, was photographed in 1880. It shows the Eagle Brewery building (right) with the Crystal Palace Saloon occupying the lower level. This saloon was a favorite of John Henry Holliday's.

One of John Henry Holliday's former haunts – the Eagle Brewery / Crystal Palace Saloon – as it looks today.

The interior of the Crystal Palace Saloon was photographed in the 1880s. It was at these tables that John Henry "Doc" Holliday spent much of his time gambling. This photograph, no doubt, was taken by the town's venerable photographer, Camillus S. Fly, in whose rooming house Doc Holliday rented a room during his stay in Tombstone.

the buildings and other sites in the town associated with the Earps and Holliday, many other sites were the stomping grounds of such notables as Buckskin Frank Leslie, Bat Masterson, Texas John Slaughter, and many others.

Ultimately, in their last days in the Tombstone vicinity in 1882, Doc, Wyatt Earp, Warren Earp, Texas Jack Vermillion and a handful of close friends began what was known as "the Vendetta Ride." They were hunting down the outlaws who had killed one Earp and maimed another for life and who had been protected for years by the corrupt judicial system in Cochise County. Months later, when most of the outlaw element had been rooted out (by what many described as vigilante justice), Doc, Wyatt and Warren left forever, wandering anew, searching once again for adventure.

For the rest of their days, both Doc Holliday and Wyatt Earp did nothing more than travel and enjoy life. Neither of them ever owned a home after leaving Tombstone (Doc never owned a home at all, preferring to live in hotels and rooming houses his entire adult life), and they both literally went wherever the wind blew them.

After the Vendetta Ride, Doc, Wyatt, Warren and Texas Jack drifted east to New Mexico Territory. Eventually, Doc and Wyatt drifted up to Colorado, to the gold and silver mining towns which offered a refuge from the Cochise County, Arizona authorities, and an opportunity for gambling which both men needed to generate income.

Approximately four years later in 1886 – just a short time before he died – Doc met Wyatt one last time. It was in Denver, Colorado. Doc was extremely ill by that point, and they both knew he couldn't last much longer. According to the memoirs of Josephine Sara Marcus (Wyatt's commonlaw wife), Wyatt told Doc, *"Isn't it strange that if not for you I wouldn't be alive today, yet, you must go first."*

Josephine said that as Wyatt and Doc parted that day, Doc threw his arm over Wyatt's shoulder saying *"Good-bye old friend. It'll be a long time before we meet again."* Josephine said that at those words, the great Wyatt Earp wept as he watched his old friend walk quickly away in an unstable gait.

The Final Days

Doc finally reached the end of his travels in 1887. The tuberculosis bacteria had ruined his body, and he ultimately drowned in his own blood when the vessels in his lungs were ruptured to the point of no return. Despite movies which have portrayed him as dying in a tuberculosis sanitarium in Glenwood Springs, Colorado, the end actually occurred slightly differently.

There was no sanitarium in Glenwood Springs in 1887 – only a small town built around the site of natural warm springs which supposedly offered recuperative qualities. Doc died as he assumed he always would – in a hotel room. According to some accounts, the woman who had been his love for the past 15 years – Kate Elder – came to Glenwood Springs to care for him when he could no longer manage for himself.

Doc only lasted about six months after arriving at Glenwood Springs. According to reports, Kate, devotedly, was with him until he died. He was buried a short distance away near Linwood Cemetery in a simple grave.

Mannekins representing the participants in the gunfight at O.K. Corral have been positioned today in the approximate spot upon which the individuals stood on the fateful day, October 26, 1881. John Henry Holliday is represented by the dark figure (right rear) with the shotgun near the entryway.

The victims of the gunfight at O.K. Corral were buried in Boot Hill just outside Tombstone in 1881. Frank McLaury, Tom McLaury and Bill Clanton went to the hereafter after a quick but fierce shootout.

This gravesite appeared in the opening scene in the major motion picture "Tombstone" released in 1994. It is just one of numerous gravesites in the old cemetery at Tombstone, many of which include colorful headstone inscriptions from yesteryear.

The Last Days Of John Henry Holliday

In his day, he was one of the most feared gunmen in America. He came from a prominent family in Griffin, Georgia, was well-educated, and seemed destined for a productive life as a physician. Fate, however, dealt him a different hand.

It was the Rocky Mountains of the West which attracted the early gold-miners and animal trappers as the last frontier in America was being settled in the 19th century. And with the gold-mining towns came the gamblers.

The name "Doc" Holliday has captured the minds and imaginations of history enthusiasts, movie-goers and Western fanatics for decades now. Most people know of him as a gunman and gambler who was well-known long before he achieved even greater fame in the gunfight at O.K. Corral in Tombstone, Arizona, in 1881.

Despite the things that are known about him, John Henry is, in many ways, a mysterious individual. He traveled aimlessly throughout the West in the dying days of the old frontier. Though he was a highly-educated man, he left few writings of his experiences, so there are many gaps in his collective history. The only historic recordings of him are the few letters he sent back home, and newspaper accounts of the time which often were inaccurate and sometimes virtually fictitious.

Despite their beauty, the Rockies in Colorado must have been very taxing for John Henry – with his tortured lungs already partially destroyed by the tuberculosis eating away within him. He must have been constantly out of breath, wondering if he was going to make it to the next day.

Doc spent a good bit of time in Denver during these years. His last days, however, were spent in the mining towns of Leadville and Glenwood Springs.

When he could no longer practice dentistry (because of terrible coughing fits), Doc had become a gambler in order to create a livelihood for himself. He was adept at it too, having learned a number of tricks of the trade – including the skill of "skinning cards." This nimble trick was taught to him early in his life by a mulatto servant in his family named Sophie Walton.

Approximately six months after the shoot-out at O.K. Corral, Doc, Wyatt and Warren Earp, Turkey Creek Jack Johnson, Texas Jack Vermillion and a few others involved in the "vendetta ride" in Arizona, left that state for New Mexico and ultimately Colorado. They traveled together for a period of time, but eventually decided to split up, with Doc traveling alone to Denver. Wyatt – and presumably brother Warren – headed westward to Gunnison.

On the way to Denver, John Henry –

who always seemed to be in one kind of affray or another – reportedly met up with some other old friends in Pueblo, Colorado – Sam Osgood and an individual known only as Texas George. The men planned to attend the horse races in Denver and checked into the Windsor Hotel on the northeast corner of Eighteenth and Larimer streets.

The five-floor Windsor was a 300-room hotel – one of Denver's finest – and with its white marble floors, plush red carpeting and sixty-foot mahogany bar, it was just the type lavish establishment that John Henry enjoyed.

Unfortunately, Doc's penchant for trouble caught up with him once again. An individual named Perry Mallen, suddenly arrested Doc. Mallen identified himself as an associate and envoy of Sheriff Johnny Behan of Cochise County in Arizona, where Doc was "Wanted" on a fraudulent murder charge. This incident snowballed and it was several weeks before John Henry was rescued by an acquaintance, Barthomew "Bat" Masterson.

In a further attempt to escape his past, and to continue his livelihood in gambling, Doc left Denver and traveled approximately 125 miles southwestward to the town of Leadville. This community had been a mining boomtown since 1877 when a rich outcropping of silver ore had been discovered. By the time Doc arrived in July of 1882, mining of the precious metal had slowed, but there were still a lot of gambling opportunities at the many saloons and bordellos in town.

One can only guess today at John Henry's perception of Leadville back in the 1880s. Did he enjoy the snow, or did he simply find it to be another impediment to life? What was it like in the bleak shadows of the Rockies in a time when there was no indoor plumbing in many establishments, and no warm comfortable automobiles in which to travel? It was a different world, to be certain.

John Henry Holliday as he appeared in the later years of his life. Gone was the vitality of youth even though he was only in his thirties, age-wise. (Photo courtesy of the Colorado Historical Society)

Though she was called "Big Nose" Kate Elder during her years with Holliday, Mary Katherine Harony was an attractive female in her younger years. According to Karen Holliday Tanner, a cousin of Doc Holliday's, Kate nursed the ailing gunfighter in his last days, courageously and lovingly using her meager savings to sustain the couple until he died.

When he arrived in Leadville, John Henry Holliday found employment as a faro dealer at Cyrus "Cy" Allen's Monarch Saloon which was located at 320 Harrison Avenue, but he didn't last long there. He probably was heavily dependent upon alcohol by this time, and it no doubt affected his ability to perform his job. One must remember that by this time, Doc's best years were behind him. Whatever the circumstances, John Henry left his employment at Allen's Saloon.

According to reports, Holliday found new work nearby as a faro dealer in one of the clubrooms of Hyman's Saloon owned by Mannie Hyman. It was located at 316 Harrison Avenue next door to the Tabor Opera House. Doc apparently decided this was a good spot to put down some roots, and he was able to obtain a room upstairs on the northwest corner of this building. This structure still stands today in this historic mining town.

Doc's tiny room – seven by fourteen feet – was his refuge in these final years. It gave him a view of the snow-covered peaks of the Rockies. However, when he wasn't sleeping, Doc almost always could be found in Hyman's saloon, dealing the faro games, or, across the street at John G. Morgan's Board of Trade Saloon where he often sat on the player's side of the table, playing stud poker.

According to reports, during the years 1882 to 1886, John Henry occasionally visited most of the gambling houses along Harrison Street, plying his trade. However, by this time, his physical condition had debilitated his skills as a gambler, and his winnings had declined considerably. He was often short of money.

It seems almost pitiful to imagine Doc Holliday by this point in his life. He was very quickly succumbing to the tuberculosis ravaging his lungs and his health in general. He had always been slight in stature, but had been lightning quick with strong hands and arms, and usually capable of handling himself in a fight. His growing alcoholism, however, had affected his diet – and thus his weight and strength. He had also lost most of his stamina due to the tuberculosis in his lungs. In short, Doc Holliday was a pitiful sight in the mid-1880s.

When the whiskey – with which Doc was liberally self-medicating himself – ceased to calm the growing pain and ongoing destruction in his lungs, the once handsome dentist and gambler found another medication – laudanum. A local druggist who owned an apothecary at the corner of Sixth and Harrison streets, reportedly befriended Holliday and offered to provide the drug to him "free of charge."

His growing dependency on laudanum coupled with several bouts with pneumonia weakened John Henry even more. He was able to sustain himself with an occasional win at the card tables, but it was a meager existence at best.

As a result of his obvious weak physical state, Doc gradually became a target for predators. In his prime, he needed only to identify himself to most gunfighters – even vicious ones – in order to avoid a fight. But by the time he was living in Leadville, Doc was regularly approached by roughnecks and gamblers who wanted to make a name for themselves as the person who had killed the famous Doc Holliday in a gunfight.

Though he was weak and disabled, John Henry Holliday was never a coward, and he would not be bullied, regardless of the circumstances. For this reason, Leadville, Colorado enjoys the unique distinction of being the site of John Henry "Doc" Holliday's last gunfight.

Two of Doc's old Tombstone enemies – William "Billy" Allen and Johnny Tyler – unfortunately were living in Leadville at the time of Doc's residence there. According to Karen Holliday Tanner in *Doc Holliday: A Family Portrait,* Allen was a former Leadville policeman who had been a friend of Doc's old nemesis – Ike Clanton – during the Tombstone years. Allen had served as a prosecution witness during the O.K.

Corral shooting inquest and had testified against Doc.

". . . he (Allen) had accompanied Reuben Coleman on the day of the gunfight in Tombstone," Ms. Tanner writes. *"They had walked down Allen Street through the O.K. Corral to the front of Camillus S. Fly's Gallery (behind Fly's Boarding House). It was believed by some, and certainly by Doc, that during the fracas, Allen had fired a number of shots aimed at both Holliday and the Earps from the passageway between Fly's buildings. After coming to Leadville, Allen had been a part-time policeman and had been hired as a bartender at the Monarch Saloon."*

Ms. Tanner also explains how Johnny Tyler – after the Tombstone years – was dealing faro at the Casino Gambling Hall in Leadville. *"Tyler had not forgotten the humiliation he had suffered in 1880 when he was evicted from Tombstone's Oriental Saloon by Wyatt Earp with Doc looking on, laughing and taunting him,"* Ms. Tanner adds. *"Tyler harbored tremendous anger and resentment toward Doc and now prepared to vent it.*

"Johnny Tyler and Billy Allen plotted their vendetta. . . In August of 1884, Doc found himself in the unenviable position of owing Billy Allen five dollars. Allen, knowing of Doc's dire straits (financially), had willingly loaned the money, assuming that he would have difficulty repaying the debt. This would give Allen justification to goad the weak, sick Holliday into a gunfight. Doc had borrowed the money with the promise to repay it in less than a week. Seven days later, he had to go to Billy and humbly explain that he had not been able to collect an outstanding debt and therefore did not have the money (to repay Allen)."

For a number of weeks in Leadville, John Henry was goaded and continuously insulted by Johnny Tyler and his cohorts. In an earlier day, they would not have dared to confront and challenge him, but in 1884, Doc was only a shadow of his former persona, and his antagonizers knew it. They continuously tried to press Holliday into a

It was the warm springs and water vapors - along with the gambling opportunities in the saloons - that John Henry Holliday sought as he traveled to Glenwood Springs in May of 1887. Ironically, the surphurous vapors at the springs did more harm than good to Holliday's ailing lungs. Pictured here is a bathhouse built over old Ute vapor cave - which Holliday undoubtedly visited - at Glenwood Springs.

After he arrived in the West, John Henry Holliday spent a great deal of time in saloons at which prostitutes were usually employed. His long-time companion, Mary Katherine Harony had herself been a lady of the evening. Pictured here are reproductions of the original chits used to purchase "time" with the females in saloons from Los Angeles to Dodge City of the 1880s.

Contrary to many accounts of the last days of John Henry Holliday, the gunman did not die in a sanitarium, rather in a room in the Hotel Glenwood which once stood at the corner of 8th Street and Grand Avenue in Glenwood Springs. The hotel was photographed here circa 1887, the year Holliday died. (Courtesy of Frontier Historical Society)

Pictured to the rear of the author is the corner of 8th Street and Grand Avenue in Glenwood Springs. From 1884 to 1945, the three-story posh Hotel Glenwood occupied this corner, and it was here, in 1887, that John Henry Holliday died in one of the upstairs rooms. (Photo by Judy Jackson)

Today, locales such as Vail, Aspen and Breckenridge, Colorado – just a short distance from Glenwood Springs – offer a variety of tempting opportunities for vacationing and enjoyment. (Photo by Olin Jackson)

gunfight, but by this time, Doc no longer even carried a gun. He was virtually destitute, and could not afford to pay a fine for possession of a weapon. After having been stopped and searched a number of times by the Leadville police, he was very careful not to violate the city ordinance by carrying a gun anymore.

"*Words passed between he and Tyler and his cronies at Hyman's Bar, and several of them called him to 'pull his gun,'*" a local Leadville newspaper reporter wrote at the time. *"He said he had none, and as he passed outside, he was called filthy names. . . Next day, he told this writer, with tears of rage coming to his eyes as he talked, that they were insulting and humiliating him because they knew he could not retaliate."*

Billy Allen, who had been waiting for his opportunity, finally issued Doc an ultimatum: Pay the debt by noon of the following Tuesday or face the threat of violence.

"When Tuesday arrived, some of Doc's friends went to his room and told him that Allen was looking for him with a gun," Ms. Tanner continued. "*. . . On the stairway down into the saloon, Doc asked Mannie Hyman to get an officer for protection. He continued into the saloon but did not find Allen. He asked his friend and fellow boarder Frank Lomeister, who was working the day shift as bartender, to get Capt. Edmond Bradbury of the Leadville Police Department or Marshal Harvey Faucett, adding that he did not want to sit around for the afternoon unprotected.*

"Doc then returned to his room, where he stayed until about five o'clock in the afternoon. He sent a friend down to the saloon to conceal his Colt's .41 revolver behind the end of the bar. Doc knew he could not afford the fine if he were found carrying a weapon. Soon thereafter, he arrived and stationed himself by the cigar case, near the end of the bar and the hidden gun."

It was obviously a very dramatic setting, one more characteristic of Doc's earlier days in Dodge City or Tombstone. According to reports of the incident, Billy Allen eventually did enter the saloon, and he had his hand in his pocket as if holding a weapon.

That was all the threat Doc needed. When he saw the hand in the pocket, he immediately grabbed his own pistol and fired a round at Allen. It struck the unfortunate victim in the fleshy part of his upper arm and severed an artery. When Allen fell to the floor, Doc fired at him again. He meant to end this threat once and for all. This round struck the door sill, barely missing Allen's head. Before he could get off another shot, Doc was grabbed by Henry Killerman, and this most assuredly saved the life of one Billy Allen.

Doc was arrested and charged with *"Assault with intent to commit murder."* He was locked up in the jail and his bail was set at five thousand dollars. In an earlier day, John Henry could have easily raised that amount to bail himself out of jail, but by the time of his days in Leadville, Doc was living virtually hand-to-mouth. For that reason, $5,000 was an impossibly high bail for him to raise, and he must surely have thought he was going to be incarcerated until his trial date arrived.

Interestingly, though it has seldom been publicized, John Henry Holliday had many good friends in his later years. Two of these stepped forward immediately. John G. Morgan and Samuel Houston, co-owners of the Board of Trade Saloon, arrived the next morning and posted bail for Doc.

In the trial that followed, a number of witnesses testified to the threats that had been issued at John Henry, and the circumstances of the shooting that had followed. Doc took the stand on his own behalf and explained the details of the loan and the subsequent threat.

According to his testimony, Doc explained that *"I saw Allen coming in with his hand in his pocket, and I thought my life was as good to me as his was to him. I fired the shot and he fell on the floor, and (I) fired the second shot; I knew that I would be a child in his hands if he got hold of me; I weigh 122 pounds; I think Allen weighs 170; I have had pneumonia three or four times. I don't think I would have been able to protect myself against him."*

The jury ultimately returned a verdict of *"Not Guilty"* in the case of *People vs John Henry Holliday*. Following this last gunfight, the curtain essentially came down on the life of Doc Holliday, and it ended completely his gunfighting days. He was never again involved in a shooting incident.

Not too long after the trial, John Henry Holliday must have felt the urge to move on to another town. He had heard of the steamy sulphur waters at Glenwood Springs in northwestern Colorado. This town, no doubt, was doubly attractive, since it was known as a health resort (where he might get treatment for his ailing lungs) and it also was a mining town, offering a variety of gambling opportunities.

Today, the town isn't much larger than it was in Doc's day in 1887. The warm springs are still active and frequented by many individuals interested in the curative qualities of the waters.

Doc traveled to the town in particular to breathe the sulphur vapors in a mistaken assumption that they would help his sick lungs. Ironically, rather than curing Doc's ills, the acidic and acrid vapors caused him to cough even worse, hastening his demise.

Doc had traveled by stagecoach from Leadville to Glenwood Springs. When he reached town, his appearance, according to a newspaper article of that day, reportedly was that of an individual well-advanced in years, with silver hair and an emaciated stooped posture.

His spirits understandably were low, and, according to Karen Holliday Tanner, Doc had written to his former consort – Mary Katherine "Kate" Harony in Globe, Arizona – telling her he was traveling to Glenwood Springs, and asking her to join him there. By this point, Doc must have known he was fast approaching the time when he would need someone to physically assist him with the rudimentary tasks of daily life. He knew of no one to call upon except Kate.

Doc and Kate had traveled many miles together earlier in their lives. They had enjoyed many adventures across the West in places like Tucson, Dodge City and Tombstone. This bond no doubt held them together as Doc fought for life in his final year of life.

Doc and Kate took rooms at the Hotel Glenwood on the northeast corner of Grand Avenue and Eighth Street in Glenwood Springs. This fine hostelry had just recently been built (1886) and offered among its amenities electric lights and both hot and cold running water in every room. The water was pumped directly from the Grand (later renamed Colorado) River, since there was no water system in the town.

Once again – at least for a short while – Doc plied his living as a gambler and faro dealer around town in the gambling houses. Most of the old saloons and gambling establishments are gone today, replaced by more modern structures. Tragically, the Hotel Glenwood burned to the ground on December 14, 1945, killing five people, and destroying forever the last home ever known by John Henry Holliday.

Though Glenwood Springs seems to have paid little heed toward historic preservation over the years, the community yet retains a somewhat scenic air, unique with its warm springs. The stark Rockies can be beautiful, even breath-taking, but they must have been cold and forbidding to Doc in his dying days.

According to accounts, John Henry was admired by the residents in town, and even in the short year that he was there, he cultivated many friends. One man in Glenwood Springs who observed Doc said, *"He walked down the street with a feeble tread and a downcast look. If he heard a (gun)shot, he raised his head with eager attention and glanced this way and that."*

During the last 57 days of his life, John Henry Holliday reportedly rose from his bed at the Hotel Glenwood only twice. He and Kate relied upon the bellhop to serve them their meals so that Kate did not have to leave his bedside.

It is poignant to imagine Kate attending to him in his last days. She easily could have ignored his request to join him in Colorado. She must have known the task of caring for him would not be pleasant. She reportedly never wavered from her duties however, and even used her meager savings to support them after Doc could work no longer. In her later years, she said she considered her relationship with Doc to be a marriage.

All the years of smoking, drinking, thin air, late hours, pneumonia and tuberculosis finally caught up with fabled John Henry Holliday. By the third week in October of 1887, he was delirious, and by Monday of November 7, he reportedly was unable to speak. He died on November 8, 1887.

Contrary to popular myth and modern movie portrayals, Doc Holliday did not die in the Glenwood Springs Sanitarium. There was no sanitarium in Glenwood Springs in 1887. Doc died in the Hotel Glenwood, with the devoted Kate by his side.

Mystery seems to follow Doc right into the grave. The actual site of his burial is not known today. There is a Doc Holliday gravesite in Linwood Cemetery in Glenwood Springs, but it is an acknowledged fact that Doc Holliday is not buried there. Records state only that it is believed that he is *"buried somewhere in this cemetery."*

On the day of Doc's funeral, the weather was cold and wintry. Along with John Henry, one other recently-deceased gentleman was to be buried in Linwood Cemetery on the same day. On the day of the burial, the trail up to the cemetery was impassable, and, as a result, Doc and the other deceased individual were buried by the side of the road somewhere *along the route up to the cemetery*, the intention being that they would be exhumed in the spring and re-buried in the cemetery.

The following spring, however, things changed a bit. The individual buried beside Doc had family in the Glenwood Springs area who readily paid to have their loved one dug up and re-buried in Linwood. Doc, however, had no family in the area, and according to reports, no one was forthcoming to pay the fee to have him exhumed and re-buried. He, therefore, was left buried beside the road.

As time passed, local residents came and went and the grave of John Henry Holliday reportedly was forgotten. It was only in the mid- to late-20th century that local residents – realizing the historic and tourism-related value of Doc's burial site – began trying to locate his grave again. Despite some efforts however, the gravesite remains a mystery. Today, the mortal remains of Dr. John Henry Holliday quite possibly exist beneath someone's back porch or in someone's yard on the route up to Linwood Cemetery.

Other accounts differ with the above scenario. According to one, Doc's remains were indeed later dug up and re-buried in Linwood Cemetery, where they exist today. Another account maintains that they were dug up, but were transported – via the new railroad in Glenwood Springs – back to Georgia in the late 1880s, where they were re-buried in an unmarked grave in Griffin, Georgia, Doc's birthplace.

Interestingly, Doc's consort for all those years in Arizona and Colorado – Mary Katherine Horony – reportedly gathered up Doc's belongings from his room after he died, and shipped them to Doc's one true love – his cousin, Sister Mary Melanie of the Order of the Sisters of Mercy – who had entered a convent to become a nun after Doc left Atlanta, Georgia for the West.

After she had disposed of Doc's last possessions, Kate then left the sadness in Glenwood Springs forever, but remained for a time in the Crystal Valley region of Colorado. On March 2, 1890, she married George M. Cummings in the mining town of Aspen, Colorado, a well-known ski resort today. The couple moved about before finally settling in Bisbee, Cochise County, Arizona in 1895, just a few miles from Tombstone where Doc had gained so much fame in 1881-1882.

This marriage lasted approximately nine years before Kate left Mr. Cummings who was an alcoholic. On June 2, 1900, she accepted employment as the housekeeper of John J. Howard of Dos Cabezas, Arizona. She remained in his employ until Howard's death in 1930. On June 13, 1931, Kate wrote to Arizona Governor George W. Hunt requesting permission to live in the state-owned Arizona Pioneers Home in Prescott.

Governor Hunt reportedly granted Kate's request. For the last nine years of her life, Mary Katherine Cummings (nee Horony) – also known by many as "Big-Nosed Kate" – lived out her life in the town where, in 1880, she and Doc had spent time together just prior to his Tombstone days. She died on November 2, 1940, and was buried at the Pioneer Cemetery in Prescott.

Today, one can only imagine how John Henry Holliday felt in his last days, separated from his family and friends back in Georgia, as well as his surrogate family – the Earps – who, by that time, were scattered from Arizona to California. Thankfully, he did have Kate in his last days. She no doubt brought him much comfort in his final hours.

It, however, seems a pity the last remains of one of the most famous and fabled of all the individuals of the Old West, lie in an unknown and unmarked grave today, mysterious and yet respected even in death. Ironically, that's probably just the way Doc would have wanted it. His lonely wandering soul is finally at peace.

Where Lie The Bones Of John Henry 'Doc' Holliday?

He is one of the most celebrated figures of the American West, but today, the final resting place of John Henry "Doc" Holliday is unknown. . . or is it?

John Henry was born in Griffin on August 14, 1851. That's a documented fact. The location of Holliday's last remains, however, is a mystery to historians today.

Holliday's parents – Henry Burroughs Holliday and Alice Jane McKey – were from South Carolina. They provided a good education for their son, but his primary interest was the great outdoors. Nothing interested young John Henry more than hunting, fishing and horseback riding. In time, this came to include the use of firearms.

In 1861, Henry Burroughs Holliday accepted a presidential appointment from Jefferson Davis to serve as quartermaster in the 27th Georgia Infantry, Confederate States of America. After the Battle of Manassas, Henry Burroughs was promoted to the rank of major and fought in the Peninsula Campaign as well as in the Battle of Malvern Hill.

In 1862, a short time after fighting at Malvern Hill, Major Holliday was forced by ill health to leave the army and return to his family in Griffin.

As the war ground on and moved steadily nearer to Georgia, Major Holliday sold most of his holdings in Spalding County and moved his family southward to Lowndes County, Georgia, where they settled on a 2,450-acre farm seven miles northwest of Valdosta. Henry Burroughs was hoping to find a safe haven from the war for his wife and child.

Doc Holliday's life contradicts the myth of the man.

By 1864, Generals John Logan and William T. Sherman had successfully devastated much of Georgia – including the state's heart – Atlanta. Plantations, farms, homes, factories and businesses were put to the torch and destroyed. Wells were poisoned. Personal property and stores were pillaged. This devastation had a life-long impact on young John Henry Holliday and gave him a determination for life which would serve him through many hard times.

In 1872, John Henry graduated from the Pennsylvania School of Dental Surgery. He returned to Georgia and shortly thereafter began a dental practice in Atlanta in the offices of Dr. Arthur C. Ford. It was only a short time later that John Henry was confronted with his first real test in life. He was diagnosed with tuberculosis and advised to move to a dryer climate such as that offered by the American West.

Many say that John Henry Holliday left Georgia and rode off into those make-believe Hollywood Westerns that made him a legend. In the movies, he appeared to be a fearless gunman and a killer. In reality, however, by this stage in John Henry's life, he was a sick man looking for a way to survive and enjoy his last remaining years.

He took up gambling for a livelihood after his tubercular cough became too pronounced to allow him to practice dentistry anymore. According to personal letters and fleeting comments made along the way, he secretly longed for his Georgia home to which he knew he could never return.

During his lifetime, John Henry was credited with the shooting of a number of men who were actually shot by other individuals.[1] The newspapers of that day, however – in the absence of factual information – seemed to fabricate much of the details of Holliday's life out west.

With its usual artistic license, Hollywood also created a false image and persona for John Henry Holliday. In most instances, it portrayed him as a bloodthirsty and cold-blooded killer.

Two unmarked graves in the Thomas family plot at Oak Hill Cemetery in Griffin, Georgia. Is this the final resting place of John Henry Holliday and his father? **(Photo by Edward Jordan Lanham)**

In reality, many of the shootings in which Holliday was involved occurred because much larger and stronger men – who viewed John Henry as weak and vulnerable – tried to increase their own stature at his expense. These instances invariably ended in a gunfight when the men tried to manhandle John Henry. Holliday was weak physically, but he was blessed with very fast hand speed and deadly accuracy which he demonstrated on a number of occasions – the last time of which occurred in a barroom in Glenwood Springs, Colorado.

Doc Holliday's life contradicts the myth of the man. He was not a sorrowful man, nor was his life a sad one according to many accounts. "When any of you fellows have been hunted from one end of the country to the other, as I have been, you'll understand what a bad man's reputation is built on," John Henry is reported to have once said.

Inaccurate information seemed to plague John Henry in death just as it had in real life. His obituary was printed in a variety of newspapers, but none of them agreed on the facts. The local newspaper in Glenwood Springs, Colorado (where he died), stated that Doc was buried in Linwood Cemetery, Glenwood Springs, Colorado, at 4:00 p.m., November 8, 1887. However, the steep trail that led to the cemetery – which exists on a hilltop – was impassable due to snow and ice at the time. According to records, Doc Holliday was buried in a temporary grave at the foot of the hill, and no one knows – with even a measure of certainty – exactly where he is buried today.

The same Glenwood Springs newspaper also stated that many friends attended Holliday's funeral, but since he was buried the same day he died, this too is doubtful.[2] Further, both a monument and Holliday's headstone in Linwood Cemetery contain numerous mistakes. It was almost as if his detractors were attempting to harass him even in death. Tombstone, Arizona historian Ben Traywick seems to state it best: "It is difficult to see how so many mistakes could be made on a headstone without trying."[3]

Today, Linwood Cemetery – overlooking Glenwood Springs – contains a headstone and a monument to the memory of Holliday. Supposedly, he was buried there, but most historians are convinced he was not. One account maintains that following the spring thaw in 1888, a relative of Holliday's traveled to Glenwood Springs, retrieved the gunfighter's body, and returned with it to Georgia.

Interestingly, current research indicates John Henry Holliday quite possibly is buried in his hometown of Griffin, Georgia, in Oak Hill Cemetery. Mr. Bill Dunn who heads up the Doc Holliday Society and is a distant relative of the gunfighter, has been engaged in extensive research on the Holliday family for a number of years.

"There is no doubt in my mind why the people in Glenwood Springs don't know exactly where Doc is buried," Dunn said in an interview in 1999. "He isn't there. Doc is buried right here in his hometown of Griffin. He was originally buried in Linwood Cemetery, but he is not there now. You just don't lose the grave of a man who held his celebrity status."

Some researchers believe that Doc's father, Major Henry Holliday, C.S.A., traveled to Glenwood Springs and claimed his son's remains. Money was not an issue for Major Holliday who was a man of substance and wealth. Transportation of the coffin and remains could have been accomplished relatively easily too, since the train depot in Griffin was within a mile of the cemetery.

"You just don't lose the grave of a man who held his celebrity status."

Dunn says he believes that if Major Holliday did not retrieve his son's remains himself, he had his nephew, Robert Alexander Holliday, perform the task. Doc's companion – Mary Katherine Haroney, also known as "Big Nose" Kate Elder – recalled that one of Doc's cousins visited him in Tombstone after the shootout at O.K. Corral. Dunn says he believes this man was cousin Robert.

Strangely coincidental – or maybe not – is the fact that the final resting place of Major Holliday – Doc's father – is also unknown today. Considering the fact that Major Holliday was a wealthy landowner, a decorated veteran of three wars, and the mayor of Valdosta, Georgia, it is highly unusual and surprising that his final resting place is not marked – or definitely known – today.

Major Henry Burroughs Holliday outlived his son by several years. He died on February 22, 1893 in Valdosta. Despite many years of searches, the location of his grave has eluded researchers.

Bill Dunn maintains that he has located a marked grave for every Holliday family member in Valdosta and Griffin – all except for Major Holliday and his son, Doc. Dunn says he now believes without a doubt he has found the unmarked graves of both in Griffin's Oak Hill Cemetery.

The two graves which Dunn says belong to Henry Burroughs and John Henry Holliday are located in the Thomas family plot. The families enjoyed a very close relationship, and Dunn says he believes the Thomas family may have agreed to an anonymous burial of Doc in their family plot to avoid vandalism of his grave.

"I believe they buried Doc in Oak Hill when he was brought back from Glenwood Springs, and Major Holliday was buried there when he died," Dunn remarks. "Why would a plot containing expensive marble markers of the Thomas family contain two concrete slab graves with no marking or identification? Could it be that they wanted them to remain anonymous?"

Osgood Miller, an employee of Clark Monument Company for forty-six years, adds credence to Dunn's claim. He says he remembers the late Charlie McElroy, who was cemetery superintendent during the 1930s, telling him that Doc Holliday was buried in Oak Hill. Osgood says Charlie pointed in the direction of the Thomas plot when he made the statement. Several years later, the late Griffin historian Laura Clark pointed out the same area as Doc's final resting place.

In 1906, the *Washington Post* stated, *"Doc Holliday was a native of Georgia and take him all in all, he was possessed of the most daredevil and reckless bravery of any of his associates."* It is one of the few times in which Holliday was attributed the acclaim to which he is entitled, for he was a very brave man indeed to have faced what he faced in the American West of the 1880s.

Wyatt Earp, who was probably the closest friend John Henry Holliday ever had, died in 1929. Ironically, after all the gunfights in which he was involved, Earp was never even wounded. He died in bed from what undoubtedly was prostate cancer (listed as prostatitis on his death certificate). While he and Doc were both still alive, he was quoted as saying *"Doc Holliday is the nerviest, fastest, deadliest man with a six-gun I ever saw."*

If anyone knew about Doc Holliday's capabilities, it was Wyatt Earp. One can only marvel today that the final resting place of such a celebrated figure of the Old West is, for all intents and purposes, unknown.

ENDNOTES

1/ *John Henry* by Ben T. Traywick

2/ Ibid

3/ Ibid

Moonshining, And The Murder Of Sheriff William Shirey

An ambush was waiting when Troup County's top lawman led a party of officers to an illicit liquor "still" on February 26, 1917. Shots rang out as Sheriff William Brewer Shirey was destroying the still. The beloved official died minutes later from a gunshot wound, and the county suddenly was thrown into turmoil.

Troup County and its government seat at LaGrange were under the "bone dry" law in 1917, but "wet spots" still dotted the countryside, making the issue of Prohibition a much-discussed topic. Early that same year, a tragic incident had occurred as a result of illicit liquor trafficking which underscored the need for a resolution to the growing problem.

Many other counties and municipalities in Georgia had outlawed alcohol as well, and they also struggled with the problem. In Troup, it was illegal to make or sell any alcoholic beverages, but "wildcat stills" could be found in most communities, and law-abiding citizens considered them a blemish on their otherwise tranquil locale.

While devout ministers preached sobriety in 1917, LaGrange and Troup County news reports often revealed that the ministerial efforts were in vain. The lawlessness which occurred in the region was attributed to "demon gin," a threat to peaceful living that was echoed throughout the state of Georgia and the nation.

By year's end, on December 18, 1917, the U.S. Congress had passed the 18th amendment to the Constitution outlawing the manufacture, sale or transportation of alcoholic liquors. The amendment was ratified on January 29, 1919, ushering in the formal Prohibition era. Ironically, as it sought to reduce lawlessness, Prohibition actually was the catalyst for a new wave of American crime in the 1920s, most notably that of organized crime in larger municipalities such as Chicago and New York. Included in this crime-wave was the production of illicit liquor which was pervasive throughout the nation – particularly in the deep South.

Sleeping Volcano

In the March 1, 1917, edition of *The LaGrange Graphic*, an editorial call-to-arms suggested that the corruption that accompanies illicit liquor had been a problem brewing locally for some time.

"Our people have been sleeping over a volcano for the last several years," the *Graphic* intoned, "secure in the belief that our county was safe from the things which had made other sections of the country notorious for lawlessness. The volcano has erupted at last..."

The sleeping volcano had indeed erupted four days earlier, and the news account trumpeted the cold-blooded shooting of Sheriff W. Brewer Shirey, who was left bleeding and dying in the Troup County back-country. It was termed "one of the most dastardly crimes ever committed in the state." The assassination of Sheriff Shirey sent chills throughout Troup County and the state of Georgia.

The following account was compiled from articles in *The LaGrange Graphic* and *The LaGrange Reporter* newspapers; from interviews with Troup County natives who remembered the case; and from a summary of the crime by Troup County Archives Director Kaye Minchew who used newspapers, Superior Court records and interviews to research the case in 1983.

In February of 1917, local law enforcement authorities received information about several illicit moonshine distilleries in the Oak Grove community in the southern section of Troup County. In addition to requests that the "stills" be destroyed, the sheriff's office also had received written threats demanding they stay away from certain stills in the southern part of the county.

Ignoring the threats, Sheriff Shirey, U.S. Deputy Marshall J.A. Henderson and Deputy Sheriff S.A. Smith set out on the morning of February 26 to the suspected location of several of the stills. After searching a wooded area near Flat Shoals Creek for a short time, the officers happened upon

LAGRANGE, GEORGIA, MARCH 1, 1917

SHERIFF W. B. SHIREY FOULLY ASSASSINATED

The March 1, 1917 issue of the LaGrange Reporter announces the murder of Sheriff William Brewer Shirey.

LIQUOR LAIR – Large wooded stretches – reminiscent of the early 1900s when a vast wilderness provided ample room for the surreptitious production of illegal liquor – still remain along South Thompson Road in Troup County's Oak Grove community. (Photo by Jackie Kennedy)

what proved to be a relatively large still, capable of producing about 350 gallons of moonshine per run. In addition, they discovered more than 20 barrels of beer at the site.

In their haste to quickly deal with the situation at the still, the trio of lawmen quite possibly ignored one fact that might ultimately have saved Sheriff Shirey's life. According to the initial account of the ambush recorded in the March 1, 1917 edition of *The LaGrange Graphic*, the still was "fired up" when the officers found it, with everything in place for one to begin making a run of corn liquor. The readiness of the still should have tipped off the lawmen to the dangerous presence nearby of the moonshiners. Had the still been silent and inoperative – with its workers in the fields or at home – the officers' job would have been much safer.

Disregarding the still's state of operation, the sheriff, marshal and deputy began pouring out beer from the barrels and destroying the still. Most of the beer had been emptied and Sheriff Shirey had just opened the still to drain its contents when the first shots were fired.

According to a newspaper account of the incident, several shots were blasted in rapid sequence by someone in ambush about 35 or 40 yards from the still. Because the shots rang out so rapidly, no one could tell with certainty exactly how many shots had been fired.

Marshal Henderson and Deputy Smith later said they believed it was the first shot that struck their partner, the bullet entering the sheriff's right breast, passing through his body and exiting under the left arm. The bullet was thought to have passed straight through his heart.

Dazed from the moment he was shot, the sheriff died about 30 minutes later. Neither of the other officers was injured.

Sheriff William Brewer Shirey was 42 years of age at the time of his death. He had been Troup's sheriff for three years. He left a wife and two daughters and, according to newspaper tributes, an undying heritage to his bereaved.

Arrests

Emotions ran high as word spread throughout the county that Sheriff Shirey had been shot and killed. A posse was formed early in the evening of February 26 with plans to raid that night the settlement at which the tragedy had occurred. More level-headed and responsible individuals, however, overruled the planned raid, and the decision was made to wait until Tuesday morning, at which time arrest warrants would be issued for the suspects.

The next morning, S.A. Smith – who had been sworn in as acting sheriff the previous evening – deputized several officers and, armed with warrants, headed to Oak Grove where the posse arrested 11 men – nine white and two black – who were placed in the Troup County Jail.

Emotions ran high as word spread throughout the county that Sheriff Shirey had been shot and killed.

While Smith and his deputies were making their arrests, other U.S. deputies from several adjoining counties made their way to the ambush site where they soon discovered and destroyed two more liquor stills nearby. Tuesday evening, another pair of "wild cat" stills were located and demolished.

Within days, a sizeable reward had been offered for information leading to the arrest and conviction of the guilty parties. The governor himself offered $500, which was equal to the amount being offered by the Troup County government. The Department of Justice pitched in an additional $200 and local businessmen pledged a "considerable sum."

Wildcat Stills

Troup County and LaGrange residents were outraged. Their sheriff was dead and his family had been left virtually destitute.

Editors of *The LaGrange Graphic* spoke the sentiments of many: "The law abiding people of LaGrange and Troup County stand appalled – horrified – that lawlessness has endeavored to override the law and plant its banner of defiance upon the hills of Troup County."

When local citizens learned of the "foul assassination" of Sheriff Shirey, according to the editorial, they "stood aghast, dumbfounded and awestruck at the boldness of the deed. They could scarcely be made to realize that such a thing could have happened in Troup County. But it has happened, and the citizens of our county stand face to face with a condition that must be blotted out at any cost."

A town meeting was set for March 5 at the Troup County Courthouse to discuss ways to suppress illicit stills and the unlawful sale of liquor. All districts in the county were encouraged to send large delegations. An estimated 400 citizens attended the mass meeting, all determined "to rid Troup County of wildcat stills and blind tigers."

Wildcat stills were those illicit distilleries that often were quickly built, and which could be quickly disassembled and moved

NEW LAWMAN – S.A. Smith was sworn in as acting sheriff on the evening of February 26 as the manhunt began for the murderers of Sheriff Shirey. Smith later won a special election for Troup County Sheriff in early April and regularly appeared on the pages of the local newspaper as he led the effort to eradicate illicit liquor distilleries in the county. In reality, he was no more successful in slowing the efforts of the "moonshiners" than were any of his contemporary sheriffs all over the Deep South.

NOTORIOUS CONVEYANCE – The aged steel bridge at Flat Shoals Creek on Salem Road in southern Troup County has remained unchanged for well over 85 years. The illegal liquor distillery at which Sheriff Shirey was assassinated once existed a short distance up the creek from this point.
(Photo by Jackie Kennedy)

Flat Shoals Creek has changed little since the early 1900s when illegal liquor distilleries proliferated up and down its length. (Photo by Jackie Kennedy)

Sheriff Shirey's funeral was conducted at his church - East Vernon Baptist Church - in rural Troup County. (Photo by Jackie Kennedy)

to another location. They dotted the map across Troup County.

Blind tigers were houses at which a knowing individual could obtain – for a fee – illegal moonshine whiskey.

Convictions

A special session of Troup County Superior Court was convened on April 30, 1917, to try the men arrested after the ambush. Following a grand jury investigation, two of the 11 – John Thompson and Walter Easterledge – were charged with the murder of Sheriff Shirey. Two others – Lewis and Lon Hart – were charged with and ultimately convicted of illicitly distilling and possessing an illegal amount of liquor, and each was sentenced to two years imprisonment. The remaining seven suspects – including both blacks – were not charged.

Thompson and Easterledge faced separate trials that attracted much attention and were attended by large numbers from Troup and surrounding counties. Both defendants were found "Guilty" of murder, and Easterledge was sentenced to life in prison after his jury recommended leniency.

At Thompson's trial, a "large number of witnesses" for the State were put on the stand while the defense introduced no witnesses, relying solely upon the statement of the accused. Subsequently, Thompson was found "Guilty" and sentenced to hang on June 29, 1917.

The 21-year-old farmhand appealed his murder conviction, citing irregularities that occurred during the trial and the presence of an incompetent and biased juror. Thompson claimed the irregularities included the use of a confession obtained by force. He also maintained that one juror, who publicly stated prior to the trial that he hoped Thompson would hang for his crime, was clearly biased.

On June 12, 1917 – less than three weeks from his execution date – Thompson's request for a retrial was denied and construction was begun on a scaffold for the impending execution. At the last minute, the Georgia Supreme Court agreed to hear the case and postponed the hanging.

Execution

When he received word of his "Stay of Execution," Thompson undoubtedly heaved a sigh of relief. His appeal gained him an extra year of life, but it ultimately did not save his life. On July 26, 1918, at the age of 23, he was hung from the gallows at the Troup County Jail – exactly one year and five months after the shooting of Sheriff Shirey.

Interestingly, John Thompson had the distinction of being the last legal hanging in Troup County history. A tragic twist to the story involves rumors which circulated for years following Thompson's execution for the crime.

Thompson, who pled "Not Guilty" to the crime, maintained his innocence right up until his execution. Troup County Sheriff Lem Bailey, who headed the department from 1952 to 1980, said it was rumored that Thompson actually *was* innocent, and that the boy's *father* was the one actually responsible for murdering Sheriff Shirey.

Thompson's father was not among the 11 men arrested in the case but, less than five months after his son was hung, the elder Thompson committed suicide.

Aging family members in the 1980s continued to maintain the innocence of both John Thompson and his father, saying the father's grief was due to the hanging death of his son, not remorse over the commission of a crime for which he had allowed his innocent son to be executed.

At the young age of 23, John Thompson went to the gallows and was hung by the neck until dead in old Troup County Jail in downtown LaGrange. It was the last legal hanging in the county. Today, this structure houses the offices of Chattahoochee Valley Art Museum. (Photo by Jackie Kennedy)

Lingering Vestiges

While the shooting death of Sheriff Shirey created unity among citizens in the public efforts against the illicit manufacture and sale of moonshine, the county's problems with bootleg liquor and moonshine stills persisted.

In the year of 1948 alone, 192 liquor stills were dismantled by county police with a total of 54,620 gallons of mash and 578 gallons of liquor destroyed.

In 1965, Sheriff Bailey reported that his department had destroyed the largest liquor still on record in Troup County. According to an article in the January 30, 1965 edition of *The LaGrange Daily News*, the sheriff said the sophisticated operation was capable of producing 500 gallons of whiskey per run, giving moonshiners the opportunity to make $3,000 per run.

In 1972, after great debate by the mayor and city council, the officials decided to grant a business license to the first liquor store in LaGrange. It opened its doors at noon on September 15, an act which ironically put a huge dent in the illicit liquor business in Troup County.

The Last Hanging In White County

On a sorrowful day in the autumn of 1906, the last hanging in White County – and indeed, possibly all of north Georgia – was conducted on a hillside fronting the Clarkesville Highway, just beyond what today is Truett-McConnell College in Cleveland, Georgia.

AUTHOR'S NOTE: The incident detailed on the pages which follow is true, and all names are the actual names of the individuals involved. The names of the victim and her family, however, have been omitted at the request of surviving family members.

The hanging of Bob Moore, September 10, 1906, on the outskirts of Cleveland, Georgia, was a legal execution carried out by duly elected county officials. Moore was a thirty-six-year-old black male who had been convicted of the rape of a seven-year-old white girl.

When compared to today's judicial system, Moore's speedy trial and execution, as well as the carnival atmosphere that prevailed at his execution, seem to have been a travesty of justice – a sad day in the history of White County, Georgia. Certainly, from the moment of his arrest, Bob Moore was a doomed man. However, when viewed within a historic perspective of the times, a different picture emerges; a picture which shows the judge and sheriff acting in a most courageous manner under difficult and very dangerous circumstances.

Perhaps Bob Moore received as fair a trial as any black man could have received in the South at that time. In 1906, just forty-one years after the end of the Civil War, no crime – not even murder – was considered more heinous by the white population than the assault of a white woman by a black man. It is a dark period of Southern history in which many a black man, convicted (or many times just accused) of a similar crime, met his fate at the end of a lynch rope.

In many instances, even more brutal and sadistic measures were used instead of lynching. In a throwback to the Middle Ages, burning at the stake was another form used to extract as much pain and suffering as possible from the accused before his eventual death.

As of this writing (1989), first-hand

remembrances and knowledge of the execution of Bob Moore are just now receding into the mists of history. Hardly anyone who actually knew him was still alive at the time this article was penned. There are, however, still many people in the White County area one generation removed, to whom details of Moore have been passed down by their parents and older relatives.

By most accounts, Bob Moore was a good, hard-working family man. He had worked for the family of the victim for some twenty years (all of his adult life) and was regarded almost as a member of the family.

Moore also had a family of his own. They were listed in the 1900 Federal Census of White County in the Nacoochee District, House #74: Moor(e), Bob, born Feb. 1870, age 36; wife Nancy S., born June 1872, age 27; son Logan, born August 1888, age 11; son Richard, born May 1890, age 10; daughter Jennie, born August 1894, age 5; and son Edker, born April 1897, age 3. Bob and Nancy had been married twelve years.

Moore's most consuming vice – and certainly a contributing factor to the incident which ultimately cost him his life – was his fondness for alcohol. And good moonshine whiskey was not hard to obtain in Nacoochee Valley in the early 1900s, when many a farmer found that it was easier to transport his corn to market by the gallon than by the bushel.

The family for whom Bob Moore worked was one of the first families to settle in White County. The father of the victim was one of the four brothers that owned adjoining farms in the Sautee-Nacoochee area. They were very prosperous, influential, and highly regarded members of the community.

Today, no transcript of the trial can be found at the White County Courthouse. As a result, many of the details of the crime must be found in newspaper accounts which, although somewhat inflammatory, appear to be reasonably accurate.

The incident which would shortly cost Bob Moore his life occurred Saturday, August 18, 1906, at the farm of Moore's employer. The victim – who had just reached the age of seven only two months earlier – and her four-year-old brother, were customarily following Moore around as he did his work.

The *Dahlonega Nugget* newspaper of August 24, 1906, provides the following version of the circumstances:

"It occurred in the potato patch off out of sight of the house. The negro went to pull some weeds and this little child and her small brother were allowed to go with him. In a short time, the boy returned, saying that the negro told him he could not cross the creek, but the mother thought nothing of it for she felt confident that the trusty negro would take care of her little daughter.

"After awhile, the negro and child returned. And when supper was announced ready, the little thing was lying down who said that she was sick and did not want to eat any. And still nothing was suspicioned.

"That night, the little girl cried in her sleep, and the next morning after the mother found bruises on her child, she was informed

In many instances, even more brutal and sadistic measures were used instead of lynching.

DEATH SENTENCE – The old White County Courthouse, which still stands as of this writing on the town square in Cleveland, Georgia, was photographed (above) from the southeastern side, at approximately the same time (circa 1897-1905) as the trial of Bob Moore. Moore was convicted of rape in this courthouse and sentenced to death by hanging. This photo evidently was taken from the old Henderson Hotel which once stood on the square. (Photo courtesy of Jean Gilreath and Gil Colnot)

by her how it occurred, saying that the negro said he would kill her if she ever told it.

"The father was notified of the fact by his wife who plead to him not to kill Bob, but to let the law take its course. Mr. _______ secured the services of a neighbor and the two carried the fiend ten miles to Cleveland and turned him over to Sheriff Jackson.

"The news spread like wild-fire, and by night, men came in from all parts of the county and stood around in crowds of a dozen or so in a place talking low."

The sheriff of White County was forty-year-old William Andrew Jackson who had served as sheriff since 1898. The judge of the Northeastern Circuit, of which White County was a part, was John Johnson Kimsey. Judge Kimsey, born May 23, 1849, had been admitted to the bar in 1873, and was elected White County's representative to the Georgia General Assembly in 1877, 1880, and 1883. On October 29, 1894, he was elected judge of the Superior Court Northeastern Circuit, and had held that post continuously ever since. He was one of the most highly respected judges in the state.

Although court was not in session at the time of Bob Moore's arrest, Judge Kimsey, who made his home in Cleveland and realized that there was going to be serious trouble, ordered that Moore be carried to Hall County for his protection and instructed that a special term of court be convened to try him.

According to a news account of the incident in *The Dahlonega Nugget*:

"That night when the sheriff started off with the negro, it is said that at least fifty shots were fired close by, some of the balls throwing mud on the sheriff's back, but instead of stopping, Jackson increased the speed of his team and was soon out of reach.

"On Monday, people came flocking into Cleveland from all parts of White and many adjoining counties, and by 3:00 o'clock, the time the sheriff returned with his negro, the crowd in town numbered at least 1,500. One man grabbed at the negro as they were taking him out of the hack, but was stopped in time to save trouble."

In an attempt to give Moore as fair a trial as possible, Judge Kimsey appointed all four of the local attorneys for Moore's defense. These four attorneys, Charles Herbert Edwards, Joseph W.H. Underwood, George S. Kytle, and William J. Oakes, were all respected in their profession, and all had successful careers in law and other public service. For the prosecution, W.A. Charters of Gainesville, Georgia, was the Solicitor General (present-day office of District Attorney).

After the Grand Jury, with John H.

Stovall, foreman, issued a True Bill for "Rape," a Traverse Jury of twelve citizens of the community was selected. All twelve were white males which certainly did not help any chance, however slight it may have been, that Moore may have had for acquittal or leniency. The twelve jurors were: 1/ C.L. Franklin; 2/ F.L. Smith; 3/ Frank Miles; 4/ J.E. Pardue; 5/ G.B. Irvin; 6/ J.H. Brackett; 7/ Lenwood Edwards; 8/ W.F. Taylor; 9/ J.M. Allison; 10/ J.W. Westmoreland; ll/ J.T. Curtis; 12/ Jesse Conner.

The defense presented by Moore's attorneys has not been preserved for posterity. In any event, they most certainly did not have adequate time to prepare their case.

The day of the trial, the little seven-year-old victim was carried into the courtroom upon pillows, to testify for the prosecution. In a little over an hour and a half from the time the trial began, a verdict was reached: "Guilty, With No Recommendation For Mercy" was the decision handed down by the jurors. When the verdict was read, it brought a cheer from the spectators in the courtroom.

As a result of this verdict, Judge Kimsey issued the following sentence:

". . . on the tenth day of September, 1906, between the hours of 1:00 o'clock a.m. and 4:00 o'clock p.m., he be taken from said common jail by the sheriff of said county, and a sufficient guard to such place within one mile of the courthouse in said county as may be provided by the proper authority of said county whereas when the said defendant shall then and there be hung by the neck until he is dead."

The last part of the sentence ordered:

"The execution of this sentence shall be in private and witnessed only by the executing officer, a sufficient guard, the relatives of said defendant, and such clergymen and friends as

Old White County Jail, photographed here in the 1990s, still stands as of this writing, and currently serves as the Cleveland-White County Chamber of Commerce building. It was in this jail that Bob Moore was confined during his trial in 1906. In the distance up the street stands historic White County Courthouse – in which the trial took place. (Photo by Olin Jackson)

LAST MOMENTS – Bob Moore, with the noose already around his neck, stares solemnly at the photographer's lense moments before his execution on September 10, 1906. The grim visages of the officials conducting the execution leave no doubt that it was a traumatic experience. The individual standing on the left side of the gallows wearing a dark hat is John Jackson. Standing beside him is Deputy Sheriff Frank Carroll holding the hood that was placed over Moore's head. Sheriff William Andrew Jackson stands behind Moore with one hand holding the noose. Two of the other four men were Newt Blalock and Floyd Shelnut. (Photo courtesy of Jimmy Anderson)

he may desire.

"Sentence pronounced and signed this the 20th day of August, 1906.

W.A. Charters, Sol. General

J.J. Kimsey, Judge of the Supreme Court for the Northeastern Circuit"

After the trial, Moore was taken back to the old White County Jail which still stands today one block north of the old town square in Cleveland. He reportedly awaited his execution there in silence. If any appeals were filed on his behalf, they were rejected.

The site selected for the execution was just off the Clarkesville Highway, a short distance past what is today Truett-McConnell College. Shortly after 10:00 a.m., Monday morning, September 10, 1906, Bob Moore was conveyed – under heavy guard – to the gallows that had been erected. He rode in a horse-drawn wagon, sitting on the pine coffin that would very soon contain his lifeless body.

As the following news article from the September 14, 1906 *Dahlonega Nugget* will attest, the execution was in no way the private affair that Judge Kimsey had ordered:

"Bob Moore, the negro who assaulted the little seven-year-old daughter of ________ in the county of White, was hanged last Monday at 11 o'clock, just twenty-one days from the time the deed was committed.

"'Dead and on his way to heaven,' so the negro said through a minister. The idea of a negro or any one else going to heaven, after committing such a horrible crime as this and then be put on a seat up there by the side of some good old person who lived and died a Christian, we don't believe it.

"At any rates, Bob Moore paid the penalty in the presence of three or four thousand persons, and is now covered up with earth. A number of people were present from Dahlonega, including City Marshall Walker, who assisted in tieing (sic) him for the hanging.

"At about 11:00 o'clock, he was brought out from the jail by Sheriff Jackson and carried about a mile to the place of execution under a strong guard. There was nothing around the gallows except a piece of black calico fastened to a rope, and men, women and children, both white and black, could all see the criminal alike.

"A white minister, whose name we did not learn, read the negroe's confession and so-called profession made by him the night before – the negro didn't utter a word on the scaffold.

"Then, when everything was arranged and ready, the sheriff sprung the trigger and a great cheer went up from the crowd as the criminal fell. A rush was made and in a very few minutes, the rope and calico surrounding the scaffold were cut and torn into little bits of pieces, and in the pockets of all those who enjoy getting hold of such things at a hanging.

"While this wild rush was being made for the calico and rope, Jerry Mingo, a Spaniard who has been living in Cleveland for a number of years, ran up on the scaffold where there was a bucket of drinking water, saying, 'Let's baptize him,' who then quickly dipped his hand into the bucket and threw what water he could hold in it three times down on the negroe's body below, just as the thread of life had snapped.

"After life was extinct, all were allowed to march round and view the corpse, ladies first. Then, all was over, and the occurrences passed into history."

Bob Moore finally was laid to rest. The *Dahlonega Nugget* printed one last item which became a sort of macabre footnote to the entire event:

"We saw a White County man in Dahlonega last week who wore a piece of the rope that recently stretched the neck of Bob Moore in that county. . ."

A Retreat From Tragedy:

Nacoochee Valley's 'West End,' And The James Hall Nichols Family

A sense of mystery and a tragic legacy pervade the historic old home built by Capt. James Nichols (CSA) in White County shortly after the U.S. Civil War.

Below Sal Mountain, at the junction of U.S. Highway 17 and GA Highway 75 in north Georgia's White County, an imposing Italianate villa looms in the edge of the fabled Nacoochee Valley. For over a century, the home has been as much a part of the Nacoochee as have the broad fields, the song of the Chattahoochee, and the blue foothills enfolding into the mountains.

Since the days of the Cherokee, legends – handed down through folklore, poetry, and the passion of moon-struck bankers – have haunted the Nacoochee. Included among these legends is the story of James Hall Nichols, builder of the impressive home which he named "West End."

Born in Milledgeville on February 17, 1835, Nichols lived in the Midway community there, and married Kate Latimer on April 30, 1856. He was a merchant in Milledgeville – a druggist.

Prior to the U.S. Civil War in 1861, James and Kate Nichols became the proud parents of a daughter – Anna Ruby – whose name has found a lasting permanence attached to the nearby tempestuous mountain waterfall a few miles north of Nacoochee Valley in Unicoi State Park.

At the outbreak of war, Nichols was elected captain of the elite "Governor's Horse Guard" in Georgia. The cavalry unit saw action in northwestern Virginia and then along the South Carolina coast where Nichols may have first contracted the malaria which plagued him the rest of his life. In early 1862, the unit was moved to a site near Richmond, where it became Company A of Phillip's Legion, Stuart's Cavalry, in the Army of Northern Virginia.

At the outbreak of war, Nichols was elected captain of the elite "Governor's Horse Guard" in Georgia.

Nichols was in Virginia when the tragedy that was to darken his life occurred. In November of 1864, Gen. William T. Sherman burned Atlanta, and set off on his campaign to "make Georgia howl." According to accounts, when Union troops neared Milledgeville, two blue-coated soldiers forced their way into the Nichols' home in the isolated Midway community. Young Anna Maria Green, a resident of the area, penned the following lines in her diary that November:

"The worst of their acts was committed to poor Mrs. Nichols. . . an atrocity committed that ought to make her husband an enemy unto death. Poor woman, I fear she has been driven crazy."

Rape was a subject which polite 19th century Georgians did not discuss. Insanity was another. And from the time of her tragic misfortune in Milledgeville, right up until her death, Kate Latimer Nichols virtually disappeared from the public scene, receding almost into nonexistence.

By April 9, 1865 when he surrendered at Appomattox, James Nichols had advanced to the rank of colonel of the cavalry unit he commanded. Weakened from the debilitating effects of malaria, and no doubt scarred by defeat, Nichols was forced to endure the additional pain and suffering resulting from the tragic situation he faced when he finally reached home at Milledgeville. We know nothing of his reaction to the discovery of his wife's tragedy. One can only imagine his despair.

From war's end until 1868, Nichols remained at his Milledgeville home, recuperating in health and fortune. And although legend credits malaria with his eventual removal to the mountains, Kate's condition may well have been a factor in his decision to relocate the family residence to the isolation of Nacoochee.

According to one anonymous account, Nichols was visiting a popular resort of the day outside Gainesville, Georgia, called White Sulphur Springs *(Readers please see A North Georgia Journal Of History, Volume I, "White Sulphur Springs Resort")* when his malaria flared again, forcing him to his sickbed. He reportedly lingered on the point of death for weeks before recovering. Finally, intent upon pushing into the Blue Ridge Mountains for health reasons, he reached the Nacoochee Valley. Later, with funds from a family fortune which had fallen into his hands through the death of an unspecified relative, Nichols purchased his property in the Nacoochee.

Author George Chapin's description of the valley in 1892 probably closely coincides with what Nichols felt: *"A view of this lovely valley bursts upon us – a view once seen, never to be forgotten. . ."*

Beginning in November of 1868, Nichols began purchasing the land that was to comprise his 2,600-acre estate known as "West End." And on February 17, 1869, he purchased the 473 acres in the Nacoochee that were to be the center of his mountain empire, and the center of social life in the valley for two decades.The exact date of the construction of Nichols's Nacoochee home is unknown, but it is unlikely that he completed it before 1870. George W. Williams's *Sketches of Travel In The Old And New World,* (1870), describes the Nacoochee in detail, but fails to mention West End.

Nichols was in Virginia when the tragedy that was to darken his life occurred.

To build the impressive dwelling, Nichols demolished a homestead on the site constructed years earlier by pioneer Daniel

Brown. He also leveled the top of the Indian mound in the large field in front of the home, in order to build a "summer house" at the site.

Nichols may have modeled his West End home after his former residence in Midway. It rises majestically into the edge of the hillside, almost like an Andrew Jackson Downing painting; an Italianate country residence, weather-boarded, and painted white, with a distinctive square central cupola, and fine detailing throughout.

The residence enjoys fresh mountain water from a spring at the rear of the home. Italian marble filled the rooms of the home at one time; marble basin and wash-stand lavatories graced each bedroom, as did an unusual abundance of closets.

Twenty-two years later, George Chapin admired:

"The dwelling is spacious, surrounded by broad piazzas, over which are entwined flowering vines, and here Captain Nichols has gathered around him everything that makes life pleasant, a large farm, well-stocked rich fields, trained hounds, and plenty of game, fish ponds, a choice library, billiard room, pure spring water throughout, greenhouse, fountains, and nearby on a rise of land, shaded by beautiful oaks, the captain has erected a charming little church finished in natural woods from the trees of the forests of Nacoochee Valley, comprising many different shades and colors which beautifully harmonize, and this gem of a church Captain Nichols has deeded to the trustees of the Presbyterian Church. . . many acres of rich interval are now in waving crops, presenting a scene of rare loveliness. . . The whole forming one of the most perfect country seats in the South."

A raised, covered walkway led to the one-story kitchen at the rear of the Nichols home, and a bridge connected the house to the two-story game room with its scalloped wood-working. When completed, West

Photographed during happier days, Captain James Hall Nichols is seen on the rear porch of West End, teasing his hunting dogs with some treats. Notice the bird – either a falcon, pigeon or dove – on the perch to Nichols' right. (Photo courtesy of Gladys Payne Gausmel Martin, granddaughter of Nichols)

End included a magnificent two-story dairy barn, game pens, servants' quarters, a spring house, and more. Nichols operated the dairy, as well as his gristmill – which was nearby on the river – while farming the fertile river-bottomlands.

On the Indian mound, Nichols built a "summer house," complete with table and chairs for reading, writing, and reflecting. From the spring and the willow-draped pond, he ran water through pipes to the mound.

While plowing near the mound in June of 1870, Nichols discovered a number of large stone slabs several inches below the surface of the field. After removing the slabs, he discovered three stone graves. *(Readers please see A North Georgia Journal Of History, Volume I, "The Underground Village At Duke's Creek").*Charles C. Jones studied the site and discussed it in *Antiquities of the Southern Indians. "So far as we are informed, these are the first ancient stone graves which have been observed within the geographical limits of Georgia,"* he said.

Breathtaking and soothing, the Nacoochee was an isolated paradise. Mail

Captain Nichols loved to explore the Blue Ridge Mountains with his daughter, Anna Ruby, after whom he named the beautiful water falls near his home. (Photo courtesy of Gladys Payne Gausmel Martin, granddaughter of Nichols)

Mr. Calvin Hunnicut was the second owner of the West End property and home, owning it during the 1890s. This photo shows Hunnicut and his family on the front porch of the main house during the summer of 1897. (Photo courtesy of George Gillon, Atlanta, Hunnicut descendant)

was delivered only once a week. Farming and gold mining were the main occupations. Perhaps naturally, Nichols assumed the role of patron, perfectly happy to be reduced in rank back to the title of "Captain" as he was known by the mountaineers, and charmed by their respect for him.

From Midway, Nichols brought his Scotch coachman and three black and one white house servants. Augusta Latimer, Kate's mother, lived also at West End, and designed the lovely flowers and gardens there . . . and probably cared for her daughter too.

Kate, by this time, quite likely bordered on madness, yet the Captain was a Sphinx to his neighbors. Invariably, the few recorded accounts of him throughout his life raise more questions than answers. One visitor to West End likened James Hall Nichols to Orion, the mythological hunter.

Georgia Walton Williams termed Nichols *"that liberal-hearted Christian gentleman. . . who has expended more than a hundred thousand dollars in making this valley 'as lovely to the eye and hand of Art, as it comes to Art beautiful from the hands of Nature.' "* A stable-keeper – John Jones – of Clarkesville once declared:

"Ah sir. Captain Nichols is a good man. God, I think, never made a much better one. He is not one thing to one man and another thing to another, but the same today as yesterday, and an honest man to all!"

Captain Nichols was an avid hunter with hounds, and had at one time a game park, bear pens (the heavy steel bars are still in place in the basement of the horse barn), and trophies inside West End. His abundance of leisure-time pursuits were in keeping with those of a man of his wealth and social standing, but he also served as a trustee of the lunatic asylum in Milledgeville, a preoccupation which some of his contemporaries undoubtedly considered unusual for a man of wealth who resided a substantial distance away in north Georgia.

In July of 1879, Nichols granted the house and grounds of West End to Kate and Anna Ruby, with the provision that he was to serve as trustee and retain possession during his natural life.

In 1885, Anna Ruby married George Frederick Payne of Macon, and what almost certainly had become the light of Nichols' life – his daughter – was suddenly gone. The magic of West End, no doubt, was now

SUMMER GOVERNOR'S MANSION – Georgia Governor Lamartine G. Hardman (center), who purchased the West End property in 1903, is surrounded by family members on the front porch of the main house at the property during the summer of 1930. Hardman was governor of Georgia from 1927-1931, and during his tenure, West End became known as the summer governor's mansion.

quickly diminishing with each passing year for Nichols.

Kate, undoubtedly, was worsening by this time too. Was she mad enough that Nichols kept her hidden now? How much did Anna Ruby know about her mother? Of these questions, one can only guess at the answers.

Whatever the circumstances, on July 24, 1893, Nichols apparently had decided another change was necessary. He sold 604 acres in White County, including the house and grounds, 18 head of cattle, growing crops, farm implements, wagons and harness, and "all household and kitchen furniture except bed and table linen," for $22,500, to Calvin W. Hunnicutt of Atlanta. The new owner was a former Fulton County commissioner, and wealthy gas and plumbing fixture dealer with Hunnicutt & Bellingrath.

After the sale, Nichols purchased two

The historic main house at West End in the Nacoochee Valley is little-changed from the way it appeared in the days of Capt. James Hall Nichols (CSA). (Photo by Olin Jackson)

The lovely little church built by Capt. Nichols near his home at West End still stands and is still used today. (Photo by Olin Jackson)

GLENN HOUSE – Taken from a postcard from the early 1900s, this photograph shows the Glenn House, known today as the Glenn-Kenimer-Tucker House or "Grandpa's Room" in Nacoochee Valley. This structure was built in the early 1870s by James Glenn and E.P. Williams, and was operated for many years as a mountain inn, a tradition continued as of this writing. The structure is located a short distance down Georgia Highway 17 from the Nichols-Hardman (West End) home, and local folklore maintains it was the Glenn House at which Captain James Hall Nichols suffered his fatal heart attack following a meal there on November 23, 1897. (Photo courtesy of Libby K. Tucker)

lots in Atlanta on Linden and Williams Streets, and one on West Peachtree Street, including the C.W. Hunnicutt homeplace on Spring, opposite the Baltimore Block.

Tannie Williams Lumsden wrote:

"I suppose you have heard Capt. Nichols has sold his home in the Valley. I think that he exchanged it for property in Atlanta. Captain has lived here so long we will miss him very much when he leaves."

Perhaps the Nacoochee was losing the isolation that Nichols had craved initially. In the 1890s, the mail was delivered daily, and there was talk of a rail line. Summer boarders now filled the handsome cottages strung along the Unicoi Turnpike. The haunting loveliness of the valley in the shadow of the Blue Ridge Mountains was no longer a well-kept secret.

Perhaps also, Nichols's decision to leave hinged upon the stability of his wife. On August 5, 1895, he was appointed guardian for the person and property of Kate L. Nichols, who, according to the 1895 White County Estate Records, was "now in the Lunatic Asylum."

Today, much of what is remembered about Kate in the old home centers around a hook suspended from the upper bedroom ceiling. Local folklore maintains that Kate's cot reportedly hung from this hook, and that she often was confined in this spot. Additional details concerning her illness and the circumstances of her years at West End have faded into the mists of time.

Captain Nichols, following the move, involved himself in Georgia's exhibit in an exposition in Nashville, Tennessee in the summer of 1897. The malaria that had first driven him to the Nacoochee Valley struck again in Tennessee. By the time the exposition closed and he arrived back in Atlanta, he was in feeble health.

In an apparent bid to repeat his earlier remedy, Nichols decided to return to West End to restore his health. At first, he did in fact seem to recover, but on a cold Wednesday evening on November 23, 1897, after eating a hearty supper, he suffered a massive heart attack, and reportedly died within minutes.

Nichols's remains were brought to Milledgeville for interment in the family vault there. Accompanied by his son-in-law, they arrived at 3:00 p.m. on Friday.

Nichols's old cavalry comrades served as his pall-bearers. The *Union Recorder* reported: *"Captain Nichols was a noble cultured christian gentleman – a gallant soldier, an upright citizen, a noble man."*

Dr. Lamartine G. Hardman, a future governor of Georgia, purchased West End from Hunnicutt in November of 1903. He renamed it "Elizabeth On The Chattahoochee" in memory of his mother. During his tenure as governor (1927-1931), the site served as the summer governor's mansion.

It might almost be considered poetic justice that James Hall Nichols departed this life prior to the turn-of-the-century, for he undoubtedly would have despaired the destruction of the beauty he so enjoyed in his beloved Nacoochee Valley. Sawmilling, which plundered the beautiful mountainsides, soon spoiled the lovely land.

The first big mill came in 1907, and primarily because of the mills, tracks for the Gainesville and North Western Railroad were laid into Nacoochee in 1911, increasing the fury of the logging industry there. The mills stripped the hills and mountains bare, violating the once breath-taking beauty of the valley. After the timber was gone, the railroad departed with it. The tracks were pulled up from the Nacoochee Depot in 1931, and a peacefulness descended upon the valley once again.

Interestingly, in 1912-13, St. Louis-born John E. Mitchell had laid out a tiny new community not far from Nacoochee Depot. In 1915 the Mountain Ranch Resort was built there, setting the stage for later growth in the little community named "Helen." Ironically, rampant development today in Helen poses what could be a greater threat to the scenic beauty of West End.

For the Nichols family however, the future in the Nacoochee Valley ended long ago. At the junction of U.S. Highway 17 and GA Highway 75 today, the old white weather-boarded villa still looms behind the magnolias. Immense, impressive, and silent. . . its past shrouded in a mist-like secrecy forever.

Editor's Note: *The former Nichols home at West End is privately-owned property today, and as such, is not open for public viewing or visits. The home is listed in the National Register of Historic Places, and is included as a portion of the Sautee-Nacoochee Valley Historic District. Nichols's former grist mill however, (called Nora Mill as of this writing) on the Chattahoochee River near the home, is open to the public, and still grinds meal which is sold to the public today.*

REFERENCES:

1) *The Diary Of A Milledgeville Girl*, 1861-1867, from the diary of Anna Maria Green, edited by James C. Bonner.
2) *Health Resorts Of The South*, 1892, by George Chapin.
3) *Health Resorts Of The South*, 1892, by George Chapin.
4) *Nacoochee And Its Surroundings*, 1874, by George Walton Williams.
5) *Augusta Chronicle*, July 20, 1883.
6) Estate Records of White County, 1860-1895.
7) The Lumsden Papers, Josephine Hardeman.
8) Estate Records of White County, 1860-1895.
9) Lumsden Family History, Susan Lumsden.
10) *History Of The Nacoochee Valley*, 1979, by Tom Lumsden.
11) Sautee-Nacoochee Valley National Register Nomination information, Georgia Department of Natural Resources..
12) *Sketches Of Travel In The Old And New World*, 1870, by George Walton Williams.

The Murder Of Joseph Standing

The founding fathers of the United States of America viewed religious freedom as sacrosanct and a cornerstone of our nation's development. On a warm summer morning in 1879, however, an appalling act demonstrating how easily human rights can be violated, took place on a lonely mountain backroad in northwest Georgia.

Joseph Standing awoke with a start, worry creasing his otherwise seamless brow. The dream had been so vivid – so real. Had he witnessed his last day?

The next morning, the 26-year-old Mormon elder and missionary, visibly agitated, shared his premonition. "I thought I went to Varnell's Station, when suddenly, clouds of intense blackness gathered overhead and all around me," Standing told his 22-year-old partner, Rudger Clawson. "I visited a family who were connected with the Church. The moment I entered their house the most extreme consternation seized them, and they made it clear beyond any possibility of doubt that my presence was objectionable. They appeared to be influenced by a sense of great fearfulness. There was no clearing away of the clouds nor abatement of the restlessness of the people, when I suddenly woke, without my being shown the end of the trouble."

It was the summer of 1879, a time of great strife for Mormons all over the country, and especially in the South. In the small towns of Georgia, fundamentalist ministers preached with fanatical zeal against the Mormons and their polygamous beliefs. The Ku Klux Klan tried to scare Mormons from back-country neighborhoods. One Mormon missionary wrote in *The Desert News* in Salt Lake City, *"In our travels we frequently find sign seekers who request us, as a proof of our ministry, to drink deadly poison, to carry serpents in our bosoms, to walk on the water and fly through the air."*

Joseph Standing, an intense, stout young man with light brown hair who had been called to north Georgia the year before, was becoming increasingly concerned about the air of open resentment toward Mormons. Sent to the area in 1878 because of his gentle disposition, maturity and experience, he had quickly founded a branch of the church in Varnell Station (also known as Red Hill, Varnell's Station or simply Varnell) in Whitfield County, a frequent stopping place for Mormon missionaries traveling through Georgia.

The *Atlanta Constitution* newspaper reported that the hostility against the Mormons gathered in Varnell Station actually began in late 1878 "when two Methodist preachers and two or three

Baptist preachers who were residing at short distances from the place, came in and commenced circulating false reports which usually form the staple of arguments of their tribe against 'Mormonism' and incited that people to drive out the elders by violence."

Other missionaries were being attacked by armed mobs. By June of 1879, Standing had become concerned enough to write and ask the governor for protection. J.W. Warren, secretary to Gov. Colquitt, responded with a promise to look into the matter. According to state records, the governor never attempted to answer Standing's request.

On Sunday, July 20, 1879, Standing and Clawson set out on foot for a conference in Rome. It was near 9:00 p.m. when they stopped at Varnell Station, but the men felt certain some church members they knew would give them a place to rest for the night. When they got to the house, however, their friends were anything but hospitable.

"They said that threats had been made against the brethren, and the feeling toward them in the neighborhood was bitter and murderous," chronicled *The Journal of Church History*, a daily organizational diary kept by the Mormon Church historians. "They declined to allow the two men to stop overnight, because if anything happened they would have to share the trouble."

It is not known how Standing reacted, but it is said that Clawson shivered in recognition of his partner's dream.

The missionaries did find shelter that night at the home of a non-Mormon named Henry Holston. Despite being hospitable, their host told them the same thing: "There is danger in the air – threats of mobbing, whipping and even killing."

Joseph Standing harbored an intense, almost obsessive fear of being beaten. Anxious and pale, he slept that night with an iron bar propped by his bed.

The next morning, which, by church accounts was *"clear and beautiful,"* Standing and Clawson headed back to the first family's home to retrieve some belongings they'd

Rudger Clawson (l) and Joseph Standing (r) prepared for travel.

left there in their hasty departure the previous night. The road was densely wooded on both sides. The pair had traveled only a short distance when suddenly a mob of twelve men – three mounted on horseback – appeared in the road. They were armed.

The blood-thirsty crew cursed the two missionaries and commanded them to follow them. Standing and Clawson pleaded with the kidnappers. "It is not our intention to remain in this part of the state," Standing reportedly told the men, then added, "We use no inducements to persuade people to join our church."

The mob, however, was unmoved, and continued to taunt the young Mormons, striking them from behind with blunt weapons. Clawson later told reporters that at one point, one of the men said smugly, "The government of the United States is against you, and there is no law in Georgia for Mormons."

Twice the group passed other travelers

The modest brick enclosure covers the spring where a mob overtook Joseph Standing and Rudger Clawson. Standing reportedly was killed at this spot.

Joseph Standing Park was commemorated in 1952.

– first a local man named Jonathan Owensby, then Mary Hamlin – the daughter of a Mormon family who had been sent – too late of course – to warn Standing and Clawson of the potential danger.

Three members of the mob temporarily veered off from the gang and the remaining members led the captives to a secluded spring near Elledge's Mill. According to reports of the incident, the apparent leader of the group – James Faucett – was approximately 60 years in age, and spoke from his mount. "I want you to understand that I am the captain of this party, and that if we ever find you in this part of the country we will hang you by the neck like dogs."

There are several accounts of what transpired next. Clawson first told authorities that Standing was shot down when he seized a pistol from one of the mobsters. Clawson, however, later testified at the trial that Standing was merely attempting to bluff the mob into thinking he had a weapon.

According to Mormon Church records, Standing jumped up, commanded the gang to surrender, whereupon "a man seated close to him pointed his pistol at him and fired." Standing was shot through the eye. An article in the *Southern Star* dated December 31, 1898, stated that the young man died instantly, while other accounts indicate Standing was unconscious but still alive for some time.

As soon as Standing had fallen, one gang member pointed at Clawson and declared "Shoot him." Clawson, however, amazingly maintained his composure, and was able to convince his captors that someone needed to bury the body.

"It is a burning shame to shoot a man down in this way and leave him to die in the woods. Either go and get help or let me go," church records quote him as saying.

Following his release, the shaken but courageous young missionary then made his way back to Holston's where he borrowed a horse and rode to the coroner's office. He arrived in Salt Lake City 10 days later, with Standing's body, which had, by the time Clawson retrieved it from the murder site, been riddled with more than 20 bullets. Standing was buried in the old Salt Lake Cemetery amid much ceremony and mourning.

Back in Georgia, a jury ordered the arrest of David D. Nations, Jasper N. Nations, A.S. Smith, David Smith, Benjamin Clark, William Nations, Andrew Bradley, James Faucett, Hugh Blair, Joseph Nations, Jefferson Hunter and Mack McClure. A Whitfield County Grand Jury later indicted Jasper N. Nations, Bradley and Blair on charges of "First Degree Murder," "Manslaughter" and "Riot," and set bail at $5,000 each.

Area newspapers, hardly objective in those days, carried conflicting accounts of the murder and the circumstances surrounding it.

"It appears that two Mormon preachers

have been in that portion of the county for several weeks proclaiming their plurality of wives doctrine, with a view to working up a colony of women to send back to Utah," wrote a reporter for Dalton's *North Georgia Citizen* in an article which appeared July 24, 1879, three days after Standing's death. *"The boldness with which they proclaimed this doctrine incensed the men of that neighborhood against them, so much so that they were warned to leave the county."*

The Daily Constitution in Atlanta which had previously described the murder as a *"cold and premeditated one, no cause having been given other than that the Mormons had made some converts and created some disturbances in families in the neighborhood,"* did an about-face on August 24 when it ran an un-bylined story entitled "The Lustful Lout." In this article, Standing is accused of having *"succeeded in accomplishing the ruin"* of two women in Walker County. In example after example, he is cited as a seducer of young ladies, including a daughter of one of the murderers.

The Catoosa Courier also rationalized the killing: *"Mr. Standing's preaching and teaching have been of such an immoral character that the good citizens . . . could not stand any longer the bad influence that his preaching had upon the female portion of the neighborhood."*

A few news accounts, however, were much less negatively biased, perhaps even a bit sympathetic toward Standing and his fellow Mormon missionaries in Georgia. *"Their policy is not, as has been supposed, to take all their converts to Utah,"* wrote a reporter for *The Macon Telegraph and Messenger*. *"They do not attempt to practice under Georgia laws the polygamic part of their creed."*

A Dalton correspondent of the *Chattanooga Daily Times* wrote, *"So far as the reports in regard to Standing's immoral influence over his female converts is concerned, I find no proof to support the rumor."*

Several months after the murder, Clawson was summoned back to Dalton to testify against Nations, Bradley and Blair. So many Whitfield County residents were reluctant to testify against the three men that 150 people were interviewed before a jury was selected.

On October 16, the first day of the trial, Whitfield County Superior Court was packed with curious onlookers eager to hear the case against Nations. To Clawson's dismay, as well as the rest of the Mormons in the area, the jury rendered a "Not Guilty" verdict.

Later that same week, the prosecution dismissed the murder charges against Bradley and Blair. On Thursday, October 23, the last charge of "Riot" was dismissed. Sadly, it has been proven throughout our nation's history that one's cultural and ethnic identity can make it difficult to obtain a fair trial in the U.S. legal system.

Today, a memorial park lined with maples, poplars and weeping willows marks the spot where Standing was killed. The site remains much as it might have been when Standing and Clawson traveled this winding back-road near present-day Varnell.

The persistent drilling of a woodpecker echoes through the lonesome woods, and a "Bob White" partridge calls mournfully in the distance. The spring where the mob stopped with their young Mormon captives still trickles over a moss-flanked bed of rocks.

At the park's entrance, an unobtrusive dark wooden marker, low to the ground, reads simply: "Joseph Standing Monument." Further on, a small square stone with the initials "J.S." identifies the spot where Standing reportedly died.

Dalton resident W.C. Puryear donated the tract of land to the Mormon Church in the early 1950s, and in May of 1952, a special church ceremony was held at the spot to honor the first Mormon missionary killed in the U.S.

The story of Standing's murder is occasionally retold at the site by members of the Mormon chapters in Chattanooga and Dalton. Today, the hidden park, which has been beautifully maintained by the Chattanooga ward since the 1970s, offers a haven for modern-day Mormons to remember and honor their past.

The Mysteries Of Old Gordon Springs

A forgotten mountain community was the childhood home of one of Georgia's most famous soldiers. It was also the site of a mysterious, brutal, murder which remains unsolved to this day.

McCutcheon's Cove is a scenic valley nestled between the steep, rocky slopes of Taylor's and Dick Ridges in the mountains of northwestern Georgia. Although one would be hard-pressed to find evidence of it today, a bustling farm community once occupied this site at the turn of the century – and a heinous crime was committed there on a hot June afternoon in 1895.

Mollie Houston's Final Journey

Mollie Jones Houston, a pretty 29-year-old widow, was well-known to the residents of McCutcheon's Cove. Following the death of her husband several years earlier, she had returned to the cove to live with her parents. Her father, Rev. Ransom Adolphus Jones, owned a farm near the wooded ridge that separated McCutcheon's Cove from the more populous community of Gordon Springs two miles to the south.

Mollie Houston often walked to Gordon Springs on a narrow, winding path across that ridge. On the afternoon of June 28, 1895, she set out along the path alone, carrying a pail of blackberries that she hoped to sell at Neal and Keowns' Store in Gordon Springs.

Today, one can only imagine Mollie's discomfort as, clad in a lengthy skirt, she made her way up the mountain path in the sultry, summer afternoon heat. At the crest of the ridge, she likely paused to catch her breath, setting down the pail of heavy, succulent fruit, momentarily enjoying a refreshing breeze.

It was into this wilderness, that the Reverend Gordon brought his wife and family in the late 1830s.

Here, Mollie would have had a panoramic view of the spacious valley below which had once been occupied by the old Gordon Springs resort which was in decline in 1895. She would have been familiar with the colorful history of this once-popular travel destination, and the pioneer family which had established it.

For reasons unknown today, however, Gordon Springs had seen its best days long before Mollie passed by.

Early Settlement At The Springs

Following the removal of the Cherokee Indians in 1838, Reverend Zachariah Gordon moved his family from Upson County to the mountain wilderness of northwestern Georgia. There, he purchased most of the land in a unique valley completely surrounded by Taylor's and Dick Ridges.

The only access to Gordon's valley was via a gap through Dick Ridge to the east, and, to the west, through Gordon Springs Gap high atop Taylor's Ridge.

It was into this wilderness, that the Reverend Gordon brought his wife and family in the late 1830s. His brood would eventually grow to include some twelve children.

The Gordons' fourth child, eight-year-old John Brown Gordon, was delighted with his new home. He explored the surrounding forests and mountains by foot and on horseback, venturing as far away as Cherokee Chief John Ross' old house at Rossville. Years later, he would fondly recall having found *"fresh relics of the redskin warriors, who had fished in Chickamauga's waters and shot deer as they browsed in herds along its banks."* [1]

Zachariah Gordon was a stern, though loving, father who instilled in his children strong religious values. He established a small church at Gordon Springs and served as its pastor for some time. His small congregation must have occasionally included Cherokees, for it was later said that he *"preached to the Indians with such eloquence that at times he moved them to tears."* [2]

Gordon also founded a school and employed a graduate of Princeton University to teach. Young John Gordon was a bright student and he later attended prestigious Chattooga Academy, a boarding school in LaFayette which still stands today. He usually made the ten-mile trip across Taylor's Ridge to LaFayette on foot.

Zachariah Gordon built a successful hotel and resort at the foot of Taylor's Ridge where numerous mountain springs dotted the landscape. A visitor in the 1840s noted that there were at least twenty springs, twelve of which were crowded into a space of less than a half-acre. These springs had been frequented by the Cherokees – as many as 300 to 400 at a time – and were reported to contain chalybeate, sulphur, magnesium, and other healthful minerals.[3]

At the height of its popularity in the 1850s, Gordon Springs attracted visitors from as far as Memphis and Charleston. It was *"the resort of northwestern Georgia"* said Sybil Tate, a life-long resident of Gordon Springs and author of *A Short Story Of Dogwood Valley: 1830 – 1950* (a history of the area).

Many women visitors to the resort contributed to a quilt that was pieced together from 1854 to 1856. Each square has the name and hometown of its maker embroidered on back. Among the 44 contributors were "Little Sallie Tuskna" of Liberty County, Georgia, and Fannie Haralson Gordon (wife of John Gordon). This quilt is displayed today at the Atlanta History Center in Atlanta.

Other activities at the resort included horseback riding and bathing in the springs by day, and dining, dancing and entertainment at night. According to long-time resident Harry Copeland, whose grandparents resided in Gordon Springs during its heydays, the Ringling Brothers Circus regularly performed at the resort.

Copeland's great-grandmother, Susan

Beasley, was an early physician at Gordon Springs – and one of the first female doctors in northwestern Georgia. Her career was cut short, however, by a tragic accident. While riding through Gordon Springs Gap to see a patient, she was thrown from her horse – which had been spooked by a covey of quail – and mortally wounded when her head struck a stone.

In addition to preaching and innkeeping, Zachariah Gordon was also involved in several business ventures. His coal mining operations in northeastern Alabama, in particular, required ever-increasing attention and, in 1855, the Gordon family moved to Jackson County, Alabama, to be closer to the mines. A few years later, just after the outbreak of the Civil War, Zachariah sold his Gordon Springs property.

None of the long-time residents of Gordon Springs that were interviewed for this article can recall having seen or heard of a photograph of the once-grand hotel and resort. Fortunately, however, a description of the resort did appear in an 1862 advertisement which ran in *The Southern Confederacy*:

"A fine hotel containing thirty rooms, together with all necessary out-houses, four cottages with four rooms each, and one larger one-story building with thirty rooms. . . A fine Stock Farm is attached to the Springs, of between 300 and 400 acres, cultivated in grain, of which two hundred acres are creek bottom land. A portion lies on the mountain side, suitable for a vineyard, while near the Hotel is an Orchard, with fruit of almost every description. These Springs are on the Western & Atlantic Railroad and easy of access, being convenient to those desiring a pleasant or summer residence." [4]

The Civil War Years

The sons of Zachariah Gordon were, like their father, ardent supporters of the Confederacy. John B. Gordon, for instance, recruited men from the iron mines of Lookout Mountain to serve in an infantry unit called "The Mountain Rifles." When they reported for duty wearing raccoon skin caps, however, they were quickly dubbed "The Raccoon Roughs."

Despite his lack of formal military training, John Gordon quickly rose in rank. Known for his courage under fire, he bravely led his troops in many of the war's most famous battles – including Chancellorsville, Gettysburg, The Wilderness (where his brother Gus was killed), and Spotsylvania Courthouse.

In 1864, Gordon was promoted to the rank of major general and soon became one of Robert E. Lee's most trusted lieutenants. In fact, Gordon was in command of half of Lee's Army of Northern Virginia when it surrendered at Appomattox in April of 1865.[5]

Credited with saving Lee's life at Spotsylvania, and known for his courage under fire, Gordon is widely considered to be Georgia's most distinguished soldier from the war.

After the Civil War, Gordon served in the United States Senate and as Georgia's governor. In 1890, he was elected commander of the newly-formed United Confederate Veterans – a post he held until his death in 1904.

Gordon's old home-place did not escape the war unscathed. Federal cavalry under the command of Major General Judson Kilpatrick occupied Gordon Springs from May 7 to 10, 1864.[6] Sybil Tate, whose grandfather was 15 years of age when these cavalrymen arrived, remembers his stories about the occupation.

"To prevent spying," she says, *"local residents – including my grandfather and great-grandfather – were forced to spend each night at the Federal camp under guard. They were told that they would be tracked down and shot if they failed to report on time."* Mrs. Tate has a cannonball recovered from the site of this camp.

Less than a week after Kilpatrick's

departure, the 15th Corps of the Federal army – 12,500 men under the command of Major General John A. Logan – crossed Taylor's Ridge at Gordon Springs Gap and marched through the springs toward Resaca and, ultimately, Atlanta.

Decline Of Gordon Springs

The buildings at Gordon Springs were not damaged by Union soldiers during the war. Afterwards, however, the resort rapidly declined, no doubt due at least in part to the poverty-stricken conditions in the South at that time. In the years immediately following the war, no one had the time to travel to mountain resorts and enjoy good times anymore. They were too busy trying to find a way to survive.

The exact cause, however, and time-period of the resort's final demise are a mystery today, even to long-time residents of the area. Whatever the reasons, the resort had ceased operations by the 1890s. A visitor at that time noted:

"These springs supply a good chalybeate water, and enjoyed an extensive reputation before the war, but the resort has since been allowed to decline. It is hoped that they will again be opened to the public, as, in addition to the advantages of the water, is added a pleasant and salubrious climate." [7]

The visitor's hopes, however, went unfulfilled, as, one by one, the resort's structures were abandoned, then destroyed, over the ensuing years. A visitor today will, with one exception, find that every trace of Zachariah Gordon's resort has disappeared.

The exception is a forlorn, dilapidated house which stands alongside the dusty road leading to Gordon Springs Gap. Initially built for lumbermen working in the valley, it was later occupied by several families. Its final occupants were W.H. and Ruby Crawford, who raised cotton, corn, vegetables and goats at Gordon Springs in the 1930s and '40s.

A farmer's life was difficult at best in those days, recalls Ruby Crawford, who was 85 as of this writing. When she recounts the long, hot days spent plowing, planting and tending to crops, it is without a trace of longing for the so-called "good ole days."

Ruby Crawford and her husband were the last residents at the site of Zachariah Gordon's old resort. With their departure, traffic on the old road through the gap all but ceased. Judging from the size of the pine and cedar trees now growing in the old wagon ruts, the road appears not to have been used by vehicles since the Crawfords left the valley in the 1940s.

As recently as the 1920s, this road had been a primary travel route across Taylor's Ridge. Sybil Tate recalls that her husband, Tom Tate, travelled by wagon across Gordon Springs Gap in 1920 when his parents moved from LaFayette to Gordon Springs.

The fate of Zachariah Gordon's church, like that of his resort, also puzzles long-time residents of the area. Even the name and precise location of the church have been lost through time.

Ruby Crawford and Sybil Tate believe, however, that the church was situated near a small, unkempt cemetery atop an isolated knoll near the eastern entrance to Gordon's valley. Although time has nearly erased the words engraved on the cemetery's headstones, one can still discern a few names – including that of Washington K. Gordon. This cemetery, now overgrown with briars and brush, was used from 1842 to 1875.

Gordon's church was probably named "Medicinal Springs Baptist." Early maps refer to the resort as "Medicinal Springs," and Sybil Tate, while researching old records for her history of Dogwood Valley, found a document in which Gordon is mentioned in connection with a church by that name.

Other than the cemetery and the solitary ruins of the old Crawford house, however, nothing remains today of the once-thriving resort at Gordon Springs. Most of the valley is now owned by a forest products company and is, with the exception of a residence near the valley's eastern entrance, uninhabited.

The Murder Of Mollie Houston

So the old resort had already begun its slide into oblivion when Mollie Houston passed nearby on that fateful afternoon in June of 1895. She never, however, completed her journey to the resort.

When Mollie didn't return, as promised, by sun-down, her father went looking for her. He found her lying on the dusty trail atop the ridge, her skull crushed by a rock. Mollie Houston had been murdered.

Investigators called to the crime scene from LaFayette and Dalton were puzzled by the lack of evidence. There wasn't any sign of a struggle and, because her hand still clutched 40 cents and the pail of berries stood by her side undisturbed, they concluded that Mollie Houston must have known her assailant. Perhaps, they speculated, she had stopped to speak with this acquaintance and was struck from behind as she resumed her journey.

The community was shocked by this savage deed. Some believed that she had been killed to prevent her from inheriting the estate of her deceased husband. Others suspected that the killer was an itinerant laborer. Despite the efforts of the investigators, however, the crime was never solved.

A century has passed since Mollie Houston's death. The grandchildren of her brothers and sisters are now in their 70s and 80s. Although they concede that the identity and motive of her murderer will never be known, they have not forgotten their ancestor whose life was so abruptly and brutally ended.

In a recent interview with this writer, Sybil Tate, Mary Nan Greeson, and Eunice Thomason – Mollie Houston's great-nieces – recalled her final hours.

On the morning of her death, Mollie and her young niece, Ethel Capehart (Sybil Tate's aunt), heard an unusual sound in the nearby forest while they were picking berries. Although they didn't think anything of it at the time, in later years, Ethel Capehart often wondered whether the sound had been made by the murderer who, even then, was stalking Mollie Houston.

Later that afternoon, Ethel's father quite possibly saved her life unknowingly when, as Mollie set out for Gordon Springs, he refused to allow Ethel to accompany Mollie because she still had chores to complete. Ethel must have been devastated by her aunt's death and the realization of her own narrow escape from a similar fate.

Mollie Houston was buried in the Dunagan Church cemetery near Gordon Springs. Soon afterwards, her father returned to the site of the murder and marked it with an upright slab of rock.

A family friend later chiseled a simple epitaph onto the face of the stone slab:

"Mollie E. Houston. Died June 28, 1895." This grim monument still stands atop the ridge alongside the forsaken path linking the ruins of Gordon Springs and McCutcheon's Cove.

ENDNOTES:

1/ Gordon, John B., 1903. *Reminiscences Of The Civil War* (Charles Scribner's Sons, New York), p. 198.

2/ *The Georgia Historical Quarterly, 1952.* (University of Georgia, Athens, Georgia), Vol. XXXVI, p. 237.

3/ White, George, 1849. *Statistics Of Georgia,* pp. 584-585.

4/ Tankersley, Allan P., 1955. *John B. Gordon: A Study In Gallantry* (The Whitehall Press, Atlanta, Georgia) pp. 30-31.

5/ Another Georgian, General James Longstreet, was in command of the other half.

6/ Union cavalry under the command of General Judson Kilpatrick camped at Gordon Springs from May 7 to 10, 1864. Davis, Major George W., 1897. War Of The Rebellion: Official Records Of The Union And Confederate Armies (U.S. Government Printing Office, Washington, D.C.) Series I, Vol. 38, Part 1, p. 140.

7/ Crook, James K., 1899. *The Mineral Waters Of The United States And Their Therapeutic Uses* (Lea Brothers & Co., New York), p. 212.

Mystery Of The Gold Coins At Chenault Crossroads

During the closing days of the U.S. Civil War, a fortune in gold and silver was stolen by outlaws in a daring early-morning raid at Chenault plantation, and much of it was never recovered. For over 130 years, legends of this treasure have haunted the back-roads of Wilkes County.

As far back as I can recall, my father was obsessed with finding what he called "the lost Confederate treasury." He wasn't the first and he won't be the last. It's only natural, I suppose, because the local folklore has been alive with tales of the missing millions since the spring of 1865.

In May of that year, Confederate President Jefferson Davis had crossed the Savannah River at Petersburg on the southern fringe of Elbert County, carrying gold worth millions of dollars today. Defiant to the last, Davis, according to a misguided legend, had thrown the solid silver Great Seal Of The Confederacy into the Savannah (other tales maintain it was a well) so that it could not be recovered and destroyed by Federal authorities.

Also according to various legends, Davis' escape hinged upon his ability to lighten his load, and he thus had cached (in a secret place) the millions that his refugee government had spirited out of Richmond. And so the stories have gone for generations. And it all had happened within a twenty minute drive of our house!

I long ago lost count of the Sunday afternoons my father spent tracing down clues and possible hiding places mentioned in his well-thumbed copy of Ernest M. Andrews' *Georgia's Fabulous Treasure Hoards.* The book itself went from dog-eared to debris as he read and re-read it again and again in his constant search for clues to the mystery of the gold and silver treasure. After all, many legends are woven around a kernel of truth. The trick is locating the kernel.

My father never gave up. Why should he? After all, some of the treasure had already been found. Some boys had seined up a few coins from a creek where a wagon-load of the treasure supposedly had turned over. Everybody knew that; everyone remembered it. They just couldn't remember exactly when – or exactly where – or exactly who had even found the coins.

Most of the treasure however, must still be where Davis hid it. . . Right? Still waiting there for the farmer's plow point to

This Civil War engraving depicts federal soldiers looting a Southern farm. Note the pathos in the faces of the women of the farm, and the sly grin on the face of the soldier to whom the slave is whispering information. (Courtesy of the author)

CHENAULT CROSSROADS – Chenault mansion is faintly visible behind the trees in the distance to the right. The road in the foreground is the same one traveled by the wagon-train carrying the gold bullion in 1865. The site of the fenced horselot was the small field on the right (just beyond the stop sign).

New Ford Creek ford was the spot at which one or more of the raiders supposedly dropped a portion of the gold coins. Fishermen seining the creek reportedly recovered a few of the coins in more recent times.

expose it, or for the idle rambler like my father to finally put the pieces of the puzzle together to unravel this mystery.

Later on, I joined in the hunt myself, but instead of taking to the countryside, I took to the libraries and archives. There, after some digging, I found most of the treasure. And it wasn't where one would necessarily have expected to find it.

Separating Fact From Fiction

Though stories of the Great Seal Of The Confederacy being dumped into the Savannah and into a well in Petersburg have been perpetuated for a century, in actuality, the heavy sterling silver Seal was left behind by Davis and his cabinet as they fled Richmond. Secretary of State Judah Benjamin had given the Seal to his chief clerk, William J. Bromwell, and had instructed Bromwell to hide the Seal until a later date when it would be retrieved. In the years which followed, the Seal was eventually returned to Richmond. It is on display today in the rotunda of the Museum of the Confederacy.[1]

The demise of the Confederate Treasury is similarly explainable. Jefferson Davis – more concerned about capture than he was about the safety of the Treasury (which amounted to approximately $250,000 at that time), traveled on ahead of the slower-moving Treasury wagons. John C. Breckinridge – a former vice-president who had resigned his seat in the United States Senate to become the secretary of war for the Confederacy and a brigadier general in the Confederate Army – had remained behind, trying to suppress a mutiny by the rear-guard protecting the Treasury wagons.

The unpaid, demoralized cavalrymen guarding the Treasury were threatening to seize the wagons carrying the fortune in gold and silver coins. Most of the men considered the war to be well over, and well lost, and they didn't want to pursue the lost cause any further. They demanded to be disbanded, and they demanded to be paid. The degree of force they used to cause these demands to be fulfilled is unknown today.

In any case, Breckinridge, unable to placate the rebellious soldiers, agreed to pay them their back-wages, distributing to the men a total of $108,322.90, an act for which the punctilious acting treasurer secured receipts. This process took several hours, and Breckinridge did not arrive in Washington, Georgia (to whence Davis had earlier traveled) with the remaining Treasury funds (approximately $143,000), until the afternoon of May 4.[2]

In Washington, Jefferson Davis convened what proved to be the final cabinet meeting of his administration. Among those present were Davis, John H. Reagan, Colonel William P. Johnston, and Colonel Frank R. Lubbock.

Davis's last official act was to appoint Captain Micajah H. Clark as Acting Treasurer. Then, realizing that their cavalry escort was no longer dependable, the men agreed to disperse and attempt escape in small inconspicuous groups.

Plans were quickly made to depart Washington. An aide sewed Davis's private letters and journals into bedding that would be hidden in Washington. Clark and Reagan distributed the remaining Treasury funds among cabinet members, trusted aides, and Confederate Army officers for transportation to Texas or abroad.[3]

The disbursing officer, Acting Treasurer Micajah Clark, was so scrupulous with his accounts that most of the Treasury can be accounted for with signed receipts. Only in folklore is the Treasury's fate a mystery. . .

This, however, certainly doesn't mean there isn't a "lost treasure. . . " There was yet another – even more valuable – hoard of gold and silver in this same area in May of 1865, and over half of it did disappear amid bizarre circumstances. The unending search for the mythical Confederate Treasury, however, has largely pushed these goings-on into history's footnotes.

The Real Treasure

Brought to light, what emerges is a tale of high finance gone awry, of desperate flight, of robbery, of a local reign of terror, of intrigue, and, finally, of an unbelievable theft in broad daylight by the U.S. government. All of this is wrapped up in yet another bundle of tall tales and mysteries which have been handed down through generations of story-tellers.

The origins of this almost unbelievable story rest with the old Chenault plantation home once owned by Reverend Dionysius Chenault. The two-story Georgian mansion still exists today atop a rise overlooking the crossroads of state highways 44 and 79, about 14 miles northeast of Washington, Georgia. Even today, the vicinity of the Chenault plantation is a quiet bucolic community amid low, rolling hills that fall away toward Lake Thurmond on three sides.

Where the sounds of the plantation once echoed, the peace is seldom broken today in this quiet rural setting. Few individuals pass the house these days. Other than the scattering of locals, most passersby are either fishermen heading for the lake or travelers who took a wrong turn.

In 1865, however, the road winding by the house (present-day GA 44) was the main thoroughfare between Washington and what remained of the once-thriving riverport town of Petersburg, where a pontoon bridge had been laid across the Savannah. That spring, the road carried a

When he saw Confederate President Jefferson Davis (above) and his small entourage ride into Washington, Georgia, William W. Crump knew that the tiny town would be a poor place to try to shelter the Bank of Virginia gold bullion from Union seizure. He then headed back out of town toward Chenault Crossroads. (Photo courtesy of the Georgia Dept. of Archives & History)

steady stream of paroled Confederates heading for Washington and its rail spur, bound for home. Nearly all were ragged and for most, the skimpy army rations of wormy cornmeal and tainted side meat would have then seemed a banquet.

The Reverend Chenault and his family shared with the travelers whatever he and his family could spare. A meal, a shuck mattress instead of the hard ground, maybe a dollar or two if the man had far to go. No one was turned away.

"We had so many most of the time that there wasn't room in the big house," the reverend's niece, Mary Ann Chenault Shumate recalled later in an interview, *"so we fixed up out-houses and slept them there."*[4]

As dusk fell on May 24, a squad of Federal cavalrymen and a coterie of well-dressed Southern civilians plodded up the dusty road from Washington. The riders' pace was set by the five heavily-loaded wagons they escorted and over which they seemed to be cautiously watching.

The men were bankers from Richmond, the Southerners told the reverend. They were returning their banks' assets to Virginia, heading now for the railhead at Abbeville, South Carolina. The men explained that since their departure from Washington, Georgia, that morning, they had been shadowed by an unknown party believed to be Confederate renegades.

The bankers said they had hoped to be able to make Petersburg by nightfall, but it was clear now that darkness would catch them in open country. They said they would be much obliged if they could camp at the Chenault home for the night.

If the Reverend Chenault had any misgivings about this unlikely band after hearing their story, he didn't betray them. In any case, he welcomed these travelers as he had all the rest. It was a decision the good man would come to regret.[5]

As the Chenaults busied themselves readying food and beds for the new arrivals, the sergeant commanding the Federal escort probably looked back the way he'd come and cursed the coming of night. History doesn't record the name of this sergeant from the 22nd Iowa Volunteer Cavalry, but his actions no doubt mirrored his thoughts.

In the gathering twilight, the sergeant couldn't make out the wispy haze of dust that he'd watched rise higher and higher since before midday. (*Rebs. . . .*) he thought to himself. . . (*Had to be.*) How many, he couldn't tell, but by late afternoon, they had raised enough dust for Bedford Forrest's whole cavalry.

Washington had been full of ex-Confederate soldiers – most Kentuckian and Tennessean cavalrymen. Paroled, but still hard men, they had seen the wagons roll out that morning, and they knew what they were carrying. It was enough gold to make an honest man – let alone a desperado – think twice about taking it by force.

The sergeant in charge of the 10-man Iowa Cavalry knew his men couldn't put up much of a fight against a concerted assault. If the Rebs were coming, he knew they would probably wait until it was good and dark before making their move.

If they came, the sergeant was determined not to be caught flat-footed. He ordered the teamsters to drive the wagons into the Chenault's fenced horse-lot and to draw the wagons into a circle. The bank officers and cashiers could take beds in the house, but the cavalrymen, teamsters and the junior tellers would bivouac with the wagons.

Surprise Attack!

Into the late hours, the Federal pickets watched the flickering of campfires through the trees in the distance. Did the pickets eventually foolishly drift off to sleep? We'll never know today.

It is known, however, that in the wee hours of morning, the Chenault household was roused by the tremendous din of countless hoof-beats followed by shouts and the blood-chilling Rebel yell, all punctuated by gunshots. The Chenaults and the bankers, rushing from their beds, were appalled by the macabre scene which greeted them.

The horse-lot was a center of pandemonium. Figures on horseback – spectral shadows in the pale moonlight – waved and

The Heard Building in Washington, Georgia, was a branch office of the Bank of Georgia into which William Crump had stashed nearly half a million dollars in gold coins from the Bank of Virginia. This building ironically was also the site of the final cabinet meeting of Confederate President Jefferson Davis, and Crump requested a meeting with Davis which never came to pass. The Wilkes County Courthouse was built on the site of the Heard Building after it was demolished in later years. (Photo courtesy of Mary Willis Library, Washington, GA)

In what is perhaps the height of irony, the community in which William Crump chose to hide the Bank of Virginia gold coins was a hotbed of Confederate leaders' homes and activities. Robert Toombs, secretary of state of the Confederacy, was one of those residents. His home (above) still stands today in the community. Toombs was arrested by Federal troops who threatened to hang him from an oak tree which still stands in the front yard. Toombs, however, amazingly escaped and spent several years in exile in France. (Photo by Daniel M. Roper)

fired their revolvers, horrifying their victims. Horses whinnied, shied, reared and bolted. Figures on foot teemed around the wagons, dark figures hacking and slashing at the tarpaulins and the containers therein.

Forty? Fifty? Sixty? Maybe more? They skittered over the wagons, over each other, cursing and shouting, grabbing at the booty like lions on a fresh kill. They splintered open boxes and kegs. They *"waded ankle-deep in gold and silver. [They] filled their haversacks and pockets. They tied bags of gold and silver to their saddles."*[6]

And then they were gone, almost as quickly as they had come. Aghast, the Chenaults and the bankers watched them scatter into the darkness. The riders spurred and whipped their mounts up the roads and across the fields, toward the river and the creek fords, the lathered horses galloping to the jingle of golden coins.

Surprisingly, not a drop of blood was spilled in the entire diabolical incident. The Iowan troopers and the teamsters were nowhere to be seen. They had departed in terror in the face of the raiders' sheer numbers, and where and when they stopped running, history doesn't record. The young bank tellers had been tied up, but none of them were any the worse for wear.[7]

With the first rays of the dawning sun, the Virginians took stock of their predicament. The horse-lot and the Chenaults' yard glittered with stray silver dollars and five-, and 20-dollar gold pieces. So did the roads and fields. According to records, the bankers managed to collect a little more than $40,000 in odd coins lying about on the ground.[8] Seven weeks earlier, they had left Richmond with $450,000.

The horse-lot and the Chenaults' yard glittered with stray silver dollars and five-, and 20-dollar gold pieces.

Origin Of The Treasure

How did $450,000 in gold and silver coins (specie) from Virginia banks come to be in wagons at a quiet Georgia backwater. Why was it there? Who stole it?

The answers are rooted in the twilight days of the Confederate government. On March 14, 1865, the Virginia State Legislature authorized a loan of $300,000 in hard money to the Confederate government which was in dire need of funds. The state of Virginia itself would have to borrow the funds, and that would be authorized only when the loan was secured by two million pounds of cotton held in various warehouses.

The banks which handled Virginia's finances – The Bank Of Virginia, The Farmers' Bank of Virginia, and The Exchange Bank of Richmond – began scrambling to borrow the hard money from smaller banks and private holdings. At the helm of this wheeling and dealing was Judge William W. Crump, president of The Bank Of Virginia and Assistant Treasurer of the Confederacy. Shrewd and competent, Crump made easy work of a hard job. Swirling events, however, soon made him regret his assumption of this task.[9]

Richmond, Virginia, soon was under siege by the Union Army. *"It is just a matter of time,"* Lee wrote to Jefferson Davis.[10] Despite still-high hopes in some quarters as March waned, a gloomy reality began taking hold of the Confederate capital. With the city's fall imminent, the Confederate Congress adjourned and fled – without authorizing surety (the two million pounds of cotton) for Virginia's loan. As a result, the deal collapsed, leaving the bankers flustered, but flush with hard money.

The bankers then had hundreds of thousands of dollars in gold and silver, and their enemy was poised to sweep into their city. What would one expect them to do? Crump knew the Confederate Treasury Department had plans to remove the government's specie and bullion reserves and so he made arrangements to spirit the Virginia banks' funds out at the same time.

As Richmond was being burned and looted, Crump and his hand-picked cadre of bankers gathered their banks' hard money – a sum amounting to approximately $450,000 – and smuggled it through the bedlam, loading it into the same railroad boxcar into which the Confederate Treasury was loaded. Near midnight, the treasure train creaked out of the dying city. Dawn would find a Union flag flying over the former Confederate capitol.

Interestingly, the train traveled under the authority and protection of the Confederate Navy. In this case, that meant Lieutenant William H. Parker, superintendent of the Confederate Naval Academy, ten officers of his faculty and fifty of his midshipmen – cadets ranging in age from seventeen to twelve.

These young guards probably never inspired Judge Crump with confidence, but Parker's fledglings proved to be the most reliable protection the banks' funds would ever have.

The intrepid Parker pushed his command steadily southward, staying well ahead of the Federal cavalry sweeps out to net the fleeing Jefferson Davis who was moving his refugee government along the same route. When the rail lines ran out, Parker switched the treasure to wagons and moved on the back roads.

The lieutenant quickened his pace as rumors of what – and how much – he was carrying nipped at his heels. The tales grew taller in the telling, and the farther south Parker moved, the more he came to fear renegade Confederates more than he feared Yankees. He remained confident, however, as he noted in his memoirs, that if attacked, by anyone, that *"we could give a good account of ourselves."*[11]

Crump and his bankers traveled with Parker as far as Augusta, Georgia, arriving on April 18. In Augusta, Parker received orders to disband his command. This he declined to do, refusing to abandon his duty to guard the Treasury.

Instead, Parker decided to retrace his route in the hope of meeting Davis and turning the Treasury over to him. Crump decided to keep his party and their funds in Augusta.

Finding A Safe Stash

It wasn't long, however, before Crump reconsidered his stay in Augusta with the bank funds. Officers of twelve Tennessee banks were already hiding over $500,000 in specie in Augusta, and they feared Union forces already had them targeted. Washington, Crump decided, which they had passed through en route to Augusta, was a better place to lie low.

Avoiding the railroads, the bankers moved their trove through the back country, arriving in Washington, Georgia, on May 3. The small, remote town of 2,200 was the political and commercial center of a fairly wealthy farming district.

The community itself had been little touched by the war. General William

Sherman's bummers hadn't quite reached out so far. The converging roads and the Georgia Railroad spur line made Washington a natural way station for anyone bound for someplace else. In the full flower of spring, the hamlet offered memories of happier times to the many war-weary Confederates passing through it..[12]

Given his desperate situation, Crump can almost be excused for misjudging Washington's virtues. Almost. But if he had weighed the little town's assets and liabilities with his usual shrewd banker's eye, he almost certainly would not have found it to be so comforting a haven.

Robert Toombs, the former Confederate Secretary of State, Brigadier General and all-around secessionist firebrand had been nursing his bruised ego in Washington – his hometown – for over two years. Confederate Vice-President Alexander H. Stephens had been sulking in his home only a few miles away for some time also. Judge Crump should have figured both men as certain targets of Federal dragnets. What's more, he ought easily to have reckoned that Washington's road hub would likely draw Jefferson Davis there as well – and Crump knew that Davis had Federals on his heels.

As it happened, a few hours after Crump and his party had stored their specie in the Washington branch of the Bank of Georgia, Davis and what remained of his government rode into town. Judge Crump requested a meeting to discuss his dilemma, but it never came off. Davis had enough problems of his own.

Since the assassination of Lincoln, the Federals were pursuing Davis with renewed vigor, and he knew he would have to lighten his load if he were to have any hope of escaping his pursuers. Thus he divided what remained of the Confederate Treasury between his cabinet members. They then rode off in separate groups, supposedly planning to regroup at a later date in Texas.

Crump and his bankers now knew that Washington would soon be overrun with Federals searching for Davis. And even before Davis had departed, Crump had learned even more disturbing news. Some of Davis's escort had mutinied and seized part of the Confederate Treasury soon after crossing the Savannah. Crump knew his problems were mounting by the day.

On May 5, Federal cavalry entered Washington, Georgia, and seized any property with even a whiff of the Confederate government about it. The $450,000 sitting in the Bank of Georgia fairly smelled to high heaven. After all, the Federal Secretary of War, Edwin M. Stanton, had electrified the pursuit of Davis by announcing that Davis carried millions in gold with him – money that was up for grabs when Davis was caught.

On the advice of his host, Judge Garnett Andrews, Crump left hurriedly for Virginia and a meeting with Federal provost authorities. He hoped to establish the $450,000 as private property and, in doing so, regain possession of the money.

On May 18, two more bank officers from Virginia reached Washington. They carried instructions from Judge Crump and letters of transit signed by Major General Marsena R. Patrick, the Federal Army's Provost Marshal General. Against seemingly long odds, Crump had come through! The bankers could transfer the specie back to Richmond and return it to its rightful owners. General Patrick's authorization would guarantee safe conduct.

Presented with the documents, the commander of the local garrison, Captain Lot Abraham of the 22nd Iowa Volunteer Cavalry, released the specie, but could spare only a token guard to accompany the coins back to Virginia. He had received orders to shift his command to Augusta.

The Secret Is Out

Happy to have their money back and eager to set off for Virginia, the bankers were undeterred. They hired teamsters and wagons, and near dawn on May 24, set off for the rail head at Abbeville, South Carolina.[13]

If they hoped to steal away unnoticed, Crump and the bankers failed miserably. Years later, Lewis Shepard, a Tennessean from Vaughn's brigade, recalled what happened when the word spread (but without owning up to any participation in the events himself):

". . . Some of the officers and men of Vaughn's brigade became appraised that a train of specie was being carried North under Federal guard, and they jumped to the conclusion that it was the property of the Confederate government which the Federals had captured. They concluded that their. . . hard service for the Confederacy entitled them to a share of this gold and silver provided they could. . . . [succeed] in securing it from the Federal guard. . . . They organized an expedition with the view of capturing this money and followed the [wagon]-train until a favorable opportunity of attack presented itself. . . [14]

Sincere or not, this belief that they were merely reclaiming the Confederate Treasury became the raiders' justification for the robbery. Furthermore, it seems that the presence of the Federal guard served only to reinforce this opinion.

Like gathering storm clouds, the raiders scuttled over the countryside, picking up any locals who wanted to join them. Meanwhile, the wagon-train plodded toward the Savannah River and an ultimate date with destiny. Later that night, the bandits were soon high-tailing it across the countryside, hurrying away to enjoy their ill-gotten gains from the treasure train stopped at Chenault plantation.

Partial Recovery Of The Gold

In the early afternoon of May 25, Brigadier General Edward Porter Alexander and a band of paroled Confederates cantered toward the Chenault plantation. Following the trauma of the assault and robbery, the bankers and Judge Andrews had contacted Alexander to help them regain the stolen gold and silver. The brilliant 30-year-old engineer had returned to Washington barely three weeks previous from Appomattox. His handling of the artillery for Longstreet's Corps had made him one of the Confederacy's most respected soldiers, and a near-legend around his hometown. His reputation for integrity and bravery was sterling. If there was one man in the community who might carry weight with any raiders remaining in the area, it was Alexander.

The young general had gathered six members of the local Irwin Artillery and had pushed on immediately for the Chenault place, adding eight more recruits to his band as they passed through the Danburg community. Also along was Judge William M. Reese, the local magistrate, to provide warrants and official sanction if Alexander had to make arrests and take back the loot by force.

"We came on a party of guerillas who had about $80,000 of the money in charge," Alexander recalled in an 1881 interview. *"They said they did not know it was private property; believing it to belong to the Confederacy, they thought they were as much entitled to it as anyone else. . . . but being convinced that it was private property, they were willing to surrender it".*[15]

This confrontation took place with pistols drawn, but luckily, no shooting occurred. Alexander could see other raiders gathering, watching, and he was certain there were others he could not see. He wanted the money, not bloodshed, and he realized at a glance that his force was far too small to take back any of the loot that was not voluntarily surrendered. Any attempt to make arrests, he also decided, would be imprudent at best. Besides, money or no money, Alexander had little taste for arresting Confederates – even guerrillas – who would ultimately face Federal martial law.

When he had collected all of the gold and silver that the men were willing to surrender, Alexander returned to Washington to report to Crump. All told, the bankers now had recovered approximately $120,000. Though he was far short of the original sum, Crump undoubtedly didn't feel quite as bad. However, had he been able to see a bit into the future, his heart would have sunk.

A Damned Yankee

Brigadier General Edward A. Wild was that sort of "damned Yankee" whose very name Southerners for three generations after the war couldn't hear uttered without feeling compelled to spit. A rabid abolitionist from Massachusetts, Wild held a deep, burning hatred for all white Southerners, slave-holders or not. He had lost an arm at Gettysburg, and the wound fostered an addiction to laudanum (opium) that twisted his mind and stoked his hatred to a white heat. Wherever he served, he cut a swath of wanton cruelty against prisoners and civilians alike. . . it just didn't matter to him.

In Virginia in 1864, several random hangings of Confederate prisoners, with Wild personally acting as hangman, prompted his then commanding officer, Major General Benjamin F. Butler to write Secretary of War Stanton: *"I wish Wild were elsewhere. He has no common sense."*[16]

Wild had come to Washington, Georgia, to investigate several lynchings, but when he learned of the looted treasure train, the lynchings were forgotten. He became fixated upon the money and the capture of the raiders. The local population soon fell victim to Wild's cruel hand.[17]

For a start, the twisted brigadier general arrested the Virginia bankers and confiscated their specie, despite their legitimate Letter of Transit issued earlier by Union Provost Marshal General Marsena R. Patrick. Wild filled the county jail and several temporary jails with suspects. For several weeks, he and his men ravaged the countryside in an effort to root out any of the booty still in local hands. However, if it was still there, it was well hidden, and Wild was unsuccessful in his efforts.[18]

But the demented general's most brutal actions were yet to come. In mid-July, a former slave once owned by John Chenault made her way to Wild's headquarters, possibly seeking revenge against her former owner. She accused John and Dionysius Chenault not only of taking part in the raid, but also of hiding a great deal of the loot. With the woman, Angelina, in

This confrontation took place with pistols drawn, but luckily, no shooting occurred.

tow as a guide, Wild led a detail to the Chenault plantation.

Brutal Torture

When they arrived, Wild's men opened accounts by killing the Chenault children's dog, shooting and stabbing the poor animal to death. They ignored the desperate cries and pleas from the children, "laughing and hoorahing" as they pursued their grisly deed.

For his part, Wild arrested John and Dionysius, as well as John's 16-year-old son, Frank, and set about torturing the three in order to extract confessions and the hidden loot's location. The prisoners were herded into a nearby wood-lot where the first punishments were to be meted out.

"They tied their hands behind them and hung them up by their thumbs, with their feet off the ground," explained Mary Ann Chenault Shumate in a later interview and who was seventeen at the time. *"They said the pain was so great that after the first time they begged the Yankees to shoot them dead rather than suffer so again. . . . Their hands were so black and swelled up that it was a long time before they could use them again."*[19]

The torture reportedly went on for the remainder of the day and into the night. When torturing the Chenaults proved futile, Wild tortured John Chenault's body servant, Tom, who was Angelina's son, (an eventuality which no doubt caused Angelina to regret her accusations).

Meanwhile, back at the plantation house, the rest of Wild's men and Angelina heaped abuse upon the other Chenaults. *"Some of the soldiers came to the house and began cursing and abusing Ma and the children,"* Mary Ann Chenault Shumate continued. *"They took Ma and me and Aunt Deasy [Ardesia (Mrs. Dionysius) Chenault] and shut us up in a room. . . and forced us to strip off our clothes while Angelina came in and searched us."*[20]

The servants managed to get the younger children away to the neighbors or to their own cabins. In the end, all that Wild could seize were the Chenault women's few pieces of jewelry and $150 in coin the Chenault brothers had accumulated. All six Chenaults – John, Dionysius, their wives, Mary Ann and Frank – were hauled back to Washington and imprisoned.

The Chenaults remained in jail for several days while Judge Garnett Andrews traveled to Augusta to plead their case before Wild's superior, General Steedman. Andrews, much respected in Washington though he had remained a staunch Unionist, was perhaps the only person in a position to offer the Chenaults any hope. He returned to Washington with Col. E.L. Drayton of Steedman's staff.

"Colonel Drayton behaved very gentlemanly and sent us back home, just as soon as he could finish investigating the case," Mary Shumate recounted. Drayton also returned the Chenault's money and jewelry as well. He also freed the rest of Wild's prisoners, including the Virginia bankers, but he didn't return the bankers' money.[21]

In the meantime, Wild had been recalled to Augusta and shipped off to yet another post. However, his torture of the Chenaults had served as what was perhaps its real purpose all along. *"A good many others* [who did have part of the gold and silver coins], *when they saw how things were going, got uneasy and gave up their share,"* Mary Shumate recalled, *"and so the Yankees got a good deal of it back."*[22]

Bank Funds Stolen By The Federals?

By late August, the dribbles of gold and silver coins had stopped trickling in and the recovered loot amounted to nearly $200,000. Under orders from Secretary of War Stanton, General Steedman transferred the large sum to Augusta and turned it over to Treasury officials who in turn transferred it to Washington, D.C.

The Richmond banks petitioned President Andrew Johnson and the Secretary of the Treasury to have the money returned, in keeping with Judge Crump's agreement with Provost Marshal General Patrick. After a full investigation, President Johnson, the Secretary of the Treasury and the Attorney General held forth in March of 1867 that the specie was private property and that the banks were entitled to have it returned.[23]

Surprisingly, however, Secretary of War Stanton swung into action, calling upon his "Radical Republican" allies in Congress. On March 22, 1867, the U.S. House of Representatives passed a resolution claiming the money for the U.S. Treasury. The Senate passed an identical resolution the next day. In both cases, the margins of victory in the votes clearly signaled to Johnson that he would lose a fight to sustain a veto if he pressed the issue and forced Congress to pass the resolutions as formal bills.[24]

This was just one skirmish in a political war that had flared between Johnson and Stanton almost from the moment John Wilkes Booth had squeezed the trigger behind Abraham Lincoln's ear. In just a few more months, after a few more skirmishes, Johnson would try to remove Stanton from office, triggering his own impeachment.[25]

The seizure of the Virginia bankers' specie fit a pattern Stanton had laid down in the war's waning days. On May 14, 1865, he had cabled Major General James H. Wilson, then occupying Macon, Georgia, instructing him to move at once against Augusta and confiscate the assets of the various Tennessee banks known to be there. After that, any funds to which a Unionist Tennessean could establish claim were returned to that individual; the rest was shifted to the U.S. Treasury. This pattern was played out all over the Confederacy. It was outright theft, but there was no way to fight it.[26]

The legal fight over the Virginia banks' funds didn't end with the acts of Congress. Lawsuits ground on for twenty-six years as first the banks, and then their receivers brought claims for the money. The suits were finally resolved on June 22, 1893, when the United States Court of Claims ruled that the receivers of the Bank of Virginia were entitled to recover $16,987.88.[27]

In the end, after all the suffering and legal wrangling, only the renegade Rebels who had taken (and not returned) the gold and silver coins back at Chenault plantation, stood vindicated. And it is they who left the most enduring mark in the folklore of the Washington, Georgia area.

A Legend For The Ages

Almost from the moment the echoes of the raiders' din died away, the tales of lost treasure began growing in the community as thick as the cotton which once grew in the fields. The legend of the roughly $250,000 in gold and silver taken (and never returned by the raiders) on that summer night has grown with each passing year.

A wagon-load (or two) possibly turned over in a creek before the wagon train even reached the Chenault plantation. Or could the double eagles discovered in the young boys' seine years later have been lost from the bags of raiders as they spurred their frantic horses through the rocky shallows of creek fords in the dark of night? Almost every tale has a plausible explanation.

Lewis Shepard in his time claimed to know many raiders who had fled with tens of thousands of dollars in gold coins to places as far away as Missouri and California. But he didn't mention any names.

In the Chenault community today, you hear other tales. *"That gold didn't go missin'. . . That's how So-and-So's great-granddaddy got his start. . . That's how they come by all that land. . . .Ol' Jim Smith was one-ah the raiders, ya know. . . . That's how he got what he had."*[28]

James Monroe Smith, governor of Georgia from 1872 to 1877, owned a cotton and cattle farm that covered about 3,000 acres of nearby Oglethorpe County. Weighty evidence places him in Tennessee in May of 1865, so the odds of his having been involved in the raid at Chenault plantation are slim to none.

Therefore, the snippet of folklore involving Smith in the raid can probably be dismissed outright. But the rest of the tales are alive and thriving. The lure of the treasure still pulls visitors to Chenault crossroads just as strongly as it pulled the raiders in 1865.

Today, the old Chenault plantation can be reached either by driving northeast out of Washington on GA 44 or by turning south onto GA 79 off of GA 72 twelve miles east of Elberton. The old home was recently restored and is privately owned today.

The stately house and quiet community still whisper of the mysteries they haven't given up in almost a century and a half. Are there still hidden treasures about? We may never know. It is fun, however, to visit the site today, and imagine what transpired on a summer's eve long ago, when the grounds around the Chenault home were left "twinkling" with the awe-inspiring glitter of gold and silver coins.

ENDNOTES

1/ Burke Davis, *The Long Surrender* (New York: Vintage Books, 1985), pp. 127-130

2/ William H. Parker, *Recollections Of A Naval Officer, 1841-1865*, (New York: Charles Scribners' Sons, 1883), pp. 122-124.

3/ *Flight Into Oblivion*, (Johnson Publishing Company), pp. 88-93 and Ibid, Note #1, *The Long Surrender*, pp. 123, 129-130.

4/ Otis Ashmore, "The Story Of The Virginia Bank Funds," *The Georgia Historical Quarterly*, 4 (December, 1918), p. 179. Ashmore cites letter from Mary Ann Chenault Shumate.

5 *Official Records Of The War Of The Rebellion, Series I*, Vol. 49, Part II (Correspondence), p. 880.

6/ Ibid, p. 185.

7/ Presumably, the Iowans made their way back to the 22nd Iowa, then en route to Augusta. However, a search of the Official Records turns up no report filed by Captain Abraham referring to the incident or the fate of the detail.

8/ Ibid, Burke Davis, p. 185.

9/ Ibid, Otis Ashmore, p. 190.

10/ Ibid, Burke Davis, p. 17.

11/ Ibid, William H. Parker, p. 379.

12/ Ibid, Burke Davis, p. 114-115.

13/ Ibid, p. 184.

14/ Robert M. Willingham, Jr., *No Jubilee: The Story Of Confederate Wilkes County*, (Washington, GA: Wilkes Publishing Co., 1976), p. 197.

15/ Ibid, Otis Ashmore, pp. 174-175.

16/ Dick Nolan, *The Damndest Yankee: Benjamin Franklin Butler*, (Presidio Press, 1991), pp. 242-243.

17/ Diary Of Eliza Francis Andrews

18/ Ibid, Burke Davis, pp. 186-187.

19/ Ibid, Otis Ashmore, pp. 180-181.

20/ Ibid, p. 181.

21/ Ibid, p. 182.

22/ Ibid, p. 183.

23/ Ibid, pp. 186-188.

24/ Ibid, pp. 190-197.

25/ Brooks D. Simpson, *The Reconstruction Presidents*, (University Press Of Kansas, 1998), pp. 80-88.

26/ *Official Records Of The War Of Rebellion, Series I, Vol. 49, Part II* (Correspondence), p. 799. General Wilson acknowledges cable from Stanton, and discusses its contents.

27/ Ashmore, pp. 196-197.

28/ Ashmore, p. 172.

The Chase And Capture Of Jefferson Davis

With the Confederacy in a shambles around him, Confederate President Jefferson Davis made a desperate attempt to reach Texas, where he hoped to reorganize his government and armies. First, however, he had to get across the state of Georgia, fleeing with his family, trusted lieutenants, and hundreds of thousands of dollars-worth of gold bullion, a treasure which would be worth millions today.

At dawn on May 3, 1865, Confederate President Jefferson Davis stood on the east bank of the Savannah River, gazing across the body of water at his destination – Petersburg, Georgia. Behind him lay the charred ruins of Richmond – the former capitol from which he and the remainder of the Confederate government had abruptly fled just one month earlier. He undoubtedly suspected the trip across Federally-occupied Georgia would not be easy – and he was correct.

Davis's destination was Texas. He intended to reorganize the government for the Southern states and its armies there. First, however, he had to traverse the broad expanse of Georgia, and the first leg of the trip included crossing the Savannah and entering Petersburg.

Pioneer Community

Petersburg was a unique township, and continues to intrigue historians even today. After the American Revolution, hundreds of tobacco farmers from Virginia and the Carolinas moved into what then was the wilderness of north Georgia. Many settled in the Broad River valley, attracted by its fertile soil and favorable climate.

Within a few years, these hardy settlers had established a flourishing tobacco industry. And because of its "refreshing, healthful location," Petersburg was also a popular summer resort among residents of coastal Georgia, well-known for its "social life."[1]

During the early 1800s, Petersburg had more than 2,000 residents, two taverns, a post office, market place, town hall, several churches, and at least 40 stores and warehouses – enough to classify it as the third-largest city in Georgia, behind only Savannah and Augusta.

According to Bobby Brown State Park Superintendent Danny Burt who was interviewed for this article, in the late 1700s, the state of Georgia required that tobacco be weighed and inspected at state-chartered warehouses before it could be exported for sale abroad, and one of these warehouses was located at Petersburg.

As a result, the community grew and prospered, but by the 1820s, the burgeoning tobacco market had been supplanted by a new cash crop which ultimately helped shape the identity and destiny of the 19th century southern United States. That new crop was cotton, and since the state of Georgia did not require cotton to be inspected, it could be loaded onto ships from any convenient riverside landing.

As more and more farmers in upper Georgia turned to the production of cotton instead of tobacco, Petersburg quickly declined in importance as a commercial center. Its main source of commerce had been replaced by a new cash crop, and businesses and families moved to other cities to begin anew.

"By the 1850s," said Superintendent Burt, "the post office was the only remaining business, and the members of the Cade family were the only residents."

A visitor to the site in the 1870s noted: *"Now sunken wells and the mounds of fallen chimneys are all that attest to the former existence of the town. . . Extensive fields of corn and cotton have obliterated all traces of warehouse, shop, town-hall, church, and dwellings. Beneath the conserving shadows of tall trees which mark the outlines of the old cemetery on the left bank of the Broad River may still be seen numerous graves, fresh and green when the town was replete with life, but neglected and overgrown with brambles now that the village too is dead."*[2]

Adding insult to injury, Petersburg was virtually erased by modern-day development. In the 1950s, the U.S. Army Corps of Engineers impounded the Savannah River creating Clark Hill Lake. The historic community now lies beneath 20 feet of water.

"Just before the dam was completed," Burt adds, "the caskets in the Petersburg cemetery were exhumed by the Army Corps and re-interred in nearby church cemeteries."

Desperate Confederate Flight

Today, Petersburg is just a footnote in Georgia history, but in 1865, it was a destination which was tantamount to freedom for Confederate President Jefferson Davis. The Confederate armies east of the Mississippi River – including those commanded by Robert E. Lee and Joseph E. Johnston – had surrendered.[3] The victorious Federal forces had therefore turned their attention towards the capture of the remaining "plums." – Davis and his cabinet members – who had eluded capture.

By May 3, 1865 – the same date Davis had reached the Savannah – Federal troops had already occupied most of Georgia, and were fanning out across the countryside to cover likely escape routes. To increase the odds of capture, President Andrew Johnson had issued a reward for Davis's capture.[4]

Other extraordinary measures were also taken to capture Davis. Allen Pinkerton, then America's most famous detective, was hired by a Union general to "capture the murderer of Lincoln and to capture Jeff Davis."[5] At that time, it was

Jefferson Davis was the first and only president of the Confederate government.

Looking east across Clarke Hill Lake from Bobby Brown State Park. It was here in the pre-dawn hours of May 3, 1865, that Jefferson Davis crossed the Savannah River on a pontoon bridge and entered Petersburg, Georgia. The ruins of Petersburg now lie beneath the waters of the lake just south of this location. (Photo by Daniel M. Roper)

widely believed Davis and his cabinet were involved in Lincoln's assassination.

Davis's family – including his wife Varina and their four children – were already in Washington, Georgia, in the care of Colonel Burton N. Harrison, Davis's personal secretary. A wagon train carrying the Confederate treasury, guarded by Captain William H. Parker and 60 cadets from the Confederate Naval Academy, had crossed the Savannah several days earlier and had arrived safely in Augusta.

However, worried that marauders (of whom there were many in the 1860s) might attempt to seize the treasury, Augusta officials had convinced Parker that the city was not secure. The wagon train, along with its escort, had plodded back to South Carolina where it rejoined Davis's party.

Davis's group included Secretary of War John C. Breckinridge, Secretary of State Judah P. Benjamin, Secretary of the Navy Stephen R. Mallory, Postmaster General (and acting Secretary of the Treasury) John H. Reagan, a number of aides and attendants, and an escort of 2,000 cavalry. Several other cabinet members had resigned as the government had made its way south through the Carolinas.

Crossing the Savannah on a pontoon bridge, Davis entered Petersburg which was little more than a ghost town in 1865. According to Bobby Brown State Park Superintendent Danny Burt, local folklore maintains that Davis disposed of the heavy Official Seal of the Confederacy by dropping it into a Petersburg well.

In actuality, the heavy sterling silver Seal was left behind by Davis and his cabinet as they fled Richmond. Secretary of State Judah Benjamin had given the Seal to his chief clerk, William J. Bromwell, and had instructed Bromwell to hide the Seal until a later date when it would be retrieved. In the years which followed, the Seal was eventually returned to Richmond. It is on display today in the rotunda of the Museum of the Confederacy.

At the time of his flight, Jeff Davis probably gave little or no thought to his lack of an official governmental seal. He had proceeded on horseback, stopping for breakfast at a farmhouse near the Dionysius Chenault plantation.

Davis reportedly arrived in Washington at 11:00 a.m. While in the city, he was the guest of Dr. J.J. Robertson (cashier of the local branch of The Bank of Georgia), staying in Robertson's apartment above the bank.

Other members of Davis's party were also given rooms by prominent Washingtonians. John Reagan, for example, stayed in the home of Robert Toombs (a state historic site today).

Two cabinet members left Davis's party before its arrival in Washington. Judah Benjamin decided to make his escape alone, assuring Davis that he would rejoin him in Texas. Privately, however, Benjamin told John Reagan that he was "going to the farthest place from the United States if it takes me to the middle of China."[6] Stephen Mallory resigned and headed to his sister's home in LaGrange, Georgia.[7]

Lost Confederate Treasure

John Breckinridge – a former vice-president who had resigned his seat in the United States Senate to become a brigadier general in the Confederate Army – had remained behind, near the Chenault plantation, trying to suppress a mutiny by the rear-guard. These unpaid, demoralized cavalrymen were threatening to seize the wagons carrying the Confederate treasury assets.

Unable to placate the rebellious soldiers, Breckinridge finally agreed to pay back-wages, distributing to the men more than $100,000 – a large sum even today, and a huge amount in 1865. This process took several hours, and Breckinridge did not arrive in Washington with the remaining treasury funds – $143,000 – until the afternoon of May 4.

Through dispatches from Breckinridge, Davis learned of the mutiny. The next morning, the fleeing president convened what proved to be his final cabinet meeting. Among those present were Davis, Reagan, Colonel William P. Johnston, and Colonel Frank R. Lubbock.

Davis's last official act was to appoint Captain M.H. Clark as acting treasurer. Then, realizing that the cavalry escort was no longer dependable, they agreed to disperse and attempt escape in small inconspicuous parties.

Plans were quickly made to depart Washington. An aide sewed Davis's private letters and journals into bedding that would be hidden in Washington. Clark and Reagan distributed the remaining treasury funds among cabinet members, trusted aides, and Confederate Army officers, for transportation to Texas or abroad.[8]

The fate of the Confederate treasury funds has often been (and should not be) confused with the theft of the assets of the state banks of Virginia and Louisiana. These assets, consisting of one-half million dollars in gold and jewelry, had been brought to Washington (Georgia) along with the Confederate treasury funds and were deposited in the vault of The Bank of

The Heard Building in Washington, Georgia, housed a branch office of The Bank of Georgia, and was the site of the last Confederate cabinet meeting. (Courtesy of Mary Willis Library, Washington, GA)

The home of Robert Toombs, Davis's first secretary of state. Toombs was arrested by Federal troops who threatened to hang him from an oak tree (which still stands as of this writing) in the front yard of his home. Toombs, however, managed to escape, and spent several years in exile in France.

The interior of Warthen's Store, photographed circa 1913. Heading south from Washington, Georgia, Jefferson Davis and his party purchased supplies in Warthen, and set up camp the evening of May 5 at Griffin's Pond. (Photo courtesy of GA Dept. of Archives & History)

Georgia.

When (Jefferson) Davis left Washington, bank officials attempted to ship the assets back to Richmond. The shipment was seized, however, near the Chenault plantation by (depending upon the source) Confederate Army deserters, Union Army deserters, or destitute Wilkes County farmers and ex-slaves.

In an attempt to locate the missing funds, Union cavalrymen hung members of the Chenault family by their thumbs, torturing them at length in excruciating pain. Only $111,000 of the missing state bank funds was ever recovered by the authorities, however, and even today, one hears rumors of buried "Confederate" treasure in this remote corner of Wilkes County.[9]

Meanwhile, Jefferson Davis was continuing to flee southward. He asked for and received ten volunteer Kentucky cavalrymen to serve as his escort. Then, accompanied by Reagan, Johnston, Lubbock, and several other aides and attendants, he hurriedly continued his flight.

General Breckinridge, after paying off the mutinous cavalrymen, arrived in Washington just after Davis had departed. He assisted Clark in the distribution of the treasury funds, disbanded the War Department, and directed the cavalry to leave Washington by several roads in order to confuse the pursuing Federal troops. Breckinridge then headed south himself, determined to escape on his own.[10]

The Federal Pursuit

Michael Lightner left Washington soon after Davis and Breckinridge. Lightner, a soldier in the 54th Pennsylvania infantry, had infiltrated Davis's party – dressed in a Confederate uniform – to spy.

He had accompanied Davis from the Catawba River in North Carolina to Washington. The next day, he reported to the Federal commander in Atlanta that Davis was in Washington with 1,500 cavalry and had.

"$15,000,000 in coin, and wagons, perhaps fifty."[11] Despite this report, however, Davis succeeded in shaking federal surveillance.

By May 6, Davis was aware that Federal troops controlled the escape routes north of Macon. He had decided to head south, towards the Florida coast, where he hoped he might obtain a boat to sail to Texas. He passed through Sandersville and, as dusk approached, prepared a camp on the east bank of the Oconee River at Ball's Ferry.

Meanwhile, in Macon, forty miles west of Ball's Ferry, Major General J.H. Wilson was trying to organize his troops to pursue Davis. In a dispatch to one of his field commanders – Colonel Robert H.G. Minty – Wilson instructed him to deploy his troopers at each of the Ocmulgee River crossings, surmising that Davis was headed south. Minty, in turn, sent a detachment of the 4th Michigan cavalry, commanded by Lieutenant Colonel Benjamin Pritchard, to patrol south of Hawkinsville, and 150 troopers from the 1st Wisconsin, commanded by Lieutenant Colonel Henry Harnden, to attempt to strike Davis's trail near Dublin.

Back at Davis's camp, the fatigued Confederate president received an alarming report from the ferryman that a band of desperadoes planned to attack his wife's party – which had crossed the river earlier that afternoon. Davis immediately broke camp, crossed the river, and then spent hours crisscrossing the dark, lonely countryside in search of his family. Finally, near dawn, he found them at the E.J. Blackshear plantation, ten miles north of Dublin.

This pontoon ferry on the Oconee River was photographed circa 1914. It was by a ferry just such as this that Davis crossed the Oconee at Ball's Ferry on May 6 of 1865. (Photo courtesy of GA Dept. of Archives & History)

The historic Chenault plantation house is owned today by Jim Hamilton, a developer from Virginia.

After a brief, emotional reunion, the combined parties proceeded to Dublin, arriving there early on Sunday morning, May 7. Although it was the Sabbath, Judge F. H. Rowe – recognizing the distinguished visitors – agreed to open his store. Having re-supplied themselves, Davis and his party then separated and resumed their journeys southward. Davis camped on Alligator Creek four miles south of Eastman.

The next evening, Harnden's detachment of Wisconsin cavalry arrived in

Dublin. Receiving conflicting information about Davis, Harnden was unsure what to do until, at midnight, a former slave told him that Davis had headed south towards Eastman. Having finally struck Davis's trail, Harnden set off in pursuit.

Unaware that Federal cavalry was closing in, Davis's party plodded south along muddy roads. After enduring a thunderstorm and crossing the rain-swollen Ocmulgee River at Poor Robin Ferry, the party established camp in Abbeville. Early the next morning (May 9), Davis's party broke camp and resumed the journey to Florida – now just 75 miles away.

The Capture Of Jeff Davis

As evening approached on the 9th, the separated Davis parties reunited and prepared to camp in a pine grove one mile north of Irwinville.

While Davis's party was preparing supper, Union Lt. Col. Pritchard received a report that a party with tents and wagons had passed down the Irwinville road earlier that afternoon. Since Lt. Col. Harnden's detachment did not have wagons, Pritchard deduced that it must be Davis's party.

According to Roy Rowe, present-day superintendent of the Jefferson Davis Memorial Park at Irwinville, Pritchard sent one of his troopers into the little town – dressed as a civilian – to inquire into Davis's whereabouts. "This soldier," Rowe says, "learned that a party had camped just north of town on the Abbeville Road."

Back at the Davis camp, the travel-weary band finished a quick meal and retired for some much-needed sleep. They made one mistake, however – they failed to post a guard that night.

Meanwhile, acting on the information he had received, Pritchard sent a party to scout the road north of Irwinville. The suspect camp was quickly discovered and, by 2:00 a.m. on May 10, Pritchard had deployed his detachment around the camp of the fleeing president of the Confederacy.

The efficiency of the Federal troops in capturing their prey left something to be desired. As Pritchard encircled the Davis camp, his troops encountered Harnden's detachment – which had also arrived at the Davis camp – in the pre-dawn twilight. Each, unfortunately, mistook the other for Confederate cavalry, and a sharp skirmish erupted between the two.

At about the time of the skirmish, Pritchard and a portion of his troopers had entered Davis's camp – encountering no resistance – and had been in the process of taking the group into custody when the shooting began. Leaving one soldier to guard Davis, Pritchard hastened toward the skirmish taking place north of the camp.

Davis and his wife had been in their tent when Pritchard's men arrived. Davis had quickly dressed, grabbed for his raglan (a sleeveless overcoat) – but mistakenly took his wife's – throwing it around his shoulders as he left his tent. Intending to escape into the swamp, Davis stopped when he realized that Federal troops had occupied the camp. But, when the skirmish erupted and Pritchard's men departed, Davis again moved towards the swamp. The remaining soldier, however, ordered him to stop, and Davis complied.

A rumor that Davis had attempted to escape in his wife's hoopskirt, shawl, and bonnet, was circulated by two Michigan troopers, spread by General Wilson, and then widely reported by the Northern press.[12] In point of fact, this rumor was just that – a baseless claim. During the ensuing years, most of the actual participants in the affair – both Northern and Southern – steadfastly maintained that Davis had acted honorably during his capture, and had been wearing a man's suit and a somewhat small, sleeveless overcoat.

When Pritchard returned to the camp, Davis informed him that there were not any Confederate soldiers present. Realizing that a mistake had been made, Pritchard ordered his men to cease-fire. Unfortunately, by the time order was restored, two of his men – John C. Rupert and Corporal John Hines – lay dead, and several other men from both detachments had been wounded.

The prisoners were quickly searched and disarmed. Many of their possessions became souvenirs for their captors. The prisoners were then taken to Abbeville, where Pritchard dispatched a report that informed the nation of Davis's capture:

"I have the honor to report that at day-light yesterday at Irwinville I surprised and captured Jeff. Davis and family. . ." [13] General Wilson ordered Pritchard to bring Davis to Macon.

Rupert and Hines – among the last casualties of the war – were buried in Abbeville, but were later re-interred at the United States Cemetery in Andersonville.

Pritchard and twenty troopers later took Davis by train to Augusta, via Atlanta, and from there by steamship to a prison in Virginia. The harsh treatment which Davis received during his imprisonment made him a martyr in the South.

Finally cleared of involvement in Lincoln's assassination, Davis was released in 1867. He spent several years in exile in Canada and Europe, returning to the United States in late 1869. He died in New Orleans in 1889.

ENDNOTES

1/ McIntosh, John H., 1968. *The Official History of Elbert County*, Cherokee Publishing Company, Atlanta, GA, p. 37.

2/ *Collections of the Georgia Historical Society, 1878.* Morning News Steam Printing House, Savannah, Georgia, p. 238.

3/ The last – General Richard Taylor's command in Alabama – was in the process of surrendering as Davis entered Georgia. Taylor, coincidentally, was Davis's brother-in-law.

4/ Davis, Major George W., 1897. *War Of The Rebellion; Official Records Of The Union And Confederate Armies* (Government Printing Office, Washington, D.C.), Series I, Vol. 49, Part II, p. 566.

5/ Ibid. (p. 558).

6/ Davis, Burke, 1985. *The Long Surrender* (Random House, New York, New York), p. 125; and Hanna, A.J., 1938. *Flight Into Oblivion* (Johnson Publishing Company), p. 85. Benjamin did, in fact, make good his escape. He arrived in Cuba on July 25, 1865, after a remarkable journey by horse-back across Georgia and Florida, and by boat across the Florida keys.

7/ There, on May 20, 1865, Mallory was arrested by Federal troops.

8/ Ibid, Note 6: *The Long Surrender* (pp. 123, 129-130) and *Flight Into Oblivion* (pp. 88-93). The rumors of buried treasure and highway robbery are more correctly associated with the Virginia and Louisiana bank assets rather than the Confederate treasury.

9/ August 21, 1865 issue of New York World, p. 2.

10/ Breckinridge, like Benjamin, escaped to Cuba via Georgia and Florida.

11/ Ibid. Note 4 (p. 622).

12/ Ibid. (p. 743). In his dispatch to Secretary of War E.M. Stanton, Wilson reported that Davis "hastily put on one of Mrs. Davis' dresses and started for the woods, closely pursued by our men, who at first thought him a woman, but seeing his boots while running, suspected his sex at once."

13/ Ibid. (p. 722-3)

Subject Index

A

A Breed Apart 93
A City Laid Waste 179
A History Of Rome And Floyd County 115
Aaron Palmour/Dr. Levi Russell Home 105
Abbedale 70
Abbeville Road 462
Abbeville, Georgia 462
Academic Building 75
Acworth, Georgia 84
Adairsville 30, 31
Adairsville, Georgia 315
Agents That Fly 93
Aiken Cemetery 313
Akes Station 378
Alabama Road 58
Alabama Street 399
Alligator Creek 461
Alpharetta, Georgia 127
American Board of Commissioners for Foreign Mission Schools 158
American Legion 43
American Revolution 162, 191, 456
American Union, newspaper 4
Amicalola Falls 92
Anderson (SC) *Independent-Mail* 54
Anderson's Battery of Light Artillery 214
Andrews' Raid 251
Anniston, Alabama 118
Apache Creek 104
Appalachian Mountains 277
Appalachians 94
Aragon Mill 384
Aragon, Georgia 384
Armstrong Hotel 116
Armuchee Creek 125
Armuchee, Georgia 112, 125
Ashby Street 140
Associated Press 362
ATF (Alcohol Tobacco And Firearms) 93
Athens Banner, newspaper 74, 78
Athens Normal School 168
Athens, Georgia 24, 45, 50, 74, 87, 116, 127, 132, 168, 172, 176, 212
Atlanta And Its Environs 139
Atlanta Campaign 217
Atlanta City Hall East 142
Atlanta Constitution, newspaper 44, 118, 179, 209, 357, 434
Atlanta Federal Penitentiary 44
Atlanta Fire Department 140
Atlanta Highway 178
Atlanta History Center 439
Atlanta Journal, newpaper 118, 135, 146, 185, 206, 347
Atlanta, Georgia 69, 77, 110, 139, 148, 168, 227, 268, 301, 331, 347, 393, 399, 431
Atlanta Southern Confederacy 250
Atlantic Avenue 93
Augusta, Georgia 189, 214, 389, 449, 457
Auraria, Georgia 98

B

Baldwin County 3, 194
Baldwin County Sheriff's Department 13
Baldwin Hotel 17
Ball Ground, Georgia 135, 339
Ball Of Fire 89
Ball's Ferry 461
Baltimore Block 431
Bank of Dahlonega 239
Bank of Georgia 450
Bank of Lumpkin County 233
Bankrupt Sale of 1928 73
Banner Plantation 225
Barnes Mountain 151
Barnett's Mill 114
Barrow County 280
Bartow County 24, 37, 342, 385
Battle Branch Line 217
Battle Line Branch 216, 222
Battle of Chickamauga 335
Battle of Horseshoe Bend 25, 158
Battle of Taliwa 339
Beaver Shoals 342
Belwood Road 165
Bemiss, Georgia 224
Benedict Mill 369
Berryton Mills 387
Besser Hotel 259
Beth Olam Cemetery 91
Beverly Hills 90
Bibb County 45
Big Cedar Creek 369
Big Indian Creek 53
Big Raccoon Creek 302
Big Sandy Creek 216
Big Savannah 195
Big Spring 367
Big Warriors Death 63
Blackburn Cemetery 135
Blackburn's Public House 133
Blaine, Georgia 194
Blairsville, Georgia 340

Blood Mountain 341
Blue Mountain Masonic Lodge 99
Blue Ridge Mountains 248, 428
Blue Ridge, Georgia 281
Bobby Brown State Park 457
Bolding Bridge 264
Bolding Covered Bridge 266
Bolding House 266
Bonnie Gilbert Road; 46
Borden Springs Post Office 381
Boulevard 139
Boy Scouts 144
Bradford Street 179
Branch Mint Building 240
Braswell Mountains 364
Bray Farm 164
Brenau College 178
Briartown Cemetery 104
Briartown, OK 104
Bridge Burners 251
British Fort Loudoun 341
Broad River 456
Broken Arrow 63
Brooks, Georgia 61
Bryan Street 143
Buchanan Police Department 354
Buchanan, Georgia 354
Buffington's Tavern 132
Burnt Mountain Baptist Church Cemetery 328
Burtsboro, Georgia 95
Butts County 57
Butts County Historic Society 57

C

C.C.C. (Civilian Conservation Corps) 180, 351
Cabin Creek 166
Cabin District 61
Calhoun Times and *Gordon County News* 164
Calhoun, Georgia 114, 159, 164, 260, 342
Camp Hancock 127
Camp Wheeler 15
Campus Theater 10
Campus Walk 75
Canadian River 104
Candler Warehouse 139
Canton Elementary School 73
Canton Textile Mills 68
Canton, Georgia 43, 65, 288, 339
Carnegie Hero 79
Carnegie Medal 81
Carpenter Brick House 257
Carrington's Drug Store 9
Carroll County 56, 57, 192
Carroll County Times, newspaper 208
Cartecay District 269
Cartersville Courant, newspaper 308
Cartersville, Georgia 25, 32, 34, 37, 43, 186, 270, 308, 385
Cass County 25, 31, 157
Cassville, Georgia 27, 33
Catoosa Courier, newspaper 437
Cavaliers 69
Cave Spring, Georgia 370
Cavender Creek 249
Cedar Creek 366
Cedar Creek Church 28
Cedar Valley 366
Cedartown High School 382
Cedartown Standard, newspaper 369
Cedartown's Baptist church 368
Cedartown, Georgia 43, 118, 352, 366, 378, 386
Celaqoue (Silacoa) 342
Central of Georgia Railroad 214
Central Railroad and Banking Company of Georgia 116
Chatsworth, Georgia 132
Chattahoochee High School 173
Chattahoochee River 56, 133, 202, 339
Chattanooga Daily Times, newspaper 437
Chattanooga, Rome and Columbus Railroad Company 116
Chattooga Academy 439
Chauga Creek 260
Chenault Crossroads 443
Cherokee Advocate 134
Cherokee Agency 259
Cherokee Constitution 159
Cherokee County 65, 132, 284, 313, 342
Cherokee County High School 70
Cherokee County Historical Society 73
Cherokee Indian Territory 366, 377
Cherokee Indians 24, 67, 191, 258, 366
Cherokee Iron Company 378
Cherokee Mounted Volunteers 162
Cherokee Nation 132, 156, 194
Cherokee Nation vs. Georgia 196
Cherokee Nation vs. the State of Georgia 193
Cherokee Phoenix, newspaper 164
Cherokee Street 84
Cherokee Supreme Court 159
Cherokees 26, 31, 98, 132, 156, 339, 427, 439
Chestatee River 264, 266
Chestatee Street 249
Chicago 84
Chicago Times, newspaper 324

Chickamauga, Georgia 288
Chieftains Museum 164
Chote Village 341
Church Street 86
Cincinnati Enquirer, newspaper 50
Citizen's Bank 179
City Auditorium 142
City Motors 44
Civilian Conservation Corps (CCC) 180, 351
Claiborne Parish, Louisiana 7
Clark Hill Lake 457
Clark's Drug Store 2
Clarke County 75
Clarke County Grand Jury 82, 196
Clarkite Party 196
Clayton Tribune, newspaper 390
Clayton, Georgia 170, 392
Clermont, Georgia 172
Cleveland, Georgia 262, 422, 426
Cliff House, 169
Climb The Hills Of Gordon 164
Coal City 347
Cobb County 84, 356
Cobb County Jail 152
Cochran's Funeral Home 362
College Avenue 74
Colorado State Historic Society 105
Columbus Enquirer, newspaper 327, 328
Company C of the 52nd Regiment of the Georgia Volunteers, Barton's Brigade 250
Company C, 65th Regiment, Georgia Infantry 250
Company F of the 12th Georgia Cavalry 32
Company I of the 1st Georgia Regulars 3
Conasauga Creek 270
Conasauga River 133
Confederacy 3, 268, 287, 306, 332, 345, 370, 440, 444, 456
Confederate 148, 156, 222, 249
Confederate Army 3, 156, 211, 282, 287, 305, 370, 444, 457, 459
Confederate Congress 3, 449
Confederate Naval Academy 449, 458
Confederate Navy 449
Confederate POWs 291
Confederate Treasury 444, 459
Confederate Veterans of Camp Troup 228
Confluence Park 105
Connasauga River 159
Conner House 239
Cook Armory 217
Cooper Manufacturing Company 178
Coosa Creek 340
Coosawattee River 159, 348
Coosewattie District 159
Corbin Hill Road 154
Cornelia, Georgia 168, 348, 390
Cornell University 19
Cotton Avenue 196
Covington Gang 335
Coweta County Jail 110
Creek Indians 191
Creek Nation 56, 158
Creeks 339
Crescent Farm 67
Crumby District 249
Cumberland Mountains 265
Cumming, Georgia 136, 274
Curryville, Georgia 114

D

D's Tavern 391
Dade County 347
Daffodil Farm 164
Dahlonega Gold Museum 239, 241
Dahlonega Mint 241
Dahlonega Nugget, newspaper 186, 423
Dahlonega Signal, newspaper 152, 243
Dahlonega Town Square 236
Dahlonega, Georgia 95, 147, 186, 233, 240, 248, 249, 254, 279
Dallas New Era, newspaper 299
Dallas, Georgia 301
Dalton Daily News, newspaper 136
Dalton Street 154
Dalton's North Georgia Citizen, newspaper 437
Dalton, Georgia 248, 251, 283, 290, 437
Daniel S. Printup, locomotive 120
Darnell Creek 344
Davistown Road 42
Dawson County 92, 274, 276, 289
Dawsonville City Cemetery 96
Dawsonville Highway 178, 266
Dawsonville Poolroom 92
Dawsonville, Georgia 92
Daytona 500 93
Daytona Beach, Florida 93
DC-4 cargo plane 353
Decatur Street 139
Decatur, Georgia 142
DeKalb County 31, 192
Democratic Party 147
Democrats 269, 318, 331
Department of Defense 357
Department of Justice 419
Dial, Georgia 149

Dick Ridge 438
Dixie Hunt Hotel 186
Doaksville 166
Dogwood Valley 441
Don's Convenience Store 391
Double Cabins 61
Double Springs 161
Doublehead Gap 147
Doughboys 127
Douglasville, Georgia 348
Du Pont Powder Company 144
Dublin, Georgia 461
Due West Road 91
Dunagan Church Cemetery 442
Duncan's Farm 215, 222

E

Eagle Hotel 254, 259
East Avenue 367
East Clayton Street 74, 81
East Damascus Church 152
East Point, Georgia 142
East Side Elementary School 360
East Spring Street 179
East Vernon Baptist Church 420
Eastman, Georgia 461
Edgewater Hall 67
Edgewood Avenue 140
Elbert County 443
Elberton, Georgia 455
Elgin Church 61
Elizabeth On The Chattahoochee 432
Elledge's Mill 436
Ellijay Courier, newspaper 322
Ellijay, Georgia 154, 236, 270
Emory University in Atlanta 71
Engine 345 299
Engine Thieves 251
Esom Hill Trading Post 378
Esom Hill, Georgia 353, 377
Eton, Georgia 132
Etowah River 25, 65, 99, 339
Euharlee Presbyterian Church 39
Euharlee, Georgia 40
Everett Springs, Georgia 112

F

Fairmount, Georgia 315, 348
Fannin County 147, 249, 251, 269, 280, 321
Fanny Gresham Branch 53
Farill Plantation 122
Farmer's Cemetery 124
Fayette County 61, 106
Fayette County Courthouse 110
Fayette County News, newspaper 110
Fayetteville Academy 394
Fayetteville, Georgia 110, 393
FBI 34, 44
Federal Aviation Administration (FAA) 358
Federal Circuit Court 347
Federal District Court 268
Federal Road 24, 132
Federal Union, newspaper 6
Field and Fireside 330
Fifth Regiment and the Governor's Horse Guard 143
1st Georgia Confederate "Volunteer" Cavalry Regiment 307
1st Georgia Regulars 251
1st Georgia State Troop Volunteers 292
1st Georgia U.S. Infantry 298
First Baptist Church 153
First Georgia State Line 213
First Georgia Volunteer Infantry 249
First Methodist Church 180
First National Bank 44
First National Bank of Cartersville 40
First National Bank of Polk County 369
Flamingo Hotel 85
Flat Shoals Creek 417
Flint River 61
Floyd County 111, 120, 124, 378
Floyd Creek 43
Floyd's Creek community 257
Flying Squadrons 385
Folsom School 30
Folsom, Georgia 24, 33
Forrest Carter Conner 349
Forrestville Station 120
Forsyth County 31, 132, 266
Forsyth, Georgia 127, 199
Fort Gibson 156
Fort McPherson 143
Fort Street 139
40th Georgia Infantry 28
42nd "Rainbow" Division 130
Franklin, Georgia 202, 207
Frog Mountain 270
Fullwood Springs 352
Fulton County 127, 431

G

Gainesville and North Western Railroad 432

Gainesville Bank 179
Gainesville, Georgia 175, 176, 182, 191, 266, 279, 290, 428
Gainesville-Midland Railroad 177
Gammage Funeral Home 368
Gaylesville, Georgia 284
General Courtney Hodges Boulevard 52
Georgia Bar 13
Georgia Bar Association 18
Georgia Bureau of Investigation (GBI) 352
Georgia Bureau of Investigation Crime Lab 239, 391
Georgia Cavalry 103
Georgia College & State University 15
Georgia Confederate Reserve Force, 221
Georgia Convention 334
Georgia Department of Archives & History 110, 194, 292
Georgia Department of Corrections 18
Georgia Division of Southern Railway 301
Georgia Division Safety Committee of Southern Railway 302
Georgia Factory 46
Georgia General Assembly 192, 424
Georgia Gold Rush 98
Georgia Guard 192
Georgia Historical Commission 136
Georgia Historical Quarterly 55
Georgia House 270
Georgia Journal, newspaper 194
Georgia Magazine 236
Georgia Military College 19
Georgia Militia 211
Georgia Public Safety Memorial 199
Georgia Public Safety Training Center 199
Georgia Railroad 146, 212, 450
Georgia State Legislature 3, 18, 148, 270
Georgia State Memorial Book 131
Georgia State Patrol 43, 73
Georgia State Penitentiary 149
Georgia State Superior Court 194
Georgia Supreme Court 51
Gilmer County 65, 147, 150, 270, 318, 346, 348, 351
Glade Cemetery. 26
Glenn-Kenimer-Tucker House 432
Gold Diggers Road 99
Gone With The Wind 142
Goodyear Mill 361
Goodyear Mill Number 3 385
Gordon County 114, 159, 307, 316, 342, 346
Gordon Springs 438
Gordon Springs Gap 440
Governor's Horse Guard 427
Governor's Mansion 2
Grady Hospital 140
Grandpa's Room 432
Gray 18
Great Depression 84, 94
Great Seal Of The Confederacy 443
Great Smoky Mountains 287
Green Street 176
Greenwood Avenue 139
Griffin, Georgia 61, 224, 399, 413
Griswoldville Battlefield State Park 217, 222
Griswoldville, Georgia 211
Gulf of Mexico 24
Gwinnett County 185, 192

H

Habersham County 168, 192, 249, 341
Hall County 148, 172, 192, 264, 266, 424
Hall County Police Office 185
Hall House 234
Hall's Block 235
Hancock Street 2, 8, 10
Hang Hollow 154
Hannah 71
Haralson County 199, 353, 374, 378
Haralson County Jail 354
Haralson County Sheriff's Department 354
Haralson County Tribune, newspaper 199
Harness Racing Hall of Fame 70
Harper House Hotel 9
Hawkins Street 236
Hawkinsville Courthouse 53
Hawkinsville, Georgia 53
Hays Cemetery 28
Hazzard District of Bibb County 48
Head-of-Coosa 24
Heard Building 447, 460
Heard County 202, 207
Heard County Historical Society 206
Heard County Jail 204
Heard County Superior Court 203
Helen, Georgia 341, 432
Henderson Mountain 314
Henry Grady Hotel 87
Hightower (Etowah) River 135, 157
Hightower Falls 369
Hightower Mission 25
Hightower River 340
Hillabatchee Creek 207
Hilliard Street 140
Hinton Cemetery 316

Hinton, Georgia 306
History of Lumpkin County 246, 254
HMF&P 345
Hodge's Drug Store 85
Holland Hotel 74
Holliday-Dorsey-Fife House Association 393
Hollywood 84
Holton, Georgia 47
Home Guard 288, 309, 335, 371
Honey Creek 163
Hooker's Army of the Cumberland 29
Hospital Corps 144
Houston County 51
Houston County Courthouse 53
Houston Street 140
Howard Street 116
Huerfano Valley 104
Hunnicutt & Bellingrath 431
Hurricane Club 87

I

In Search of the Hollidays 223
Indian Spring 57
Indian Territory 156, 160
Inferior Court of Gilmer County 69
influenza epidemic 124
Integrated Products 388
Internal Revenue Service 18, 91
Interstate Commerce Commission (ICC) 360
Iron Front Building 399
Irwinton 18
Irwinville, Georgia 462

J

J.B. Adcock & Brothers 29
J.R. Williams, ferryboat 156
Jackson County 74, 147
Jackson Herald, newspaper 80
Jackson Street 139
Jarrett Toll Bridge 255
Jasper Elementary School 338, 351
Jasper, Georgia 306, 313, 317, 318, 329, 333, 336, 347
Jefferson, Georgia 74, 75
Joe Brown's Pets 211
Johns Creek 114
Johnson County 18
Jones County 47, 214, 222
Jonesboro, Georgia 358
Judkin's Mill 369
Justice Department 357

K

Kansas Territory 99
Keithsburg Community 313
Kennesaw Avenue 145
Kenwood Road 106
King Cotton 306
King Hardware Company 143
King Street 140
Kingston, Georgia 32
Kite Bridge Road 107
Kite Lake Road 107
Kite Road 106
Know Nothings 345
Ku Klux Klan (KKK) 345, 434

L

L&N Railroad 73
LaFayette, Georgia 439
LaGrange County 416
LaGrange Daily News, newspaper 421
LaGrange Graphic, newspaper 416
LaGrange Reporter, newspaper 417
LaGrange, Georgia 416, 459
Lake Lanier 266
Lake Tobesofkee 55
Lakewood 100 95
Lakewood Park 143
Lakewood Speedway 95
Lansdown, Georgia 328
Las Vegas 85
Lawrenceville, Georgia 196
Laws of the Cherokees 134
Lawson and Poole Funeral Home 351
Leather's Ford, Georgia 98
Lewis and Sons 29
Liberty Church 61
Liberty County 439
Life magazine 351
Limestone Prairie 157
Lindale, Georgia 115
Linden Street 431
Line Creek, 62
Little Dry Creek 102
Little Sandy Creek 215
Living Atlanta 146
Living Atlanta: An Oral History Of The City 146
Long Branch Road 185
Long Swamp Cemetery 328, 331
Long Swamp Creek 339
Lookout Mountain 251, 440

Los Angeles Times, newspaper 90
Loyalists 342
Lowell, Georgia 61
Lowndes County Agricultural Society 228
Lowndes County Courthouse 226
Lowndes County Historical Society 223, 229
Lullwater Farms 71
Lumpkin County 148, 185, 233, 248, 254, 275, 276
Lumpkin County Courthouse 237
Lumpkin County High School 244
Lumpkin County Jail 186, 237
Lumpkin Superior Court 238

M

Macland Cemetery 33
Macon & Western Railroad 212
Macon Auto Club 55
Macon County 215
Macon Evening News, newspaper 50
Macon Telegraph and Messenger, newspaper 437
Macon Telegraph, newspaper 23, 48, 220, 328
Macon, Georgia 15, 19, 46, 212, 430, 454, 461
Madison, Georgia 367
Main Street 369
Manhattan Cafe 74
Maple Street 180
Maplewood Inn 168
Marble Hill, Georgia 346
March To The Sea 371
Marietta Country Club 87
Marietta Daily Journal, newspaper 84
Marietta Journal, newspaper 322, 326
Marietta, Georgia 84, 152, 290
Masonic Hall 2
Masonic Lodge 155
McClure Cemetery 102
McCutcheon's Cove 438
McIntosh High School 61
McIntosh Opry 61
McIntosh Road 61
McIntosh School 61
McIntosh Street, 61
McIntosh Trail 62
McIntosh's Ferry 61
McLemore Cove 251
Meaders Corner 235
Medical College of Georgia 128
Medicinal Springs 441
Medicinal Springs Baptist 441
Memory Hill 190
Merrill's Mill 207
Merrill-Roop Cemetery 210
Mexican War 224
Miami 85
Midway community 427
Milledge Avenue 51
Milledgeville 1, 8, 10
Milledgeville Memory Hill Cemetery. 9
Milledgeville Police Department 13
Milledgeville Southern Recorder 1
Milledgeville, Georgia 189, 194, 427
Milledgville Union Recorder, newspaper 7, 9, 11, 23
Missionary Ridge 28
Missouri State Penitentiary 34
Montgomery Street 34
Montgomery, Alabama 3
Moonshine 92, 107, 147, 377
Moonshine War 147, 268
Moonshiners 345
Moonshining 275, 311, 379, 416
Moore & Co. 1
Moravian Church 157
Moravian Mission 159
Moravian Mission Schools 158
Moravian missionaries 135
Morgan County 367
Mormon Church 435
Mormons 434
Morning Creek 107
Morrow Cemetery 165
Mosteller & Scott 29
Mount Etowah 67
Mountain City, Georgia 389
Mountain Creek 339
Mountain Ranch Resort 432
Mountain Signal, newspaper 262
Mrs. Abbott's Boarding House 89
Mt. Hope Cemetery 263
Mt. Pisgah Cemetery 351
Mt. Pleasant Church 149
Mt. Vernon Baptist Church 111
Mt. Vernon Church 61
Murphy Avenue 139
Murray County 346
Murrell's Gang 266
Museum of the Confederacy 444, 459
Myrtle Hill Cemetery 131

N

Nacoochee Depot 432
Nacoochee Valley 260, 423, 427
NASCAR 92
Natchez Trace 265

National Archives 272, 310
National Cemetery 290
National Council at "Broom's Town" 134
National Guard 35, 143, 385
National Guard Armory 73
National Historic Landmark 164
National Recovery Administration (NRA) 385
National Register of Historic Places 66, 123, 206, 317, 336
National Trust for Historic Preservation 73
Native Americans 24, 98, 191
Neal and Keowns' Store 438
New Armuchee Baptist Church 124
New Armuchee Cemetery 129
New Echota 157
New Echota State Historic Site 159
New Ford Creek 444
New Holland, Georgia 178
New Hope Baptist Church 114
New Town 159
New York Cafe 74
New York City 87
New York Globe, newspaper 325
New York Herald, newspaper 324
New York Times, newspaper 50, 87, 328
Newnan, Georgia 61, 110
News And Banner, newspapr 204
Newton County 189
Night Riders 274, 312, 318, 345
Nimblewill, Georgia 186, 239
1913 Rosedale Twister 111
1933 World's Fair 84
Norfolk-Southern Railroad 300, 359
North Avenue 145
North Chestatee 236
North College Street 368
North Georgia Agricultural College 240
North Georgia College 233, 240
Norton Cemetery 326
Nottely River 340
Nullification Crisis 333

Oak Grove 417
Oak Hill Cemetery 413
Oak Hill, Georgia 151
Oakland Avenue 143
Ocfuskee 57
Ocmulgee River 51, 461
Oconee County 260
Oconee Hill Cemetery 51
Oconee River 461
Oconee, Georgia 190
Official Seal of the Confederacy 458
Oglethorpe County 342, 455
Ohio State Penitentiary 34
Old College building 75
Old Fort Wayne 161, 166
Old Fountain Drive-In Restaurant 281
Old Madison Alabama Stage Road 61
Old South 6
Old Wheat Street 140
102 Railroad Street 31
Oostanaula (Ustanaula) 342
Oostanaula River 111, 159, 340
Oothcaloga 157
Oothcaloga Creek 165
Oothcaloga Mission Station 159
Oothcaloga Valley 159
Orange Hill Cemetery 53

P

Park Hill 166
Parkway Drive 142
Particular Baptist 32
Patriot 342
Paulding County 43, 299, 366, 377
Pea Ridge 163
Pea Ridge Civil War Battleground 166
Pea Ridge Road 151
Peachtree City, Georgia 61
Peachtree Street 142
Pearsons Creek 61
Pendley Creek 344
Pennsylvania College of Medicine and Surgery 99
Peoples Bank of Bartow County 39
Petersburg Cemetery 457
Petersburg, Georgia 443, 456
Philadelphia Church 351
Philippi Community 249
Philosophical Hall 74
Pickens County 147, 194, 269, 288, 305, 311, 318, 329, 332, 336, 339, 345, 348
Pickens County Courthouse 325
Pickens County Jail 325, 330, 336, 347
Pickens County Progress, newspaper 313
Pickens County Superior Court 320, 335
Pickens District 260
Piedmont 373
Piedmont Park 139
Piedmont Republican, newspaper 332
Pigeon Mountain 251
Piggly Wiggly 19
Pine Log 30

Pine Street 145
Pit Stop Grocery 281
Pittsburgh Dispatch, newspaper 54
Polk County 38, 43, 352, 353, 359, 366, 377, 384
Polk County Civil Defense 354
Polk County Courthouse 367, 370
Polk County Police 353
Polk County Sheriff's Department 383
Polk Street 86
Polson Cemetery 166
Ponce de Leon 302, 359
Ponce de Leon Avenue 139
Ponce de Leon Park 142
Ponce de Leon Woods 142
Poor Robin Ferry 462
Price Memorial Hall 240
Prince Avenue 45
Prior Mill 371
Prior Station 372
Prohibition 94, 379, 416
Providence Canyon Cemetery 213
Pruitt-Barrett Hardware 176
Pulaski Street 45
Pumpkinvine Creek 300

Q

Queen Nab 71

R

Rabun County 192, 389
Rabun County Sheriff's Office 392
Racing Hall Of Fame 97
Radical Reconstruction Government in Georgia 4
Radical Republicans 6
Railroad Street 70
Ralston's Creek 100
Raymond, Georgia 61
Raynes' Station 121
Reconstruction 147, 150, 226, 269
Reconstruction Georgia 3
Red Cross 144, 180, 348
Red Hill 434
Red Hill Cemetery 253
Red River 157
Red Stick Creeks 158
Republicans 269, 331, 332
Resaca, Georgia 275, 281, 441
Ridge Cemetery 166
Ringgold Church 61
Ringling Brothers Circus 439
Rio, Georgia 61
Road Laboratory Building 74
Robert M. Moore Building 238
Robinson Annex 168
Rock Barn 66
Rockmart School 362
Rockmart, Georgia 37, 251, 300, 359, 387
Rome & Northern Railroad 125
Rome and Decatur Railroad, 118
Rome News Tribune, newspaper 125. 362
Rome Tribune-Herald, newspaper 111, 125, 129
Rome, Georgia 24, 43, 70, 114, 116, 124, 304, 348, 361, 369, 384, 435
Rome, Georiga 382
Ron's Barber and Style Shop 200
Roopville, Georgia 61, 208
Rose Hill Cemetery 45
Rosedale, Georgia 111
Rotherwood, Georgia 61
Round Heads 69
Round Top 151
Round Top Mountain Road 151
Royal Palm 302, 359
Rusk Center 82
Russell's Gulch 102
Rutherford County 257
Rutherfordton Gazette, newspaper 261
Rutherfordton Sun, newspaper 261
Ryman Auditorium 66
Ryman Steamboat Lines 66
Ryo, Georgia 152

S

Sal Mountain 427
Salacoa 24
Salem Baptist Church Cemetery 9, 381
Salem Road 419
Salt Peter Cave 25
Salvation Army 131, 144
Sand Street 154
Sandersville Courier, newspaper 326
Sandy Plains 61
Sanford Building 11
Sara Hightower Regional Library 125
Sautee-Nacoochee 423
Savannah Avenue 226
Savannah Plantation 99
Savannah River 340, 443, 456
Savannah, Georgia 457
Scarecorn Campground 305
Scarecorn Methodist Church Campground and Tabernacle 306
Schofield's Army of the Ohio 29

Sea Field 346
Secession Convention 334
Seed Tick Road 105
Seminole and Creek Indian Wars 3
Seminoles 58
Senoia, Georgia 61
Sergeant Building 234
Sergeant's Hotel 186
Seventh U.S. Infantry and the Officers Training Camp 143
Sharp Mountain 342
Sharp Top Mountain 318, 346
Sharpsburg, Georgia 61
Sharptop District 346
Sharptop Militia District 345
Shiloh Baptist Church 377
Shiloh Cemetery 378
Shirley Hotel 168
Shorter College 127
Sigma Alpha Epsilon (SAE) 46
Silacoa (Celaqoue) 342
Silas Palmour-Green Russell Home 102
Sixes Gold Mine 69
Slaughter Mountain 341
Smithsonian Institute 67
Social Circle, Georgia 280, 386
South Broad Street 197
South Broad Street Bridge 340
South Kite Road 107
Southern Baptist Seminary 362
Southern Railway 300, 359, 369
Southern Railway and Express 185
Southern Railway Depot 302
Southern Railway's Train No. 36 182
Southern Star, newspaper 436
Southern States Portland Cement Plant 359
Spalding County 61, 399, 413
Spanish influenza 124
Sparta, Georgia 283
Spring Place 133, 158
Spring Place Mining Company 249
Spring Place, Georgia 24
Spring Street 154, 431
St. Louis 85
State Prison Board 189
State vs. George Tassels 194
State's Rights 191
States Rights 333
Stembridge Banking Company 14
Stephens County 255
Strawhill Cemetery 253
Summerville, Georgia 387
Superior Court Northeastern Circuit 424
Swainsboro, Georgia 199

T

Tahlonteskee Museum 166
Talking Rock School 349
Talking Rock, Georgia 194, 335, 351
Talladega, Alabama 58
Tallapoosa City Hall 199
Tallapoosa Jail 200
Tallapoosa Police Department 200
Tallapoosa River 57, 158
Tallapoosa, Georgia 199
Talley Mountain 341
Tallulah Falls 167
Tallulah Falls Railroad 167
Tallulah Falls School 167
Tallulah Falls, Georgia 167
Tallulah Gorge 171
Tallulah River 167
Talmadge Community 314
Talona Creek 349
Talona Valley 349
Taloney, Georgia 194
Tanyard Branch 366
Tariff of Abominations 191
Tate, Georgia 69, 338
Taylor Bridge Road 165
Taylor's Ridge 438
Taylor's Ridge 125
Taylorsville Bank 38
Taylorsville, Georgia 37
Telamon Cuyler Collection 62
Texas Valley, Georgia 112
The Athenian, newspaper 197
The Atlanta Constitution, newspaper 271, 322, 329, 338, 348
The Atlanta Georgian 362
The Atlanta Historical Bulletin 146
The Bank of Cherokee 73
The Bank of Georgia 459
The Bank Of Virginia 448
The Brewster Mercantile Company 378
The Cherokee Land Lottery 165
The Dahlonega Nugget, newspaper 237
The Daily Constitution, newspaper 240, 437
The Exchange Bank of Richmond 448
The Farmers' Bank of Virginia 448
The Grand Ole Opry 66
The Honest Man's Friend & Protector 312, 345
The LaGrange Reporter, newspaper 210
The Lucy Cobb Institute 51
The McKinney Plantation 68
The Mountain Rifles 440

The New York Times, newspaper 232
The Night Riders 71
The Nullification Crisis 192
The Old Mill Restaurant 369
The Pandora 82
The Raccoon Roughs 440
The Slicks 283
The Sons Of Confederate Veterans 164
The Southern Confederacy, newspaper 440
The Strand Theater 82
The Tack Room 69
The Tallapoosa Journal, newspaper 201
The Valdosta Times, newspaper 227
39th Georgia Confederate Infantry 298
Thomaston Road 46
Thunder Road 274
Thyatira Church 81
Thyatira Church Cemetery 75
Tift College 127
Tiger, Georgia 391
Toccoa, Georgia 167, 255
Tookabatchie 57
Tories 342
Towes Chapel 33
Trail of Tears 160, 344
Train Number 81 300
Traveler's Rest 255
Treat Mountain 355, 379
Treat Mountain Airport 358
Treaty of Indian Springs 56
Treaty of New Echota 160
Treaty of Tellico 132
Tribal Council 162
Troup County Courthouse 419
Troup County Jail 418
Troup County Superior Court 420
Troup County' 416
Troupite Party 196
Truett-McConnell College 422
Tugaloo River 255
Turin, Georgia 61
Turkey Mountain 112
23rd Georgia Volunteers 333
Twiggs County 310
Tyrus, Georgia 61

U

U.S. Army Corps of Engineers 457
U.S. Branch Mint 241, 254
U.S. Civil War 29, 33, 37, 46, 65, 98, 102, 111, 147, 150, 156, 182, 211, 224, 241, 248, 268, 282, 287, 305, 311, 332, 366, 369, 427, 443
U.S. Congress 197
U.S. Department of Revenue 153
U.S. Expeditionary Forces in France 79
U.S. House of Representatives 454
U.S. Postal Service 106, 156
U.S. Supreme Court 52, 191, 193
U.S. Treasury Department 93, 242, 346, 454
U.S. Veterans Bureau 130
U.S. Weather Service 111
Underground Atlanta 120, 399
Unicoi Gap 260
Unicoi State Park 427
Unicoi Turnpike 431
Union 148
Union Army 29, 103, 148, 157, 212, 249, 282, 288, 305, 335
Union Church 61
Union County 276, 289, 341, 392
Union Grove Road 165
Union Recorder, newspaper 190
Union Station 119
Unionist 3, 147, 332
United Confederate Veterans 440
United Merchants & Manufacturers 388
United States Cemetery in Andersonville 463
United States Court of Claims 454
United States Senate 160, 459
United Textile Workers' Union (UTWA) 387
University Bookstore 82
University of Georgia 46, 62, 74, 127, 240
University of Georgia School of Law 13
University of Georgia's Hargrett Rare Books and Manuscripts Library 194
Upper Cabin Road 61
Upson County 439
Ustanaula (Oostanaula) 342

V

Valdosta City Council 227
Valdosta Daily Times, newspaper 230
Valdosta Institute 226
Valdosta, Georgia 223, 393, 399, 415
Valley City 125
Vann's Mill Creek 133
Varnell's Station 434
Varnell, Georgia 304
Vaughn, Georgia 61
Vicksburg, Mississippi 28

W

W.F. Dorsey Funeral Parlor 81

Wage Stabilization Board 387
Walker County 437
Waltham, Georgia 61
Walton County 280, 386
Walton's Ford 260
War Between The States 4
War Department 460
War Path 339
Warthen's Store 460
Washington City (D.C.) 165
Washington Seminary 142
Washington to Milledgeville to New Orleans Highway. 24
Washington, D.C. 19, 24
Washington, Georgia 446, 459
Wayne Street 1, 8
West Avenue 369
West End 140, 428
West Peachtree Street 431
West Spring Street 181
Western & Atlantic Railroad 119, 217, 440
Wheeler's Confederate Cavalry 289
Whig 342
Whiskey Bill Mountain 280
White County 148, 262, 276, 283, 422, 427
White County Courthouse 423
White Sulphur Road 187
White Sulphur Springs 428
White Sulphur Station 182
Whitecaps 274
Whitehall Street 399
Whitesburg, Georia 60
Whitestone, Georgia 348
Whitfield County 251, 346, 434, 439
Whitfield County Superior Court 437
Wilkes County 342, 443
Wilkes County Courthouse 447
Williams Street 431
Willingham-Little Stone Company 349
Winder, Georgia 280
Wolffolk Road 389
Women's College of Georgia 15
Woodbine Cemetery 75
Woodruff Library of Emory University 326
Woodward Avenue 140
Worcester vs Georgia 198
Works Progress Administration (W.P.A.) 180, 351
World War I 13, 73, 124, 139, 146, 180, 351
World War II 79
Wrightsville 18

Y

Yankee POWs 251
York Street 140
Young Men's Christian Association (Y.M.C.A.) 78, 144, 244

Name Index

A

Aarnhart, Sgt. William A. 294
Aaron, Jesse 308
Abbott, Belle K. 194
Abercrombie, Bonnie 351
Abercrombie, Thelma 351
Abraham, Captain Lot 450
Adams, L.L. 206
Adcock, Mrs. Alton 30
Adonis, Joe 85
Alexander, Arthur 107
Alexander, General Edward Porter 451
Allen, Cyrus "Cy" 406
Allen, David 292
Allen, J.C. 152, 323
Allen, Sgt. Jesse 292
Allen, William "Billy" 406
Allison, J.M. 425
Allred, Elias R. 296
Allred, Felix 338
Allred, Lemuel 332
Allred, Lemuel J. 273
Allred, Rev. Elias 335
Almond, C.H. 78
Amos, Walter 200
Anderson, Anderson 39
Anderson, Benjamin 249
Anderson, Benjamin Harrison 251
Anderson, Capt. Ruel W. 217
Anderson, Charles Martin 251
Anderson, Cordelia 252
Anderson, George 182, 252
Anderson, Grover 95
Anderson, Henry 249
Anderson, Henry Clay 252
Anderson, Henry Franklin 251
Anderson, Isaac 249
Anderson, Jimmy 248, 260
Anderson, John 249
Anderson, John W. 292
Anderson, Jordon 295
Anderson, Margaret 249
Anderson, Mary "Mollie" Rebecca 252
Anderson, Mary Georgia Ann 251
Anderson, Maud Josephine 251
Anderson, Robert 343
Anderson, Thomas Abraham 249
Anderson, Thomas Jefferson 248
Anderson, Viola 251
Anderson, William 100
Anderson, William Arthur 251
Anderson, William H. 249
Anderson, William M. 249
Anderson, William, Jr. 295
Anderson, William, Sr. 295
Anderson, Woodrow 95
Anderson, Woodville B. 296
Andrews, Cleveland 290
Andrews, Ernest M. 443
Andrews, Garnett 450, 453
Andrews, Louis 11
Angelina 452
Archer, Russell 40
Arnold, Obadiah 4
Ash, Henry 292
Ash, Wallace 35
Ash, William 35
Ashworth, Col. J. H. 289, 298
Axtell, A.E. 232
Ayers, Elijah 294

B

Bading, Otto F. 179
Bailey, Alvin 380
Bailey, Clayton 380
Bailey, Lem 421
Bailey, Warren 380
Baird, James L. 295
Baldwin, Shep 13
Bandy, B.J. 137
Barker, Harrison 274
Barnes, Harve 69
Barnes, Matt 150
Barnett, Monroe 113
Barrett, E.W. 118
Barrett, Gilbert 172
Barrett, Thomas 292
Barton, Henry Bomer 30
Barton, S.G.H. 30
Barton, Ted 114
Bateman, R.L. 363
Bates, Samuel 100
Battey, Dr. Henry 119
Battey, George 372
Battey, George M. 115
Baxter, Carolina 256
Baxter, James Newton 256
Baxter, Andrew 258
Baxter, Ester McDowell 257
Baxter, James Newton 258
Baxter, James P. 257
Baxter, Joseph 261
Baxter, William Jr. 256
Baxter, William Sr. 257

Bearden, Ancil 296
Bearden, Jackson 148
Bearden, Sgt. Nelson 294
Bearden, William M. 296
Beardon, R.M. 294
Beasley, Susan 440
Beck, Eugene 245
Beck, John 100, 295
Behan, Johnny 405
Bell, H.P. 324
Bell, Hiram P. 152
Bell, Sarah (Sallie) Carolina 160
Belnap, Gen. 243
Benjamin, Judah 444, 458
Bennett, Corp. Robert Jr. 292
Bennett, Jackson 295
Bennett, Robert 295
Bennett, William 295
Bennette, Hiram 296
Bergwall Family 127
Bergwall, Carl 130
Bergwall, Elizabeth 131
Bergwall, Ellen A. 125
Bergwall, Ellen Saul 131
Bergwall, Ernest 130
Bergwall, Everett 130
Bergwall, John 131
Bergwall, Olaf 130
Bergwall, Signa 131
Bergwall, Sigrid 130
Bergwall, William Saul 131
Bergwall, Eric 124
Bergwall, John 124
Bergwall, Matilda 124
Bergwall, Ragland 124
Berry, M.A. 270
Berry, Milas D. 296
Berry, Sgt. Martin P. 293
Berry, William A. 296
Berry, William J. 296
Bertram, Wyatt-Brown 7
Bingham, J.F. 148
Bird, Georgia 47
Bishop 374
Bivens, Stephen "Pete" 13
Black Fox 134
Blackburn, Jesse W. 295
Blackburn, Lewis 133
Blacker, Charles B. 269
Blacker, Deputy Marshal 274
Blackshear, E.J. 461
Blackwell, Daniel 292
Blackwell, Sidney 292
Blair, Hugh 436
Blalock, Newt 425
Bleckley, Wilma 391
Bledsoe, Charlie 205
Bledsoe, Virgil 204
Bolt, Frank 111
Bolt, Henry 111
Bolt, Ruth 111
Bolt, Stella 111
Bolt, Viley 111
Bomer, Dr. Henry 30
Bonner, James C. 7
Bonney, William "Billy the Kid" 401
Booth, John Wilkes 454
Borden, Lizzie 54
Boudinot, Elias 157
Bowman, Benjamin 25
Bowman, Bersheba 25
Bowman, James L. 25, 198
Bowman, John 25
Bowman, Martha 25
Bowman, Sherrea 25
Box, Dr. J. Brent 164
Boyd, Christina Bolt 113
Boyd, Mattie 245
Bozeman, Henry B. 296
Bozeman, William A. 296
Brackett, J.H. 425
Bradbury, Capt. Edmond 408
Braden, Elias W. 295
Bradley, Andrew 436
Bradley, Dr. Richard 30
Bradley, Edward 286
Braidy, Braxton 292
Braidy, Lewis 292
Bramblet, Jesse 292
Bramblet, Reuben E. 292
Bramlet, Rachel 318
Bramlet, William 319
Brasil, Roy E. 387
Bray, Nancy 23
Bray, Rev. Bannister 164
Breckinridge, John C. 444, 458
Brewer, Jim Downey 180
Brewer, W.H. 362
Brewster, Fred 379
Brewster, Gordon 379
Brewster, J.P.S. 378
Brewster, Rev. V.A. 378
Brice, W.M. 179
Bright, Hiram 25
Brittain, Judge 262
Brock, John J. 296

Bromwell, William J. 444, 458
Brooks, Aaron T 295
Brooks, Alexander 296
Brooks, Hiram 290
Brooks, Isham A. 296
Brooks, Jacob R. 25
Brown, Bobby 458
Brown, Daniel 428
Brown, Gov. Joe E. 211, 332, 371
Brown, James G. 288
Brown, Joseph N. 292
Brown, Lawrence 200
Brown, Marjorie 376
Brown, Melvin 107
Brown, Robert S. 296
Brown, Russell "Napp" 384
Brown, Samuel 296
Brown, Thomas C. 296
Brown, William 292
Brown, William G. 296
Brown, Wofford L. 150
Bruce, Madison 296
Bruffey, Edward C. 119
Brumbelow, Wesley 384
Bryant, Wilson 148
Buckingham, James Silk 255
Bud, George 182
Buffington, Tom 133
Bulllis, H.E. 363
Bundy, B.J. 136
Burlison, William 294
Burlison, William Washington 290
Burrell, Bertha 168
Burrell, Vernie 391
Burt, Danny 457
Butler, General Benjamin F. 452
Butler, Tod 298
Byess, Dallas 321

C

Caffrey, Raymond J. 35
Cain, Andrew 246, 254
Cain, Sarah C. 283
Calhoun, John C. 116
Calhoun, Patrick 116
California Billy 182
Calloway, Corp. 270
Cameron, Alexander 342
Camp, A.A. 378
Camp, Charles 303
Camp, J.W. 378
Campbell, Col. Duncan G. 62
Campbell, Shelva 41
Candler, Asa 143
Candler, Walter 71
Cantrell, Andrew J. 294
Cantrell, Peter 307
Cape, Hobert 313
Cape, Levi 313
Cape, W. Lee 311
Cape, Waldo 313
Capehart, Ethel 442
Capone, Al 85
Carlisle, John 295
Carmichael, Pete 186
Carnes, Marshall 295
Carnes, Tandy W. 295
Carney, Absolem 295
Carney, Edmond 296
Carney, L. B. 296
Carney, S. 296
Carpenter, Judge George 16
Carroll, Frank 425
Carroll, John 88
Carroll, Lt. Henry L. 292
Carson, Frank 28
Carson, Henrietta "Aunt Connie" 28
Case, Dr. 5
Cason, "Boss" 199
Cassidy, Butch 401
Castleberry, Mark 195
Castner, Ralph 35
Catterson, Col. Robert F. 219
Cauthen, Rainey 107
Chamber, Joseph M. 295
Chambers, Barak 295
Chambers, James 296
Chambers, Phillip 295
Chambers, William B. 296
Champion, Oscar 338
Chandler, Joe Ben 381
Chandler, Will 381
Chapin, George 428
Chapman, John 296
Charters, W.A. 424
Chatlin, Lt. Henry B. 293
Chatlin, Sgt. Thomas 293
Chenault, Ardesia 453
Chenault, Frank 453
Chenault, John 452
Chenault, Reverend Dionysius 445
Chester, Ed 351
Chief Still 67
Childers, Rufus 70
Chumbley, Thompson 295

Chumbly, William A. 295
Chumley, Mac 353
Chupp, C. Gregory 73
Claiborne, Billy 396
Clanton, Billy 396
Clanton, Ike 396, 398, 407
Clark, Benjamin 436
Clark, Captain Micajah H. 445, 459
Clark, Laura 415
Clarke, Lt. Col. Elijah 342
Clawson, Rudger 434
Clayton, Augustin Smith 192
Clayton, Elias 294
Clements, Hal 361
Cleveland, Frances Folsom 24
Cleveland, President Grover 24
Clifton, George C. 286
Clifton, Leon A. 286
Clumbley, Jane 172
Clumbley, Kermit 172
Cobb, Gen. Howell 220
Cochran, Corp. Jeptha 294
Cochran, Francis M. 294
Cockran, James 292
Cody, W.C. 142
Coffee, Gen. John 25
Coffey, Martin V. 296
Coggins, Alfred B. 65
Coggins, Augustus "Gus" Lee 65
Coggins, Thomas Raleigh 66
Coggins, Tom 70
Colbert, James 292
Cole, J.W. 109
Collins, Bell 308
Collins, Berry 309
Collins, Boswell 309
Collins, Capt. Miles 309
Collins, Miller 309
Collins, Ruth 69
Colquhoun, Louis 182
Colquitt, Gov. Alfred 273, 326, 331
Colquitt, Jack 283, 372
Compton, Mrs. C. W. 2
Conger, Judge A.B. 19
Conkle, Ellen 36
Conner, Claude 351
Conner, Eugene 351
Conner, Flora Sue 351
Conner, Forrest Carter 349
Conner, Forrest Jr. 351
Conner, Harold Bud 351
Conner, James 351
Conner, Jesse 425
Conner, Martha 351
Conner, Mildred 351
Conner, Oleta 351
Cook, Lemuel 296
Cook, Lucious Riley 210
Cook, Maj. F.W.C. 218
Cooper, Richard 15
Cooper, Sheriff 49
Cooper, Simon 54
Copeland, Harry 439
Coppe, Carl 93
Corn Tassels, George 191
Corrie, Arthur M. 359
Cotter, William Jasper 197
Coulter, E. Merton 326
Coulter, Merton E. 55
Cowan, Lillie 54
Cowart, Frances M. 296
Cowart, Taylor S. 318
Cowart, Thomas A. 296
Cox, Jesse C. 298
Cox, John 303
Cox, Sheriff Dennis 12
Craine, Yerba 294
Crane, Fannie Moore 46
Crane, John Ross 46
Crawford, Ruby 441
Crawford, W.H. 441
Crisp, William 148
Crow, W.A. 185
Crump, William W. 448
Cummings, Capt. Joseph P. 335
Cummings, George M. 411
Cummings, Mary Katherine 411
Cunningham, Henrietta 333
Cunningham, Robert 296
Cunyus, Lucy Josephine 30
Curry, Capt. Wm. F. 298
Curtis, Gen. Samuel R. 163
Curtis, J.T. 425

D

Dadisman, Howard 75
Dadisman, Howard Dean 81
Daniel, Albert 292
Darnel, Capt. Elias 294
Darnel, Joshua 297
Darnel, Sion A. Sen. 297
Darnel, William J. 297
Darnell, S.A. 323
Darnell, Thomas 295
Davenport, John 272

Davidson, Victor 18
Davis, Abner 106
Davis, Anna Lou 367
Davis, Benjamin 292
Davis, Burke 305
Davis, Dick 228
Davis, Dock Heard 206
Davis, Georgia M. 375
Davis, James 298
Davis, Jefferson 412, 443, 456
Davis, Jim 186
Davis, Joe 186
Davis, John 112
Davis, Kay 112
Davis, Raymond 152
Davis, Robert S. Jr. 292
Davis, Rufus 186
Davis, Varina 458
Davison, Robert E. 189
Day, Sherman 246
Day, W.T. 323
De-gado-ga 157
Dearing, Reubin 297
deBaillou, Clemens 136
DeLong, Johnnie 173
Dempsey, E. F. 294
Denman, Felix 28
Denman, Matt 29
Denmark, Dr. Leila 127
Denney, Doug 96
Denny, Elisher 294
Denson, Corp. Jacob 292
Denson, George W. 295
Denson, Jethro 295
Denson, Joseph 295
Dexter, Pete 13
Dickson, Elwood 115
Dilbeck, Mary "Mollie" Rebecca 251
Dill, Milton 148
Dingler, Hoyt 353
Dorsey, William 39
Dosser, J.W. 363
Dotson, William 292, 294
Dougherty, Cornelius 194
Dougherty, John 195
Dowdy, James R. 292
Dowie, W.I. Jr. 363
Downing, Andrew Jackson 428
Dozier, W.T. 119
Drayton, Col. E.L. 453
Ducket, Sgt. Henry 292
Duggar, Rep. B.C. 273
Dukes and Pearson 378
Duncan, Cleveland 234
Dunn, Bill 414
Dutton, Oscar 107, 108
Dykes, Dr. 30
Dynes, W.L. 362

E

Early, John 249
Earp, George 231
Earp, Morgan 396, 397
Earp, Virgil 396, 397
Earp, Warren 397, 404
Earp, Wyatt 231, 395, 397, 404, 415
Easterledge, Walter 420
Eavens, George 293
Eberhart, Jacob 196
Eberhart, Susan 324
Eby, Robert 357
Echols, Elmer 33
Echols, Emily Elizabeth Gaines 33
Echols, Mamie 33
Edge, Bart 249
Edmonson, H.A. 378
Edmonson, Thomas 293
Edmonson, William 293
Edwards, George 182
Edwards, Ida 27
Edwards, Lenwood 425
Edwards, Rev. 155
Edwards, Yancey 18
Elder, Kate 229
Elder, Katie 396, 403, 405, 414
Elkin, Corp. William 292
Elkins, Jordon 295
Elkins, William 295
Elliott, Bill 92, 246
Elliott, Ed 201
Elliott, George 246
Ellis, Frank 109
Ellis, Police Chief Eugene 13
Emory, John 269
Ennis, Marion 11
Epstein, Joe 85
Evans, Col. Beverly D. 217
Evans, David 388
Evans, Frank 17
Evans, G. M. 297
Evans, Hoyt 314
Evans, John 294, 295
Evans, L.B. 362
Evans, Lindsey 314
Evans, Mirey 297

Evans, Nehe M. 295
Evans, Will 314
Ewards, Thomas 294

F

Fagala, John 300
Fair, Judge Peter 1
Falling, John 133
Falling, Nancy 133
Fant, David J. 182
Faucett, James 436
Faucett, Marshal Harvey 408
Faulkner, Jake 175
Featherstonhaugh, G.W. 333
Felton, Dr. Howard 27
Felton, Dr. William 27
Ferguson, Clyde R. 343
Fields, Elizabeth "Betsy" 160
Fincher, Marvin 203
Findley, Catherine 147
Findley, Col. James J. 147, 289
Findley, Deputy Marshal 274
Findley, James A. 269
Findley, James R. 147
Findley, Walter Webster “Web” 147, 321, 329
Finlay, Mrs. J.J. 363
Finney, Thomas 8
Finney, W.O. “Bill” 8
Fisher, Jay 390
Fitts, Arthur L. 245
Fitts, Ralph 244
Fitzgerald, Annie 394
Fitzgerald, John 298
Flanigan, James C. 195
Flocks, Bob 96
Flocks, Fonty 96
Flocks, Tim 96
Floyd, Charles "Pretty Boy" 31
Floyd, Duff 34
Floyd, E.W. 34
Floyd, Jack Dempsey 34
Floyd, Katherine Murphey 31
Floyd, Patience Pinson 31
Floyd, Redding 31
Floyd, Samuel 31
Floyd, Walter 33
Fly, Camillus S. 407
Flynn, W.M. 237
Ford, Charles 42
Ford, Dr. Arthur C. 399, 413
Ford, John 293
Forest, Gen. Nathan Bedford 305
Forrest, Bedford 447
Forrester, Mrs. Mark 348
Forsyth, Robert 199
Fouts, Fouts 290
Fouts, John 295
Fowler, Dr. Ralph Sr. 87
Fowler, James B. 298
Fowler, Johnson 293
Fowler, Narcissa “Sis” A. M. 318, 329
Fowler, Ralph Jr. 86
Franklin, C.L. 425
Franks, Kenny A. 157
Free, Ebenezer 293
Fricks, John D. 148
Frink, Lucian Frederick 227
Frix, Pleasant 294
Frost, J.E. 362
Fultz, John 35

G

Gable, George 200
Gailey, Homer M. 173
Gaillard, B.P. 245
Gaines, R.J. 209
Gambold, John 165
Gandee, Sherman 34
Garman, James 294
Garrard, Joseph 243
Garrett, Charmaine 40
Garrett, Franklin 139
Garrett, Joseph 293
Garrett, Martin L. 293
Garrett, Pat 401
Garrett, Robert 293
Garrison, James T. 387
Garrison, William 210
Gatewood, John P. 282
General Steedman 453
Gentry, William 151
George, James 297
Giffett, Brooks 286
Gillem, Gen. Alvan Cullem 282
Gilmer, Gov. George R. 192
Gilrith, John 293
Gladden, William 294
Gladen, William 293
Gladney, James E. 206
Glenn, James 432
Goble, Anthony “Tone” 150
Goff, Dr. John H. 340
Gold, Harriet 159
Goode, Abram 297

Goode, M.H. 297
Goode, Silome 297
Goodson, Hugh 206
Gordon, Fannie Haralson 439
Gordon, Gov. John B. 118
Gordon, John Brown 439
Gordon, Reverend Zachariah 439
Gordon, Washington K. 441
Gore, Vilwon Cook 208
Gov. Colquitt, 435
Grady, Henry W. 326, 329
Grant, Gen. Ulysses S. 212
Grant, John W. 22, 23
Grant, Pres. Ulysses S. 269
Grant, Willliam 25
Gravely, Edy 308
Gravely, Frank 308
Graves, James 198
Green, B.L. 350
Green, Garland S. D. 297
Green, J.C. 22
Green, Judge Robert 15
Green, Pete 68
Green, Robert 17
Green, W.H. 273
Green, W.S. 206
Greene, W. 343
Greer, T.F. 323
Greeson, Mary Nan 442
Grey Fox 189
Griffeth, Robert 297
Griffith, Ben 379
Griffith, John 293
Griffith, William 293
Griggs, Corp. James L. 294
Grinsmith, Leab 284
Griswold, John 320
Griswold, Samuel H. 215

H

Haas, Marron 41
Hackney, Robert 380
Haithcock, Josiah W. 295
Hale, Dr. P.T. 362
Hall, Frank W. 239
Hall, R.M. 245
Hall, Roy 92
Hall, Sheriff Dewey 18
Hambleton, John 25
Hambleton, Joseph 25
Hambleton, William 25
Hambrick, Amazilla 319
Hambrick, John 318
Hambrick, Kate 318
Hamby, Mrs. Theodore 27
Hamlin, Mary 436
Hampton, John 100
Hancock, Thomas 308
Handford, James 184
Hanie, Milton H. 369
Hansel, William Y. 193
Hardee, Gen. William J. 214
Hardeman, Col. Thomas 220
Hardgrave, Wilma Ruby 34
Hardman, Dr. Lamartine G. 432
Hardwich, Joseph 286
Hardy, Mrs. George 363
Harnden, Colonel Henry 461
Harony, Mary Katherine "Kate" 229, 409, 414
Harper, Lt. 309
Harrington, Hugh T. 7, 9, 23
Harrington, Susan J. 9
Harris, Clayton J. 40
Harris, John M. 237
Harris, Judge Iverson L. 2
Harris, T.B. 106
Harris, Thomas H. 193
Harris, Woodrow 108
Harrison, Colonel Burton N. 458
Hart, Lon 420
Hartsfield, William B. 142
Harvey, Gussie 168
Hawkins, Benjamin 344
Hawkins, Jane 62
Hawkins, Samuel 57
Haygood, Dr. Murl 87
Haygood, Zeb 351
Haymes, John 323
Haynes, John 319
Head, Sylvia Gailey 172, 176
Heard, John 68
Heath, Griffin 297
Henderson, Charles K. 369
Henderson, J.A. 417
Henderson, Lillian 7
Hendricks, Delia 115
Hendrix, John 297
Henry, Alexander 295
Hertz, Dr. 5
Hess, Capt. Levi M. 335
Hickok, James Butler "Wild Bill" 401
Hicks, Charles 134
Hicks, Eli 160
Hicks, Isabella 160
Hidalgo, Francisco 224

Hightower, Elias 369
Hill, Belle 75
Hill, Bud 148
Hill, Chick 87
Hill, Cotton 87
Hill, Fred 336
Hill, Henry Hoyt 81
Hill, J.B. 69
Hill, James 286
Hill, Lawrence Herndon 81
Hill, Mack 84
Hill, Margaret 84
Hill, Virginia 84
Hill, William Thomas 81
Hillhouse, David 167
Hilty, Robert 363
Hines, John 463
Hix, James 293
Hix, John 295
Hodge, W.W. 109
Hodges, Bessie Dodd 146
Holcomb, Sargent M. 298
Holcombe, Elizabeth 25
Holder, Emmie L. 124
Holder, J.T. 124
Holder, John 125
Holder, Louise 125
Holliday, Alice Jane McKey 226, 412
Holliday, Dr. A.C. 78
Holliday, Dr. John Stiles 393
Holliday, Henry Burroughs 412
Holliday, John Henry "Doc" 223, 229, 393, 397, 404, 412
Holliday, Maj. Henry B. 224
Holliday, Martha Anne "Mattie" 395
Holliday, Robert Alexander 414
Holliday, Sister Mary Melanie 230
Holliday, Tom 75, 81
Holt, James 272
Honea, Cora Belle 379
Honea, George M. 297
Honea, James 320
Hood, Samuel 297
Hood, Tate 297
Hooper, John W. 198
Hooper, Judge John W. 27
Hopper, Charley 293
Houston, Mollie Jones 438
Houston, Samuel 409
Howard, "Doc" 249
Howard, Gen. Oliver O. 212
Howard, John J. 411
Howard, John L. 297
Howard, Lucille 129
Howard, Maj. Dewitt C. 288
Howard, Margaret 129
Howard, Mattie E. 46
Howard, Samuel 297
Howard, Thomas 129
Howell, Bob 322
Howell, Russell 297
Hudgens, H.E. 183
Hughes, R.V. 148
Hughes, Ray 42
Hulsey, Jim 173
Hulsey, Vallie 173
Hunnicut, Calvin 430
Hunt, George W. 411
Hunter, Charlie 184
Hunter, Jefferson 436
Hunter, Oscar 251
Hurtel, Gordon N. 119
Hyde, Asa A. 295
Hyde, Henry C. Jr. 306
Hyman, Mannie 406

I

Ingersoll, Mary 310
Ingram, John 293
Irvin, G.B. 425
Isbell, Jeremiah "Jerry" 378
Isbell, Laura Jane 378

J

Jackson, Andrew 158
Jackson, Capt. Henry 117
Jackson, Gen. Andrew 25
Jackson, George 18
Jackson, John 425
Jackson, Lt. Col. Issac 342
Jackson, President Andrew 198
Jackson, William Andrew 424
James, Jesse 401
James, Thomas G. 286
Jarrard, Lt. Joseph 245
Jarrett, Devereaux 255
Jenkins, Gov. Charles 4
Johnekin, Emma 16
Johnson, Abda 32
Johnson, Dr. David 228
Johnson, Dr. James R. 153
Johnson, Elijah 272
Johnson, James E. 75
Johnson, Leon 39

Johnson, Mamie 79
Johnson, Morris 44
Johnson, President Andrew 454, 457
Johnson, Robert D. 75
Johnson, Rufus 183
Johnson, Sharon 239
Johnson, Turkey Creek Jack 404
Johnston, Col. L. 289
Johnston, Colonel William P. 445, 459
Johnston, Gen. Joseph E. 457
Jones, Ayers 147, 270
Jones, Carter 317
Jones, Charles C. 429
Jones, Charles C. Jr. 220
Jones, Charles Harry 233
Jones, Dr. C.H. 233
Jones, Elizabeth Coggins 67
Jones, Rev. Ransom Adolphus 438
Jones, Rube 71
Jones, Seaborn 359
Jones, Theodocia 233
Jones, Tom 272
Jones, Wanda 233
Jones, William 153
Jordan, Capt. Benjamin F. 290
Jordan, John G. 297
Jordan, Simeon 286
Jordon, John 298
Jossey, James 23

K

Kefauver, Senator Estes 91
Keith, S.J. 364
Kelley, Pollard 295
Kelley, William 295
Kellogg, Col. John A 290
Kelly, John 294
Kelly, Pollard 295
Kenan, Augustus H. 3
Kenan, Col. A.H. 6
Kenan, Henrietta Alston 3
Kenan, Lewis 1
Kenan, Sarah Barnes 5
Kendall, Elbert 186
Kendricks, Art 232
Kennard, Moody 63
Kerby, William 293
Kerlin, Sheriff 107
Kerlin, Tom 106
Kidd, Culver 16
Kidwell, R.P. 303
Killerman, Henry 409
Killett, Joseph 286
Kilpatrick, Gen. Judson 440
Kimsey, John Johnson 424
Kimsey, William 149
King, Jack 117
King, Ralph 336
Kinney, Bill 84
Kinsland, Bill 249
Kuhn, Will 363
Kytle, George S. 424

L

Lacky, Wm. 293
Lamar, Peter 389
Langston, James C. 106
Latimer, Augusta 429
Latson, Edward J. 285
Lawless, Lt. Calvin J. 294
Ledbetter, Cora 167
Ledbetter, Joseph 295
Ledlow, C.W. 200
Lee, Gen. Robert E. 440, 457
Leslie, Buckskin Frank 398
Lester, D.P. 323
Lester, Judge George N. 323, 329
Lewis, David W. 240
Lewis, Hart 420
Lewis, Marshall 27
Lewis, Tarleton 136
Lewis, Willie 242
Lightner, Michael 460
Lincoln, President Abraham 305, 454, 457
Lindsay, John 321, 330
Lindsey, Carl 350
Lindsey, Howard 349
Lingefelt, John 294
Lingo, Deputy Buford 21
Lipford, R.M. "Mac" 203
Lipford, Thomas 202
Little, Grover 200
Little, J.B. 200
Lively, John 294
Lively, Lewis 298
Lobrugh, Dan 363
Locket, Green 47
Logan, Gen. John 412, 441
Logan, Mary Louise 155
Long, Bernard G. 94
Long, Connord 293
Long, Henry 293
Long, James M. 293
Long, James, Jr. 293

Long, James, Sr. 293
Long, Jasper 148, 293
Long, John 293
Long, Joseph 293
Long, Nathaniel B. 293
Long, William 293
Looney, Eleanor 160
Lott, Frank Jr. 382
Lott, Frank Sr. 382
Loveless, Abner T. 297
Loveless, C.C. 297
Lovengood, William 293
Lovin, Reubin 297
Lowe, Maj. C.B. 119
Lubbock, Colonel Frank R. 445, 459
Luciano, Charles "Lucky" 88
Lumpkin, Gov. Wilson 25
Lumsden, Tannie Williams 431

M

MacAllister, Virginia Ash 244
Maddox, Robert E. 67
Maddox, Robert F. 68
Maegar, Tom 200
Maegar, William H. 199
Mallen, Perry 405
Mallory, Stephen R. 458
Manes, Harland F. 34
Manley, Julius C. 297
Manly, Lewis F. 297
Mann, Emsly O. 297
Manning, William "Billy" 201
Marcus, Josephine Sara 403
Marks, Paula 396
Marshall, Justice John 196
Marshall, Mrs. George O. Jr. 376
Martin, Capt. William 249
Martin, Loucille 111
Martin, Morgan 295
Martin, Pee Wee 96
Martin, Rachel 226
Martin, W.M. 113
Martin, William P. 297
Masis, Henry H. 298
Massee, Sheriff Bill 23
Masterson, Bat 231, 396, 398, 405
Mathews, Sgt. Thomas N. 293
Mathis, Louise 130
Matthews, J.D. "Shug" 175
Matthews, Mickey 178
McAfee, Joseph 100
McClain, Clark 318
McClintock, J.C. 286
McCloud, William M. 293
McClure, Mack 436
McClure, Reba 27
McCoker, J.M.P. 286
McCormack, M.E. 378
McCoskey, John 249
McCoskey, Walter 250
McCrarey, Corp. Willis 292
McCrarey, Lt. Leander 292
McCrarey, Sgt. Harper 292
McCrary, Capt. George W. 289
McCrary, Julius 295
McCravey, D.S. 297
McCravey, William 297
McCutchen, Lt. Robert B. 296
McDaris, Mrs. Tom 27
McDonald, Hugh 140
McDonald, Paul 300
McDugle, John C. 294
McElroy, Charlie 415
McFarland, Willie Pickett 313
McGuire, Alma 236
McGuire, George Henry 237
McHan, Alfred 297
McHan, Henry 297
McHan, W. M. 297
McHan, Wilkie 297
McIntosh, Chief William 56
McIntosh, Chilly 58
McIntosh, Peggy 62
McIntosh, Susannah 62
McIntyre, Lt. Augustine 270
McKinney, James 68
McLaury, Frank 396, 398
McLaury, Tom 396, 398
McMillan, Ernie 376
McSpadden, Samuel 286
McWhorter, Frank 210
Meaders, Maggie 234
Meaders, R.C. "Mr. Bob" 234
Mealer, Mary 319
Mercer, J.S. 378
Meriwether, Major James 62
Merrill, Carrie Lee 208
Merrill, Henry Albert 208
Merrill, Lula Miller 208
Merrill, Robert 208
Merrill, Sara 208
Milam, Agent 106
Miles, Frank 425
Miller, Charles 237
Miller, Dr. Wilbur R. 274

Miller, Osgood 415
Miller, S. Young 206
Miller, Tom C. 175
Miller, Vern 35
Miller, Walter B. 183
Miller, Wilbur S. 274
Miller, William "Baby Face Billy" 35
Millsaps, Stephen S. 295
Millsips, Solomon 295
Minchew, Kaye 417
Mincy, James 294
Miner, Bill 182, 239
Minty, Colonel Robert H.G. 461
Mintz, Duane "Cowboy" 300
Mintz, H.D. "Cowboy" 365
Mintz, Leonora 359
Mitchell, John E. 432
Mitchell, Margaret 142, 394
Mitchell, Maybelle 142
Monroe, Daniel P. 295
Monroe, Samuel L. 295
Monroe, Vanburen H. 295
Monroe, Virgil D. 294
Montgomery 374
Mooney, James 339
Mooney, Walter T. 183
Moore, Bob 422
Moore, Edker 423
Moore, Jennie 423
Moore, Joseph 293
Moore, Logan 423
Moore, Nancy S. 423
Moore, Richard 423
Moore, Susan 46
Moore, Thomas 46
Moore, Tom H. 189
Morgan, Cunningham 294
Morgan, George 182
Morgan, John G. 406
Morgan, Sam 152
Morris, Joseph 296
Morris, Mary Ann Camp 28
Mosley, Albert 297
Moss, Felix 68
Moss, H.R. 362
Moss, John 297
Mosteller, David 29
Mosteller, George 28
Mosteller, Jacob 29
Mullins, George R. 297
Mullins, Green D. 297
Mullins, James P. 297
Mullins, Martin B. 297
Murphey, C.M. 33
Murphey, Frances 31
Murphey, John 31
Murphey, Matthias 32
Murphey, Roger Jr. 31
Murrell, John A. 264
Murrell, Rev.William 265
Musick, Michael 298

N

Nally, Bailey M. 307
Nally, Benson M. 307
Nally, Elijah 307
Nally, Gracy Ann 309
Nally, Jerry 310
Nally, Jesse 309
Nash, Frank 35
Nations, David D. 436
Nations, Jasper N. 436
Nations, Joseph 436
Nations, William 436
Nelms, Capt. J.W. 327
Nelson, Henry 295
Nelson, William J. 297
Newberry, Cub 148
Newberry, Hegga 294
Newberry, Jackson 293
Newborn, R. Seab 314
Newman, Frederick E. 269
Newman, James 286, 297
Newton, Ebenezer 135
Nichols, Anna Ruby 427
Nichols, James Hall 427
Nichols, Jim 299
Nichols, Kate Latimer 427
Nix, Sgt. Milton 292
Nobles and Adkins 378
Noyes, Col. Charles R. 143

O

O'Grady, William 269
O'Kelley, Harold E. 251
Oakes, William J. 424
Odum, Julian 18
Oliver, Robert 390
Osgood, Sam 405
Owen, Dr. John 246
Owensby, C.W. 349
Owensby, Jonathan 436

P

Padget, Alfred L. 297
Padget, Isaac 297
Padget, John 297
Padget, William J. 297
Page, Don 392
Pardue, J.E. 425
Parham, J.H. 210
Paris, Lt. Hezekiah M. 296
Parker, Capt. William H. 458
Parker, Lt. William H. 449
Parker, Robert 199
Parttiss, Lee 20
Path Killer 134
Patrick, Gen. Marsena R. 450, 452
Patterson, Asa 297
Patterson, E.D. 297
Patterson, Edward 297
Patterson, Hix 297
Paxton, John H. 307
Payne, Ambrose 295
Payne, George Frederick 430
Payne, George W. 293
Payne, John 293
Payne, John W. 297
Payne, Rev. Walter 349
Payne, Thomas 295
Peacock, C.H. 316
Pendergrass, Alva 75
Pendleton, Albert 223
Pendleton, Louis 225
Perry, H.H. 245
Perry, W.J. "Bill" 37
Petit, Susan 320
Petty, Lee 96
Pharr, Dott 314
Phillips 373
Phillips, Charles D. 270
Phillips, Charles H. 152
Phillips, Gen. Pleasant J. 214
Phillips, Jack 379
Pickens, Andrew 343
Pickens, David 343
Pickens, Gen. Andrew 339
Pickett, Mrs. J.W. 367
Pierce, Bobby 112
Pierce, Robert M. 362
Pines, Phillip 70
Pinkerton, Allen 457
Pinkerton, William 189
Pinyan, Abraham D. 295
Pinyan, Jacob 297
Pinyan, James H. 297
Pinyan, Jeptha 295
Pirkle, Sanford 147
Pitts, Mortimer 325
Platt, James C. 387
Ponder, Will 349
Pool, William 297
Poole, D.P. 336
Pope, Henry C. 200
Pope, Nell M. 179
Porch, Rosa "Lizzie" 109
Presley, J. Marion 297
Prewitt, William A. 298
Price, Col. William Pierce 241
Prince, Archibald A. 294
Prince, Capt. Alvin W. 293
Prior, Ann M. 367
Prior, Asa 367
Prior, Haden 369
Prior, James 372
Prior, John 372
Prior, John T. 367
Prior, John Thomas 372
Prior, Sally 367
Prior, Sarah 368
Prior, William H.C. 370
Pritchard, Col. Benjamin 461
Proctor, John 195
Proctor, Letty 194
Proctor, Rev. Issac 195
Purvis, Melvin 36
Puryear, W.C. 437

Q

Quilliams, Rev. J.C. 390

R

Rackley, Willis 149
Ralston, Lewis 100
Ramsaur, L.B. 245
Rankin, William Robert 270
Raum, Green B. 274
Ray, Archable 293
Ray, Archibald 294
Ray, John D. 293
Ray, Joseph 293, 294
Ray, Martin 293
Ray, Pearl 237
Ray, Thomas 297
Ray, Tom 235
Reagan, John H. 445, 458

Reece, A.J. 294
Reece, Glen 151
Reece, Homer 151
Reece, Jackson T. 294
Reece, Lt. James M. 293
Reece, William 294
Reed, Corp. John 294
Reed, Jack 115
Reed, John 111
Reed, Robert G 294
Reese, William M. 451
Reeve, Jewell B. 164
Rice, Erskine 245
Rice, George Erskine Sr. 245
Rice, Judge 335
Rice, Nathan 25
Richardson, Bill 69
Richardson, Jack 70
Richardson, William E. "Bill" 70
Richetti, Adam 35
Richetti, Adam "Eddy" 35
Rider, Corp. Joseph 294
Rider, Henry 294
Ridge, John 158
Ridge, Major 158
Ridge, Susanna 159
Ridley, Harmon 208
Riley, Harrison W. 254
Ringo, Johnny 398
Rivers, Marvin 106
Roberts, Bud 148
Roberts, Fireball 96
Robertson, Dr. J.J. 459
Robinson, Andrew J. 295
Robinson, George R. 290, 296
Robison, Richard 298
Rockwell, Samuel 193
Roe, Ancil C. 297
Roe, Solomon 100
Rogers, Dr. Lee 180
Rogers, Guy 392
Rogers, John 176
Rogers, Joseph 293
Rogers, Oma 178
Rogers, Ruth 180
Roop, Benjamin Jocephus 208
Roop, Bula 208
Roop, Ella 208
Roop, Georgia Merrill 208
Roop, Homer 208
Roop, Martin 208
Roop, Thomas 208
Roosevelt, Franklin D. 179
Roper, Ed 179
Ross, Chief John 158, 197
Ross, John 439
Rouse, Carleen 94
Rowe, F.H. 461
Rowe, Roy 462
Rowland, Judge Roy 18
Ruddell, Clifford 136
Rupert, John C. 463
Russell, Frances 103
Russell, James 98
Russell, Jane 103
Russell, John 297
Russell, Joseph Oliver 98
Russell, Levi 98
Russell, Meager 298
Russell, Susan 104
Russell, William Greenberry "Green" 98
Rusts, Corp. Gus 363
Rutherford, John C. 51
Ryman, Daisy 66
Ryman, Pearl 66
Ryman, Thomas Green 66

S

Samuels, George B. 109
Satterfield, Marvina 39
Saye, Dr. John 168
Scoogins, Mathew 294
Scott, Benjamin 28
Scott, Fr. Philip P. 30
Scott, Henry Bomer 26
Scott, Jeff 27
Scott, Rebecca Franklin 26
Seaborn, John 25
Seay, Garnett 95
Seay, Gov. Tom 118
Seay, Lloyd 92
Seibert, L.I. 363
Sergeant, John 186
Sevier, John 344
Shadburn, Don L. 133
Shear, Forrest 146
Shelley, Frank 388
Shelnut, Floyd 425
Shepard, Lewis 451
Sherman, Gen. William T. 29, 212, 332, 412, 427, 450
Sherman, Otto 71
Sherman, T.R. (Rex) 316
Sherrill, Ernest 136
Shirey, William Brewer 416

Shirley, C.H. 183
Shirly, Nathan 297
Shoemaker, Bob 303
Shook, William G. 286
Shoup, Lieutenant 103
Shumate, Mary Ann Chenault 446, 453
Sibley, judge Edwin 12
Siegel, Benjamin "Bugsy" 85
Simmermon, Jacob 296
Simmermon, James 296
Simmons, James 334
Simmons, S.J. 148
Simmons, W.H. 323
Sister Mary Melanie 411
Sitton, James 270
Sizemore, A. 297
Slaughter, Texas John 398
Sloan, Eva 17
Slocum, Gen. Henry W. 212
Smith, A.S. 436
Smith, Ben 308
Smith, C.L. 314
Smith, C.L. "Seal" 317
Smith, Charles 148
Smith, Chester 36
Smith, Col. Jack T. 326
Smith, Collins 296
Smith, David 436
Smith, F.L. 425
Smith, Gen. Gustavus W. 214
Smith, Gov. James M. 3, 324, 455
Smith, Harry 365
Smith, J.R. 109
Smith, Jackie 41
Smith, James F. 165
Smith, John Hogg 198
Smith, John I.P. 153
Smith, Judy 123
Smith, S.A. 417
Smith, Verna Cook 210
Smith, Will 380
Smith, William 380
Smyth, Chester 252
Smyth, Jack 252
Smyth, Lewis 252
Smyth, Robert Henry 252
Smyth, Robert Lee 252
Smyth, William 252
Smyth, William E. 248
Snelling, Col. C.M. 78
Snider, Jane 389
Sorrells, Henry 365
Soseby, Gober 92
Southern, James 322
Southern, Kate 147, 318, 329
Southern, Miles 322
Southern, Robert 318, 329
Southern, William 322
Southers, Ramsey 276
Sparks, George 148
Spriggs, Corp. John T. 294
Standing, Joseph 434
Stanley, Bill 8
Stanley, Braxton 293
Stanley, Elisha 293
Stanley, Julian 8
Stanley, Reculious 293
Stanley, Samuel 293
Stanley, William, Jr. 293
Stanley, William, Sr. 293
Stanton, Edwin M. 450
Steedman, Gen. James B. 289
Stembridge, Marion 10
Stembridge, Roger 13
Stembridge, Sarah 15
Stepenson, Joe 200
Stephens, Alexander H. 450
Stevens, Robert L. 369
Stewart, Andrew B. 298
Stewart, Millie 54
Stiles, George 70
Stockton, V.D. 391
Stockum, Jean 21
Stokes, Henry Bomer 30
Stokes, J.H. 25
Stone, C.D. 385
Stone, Deputy Sheriff 380
Stone, James J. 297
Stone, Jeptha 296
Stone, Jordon 296
Stovall, John H. 425
Stratigos, James 96
Strother, Edward L. 7
Strother, John 1
Stuart, Iley T. 289
Stuart, John A. 148
Styles, Carey W. 323
Styles, Col. Carey W. 325
Sundance Kid 401
Susan J. Harrington, 7
Suttle, George 257
Suttle, Nancy 257
Sutton, Amos 296
Swaney, James C. 294
Swann, F.W. 363
Swoffered, William M. 298

T

Ta-ker-taw-ker 157
Talburt, Eileen 376
Talley family 341
Tally, John 298
Talmadge, Gov. Herman 10
Tanner, Big Boy 276
Tanner, Karen Holliday 406
Tate, Luke E. 332
Tate, Sam 316
Tate, Sybil 439
Tatom, Horatio 296
Tatum, John 295
Taylor, Bob 38
Taylor, Cicero 298
Taylor, Henry Lee 203
Taylor, Lewis 298
Taylor, Thomas 296
Taylor, W.F. 425
Taylor, William 298
Teague, William 148
Terry, Sam 17
Terry, Sarah Jordan 15
Tesseneer, James 296
Texas George 405
Thomas, Gen. George H. 288
Thomas, L.H. 8
Thomas, Susan McKey 223, 229
Thomason, Bill 40
Thomason, Eunice 442
Thompson, David 262
Thompson, E.P. 298
Thompson, Howard 188
Thompson, James 293
Thompson, John 420
Thompson, Leander J. 298
Thomson, Lt. Archibald H. 282
Thornton, William 237
Tierney, Luke 101
Tilly, Benjamin M. 148
Tipton, Claude 276
Tipton, Dora 280
Tolbert, Oscar 200
Tollison, A.B. 136
Tompkins, Judge H.B. 119
Toochalar 134
Took, George 25
Tooke, George 198
Toombs, Gen. Robert 211
Toombs, Robert 450, 459
Touchstone, Loretta 125
Touchstone, Oscar 125
Townsend, David 298
Townsend, W.B. 238
Traywick, Ben 414
Tripp, W.D. 38
Trippe, Turner H. 196
Troup, Gov. George 56
Trudeau, Noah Andre 305
Tucker, Nellie 387
Tumlin, Sheriff Lewis 25
Tuner, William 293
Turner, Capt. George H. 296
Turner, Corp. W.P. 294
Turner, David 298
Turner, Fielden 298
Turner, H. Green B. 298
Turner, James 298
Turner, Martin 298
Turner, Memory 298
Turner, O.P. 294
Turner, Tandy W. 296
Turpen, Drucy 168
Turpen, Rev. Jim 170
Tuskna, Sallie 439
Tustinugee, Toma 59
Twigg, William A. 289
Tyler, Johnny 406

U

Ulio, Lt. James 271
Unakayah-wah 26
Underwood, Curtis 275
Underwood, Joseph W.H. 424
Underwood, Judge William H. 193
Une'ga-tehee 198

V

Van Dorn, Gen. Earl 163
Vandergriff, J.W. 148
Vann, Chief James 132
Vann, J. Raymond 135
Varnedoe, Samuel McWhir 225
Vaughters, Lindsey 290
Vaughters, Linza 296
Vermillion, Texas Jack 402, 404
Vineyard, Tablah 298

W

Wade, Agnes Palmour 178
Wafford, James 339
Walcutt, Gen. Frank 215

Walden, William 298
Waldrop, Lloyd 206
Walker, Bert 34
Walker, Robert 245
Wallace, David Duncan 262
Wallace, Maj. Campbell 68
Waller, Charlie 106
Waller, Crash 96
Waller, John 106
Walraven, Bob 114
Walraven, Jasper 114
Walraven, Lester 114
Walthall, Linton 366
Walton, Sophie 404
Ward, Marie 180
Warren, J.W. 435
Warren, Jeremiah 298
Warren, Mary B. 30
Waters, Col. Thomas 342
Watie, Buck 157
Watie, David 157
Watie, Isabella 165
Watie, Stand 156
Watie, Susannah 159
Watkins, Elias 298
Watkins, Sam R. 216
Watkins, Virginia 88
Watts, David 391
Watts, George 369
Watts, Jimmy 17
Watts, John B. 189
Weaver, James M. 298
Weeks, Eve B. 30
Weems, Charley 93
Welch, George W. 390
Wells, Edward P. 269
West and Hackney 378
West, Columbus J. 298
West, Jim 358
West, Matilda 376
West, T.J. 378
West, Temperance 48
West, W.P. 378
West, William E. 369
Westcot, Sheriff 49
Westmoreland, J.W. 425
Whatley, Hampton 366
Whatley, W.O.B. 367
Wheeler, C.M. 378
Wheeler, Gen. Joseph 283
Wheeler, Jim 39
Whelchel, Frank 181
Whisenhunt, J.W 363
Whitaker, Mrs. J.W. 362
White Man Killer 198
White, J.W. 115
White, Samuel 148
White, Son 146
Whitmore, Charles 296
Whitmore, Henry T. 296
Whitmore, William 296
Whittle, E.E. (Emmett) 300
Whittle, J.W. 189
Whittle, Ora 107
Wiggins, W.M. 190
Wigington, James S. 298
Wilcox, Victoria 393
Wild, General Edward A. 452
Wilder, Thomas Y. 286
Wilder, William D. 286
Wilkes, Nancy 391
Willey, John 296
Williams, Alice 363
Williams, Col. Samuel C. 273
Williams, E.P. 432
Williams, George W. 428
Williams, Glenn 41
Williams, Goldie 363
Williams, Ruth 388
Williams, Wm. W. 294
Williamson, Capt. John D. 116
Williamson, Gen. Andrew 342
Willis, Liz 5
Wilson, Carter 317
Wilson, Dr. Bob 23
Wilson, Gen. James H. 454, 461
Wilson, John 369
Windencamp, W.J. 190
Windham, Melvin 107
Wirt, William 193
Wisdom, Francis 298
Wiseman, Edward 363
Wofford, Gen. William T. 291
Wofford, Nathan 25
Wood, Byrd 210
Woods, Capt. Martin V. 291
Woods, Jim 379
Woody, Arthur 180
Woody, Robert 293
Woody, Robert P. 148
Woolfolk, Annie 48
Woolfolk, Charles H. 48
Woolfolk, Floride 46
Woolfolk, Lillie 46
Woolfolk, Pearl 48
Woolfolk, Richard Franklin 46

Woolfolk, Rosebud 48
Woolfolk, Thomas "Bloody Tom" 46
Wright, A.J. 329
Wright, Patti 23
Wyley, William 28

Yancy, Obadiah 298
Yeager, Rev. 136
Yeager, Wayne 135
Yeargin, John 286
York, Chester 392
Young, Wilson Abercrombie 298

Z

Zbar, Jack 136